A HISTORY OF THE UNITED STATES
SINCE THE CIVIL WAR

A HISTORY

OF

THE UNITED STATES

SINCE THE CIVIL WAR

BY

ELLIS PAXSON OBERHOLTZER

IN FIVE VOLUMES
VOLUME IV: 1878–88

NEGRO UNIVERSITIES PRESS
NEW YORK

Originally published in 1917-37
by The Macmillan Company, New York

Reprinted 1969 by
Negro Universities Press
A DIVISION OF GREENWOOD PUBLISHING CORP.
NEW YORK

SBN 8371-2645-2

CONTENTS

CHAPTER XXV

UP FROM PANIC AND DEPRESSION

CHAPTER XXVI

GARFIELD AND ARTHUR

CHAPTER XXVIII

THE CHINESE

CHAPTER XXIX

PRESIDENT CLEVELAND

CHAPTER XXX

WAR UPON THE PRESIDENT

CHAPTER XXXI

THE NEW SOUTH

CHAPTER XXXII

IN THE WEST

A HISTORY OF THE UNITED STATES
SINCE THE CIVIL WAR

A HISTORY OF THE UNITED STATES SINCE THE CIVIL WAR

CHAPTER XXV

UP FROM PANIC AND DEPRESSION

In no body of human knowledge, except probably in medicine, does the quack intrude so insolently as in that science which Adam Smith organized under the name of "The Wealth of Nations." In few other fields does he find so interesting a refuge as in that one which concerns itself with the production of wealth, the distribution of wealth, taxation and the function and character of money. In economics, as in religion, the emotions are considered to have equal authority with reason. Further than this, since political economy affects and should govern the course of the state, its principles may be betrayed by demagogues, ready in a democracy to ride the masses of the people for the advancement of their selfish ends. To tell a mob of men who possess the vote that their material burdens will be lifted and their way in the world will be made the easier by some misapplication of economical laws is to excite them to a frenzied support of it. The ignorant, or the crack-brained leader of the ignorant, enforced by the politician, skilled in chicane, has time and again shaken people and commonwealth. The electorate, enlarged after the war to include practically all the males in the republic, black and white, past twenty-one years of age, barring Indians and Chinamen and those who were too recently arrived through our ports of immigration, was to be played upon by writer and orator. To this contentious rabble must the country look for a determination of the currency question. Should it have paper money or specie as a medium of exchange and for the payment and collection of private and public debt? To this

1

problem, which incompetents and knaves had labored with
ever since the war, was to be added now a choice of the kinds
of specie. Should it be gold, or the silver which was being
taken out of the earth in too great a quantity for profit so
long as it was used only in the manufacture of teapots, knives
and forks, meat platters, candle sticks and thimbles, unless
the mines could sell it to the government for mintage? Angrier
discussion of a political subject has scarcely ever been seen
than that which had been already, and would continue inter-
mittently, for many years, to be waged about this one.

The agreement of Congress in 1875 upon a plan for the assignment of the greenbacks to a more correct place in our
monetary system, and the resumption of specie payments was
a makeshift measure adopted amid mad opposition. The
date of the event was set far forward, in 1879. The most
optimistic were not hopeful that the promise of the law could
be fulfilled even when the day should arrive. A number of
elections would intervene. Other Congresses could undo what
the Forty-third had done. The way must be found by administrative officers, yet unnamed, and without skill or courage
enough, in all likelihood, to compass such an end.

The progress of that enterprise, of which so much in economy
was expected—the refunding of the debt into bonds bearing
a lower rate of interest—met a number of obstructions, which
at times were referable to "politics" and again to the general
financial situation. A "syndicate" directed by Jay Cooke had
successfully concluded a negotiation in 1871. Another movement of the same kind, conducted by associated bankers in
this country and Europe, broke down on the eve of the panic
in 1873.[1] Prior to that calamity the debt, bearing 6 per
cent interest, Secretary Richardson observed, had been reduced, through conversion into five per cents, by about $100,-
000,000, at a saving to the government of $1,000,000 a year,
and the whole conversion since the passage of the refunding
acts of 1870 and 1871 was declared to be $300,000,000.[2] That

[1] Oberholtzer, Life of Jay Cooke, vol. ii, pp. 359–74.
[2] Report of Sec. of Treasury for 1873, pp. ix–x.

our credit as a nation remained high in spite of the shock
suffered by private finance was proven in July, 1874, when
Secretary of the Treasury Bristow received bids from the
Rothschilds, Seligmans, Morgans and their associates for
$55,000,000 of 5 per cent bonds to be taken prior to February 1,
1875, when they might avail themselves of an option granted
them with reference to the remainder, some $122,000,000, of the
loan.[1] This course was chosen, upon the approach of the nominated time, and Secretary Bristow, in his report in December,
1875, was able to say that the sale of the "new fives" had been
completed—$500,000,000 of the 6 per cent bonds had been re-
funded at a saving of $5,000,000 annually to the government.

The next task was the conversion of the sixes into bonds
bearing 4½ per cent interest, an operation which Congress
had authorized the Secretary of the Treasury to undertake,
when the "fives" should have been distributed. But the new
loan was to run for only 15 years. In order that the conversion could proceed, Mr. Bristow recommended that Congress
should extend the time of redemption to 30 years from the
date of issue.[2]

In August, 1876, the same associates agreed to take $40,-
000,000 of the 4½ per cent bonds, with an exclusive right to
subscribe to the rest of the issue, amounting to $26,000,000,
on or before June 30, 1877,[3] subject to a revocation of the contract, on ten days notice, after March 4, 1877, when Grant's
term would end and another's would begin.

Excited minds were now turning their attention from the
greenbacks to the use of silver in the currency. So much silver had been found in the Comstock Lode in Nevada during
the course of the war that its battles could scarcely drown the
din which attended the discovery of the bonanza. In one year,
1863, 3,000 mining companies, with a nominal capital of one
billion dollars, were organized in San Francisco to exploit
the region.[4] In 1873, a new body of ore was discovered in the

[1] Report of Sec. of Treasury for 1874, pp. ix–x.
[2] Ibid. for 1875, pp. xi–xii.
[3] Ibid. for 1876, p. xi.
[4] Report of Silver Commission, p. 17.

Comstock Ledge, the mines of which, all taken together, accounted for more than one-half of the whole silver production of the United States.[1] Large and important as the output presently grew to be, the annual yield, as well as the amount in sight but not yet taken from the earth, was greatly exaggerated,[2] with signal effect upon the price of silver. The fall began in 1874, becoming abrupt in 1875. The depreciation in July, 1876, had reached 21 per cent.[3]

In those civilized countries which were still using silver in conjunction with gold as a standard of value (it was no matter to uncivilized countries not in close commercial relationships with the world) the prospect was highly disturbing. Germany, which had come under Bismarck's intelligent guidance, had demonetized silver. Denmark, Norway and Sweden followed. The members of the so-called Latin Union, consisting of France, Italy, Belgium and Switzerland, which had been acting together in the joint and concurrent use of gold and silver, in conformity with the monetary treaty of 1865,[4] were hurriedly formulating plans to protect themselves from the derangements which impended. Coincidently England's purchases for making payments in India, which were so great while she was buying cotton there during our Civil War, and subsequently for a time in building railroads and public works in that country,[5] had practically ceased, and China, Mexico and other lands, into which our silver salesmen wished to discharge their product at high prices, offered but small prospects to their eager minds.

[1] Report of Silver Commission, p. 19; cf. A. D. Noyes, Forty Years of American Finance, pp. 37–8.
[2] Report of Silver Commission, p. 2.
[3] See N. Y. Nation, Aug. 17 and Dec. 14, 1876. Representative Payne said in Congress on July 13, 1876: "Owing to the remarkable decline in the price of silver within the last few months and its more remarkable decline within the last ten days the silver dollar of 1861 is now worth less than 80 cents in gold. . . . It will be observed that this silver dollar at its present discount of 20 per cent, is worth nearly ten per cent less than greenbacks."—Cong. Record, 44th Cong. 1st sess., p. 4551.
[4] House Ex. Doc., 45th Cong. 3rd sess., pt. 7, no. 1, p. 2. Later, in 1868, joined by Greece.
[5] Report of Silver Commission, p. 142.

The miners in the Rocky and Sierra Mountains, together with such Eastern capitalists as were pecuniarily interested in the mines, and their agents in Congress and in the newspaper press, were joined by the hazy theorists who called themselves bimetallists. To their ranks gravitated a much more numerous body of men. Now that the silver dollar was worth less than the greenback an attractive scene unfolded—those who were in debt had wanted to pay in paper; here was money that was cheaper than paper.[1] The silver men were greenbackers and the greenbackers were silver men.[2]

Then, too, there was a benevolent element, sometimes named Socialist, with pity and sympathy for the masses of the people as against the money lending and capitalist class who were pictured by lively fancy as oppressors and exploiters of the poor. All together said that silver must be "remonetized"—it must be restored to its place as currency in the United States by law of Congress. Many demanded that the resumption act be repealed, since it was "hopeless of execution and a standing threat to our prosperity."[3] Anyhow "resumption must wait upon remonetization."[4]

In point of fact silver in this country had never been consciously or formally "demonetized"—what came to be called by the silver men "the crime of 1873" had never been committed.[5] While coin in the United States, it is true, had meant either gold or silver, and our money standard thus, in theory, was bimetallic, silver had never been an obtrusive factor in our financial system. In 1792, Congress had undertaken to establish a ratio of 15 to 1 between the two metals, which is to say that 15 ounces of silver were to be held to have the

[1] N. Y. Nation, Aug. 10, 1876. Such a movement as the silver movement was supported, said Garfield, by "an innate desire in the human mind to cheat somebody."—Cong. Record, 44th Cong. 1st sess., p. 4561.

[2] On November 8, 1877, the New York Nation declared that silver had so far replaced irredeemable paper in the minds of the inflationists that the greenback movement was "practically dead" (cf. issue of Jan. 24, 1877), though this was a premature announcement.

[3] The words of Representative S. S. Cox, August 5, 1876, in Cong. Record, 44th Cong. 1st sess., p. 5219.

[4] Groesbeck in Report of Silver Commission, p. 133.

[5] Cf. N. Y. Nation, Feb. 21, 1878.

.value of one ounce of gold for purposes of coinage. But because gold had become more valuable than silver gold was exported, and in 1837 a correction had been made in the ratio— which thereafter would be 15 98/100 to 1, practically 16 to 1. In the new price relation of the two metals, silver, since it had the greater value, was either sold abroad or hoarded: it was automatically demonetized—gold becoming the standard of the country.

In 1853 a new policy was adopted. Silver, it was determined, should thereafter be used only in the form of fractional currency, and to a limited degree—it should be legal tender for the payment of debts in sums not exceeding five dollars. For this purpose the ratio was adjudged to be 14.88 to 1. The act did not mention the silver dollar, which from 1792 until 1874 had had a greater intrinsic value than the gold dollar, at the ratio fixed by Congress in 1837. Only some 2,500,000 silver dollars were issued prior to 1853—the whole issue of this coin, nearly altogether for exportation, was only about 5,500,000 pieces in the next 20 years, or up to 1873, at which time the "old silver dollar" was never seen by the people outside of numismatist's collections. Even on the Pacific coast, where coin was the sole currency in circulation, the silver dollar was unknown.[1]

The act of 1873,[2] which was to become the subject of so much intolerant rage in writer and orator throughout two decades of our national history, provided that some millions of fractional silver currency, under limitations which were wise, should be issued. Provision was made, too, for the coinage of a new "trade dollar." Our commerce with China had a considerable volume and to pay our balances we were buying and shipping thither Mexican silver dollars, which were highly esteemed as a currency in that country.[3] But the government of Mexico had laid an export duty on its silver money and the Californians, who were largely engaged in the China

[1] John Sherman's Recollections, pp. 615–7.
[2] Approved on Feb. 12, 1873.
[3] House Mis. Doc., 45th Cong. 2nd sess., no. 44, pp. 1 and 10; H. R. Linderman, Money and Legal Tenders in the U. S., chap. x.

trade, asked for the coinage of a dollar of the same size and value. Accordingly it was specified in the law of 1873 that anyone bringing silver bullion to the mints of the United States might have it coined at the cost of manufacture into dollars for export of a weight of 420 grains Troy. At the time such a dollar had a market value of $1.02 13/100 in gold. But the silver dollar of 412½ grains as a national coin, with which no one had daily acquaintance and for which people, press and Congress at the moment felt and expressed no concern, ceased to be a product of our mints.[1]

It was in this manner and under these circumstances, said the "silver men," as they contemplated in retrospect the course of events, that the step on the road of error had been taken and that they had been betrayed. Silver had been "demonetized," though at the time we had no "silver men," and we had no silver to demonetize,[2] since 3 per cent could be made by exporting it.[3] The deed had been done "stealthily," said Congressman Richard P. Bland, one of the most voluble of the oracles of the new political economy;[4] the scheme was "stolen through Congress," said another representative of the people in that body.[5] By trickery and fraud the Scriptural money of Abraham, Isaac and Jacob, "the dollar of the fathers," the "money of the Constitution"[6] had been taken away from "the honest yeomanry of this country."[7]

Bland, as chairman of the House Committee on Mines and Mining, made himself, in the Forty-fourth Congress, the sponsor of a bill for the free and unlimited coinage of the old silver dollar of 412½ grains,[8] and this "bold and startling proposition," as Mr. Chittenden of New York described it in the House,[9] was one of the many subjects to be taken to the people

---

[1] N. Y. Nation, Nov. 8, 1877.
[2] Ibid., Nov. 1, 1877.
[3] Ibid., Nov. 29, 1877.
[4] Cong. Record, 44th Cong. 1st sess., p. 5234.
[5] Ibid., p. 4553.
[6] N. Y. Nation, Nov. 8 and Dec. 6, 1877.
[7] Cong. Record, 44th Cong. 1st sess., p. 5235.
[8] Ibid.
[9] Ibid., p. 5224.

in 1876, though it would but little disturb them in the presence of issues with which they were more familiar and for which
they would yet, for a while, feel a more immediate concern.
Bland, and those who thought and spoke as he, were dismissed
at this session with a small additional issue of subsidiary silver coin,[1] and a resolution, passed by Congress, shortly before adjournment, on August 15, 1876,[2] creating a commission,
to consist of three senators and three members of the House
of Representatives, and "experts not exceeding three in number," to study the silver question with a view to a "restoration of the double standard in this country." To this body
more general duties were assigned, with regard to the investigation of monetary matters, but these were little considered—
it at once came to bear the name of the Silver Commission.

The money question was in this position when, on March 4,
1877, the Treasury passed to the direction of John Sherman,
who, seeing an opportunity for more favorable arrangements
with the syndicate engaged in refunding operations, which
was selling 4½ per cent bonds, announced that he would
limit the sale of this issue bearing this rate of interest to $200,-
000,000 in all. Acting in conformity with the provisions of
the law governing the return to specie payments he used but
$185,000,000 of the sum received from the sales in redeeming
the 6 per cent "five-twenties" and kept $15,000,000 in gold
in the Treasury. He would now offer the four per cents. It
was a bold measure taken in the interest of resumption, which
was to be Sherman's service to his countrymen. With the
syndicate, in June, 1877, he entered into a contract for the sale
at par of four per cents, and the distribution in the summer and
autumn of 1877 advanced rapidly until $75,000,000 of bonds
of this kind had been subscribed for. Of the proceeds $50,-
000,000 were applied to the redemption of six per cents, while
$25,000,000 in coin were held in the Treasury for resumption
purposes. From time to time Sherman was redeeming, retiring and canceling greenbacks.

---

[1] By resolution of July 31, 1876.
[2] Cong. Record, 44th Cong. 1st sess., pp. 5219, 5240, 5667.

Meanwhile as August Belmont, who represented the Rothschilds in the bond sales, declared, when our funded debt was
selling, "equal to that of any other public security in the
world," [1] business conditions were growing better. The foreign
commerce of the country was increasing, showing a favorable
balance of trade, the exportation of bullion was arrested, the
revenues of the government were in excess of its expenditures
so that a surplus was accumulating in the Treasury, [2] which
not only contributed sentimentally to an improvement of the
public credit but also practically strengthened Sherman's hand
for the tasks which confronted him. In proof of the stability
of the country's economic position and the buoyancy of public feeling, greenbacks in October, 1877, had a quoted value
of 97³/₈ cents in coin—they were nearing the long desired
parity with gold. [3]

Quiet might well have been the part of those men who had
been industriously fomenting a feeling of dissatisfaction with
their governors as well as with the entire social order. Hard
times there had been for four years. There were unemployment, poverty and a considerable amount of real distress among
workers in the factories, as well as farmers. A class of vagrants,
usually called "tramps," appeared and the "loafer," at odds
with society, became a figure in country and town. [4] Fortunes
had been dispersed by the panic, capital had been made timid.
Recovery, though on the way, was slow and many classes of
the people were visibly impatient. It was an opportunity for
the demagogue, and he used it actively. The blame was laid
at the door of the banker and the moneyed man of whatever
description. The poor and unreflecting parts of the population were being stirred to resentment at their employers for
many ills which the profligate living and arrogance of these

---

[1] Sherman's Recollections, p. 605.
[2] The surplus revenue over expenditures was $30,000,000 for the
fiscal year ending June 30, 1877.—Report of Sec. of Treasury for 1877,
pp. iii–iv.
[3] Ibid., for 1877, pp. vii–xii; Sherman's Recollections, pp. 608–609;
N. Y. Nation, Oct. 11 and 18, 1877, and later week by week.
[4] Gompers, Seventy Years of Life and Labor, vol. i, p. 140.

employers, as the workingman believed, had laid upon him [1]—
the rate of wages, the hours of labor, the scarcity of work.
It went farther—it was leading to the spread of communistic
theories on the subject of property, such as railroads, factories,
mines, which were to be confiscated and put somehow to the
uses of the poor.[2] Physical violence was advocated and was
not far away.

This social rising reached picturesque and formidable proportions in California where an Irish ruffian named Denis
Kearney made himself its leader. It included a use of the prejudices aroused against the Chinese as competitors of the white
workingman and, throughout, was such a ferment as calls
for consideration at length in a separate place.

Of this character, too, were the activities of the Molly
Maguires,[3] a band of terrorists who were active in the anthracite coal mining districts of Pennsylvania. This organization had connections with a parent society with headquarters,
for the state, in Pittsburgh and, for the United States, in New
York, under a higher controlling authority called the Board
of Erin in Great Britain.[4] Its purposes were socialist and anarchist. It first drew attention to itself in Pennsylvania through
the resistance which it offered to the draft during the Civil
War,[5] and was an outgrowth of the feeling that burst forth
periodically in miners' strikes which were organized and directed by the labor unions. The Molly Maguires fortunately
did not always control the unions; [6] but they entirely captured
the official machinery of the Ancient Order of Hibernians,

[1] Cf. article on "Fair Wages" in North American Review, Sep.–Oct.,
1877.
[2] N. Y. Nation, May 9, 1878.
[3] A name which seems to have come from Ireland, because of the disguise there of such men in women's dress.—F. P. Dewees, The Molly
Maguires, p. 44; J. T. Morse, Am. Law Review, Jan., 1877, p. 237.
[4] F. B. Gowen in Report of the Case of the Commonwealth vs. John
Kehoe, p. 176; Morse, loc. cit., p. 253.
[5] Dewees, op. cit., pp. 46–9.
[6] However they seem to have had the sympathy of labor unionists
everywhere (Samuel Gompers, Seventy Years of Life and Labor, vol. i, p.
139) as well as of the element which as socialist, communist or whatever
its name took the "Labor" cause into politics.—Cf. N. Y. Nation, May 9
and 16, 1878.

through which they acted in the spread of their influence.[1] Thus they entered politics. They sought and held public places that they might rob the taxpayers and plunder town and county treasuries,[2] and, by electing their members to disciplinary and judicial positions, saved themselves and their friends, at need, from merited punishment for worse crimes.[3]

Meanwhile the Philadelphia and Reading Railroad Company and its affiliated Coal and Iron Company came under the presidency of an able and a determined man, Franklin B. Gowen. He himself for a time had been a coal operator, later studying and practicing law, in which he displayed brilliant powers. He was intent upon exterminating this band of outlaws who made the conduct of the business of his companies difficult and dangerous. He stated the case to the officers of a leading detective agency, the Pinkertons, and they set a young Irishman, James McParlan, at the task of assembling the evidence to convict the perpetrators of the outrages, not one of whom had ever felt the hand of the law. McParlan seems to have had the qualities fitting him for the social companionship of such black-hearted men. He was assigned to his duties in October, 1873, and, disguised under the name of McKenna, became a "Molly" in the sight of every one in the coal regions. He continued his strange double life, gaining access to all the secrecies of the order and facing the gravest personal dangers[4] through the year 1874, at the end of which the miners began what was called the "long strike." During the entire period of nation-wide depression they had not felt any of its effects, for the coal carrying companies had been able to keep up the price of coal.[5] In a resolution, under necessity, to reduce wages, the companies remained firm and the men who had stopped work in a body, and their families, in

[1] Dewees, op. cit., pp. 31, 38.

[2] J. F. Rhodes, Hist. of the U. S. from Hayes to McKinley, pp. 56–7; cf. ibid., Am. Hist. Review for April, 1910.

[3] J. T. Morse, loc. cit., pp. 238–9.

[4] Only by a miracle was he, on one occasion, saved from assassination. For services of this kind his employers paid him $2 a day.—The Great Molly Maguire Trials in Carbon and Schuylkill Counties, p. 37.

[5] Dewees, pp. 108–10. Another view in Dacus, The Great Strikes, p. 149.

the winter of 1874–5, began to suffer. Disorder and crime increased. Railway and mine property was destroyed. Train hands and other men usefully serving their employers were beaten, stoned, shot, stabbed and robbed. Such outrages were of daily occurrence not in one place but throughout the district.[1] On June 1, 1875, the union was finally vanquished, leaving the miners in such a frame of mind that their excesses grew more than ever intolerable. Several murders in cold blood and in broad daylight followed, attracting country-wide attention. The governor of Pennsylvania was called upon for troops and he sent to the scene a regiment of militia under the protection of which, aided by a body of the company's private guards called the "Coal and Iron Police," the operators were enabled again to take coal out of their mines and send it to market. Late in the summer of 1875, the first arrests were made and in January, 1876, three fiends were put on trial at Mauch Chunk. One turned informer to be a very useful witness for the state, the other two were convicted and sentenced to be hanged.[2] More followed. Dozens of the villains were soon in custody to be brought promptly into court to answer for their sins either at Mauch Chunk or Pottsville, the seats of justice of the two counties in which most of the crimes had been planned and perpetrated. Gowen himself acted as one of the prosecuting attorneys.[3] McParlan, throwing off his disguise at last, dramatically confronted his old companions to testify as to their awful guilt. Throughout the Centennial year the record of this organized body of assassins[4] was unfolded and, before it was done, a dozen were sentenced to the gallows, while many more were sent to prison for per-

[1] For a record of these outrages see Dewees, op. cit., appendix.

[2] The Great Molly Maguire Trials in Carbon and Schuylkill Counties, p. v.

[3] For an example of Gowen's brilliant oratory see his argument in the Kehoe trial. Report of the Case of the Commonwealth vs. John Kehoe, pp. 176 et seq.; cf. Morse, op. cit., p. 254.

[4] " Never since the world began has there existed a more villainous society or more horrible organization" than this one.—George R. Kaercher, district attorney of Schuylkill County in Report of the Commonwealth vs. Kehoe, p. 218.

jury committed in the business of protecting their evil mates, for assault and battery and minor offenses not calling for capital punishment, and still others fled the country never to return. Appeals to the higher courts and to the governor of Pennsylvania were of no avail and on a day in June, in 1877, four Mollies were hanged for murder at Mauch Chunk, while simultaneously six more paid a similar penalty for their iniquities at Pottsville.[1] Three on a later day were made to feel the halter of the law at Bloomsburg, the county town of Columbia county. The "reign" of the Molly Maguire was being rapidly brought to an end. The movement to rout this body of criminals culminated in the execution of "Big Jack" Kehoe, the county delegate for Schuylkill county, and one of the most crafty and adroit of its leaders, in the jail yard in Pottsville on December 18, 1878.[2] In all nineteen were led to the scaffold and were hanged.[3]

The employees of the principal railroads, like the miners, had, after the panic, suffered little if any reduction in their wages. While carpenters who, on May 1, 1872, received $4 for an eight hour work day now accepted $2.25 and $2.50 for ten hours labor at their trade, while masons and plasterers in the same time had found their daily returns reduced from $5.50 and $6 to $2 and $2.50, and the compensation of mechanics and laborers generally had fallen from 37½ to 60 per cent, the pay of locomotive engineers, firemen, train conductors and brakemen remained practically what it had been.[4] The wages of railway employees, indeed, were higher than in 1861, at the outbreak of the war.[5] Widely varying rates prevailed on the different roads but the average per month for an engineer was about $85. None received more than $115, none less than $60. The man on the other side of the cab who stoked

[1] Public Ledger, Phila., June 22, 1877; N. Y. Tribune, June 21, 22, 23, 25, 26 and July 7, 1877; cf. A. K. McClure, Old Time Notes of Pa., chap. xc.
[2] Phila. Inquirer, Dec. 18 and 19, 1878.
[3] J. F. Rhodes, Am. Hist. Review, April, 1910, p. 560.
[4] N. Y. Nation, Aug. 16, 1877; cf. Dacus, p. 43; Gompers, Seventy Years of Life and Labor, vol. i, pp. 139–40.
[5] Statement of vice-president of B. & O. R. R. in E. W. Martin, History of the Great Riots, pp. 47–8.

the fires, and the brakeman, whose services were considered to require not more skill than a day laborer's, would average about $45 and $42 a month respectively.[1]

While these facts must be admitted it was alleged that the cost of living, in rents, food, clothing and other necessities, had increased. In most respects this could be denied. Coal, flour and kerosene were cheaper than in 1873. Prices in general, after the orgy with the greenback had ended, had returned to approximately what they had been in 1860.[2]

The interests of the engineers were defended vigorously by a powerful labor union, the Brotherhood of Locomotive Engineers, which had come to include some 13,000 members, nearly 90 per cent of all the locomotive engineers in the country. From a body with social and benevolent purposes it was developed, in 1874, into an instrument to foment a spirit of discontent in the men with reference to the corporations which they served. The organization stood under the direction of three salaried officers with headquarters in Cleveland, one of whom, the "Grand Chief Engineer," a Scotchman by birth, P. M. Arthur, became a militant figure in trades unionism.[3] He was an advocate of abandoning trains, blocking tracks and interrupting travel and trade, when employers refused to heed his demands. Late in 1876, and early in 1877, he had organized successful strikes on the New Jersey Central, Grand Trunk and two other railroads, turning then to the Boston and Maine, an enterprise in which he was discomfited.[4] In April, 1877, an effort was made to cripple the Philadelphia and Reading Railroad, but the labor leaders were circumvented by President Gowen.[5] In the summer of 1877, the companies generally, their business calling for retrenchment, a situation which they had done much to bring upon themselves by competitive rate "slashing" and "wars" in freight charges and passenger

[1] N. Y. Nation, Aug. 16, 1877.
[2] Ibid.
[3] For an account of Arthur see Allan Pinkerton, Strikers, Communists, Tramps and Detectives, chap. viii.
[4] N. Y. Nation, March 15 and 22, 1877.
[5] Ibid., May 3, 1877; also Pinkerton, op. cit., pp. 107–15.

fares,[1] posted a reduction in wages of 10 per cent to take effect on July 1st. This step on their part precipitated a great strike which involved the entire eastern part of the United States, barring the South and New England. The roads farther west escaped only because most of the managers compromised the issue.

The first outbreak, instigated by firemen whose pay running from $1.75 down to $1.50 a day, according to their efficiency, was to be reduced to a level of from $1.58 to $1.35 a day,[2] occurred on July 16th among freight train hands of the Baltimore and Ohio Railroad at Martinsburg, W. Va., where extensive repair shops were located. The disorder soon spread to other places on the lines of the same company in Maryland, West Virginia and Ohio, until the strikers were in complete control and no trains, whether in the passenger, postal or freight service, were permitted to move. Soon the Pennsylvania Railroad was involved at Pittsburgh. The strike ran east and west along that line of railway, extending to the Erie and other trunk line systems. The places of the men could have been filled but this was to be prevented at any cost. Mobs were formed, applicants for the positions held by the strikers were intimidated, if not subjected to bodily injury, railroad stations and freight sheds were set on fire, tracks were torn up, cars and locomotives were wrecked. Traffic was obstructed in all directions.

Militia companies, ordered to Martinsburg by the governor of West Virginia, were repulsed in some opera bouffe encounters—the soldiers joined the strikers with whom they were in sympathy. Deserted by the few companies of troops with which the state was provided,[3] and unable to assert his authority he, on July 18th, appealed to the President of the United States.[4] Hayes issued a proclamation commanding the rioters to disperse,[5] and sent Federal troops to Martins-

[1] See vol. iii of this work, pp. 99–101, and vol. iv, chap. xxix; cf. E. W. Martin, History of the Great Riots, p. 48.
[2] Dacus, op. cit., p. 27.
[3] E. W. Martin, History of the Great Riots, p. 25.
[4] Dacus, op. cit., pp. 37–8.
[5] Richardson, Messages and Papers of the Presidents, vol. vii, p. 447.

burg to enforce his command. Order was about to be restored
there when the Maryland militia were called out by Governor
Carroll of that state to deal with the situation at Cumberland.[1] They were hooted and jeered as they assembled at
their armories in Baltimore and responded slowly and without enthusiasm. It was the 20th of July. The strikers, and
the ruffians who swarmed out of every alley and from the
docks, to join them, filled the streets and, when the militia-
men were ready to march to the railway station, they were
pelted with stones. The volunteers fired into the mob killing
and wounding several men, but were practically held prisoners
in the Baltimore and Ohio Railway station during the night,
while the mob ravaged property on all sides. President Hayes
being called upon for aid by the governor of Maryland issued another proclamation[2] and sent General Hancock with regulars
from New York to the scene of the disturbance. That was the
end of rioting in that quarter.

At Pittsburgh, too, the strikers had the sympathy of a
large part of the population. Thomas A. Scott, the president,
and other officers of the Pennsylvania Railroad did not enjoy
the good will of the community because of a belief that the
city was being discriminated against in freight rates and suffered other disadvantages which were laid at the door of the
company. The mayor and the police were appealed to, with
little response,[3] and soon the work of guarding property and
preserving the peace passed to the Pennsylvania militia.
Governor Hartranft was on his way to the Pacific coast but
the adjutant-general, as commander-in-chief of the military
arm of the state government, ordered three regiments and a
battery, whose headquarters were in Pittsburgh, to take the
field. A part of these forces were dilatory in assembling and
apathetic when under arms, because of their want of interest
in the task to be performed, and it was necessary to import

[1] Dacus, pp. 62–4.
[2] Richardson, vol. vii, p. 448.
[3] The strike, it has been said, was not "properly" this but "a revolt of
the community against the Pennsylvania Railroad."—N. J. Ware, The
Labor Movement, p. 48.

units of the "National Guard" from Philadelphia. It was Saturday afternoon, July 21st, when the Philadelphians, including many young men drawn from the leading families of the city, arrived to meet a mob which had grown to immense proportions. Without support on any side and in danger of being disarmed they reluctantly fired on the crowd, killing a score and wounding many more. As night advanced the fight was on in earnest. The Philadelphians who had taken shelter in a round house were besieged. When it was set on fire they, exhausted by loss of sleep and hunger, withdrew with what order was possible, harried by the mob, to the suburbs.[1] A veritable reign of terror continued through Saturday night, July 21st, and Sunday, the 22nd.[2] The strikers and the rabble which joined them sacked freight cars,[3] tore up tracks and, with the assistance of oil in tank cars in the freight yards, burned station buildings, machine shops and rolling stock. Riots were in progress at the same time in Altoona and Harrisburg, where mobs were assembled to prevent the passage of troops and obstruct traffic.

The visionary, as well as the idle and vicious, came everywhere to the support of the strikers. The "International Association of Workingmen" brought forward its various agents and exhibited its power. Never before in the United States had its hand been so clearly seen.[4] Trades union influences in every branch of industry, incipient and feeble as they yet were, in comparison with the force which they were to gain in a few years, came to the defense of the workers on the railroads.[5] On Sunday in the principal cities meetings were held in labor union halls; demagogues mounted boxes and barrels

[1] Cf. J. W. Latta, History of the First Regiment, pp. 219–26.

[2] "The dreadful events of that awful Sunday." (R. B. Hayes in his Diary and Letters, vol. iii, p. 440.) For twenty-four hours Pittsburgh was "such a scene of riot, arson and bloodshed as can never be erased from the memory of its people."—T. A. Scott in North American Review for Sep. and Oct., 1877, p. 352.

[3] The contents of over 1,800 cars were despoiled.—T. A. Scott in North American Review for Sep. and Oct., 1877, p. 357.

[4] Dacus, The Great Strikes, pp. 23, 25.

[5] Cf. Gompers, Seventy Years of Life and Labor, vol. i, chap. vii.

at the street corners animating the men to new disorders. To a young labor leader like Samuel Gompers the sky at Pittsburgh, reddened by fire, brought "the message that human aspiration had not been killed or cowed."[1] The government should own the railroads and the workingmen should constitute the government. They should have employment; they had families to keep; they must have a living wage. Under the spur of agitators the employees of a half dozen more roads joined the strike, the managers of some having made the situation worse by acceding to the demands of the men. Other companies, intimidated, made no attempt to operate their equipment. Mobs occupied the streets in a hundred towns and cities. The strikers thus gained courage. Grave conditions prevailed in Reading, Pa., where in a collision with the militia a number of people were killed, in West Philadelphia, in Buffalo, Columbus, Hornellsville, N. Y., Corning, N. Y., Columbus, Fort Wayne, East St. Louis, Chicago, where Sheridan with regulars was called upon to preserve the peace. President Hayes ordered Hancock to Philadelphia.[2] All available United States troops were brought on from the South and from the plains; garrisons everywhere were drawn upon for soldiers who were hurried to critical points. The militia of ten or a dozen states were under arms.[3] Governor Hartranft of Pennsylvania, an officer who had displayed his bravery on many fields in the war, had been intercepted in Wyoming. He telegraphed, ordering out all the volunteer forces of his state, appealed to the President who issued another proclamation[4] and took the first train for the East. He reached Pittsburgh on the 24th and took command of his militia in person. Hastening to Philadelphia for a conference with Hancock and Schofield, who had come on from Washington to assist in the restoration of peace, he set out on the 26th with reinforce-

[1] Cf. Gompers, Seventy Years of Life and Labor, vol. i, p. 140.
[2] E. W. Martin, History of the Great Riots, p. 146.
[3] Dacus, op. cit., p. 24.
[4] Richardson, vol. vii, p. 449. The President's proclamation for West Virginia was issued on July 18th, for Maryland on July 21st and for Pennsylvania on July 23rd.

ments for Pittsburgh, with the resolution of opening the lines of the Pennsylvania Railroad. He established his headquarters in a Pullman car and, supported by several hundred regulars, he was ready for any emergency. Hartranft told the officers of his militia to order the rioters to disperse. If they refused, the command to fire should be given, and every soldier should "fire with effect."[1] At sight of such intrepidity the mobs slunk away and the railroad company could begin the work of repairing its tracks. In a few days trains were once more running through the state and in a fortnight the strike everywhere was at an end.

Miners in the anthracite coal fields of Pennsylvania seized this opportunity again to embarrass their employers. Reading, where the railroad strike had led to riots, was near the Schuylkill coal mining district. A posse assembled by the burgess dispersed a mob in Shamokin. At Pottsville the leaders failed to create violent disturbance, but in the Lehigh, Lackawanna and Wyoming valleys, where the railroads were in the hands of the strikers, who intimidated all who would not join them, and who soaped the tracks, when they did not lift the rails and stop traffic, the outlook was more grave. During the obstruction to transportation mills and factories were compelled to suspend work—their employees increased the idle throng. Out of this situation came a great strike in the coal mines in and around Scranton. Miners were receiving from $15 to $20 a month and they asked for an advance in wages of 25 per cent.[2] In a short time 30,000 to 40,000 men were involved. The strikers even compelled the pumps to be stopped to the serious injury of mine property.

As the mayor of Scranton passed through the streets of his city he was murderously assaulted with a club and he narrowly escaped with his life. A posse fired into a mob and Governor Hartranft, who was still in Pittsburgh, was appealed to for a military force. He instantly transferred his head-

[1] E. W. Martin, History of the Great Riots, p. 155.
[2] N. Y. Nation, Aug. 16, 1877. Wages were distressingly low—see R. P. Porter in Galaxy, Dec., 1877.

quarters to the new center of turbulence, and, with some regulars furnished him by Hancock, was employed in August, 1877, in restoring quiet.

In the midst of these disturbances politicians in states which were troubled with elections in 1877 were preparing for the campaigns. The panic, the unemployment and poverty of the few years past, the reduction of wages, the strikes were all ascribed, of course, to the "scarcity of money." [1] The greenbacks should not be retired and canceled, gold did not exist in sufficient quantities for use as currency, silver must also be coined. Money that was good enough for the people was good enough for the bondholder and to pay off the national debt.

The silver "mania" was neither Republican nor Democratic, though it was largely Western and Southern, and, in general, the Democrats displayed the most haste and zeal in embracing the cause. [2] The idea was powerfully represented in the ranks of both parties and it was useless to argue with those under the strange influence of the craze. [3]

In Ohio a governor was to be elected to succeed Hayes, who had left the office in March to become President, and a legislature, which would reëlect Stanley Matthews, Sherman's successor, by appointment, in the United States Senate, or would put a Democrat in the place. The people boiled with excitement—they had all but lost command of their reasoning faculties, and they were not calmer of temper nor better fitted for their political tasks in several other Western commonwealths. The legislature of Ohio in May had before it a bill making silver legal tender in that state after the 1st day of July, 1877, all the rest of the country to the contrary, notwithstanding. [4] In Illinois the legislature actually adopted such a measure which, however, met the veto of the governor. [5] A Cleve-

[1] Gompers, Seventy Years of Life and Labor, vol. i, p. 135.
[2] N. Y. Nation, Nov. 8, 1877; A. D. Noyes, Forty Years of American Finance, p. 40.
[3] N. Y. Nation, Feb. 14, 1878.
[4] Ibid., May 10, 1877.
[5] Ibid., May 10 and 31 and June 7, 1877; McPherson's Handbook of Politics for 1878, pp. 139–40; A. B. Hepburn, History of Currency in the U. S., p. 283.

land, O., correspondent wrote to the New York Nation— [1] "The hold which this madness has obtained upon public opinion in this state is very strong. Scores of men who two years ago did earnest work for a sound currency are now carried away by this delusion and it has a large following even among bankers and professional men." Another, in a town in Illinois, wrote that he there stood alone in opposition to the craze, for which he was roughly proscribed by the entire community as a "bullionist" and "the poor man's enemy." No such intolerance of opinion had been experienced since "the old anti-slavery days," when his father had stood unsupported in a town in New York state in opposition to slavery.[2] In some states, where enough men of sound views were at hand, they formed themselves into "Honest Money Leagues."[3]

Both parties in Ohio held their conventions while the strike was in progress. The Democrats wanted, they said in their platform, no contraction and no resumption. Greenbacks and gold and silver were to be equal as legal tenders and interconvertible. The Republicans followed. They were in favor "of both silver and gold as money," and "the remonetization of silver." Thoroughly scared they resolved to say nothing about resumption.

The Republicans nominated a man named West. Seeking the votes of the strikers and their sympathizers, he boasted that, in his youth, he had blown the bellows and wielded the sledge. He was not a railroad officer, he owned no railroad bonds or stocks, no government bonds or bank stocks—he never had done so and never would do so. He unfolded plans for giving wages to labor sufficient for the "sustenance of the laborer." Railroad companies must be prohibited from reducing their rates "by ruinous competition" to such a degree "as to disable themselves from paying a just compensation to their operators." There should be a "minimum of prices" for labor. The eager candidate developed a profit

[1] Issue of Nov. 1, 1877.
[2] N. Y. Nation, Feb. 7, 1878.
[3] Ibid.; Sherman's Recollections, p. 646; Smith, Life of Garfield, p. 672; Diary and Letters of Hayes, vol. iii, p. 508.

sharing plan. Employers, after an audit of their accounts, at the end of the year should divide the gain with their men.[1]

Stanley Matthews, earlier a respected figure, was not better than West, with whom he vied in demagogic declarations in a quest for popular acclamation. At political meetings he would hold up a silver dollar for the crowd to see; he would coin, he said, as many of these dollars as might be necessary, with the aid of gold and greenbacks, "to oil the machinery" of business, so that every man should be "busy in keeping up with the wheels of industry."[2] Sherman entered the canvass in a speech marked by equivocal statements, evasions and silences.[3]

The Republican party was defeated, as it deserved to be, on such a platform, under the leadership of candidates who thus fell over their enemies in their haste to surrender their principles. Stanley Matthews was succeeded as a United States senator by Pendleton, whom all knew for what he was on the money question, Matthews being saved to the public service by Hayes, who appointed him a justice of the Supreme Court.

While the price of silver was falling in 1876 until 420 grains Troy, the amount contained in the "trade dollar," was worth less than a paper dollar, that coin had come into circulation in our currency, on which account Congress, on July 31, 1876, by joint resolution authorizing an additional issue of fractional silver, declared the "trade dollar" not thereafter to be a legal tender and instructed the Secretary of the Treasury, at his discretion, to limit the mintage of it to a quantity sufficient to meet the foreign demand.[4] When the price of silver rose in London, because of a renewal of purchases for India and China, the excitement abated—silver offered the cheap money men less advantage than they had anticipated, and their enthusiasm for bimetallism waned.[5]

[1] N. Y. Nation, Aug. 9, 16, 23, Oct. 18, 1877, June 27, July 18, 1878.
[2] Ibid., Aug. 9, 1877.
[3] Ibid., Oct. 18, 1877.
[4] Report of Sec. of Treas. for 1877, p. xx; Cong. Record, 44th Cong. 1st sess., pp. 4458, 4553, 4565, 5028.
[5] N. Y. Nation, Dec. 14, 1876. In February, 1877, the "trade dollar" was worth 97⅝ and the greenback 94 cents in gold.—Ibid., Feb. 1, 1877.

But quiet was short-lived. So much silver was being presented at the mints in the early months of the Hayes administration, since the profit accruing to the owners of bullion continued to be large, and so much came into circulation that Sherman, in October, 1877, when some $30,000,000 had been issued, directed, as it was his right and duty to do, that no more be received for manufacture into this coin until an export demand for it should again arise.[1]

The Silver Commission had been the device of the last Congress for ridding itself of the money question. As members Senator Jones of Nevada, silver miner and representative of "silver kings," Bogy, a senator from Missouri, and an inflationist, and Boutwell of Massachusetts, without insight into financial questions, as his career as Secretary of the Treasury gave proof, had been appointed on the part of the Senate; Bland, George Willard, a newspaper editor in Battle Creek, Mich., whose voice had been raised for inflation, and Randall L. Gibson, an intelligent Democrat who had just reached Congress from Louisiana, on the part of the House of Representatives,[2] while as "experts," after advances had been made to some who would not serve,[3] William S. Groesbeck of Ohio and Francis Bowen of Massachusetts were named.

The sessions began in New York and continued in Washington. Circulars were sent out to individuals and bodies of men in the United States and in foreign countries in search of light on the great subject under discussion. A mass of material—correspondence, essays, reports and transcribed oral testimony—was accumulated and considered worthy of publication at the expense of the government.[4]

Though a summary of the conclusions of the commissioners had been given out in March, the occasion of the meeting of Congress in its special session, made necessary for want of

[1] Sherman's Recollections, pp. 613–4.
[2] Cf. N. Y. Nation, Sep. 14, 1876.
[3] Ibid., Oct. 19, 1876.
[4] It had reached Congress and was ordered to be printed on March 21, 1877. Cong. Record, 44th Cong. 2nd sess., p. 2125; N. Y. Nation, March 8, 1877; cf. ibid., Nov. 1, 1877.

an appropriation by the last Congress for the support of the army, and which Hayes, upon coming to office, had delayed convening until October, 1877, was chosen for the publication of the document. Jones of Nevada, perfectly voicing the aspirations of the owners of the silver mines, Bogy, Bland, Groesbeck and Willard presented the majority report in favor of the unrestricted coinage of silver. Jones, Bogy and Willard proposed that the ratio be 15½ to 1, the relation established by the Latin Union, though by the fall of the price of the metal in July, 1876, it had actually been 20 to 1.[1] Mr. Groesbeck's course had several times earned him the respect of his countrymen, but he was patently without instruction on the money question. He dissented from the opinion of his associates only to the extent of urging that the relation of weight in coinage should be 15.98 to 1, as in the old silver dollar,[2] on which point Bland seemed to be in concurrence with him.[3]

Here were five of the eight members of the commission who favored and advocated "free coinage." There was, they said, "a shrinking volume of money," to which all the economic troubles of the country, since the panic, were to be ascribed. Three million men who were willing to work were idle.[4] This "vast poverty stricken army," though unemployed, must live somehow; should the cost of their support be reckoned at only one dollar a day the whole would be enough in two years to discharge the national debt.[5] The depression of business, instead of diminishing, would become "more deathly"; the number of idle laborers would "indefinitely multiply"; money would still "rise in value" and prices would continue to fall, if "the policy of chaining the industry and commerce of the world to a single metal" should be persisted in.[6] Such gammon was uttered in spite of the fact, as was daily said and as might have been clearly enough perceived, that the country was not then on a gold basis and, since the adoption of the legal tender acts during the war, had not, except in

[1] Report of Silver Commission, p. 139.
[2] Ibid., p. 131.
[3] Ibid., p. 133.
[4] Ibid., pp. 55, 121.
[5] Ibid., pp. 58-9.
[6] Ibid.

California, used this standard of value. All domestic exchange
was conducted on a paper money basis, as it would continue
to be, until January 1, 1879, and, perhaps, for a longer time,
if such influences were to direct the course of the government
on the money question.[1] So much was said also in spite of
the patent fact that commerce and industry were undergoing
a marked revival, as every intelligent observer might see.[2]

Boutwell from Massachusetts, in some degree controlled
by good opinion, fearful of the result to him personally of his
joining the "bimetallists," took refuge in the suggestion of
an international conference, an agreement among the countries, before we should commit ourselves to the policy.[3] The
out and out "free coinage" men would have silver money in
spite of the rest of the world. Ignorant of international exchange, indeed of any of the rudimentary principles of political economy and finance, they pretended to believe that the
mere fiat of the Congress of the United States would give
whatever value was desired to silver currency. A chance phrase
of Stanley Matthews in debate in the Senate "What have we
got to do with abroad?"[4] was made to be expressive for a
generation, somewhat to their discomfiture at times, of the
attitude of mind of the silver fanatics, as well as of that body
of kindred reasoners in political philosophy, the high tariff
men, soon to appear in power upon the scene. Only Professor
Bowen, who had once been the editor of the North American
Review, for years a professor in Harvard University, a New
England scholar of judgments made ripe by reading, travel
and correct reflection,[5] evidenced a sound understanding and
presented valuable views about the matter under consideration.

[1] Report of Silver Commission, p. 121.
[2] Ibid. We were "on the threshold of a new industrial era," said Senator
Dawes. We were developing our vast national resources, and our manufacturers were so far advanced that they were "turning to foreign markets
for relief."—Cong. Record, 45th Cong., 2nd sess., p. 646.
[3] An international conference was proposed by the Finance Committee
of the Senate in January, 1877.—N. Y. Nation, Jan. 25, 1877.
[4] Cong. Record, 45th Cong. 2nd sess., p. 91.
[5] The "only man" on the commission "whose mind entitled him to be
there or made his conclusions of any consequence."—N. Y. Nation, Nov. 8,
1877.

He was supported by Mr. Gibson. With the use of both metals they foresaw very well that gold would be driven out of circulation by a cheaper currency. Silver, they said, in their minority report, had become "entirely unfit for use as a standard of value," as was proven by the course regarding it recently taken by enlightened European governments. The "so called double standard" was "an illusion and an impossibility." Silver was required in any monetary system only as a subsidiary or token currency.[1]

The special session was certain to be full of rebellion. The hostility of the Stalwarts to the President because of his course regarding the civil service and his withdrawal of the troops from the South left him practically without a party. The great electoral dispute in the winter of 1876–77 had not prevented Bland from pursuing his free coinage bill, and it was passed by the House, after brief debate, on December 13, 1876.[2] It went no farther.[3] Now, at the special session, action was to be definite and prompt. A score of bills for the repeal of the resumption law of 1875 and for the remonetization of silver instantly appeared in the House and the Senate. The political campaigns were in progress and many of the members, as they rose in their places in Congress, thought themselves on the stump in the Western states. For many months now bankers, business men of sagacity, men who controlled capital and employed labor had been denounced as "wreckers," "bloated bondholders," "robber capitalists" and "money sharks." Those who stood on solid ground and defended correct principles of finance were "agents of the money sharks," of the "money kings," whose "silvern and golden slippers" muffled the steps of dangerous figures, seen in fancy in the lobbies and halls of the Capitol.[4] The people were "to dance to the caprice of Shylocks."[5] The workingman had been re-

[1] Report of Silver Commission, pp. 159–60.
[2] By a vote of 167 to 53.—Cong. Record, 44th Cong. 1st sess., p. 172.
[3] N. Y. Nation, Jan. 25, 1877.
[4] Bland in Cong. Record, 44th Cong. 1st sess., p. 5235; cf. ibid., 45th Cong. 1st sess., p. 626.
[5] Ibid., 44th Cong. 1st sess., p. 4554.

.duced to "beggary and want" because of a contraction of
the currency; a great mining interest was being destroyed for
the advantage of "gold gamblers and bondholders." [1] The
"distress of the country" was "beyond all historical compari-
soh." It would require "but a few more turns of the wheel
to submerge the majority of the body of the people into hopeless bankruptcy." [2] Whoever would deny silver its place as
money, and thus restrict the money supply, was an enemy of
"the toiling millions," who were "earning their bread in the
sweat of their face." [3]

The "people" pleaded for mercy. If it were not granted
them they would gain it by other means. The "pulpy worm"
would turn upon the foot which pressed it. Men in the rich
Eastern cities who were "dreaming of an empire," with them-
oolvos as its "moneyed aristocracy," could remember that
republics turned not into empires "except through a baptism
of blood." [4] Some of the editors of newspapers who had proven
themselves wise mentors on the subject of irredeemable paper
had succumbed to this new craze. The Chicago Tribune,
now returned to Medill's unsettled direction, and the Cincinnati Commercial, where Murat Halstead's want of fundamental instruction served him ill, though both had seen the
greenback in its true light, lent their columns to the propagation of the fallacy. [5]

No time was to be lost in the House on the subject of silver.
The rules were suspended, thus cutting off debate of the bill,
and in a few minutes, on November 5, 1877, on an issue between what Garfield said was, on the one hand, "public honor,
and, on the other, the deepest public disgrace," [6] the lower
branch of our national legislative assembly chose the evil al-

[1] Cong. Record, 44th Cong. 2nd sess., pp. 165-6.
[2] Ibid., p. 91.
[3] Bland in Cong. Record, 44th Cong. 1st sess., p. 5235.
[4] Cong. Record, 45th Cong. 1st sess., pp. 280-81.
[5] N. Y. Nation, Aug. 10, 1876, Nov. 22, 29, Dec. 20, 1877, Jan. 3, 1878;
Williams, Life of Hayes, vol. ii, pp. 122-3.
[6] On July 13, 1876—Cong. Record, 44th Cong. 1st sess., p. 4560. He had
never known a scheme that "contained so many of the essential elements
of vast rascality, of colossal swindling as this."—Ibid., p. 4561.

ternative by a vote of 163 to 34,[1] authorized, for any owner
of bullion who would present it at the door of any United States
mint, the free coinage of a silver dollar of 412½ grains Troy,
the weight of the old silver dollar of 1837, worth now for a
year past not more than 90 or 92 cents in gold, and made the
coin legal tender without restriction of any kind. Silver, by
order of Congress, was to be given a place in the monetary
system of the country equal to that of gold. This done, the
House instantly again suspended the rules and, by vote of
143 to 47, passed a resolution to proceed, on an early subsequent day, to the repeal of the resumption act.[2]

But men of sense, Garfield, S. B. Chittenden and Abram S.
Hewitt among them, were first to be heard in debate. Attempted
resumption, Mr. Chittenden said, was no more responsible
for the prostrated enterprise of the past four years and the
present sufferings of the people than for the frozen feet of the
Turks in the Shipka Pass.[3] The repeal of the law was a scheme,
he declared, for "downright repudiation." The greenback was
"the most powerful enemy" the country had ever encountered,
"slavery only excepted." The "legal tender" note was not
money but a "device"; it was a "fraud" and a "sham."
Should the "credit and honor and integrity of the United
States" be "sacrificed in the presence of all mankind and sunk
into a bottomless pit of disgrace?" That was the question
which Congress must answer.[4] Abram S. Hewitt said that
movable capital would "quit the country" if the silver and
anti-resumption bills were passed. Values would fall, creditors would take "the remnants of their fortunes and go to some
clime where property is respected and plighted faith is kept."[5]
Garfield spoke with singular effect. We were bound to resume
specie payments, he said, for "three great reasons"—the sanc-
tity of the public faith required it; the material prosperity

[1] Cong. Record, 45th Cong. 1st sess., p. 241; N. Y. Nation, Nov. 8, 1877.
[2] Cong. Record, 45th Cong. 1st sess., p. 242; N. Y. Nation, Nov. 8 and
29, 1877.
[3] Cong. Record, 45th Cong. 1st sess., p. 382.
[4] Ibid., pp. 382, 383, 384, 405.
[5] Ibid., p. 495.

of the country demanded it; future prosperity was conditioned
on a cessation of the agitation—a safe and permanent basis
must be found for financial peace.[1] It was November 23rd
when the House, though somewhat cooled for its task by such
plain speech, voted to repeal the resumption law.[2]

The effect was instantaneously disastrous to the operations
which Sherman had in hand and to the hopes of all intelligent
Americans. August Belmont, at the head of the syndicate
of bankers which was selling the four per cent bonds, at once
wrote, saying that "to remonetize silver upon the old standard and make it a legal tender" would be considered by "the
whole civilized world as an act of repudiation" on the part
of the government. It would "cast a stain upon our national
credit." It was a "blind and dishonest frenzy" which had
taken hold of Congress. The quoted price of "fours" in the
market had fallen to 98¾. The negotiation must be abandoned.[3]
No one in Europe or America would buy a bond at par in
gold in view of the overwhelming vote in the House, and the
assurance which it betokened of the enactment of the silver
bill into law.[4] The Senate, where there were some sound heads
and stout hearts, was to be heard from, indeed, and the President; but the unsettlement of mind of the members of one
house was nearly equal to that of the members of the other,
and a veto of the President, in the state of public sentiment
and party organization, it was predicted, would quite certainly
be overridden.

Secretary Sherman's first report and the President's message
when Congress met in its regular session in December, 1877,
were firm in tone. Though wrath and indignation came to
expression in the West, in newspaper and at public meeting,
the valuable and respected part of the press in the East supported Hayes; the heads of banks, trust companies and mer-

[1] Cong. Record, 45th Cong. 1st sess., p. 465. Garfield's speech against
the bill, said the New York Nation, "showed him to be a debater of uncommon powers."—Issue of Nov. 22, 1877; cf. T. C. Smith, Life of Garfield, pp. 660–61; C. S. Olcott, Wm. McKinley, vol. i, p. 199.

[2] By a vote of 133 to 120—Cong. Record, 45th Cong. 1st sess., pp. 632–3.

[3] Sherman's Recollections, pp. 604–5.

[4] Ibid., p. 607.

cantile business in New York, Boston, Philadelphia, Baltimore, New Orleans met and passed resolutions; delegations
of them visited Washington to present their views in protest
against legislation so injurious and demoralizing.[1]

The crystallization of opinion was proceeding slowly.   In
the Senate, Morrill of Vermont called it "a fearful assault
upon the public credit," [2] Dawes of Massachusetts "a blot
upon our honor" as a nation.   Here was inflation, said Dawes,
in its "most insidious and dangerous form." [3]   Lamar of Mississippi, who acted in disregard of definite instructions from
the legislature of his state,[4] maintaining his right to exercise
and express his individual judgments,[5] and Bayard of Delaware
spoke in similar tones—they gave proof to the country that
good sense and bravery, in the face of popular storm, had not
departed from all of the leaders of the Democratic party.
Sherman wrote to Allison of Iowa, who was chairman of the
Finance Committee of the Senate, a position which the Secretary of the Treasury had so lately vacated.   Allison's state
was in the "infected area"—his principles on this subject
were lightly held—he was earnestly implored to avert the
impending calamity.[6]   The plea was heard; the issue would
be compromised; the bill was amended, and it was finally
passed in the Senate, after an all night session, on February 15,
1878, by a vote of 48 to 21.   Dawes and Hoar, Edmunds and
Morrill, Bayard and Lamar, Blaine [7] and Conkling voted
against the bill.[8]   Instead of free coinage it was agreed that
not less than $2,000,000, nor more than $4,000,000 of silver

[1] N. Y. Nation, Jan. 10 and 17, 1878; Sherman's Recollections, p. 606.
[2] Cong. Record, 45th Cong. 2nd sess., p. 607.
[3] Ibid., pp. 644, 645.
[4] Sess. Laws of Miss. for 1878, p. 250.
[5] In which he "honored himself and the South."—N. Y. Nation, Jan. 31,
1878; cf. ibid., Feb. 21, 1878; Cong. Record, 45th Cong. 2nd sess., p. 1062;
Mayes, Life of Lamar, pp. 330–48; Hoar, Autobiography of Seventy Years,
vol. ii, pp. 176–7.
[6] Sherman's Recollections, pp. 620–21.
[7] After having tried to follow a temporizing course in order to win favor,
if he could, with the silver men.—Cf. N. Y. Nation, Jan. 31 and Feb. 14,
1878.
[8] Cong. Record, 45th Cong. 2nd sess., p. 1112.

should be purchased for coinage monthly. "Silver certificates" were to be issued against silver coin deposited in the Treasury of the United States to take their place in the country's paper currency, and to be the equal of coin in the payment of customs and other public dues. The President was authorized to appoint three men, at $2,500 each and their expenses, to attend an international conference of representatives of countries composing the "Latin Union" and other European nations to be convoked in the interest of bimetallism.

The fanatical group in the House to which the bill was returned made a great ado about the mutilation of their free silver scheme. The amendments must be accepted, said Bland, as "one step in the right direction." But he vowed angrily "here and now" that his war would never cease, so long as he had a voice in Congress, until the rights of the people were fully restored and the silver dollar should take its place alongside of the gold dollar. If he should fail, then, said he, amid applause, he would be in favor of issuing enough paper money "to stuff down the bondholders until they were sick."[1] Garfield and others in the small band of sound money men in the House made an attempt to lay the bill upon the table, but ineffectually,[2] for, on February 21, 1878, the House concurred in the Senate amendments and the bill went to the President. There was reason to believe that Hayes would veto it,[3] though public opinion for it was organized and brought to bear upon him through party leaders and the newspapers.[4] Men full of sound and fury visited him.[5] There were influences at work around him which would have shaken a feeble man. Some of his friends, Stanley Matthews among them, had completely lost their intellectual bearings on this great matter. Matthews

[1] Cong. Record, 45th Cong. 2nd sess., pp. 1250–51.
[2] The vote on this proposal was 71 to 205. (Ibid., p. 1283.) Garfield stood alone in the Ohio delegation and almost alone among the members in the House from the Mississippi Valley.—T. C. Smith, Life of J. A. Garfield, p. 663.
[3] Cf. Diary and Letters of Hayes, vol. iii, p. 459.
[4] Ibid., pp. 465–6.
[5] Williams, Life of Hayes, vol. ii, pp. 122–3.

was for paying the national debt in silver.[1] The legislature of Ohio had demanded "the restoration of the silver dollar to its former rank as lawful money,"[2] and "instructed" its senators and "requested" its representatives in Congress to vote for free coinage.[3] The recent campaign had revealed the temper of the population in the President's own state. But he was never in doubt. He would veto the bill. He had "no misgiving," he wrote in his Diary. The nation "must not have a stain on its honor"; its credit must not be "tainted." The "first and great objection" to the scheme he found to be the fact that it was "a violation of the national faith."[4] Gold would be expelled from the country in the presence of depreciated silver.[5] The bill must be disapproved because it authorized what was "dishonest."[6] It was "sound currency" on one side and inflation, irredeemable paper, "cabbage leaves," on the other.[7] The question involved, and facing him, transcended "all questions of profit and of public advantage." If silver dollars were to be issued they must be of full value, "which would defraud no man."[8]

The President prepared his message and read it to the cabinet. Mr. Thompson, who had been appointed Secretary of the Navy to satisfy Senator Morton of Indiana, was, like his sponsor, an advocate of cheap money. All the others led Hayes to think that they were in accord with him in his resolve to disapprove the measure, though Secretary McCrary of Iowa wavered and, under direction, less firm than the President's, would have been found on the other side.[9] The President inferred that his Secretary of the Treasury was opposed to the approval of the measure,[10] but Sherman's sincerity was

[1] See his concurrent resolution—Cong. Record, 45th Cong. 2nd sess., p. 47.
[2] Sess. Laws of Ohio for 1877, pp. 537–8.
[3] Cong. Record, 45th Cong. 2nd sess., p. 1062.
[4] Diary and Letters of Hayes, vol. iii, p. 440.
[5] Ibid., p. 459.
[6] Ibid., p. 462.
[7] Ibid., p. 466.
[8] Richardson, vol. vii, pp. 486–8.
[9] Diary and Letters of Hayes, vol. iii, p. 461.
[10] Ibid.

brought into question again, as it had been before, when he must choose between what he knew to be right and the favor of the people, particularly in the state of Ohio, at this particular hour. His knowledge of fiscal subjects was very considerable, but in a crisis his personal ambitions made havoc of his courage. If he were ever to be President—a vision constantly before his eyes—he must, he believed, cringe and temporize, which was one of the reasons, perhaps, if he could have known it, that no greater honors than were his would be conferred upon him by his countrymen. When he wrote Allison about the silver bill it was but in behalf of its amendment. It should be modified because it arrested "funding and resumption operations," and in doing this it would damage the administration and "our party." He was "as much in favor of the silver dollar as any one." He said nothing of right or principle, and, when the bill was changed, allowing limited purchases of silver bullion, his objections were answered, and he was ready to declare now, outside of the cabinet room, if not in it, and afterward, that he was in disagreement with Hayes and would have had the President sign the measure.[1]

Hayes forwarded his veto on the last day of February. His "manly and courageous"[2] protest deserved to be heard, but Congress hurried to the task of repassing the bill the same day his message was received,[3]—in the House by a vote of 196 to 73,[4] in the Senate by a vote of 46 to 19,[5] — and thus it became a law.

The bill to repeal the resumption act was still to claim the attention of the Senate, and the paper money men and their silver allies in the House viewed its progress impatiently. Having gained their ends, at least partially, in the enactment of the

---

[1] Sherman's Recollections, p. 623. The law had "satisfied a strong public demand for bimetallic money and in a government like ours it is always well to obey popular current," he said to the Senate Committee on Finance on March 19, 1878. See N. Y. Nation, March 28, 1878; cf. A. D. Noyes, Forty Years of American Finance, pp. 41–2.

[2] N. Y. Nation, March 7, 1878.

[3] February 28, 1878.

[4] Cong. Record, 45th Cong. 2nd sess., p. 1420.

[5] Ibid., pp. 1410–11.

Bland bill and having set the mints at work coining what were
very appropriately and generally called "Bland dollars" which,
jingling like tinware in, and straining at, the pockets of all
who would receive this new money from the banks, most un-
pleasurably impressed the people,[1] the inflationists returned
to their old scheme of paying the national debt in greenbacks.
They had not mustered as much strength in the House in
November for the repeal of the resumption law as they had
reckoned on. Public sentiment was gathering strength and
it was not so clear, even in minds which were in great unsettlement, that the slowly developing plans for resumption should
now be summarily abandoned.

Sherman's dalliance with all the factions in his party and
his evasive and pliant nature as a public man stood him now,
it is likely, in good stead,[2] for he approached leaders, both
Democratic and Republican, in the House and the Senate,
where his acquaintance was large, and stated what were his
objects in reference to resumption and how they were to be
attained. He, aided by others, won over, or at any rate allayed
the hostility of, men of great influence. By repeated and
prolonged conferences, conversations and explanations privately given and in testimony in committee rooms,[3] where
he continued to play the part of Mr. Facing-both-ways on
the silver question,[4] the cause was advanced to such a point
that the determination to throw all again into confusion and
put the date for resumption forward to some indefinite time
lost many friends.[5] The scheme for repeal was defeated in the
Senate Finance Committee by a majority of one,[6] a result, in
some degree, acquiesced in by the inflationists because of a conviction still held by many of them that, anyhow, the end in view
could not be attained.

[1] "Cart wheels" to the people who, accustomed only to paper money
looked with little favor on the prospect of carrying about such currency.
[2] N. Y. Nation, March 28, 1878.
[3] Cf. House Mis. Doc., 45th Cong. 2nd sess., no. 48.
[4] Cf. N. Y. Nation, March 28, and April 4 and 11, 1878.
[5] Sherman's Recollections, pp. 629-35-646-8.
[6] Ibid., pp. 646-7.

The repeal of the resumption law, like free coinage, was to be the subject of a compromise—the principal feature of the plan being a proposal which it was believed might satisfy the prejudices of the greenbackers and the silver men in regard to "contraction" and "making money scarce." It was a "frightful abyss of ruin" which impended if the country should not turn back on its path, said Senator Maxey of Texas.[1] Voorhees of Indiana found that within a few years the East had placed $300,000,000 in mortgages on Western farms.[2] Everywhere was heard the "cry of the sheriff's sale," everywhere was seen the "flag of the auctioneer." The repeal of the resumption act was necessary "for the benefit of prostrate business and destitute labor."[3] The rich, "while preaching economy to the industrial classes," sat down each day to banquets "such as Dives presided over when Lazarus lay at his gates begging for bread." The whole "heavens" were black. One form of slavery had been swept from American soil, but another was seen in its place.[4] Nothing since the advent of peace at Appomattox would be "hailed with such joy" as would "ring through the land," from the Atlantic to the Pacific, on the day of the repeal of this "pernicious law—the deadly upas tree of American legislation."[5]

With such commotion in the public mind the Finance Committee sought and found its *pis aller*. On April 17th, in reporting the House bill for the repeal of the resumption law it developed a plan for the receipt at once of greenbacks in payment of the four per cent bonds which Sherman was offering for sale in gold, and for the acceptance of greenbacks for customs dues after October 1, 1878, thus entirely depriving the Treasury on that date of its coin revenues. He would be compelled, furthermore, to bring to an end the operation in which he was engaged, under the terms of the resumption act, of canceling the greenbacks. The amount outstanding on October 1st should be reissued and kept in circulation and no more

[1] Cong. Record, 45th Cong. 2nd sess., p. 3466.   [4] Ibid., p. 3086.
[2] Ibid., p. 3085.   [5] Ibid., p. 2087.
[3] Ibid., p. 3087.

should be retired.[1] The bill made progress through the Senate but slowly and, when it was passed finally, on June 13, 1878,[2] its form had been greatly altered and it was too late to secure concurrence, so it fell by the way.[3] Anyhow interest in it by this time had diminished, since the House had passed a bill, sponsored by a representative from Illinois, under suspension of the rules, commanding the Secretary of the Treasury to put an immediate stop to the work of retiring "legal tenders." [4] This measure was approved by the Senate on May 28th, by a vote of 41 to 18,[5] to be signed by President Hayes, to the regret of many of his friends,[6] following the advice of Sherman.[7]

Once again the work of retiring the greenbacks, always interrupted whenever it was begun, came to an end. The progress of the scheme was resisted by the small body of sound money men in Congress, including Morrill, Dawes and Bayard in the Senate and Garfield and Hewitt in the House. The measure was condemned unreservedly in the intelligent press as one of the gravest of errors.[8] But whether the operation should cease or not was a matter of less importance than it had been, in view of the fact that the Bland silver dollars were now issuing from the mints by the million each month. That there was no popular demand for such money, that it would gain no circulation except in a few rural districts was everywhere remarked. Even in obscure hamlets it was not liked and the anomalous sight was witnessed of the grocer or the butcher refusing, since he could not deposit it in bank, a "trade dollar," which contained 420 grains of silver, when he must

---

[1] Cong. Record, 45th Cong. 2nd sess., p. 2599.
[2] Ibid., p. 4549.
[3] For summary of votes see McPherson's Handbook for 1878, pp. 143-9.
[4] By a vote of 177 to 35.—Cong. Record, 45th Cong. 2nd sess., pp. 2928-9.
[5] Ibid., p. 3871; cf. McPherson for 1878, pp. 149-50.
[6] N. Y. Nation, June 6, 1878.
[7] Williams, Life of Hayes, vol. ii, p. 130; cf. ibid., p. 140; Cong. Record, 45th Cong. 2nd sess., p. 4039. That Hayes himself sincerely wished to bring about the retirement of the greenbacks is clear from his next ensuing annual message of December 1, 1879. (Richardson, vol. vii, p. 559.) Sherman on the other hand, pretended to the end that this paper was a good form of currency.—Recollections, vol. vii, p. 559.
[8] Cf. N. Y. Nation, May 30, 1878.

accept the "Bland dollar" of only 412½ grains.[1] All the silver which the government put out at once returned to the Treasury where it rapidly accumulated. One hundred thousand dollars released by Secretary Sherman in New York were again, the next day, in the vaults of the government. Being available, like gold, for the payment of customs dues, silver, after serving this purpose, resumed its place in the Treasury.[2] The idea that a liking for silver coin would be displayed, either because of a sentimental interest in the double standard, or as a patriotic duty, was exploded in the first days of the experiment.[3] Though efforts to distribute the Bland dollars continued[4] these were vain until Sherman withdrew many millions of one dollar bills from circulation and thus created a void which coin must fill.[5]

In 1878 the country was again in the midst of campaigns in all the states for the election of representatives in Congress—in some for the choice of governors, and legislatures which would elect United States senators. The money question was again a leading issue in the East as well as in the West. On Washington's Birthday, 1878, the Labor Reform party, stronger in the East, and the Greenback party which had been developing in the West with similar aims, although they had been acting separately, came together in a conference in Toledo. Some 800 delegates from 28 states were in attendance.[6] They resolved to call the United Greenback Labor party the National party and all of the ills of society they ascribed to the resumption law, the national banking law, the demonetization of silver, the retirement of the greenbacks and the payment of the public debt in gold. These things were "crimes against the people."[7] In many states the Greenbackers put tickets in the field, their

[1] Cf. N. Y. Nation, Aug. 22, 29, Sep. 19, 1878.
[2] Cong. Record, 45th Cong. 2nd sess., p. 3868; cf. N. Y. Nation, May 30, 1878.
[3] N. Y. Nation, July 11, 1878; cf. Davis R. Dewey, Financial History of the U. S., p. 408.
[4] N. Y. Nation, Sep. 12 and 19, 1878.
[5] Ibid., Nov. 7, 1878.
[6] Haynes, Third Party Movements, chap. x.
[7] McPherson's Handbook for 1878, pp. 167–8.

candidate for governor in Massachusetts being Benjamin F.
Butler, who at last, failing of the preferment which he had
coveted at the hands of the Republicans, captured the Democratic nominating convention [1] and, with the indorsement of
the Greenbackers, organized the ignorant parts of the electorate for his uses. In the main, their platform of principles
was that all debts, public and private, should be paid with
paper and that this paper should not be paid with anything.[2]
Men in the West broke up mowing and reaping machines
which, it was said, threw farm hands out of work. Barns and
haystacks of farmers who used such machinery were burned.[3]
A demagogue leading a rabble spoke from the steps of public
buildings in Washington and went about counseling laborers
who were receiving less than $1.50 a day to quit work.[4] A mass
meeting of workingmen in Nashville, Tenn., demanded the issue
of ten millions of greenbacks monthly until popular distress
should be relieved. A member of Congress actually advocated
the digging of a ship canal from New York to San Francisco to
employ idle laborers—then the printing press should be set in
motion to make the money with which to pay their wages.[5]

In the election in Maine in September the Greenbackers
disclosed an alarming strength. The state convention of the
party had brought forward as its chairman a picturesque yokel
named Solon Chase. Things had come to such a pass that
"the farmer's grass grows backwards," said this wiseacre.
"Inflate the currency," he observed, "and·you raise the price
of my steers,[6] and, at the same time, pay the public debt."
He declared that the Greenbackers were going "to throw a
vote" in Maine that would "strike both parties like a stroke
of chain lightning." [7] Their strength was surprising. No
candidate for governor was elected and the choice devolved

[1] N. Y. Nation, Sep. 9, 1878.
[2] Ibid., Aug. 1, 1878.
[3] Ibid., July 11, 1878.
[4] Ibid., Sep. 26, 1878.
[5] Cong. Record, 45th Cong. 1st sess., pp. 625–6.
[6] The newspapers made "them steers" famous.—Haynes, Third Party
Movements, p. 128.
[7] App. Ann. Cyclop. for 1878, p. 514.

upon the legislature. In the interest of party success at the October and November elections President Hayes visited the West and Northwest where he was warmly welcomed, speaking in unmistakable tones for sound money.[1] Sherman and Garfield appeared on a number of platforms. Butler in Massachusetts, whom Hayes denominated "the most dangerous and wicked demagogue we have ever had,"[2] sustained defeat. The results generally were such as to give satisfaction to the friends of "honest money," though the Greenbackers and their Labor Reform allies polled in the various state campaigns upwards of a million votes, a number greatly in excess of their record in any earlier or subsequent years.[3] They elected fifteen members of Congress.[4] It was a verdict, President Hayes declared, in favor of resumption and of "a currency equal to gold."[5] It changed "the face of the political sky," said Garfield.[6] If this were so, the Democrats, nevertheless, remained in control of the House and for the first time since the war gained a commanding majority in the Senate.

The preparations for resumption were checked—that they could proceed at all was subject for surprise. The contract with the syndicate for the sale of four per cent refunding bonds was terminated.[7] It remained Sherman's task to bring gold into the Treasury. After the policy of Congress was defined, with the return of some settlement of the public mind, he was enabled again to face his responsibilities. He visited New York and called representative leaders of that financial center to him for conference. He met Belmont, Seligman, the men who had learned their lessons with the house of Jay Cooke and Company, now connected with the First National Bank,

[1] Diary and Letters of Hayes, vol. iii, pp. 500–01, 508; Williams, Life of Hayes, vol. ii, pp. 255–262.

[2] Diary and Letters of Hayes, vol. iii, p. 508.

[3] Haynes, Third Party Movements, pp. 124–5; cf. App. Ann. Cyclop. for 1878, p. 808.

[4] McPherson's Handbook for 1880, p. 98. Haynes says fourteen.—Third Party Movements, p. 131.

[5] Diary and Letters of Hayes, vol. iii, p. 509.

[6] Smith, Life of Garfield, p. 671.

[7] Sherman's Recollections, p. 627.

and others who had been active in the international syndicate, the operations of which had broken down during the excitement created by the appearance in Congress of the Bland bill; also a group of presidents of national banks who represented domestic financial interests. It was agreed that no more need now be said about four per cent bonds, and the discussion turned to four and a halfs. Sherman required $50,000,000 in gold to make his position safe for the work of January 1, 1879, when the government was to begin to pay out specie for greenbacks. Both the foreign and the New York bankers made proposals. It was on April 11, 1878, that Sherman entered into an agreement with the international syndicate—the Rothschilds, the Morgans, the Seligmans, the Morton firms and the First National Bank and their associates—their proposal being the most advantageous, for the sale of the four and a half per cent bonds at 101½ in gold for a commission of one-half of one per cent, $10,000,000 at once, and at least $5,000,000 monthly through the rest of the year, thus assuring him of the necessary resources for resumption with the advent of 1879.[1]

The interruption of the work of retiring the greenbacks had left in circulation $346,000,000 of these notes. Since the coin reserve in the Treasury under the law must be 40 per cent of the amount of such paper money outstanding, which it was expected would have been reduced to $300,000,000, it would be necessary now for Sherman to increase his reserve in coin from $120,000,000 to $138,000,000, which added to his perplexities.[2] As the year advanced and the date for resumption drew near the leaders in the money markets of the country, as well as the theorists, watched the situation closely. The press was filled with speculation and prediction, much of it reflecting little confidence in the outcome, though the Secretary of the Treasury betrayed no solicitude and spoke, when he did speak, with the greatest assurance of a successful result.[3] The banks in New York pledged the government

[1] Sherman's Recollections, pp. 640–45.
[2] Report of Sec. of Treas. for December, 1878.
[3] Sherman's Recollections, pp. 670, 699.

their good offices and facilitated the movement. Conditions in trade and industry continued to improve. The crops in 1877 and 1878 were "enormous." [1] Railroad companies and shipping enterprises prospered. Never since the panic had there been so much healthful activity in business. The revenues of the government were sufficient—more than sufficient—to meet all its expenditures, including the payment of the interest on the public debt.

When the long expected day arrived the premium on gold had become merely nominal. At the end of the year Sherman had in the Treasury more than $140,000,000 of gold coin and bullion and on the 2nd day of January, 1879 (the first was a Sunday), when the greenbacks were presented at the Treasury or the subtreasuries, the holders, at request, were paid in gold, on which account, the knowledge spreading that so much might be had, no one wished to avail himself of the privilege. At the end of the day this message came to Sherman from the subtreasurer in New York—" $135,000 of notes presented for coin, $400,000 of gold for notes." That was all. [2] Succeeding days exhibited a like assurance in the public mind. The receipts of gold for legal tender notes were four or five times as large as the payments of gold for greenbacks. [3] For the first time in 17 years there was no gold market and the Gold Room in New York was converted to other uses. The change had come with no more shock than there is in the transition from night to day. [4]

Paper and gold were at an absolute parity, as was silver also, since this money, in the meantime, had been brought forward to complicate the operation. Though the bullion value of the silver in the silver dollar, when the Bland bill had been passed, was 93¼ cents it had fallen by September,

[1] N. Y. Nation, Sep. 20 and 27, 1877; App. Ann. Cyclop. for 1878, p. 809.
[2] Sherman's Recollections, p. 702. President Hayes wrote in his Diary—"Resumption has gone off well so far. More gold brought in for notes than notes for gold. A great event, if it sticks and I believe it will." (Diary and Letters of Hayes, vol. iii, p. 518.) Why it "stuck" is discussed in A. D. Noyes, Forty Years of American Finance, chap. iii.
[3] N. Y. Nation, Jan. 9 and 16, 1879.
[4] Ibid., Dec. 26, 1878.

1878, to 87, and in October to 83 cents. In December it was about 86 cents. Resumption was an achievement even greater than it had promised to be when the task was begun, for the monthly outpouring of silver coin at the mints must be kept at par with the other two forms of money. The value of the silver dollar, as well as of the greenback, rested upon government guaranty and public faith.

The fiscal and commercial position of the country was such, it appeared, as to enable it to defy, for the present at least, its worst enemies at Washington. Nevertheless it was not the resumption which anyone of correct judgment on financial subjects had had in view. We were well rid of the old state bank notes which had been the paper money of the country before the war and had won the national bank notes, buttressed by government bonds, the resources of the issuing institutions and the credit of the stockholders of these institutions,—a currency which, but for the prejudices of ignorant parts of the population, who unfortunately shared the task of solving a problem calling, and calling only, for the talent of a few trained and competent men, could well have been increased in volume.[1] Whatever had been gained two great wrongs remained in our public fiscal system. One of these was bound up with the United States notes. The greenbacks, based on nothing but a bare promise, we had started out to retire and cancel; we had failed—they, although finally brought to parity with gold, were to remain in circulation, a temptation in the future as in the past to demagogues, as events subsequently gave proof. This evil had been perpetuated when it should have been abolished root and branch. The other weakness was of fresh creation and it rested on the compliance of Congress with the demand of the silver men that the foolish experiment of using two metals as a standard of value should be tried, and that a dollar which was worth from ten to twenty cents less than a gold dollar should be coined and declared to be of similar value. This also pointed straightway to future conspiracies of people and politicians to work fraud on private

[1] Cf. N. Y. Nation, Dec. 12, 1878.

and public creditors. The way was being prepared for many a panic, the ruin of many an honest business, the bankruptcy of many a worthy merchant because of the want of a national wish, or of power in those in responsible places, to face the money question and adopt measures for its definitive settlement.[1]

Men said that the future might take care of itself. Public enterprise had been latent so long, the eagerness for new achievement was so great that the effect upon national and private credit of what was seen was instant. Large subscriptions to the four per cent government bonds, which for a time could not be sold, were made in all parts of the United States and in Europe. The refunding of the public debt proceeded rapidly with great saving in interest. When the operation was completed the bonds advanced in price.[2] Business which had been proceeding so uncertainly for many years felt a sudden impulse and the year 1879 was marked by evidences of prosperity, which had not been witnessed in many years.[3]

The provision contained in the Bland bill for the convocation of an international monetary conference led to correspondence in the State Department.[4] Evarts received favorable replies; the meeting would be held in Paris on August 6, 1878, at the French Ministry of Foreign Affairs, where its precursor, an international conference convened by the French government, had met in 1867.[5] As delegates from this country the President, after trying to find other men who would serve, appointed the leading anti-Conkling figure in New York state, a "weather-beaten politician," ex-Governor Reuben E. Fenton, William S. Groesbeck who had put himself on the side of the silver miners as an "expert" of the Silver Commission of 1876

---

[1] Cf. Horace White, Money and Banking, pp. 204-5.
[2] Sherman's Recollections, chap. xxxvii; N. Y. Nation, Jan. 16, 1879.
[3] Sherman's Recollections, pp. 738-9, 741.
[4] N. Y. Nation, March 21, 1878.
[5] Report in House Ex. Doc., 45th Cong. 3rd sess., no. 1, pt. 7, p. 2. Our delegate to this conference was Samuel B. Ruggles, Hamilton Fish's friend, who had gone to Paris as the commissioner of the United States to the "Universal Exposition" held in that city.—Senate Ex. Doc., 45th Cong. 3rd sess., no. 58, p. 805.

and Francis A. Walker, one of the few competent writers of the country whose theorization inclined him to the advocacy of bimetallism.[1] Leon Say, the French Minister of Finance, presided over the meetings. Most of the countries of Europe, except Germany which declined to participate in so Utopian a discussion,[2] sent representatives, England's delegation including Mr. Goschen, one of her foremost authorities on public finance. It was to Great Britain that our inflationist orators had ascribed the basest motives in imposing gold monometallism upon the world. But it appeared, as a result of this meeting, that the real obstructionists in the way of our silver missionaries were the governments of the Latin Union from which only friendly accord had been expected. The states which "in the past" had "performed this grand service to the world," *i.e.*, promoting the use of silver currency, appeared in the conference of 1878 "with a divided opinion"; it was to the influences emanating from the Latin Union that "the failure of the conference to adopt any positive measures" were "primarily to be referred." [3] Another reason for the failure of the conference, aside from the utter impracticability of giving value to money by fiat, whether national or international, was the well-grounded suspicion that the United States in convoking the meeting was seeking a market for the product of its silver mines.[4] Anyhow all the proposals of our emissaries for a general agreement among states touching the use of the two metals concurrently as a basis for currency were repelled. Since no understanding could be arrived at it was needless to enter into any parleys as to a ratio which might properly subsist between gold and silver for purposes of coinage.[5]

[1] Cf. N. Y. Nation, June 20, 1878.
[2] House Ex. Doc., 45th Cong. 3rd sess., no. 1, pt. 7, pp. 5–6.
[3] Ibid., pp. 2–3.
[4] Ibid., p. 6.
[5] Ibid., p. 10; Journal of the Conference in Senate Ex. Doc., 45th Cong. 3rd sess., no. 58.

CHAPTER XXVI

GARFIELD AND ARTHUR

AFTER Hayes had overthrown the corruptionists who were perpetuating carpetbag rule in the South, had met the issue with Conkling on the subject of the civil service and had played his part, as Congress would allow, in reference to the currency, he was left with two years of his administration for the further development of his policies. The Forty-fifth Congress had been hostile; the Forty-sixth would be as much out of sympathy with his purposes. In addition to the opposition of the enemies within his own party he would have to reckon with Democratic majorities in both houses, which would render difficult any movement that he should inaugurate. To make his way the harder and prepare the field in 1880 for a victory, of which the Democratic leaders felt themselves to have been so unfairly deprived in 1876, they, in 1878, revived the asperities of the contest waged before the Electoral Commission. Jeremiah S. Black had denounced the "Great Fraud" in the most intemperate language in the North American Review.[1] Such newspapers as the New York Sun malignantly assailed, not only the Republican leaders for their action in "stealing" the Presidency, but also Hayes in person for accepting and enjoying the stolen fruit. Mr. Tilden had gone abroad after his discomfiture. Upon his return to New York, in October, 1877, he reopened the issue bitterly.[2] All the rascals in Louisiana and Florida who had had their parts in the sordid bargaining in those states could not be satisfied with offices, and some made "exposures" and "revelations" which served to reawaken strife. The legal prosecution of members of the Returning Board in Louisiana by the Democrats renewed controversy and, on May 13, 1878, Clarkson N. Potter of New York, desig-

[1] Issue of July, 1877.
[2] Williams, Life of Hayes, vol. ii, p. 142.

nated for the task by the Democratic party caucus, presented resolutions in the House authorizing an inquiry into the "frauds" attending the election.

The measure was passed on May 17th and a select committee of eleven members with Mr. Potter as chairman was appointed. Witnesses were heard during the summer of 1878 so that their testimony might affect, in whatever way it could, the Congressional elections of that year.[1] Much now came to pass. The Potter Committee was actively engaged in its inquiries, heaping day by day innuendo upon innuendo, and evidence upon evidence, for the displeasure of the Republican party, when the "cipher dispatches" appeared. While the committees of Congress had been at work in 1877 upon the electoral contest copies of some 3,000 telegrams which had passed between the politicians during the Presidential campaign had been taken by subpœna from the files of the Western Union Telegraph Company. It was from this source that the information so unfavorable to Colonel Pelton, Mr. Tilden's nephew, and, therefore, to Tilden himself, on the subject of Oregon, had been procured while the Electoral Commission was still engaged in its arbitration of the dispute. At the end of the investigation the dispatches had been returned to the telegraph company which, it was supposed, had burned them [2] and put them out of the way.

However, while the telegrams were in possession of the Congressional committees, several hundreds of them had been abstracted by some political scamps and, unknown to the company, were retained. These related principally to Florida and South Carolina, but so far they had baffled the attempts of those who were intent upon deciphering them. They came into the hands of the New York Tribune, which was now in a fair way to usurp the title of its rival, the Times, to place as the preëminent organ of the Republican party. At length John R. G. Hassard and Colonel Grosvenor, two employees of the Tribune in its editorial department, set themselves to

---

[1] Cf. Williams, Life of Hayes, vol. ii, pp. 42–60.
[2] Cf. Bigelow, Life of Tilden, vol. ii, p. 71.

the task and found the key.[1] Bartering for the Presidency like that which had been proceeding on the subject of Oregon, it was now clear, had been engaged in with reference to Florida and South Carolina. The votes of both states were to have been purchased. Colonel Pelton, at Tilden's own house in Gramercy Park, had been conducting the negotiations. Day by day, beginning in October, 1878, the Tribune continued the publication of the dispatches, with their translations, to the amazement of the country, and the complete bewilderment of the Potter Committee and the Democratic leaders, who had reopened the controversy.[2] No effective denial was possible, though Tilden promptly and emphatically declared in the newspapers that he had had no personal knowledge of the corruption which others were promoting in his behalf.[3] He later made a statement to the Potter Committee [4] and most men tried to exonerate him of participation in such transactions.[5] Efforts to discover evidence similarly inculpating the Republican leaders failed,[6] and the whole result of the movement reacted greatly to the disadvantage of the Democratic party and, especially, of those who had led it with so little-skill and fortune in 1876.[7]

For a while the assault upon Hayes, being an assault at the same time upon the Republican party, served to quiet the opposition by the Stalwarts to his administration. The peace was short-lived, though his enemies were disarmed again during the contest which he waged with the Forty-sixth Congress on the subject of Federal enforcement of the election laws in the Southern states. The Forty-fifth Congress had ended the term of its life on March 4, 1879, after rancorous and

[1] Williams, Life of Hayes, vol. ii, pp. 161–3.
[2] Cf. Bigelow, Life of Tilden, vol. ii, p. 174.
[3] His statement appeared in the N. Y. Herald—Issue of October 18, 1878. See Bigelow, Life of Tilden, vol. ii, pp. 175–9.
[4] Cf. Bigelow, op. cit., vol. ii, pp. 179–219.
[5] Many were unable to do this. See, e.g., Williams, Life of Hayes, vol. ii, pp. 164–7; Harper's Weekly, March 1, 1879; N. Y. Times, Feb. 7, 1879.
[6] Williams, Life of Hayes, vol. ii, p. 165.
[7] Cf. McCall, Life of T. B. Reed, pp. 72, 74; D. S. Alexander, Political History of New York, vol. iii, pp. 394–5.

fruitless contention. The Democratic majority in the House had attached "riders" to the bills appropriating money to pay the army and the employees of the government in the civil service. The Senate, which still had a small Republican majority, must accept the principle of no Federal control over Congressional elections, else the House would not pass the money bills. Neither would yield and the session ended. If the wheels of government were not to be entirely blocked President Hayes must, it was said, call a special session of Congress. This would be a new Congress, Democratic in both branches, and the party thus would have the opportunity, it was conceived by some of its leaders, to strengthen its position before the country. On the issue of "freedom of elections" it might gain new friends for the Presidential campaign of 1880.

The President acted promptly. It would be a "long contest" he feared, but he did not "dread" it. The people would not "allow this revolutionary cause to triumph." [1] The day upon which the old Congress adjourned he convoked the new one in special session, beginning March 18, 1879. There was a Democratic majority of eight in the Senate without counting David Davis, who still regarded himself as an Independent, and of 19 in the House, apart from a dozen or more Greenbackers. The senators and representatives met, amid acrimonious controversy in the newspapers, which further stirred, as it reflected, the bitterness of partisan feeling throughout the country. Some of the Democrats predicted that the President, in the approaching conjuncture, would give his favor to the South. Had he not been the instrument for the withdrawal of the troops from the state capitals and the surrender of the governments to the people in 1877? This action marked him as a liberal. The Stalwarts, who were eager at heart, when not openly, for the President's undoing, could ill conceal their hope that he would espouse the cause which the Democrats now presented to the country. In a brief message to the new Congress Hayes regretted the existence of the "emergency" requiring a special

[1] Diary and Letters of Hayes, vol. iii, p. 529.

session. He directed attention to the estimates for which no provision had been made by appropriation, when it was "the general judgment of the country that the public welfare" would be "best promoted by permanency in our legislation and by peace and rest." [1]

The Democrats again joined the appropriation bills and the repeal bills, which were in the interest, as they declared, of local self-government and state rights. The first to reach the President was the army bill to which was attached the "rider" abrogating the law authorizing the use of troops "to keep the peace at the polls." This was, to be sure, a war measure; it was an inheritance of the war and was designed to meet conditions which the Democrats were pleased to say had ceased with the war. To retain such a law on the statute books was coercion of the South. It was a "force bill"; it looked in the direction of centralization and empire; it was intended to make easier the election of Republicans and to make more difficult the election of Democrats to Congress in the South.

There was never the least reason to suppose that Hayes would sign such a measure. His interest in the emancipated and enfranchised colored man in the South, and his attachment to the principle, established by Article II, section 4 of the Constitution and by the 15th Amendment, that it was the duty of the nation to protect and control national elections would have determined his action. He also, in his message returning the bill, made much of the point that such a course as was proposed by the Democratic majority was an encroachment by Congress on the powers of other departments of the government. A bare majority in the legislative body thus would become the government. He was averse to the use of the military at the polls; there was now and there had recently been no such use, but he would not surrender the Federal right to interfere, in the interest of an honest result, if the need arose, either by the employment of troops or by the exercise of civil authority, in the election of a representative in a Congressional district, whether in the North or

[1] McPherson's Handbook of Politics for 1880, p. 95.

in the South. The veto came on April 29th. It was a calm, well reasoned statement which carried an eloquent rebuke. It met with general approbation and brought the President's enemies considerable chagrin.[1]

The next scheme of the Democrats in Congress was to incorporate their principle as to the use of soldiers at the polls in a separate bill. Perhaps the President would accept so much by itself, if it were disconnected and stood apart from a bill granting supplies. On May 12th, he vetoed this measure on the ground that the use of the army was a general and well established executive prerogative, at all times in all parts of the country, which could not, with his consent, be surrendered "on certain days and at certain places." The bill, if it were approved, would be a "subordination of national authority and an intrusion of state supervision over national duties," which amounted, "in spirit and tendency, to state supremacy." [2]

Congress passed to the legislative, judicial and executive appropriation bill to which it attached a rider repealing the laws in question affecting the elections. This veto came on May 29th. While Federal "supervision" should be theoretically continued, if he should approve the proposed law, the President said, the supervisors would hereafter be mere watchmen, empowered to make report. Any original or effectual oversight by them in the future would be impossible. Such a law was not in the interest of "free and fair elections," which all people of all parties had in view. Public opinion was so far from favoring relaxation of the authority of the government that it demanded, the President believed, "greater vigor," both in the enactment and in the execution of laws framed to protect elections "from violence and corruption." Such control was needed for New York City no less than for many parts of the South.[3]

[1] Cf. Hayes to W. H. Smith in Williams, Life of Hayes, vol. ii, p. 179; Richardson, vol. vii, pp. 493–5, 531–2; McPherson's Handbook for 1880, pp. 102–7; Diary and Letters of Hayes, vol. iii, pp. 529–50.

[2] Richardson, vol. vii, pp. 532–6; McPherson's Handbook for 1880, pp. 109–11; Diary and Letters of Hayes, vol. iii, pp. 551–2.

[3] Richardson, vol. vii, pp. 536–41; McPherson's Handbook for 1880, pp. 118–21.

The summer was coming on and the Democrats were weary-
ing of their contest, especially as the country showed signs
of disfavor for their obstructive strategy. The government
must have its supplies and mere antics of politicians to prevent the attainment of indispensable objects soon led to
reactions in public feeling. The army bill was passed with
a meaningless rider as a salve for wounded dignity and the
President approved it. The legislative and executive appropriations were taken out of the civil bill and were passed and
approved. The grants of money for judicial officers, many of
whom were in service in the South, were made the subject
of a separate bill to which riders were attached repealing the
jurors' test oath law and forbidding the use of any of the money
provided in the bill for the enforcement of the election laws.
Here was the invitation for another veto which was promptly
accepted, on June 23rd. The design of this bill, the President·
said, was "to render the election laws inoperative and a dead
letter during the next fiscal year." Laws were left upon the
statute book. Congress was now making it impossible to execute
these laws by forbidding the payment of officers employed
for this purpose.[1]

Thwarted here again the Democratic leaders in Congress
presented and passed another bill providing moneys for the
judicial department, except United States marshals and their
deputies, and it was approved. The repeal of the jurors' test
oath, to which neither the President nor any other objected,
was effected in a rider attached to this measure. A separate
bill covering the marshals' salaries, with a prohibition of their
activities in reference to elections was passed, to meet the
President's veto on June 30th, the fifth of the series of vetoes
in this struggle with his contumacious adversaries.[2] Congress
adjourned on July 1st, leaving these officers without support,

[1] Richardson, vol. vii, pp. 541–4; McPherson's Handbook for 1880,
pp. 126–8.
[2] Richardson, vol. vii, pp. 544–7; McPherson's Handbook for 1880,
pp. 129–30. Two more vetoes were interposed by the President when
Congress resumed its consideration of this subject in 1880. See McPherson's Handbook for 1880, pp. 131–45; Richardson, vol. vii, pp. 591–8.

though they continued to perform their duties, in the confidence that justice would be done them at some future day.[1]

The President had won a pleasant triumph, as he had in his contests—first, with the carpetbaggers and their allies in the North, and, secondly, with Conkling and the Stalwarts on the subject of the civil service. Indeed he was warmly acclaimed by all but the most biased and implacable of his foes.[2] His own estimate of the achievement was that he had "vindicated the power of the national government over Congressional elections and the separate authority of the executive department of the government," as against the advances of the legislative.[3]

If the elections in 1878 had been, in general, favorable to the Democrats in that the party had won substantial majorities in both houses of Congress, those of 1879 indicated a swing in the other direction. Tammany refused to support the Tilden candidate for governor of New York and the Republican, a Conklingite, no other than Cornell, against whom, with Arthur, Hayes had waged his contest for the establishment of correct principles in the civil service, was elected. Similar victories indicative of some disapproval of the course of the Democratic leaders, which might be prophetic of the popular attitude on the question of the Presidency in the next year, were gained throughout the North wherever the issue was drawn. The campaign of 1880, for a new display of all the bitternesses between and within the parties, was not far away and Hayes's attitude toward it was one of unconcern, as to his personal fate, since he had made a promise to himself and to the country that he would not be a candidate for reëlection. There were few in influential positions in party management who would have desired his renomination had he offered himself to the suffrages of the people a second time. In the state of public feeling, in view of the manner of his coming

[1] Williams, Life of Hayes, vol. ii, p. 205.
[2] Diary and Letters of Hayes, vol. iii, p. 564. He had the support, and won the good opinion, seldom cheerfully accorded him, of Garfield.— Smith, Life of Garfield, pp. 673–87.
[3] Diary and Letters of Hayes, vol. iii, p. 564.

to office, he would have had but little strength as a candidate. The value of his administration, if at the time it were perceived and understood by discriminating men, was concealed beneath a weight of rancor and opprobrium from which he could have escaped in no manner.

The old proposal for connecting the Atlantic and Pacific Oceans at the American isthmus gained fresh impetus by the completion of the Suez Canal, under the direction of the French engineer, Ferdinand de Lesseps, who was soon to give his mind to the work of excavating a similar channel for ships at Panama, under circumstances to be described in another place. To quiet the opposition which the prospective activity of a French company in connection with a long cherished American project developed, de Lesseps proposed that an advisory American committee should be formed and that its president should be General Grant, or some other figure whose name was widely known. Colonel Thompson, the Secretary of the Navy in President Hayes's cabinet, was finally chosen. He, for $25,000 a year, agreed to serve the canal company, while at the same time continuing to act as the head of a great department of government at Washington. Hayes had said, when he had entered office, that no one would be appointed to a cabinet position "to 'take care' of anybody." But he had not kept his promise to himself in Thompson's case, for that venerable politician had been chosen to propitiate Senator Morton of Indiana. Thompson alone in the cabinet was willing to corrupt his country's currency to gain the votes of ignorant men. The President, through Evarts, from whom the information of Thompson's action had come, made it clear that such a connection with the canal company was tantamount to a resignation and the Secretary of the Navy accordingly left the cabinet to be replaced by Nathan Goff of West Virginia. Secretary of War McCrary, who had become a United States circuit judge, and Postmaster-General Key who had become a United States district judge, by appointment of the President, had earlier been succeeded by Alexander Ramsay of Minnesota and Horace Maynard of Tennessee.

The significant achievements of the Hayes administration, such as the reform of the New York customhouse, the return of self-government to the Southern states and the resumption of specie payments, of so much lasting virtue, were the very measures which had won him the enmity of the leaders within his party. These men were preëminently Conkling, Cameron and Blaine. Their followings included large bodies of the people who were without knowledge of the correct principles of government or responsible feeling as to the proper conduct of public affairs. They, their stump speakers and their press dismissed Hayes as one, who "regarded his election as a personal and not a party victory, who ignored the claims of, and treated with indifference, those who risk so much to secure party success." What he stood for was not Republicanism but "Hayesism." [1] To the old hacks of the party he was a "reformer," a pious nondescript at his wife's apron strings, a subject of jest if not of contempt, when he should be worth speaking about at all.[2] They would make certain that he should be returned to an obscurity from which he could never again emerge. It was no matter to them whether he wished or did not wish to serve four years more as President. They had other plans in mind which they would arrogantly impose upon the party, and Hayes, accidentally risen for a time to a kind of leadership, would have no part in the development of these plans. In the first place Blaine would, if he could, gain for himself the nomination of which he had been deprived in 1876. Conkling and Cameron, on their side, as a way back into the power which they had enjoyed during the Grant administrations, would become the advocates of a third term for General Grant.

The movement to renominate Grant at the Republican convention of 1880 was the subject of careful arrangement. Upon leaving office in 1877 he meditated a trip around the world. It was at the day a favorite advertisement on the part of steam-

---

[1] W. E. Chandler Papers in Library of Congress.
[2] He "came in by a majority of one and goes out by unanimous consent." —N. Y. Herald, March 5, 1881.

ship companies, as of railroads, to invite men of prominence
to use their lines. Several had importuned Andrew Johnson
to go abroad at their expense at the end of his term of office.[1]
There was competition among them to carry Grant to Europe
and as much farther as their facilities extended. Without
future prospects, untraveled, fond of luxury and ease, tastes
shared by members of his family, and, made vain by his recent
experiences in the Presidency,[2] he was easily enticed into
undertaking a journey which should begin at Philadelphia, embrace Europe, Asia and Africa, and bring him home again by
way of San Francisco. "Encircling the globe" was as yet a
comparatively strange adventure. It was the acme of indulgence by the very rich who, after the war, had been cast
upon the golden shores of our new society and Grant, with
his wife and son, Jesse, on the 17th of May, 1877, embarked
for Liverpool on the *Indiana*, one of the few steamships in the transatlantic service flying the American flag.
His departure from Philadelphia was accompanied by attentions at the hands of a number of wealthy men in that city
one of whom, Adolph E. Borie, would be his companion
over the greater part of the way.[3] The ministers in all the
principal foreign countries which he would visit, the consuls
in cities, were still his appointees in office and his personal
and obliged friends.[4] Mr. Evarts, as Secretary of State, informed of Grant's intention to travel, commended the ex-
President to the attention of all diplomatic and consular
officers.[5] Hayes telegraphed his good wishes,[6] and the trip
assumed an almost official character. It was made to seem
not only a kind of triumphal tour by our principal military
hero but a visit of an official representative of the government of the United States to every country to which he might

[1] Johnson Papers in Library of Congress.
[2] Blaine said that Grant liked "popular applause" more than any man
he ever knew.—Mrs. Gresham, Life of Walter Q. Gresham, p. 494.
[3] Cf. Public Ledger, Phila., May 18, 1877.
[4] Cf. Badeau, Grant in Peace, pp. 263–4.
[5] Young, Around the World with General Grant, vol. i, pp. 3–4.
[6] Ibid., pp. 6–7.

come. He had been President for eight years—he had just
left this position. It was an opportunity for our friends during
the war to show their respect for the United States, for those
who had not been our friends to reinstate themselves in the
favor of a republic, seen now to be more powerful than ever
before. It was of no note, if it were known, that Grant had
been a civil magistrate unworthy of the approval or trust of
discriminating men. He was viewed only as a victorious general and came, it appeared, as an accredited national representative.

Upon his arrival in England he was met by the mayor of
Liverpool and many distinguished citizens. Passing to other
English cities he received similar courtesies. In London he
was granted the freedom of the city, and dined with the Duke
of Wellington, the Prince of Wales and Queen Victoria, to
name no lesser personages, followed about on most occasions
by Adam Badeau, a perfect product of the Grant administrations, who was disgracing the nation while he enjoyed rich
fruits as our consul general in London.[1] A band of "old soldiers,"
assembled at Providence, R. I., interrupted the Queen's dinner at Windsor Castle with a cablegram asking her to thank
England for according Grant so kind a reception.[2]

From England the party passed to Ostend, Brussels and
the Rhenish cities of Germany, extending their trip to Switzerland and Italy, returning then to England for further visiting
in that country and in Scotland. It was late in October before
they reached Paris where honors were again showered upon
Grant. In the south of France, in December, an American
warship called for the travelers and they started away for
Naples, Palermo, Malta, Egypt and the Holy Land. Their
steps led them in March, 1878, to Stamboul, for a view of
European Turkey and Greece, from which they passed to
Rome, Florence, Venice and Milan. On May 7th Grant was
again in Paris for a view of the exposition which had just been

---

[1] Grant stayed for a time at Badeau's lodgings.—Badeau, Grant in
Peace, p. 263.
[2] Young, pp. 33–4.

opened in that city. This done, he proceeded to Holland, and, at the end of June, reached Berlin for receptions by Prince Bismarck and a military review arranged in his honor by the Crown Prince. Then the party visited Denmark, Norway and Sweden. Crossing the Baltic to Russia they returned through Warsaw, Vienna and Munich to southern France, Spain and Portugal. Again in Paris, Grant once more visited England, making a brief excursion to Ireland. It was now January, 1879; more than eighteen months had elapsed since his arrival in Europe and in a few days, joined by Fred Grant, who replaced Jesse, and by Mr. Borie, they would embark at Marseilles for the trip through the Suez Canal to India, and on around the world. They came to Hong Kong about the first of May, passed to Japan, and, after eighteen days on the Pacific, on Saturday, September 20, 1879, sailed into the Golden Gate.

A great popular reception awaited Grant in San Francisco. He had been absent from the country for nearly two and a half years. It was one of the most noteworthy tours ever undertaken by an American citizen and the prominence of his military and political position gave his movements an extraordinary significance. He returned loaded with presents and testimonials which had been bestowed upon him by kings and princes, by governments and peoples, intended for the American nation no less than for him personally. Throughout the time of his absence he had been accompanied by John Russell Young, acting as a correspondent of the New York Herald. Bennett had correctly sensed the news value of the trip, and to his paper, which was so eagerly embracing the opportunities of such an occasion for its own magnification, interesting accounts of Grant's movements were brought by each post, and by cable. While Grant and Young sat in a hotel rotunda or paced a steamer deck they talked on every subject in their minds, and, beginning with the so-called "Hamburg interview," because it was founded on a conversation held in, or at any rate was dispatched to the Herald from, that city, their companionship led to the publication of a large body of reminiscence and opinion on questions connected with

American politics and history.[1] Young made Grant articulate when he was inarticulate, but the "interviews," it was said, were submitted for approval before they were published. Casual and inexact as to fact as the conversations were, they were printed from the Herald's pages in all parts of the country, inducing, in some instances, wide comment and spirited controversy. They were brought together in two volumes with 800 illustrations, to be distributed by subscription in twenty parts. "Around the World with General Grant" attained a great sale and was up to that time one of the most widely circulated books in the history of the publishing trade in America.[2]

Nothing could have better promoted the plans of Conkling, Cameron and the "unclean horde,"[3] who wished to ride back to the power which they had held before Hayes's coming into office. The country, they said, needed a "strong man."[4] The South had again got hold of Congress and had revived the Calhoun doctrine of state rights.[5] Grant was a necessity of the situation and the popular choice. The masses of the people to whom the shame of his administration as President was but little known, and who are so often without a proper feeling on the subject of public service, wrought themselves into enthusiasm.[6] He was the hero of the war—they thought only of his military renown.[7] He had been received by the world on his tour as the first American citizen. The Republican state convention in Illinois as early as in June, 1878, demanded his renomination.[8] One politician, one newspaper after another, while he was still abroad, presented his name as the candidate of the Republican party for President in 1880.[9]

[1] Cf. Young, Around the World with General Grant, vol. ii, p. 151.
[2] In addition to Young's account of the tour its main events are summarized in Badeau, Grant in Peace, pp. 263–314.
[3] N. Y. Nation, Aug. 28, 1879.
[4] Ibid., Oct. 16, 1879; Badeau, Grant in Peace, p. 315.
[5] N. Y. Nation, Jan. 15, 1880.
[6] Cf. N. Y. Times, quoted in N. Y. Nation, Aug. 7, 1879.
[7] Washington correspondence of N. Y. Herald, Dec. 9, 1878.
[8] N. Y. Nation, July 4, 1878.
[9] Cf. ibid., Aug. 22, 1878; Badeau, Grant in Peace, pp. 316, 317.

Some said that he would not run; he must do so, said those who wished again to use him,[1] and thus the subject continued to be argued and discussed in the press and among the people.

In addition to the need, which was remarked and emphasized, of a "strong man" to maintain order in the South, where crime and outrage continued to be too prevalent,[2] there flourished, for his advantage, a persistent exaggeration of the dangers of communism. The railroad strikes of 1877 and other labor disturbances were made to appear to be the symptoms of deep-lying social disorder which any day would break out afresh. The foundations of civilization were about to be shaken by national and international organizations of workingmen and the successful commander of the war was required in a place of authority to preserve our institutions.[3]

Grant himself said nothing or spoke in monosyllables, a part in which he excelled. When he was asked in San Francisco as to his wishes and intentions he evasively replied that he did not think he was "needed as a candidate." He would "rather" have them "take somebody else." Such words meant, of course, that he would not decline the nomination, if it were tendered him by those whose duty it was to present a name to the country for the suffrages of the people.[4]

Men in the Republican party who had found value in the administration of Hayes and who cherished ideals for the state were very frankly alarmed at the exhibitions of emotion which accompanied Grant's reappearance upon the scene. Their reasons might not be understood. Their protests, founded on such reasoning, would not be heeded. But there was force in the cry which was raised about the "third term," the unwritten law since Washington's time that no President should serve for more than two terms, about the "Cæsarism" which was implied by the prolonged occupation of the office by one man. It was undemocratic—especially unsafe must it be to in-

[1] N. Y. Nation, Aug. 28, 1879.
[2] Cf. ibid., April 17, May 8 and Oct. 9, 1879.
[3] Cf. ibid., July 4, and Aug. 22, 1878, and May 8, 1879.
[4] Williams, Life of Hayes, vol. ii, p. 236.

stall a military figure in the Presidency in permanency.[1] The
Stalwarts were undisturbed and proceeded with their plans,
though sensible headway in opposition to their devices was
made by the emphasis which was put upon the dangers underlying a violation of a rule chosen by Washington for his guidance, and which all other Presidents had hitherto followed
for their own credit and for the advantage of the republic.

By good fortune the Stalwarts were not in union. Blaine's
ego was so large that it would not allow him to follow other
men. He had been a candidate for the nomination in 1876,
his ambitions remained unsatisfied, and he would present a
formidable opposition to those who reckoned without him.
His following was large. The New York Tribune's departure
from its high and enviable position as a leader among newspapers on the side of good government had been signalized,
in the first instance, when Whitelaw Reid, in the summer of
1877, found space in that journal for the laudatory articles
concerning Blaine by "Gail Hamilton,"[2] a woman holding
family relationship with Blaine, who, as a "press agent," was
of distinct value to the cause to which she so unreservedly
gave her pen. It also marked Reid's and William Walter
Phelps's abandonment of their places as "reformers." The
Tribune, in its adventure with the "cipher dispatches," had
achieved further progress in the work of making itself "regular."[3] It became the principal organ of the Republican party[4]
and it cried out in loud tones for Blaine. The Times, seeing
its ascendency in the same field menaced, took refuge behind
the cause of General Grant.

Blaine himself had lost no opportunity during the Hayes
administration to strengthen his hold upon the party, particularly through the younger elements in whose ranks his admirers

[1] The New York Nation called it an attempt "to convert the Presidency
into a peerage or estate for a successful soldier."—Issue of June 23, 1880.
[2] Cf. N. Y. Nation, Aug. 22, 1878; Reminiscences of Carl Schurz, vol.
iii, p. 391.
[3] Cf. N. Y. Nation, Oct. 24, 1878. In the process of becoming "regular"
as rapidly as possible the Tribune had supported Cornell in 1879.—Ibid.,
Oct. 23, 1879.
[4] Ibid., Oct. 2, 1879.

abounded. He was as shrewd as he was alert in taking advantage of every occasion for gaining notoriety and making votes. He was without interest in civil service reform and let it be known that the offices, if he were President, would be given to his friends.[1] All the popularity which could be achieved by "waving the bloody shirt" and pointing to the menace of a "Solid South" he added to his account whenever it was possible.[2] No other in Congress was so adept in taunting the "rebel brigadiers" whom the South had sent to the Senate and the House, and making use of their retorts for the increase of his own prestige. By other maneuvers, too, he aimed to mount the American eagle and soar over the heads of his following for their acclamation. He had adopted what he thought would be a clever measure to propitiate the cheap money elements in the West, while still holding the affection of the people of the East, during the progress of the discussion of the currency question.[3] To gain friends on the Pacific coast he had ostentatiously espoused the cause of the rabble in California as against the Chinaman, when it was a question of answering the demand for an abrogation of the treaty with China and the prohibition of immigration.[4] He, for the advertisement of his Americanism, denounced the fisheries award in 1878 as being too favorable to Great Britain,[5] and the Clayton-Bulwer treaty for the restrictions which it put upon us with reference to de Lesseps and the canal at the Isthmus of Panama.[6]

In short, upon no issue which appeared was he unmindful of himself and of the exalted aspiration which he nourished of riding the masses on his way to the White House. If his friends had not grown in number, those who had been faithful to him and saw in him the man for the Presidency in 1876

[1] Smith, Life and Letters of Garfield, p. 529.
[2] Cf. N. Y. Nation, Dec. 19 and 26, 1878; Mayes, Life of Lamar, pp. 354–62, 368.
[3] Cf. N. Y. Nation, Jan. 31 and Feb. 14, 1878.
[4] Cf. Smith, Life of Garfield, p. 677; N. Y. Nation, Feb. 20 and 27, 1879.
[5] N. Y. Nation, March 14 and 21, 1878.
[6] Ibid., Feb. 16 and 23, March 30, 1882.

were still his advocates in 1880. A "National Blaine Club" was formed. "Blaine Clubs" were organized throughout the country. They hired headquarters, flung out banners, put legions of marching men with brass bands upon the streets.[1]

Sherman had ambitions which were as high as Blaine's. In his mind, too, the hope of one day being President was never entirely quiet. He saw his opportunity now and he would present his claims to the nomination through the potential state of Ohio, where he had effective support. He had carefully done nothing to estrange himself from the cheap money elements which abounded in the Republican as well as the Democratic party, especially in the valleys of the Ohio and the Mississippi rivers. He had shifted from one foot to another so adroitly that his faithfulness to the President, whose Secretary of the Treasury he was, seemed at more than one point very questionable. He was favorable, or led the public to suppose (as he desired) that he was favorable to the scheme to coin "short" dollars from $2,000,000 worth of silver purchased from the Western miners each month. He declared that he approved of holding fast to the greenbacks instead of retiring them, a purpose which every other authority on the subject had regarded as a necessary condition precedent to a return to specie payments. Throughout the struggle to gain the result which, it is true enough, he was the instrument to achieve he had been a more or less false friend to true resumption. His compromise measures paved the way for financial and economic crises which, with more sincerity on his side at the right moments, might probably have been greatly to his country's advantage. In any case, whether, by candor, he could or could not have gained the ends which intelligent men had in view, his personal record in their sight would have been a worthier one, and he would deserve and hold a larger and more creditable place in the annals of his country's public life.[2] But he sought popularity for himself and the votes which come, it is believed, by not seeming to be out of accord

---

[1] W. E. Chandler Papers.
[2] N. Y. Nation, Feb. 26, 1880; Smith, Life of Garfield, pp. 475–6, 958.

with prevailing opinion in the electorate,[1] and was frankly, as every one knew, a candidate for the Presidency.[2]

More faithlessness than any which he had displayed in the course of his dealing with the currency question was displayed by his entering New York state to assist Conkling in the election of Cornell as governor. The achievement of most distinction in Hayes's administration, barring the removal of the troops from the Southern state capitals, was the capture of the customhouse from the spoilsmen in New York City and the President's assertion of his authority in the face of Conkling. This wrong flourished in the Treasury Department— the customhouse was under the jurisdiction of the Secretary of the Treasury. Sherman had said that he would not serve in his office if Conkling were to control the Federal appointments in New York. Cornell and Arthur were dismissed in the interest of civil service reform and honest principles in government. Conkling nursed his wrath until he could nominate Cornell for governor and take the case to the people. To elect Cornell would be to rebuke Hayes,[3] and it might have been supposed that Sherman, who had been the instrument in the humiliation of Conkling in this notable controversy, would, at least, have kept silent during the campaign. But, when the invitation came, he went to New York [4] and spoke at several places in the state for the ticket.[5] All of his errancies and divagations in these particulars, it was expected, would pass for mere shrewdness or cunning in politics and he presented himself now, and was put forward in the campaign by his friends, as the representative of the Hayes administration. He would take its honors to himself and seize such favors

---

[1] As in the campaign in Maine in 1879; cf. Hayes's views in Diary and Letters, vol. iii, p. 569.

[2] Cf. his speech at Portland, Maine, in July, 1879. (N. Y. Nation, July 31, 1879.) Also speech in Ohio.—Ibid., Aug. 28, 1879.

[3] It was a breath of defiance to the whole reform element in the Republican party.—N. Y. Nation, Sep. 4, 1879.

[4] Possibly with Hayes's assent. Cf. Diary and Letters of Hayes, vol. iii, p. 577; N. Y. Nation, Oct. 30, 1879.

[5] Sherman's Recollections, pp. 747–8. Evarts did the same, though but once, without better excuse.—N. Y. Nation, Oct. 30, Nov. 6 and 20, 1879; D. S. Alexander, Political History of New York, vol. iii, p. 425.

and advantages as entrenchment in office puts at the disposal
of a candidate, in so far as Hayes, who would not succeed
himself, could transfer these to another man.

It was near Christmas, 1879, when Grant's leisurely progress
across the continent, amid attentions on every side, as he
advanced into the East, before reserved only for kings and
emperors and the most favored of the earth,[1] brought him
back to Philadelphia, whence he had gone away on his tour
of the world. Sixty thousand people in a procession twelve
miles long greeted him in what Harper's Weekly called "one
of the grandest ovations ever given to any man in the United
States."[2] It was made very plain on this occasion, as before,
that he was to be set back in the President's chair, if possible,
with a "whoop and halloo."[3]

For the purposes of his managers Grant had returned too
soon. It had been their hope to prolong his tour for yet six
months in order that his arrival home should have more nearly
synchronized with the meeting date of the convention.[4] But
he had used a large sum of money contributed by his friends [5]
and had about exhausted his means. Against advice, he had
disarranged the plans of his industrious counselors. To make
up for such a loss, his travels, when the popular enthusiasm
at home gave signs of waning, were resumed. In January,
1880, he was in Florida. From Key West he passed to Cuba [6]
and on to Mexico. Upon his return he visited New Orleans
and the cities of the South and received another ovation in
Chicago.[7]

Where should the national convention be held? Blaine's
friends favored Cincinnati which Whitelaw Reid said would
be "the worst place in the country for Grant."[8] If they should

[1] Cf. N. Y. Nation, Nov. 27, 1879.
[2] Issue of Jan. 3, 1880; Public Ledger, Phila., Dec. 17, 1879.
[3] Harper's Weekly, Jan. 10 and 17, 1880.
[4] Badeau, Grant in Peace, pp. 317–8.
[5] Chiefly by his son Ulysses, who had married into a family enriched by
mining in Leadville.—Ibid., p. 416.
[6] Harper's Weekly, Feb. 21 and 28, 1880.
[7] J. B. Bishop, Presidential Nominations, p. 79.
[8] To W. E. Chandler, Dec. 13, 1879, in Chandler Papers.

go to Chicago, Halstead averred, it would be to "play second
fiddle in the Grant orchestra." [1] Grant's managers were of a
like opinion, on which account they made certain that the
convention should meet in Chicago—Don Cameron should be
chairman of the National Committee [2] in succession to Zachariah
Chandler, deceased.   They continued to circulate the idea
that there was an irresistible popular demand for the nomination, that no other course was open to the country, while
Grant, in a waiting state of mind, [3] continued to ride through
the streets of cities under the escort of reception committees,
to listen to adulatory speech and to grace dining rooms and
ball rooms, where men and women gathered to look into a
countenance which they seemed to think was "brighter than
the sun." [4]

The Pennsylvania state Republican convention was held
very early in February and the Camerons, though there was
vigorous opposition by the friends of Blaine, secured the adoption of resolutions instructing the delegation to vote as a
unit for Grant. [5] This was the opening of the campaign. The
convention in New York soon followed and this body, though
there was a strong undercurrent of feeling for Blaine among
the delegates, gave further impetus to the Grant "boom."
The Conkling "machine" was as powerful as it ever had been.
Its leader was in absolute control of the Republican party
organization throughout the state, as was proven by the nomination and election, aided by Tammany, [6] of Cornell to the
governorship in the preceding November. Conkling was an
embittered man. His extraordinary pride had been hurt by
the indignities put upon him in the Hayes administration.
The "malevolence of his expression" visibly increased. It
was "terrible," a woman correspondent who had studied him
in Washington declared, "to despise and hate people as much

[1] Halstead to Chandler, Dec. 16, 1879, in Chandler Papers.
[2] N. Y. Nation, Dec. 18 and 25, 1879.
[3] Cf. Badeau, Grant in Peace, p. 320.
[4] N. Y. Nation, Nov. 27, 1879.
[5] Ibid., Feb. 12, 1880.
[6] D. S. Alexander, Political History of New York, vol. iii. p. 426.

as he looks as if he did." [1] It was in the summer of 1879 that
a scandal which he never outlived was attached to his name.
The newspapers published and republished the stories of his
visit to the wife of Senator Sprague, the beautiful Kate Chase,
daughter of the Chief Justice, the reigning belle of Washington
of a few years since, on Canonicut Island, near Newport, and
of Sprague driving him off the estate with a shot gun. [2] Though
such disclosures in no manner affected his hold upon his re-
tainers it gave new color to the character of the forces [3] which
were masking their designs upon the government through the
use of a great military reputation.

The New York delegates were not bound as a unit for Grant,
but they were "called upon and instructed to use their most
earnest and united efforts" to secure his nomination. [4] Cameron
and Conkling had done their parts well; the third member of
the Grant "syndicate," Logan in Illinois, was not far behind
them. [5] The convention in that state met in May. There was
bitter and effective opposition from those who were in favor
of Elihu Washburne, and from others who supported Blaine,
but the delegation, through Logan's power, was pledged to
Grant, [6] though this alignment would be the subject of contest
in the convention. In the South, where the Republican party
was in the hands of low and corruptible elements, many delegates were instructed for the "third term" candidate. As
conventions met in this state and that, the number of men
who were to go to Chicago, and to vote for Grant "first, last
and all the time," increased to such a point that careful judges
were more than fearful of his nomination. He himself retired
to his quondam home at Galena that he might have an ap-

---

[1] N. Y. Nation, July 3, 1879.

[2] Ibid., Aug. 14, 21, 28, 1879.

[3] "Show us a Republican criminal or fugitive from justice, or Republican under a cloud of any sort," said the New York Nation, "and we will
show you a 'Grant man.'"— Issue of April 1, 1880.

[4] N. Y. Nation, March 4, 1880.

[5] Smith, Life of Garfield, p. 960; cf. Boutwell, Sixty Years in Public
Affairs, vol. ii, p. 267.

[6] N. Y. Nation, May 13 and June 17, 1880; Harper's Weekly, June 12,
1880.

parent residence in Illinois, to which state he had before been accredited. The reticence which was habitual to him was continued, though he was anxiously represented with considerable activity [1] by his son Fred, to the visible annoyance of his managers,[2] who themselves were intent upon directing the campaign in their own experienced ways.

Little was offered in recommendation of the candidate which was founded on his eight years of service as President. It was accounted sufficient to appeal to his career in a period anterior to this time, and not as a civil magistrate but as a military figure. What was said during the campaign concerning his civil capacity was said by the opposition, and this the managers dismissed as scurrilous and an outrage upon the great man to whom the country owed its salvation and its life.[3]

The Independents, the "Scratchers," as they were called in the state campaign of 1879 in New York, when they would not vote for Cornell,[4] surveyed the scene as it developed with intelligent concern. Godkin in the New York Nation was eagerly alert to see and expose the fraud, duplicity and evil designs which lay behind the movements of the politicians. No villainous purpose escaped his eye nor did his courage flag in denouncing it and those who nurtured it, and who hoped by their slyness to beguile the people into an indorsement of their projects. Curtis in Harper's Weekly, in his serener manner, was also a doughty defender of honorable ideals in government.

But there were losses since 1872 and 1876. The change of ownership in the Chicago Tribune, with Medill in charge of its destinies, was to be deplored. Halstead in the Cincinnati Commercial, so frankly revealing his ignorance in the discussion of the money question, was no longer useful to the friends of good government. The death of Bowles of the Spring-

[1] Badeau, Grant in Peace, pp. 319–20.
[2] N. Y. Nation, June 3, 1880; cf. Boutwell, Sixty Years of Public Affairs, vol. ii, pp. 271–2.
[3] N. Y. Nation, June 3, 1880.
[4] D. S. Alexander, Political Hist. of N. Y., vol. iii, pp. 424–5.

field Republican was a disaster. Of yet more importance was the departure from the path of faithfulness of the New York Tribune.[1] Having "clamored for reform" it now "turned and clamored against any reform, which might help the Democrats."[2]

But, if Whitelaw Reid and William Walter Phelps were deserters of the cause, other young men, with some comprehension of the merit of disinterested and worthy public service, were coming forward. Independent Republicans appeared before the Cameron convention in Pennsylvania, addressed it and enjoined it to remember that a "third term" candidate such as Grant, or a corrupt candidate such as Blaine, could not and would not receive their support. They procured a large body of influential signers for their paper. They would rescue the party from "degradation and impending disaster."[3]

In New York a similar body, acting in a similar spirit, addressed the Conkling convention prior to its meeting at Utica. They directed attention to the fact that about 20,000 Republicans had "scratched" Cornell. Grant and Blaine were deemed "unfit" candidates, and they could not be supported by Republicans of high, conscientious and independent minds.[4] Massachusetts soon followed with the protest of judicious Republicans in that state.[5]

In St. Louis an anti-Grant meeting was organized under the leadership of ex-Senator Henderson, who had voted against the conviction of Andrew Johnson, and had been dismissed by Grant as a prosecutor because he had played the part of an honest man in the Whiskey Fraud trials. He found "the danger of Mexicanizing the republic" to be "greater than the temporary success of the Democratic party," should it be true, as the Grant managers had said, that no other Republican candidate for President could be elected. A "third term" nomination was declared by resolutions of the meeting to be "unwise, inexpedient and subversive of the tradi-

---

[1] Cf. N. Y. Nation, Jan. 9, 1879.
[2] Ibid., July 22, 1880.
[3] Ibid., Feb. 5 and March 4, 1880.
[4] Ibid., March 4, 1880.
[5] Ibid. March 11, 1880.

tions of the government." [1] A call was issued for a national convention.[2] The friends of the movement in New York opened headquarters in that city, organized public meetings, which were addressed by Horace White, Charles Francis Adams, Jr., R. R. Bowker and others, and convoked a state conference at Albany, where delegates would be chosen to attend the national convention, which was to be held in St. Louis on May 6th.[3]

This convention was not large, but it was a significant gathering of earnest men who uttered a distinct remonstrance against the proposed nomination of Grant. While nothing was said concerning Blaine, whose strength lay in the West, that candidate also won no recommendations from the meeting. It was resolved to appoint a committee of one hundred members which, in the event of Grant's being named as the candidate, should convene at once in New York City for the selection of an independent ticket.[4]

The Republican national convention met in the Exposition Building, a huge elliptical amphitheater on Michigan Avenue, Chicago, on Wednesday, June 2nd, with Conkling, Cameron, Logan and their henchmen boasting loudly that they would nominate Grant on the first ballot. But the "triumvirs" early met with some reverses. The most active and experienced of Blaine's lieutenants was William E. Chandler, who was rather fulsomely described by a friend as the "indefatigable brains and force of the National Committee" in 1868 and 1872, and also in 1876, when, but for his genius, Tilden would have become President.[5] However this may have been Chandler was, with Hale and Frye of Maine, in Blaine's service in Chicago.[6] He had engaged a suite of rooms at the Palmer House, but the Grant men got these away from him and, with a threat to sue Potter Palmer for violation of contract which had been

[1] N. Y. Nation, March 18, 1880.
[2] Ibid., April 1, 1880.
[3] Ibid., April 22 and May 6, 1880.
[4] Ibid., May 13, 1880.
[5] To Chandler, May 5, 1879, in Chandler Papers.
[6] Cf. J. M. Forbes, Letters and Recollections, vol. ii, p. 192.

reduced to writing, he established his headquarters at a smaller hotel. Here strategy was hatched, from this place it emanated, "For God's sake save our party—anybody but Grant," one telegraphed to Chandler. "War, famine and pestilence," said another, would not be "more destructive" than the success of the "third term candidate." Blaine had a majority in the National Committee, but a "third term traitor" was its chairman. "Rule or ruin" was the maxim of the "third termers." They had hoisted the "black flag"; victory for them would be death to every Republican who opposed their schemes. "Remove tyrant Cameron!" Thus spoke the friends of Blaine.[1]

Cameron was to have been the temporary chairman of the convention and in this place he could have greatly aided Grant.[2] Chandler, who was in constant telegraphic communication with Blaine, found it to be his initial task to set Cameron aside in favor of Senator Hoar.[3] The "unit rule," by which the "third term" managers would hold the instructed delegations in leash and name their candidate in a panic of emotion, it was determined, should meet its fate in the convention after the organization of that body,[4] and there it was promptly and impressively rejected.[5] Logan's group from Illinois was shaken by the seating, amid his roars of protest, of contestants for places in the delegation that he had seized for Grant.[6] Conkling's ill nature and insolence were increased by every reverse which overtook him and his cause.[7]

There were 756 delegates, 379 of whom would have constituted a majority capable of making a choice, and, if the New York, Pennsylvania and Illinois delegations could have been held together by the enforcement of the "unit rule,"[8]

[1] Chandler Papers.
[2] Smith, Life of Garfield, p. 964; Hoar, Autobiography of 70 Years, vol. i, pp. 390–91.
[3] Smith, Life of Garfield, p. 966; Hoar, Autobiography, vol. i, pp. 391–2.
[4] Smith, Life of Garfield, p. 966.
[5] Ibid., pp. 967, 973.
[6] Phila. Public Ledger, June 5, 1880; N. Y. Nation, June 17, 1880.
[7] Cf. J. B. Bishop, Presidential Nominations, chap. xi.
[8] Cf. Smith, Life of Garfield, pp. 958–9.

it was said that Grant would have had 389, while 226 were conceded to Blaine, 80 to Sherman, 34 to Edmunds, 17 to Washburne and 10 to Windom. It was a vast assemblage— it is computed that there were 15,000 persons in the galleries.[1] Temporary chairman Hoar became permanent chairman, a post which he was to administer with great ability.[2] The commotion and tumult attending the organization of a body composed of the representatives of so many antagonistic factions [3] continued until Saturday when, late on that day, at an evening session, the names of the candidates were presented. A delegate from Michigan, James J. Joy, with the oratorical fanfare needed for the occasion, nominated Blaine. The speech was interrupted by cheering and other loud demonstrations from the friends of the "magnetic" leader.[4] After the seconding speeches had been made William Windom was brought forward by Minnesota as a "favorite son," which led to a call for New York, whereupon Conkling, lofty and supercilious of mien, stepped to the reporters' stand and, with sonorous voice, began his eulogy of Grant "from Appomattox," not unmixed with sneering references to other candidates. The pending election would be "the Austerlitz of American politics"—it would determine for years to come whether this country should be "republican or Cossack." Grant was the "most illustrious of living men"; he stood "on the highest eminence of human distinction." Alluding to his recent tour of the world he had, said Conkling, "studied the needs and defects of many systems of government." He had "never betrayed a cause or a friend"—he and he alone could carry the doubtful states. Referring to the money question Conkling spared no praise. To Grant, "more than to any other man," did the country owe it that "every paper dollar" was "as good as gold." He, "single and alone, overthrew expansion and cleared the way for specie resumption." When Conkling was done the Grant claque rocked the house

[1] Hoar, Autobiography, vol. i, p. 393.
[2] N. Y. Nation, June 24, 1880.
[3] Smith, Life of Garfield, p. 977.
[4] Cf. Gail Hamilton, Biography of Blaine, p. 464.

with noise which continued for upwards of a quarter of an hour.[1]

It was now another's turn. Garfield was the Hayes administration leader in the House. He had been the party leader there, after the advancement of Blaine to the United States Senate. His name had just been lent new prominence by his election as a senator from Ohio,[2] though he had not yet taken his seat. He himself had not been out of the public mind as a possible nominee for the Presidency.[3] He was wanting in sincere admiration for the man whose name it became his duty to present,[4] and who was plainly without the qualities adhering to an "attractive" popular figure.[5] Sherman, indeed, was not in command of the entire delegation of his state where Blaine also had friends,[6] and as many were saying that the orator himself, by reason of his happy bearing in the convention,[7] rather than Sherman, should be the candidate of Ohio, his position was far from an enviable one to occupy.[8]

Taking the place on the platform which Conkling had just held, with a finer presence, a sweeter note, Garfield made a speech for the Secretary of the Treasury. From the Austerlitz of Conkling Garfield passed to Grecian history. The battle this year would be the Republican party's Thermopylæ. The Spartans must meet all the Greeks of Xerxes, and with Sherman, said Garfield, "all the stars in their courses will fight for us." For twenty-five years Sherman had trod the "perilous heights of public duty" and, "against all the shafts of malice," he had come through, "his breast unharmed." The "blaze of that fierce light" which had been upon him had found "no

[1] Cf. Gail Hamilton, Biography of Blaine. Conkling's speech seemed to one of Sherman's friends in the convention to be "lachrymose in tone and delivered like a funeral discourse."—Moulton to Sherman. June 6, 1880, in Sherman Papers in Library of Congress.

[2] Cf. Harper's Weekly, Jan. 24, 1880.

[3] Smith, Life of Garfield, pp. 943–52.

[4] Ibid., p. 958.

[5] Ibid., p. 974. Regarded and often spoken of as a "human icicle."—Cf. Autobiography of Platt, p. 111; Williams, Life of Hayes, vol. ii, p. 234.

[6] John Sherman's Recollections, pp. 774, 775, 776, 778.

[7] J. B. Bishop, Presidential Nominations, chap. xi.

[8] Smith, Life of Garfield, pp. 965–6, 967, 969.

flaw in his armor, no stain upon his shield." It was a really
splendid *tour de force* in political eloquence [1] which was in every
hearer's mind [2] at a momentous hour, when, despairing of an
harmonious issue, the convention sought a way out of the
stalemate into which it was soon to be plunged.

Edmunds's and Washburne's names were presented, when,
near midnight, an adjournment was taken till Monday morning. Sunday was spent in active discussion of the theme which
was on every tongue. Could Grant be nominated? Could
Blaine secure enough votes to become the nominee? If not,
who would be made the party's candidate for President? The
hour came. On the first ballot Grant received 304 votes, Blaine
284, Sherman 93, Edmunds 34, Washburne 30 and Windom 10.
Nineteen in the New York delegation had disregarded "instructions" and defied Conkling, who sneered at them in announcing the vote of the state,[3] 17 being for Blaine and 2 for
Sherman. Thirty-two Pennsylvanians voted for Grant and
26 against him. Ten out of 36 delegates in Illinois challenged
Logan's leadership. At the end of the day, after 28 ballots
had been taken, when Grant's vote was 307 and Blaine's 279,
the convention adjourned until the next morning. No progress
was made until the 34th ballot when Garfield, for whom one
or two votes had been cast from time to time, and who had
won the admiration of the convention—often expressed in
cheers—[4] as he had risen before it, suddenly gained the support
of 17 delegates, a contribution mainly from Wisconsin,[5] whereupon Garfield took the floor and spoke in deprecation of their
course.[6] But to no avail. On the next ballot he had 50—
Indiana had joined Wisconsin. On the 36th ballot nearly all
of the Blaine and other anti-Grant strength was transferred
to him and his name "swept with lightning rapidity through

[1] Hoar, Autobiography of 70 Years, vol. i, p. 393.
[2] Smith, Life of Garfield, p. 976.
[3] Ibid., p. 979; Public Ledger, Phila., June 8, 1880.
[4] Smith, Life of Garfield, pp. 967–8, 972, 973; Halstead in McClure's
Mag., Feb., 1896.
[5] McPherson's Handbook for 1880, p. 191.
[6] Smith, Life of Garfield, pp. 981–2.

the convention."[1] Having received 399 votes he was declared
to be the nominee. The Grant delegates, now numbering 306,
remained a solid phalanx, while 42 of Blaine's friends were
unmoved by the collapse of factional lines. The noise, both
on the floor and in the galleries, was "terrific."[2] Garfield
went to Bateman "with apparent emotion," when he saw
what impended, to assure Sherman's principal agent, that he
had had "nothing to do with it"—he would "rather be shot
to death by the inch" than furnish his friends any just ground
for suspicion of "unfaithfulness."[3] It was "the escape of a
tired convention."[4] The banners of the states were brought
up to surround Garfield who sat motionless, onlookers have said
dazed, in his seat.[5] The crowd sang "Rally Round the Flag"
to the music of the band while, outside, cannon fired salutes.

For Conkling nothing remained but to move to make the
nomination unanimous, in which gesture he was supported
by Logan and some of the Blaine leaders, whereupon, after
a recess, the convention proceeded to name a candidate for
Vice-President. There was a scurrying about by the tacti-
cians. Many favored Washburne. He had not been out of
the public mind for the Presidency. His claims had been advanced in many parts of the country. His services to the
Germans in Paris during the Franco-Prussian War had impelled
some of their leaders to say that the "Teutons would fall in"
behind his banner. Washburne had "invented" Grant,[6] and,
but for his "romantic fidelity," which would not allow him
to let himself be brought forward in opposition to his old
friend, he might have had, it was said, the first place on the
ticket.[7] So much was not true. He had had his advocates in
the convention, his name had been formally set before it and,

[1] Warner M. Bateman, a lawyer in Cincinnati, to Sherman June 8, 1880,
in Sherman Papers.
[2] Public Ledger, Phila., June 9, 1880.
[3] Bateman to Sherman, June 12, 1880, in Sherman Papers.
[4] Bateman to Sherman, June 8, 1880, in ibid.
[5] Cf. S. M. Cullom, Fifty Years of Public Service, p. 124. A Sherman delegate said that Garfield was "thunderstruck."—Sherman Papers.
[6] A Detroit correspondent to Chandler, Feb. 10, 1880, in Chandler Papers.
[7] Washburne Papers in Library of Congress.

had there been wish for it during the deadlock, the delegates could have swung to his support. But he was not forgotten now when a name was needed for junction with Garfield's. His nomination might have been regarded as a friendly gesture in the direction of the Grant men. But it was not Grant, it was Conkling, with the New York "machine," who was to be brought to the support of the ticket.

Levi P. Morton, the New York banker, might have been chosen— [1] he was *persona grata* with Conkling and was one of the faithful who had been steadily voting for Grant. But time pressed and, with General Woodford making the speech, General Chester A. Arthur was nominated to propitiate the "Old Guard," the devoted and unyielding "306," who, during 36 ballots, had never wavered in the support of the "silent old soldier." [2] Arthur received 468 votes to 193 for Washburne and was declared to be the party's choice for Vice-President. It was to be Garfield and Arthur for the campaign of 1880 and the convention adjourned *sine die*.

Sherman had had his opportunity and, by reason of the long deadlock, it was an unusual one. Some of his advocates had procured places for themselves as delegates in the convention and others were engaged in manipulation outside. For months his candidacy had been promoted with as much energy as these men could bring to their task. They had formed Sherman committees and clubs in all parts of the country. It was a time now for explanation and the apportionment of blame. Charles Foster, it was said, had been faithless and he was hard pressed for denials, which he formulated and incorporated in letters to the Secretary of the Treasury.[3] He was "coquetting"

---

[1] A. D. White, Autobiography, vol. ii, p. 193; cf. Alexander, Political Hist. of N. Y., vol. iii, pp. 443–4; R. M. McElroy, Life of L. P. Morton, pp. 105–6.

[2] How the Ohio delegation arranged this nomination, after a conference with Conkling, is told by Halstead in a story in McClure's Magazine, Feb., 1896. Another story is in Wm. C. Hudson, Random Recollections, pp. 96–8, where it is related that Conkling, in his anger, told Arthur not to touch the ticket and to refuse the tender of a nomination; and still another in A. K. McClure, Our Presidents and How We Make Them, p. 274.

[3] See, e.g., letter of June 23, 1880, in Sherman Papers.

with the Vice-Presidency and gave Sherman no cordial or useful service.[1] Governor Dennison,[2] who was deferred to as the Sherman leader in the Ohio delegation, if he were true, was "vain and opinionated," and was by nature an "old grandmother." He did not know his own mind, made himself busy in "confusion of his own creating" and would not act at the right time.[3] Massachusetts, under Henry Cabot Lodge, who was urged to take this course by Schurz by telegraph, and on other advice, had turned to Sherman, but it was too late. With leadership better than Dennison's groups of delegates in other states, it was said, could have been added to Sherman's following at a time when such support would have been infectious and valuable. Even with one-fourth of the Ohio men hostile to the state's candidate, some of them bitterly so, more spirited direction, it was believed, would have led to other results.

Even Garfield was not spared. He had presented Sherman's name, it was said, in "a sickly manner." While Conkling had stressed Grant's part, which had been small, in protecting the currency, Garfield had found little to say in praise of Sherman's great achievement in connection with resumption and the rescue of the country from soft money. Garfield had lodged in Chicago with Foster who was on relations that were too pleasant with the Blaine leaders—Chandler, Hale and Frye.[4]

Sherman telegraphed his lieutenants in the convention. "Now give us," said he, "some first class man for Vice-President." Instead of following his instructions they, in their elation over Garfield's nomination, had "rushed" to the New York delegation and got Arthur, whom they helped to shout

[1] Foster never gave Sherman "an hour of honest service." (Bateman to Sherman, June 12, 1880, in Sherman Papers.) The result was due to "Dennison's vanity and incapacity and Foster's services for others."—Bateman to Sherman at a later date in ibid.

[2] The "War Governor" of Ohio.

[3] Various informants of Sherman in June, 1880, in Sherman Papers.

[4] The situation was this, said Chandler—that, while Foster and Garfield were willing to go to Blaine in order to defeat Grant, Dennison and Butterworth were unwilling to support Blaine on any account.—Chandler to Sherman, July 23, 1880, in Sherman Papers.

into the place, without reflecting that his dismissal as collector in New York would render his choice very unacceptable to the Secretary of the Treasury, who had been the agency in that dismissal.[1]

But other men found greater satisfaction in what had been done.[2] The Committee of One Hundred, appointed by the St. Louis convention of Independents, the "charlatans and guerillas" who "deployed between the lines and foraged on one side or the other," whom Conkling had alluded to with so much contempt in his speech nominating Grant,[3] was ready to be announced,[4] but the nomination of Garfield made such action unnecessary—the forces of decency and good order had triumphed, through the Providence which has seemed so frequently to preside over our national destinies. Grant said that he was grateful to his "friends," who were, unfortunately, the same designing men to whom, by nature, it appeared, that he was drawn, and some injudicious persons who had joined such company. He was particularly touched by the devotion of Conkling who, he averred, should have been the party's nominee.[5] Grant, by his tour abroad, had regained the public affection. But by placing himself once more in the hands of a coterie of discredited politicians he had thrown aside what he had rewon. He afforded a sorry figure now in his defeat, dragged as he had been by Conkling, Cameron and Logan through their muddy lanes.[6]

[1] Sherman Papers.
[2] A truth was stated by Mr. Chittenden, long before the convention met, when he was asked to become an advocate of Sherman's nomination. "What is the use," he said, "of being for Sherman when no one else is for him?"—Sherman Papers.
[3] Public Ledger, Phila., June 7, 1880.
[4] Ibid., May 31, 1880.
[5] N. Y. Nation, June 17, 1880.
[6] No one who ever rightly estimated the value to the country of Grant's splendid military fame, said the New York Nation, could do else than "bitterly mourn" his allowing himself to be put to "base uses" by this "paltry clique." (Issue of June 10, 1880.) "I greatly regret," wrote President Hayes, while the Chicago convention was still in session, "that Grant, our first soldier and a man of many sterling qualities, should be so humiliated and degraded as he has been by his unprincipled supporters."—Diary and Letters of Hayes, vol. iii, p. 600.

So narrow an escape from a sore misfortune made the right thinking parts of the nation unduly happy over the choice of Garfield. He was, at the moment, endowed with characteristics which he did not possess. It is true that he had borne himself so well in recent conjunctures that he outshone most of his contemporaries in our politics. But this was due in part to the accident of his living in Ohio and the West. When others around him, who should have been as firm as he, had been false he had stood in his place, a courageous witness for correct principles in public life. Particularly on the currency issue had he exhibited strength, though he had been not much less heroic in his advocacy of a lower tariff.[1] He had fearlessly defended civil service reform,[2] and was open in his condemnation of the iniquities which characterized the Grant administration.[3] His feeling toward the South also marked him as a liberal—unlike so many other leaders of the party he forebore fanning the flames of sectional hatred.[4] On all these subjects he, for many years, had been in personal conference and in correspondence with the Independents in the East, and he held their confidence and esteem.[5]

He conscientiously faced the responsibilities of public life and, though attached to his party, he had appeared to be tenacious in his defense of a position which, after study, he knew to be right and not in risk of surrendering his views for policy's or expediency's sake. His reading was wide and various, and his knowledge considerably greater than that of most men who were his associates in Congress. He was, moreover, a really splendid orator—a talent which he could the better display because of his urbanity of manner and his commanding personal appearance.[6] While Sherman, whom he had so

[1] Cf. Smith, Life of Garfield, pp. 591, 715–6.
[2] Ibid., pp. 722–7.
[3] At the time of Cox's dismissal by Grant as Secretary of the Interior Garfield did not hesitate to write of the "political vermin" which infested the government and to which the President had surrendered.—Ibid., p. 462.
[4] N. Y. Nation, June 17, 1880.
[5] Cf. Harper's Weekly, Jan. 24, 1880.
[6] Cf. Sherman's Recollections, p. 807; Smith, Life of Garfield, pp. 704–7; E. V. Smalley in Century Magazine, Dec., 1881; Autobiography of T. C. Platt, p. 125; A. D. White, Autobiography, vol. i, pp. 187–8.

impressively put in nomination in the convention, was also an orator on occasion, and also a man of knowledge of public questions, he had proven himself "of the willow and not of the oak." [1] He wanted some of the disinterestedness and sincerity with which Garfield attacked the business of government.

Deficiencies in Garfield's character were discoverable to his friends and these defects later appeared to mar the public judgment of him. At the time it was enough to know that neither Grant nor Blaine, candidates equally distasteful to those who had in view higher objects for the state, had been chosen and that one, whose career in Congress had merited and won public respect, would be offered to the people for their suffrages for President. It was plain that the presentation of the name of Arthur for Vice-President was an insolence pointed directly at men of proper political standards. [2] He was, so far as was publicly seen, nothing but a henchman of Conkling. In his contest as head of the customhouse in New York City with the President and the Treasury Department, under which he served, though he well understood that he was holding the private interest of an incompetent and a corrupt body of men above the good of the public service, he chose to be faithful to an evil system rather than perform his proper duties. He was dismissed for his contumacy under circumstances which made his fault nationally notorious. And now, for this reason and for this only, since in no other case could his name have been known to the country, he was nominated for the Vice-Presidency of the United States. His associate on the wrong side of a controversy with President Hayes had been elected governor of New York state, and his own "vindication," and that of his chief, in the conspiracy against good order, would be effected now, it was hoped, in the national elections. It is true that the nomination had been made as the price of gaining, and as a bid for, a Republican majority in New York

[1] Hoar, Autobiography, vol. i, p. 400. He "studied the popular current," said Garfield, "floated with the tide and drifted with the wind of popular opinion."—Smith, Life of Garfield, pp. 475–6.
[2] Cf. W. H. Smith to Hayes in Diary and Letters of Hayes, vol. iii, pp. 602–5.

state, and through that state in the electoral colleges of the nation at large. It was none the less an insult to President Hayes, to the whole Hayes administration, to all the moral sentiment resident in the Republican party. Yet this, too, was accepted, if it were not forgiven, in thankfulness for the escape from Grant or Blaine.

Men would vote for Garfield and "scratch" Arthur; they could not do so. They must vote for electors to choose the President and the Vice-President, not for the President and the Vice-President directly. There was no way out but to minimize the disaster, as the New York Nation sought to do in an effort to satisfy the objectors for whom it stood. There was no place, said this paper, in which Arthur's "powers of mischief" would be so small as in the Vice-Presidency. It was good to know that as the presiding officer of the Senate he would be removed, during a great part of each year, from his own field of activity. Of course, it was observed, General Garfield might, if elected, die during his term of office, but this was "too unlikely a contingency to be worth making extraordinary provision for." Anyhow Conkling had been defeated in his main purpose—his getting the nomination of Arthur for Vice-President when he wanted Grant for President, and all that this would mean, was not different from his getting "a suit of old clothes in lieu of the English mission." [1]

The interest felt and displayed by the country in the issue at Chicago had been immense. Everywhere, while the convention was in session, the fronts of newspaper printing houses and of telegraph offices were besieged with men eager for news of the balloting. Cannon were fired, bonfires were lit and celebrations were organized as soon as the result was known. Probably never before in the history of the Presidential office, unless it were in 1860, had feeling run so high. The contention among the candidates for the prize reflected great public excitement. The sectional and party bitterness which remained after the war, and which could not be so soon allayed, now in

[1] N. Y. Nation, June 17, 1880.

particular, in view of the conviction among the Democrats that they had been defrauded of their victory in 1876, would make the contest angry and keen. All the nominating speeches at Chicago had emphasized the need of a candidate who could win from a strong and an aroused opposition. The press everywhere sounded the same note, and the Democrats were not unmindful of their opportunities, though they, too, were riven by dissensions which had ensued upon their failure in the last election to gain what seemed to be so manifestly theirs. The leaders with whom they had come out of that encounter were not figures who could well hold aloft the standard in a new trial of party strength.

Tilden was in all minds. He had been elected, his party said, in 1876—what more natural or right than that he should be its candidate again? [1] But admiration for him, and confidence in him in four years had not increased. That men around him, some of them of his own kith and kin, had been engaged in a corrupt conspiracy, proof of which was found in a mass of "cipher telegrams," to purchase the Presidency for his enjoyment and use very properly repelled as well as startled the entire country. [2] That he had low standards of business honor and was unscrupulous in the making of money as a lawyer and in the stock market received further impressive confirmation in some portions of the public mind in charges which had just been uttered by Cyrus W. Field. [3] The Republican press pursued him virulently, and in many directions unjustly, with the purpose, which was successful, in placing him in an unfavorable light before the country. The Independents who had voted for him in preference to Hayes were by this time well done with their adventure. He wanted the boldness and decision, as well as the honesty of a reformer. He was seen for a "Boss" in New York state politics on the Democratic side who was in no way different from, or morally superior to, Conkling. It is true that he was still not a favorite

[1] Cf. Bigelow, Life of Tilden, vol. ii, p. 168.
[2] Williams, Life of Hayes, vol. ii, pp. 167–9; D. S. Alexander, Political History of New York, vol. iii, pp. 394–5.
[3] N. Y. Nation, Aug. 28, Sep. 4, 11, 25, Oct. 2, 1879.

of Tammany which, under John Kelly, its arbitrary leader,[1] had seceded from the party and presented a separate ticket for governor in 1879, thereby defeating Tilden's candidate,[2] and now would appoint its own delegation as claimants for seats on the floor of the convention. But his hold upon the party was despotic and his methods were the practical politician's, founded upon the gaining and distribution of offices and other valuable things. The New York Herald in the summer of 1879 had demanded his withdrawal from leadership,[3] and the discussion of the subject occupied newspapers and their readers throughout the country. The delegates, as they were named, and the sentiment in the convention, when it assembled in Cincinnati on June 22nd, gave little evidence of enthusiasm for his name and, unless a call upon him had come as a spontaneous outburst of feeling, it would have but little availed him or the party. Indeed it was plain that he could not be nominated on any terms,[4] whereupon, seeing the situation to which he had come, he, at the last moment, pleading ill health as his excuse, well enough grounded, for his strength was sorely impaired,[5] while reciting his services to the party and his public achievements, left the field as a candidate,[6] though still hoping, it is believed, that he might be brought forward by the convention, so that he could have the gratification of putting the honor behind him in more impressive terms.[7] Seymour, the reluctant leader of 1868, who was spoken of as a nominee,[8] also withdrew. The convention still had before it a number of names of possible contenders for the party's honors. Many expressed a preference for Bayard of Delaware, one of its finest leaders. Indiana supported Hendricks, who had been a candidate in 1876 and who had gone down with

---

[1] D. S. Alexander, Political History of New York, vol. iii, p. 396.
[2] Cf. Diary and Letters of Hayes, vol. iii, p. 577.
[3] Cf. N. Y. Nation, Aug. 7, 1879.
[4] Letters and Memorials of Tilden, vol. ii, pp. 599, 610–11.
[5] Bigelow, Life of Tilden, vol. ii, pp. 264–5.
[6] Ibid., pp. 266–70.
[7] Ibid., pp. 271–2; Letters and Memorials of Tilden, vol. ii, pp. 597–8.
[8] Letters and Memorials of Tilden, vol. ii, pp. 594–5; A. J. Wall, Sketch of the Life of Seymour, p. 60.

Tilden as the nominee for Vice-President in that year. Representative Henry B. Payne of Ohio who enjoyed Tilden's favor, and Thurman of the same state had their advocates. Pennsylvania had in its delegation a number of friends of General Hancock who had had residence, in boyhood, in that state and who had been its candidate in the convention of 1876, while others there had the hope of nominating Speaker Samuel J. Randall.

Judge Hoadly was made temporary chairman of the meeting and Senator Stevenson of Kentucky, the permanent chairman. The convention soon came to the balloting. There were 738 delegates and, under the two-thirds rule which governed the proceedings, 492 must vote for a candidate before he could be declared the party's choice. Hancock whose name was presented in flowing periods by Daniel Dougherty, a "silver-tongued" orator of Philadephia, received 171 votes on the first ballot, while Bayard, whose panegyrist was George Gray, had 153½. The next name below theirs was Payne's—he was supported by 81 delegates. Altogether 21 names were voted for. The convention adjourned until the next day, when, sentiment favorable to Hancock having increased during the night to such a point as to indicate that he was the most available candidate, the "soldier statesman," as Dougherty had described him, "with a record as stainless as his sword," was given 705 votes, before the excitement attending changes as the call proceeded had subsided, and was declared to be the nominee. William H. English of Indiana, who had retired from politics before the war, in which he had been a "Union man," now a wealthy banker, was nominated for Vice-President.

Here was a ticket such as the Democratic party had not presented before. In 1864 when the Union was on the brink of dissolution it had nominated a soldier, General McClellan, but on a platform declaring the war to be a failure. In 1868 it had nominated Seymour, a man who had given small support to the Union during the intersectional struggle, who did not wish to be a candidate and who was half-heartedly interested in the result of the campaign. In 1872 the party had resigned all its traditions and indorsed Horace Greeley and Gratz Brown, the strange products of the "Liberal" movement of that year. In 1876 Tilden, a cold and crafty man, who cared little for the issue of the war, sound on the currency question, running on a ticket with Hendricks who was patently wrong on this question, had been the nominee. Now there were signs that folly had run its course. Lessons had been learned. The party presented to the suffrages of the people two men of high character. There was stupidity in expecting votes to be gained in the North with candidates whose record had not been sound on the great subject of preserving the Union. Both the candidates were unquestioned "War Democrats." Hancock was a truly distinguished soldier. His services at Gettysburg, as on other fields, had won him the respect as well as the gratitude of the nation. What his capacities might be as a civil magistrate could not be clear. Since the war he had had a number of *quasi* civil administrative duties to perform in the South and West and, more lately, in connection with the Pennsylvania railway riots. In Louisiana, whither he had gone to supplant Sheridan on President Johnson's orders, he had revealed himself as a liberal who had earned the gratitude of the South, while that section was under the heel of the Radical reconstructionists of Congress. What his views were on economical and other parliamentary subjects was not clear. But he came from a part of the Union which was not given to thinking and speaking nonsense about the currency question, and for once it could be said that both the candidates on a Democratic ticket, on the most important matter which confronted the country, a matter in which the party had been, and was still, honeycombed with ignorant heresy, held enlightened opinions and were actuated by honest purposes.

The Republicans were closely followed at Chicago by the Greenbackers, who assembled in the same hall in which Garfield and Arthur had been nominated. The party which found the chief matter with the country to be a want of enough paper, silver and other cheap money, for what they conceived to be their convenience and advantage, had lost some of the reasons of existence which had given it electoral victories in 1878. Specie payments had been resumed. With large crops, a return of confidence, a measure of fiscal order, and rising prosperity, a gospel such as the Greenbackers taught was losing its force. It is true that paper which was at par with gold must be kept there without provision for even the ultimate retirement of the "legal tenders," and silver was accumulating by the ton in the vaults of the Treasury, since the people would not receive "short" dollars, or, receiving them, returned them to the government. But there was a belief that, for the time being at least, the currency question had come to settlement. A few hundreds of men, who were not of this opinion, including representatives of a variety of socialist and workingmen's factions, after having discussed the propriety of nominating "Ben" Butler or David Davis,[1] presented General James B. Weaver as their candidate for President. A fine orator, of soldierly presence, he had made his way into Congress from Iowa in 1878.[2] He had been a Republican—he was now a radical "people's man," though of a more reasonable type than many of those whose leader he became.[3] His forensic gifts, as well as the sincerity of his purpose, he was to prove in the coming campaign by no less than 100 days of speech making in the open air.[4] Those who subordinated all governmental problems to the prohibition of the liquor traffic nominated General Neal Dow of Maine, a state which for some years had been experimenting with preventive laws on this subject.

All four parties had nominated for the Presidency generals of the Union armies in the Civil War, an indication of the abundance in the land of men with military titles, and of a conviction that they could stir the popular imagination in political campaigns. The platforms, reciting the party's deeds of derry in the past and making promises for the future, were esteemed of little account. The Republicans' was a rigmarole of platitudes

[1] Haynes, Life of J. B. Weaver, pp. 158–9.
[2] Ibid., Third Party Movements, pp. 164–5.
[3] S. J. Buck, The Agrarian Crusade, pp. 92–3.
[4] Haynes, Third Party Movements, pp. 140, 143; Haynes, Life of Weaver p. 167.

which evaded much upon which it might have touched and was patently insincere in regard to some points, like civil service reform, about which it was conceived definite statement should be made. The Democrats committed their task to Henry Watterson, who wrote a paper which it was fairly said would have served as well for an editorial article in his Louisville newspaper.[1] The contest was between Garfield and Hancock, between the Republicans and the Democrats, a resumption, with every weapon, of the feud which had been adjourned for a time on the seating of Hayes.

Two scandals had been laid at Garfield's door and the transactions which had given rise to them were unworthy of such a man. He had been a preacher,[2] a teacher, a soldier and he was now a statesman. His interests were serious, his ideals for himself and the government were high. The judicious who were independent in their party ties drifted naturally into his retinue—they were in no kind of doubt as to their choice as between the two nominees. While he was a party man he was no lackey for the party, or for any man in the party. His course, during the recent very difficult experiences which all public men had had with the currency question, had been even more worthy than Hayes's, since Hayes, under Sherman's advice,[3] had approved the bill (which Garfield had voted against in the House) to stop the retirement of the greenbacks. Sherman who had vacillated that he might make no enemies, and become, if possible, his party's nominee for President, had failed to realize his ambition, while instead Garfield, who had dared

[1] Hayes was condemned as a "usurper" who, in appointing Republicans to office, was "billeting villains upon the people." The Democratic party was "the friend of labor and the laboring man"—it would "protect him alike against the cormorant and the commune."—McPherson, Handbook of Politics for 1880, p. 195.

[2] As such he commended himself to the "church people." The influences of the Methodists now for some time had been carried into politics— they had claimed Grant and Hayes. Garfield was held to be of a "religious nature"; he would be, from the standpoint of voters of "religious feeling," a worthy successor in the President's office. It was Garfield who had uttered the remembered phrase at the time of Lincoln's assassination—"God reigns and the government at Washington still lives."—Smith, Life of Garfield, p. 383.

[3] Williams, Life of Hayes, vol. ii, p. 130.

to be honest on these questions, with little regard for his political fate, was taken for the place. It was enough to awaken the enthusiasm of the Independents, and, while they deplored the shadows which were cast upon Garfield's record, though not more than he. himself did, they believed and said that the entanglements, unworthy of him as they were, had not corrupted, or in any manner influenced, his course in public life. He had not been moved, nor was he involved with the intention of being turned, from an honorable career. One of these incidents, for which he and his friends had regret, was his connection with the Crédit Mobilier scandal, and the other touched his relationship with Shepherd and the "District Ring" in Washington on the subject of a paving contract with a man named De Golyer.

The contest very soon waxed warm. Our Presidential campaigns have often been the artificial expressions of excitement, confined in the main to the politicians whose selfish objects are to be subserved by the triumph of one or another candidate. It was not so now. Man, woman and even child had the deepest feeling about the issue; they knew their minds and they were stubble for a fire which would not expire until the vote should be taken. Every crossroads hamlet with a corner store and a smithy in it, every farmhouse was in a turmoil and the population was aligned for Garfield or for Hancock, as prejudice and sympathy inclined it. The morning paper from the city, when it came, the weekly paper from the county town, conversation in the field, at the store, in the tavern, at the wayside, wherever men met together, deepened the conviction of the people that their own welfare and the future good of the whole country were involved in the result. Republican families with whom memory of the war was fresh were determined that no Democrat, though he should have been a soldier of the Union, should enter the White House as President. Democrats were as fierce in their partisanship—they would retrieve the disaster of 1876 and punish those who had robbed them of their victory.

Soon the spellbinders were on the stump; as the summer advanced and autumn came on orators appeared in every town and village to expound the issues of the campaign. Youth on all sides formed themselves into marching clubs and, drilled by some returned soldiers, officers of the war whose spirits still itched for military glory, phalanxes of tramping men were ready to fill the highways. Rude "transparencies" of muslin stretched over wooden frames were painted with quip and saw in praise of their favorite candidate and in deprecation and ridicule of him who, and the party which, it was their wish and purpose to defeat. With candles and oil lamps inside of them these lettered devices at night were borne aloft in parades which stirred the popular heart. Mounted troops of young farmers in caps and capes, carrying torches; bodies of "infantry" with lighted flambeaux treading in line to familiar war-time music of brass band or fife and drum corps; fine columns of young town fellows, dressed it may be in elegant uniforms, carrying battle axes, if they answered to the name of "pioneers," the evolutions of whose platoons, as they marched, won enthusiastic admiration; dandies out of good city families in fine attire on handsome steeds from their fathers' stables—all these, on occasion, would be brought together in processions of impressive length. The streets even of the largest cities were as yet, at this time, but imperfectly lighted and the appearance in them of thousands of men with torches, "transforming night into day," was a signal for the gathering of crowds of onlookers who might, it was surmised, be moved to vote for the party which could show the greatest numerical strength and make the better appearance when on review. Red fire and other pyrotechnical displays, and the noise of exploding powder, where gunnery was not esteemed to be dangerous, added to the zest of the marchers and their admirers. In a parade in New York on a night in October it was said that no less than 50,000 men were seen.[1] They were reviewed by General Grant. The sound of marching feet on the streets of the city was heard until four o'clock in the morning.[2]

[1] N. Y. Nation, Oct. 14, 1880.
[2] Autobiography of T. C. Platt, p. 133; Badeau, Grant in Peace, p. 326.

The Democrats pressed Garfield—the two scandals [1] in which they were pleased to involve him no one was permitted to forget.[2] The Republicans in the case of the Crédit Mobilier turned the tables upon their enemies by accepting the issue. The $329 which Garfield was said to have received from Oakes Ames became the symbol of the campaign for both parties— "329" found a place on transparencies in every parade, rustics gathered on hillsides and fired 329 shots from their squirrel rifles, boys shouted "329." Few knew what such a cabalistic shibboleth meant, nor did they care. The Republican hurled it back into the teeth of the Democrat who had brought it into the campaign and who had as little particular knowledge about it. An iniquity, memory of which was intended to confound the foe, was thus converted into a slogan for that foe to write upon its banners. It was, in truth, no great matter in the sight of any candid man who would arrive at a right estimate of the candidate. The unpleasant fact was that Garfield had apparently told an untruth about it, when he had been faced with the evidence of having taken money from Ames. Searching his memory he had reached the conclusion that he had received a sum of about $300, which, however, he averred, was not in the nature of a dividend on stock. It had been a loan from Ames to finance a vacation in Europe, which the lender had been repaid.[3] So much might possibly have sufficed as an excuse. But Garfield, to be certain of exoneration, in panic, after the exposure, had again tendered the money to Ames, action which called for further explanations.[4] Caught in the intricacies of the scandal he relapsed into silence, though he shortly prepared a rather labored apology for circulation in his Congressional district where he must soon face a contest to hold his seat.[5]

[1] With the account of the two infamies laid at Garfield's door were joined facts about the "suspension of Arthur for dishonesty and inefficiency in his office by R. B. Hayes."—See a pamphlet in Sherman Papers.

[2] The pack was diligently led by the New York Sun.—Cf. Wilson, Life of Dana, pp. 449–50.

[3] Smith, Life of Garfield, pp. 531–3, 539.

[4] Ibid., p. 534.

[5] Review of the Transactions of the Crédit Mobilier Co. by J. A. Garfield, published in May, 1873. Cf. Smith, Life of Garfield, pp. 556–7.

The more the subject was discussed the more murky did it
become, and, had the discussion been continued at once, while
the public excitement was at its height, Garfield, very likely,
would have followed Colfax, who had filled the air with pro-
testations and denials, into private life.[1] Now, however, a
more just estimate of Ames, a conviction that no important
corruptions had attended the construction of a railroad, the
large value of which was generally perceived, and a belief in
the purity of Garfield's motives as a public man, caused this
incident, after a few years of oblivion, to be regarded as a
peccadillo, when the facts about it were revived with a view
to discrediting him and the party which he had been chosen
to lead.

The De Golyer charge was not so easily dismissed. A man
of this name held patents for a wooden pavement which he
wished to cause the Board of Public Works in the District of
Columbia to select for use in Washington. Garfield was chosen
by another Congressman, who was acting as De Golyer's attorney, and who was unexpectedly called away from the city,
to present the subject at a hearing when the merits of this
and other kinds of pavement should be under discussion, for
which he received $5,000 out of a large fund set aside for this
and similar uses.[2] It was alleged that as a member of Congress
and chairman of the committee of appropriations in the House,
which had fiduciary relations with the District, he should not
have involved himself in such a business. This view was emphasized because of the scandals, most of which had come to
public knowledge at a later date, attaching to the Shepherd
government in Washington. It is certain that the agent of
the paving company employed Garfield rather than another
lawyer because of his position in Congress, and it is equally
certain that he was generously paid for the mere preparation
of a brief, and gave but little actual service to his employers.
Yet the fact remained in this case, as in the case of Garfield's
relations with Oakes Ames, that he allowed the transaction in

[1] Another view in Smith, Life of Garfield, p. 546.
[2] Senate Reports, 43rd Cong. 1st sess., no. 453, pp. 1074, et seq.

no way to influence his course as a public man. There appears, indeed, to have been no point at which he could have served the contractors corruptly.[1] One case, like the other, now for the purpose of the campaign, was dismissed as an indiscretion,[2] which, it is true, it were better not to have in the record of a candidate for President. So little a thing was outweighed by a good personal reputation in other regards, an honest courage in the great matters which had confronted him for many years in Congress, and an ability which, if it were forensic rather than in tried administrative fields, promised well for the state. The Independents were putting a high value, indeed, upon Garfield when they could accept with him a man like Arthur who was "the very embodiment of machine politics," and who loaded the ticket "heavily" in the eyes of all reformers.[3]

Hancock, though he was named "the Superb" for the figure he had made upon the battlefields of the Civil War, was unacceptable to the Republicans on various accounts. The New York Nation said that he was "a gallant soldier and honest gentleman." While it was hoped and believed that he could have nothing in common with Grant his election would be solely a reward for military service. Of "Bonapartism" the country had had enough. Its problems now were not the soldier's—"The war drum throbbed no longer and the battle flags were furled."[4] The people were done with the war and were no longer exalted, as they earlier had been, by a contemplation of its triumphs.[5] Hancock was "a good man weighing 250 pounds," said the New York Sun.[6] He did "nothing," said the Chicago Tribune, "but eat, drink and enjoy himself sensually." If he were not a major-general he would probably

---

[1] N. Y. Nation, July 1 and Aug. 19, 1880.
[2] "He is in my opinion," wrote Schurz to H. C. Lodge in June, 1880, "incapable of a dishonest act, although a shrewd lobby agent may have succeeded in placing him in an equivocal position."—Writings of Schurz, vol. iii, p. 507.
[3] N. Y. Nation, June 17, 1880; cf. R. R. Bowker in ibid., July 1, 1880.
[4] Ibid., July 1, 1880.
[5] Ibid., July 15, 1880.
[6] Wilson, Life of Dana, p. 450; N. Y. Nation, Oct. 21, 1880.

be a "country landlord," who sat around, while his wife did
the cooking and his son " tended bar." [1]

Hancock was poor—he had had humble beginnings in a
little town in southeastern Pennsylvania. But the poverty
which it was supposed might be the true password to the
Presidency was Garfield's, and the picture of his rise from the
business of driving a mule on the towpath of a canal [2] and of
"ringing the bells at Hiram" in jean clothes with calico sleeves,
i.e., at Hiram College where as a student he had been performing
janitor service,[3] was by stump speaker, in "campaign biography" and in party press industriously set before the country.
It was believed that in the emphasis of such a birth and youth
lay success.[4]

Though Hancock had had an entirely satisfactory record
as a soldier there were not wanting in the campaign many
"stories" connecting him with the "rebels." [5] These moved
nobody of solid judgment and were but the outturn of partisans
for the occasion. It is clear that Hancock owed his nomination
solely to his military reputation and that there was no promise
in any past performance of a talent for managing the problems
of civil administration. Grant had been taken from the army
and every judicious man knew what failures in eight years
had been his. The country had just escaped the disgrace
which four years more of such delinquency might have brought
to its door. It was an ill day upon which to present another
military figure for public approbation.

Garfield's own judgment, as well as that of his advisers,
led him to take the part of a composer of dispute. Taste, as
well as self and party interest, as he understood this interest,

---

[1] Quoted in N. Y. Nation, July 22, 1880.

[2] Which he had followed for a short time as a boy. (Cf. Smith, Life of
Garfield, p. 23.) "Towpath clubs" were formed, each with a captain, a
first mate, a second mate, a steersman, a toll taker, a lookout, etc.—they
would assemble votes, it was hoped, for the candidate.—Sherman Papers.

[3] Smith, Life of Garfield, p. 46.

[4] President Hayes urged it. Garfield was an "ideal candidate," because
he was an "ideal self-made man." The truth is, said Hayes, "no man ever
started so low that accomplished so much in all our history—not Franklin
or Lincoln even."—Diary and Letters of Hayes, vol. iii, p. 601.

[5] N. Y. Nation, July 22 and 29, 1880.

inclined him to act as a moderator between the factions.[1]
While it was known that he had been resolute in important
emergencies it became more and more plain, under close observation, that he was, as Hayes said, "not original, not firm,
not a moral force." [2]

It is certain that he had capacities better fitting him for
platform oratory and for debate, in which he was ready and
formidable,[3] than for administrative duties. He was somehow
wanting in executive aptitude.[4] He was more likely to be right
in the choice of a policy than in his judgments of the value
of other men for place and service. To many he seemed uncertain of mind,[5] a characteristic which others said was attributable to an investigative habit.[6] He would not stand
erect when men of stronger power of will, often selfish and
bent on their own advantage, pressed around him,[7] and now
and again would yield to escape a fight.[8] Of courteous bearing in
his contacts with other men, equable of temper, careful in
reasoning processes, skillful in argument he, nevertheless, did
not dominate. He lacked assertion. A fine parliamentary
figure, he with more fighting spirit would have been a yet finer
one. Men were much alike to him. He was prepared to think
well of them. They were brothers and friends.[9] Whether his

---

[1] He was by nature eager for friendships and fond of approbation. (Smith,
Life of Garfield, pp. 548–9.) He would try too hard, John Hay said, "to
make everybody happy." (Ibid., p. 1071.) He "leaned on others"; he "could
not face a frowning world," said President Hayes.—Diary and Letters,
vol. iv, p. 110.

[2] Diary and Letters, vol. iv, p. 110; cf. Sherman's Recollections, p. 807;
Boutwell, Sixty Years in Public Affairs, vol. ii, p. 274; McCall, Life of
T. B. Reed, p. 90; S. M. Cullom, Fifty Years in Public Service, pp. 127, 128.

[3] He was "the best popular debater of his time," said President Hayes.—
Diary and Letters, vol. iv, p. 110.

[4] He was "not executive in his talents."—Ibid.

[5] Cf. Sherman's Recollections, p. 807; Autobiography of Platt, p. 125,
A. D. White, Autobiography, vol. i, p. 190.

[6] Hoar, Autobiography, vol. i, pp. 399–400.

[7] Cf. Smith, Life of Garfield, pp. 1006–7.

[8] "He rushes into a fight," said Jeremiah Black, "with the horns of a
bull and the skin of a rabbit."—Smith, Life of Garfield, p. 936.

[9] Ibid., pp. 1081, 1148. He belonged to a queer sect of religionists who
called one another "brothers" and "sisters."—Ibid., p. 1065; cf. Halstead
in McClure's Magazine, Feb., 1896.

cramped youth made him contemplate his inferiors indulgently, or whether their flattery attracted them to him certain it is that his powers of discrimination were not well developed,[1] and such traits stood him in poor stead now that
he was to be President, with the "spoils system" entrenched
in our politics as it never had been before and with men at
his door wrangling like cab drivers and baggage agents at a
railway station or on a steamboat pier for the honors and profits
attending the business of managing the government.

In all truth he was in a difficult place. He had been no
group's or faction's "first choice"—he had been nominated
only because no one else could be.[2] Two intractable enemies,
Blaine and Conkling, had wanted the leadership, one for
himself, the other, too, for himself, through Grant, and they,
especially Conkling, were, in their wounded pride, far from
likely to give whole-hearted support to the nominee. Garfield
might have said, being without obligation to any, that he
would be independent of them all, that he would be the candidate of the people of all classes in all parts of the country of
Republican sympathies. But so much he was not minded to
do. The "practical" politicians, who surround all candidates
and who now joined his retinue, advocated concession and
compromise—along this way, they said, lay his election and
party success.[3]

He expressed a willingness to give an ear to Blaine and Conkling alike—all the elements which could be brought to his
support were heard, not without arousing Conkling's suspicions,
especially when it was known that the candidate's interests
and sympathies inclined him to favor Blaine.[4] Garfield was
told that he must almost purchase the support of the New
York "machine,"[5] or meet certain defeat. The Stalwarts
were forming "306 clubs" in all parts of the North—"306,"

[1] Smith, Life of Garfield, pp. 926–7.
[2] Cf. ibid., p. 977.
[3] Ibid., p. 994.
[4] Ibid., p. 998.
[5] That favor in that quarter came by purchase is abundantly confirmed
by Platt in his Autobiography, pp. 125–6.

the number of delegates who had stood their ground for Grant
in the convention at Chicago became, like "329," a slogan of
the campaign. Conkling and his men, if they should support
Garfield in 1880, would keep before the people the name of
Grant and the hope of winning the nomination for him in
1884.[1]

To all Garfield gave pleasant words—and he filled them
with a hope that they would have a hand in his administration
when he became President. He wrote to Grant seeking friendship and approval.[2] He was willing to have such a man as
William E. ("Bill") Chandler as chairman of the committee
to manage the campaign, though Marshall Jewell was put in
the position, and as secretary of the committee "Tom" Platt
who, however, was not chosen, since Logan, who had gone
on the rampage, desired "Steve" Dorsey to have the place.[3]

Conkling so loudly voiced his bitterness, his "machine"
was so completely in his control, he was so manifestly holding
out for a bargain which would promise him advantage, the
parties were.so nearly on a balance in New York state that
the result was shrouded in great uncertainty.[4] Advisers, such
as Chandler and Dorsey, urged Garfield to offer even more
than had been made articulate in the letter of acceptance. The
candidate must go farther to appease those who were cold
to his name.[5] He should come to New York, a suggestion at
which he balked. Jewell was asked for advice. The chairman
of the National Committee said that the question was "one

---

[1] Smith, Life of Garfield, pp. 1032, 1035. This band of brothers, the
"glorious 306," actually formed an organization and dined together, at
least once a year, for a long time after Grant's death. (Cf. Autobiography
of Platt, pp. 115–23.) Medals were struck and presented to them.—Conkling, Life of Conkling, p. 609.

[2] Smith, Life of Garfield, pp. 998–9.

[3] Ibid., pp. 990–1000, J. M. Forbes, Letters and Recollections, vol. ii,
pp. 196–8.

[4] Blaine, thanking Chandler for "everything that was done and so well
done" for him at Chicago (Chandler Papers) had accepted the result in
the hope of having an important influence in the administration. He was
hopeful; the Conklingites could not "in the end," said he, "afford to scuttle
a ship on which they are passengers."—Gail Hamilton, Biography of Blaine,
p. 487.

[5] Smith, Life of Garfield, pp. 1007–9.

of the most delicate and difficult things" that he had ever
had to decide.[1] Garfield who had been giving Conkling "time
and silence," [2] as could have been foreseen, yielded (under protest for which none cared) [3] and, on August 3rd, left his home
in Ohio for New York. He was acclaimed at the railway stations on the way to the conferences in the East in which he
should not have been involved. Blaine was present, by invitation,—Garfield wished some one to "stand by" him.[4] Conkling, indeed, absented himself from the meetings,[5] though several
of his followers, including Arthur, Platt and Levi P. Morton,
the campaign treasurer, who received what to them appeared to
be satisfactory assurances that they would be given control of
the spoils in New York state, were in attendance.[6] New ovations
at railway stations marked the candidate's return to Ohio.

Conkling, having been told by his lieutenants of the result
of the interview, now tuned up his oratorical instruments and
was ready to take the stump,[7] making in all, during the campaign, about twenty speeches.[8]   Once later, while in Ohio,
he, with Grant, visited Garfield at Mentor,[9] a meeting which,
though very distasteful to Conkling,[10] was given, for appearance's sake, great political significance.[11]

[1] To Chandler, June 29, 1880, in Chandler Papers.
[2] Garfield's words in letter to Blaine, July 21, 1880.—Gail Hamilton,
Biography of Blaine, p. 487.
[3] In asking Sherman to be present Garfield said that, "at their unanimous and urgent request," he had "reluctantly consented to attend."—
Garfield to Sherman, July 31, 1880, in Sherman Papers.
[4] Gail Hamilton, Biography of Blaine, p. 487.
[5] Platt purports to state the reasons for his master's absence.—Autobiography, pp. 126–7; cf. Conkling, Life of Conkling, pp. 612–3.
[6] Conkling, Life of Conkling, p. 612; T. C. Platt, Autobiography, pp. 127–
31; cf. Smith, Life of Garfield, pp. 1012–8.
[7] Smith, Life of Garfield, p. 1018; Cortissoz, Life of Reid, vol. ii, pp. 613–5.
[8] Conkling, Life of Conkling, p. 626.
[9] Garfield's home in Ohio.—Cf. Smith, Life of Garfield, p. 1032; Conkling,
Life of Conkling, pp. 620–21.
[10] Croly, Life of M. A. Hanna, p. 117.
[11] Cf. Platt, Autobiography, pp. 134–5. Hayes, a different man, would
have taken another course. "If there are any two men in the country whose
opposition and hatred are a certificate of good character and sound statesmanship," he said, "they are Conkling and Butler. I enjoy the satisfaction of being fully endorsed by the hatred and opposition of both of these
men."—Diary and Letters of Hayes, vol. iii, p. 638.

The Independents found little satisfaction in the catholicity of Garfield's associations and friendships as the campaign progressed, nor had they admired the spirit of evasion and of compromise pervading the letter in which he had accepted the nomination, especially in reference to civil service reform.[1] They resented Dorsey's prominence, as secretary; he, with Chandler's aid, was directing the affairs of the National Committee, since Chairman Jewell chose to play only a silent part in the campaign.[2] But finally all the elements were attached to the candidate. Grant,[3] who continued his travels to receive the homage of the people,[4] Conkling, Blaine, Logan, Sherman, Evarts, Schurz [5] were brought into the campaign to stir the Republicans to the need of doing their duty at a critical hour. Even President Hayes, with his wife and two of his sons, found the period of the campaign the occasion for a visit to the Pacific coast and, though he indulged, as he passed from place to place, in no references to the claims of the candidates, his movements were timed to help, if they could, the party cause.[6]

Almost nothing marked the early weeks of the campaign but the circulation of slanders and imputations principally evidencing the bitterness of North for South, of the "Union man" for the "rebel," until the tariff was brought forward. This subject was prolific of possibilities interesting to the politician—in money that could be taken from the manufacturer, ready to exchange it for advantage accorded him in the rates

[1] Smith, Life of Garfield, pp. 1001–6. It betrayed, said the Nation, "a want of backbone." (Issue of July 22, 1880.) It was a "cruel disappointment" to the Independents. (Ibid., July 15, 1880; Harper's Weekly, July 31, 1880.) Schurz protested. (Smith, Life of Garfield, pp. 1004–5; Writings of Schurz, vol. iv, pp. 1–5.) Horace White said that Garfield had surrendered to the New York "machine." (Smith, Life of Garfield, p. 1005.) Hayes declared that Garfield had made a "mistake" in veiling his views on civil service reform.—Diary and Letters of Hayes, vol. iii, p. 614. For the letter see McPherson's Handbook for 1880, pp. 192–4.

[2] J. M. Forbes, Letters and Recollections, vol. ii, p. 197; cf. Chandler Papers.

[3] Cf. Conkling, Life of Conkling, pp. 618–21.

[4] He was in California in October.

[5] In his own way and in a manner creditable to him.

[6] Williams, Life of Hayes, vol. ii, pp. 393–8.

of taxation upon imports, and in the votes of masses of men
settled in industrial centers, who could be told that their
employment and the wages which they received were dependent
upon the success of the party willing to accord them "protection." An attempt would now be made to inject this subject into the canvass.[1]

The Democratic platform, which Henry Watterson had
written, contained a declaration in favor of "a tariff for revenue
only."[2] This, said the Republicans, was "free trade." They,
on their side, were advocates of duties "to favor American
labor," [3] i.e., of a protective tariff, which it was plainly understood was the tariff of 1861, amended from time to time,
and still the statute governing the customs officers at our
various ports of entry.[4] But Garfield, it was known, had been
actively interested in tariff reform,[5] though he had recanted
in some degree in his letter accepting the nomination,[6] while
Hancock's position was difficult to fix. It was alleged that
about this subject the Democratic candidate knew even less
than about other questions of public policy. As the Republicans pressed the Democrats with a certain treason to American
industry and a design to dismiss labor and close the mills,
some statement from him seemed to be obligatory. He was
"interviewed," and said that his election could affect American manufacturing neither one way nor another—the tariff
was a "local affair." [7] Scorn could rise to no greater height.
Here was a candidate for the Presidency who knew so little
about public matters that he called the tariff a "local question."

---

[1] Garfield wrote to John Sherman on September 25 asking his "friends"
to "push" the "tariff question which so deeply affects the interest of
manufacturers and laborers. The argument of the 'solid South' is well
enough in its way and ought not to be overlooked, but we should also press
those questions which lie close to the homes and interests of our own
people."—Sherman's Recollections, p. 787.

[2] McPherson's Handbook for 1880, p. 195.

[3] Ibid., p. 190.

[4] Cf. N. Y. Nation, Sep. 16 and Oct. 14, 1880.

[5] Cf. Smith, Life of Garfield, pp. 454–9, 460–61, 473, 715–6.

[6] McPherson's Handbook for 1880, p. 193; Smith, Life of Garfield,
p. 1002.

[7] N. Y. Nation, Oct. 14, 1880; cf. ibid., Oct. 21, 1880.

Whatever the immediate effect of raising this issue at the eleventh hour it was a discovery of value for the future—in this direction might be found the material for improving the fortunes of the Republican party in later campaigns.

The elections in October betokened Republican success in November. In both Ohio and Indiana the Democratic candidates for governor met defeat. The Republicans were exultant and were confident of the result—they were not disappointed when the day came. All the Northern and Western states gave Garfield pluralities, except New Jersey and Nevada. California upon a final count divided its electoral vote between the Republican and Democratic candidates. Garfield's triumph seemed to be decisive, for he had 214 electoral votes which left but 155 for Hancock. Nevertheless it was clear that a few thousand votes less in New York and Indiana would have given the returns a different appearance. The plurality in Indiana was only 6,600 and, without the expenditure of $100,000, which Dorsey had taken into the state from New York, it was positively stated that Hancock and not Garfield would have won.[1] All had hinged upon New York. If 11,000 men there who had voted for Garfield had voted instead for Hancock,[2] the electoral vote would have been 190 for Hancock and 179 for Garfield.[3]

All eyes were now fixed upon the President-elect. He had conducted his campaign as a conciliator—how now would he satisfy the various elements, particularly Blaine and Conkling, and their antagonistic followers? As a beginning Blaine was to be propitiated by a proffer of the first place in the cabinet, to which he was welcomed as a leader and a "friend."[4] Such a choice was, perhaps, not difficult for Garfield, since he had been an advocate of Blaine's nomination for the Presidency

[1] N. Y. Nation, Nov. 18, 1880 and Feb. 24, 1881; Smith, Life of Garfield, pp. 1023–6.

[2] Garfield's plurality was only 21,000.

[3] N. Y. Nation, Feb. 17, 1881; cf. McPherson's Handbook for 1882, p. 187.

[4] Smith, Life of Garfield, pp. 1049, 1051–2; cf. Cortissoz, Life of Reid, vol. ii, pp. 43–4. Blaine's letter of acceptance is in Gail Hamilton, Biography of Blaine, pp. 494–5, and App. Ann. Cyclop. for 1881, p. 845.

in 1876,[1] though he earlier had expressed distrust for one given to so much intrigue,[2] an opinion to which he again and again returned,[3] when out of the range of Blaine's "magnetism." At heart Garfield still seems to have been favorable to Blaine's nomination in 1880.[4] Whatever the friendliness behind the appointment, or the tactical necessity for it, the Secretary-ship of State was a position, as was observed, for which Blaine had but small fitness. He had come into public life through journalism. He knew little of law, either constitutional or inter-national. His talents were oratorical and his tastes political in a personal and party sense. "Restless and ambitious," as he at one time had been described by Garfield, the new President was preparing the way for those difficulties which were immediately to beset his administration.[5]

With Blaine in a comfortable place what now would be done for Conkling and the New York "machine"? There had been bargaining, it was said, on that fatal journey east in August. Levi P. Morton must have the Secretaryship of the Treasury in return for his services in financing the cam-paign.[6] The place had been promised him, he said; the whole New York "machine" desired him to have it.[7] Garfield de-clared that he would be willing to make Morton Secretary of the Navy, a position which he declined to accept.[8] Opinion on the currency question in the West could not be flouted by an appearance of placing the financial affairs of the country in the hands of a man whose interests and fortunes were bound up with the "gold bugs" and "money kings" of New York.[9]

[1] Smith, Life of Garfield, pp. 596, 599–602.
[2] He had called Blaine "tricky" (Ibid., p. 467) and said that he would "bear a good deal of watching."—Ibid., p. 473; cf. ibid., pp. 584, 596.
[3] Ibid., pp. 947, 957.
[4] Ibid., pp. 974, 989; cf. Sherman Papers.
[5] Smith, Life of Garfield, p. 1053.
[6] Ibid., pp. 1047–8; McElroy, Life of L. P. Morton, p. 110.
[7] Platt, Autobiography, pp. 132–3; Smith, Life of Garfield, pp. 1053–5, 1072.
[8] Smith, Life of Garfield, p. 1077.
[9] N. Y. Nation, March 17, 1881; Smith, Life of Garfield, p. 1047. This statement of the case is substantially confirmed by McElroy, Life of Morton, pp. 119–30.

By this time Blaine's selection for the first place in the cabinet was of public knowledge and the rancor of the Conkling element was increasing,[1] especially as Blaine was talking and writing in a froward manner, indicating that he would control the administration. A United States senator was to be elected in New York to succeed Kernan, a Democrat. Blaine injected himself into the contest at Albany, which finally resulted in the election of Platt.[2] Behind the scenes he was active in formulating his designs and bringing his forces to bear upon the President-elect.[3] So eager and pugnacious was he that he urged the barring from the new cabinet of both elements, the Independents and the Conkling men.[4] Thus, too, spoke Whitelaw Reid and other men in New York who were in Blaine's retinue, and who were prolific of selfish counsel.[5] All the while Garfield was holding out hope to the Stalwarts, and assuring them that he did not stand under the influence of Blaine.[6]

Choice of a Conklingite for the cabinet, with Morton out of the way, a result which was not gained until after the angriest demands were made upon Garfield,[7] and until Platt and Cornell had made a visit to Mentor,[8] seemed to lie between Thomas L. James, postmaster of New York City, and C. J.

[1] Cf. Henry L. Davis in Century Magazine, January, 1894.

[2] Platt's election, said the New York Nation, "marked the lowest point reached by the politics of this state under the Conkling influence." (N. Y. Nation, June 9, 1881; cf. ibid., Jan. 20, 1881; Cortissoz, Life of Reid, vol. ii, pp. 49–50; Platt, Autobiography, pp. 139–41.) Blaine had friends who were indiscreet also.—Smith, Life of Garfield, pp. 1056, 1058, 1072, 1087; Cortissoz, Life of Reid, vol. ii, p. 47.

[3] He was writing Garfield unweariedly, with the journalist's fluency and freedom, full of ambitions and schemes, which were presented under the mask of undying friendship, with many a flattery for Mrs. Garfield.—Gail Hamilton, Biography of Blaine, pp. 491–4.

[4] The first he called the "unco guid," "upstarts, conceited, foolish, vain"; the other, the Conkling element, he dismissed as including "all the desperate bad men of the party." (Smith, op. cit., pp. 1059–60.) But he would not knock down the Grant men with bludgeons—"they must have their throats cut with a feather."—Gail Hamilton, Biography of Blaine, pp. 490–91.

[5] Cf. Smith, Life of Garfield, pp. 1056–7, 1074.

[6] Ibid., p. 1074.

[7] Ibid., p. 1072.

[8] Ibid., pp. 1076–7.

Folger, chief justice of the New York state court of appeals.[1]
As a solution of the problem Garfield even proffered a place
to Conkling himself, against Blaine's excited tirades of protest, with the thought, if Conkling accepted, that he might
be Secretary of State and that Blaine could be transferred
to the Treasury Department,[2] and invited the New York leader
to come to Ohio for a discussion of the subject. Conkling
arrived at Mentor on February 16th and the conferences lasted
for six hours without reaching any result except what in the
end furnished ground for new misunderstandings.[3] Folger was
called; he declined the offer of the Attorney-Generalship.[4] Garfield then, when inauguration day was drawing nigh, returned
to Morton, again offering him the Navy Department, which
the New York banker accepted, only to decline it, under pressure of friends, who got him out of bed at four o'clock in the
morning to say that the post was not of sufficient importance—
he must have the Treasury.[5] The way opened for James,
who, after Garfield had reached Washington to take the oath
of office, was telegraphed, and he agreed to become Postmaster-
General.[6] James had interested himself in good government
and had won the commendation of the civil service reformers by
his excellent administration of the New York post office.[7]
Nominally an adherent of Conkling that leader could now not
very well disown the appointee, though small satisfaction was
taken in the announcement of the choice, which was made
amid charges of treachery that Conkling and his friends, Platt
and Arthur, did not cease to pour into the President's ears.[8]

[1] Cf. Smith, Life of Garfield, p. 1075.
[2] Ibid., pp. 1078, 1081–2; Gail Hamilton, Biography of Blaine, pp. 497–8.
[3] Ibid., pp. 1082–4; Platt, Autobiography, pp. 144–5; N. Y. Nation,
Feb. 24 and May 19, 1881.
[4] Smith, Life of Garfield, pp. 1084–5; 1087.
[5] Ibid., pp. 1087, 1091.
[6] Ibid., p. 1092; House Mis. Doc., 48th Cong. 1st sess., no. 38, pt. 2,
pp. 1–2.
[7] Cf. N. Y. Nation, March 17, 1881.
[8] Smith, Life of Garfield, pp. 1093–4; see also E. B. Andrews, The Last
Quarter Century in the United States, vol. i, p. 323, where a circumstantial
account, graphically illustrated, is given of an angry final interview between
Garfield and Conkling.

The Independents were to have for their representative in the cabinet Wayne MacVeagh who would be Attorney-General. Schurz had preferred and had urged the appointment of General Francis A. Walker to carry on the work in the Department of the Interior, which Schurz was leaving.[1] But Walker was opposed by Dorsey, who said that he was "not a Republican."[2] Dorsey himself, he and his friends alleged, was offered the place and might have been Schurz's successor as Secretary of the Interior.[3] While MacVeagh, who would be Attorney-General, was a son-in-law of Simon Cameron his record as a "reformer" made him, if less acceptable to other "reformers" than Schurz was in the Hayes cabinet, a figure deserving of respect.[4]

It was thought, in view of Sherman's services in connection with resumption, which had been the subject of encomium by Garfield in the nominating speech before the Chicago convention, in view too of the friendship between the men which this act betokened and his high position as a party leader, that he might be continued as Secretary of the Treasury.[5] But this would have done Conkling great affront,[6] and would have

[1] Writings of Schurz, vol. iv, pp. 82, 85, 89, 90.

[2] Dorsey had tried to get offices in Arkansas from Walker, while the latter had been in charge of the Indian Bureau. "Non-partisans" were appointed. Dorsey told Garfield that he preferred "straight out Democrats to non-partisans."—J. P. Munro, Life of F. A. Walker, p. 204.

[3] Cf. N. Y. Nation, Sep. 6, 1883.

[4] MacVeagh and Wharton Barker had been "original" Garfield men in Pennsylvania and had been of service in the convention at Chicago. (Smith, Life of Garfield, pp. 955–6.) In this appointment Garfield believed that he would "meet two wants"—he would "satisfy Cameron and please the Independents." Gail Hamilton, Biography of Blaine, p. 498.

[5] Sherman's Recollections, pp. 789–90; Writings of Schurz, vol. iv, p. 81.

[6] Cf. Diary and Letters of Hayes, vol. iii, p. 630. Sherman, as soon as it was clear that he would not be a member of the Garfield cabinet returned to Ohio "to mend his fences." He was elected to the place in the United States Senate to which Garfield had lately been chosen but had not occupied. Once upon a visit to his farm there was a suspicion that Sherman had a political object in view. No, he said, he had simply come home to "repair his fences," and look after other matters on the estate which had been neglected, perforce, while he had resided in Washington. Thus had originated a phrase which attained a wide popular use.—Sherman's Recollections, p. 728; A. D. White, Autobiography, vol. i, p. 218.

been displeasing to Blaine,[1] who urged the appointment of
Allison of Iowa,[2] which was against Garfield's judgment,[3] since
he preferred Windom of Minnesota, who was Sherman's candidate.[4] Unable to escape Blaine's importunity the place was
offered finally to Allison who, after accepting it concluded
to decline,[5] when the way opened for Windom,[6] and Kirkwood,
the rugged old "War Governor" of Iowa, who was chosen
to be Secretary of the Interior. Windom, though he had shown
himself to be quite unsound on the money question, especially
with relation to silver,[7] and occupied a place not much higher
than Allison on this point, would be held in check, it was believed, by Garfield whose position on the opposite side had
been correct and outspoken.[8] For a Southern member of the
cabinet Garfield called upon William H. Hunt, a lawyer,
until lately of Louisiana, of good family traditions, though,
before coming to Washington to be a judge of the Court of
Claims, he had been allied too prominently with the carpetbag and scalawag politics of his state. He became Secretary
of the Navy. Sentiment was indulged and Logan of Illinois
must consider that he had been propitiated by the appointment,
as Secretary of War, of President Lincoln's son, Robert,[9] who
had been in mind in Chicago as a candidate for the Presidency
before the convention had turned its interest to Garfield.[10]

It was not until after the inaugural ceremonies, on March 4th,
that these arrangements, with the free assistance of Blaine
and Whitelaw Reid, were completed. Indeed without these
skillful managers it is difficult to see how the President's problems could ever have been solved.[11] Such asking for advice,

---

[1] Sherman's Recollections, p. 802; Smith, Life of Garfield, p. 956.
[2] Gail Hamilton, Biography of Blaine, p. 496.
[3] Smith, Life of Garfield, pp. 1060–61, 1079.
[4] Sherman's Recollections, p. 815; Smith, Life of Garfield, pp. 1061, 1080.
[5] Smith, Life of Garfield, pp. 1094–5, 1097.
[6] Ibid., p. 1098.
[7] N. Y. Nation, March 10, 1881.
[8] Ibid., March 17, 1881.
[9] Smith, Life of Garfield, p. 1080; S. M. Cullom, Fifty Years of Public
Service, p. 125.
[10] Hoar, Autobiography, vol. i, p. 398.
[11] Cortissoz, Life of Reid, vol. ii, pp. 54–7.

such doing and undoing, with which no one in the end could be wholly pleased, all as Garfield believed in the interest of harmony and peace, such uncertainty of mind, have never been seen, it would appear, in the history of men about to begin their administrations of the Presidency. The more he invited advice the deeper in the slough did he fall, [1] the more preparation was made for those misfortunes which are associated with his brief term of office. [2]

The administration of President Hayes ended quietly—its course throughout had been without notable incident. A veto on his last day in office, March 3, 1881, of a funding bill sent to him by Congress, with amendments which were designed to cripple the national banking system, [3] was his final service in the defense of sound public finance. His administration throughout consisted in a serious concern for, and an honest transaction of, the business of government at a time when such attachment to the public interest was sorely needed to cool the national blood and by way of example, if the country were to prosper and its institutions were to endure. The attacks of both Blaine and Conkling, and their factions, upon the President, with charges that he was womanish, that his course was "nerveless" and supine, that his achievements were none or inconsiderable did away with no fact regarding him. There were shortcomings, but his purposes and the purposes of most of the men whom he had drawn around him were pure

[1] Schurz reminded him that a pound of pluck was worth a ton of luck. The new President should choose his course and then "go straight ahead without fear or favor." (Writings of Schurz, vol. iv, p. 83.) Such advice he could not or would not follow. "How much trouble you would save yourself by just picking out the fittest man for each place and then going ahead to make a good administration," Schurz wrote to Garfield another time.— Ibid., p. 115.

[2] A contrary conclusion is reached in Smith, Life of Garfield, chap. xxvii, after the author has presented ample evidence on the other side of the case. Vice-President Wheeler told Hayes—"I have said forty times if he [Garfield] had one-tenth of your [Hayes's] amiable obstinacy and independence he would be a great success." All he needed was "to be firm in the right" when he would have "the whole people at his back."—Diary and Letters of Hayes, vol. iii, p. 630.

[3] Sherman's Recollections, pp. 796–801; Williams, Life of Hayes, vol. ii, pp. 138–40.

and elevated.[1] There would have been no Republican party which could have asked for public support in 1880 had it not purged itself of the "influences that had discredited it" during an administration whose clean motives and high abilities the wise clearly understood.[2] Garfield now, in turn, had the almost undivided support of citizens of discreet and independent judgment who had found good in Hayes, but early there was reason to fear that the new administration would be, as it promised to be, uncertain and fluctuating.

Garfield's inaugural address wanted a fine tone; there was in it no call to service, no prophecy of definite or great deeds. After taking the oath of office on the public platform in Washington he had kissed his mother and his wife in turn, gestures which were advertised as widely as his career on the towpath, and which stood in as much relation as that experience to the statesmanship that sagacious persons desired, if they had not expected, in the new President.[3] As for his cabinet it meant, said the New York Nation, either that Garfield had "no policy at all," or none for which he intended "to strive greatly." [4]

So it fared with the administration. Seeing that no commanding mind was at the head of affairs the office-seekers, who had made Garfield's life a misery in Ohio from the time it was known that he had been elected, pressed around him at Washington and sought to gather to themselves every available piece of patronage. The government remained without any order or system in the matter of a civil service. The prizes in the form of salaried posts and other favors of pecuniary advantage were for those who, by effrontery or brigandage, could capture them. A delegate at the Republican convention

[1] "Among the multitude of public men I have met," said John Sherman, "I have known no one who held a higher sense of duty to his country and more faithfully discharged that duty than President Hayes."—Sherman's Recollections, p. 808, cf. A. D. White, Autobiography, vol. i, p. 189.
[2] Harper's Weekly, Sep. 4, 1880; cf. ibid., Sep. 25, 1880, where it is written—Hayes's "has been one of the quietest, most efficient, most spotless administrations in our annals."
[3] Cf. N. Y. Nation, March 10, 1881.
[4] Ibid.; cf. ibid., March 31, 1881.

at Chicago, Webster Flanagan of Texas, had aptly and un-
forgettably phrased the sentiment of the day. "What are we
here for," said he, "except to get office?"[1] All that had been
gained in the Hayes administration, principally in the Department of the Interior under Schurz,[2] and the theory (faithfully
expounded, if it were not consistently practiced) of Hayes concerning the civil service generally,[3] was on the point of being
swept aside in the mad contest for the spoils of victory. Blaine
demanded everything for himself and his following. Conkling wished for all and would have all, else he would betray
the party to which he adhered—in wrathful resentment it
seemed as if he would almost overturn the government.[4] From
the first day he had been full of suspicion concerning Garfield,
who, as a spokesman in the House for Hayes, could not have
enjoyed his confidence. For Garfield even to be seen with
Schurz was sufficient to awaken Conkling's rage.[5]

Stephen W. Dorsey, it was freely stated, was corruptly
interested in postal contracts. He had been an intimate adviser
of Garfield both during the campaign and since.[6] The state of
political morals was illustrated in a memorable way when,
in February, 1881, Grant presided over, Henry Ward Beecher
invoked the blessings on God of, and Vice-President Arthur [7]

[1] N. Y. Nation, June 10, 1880.
[2] Cf. ibid., Apr. 21, and May 5, 1881.
[3] He had, in the language of John Hay, aimed to, and would, in Hay's
belief, "chasten the outrageous indecency of the present system as much as
any one could." It must be thought that he fulfilled this expectation.
(W. R. Thayer, Life of Hay, vol. i, p. 430.) President Hayes wrote in his
Diary on July 14, 1880,—"The end I have chiefly aimed at has been to
break down Congressional patronage and especially Senatorial patronage.
The contest has been a bitter one. . . . But I have had great success. No
member of either House now even attempts to dictate appointments; my
sole right to make appointments is tacitly conceded."—Diary and Letters
of Hayes, vol. iii, pp. 612–3.
[4] Cf. Diary and Letters of Hayes, entry of Hayes for April 19, 1888,
vol. iv, p. 385.
[5] Smith, Life of Garfield, pp. 997–8. For Garfield's view of Schurz expressed to Blaine see Cortissoz, Life of Reid, vol. ii, p. 43.
[6] Smith, Life of Garfield, pp. 1058–9.
[7] It was at this dinner that Arthur in remembered words, in complimentary or, at any rate, condoning phrase, alluded to Dorsey's services in
going to Indiana to "buy" the state for the Republicans. Indiana, he said,
had been "put down on the books always as a state that might be carried

and others spoke at, a public dinner at Delmonico's in New York in honor of Dorsey, so that he might have an indorsement which would enable him the more forcibly to prosecute his designs upon the new President.[1]

Grant who was to be president of the Nicaragua Canal company,[2] the Panama Canal committee, a railroad in Mexico, a world's fair company[3] and what not other speculative enterprises, and who was actually again the beneficiary of subscriptions from rich men who were advertising their generosity in the newspapers,[4] abandoned the reticence which was usually his part. Deeply injured, as it appeared, because he had not secured the nomination at Chicago,[5] he chose to consider Garfield's success as, in some measure, a personal affront.

So it was on every side. The new President was overwhelmed by men who seemed to be involved in some conspiracy to usurp his functions, and direct him in the performance of his duties.[6] In his zeal to restore "harmony," respect "claims," recognize "wings" and "sections"[7] he multiplied his difficulties manyfold.

The mischief maker at his council table was Blaine who desired to use the administration, as all competent observers had foreseen that he would, for the advancement of his own political fortunes. It was his policy to berate other men, if they were his enemies, for their insincere purposes, their incompetency to hold government office and their corruption. They were "unclean birds" who wanted "loot and booty."[8] But he would promote the advancement of men of as bad or of worse instincts, if they would, in his belief, forward his personal plans. He "ate, drank and breathed politics."[9] Every

by close and perfect organization and a great deal of—(laughter)." Some one cried "soap"—that was the missing word.—Cf. N. Y. Times, Feb. 12, 1881.

[1] N. Y. Nation, Feb. 17 and 24, 1881; Harper's Weekly, March 5, 1881.
[2] Ibid., Nov. 20, 1879.
[3] Cf. ibid., March 31, 1881.
[4] Ibid., March 24, 1881; Davis, Hist. of N. Y. Times, p. 149.
[5] Smith, Life of Garfield, p. 1175.
[6] N. Y. Nation, March 24, 1881.
[7] Ibid., May 12, 1881.
[8] Smith, Life of Garfield, p. 1085.   [9] Ibid., p. 1079.

thought of his own, every aspiration for the administration was the reward of his friends and the punishment of his foes,[1] and he pleaded with such power that it was a man of a stronger character than Garfield's [2] who could withstand his insistencies. In choosing Blaine for Secretary of State Garfield had awakened the suspicions of the Independents and forfeited right to their confidence. He, at the same time, by this token, had completed the affront of Conkling and the Conkling men. Hayes, Sherman and others warned Garfield as the scene unfolded. They urged him to be the President—he should not surrender the authority of the office to his prime minister.[3]

William E. Chandler, patently unfitted on a variety of accounts for the place, was appointed Solicitor-General over the head and against the protests of Attorney-General Mac-Veagh, in whose department the new officer would serve.[4] This appointment, which involved the removal of a faithful incumbent, was dictated by, and made as a result of, the insistence of Blaine,[5] whose hand was seen prominently again, it was believed, in appointments in New York where Conkling, after his passages with Garfield over representation in the cabinet, anxiously watched the development of the situation.

It was in the interest of pacification that Levi P. Morton, about whose name the contest with Conkling had raged in the general travail of forming a cabinet, was almost at once, on March 9th, appointed to be minister to France. So much was well. On March 20th, some two weeks after the adminis-

---

[1] Smith, Life of Garfield, p. 1148.

[2] Given an inch Blaine would take an ell. He had not entered the White House for 37 months (Gail Hamilton, Biography of Blaine, p. 503), but he would make up now for lost time. On meeting days it was his wont to precede the other members of the cabinet to the White House for private conferences with Garfield and then withdraw to enter with the rest in order to conceal from them, if he could, his activities in the guidance of the Presidential mind.—W. H. Crook, Through Five Administrations, pp. 262–3.

[3] Smith, Life of Garfield, pp. 1058–9; Thayer, Life of Hay, vol. i, pp. 441–2, 447.

[4] N. Y. Nation, April 7 and May 26, 1881. Chandler, however, was not confirmed by the Senate.—Smith, Life of Garfield, pp. 1136, 1150.

[5] Smith, Life of Garfield, pp. 1086, 1149; Gail Hamilton, Biography of Blaine, p. 502.

tration had begun, Conkling, by invitation, came to the White House to discuss the question of Federal offices in New York. Told by the President that men who had supported him at Chicago must have some of the appointments Conkling suggested that they could be sent abroad, to which Garfield replied that they did not "deserve exile, but rather a place in the affairs of their own state." [1] Almost immediately after this conversation the President sent to the Senate five New York nominations pleasing to Conkling, which aroused throughout the country, as could have been foretold, much misgiving. It was concluded and declared that the President had surrendered to the New York "machine." [2]

Blaine held this view and at once visited Garfield to express his "great distress." [3] The conference lasted two hours and was productive of instant result. The next day the President, without consulting any other person, not even the appointees, sent to the Senate the name of Judge W. H. Robertson to be collector of the port at New York,[4] the bone of contention in the Hayes administration, while Merritt, an efficient officer who was occupying the place, by Hayes's appointment,[5] was made consul-general at London to succeed Grant's friend, Badeau, who was transferred to the legation in Denmark. Grant's brother-in-law, Cramer, who was at Copenhagen was nominated to be minister to Switzerland. The collectorship was, of course, the one office about which Conkling had had the most concern, both for sentimental and practical reasons.[6] Robertson was the Blaine leader in New York. He had been the anti-Conkling candidate in the state convention in which Cornell was nominated for governor in 1879.[7] As a delegate to the national convention in Chicago he had prominently led the movement within the New York delegation against the

[1] Smith, Life of Garfield, p. 1104.
[2] Cf. N. Y. Times and Phila. Inquirer of March 23, 1881.
[3] The words are Garfield's in his Diary.—Smith, Life of Garfield, p. 1105.
[4] "The most desirable and lucrative office within the gift of the President."—Autobiography of Platt, p. 150.
[5] Cf. D. S. Alexander, Political Hist. of New York, vol. iii, p. 406.
[6] Cf. ibid.
[7] Smith, Life of Garfield, p. 963.

"unit rule." He would not himself abide by the instructions given him and he used his influence actively to induce others to throw off the Conkling yoke and vote as their preferences might dictate.[1] He had opposed the election of Platt to the United States Senate.[2]

At once the President was charged by Conkling and Conkling's friends, and in the press, with having acted under the influence of Blaine.[3] Garfield, in defense, took high ground. In letters to friends he said that he would "settle the question" whether he was the registering clerk of the Senate, or the executive of the United States.[4] If he were thus motivated it was not different from Hayes's object in the passages which that President had had with Conkling, though it is to be observed that Hayes proceeded in a manner giving rise to no one's misunderstanding of his impelling purpose. Hayes had acted with reference to the customhouse at New York in the interest of the service without consideration of faction. He had affronted Conkling with a good end in view. Garfield, on the other hand, was displacing the efficient public officer whom Hayes had established in the place, not for the improvement of the service, but to make a position, controlling valuable patronage, for an adherent of a faction which was notoriously hostile to Conkling, and for no better reason whatever. In putting down one faction he was exalting another. In attacking Conkling he was satisfying Blaine, whose insistent advice had been taken and who now made no secret of his pleasure.[5] That Robertson was an "independent," which Garfield averred,[6] was a wholly specious claim. Robertson was "independent" of Conkling, but in no fine or honest sense and the new President, by this act, at once made a complete disclosure of the infirm character which he had brought into the cam-

---

[1] Nineteen men did so. Dawes in Century Mag., Jan., 1894; Smith, Life of Garfield, p. 963; Cortissoz, Life of Reid, vol. ii, pp. 58–9.
[2] Smith, Life of Garfield, p. 1058.
[3] Cf. ibid., pp. 1106–8; Boutwell, Sixty Years in Public Affairs, vol. ii, pp. 273–5; D. S. Alexander, Political Hist. of N. Y., vol. iii, p. 471.
[4] Smith, Life of Garfield, pp. 1109, 1115, 1124; Cortissoz, vol. ii, pp. 61–2.
[5] Smith, Life of Garfield, p. 1110.
[6] Ibid., p. 1109.

paign, and which was to mark his conduct now that he was President.

MacVeagh protested Chandler's appointment as Solicitor-General and very properly offered his resignation, which the President as properly declined to receive.[1] At the same time James, as the spokesman of Conkling in the cabinet, after hearing from his "Boss" and from Senator Platt and Vice-President Arthur, who were active in the same interest, resigned as Postmaster-General. The appointment of Robertson had in no way touched James as the head of the Post Office Department. Who should collect the duties on imports at New York was a matter clearly outside of the range of his official responsibility,[2] but, at command, he said that he would withdraw. The President refused to accept the Postmaster-General's resignation, which, it would appear, marked what was nearly the end of James's patience with Conkling's course,[3] though he continued, under some bond of honor, to coöperate with his friends attached to the New York "machine" and to use his place in the cabinet for a continuance of the controversy. The Vice-President, the two senators from New York, the Postmaster-General signed a protest and gave it to the President, who, they said, had violated a solemn agreement to consult them in making appointments to Federal office in territory under their jurisdiction.[4] Grant also was persuaded to address Garfield in support of Conkling's ethical position, that to the senators of a state belonged the spoils in that state.[5]

The more Conkling considered the indignity put upon him

[1] Smith, Life of Garfield, p. 1111; House Mis. Doc., 48th Cong. 1st sess., no. 38, pt. 2, p. 52.
[2] Cf. Cortissoz, Life of Reid, vol. ii, p. 61.
[3] Smith, Life of Garfield, pp. 1111–2.
[4] Ibid., pp. 1112–3; Cortissoz, Life of Reid, vol. ii, p. 61.
[5] Smith, Life of Garfield, pp. 1132–4. Grant was "talking wildly and very unjustly," the President said. (Smith, Life of Garfield, p. 1175.) He protested against the transfer of Badeau, who was at the time engaged in writing a panegyrical "Life" of Grant, from the rich consul-generalship in London to Denmark (N. Y. Nation, May 26 and June 16, 1881) and his brother-in-law's transfer from Denmark to Switzerland instead of to some balmier clime. (Ibid., June 16, 1881; cf. Badeau, Grant in Peace, pp. 328–31.) He uttered the opinion that the President did not possess "the backbone of an angle worm."—Badeau, Grant in Peace, p. 534.

and the more irritably he discussed it the more intolerable
it became. On the other side Blaine, Whitelaw Reid and their
friends were astir lest the President should change his mind
and undo what had been done for their advantage.[1] Garfield
girded himself for the contest. He said that this would be no
"rose water war." [2] A battle he did not wish, but, if it were
brought to his door, "the bringer" would find him "at home." [3]
In the Senate Conkling had unusual powers of intimidation
which he had never scrupled to employ.[4] April was occupied
with efforts to make deals and bargains,[5] in strengthening
lines for the struggle for and against the confirmation of the
appointments, as well as in settling and unsettling the President. So ominous was the outlook, from the standpoint of
the party, that the leaders, in caucus in Washington, appointed
a "Conciliation Committee," with Senator Dawes of Massachusetts at its head, with a view to a composition of the dispute. Conkling was heard. He made to the committee an
oration of great length, eloquence and bitterness. The committee visited the President.[6] Nothing availed and Garfield,
now well fortified for his task, came to a resolution which he
executed [7] on May 5th and which consisted of a withdrawal
of a number of the nominations, Robertson's among them,
and the return of Robertson's alone. The plain purpose of
this maneuver was to bring the appointment, which had principally inspired the contest, to an issue. This step was firm
as against Conkling; it was contrived by his enemies, and was
intended to compass his downfall as the "Boss" in New York.[8]
It was very clear that the Senate would ratify the nomination.

In this conjuncture Conkling and Platt, on May 14th, after

[1] Smith, Life of Garfield, pp. 1145–6; Cortissoz, Life of Reid, vol. ii,
pp. 60–64.
[2] Smith, Life of Garfield, p. 1116.
[3] Ibid., p. 1119; Cortissoz, Life of Reid, vol. ii, p. 65.
[4] Cortissoz, Life of Reid, vol. ii, pp. 62–3.
[5] Cf. Reid's letter to Garfield, in ibid., vol. ii, pp. 63–4.
[6] Dawes in Century Mag., Jan., 1894; Smith, Life of Garfield, pp. 1121–4.
[7] Again under the influence of Blaine (Smith, Life of Garfield, p. 1125),
who, after the measure was announced, wrote "Glory to God! Victory is
yours," and more like this.—Ibid., p. 1126.
[8] Ibid., pp. 1118–9.

angry explosions, tendered their resignations to Governor Cornell of New York as the representatives of that state in the United States Senate. The august upper house of the national legislature was notified of what the twain had done and they left Washington,[1] whereupon the Senate, rid of obstruction, unanimously confirmed Robertson's nomination,[2] leaving Conkling in a position which Garfield described as "ridiculous."[3] So in truth it was.[4] Conkling believed, it appears, that this action would incite some kind of a revolution which would overset Garfield, if not the republic itself.[5] He and his henchman, Platt, issued a letter reciting their grievances. Their expectation was that they would be immediately and triumphantly reëlected by the legislature at Albany and that then they might return to the old scene for further war upon the President.[6] Their statement was so wanting in adequate reasons justifying their unusual course, and the action which inspired it was proof of so much small meanness and vanity that it met with but little of the anticipated response. The New York state legislature was filled with the creatures of Conkling; they would, on most subjects, as he knew, do his bidding. But, by this maneuver, he manifestly had overreached himself. The whole country answered the challenge and that part of the press which was Blaine's, as well as that which was "Independent," heaped ridicule upon such a coxcomb and bully. Right thinking men within the party anyhow were weary enough of his leadership and the opportunity was now at hand to tumble him back into private life.[7]

[1] Smith, Life of Garfield, pp. 1127–31, 1134–5; Platt, Autobiography, pp. 152–7. Platt has desired to take to himself the credit for this heroic measure. He says that he first proposed it, though he had qualified as a senator only a few days since, and overpersuaded Conkling into following him to the point of resignation.—Autobiography, pp. 150–51.

[2] Senate Ex. Journal, vol. xxiii, p. 87.

[3] Smith, Life of Garfield, p. 1135.

[4] Cf. Harper's Weekly, June 11, 1881.

[5] It was, said John Hay, "a freak of insanity on the part of a man who has lost sight of his true relations with the rest of the world."—W. R. Thayer, Life of Hay, vol. i, p. 452.

[6] D. S. Alexander, Political Hist. of N. Y., vol. iii, p. 477.

[7] N. Y. Nation, May 26, 1881; Harper's Weekly, June 25 and July 2, 1881.

The scene shifted from Washington to Albany where a tedious contest, attended by newspaper correspondents from all portions of the country, commenced. "Stalwarts" there had been but these were opponents of Hayes and his policy in the South by which he, so it was said, had nearly ruined the Republican party. The "Stalwart" now and, indeed so early as in the struggle to elect Platt to the senatorship six months before, in January, 1881,[1] was the man who took the part of Conkling; the Blaine men and others for whom Conkling was too strong a medicine became "Half Breeds."[2] Conkling and "Me Too" Platt, represented in newspaper cartoons as a small boy sticking out of Conkling's pocket,[3] were soon fighting for their political lives,[4] Vice-President Arthur and Postmaster-General James, with little delicacy, openly essaying to aid them.[5] Grant also brought himself into the contest in statement and "interview" in denunciation of the "outrage" which had been done so eminent a statesman as his friend Conkling.[6]

While this comedy was being played to its end another spectacle, it too a legacy of the Grant administration, was seen. The dinner to Dorsey at Delmonico's, at which Grant had presided, was no idle and unmeaning courtesy to a great man. If he had been the instrument to distribute $100,000 of campaign moneys in Indiana, thereby winning for the Republican party the election of 1880 in that state, he had done much more. In view of his career in the carpetbag politics of Arkansas he was fairly under suspicion in most men's sight when he became an officer of the Republican National Committee.[7]

[1] Platt, Autobiography, pp. 141–2.
[2] N. Y. Nation, June 16 and 23, 1881. The name "Half Breed" was in use in February, 1881.—Cf. ibid., Feb. 24, 1881.
[3] Platt, Autobiography, p. 159.
[4] N. Y. Nation, June 2, 1881.
[5] Ibid., May 19, 26, and June 9, 1881; Harper's Weekly, June 18 and July 16, 1881.
[6] N. Y. Nation, June 9, 16 and 23, 1881.
[7] Certainly not admired by his colleague in the Senate from Arkansas and fellow adventurer in the carpetbag politics of that state, Powell Clayton, who, in a letter to John Sherman on June 14, 1880, described Dorsey as "a man who has no residence in this state [Arkansas] and does not

For several years there had been rumors of irregularity in the Post Office Department which were brought to President Hayes's notice, not without his inquiring about them and urging the officers in charge to give the business of the department careful scrutiny.[1] If he had appointed one like Schurz as Postmaster-General the culprits and their crimes would have been uncovered. As it was an inexperienced and easy-going man [2] was chosen, not because of his capacity to discharge his duties, but merely to propitiate the South, and the rogues continued to practice their arts, in spite of occasional grillings by Congressional committees which were on the track of the corruption,[3] and a general conviction that there was extravagance, if not wanton dishonesty of management in the " Postal Star Service." [4]

Postmaster-General James was a man of action,[5] MacVeagh as Attorney-General supported him and they were assisted by a "crusade" in the New York Times suggestive of its service in the overthrow of the Tweed Ring.[6] Reports of inquiries earlier undertaken had been impounded and a little investigation disclosed a state of affairs which, as James said, was "truly appalling." [7] Every obstacle was put in the way of those who set out to discover the truth. "Swarms of contractors, their attorneys and beneficiaries," said the Postmaster-General, "raised a deafening clamor," attacking Garfield, MacVeagh and James with every weapon at Hand.[8]

The "Star Routes" were lines by stagecoach, buckboard and saddle horse in the West and South for the conveyance of

---

as much as pay a poll tax here, a man who is generally despised and whose unblushing corruptions are well known by our citizens."—Sherman Papers; cf. J. M. Forbes, Letters and Recollections, vol. ii, p. 197.

[1] Diary and Letters of Hayes, vol. iv, pp. 10–11, 12–3.

[2] Ibid., p. 12.

[3] Cf. House Mis. Doc., 46th Cong. 2nd sess., no. 31; House Mis. Doc., 48th Cong. 1st sess., no. 38, pt. 2, p. 1; Diary and Letters of Hayes, vol. iv, pp. 10, 49, 50–51.

[4] House Mis. Doc., 48th Cong. 1st sess., no. 38, pt. 2, p. 2.

[5] Cf. House Reports, 38th Cong. 1st sess., no. 2165, p. 2.

[6] Davis, Hist. of N. Y. Times, pp. 146–8; N. Y. Nation, April 28, 1881.

[7] House Mis. Doc., 48th Cong. 1st sess., no. 38, pt. 2, p. 3.

[8] Ibid., pp. 4, 29, 49, 70, 95, 97.

the mails, where there were no railways or steamboats for
the use of the postal authorities. They were so called because
"stars" were used to designate them in the "route registers"
or government lists.[1] It was a service fraught with difficulty.
It covered the country occupied by the Indians and the troops
stationed in forts to keep them in order, and the movement
of the mails in this wilderness invited as much delinquency
as other kinds of government activity on the frontier. But,
if a carrier in Wyoming or Montana got drunk, or another
exposed the mail sacks to the rain and delivered letters in a
damaged condition, or another failed on this or that account
to depart when he should have departed or arrive when he
should have arrived, which from time to time could be viewed
as rather inevitable occurrences, there was no word of condo-
nation to be spoken for errancies which flourished amid the
settled case and order of life in the city of Washington.

There were 9,225 "star lines" for which in 1879–80 the
annual appropriation had been about $5,900,000.[2] Over some
of them not more than three letters passed in a week, yet in
18 months an Assistant Postmaster-General, Brady by name,
a henchman of Senator Morton of Indiana,[3] Dorsey and others,
who were contractors or in league with contractors on the lines,
aimed to have, and succeeded in having, the service on 93 of
these routes "improved," or made more frequent, thus raising
the cost of them from $762,858 to $2,723,464,[4] which left
only about $3,000,000 for the other 9,000 and more routes.
Thus was created a deficit which Congress must meet,[5] and
which did not escape suspicious notice.[6] But in this body the
scheme had its friends and so, until now, the corruption had
continued.[7]

[1] Report of P. M. General James, House Ex. Doc., 47th Cong. 1st sess.,
no. 1, pt. 4, p. 470.
[2] Ibid., p. 468.
[3] N. Y. Nation, April 28, 1881.
[4] Report of P. M. General James, House Ex. Doc., 47th Cong. 1st sess.,
no. 1, pt. 4, p. 486.
[5] House Mis. Doc., 46th Cong. 2nd sess., no. 31.
[6] House Reports, 48th Cong. 1st sess., no. 2165, p. 1.
[7] N. Y. Nation, April 28, May 5, 12, 19 and 26, 1881.

The deeper the investigation went the more open and shameless did the fraud appear.[1] Bids of politicians and their confederates were tendered and accepted. Contracts were sublet, the politicians pocketing profits without turning a hand. Contracts were sold. Then extensions, increases and further advantages were secured and new sums were collected for their own uses by the rascals who were involved in the traffic. Some contractors who were paid did not provide any service to the public. Men said that Dorsey would go to the penitentiary.[2] The jails could have properly received him as well as other men involved in the scandal.

Powerful influences were active in behalf of the culprits and the President was told early in the progress of the investigation that it would touch leaders of high position in the Republican party. He is entitled to no praise for declining to withhold his hand.[3] "Cut the ulcer out," he said, "no matter whom it hurts. I have sworn to uphold the Constitution and the laws. I shall do my full duty."[4] An aggressive policy was instituted at once and the work proceeded. Brady, now out of office, retorted with a letter to a man named Hubbell,[5] written during the recent Presidential campaign which, or another like it, Conkling had earlier flourished over Garfield's head[6] and which seemed to imply that he had received, or would be glad to have, assistance in money from the "Star Routers."[7] It was an unfortunate disclosure and did not admit of denial, though it necessarily pointed to no knowledge on the candi-

[1] "The boldness of the men who conspired to defraud the government," said A. M. Gibson, appointed by MacVeagh to investigate and report upon the case, was "amazing."—House Ex. Doc., 47th Cong. 1st sess., no. 1, pt. 4, p. 487.

[2] N. Y. Nation, May 19, 1881.

[3] Smith, Life of Garfield, p. 1158; House Mis. Doc., 48th Cong. 1st sess., no. 38, pt. 2, pp. 5–6.

[4] House Mis. Doc., 48th Cong. 1st sess., no. 38, pt. 2, p. 335.

[5] A politician in Michigan, chairman of the Republican Congressional Committee, of which Wm. E. Chandler was secretary.—See Chandler Papers in Library of Congress.

[6] E. B. Andrews, The Last Quarter Century in the U. S., vol. i, pp. 340–41; Smith, Life of Garfield, pp. 1122, 1123, 1124.

[7] Smith, Life of Garfield, pp. 1023, 1159; N. Y. Nation, May 12, 1881.

date's part of this "gigantic robbery."[1] Dorsey was similarly bold and active in attending to his own defense, filling the President with doubt as to the justice of the pursuit of him for his portion of the guilt.[2]

It was in this whirl of mischief that tragedy came. Man was contending with man for favors and immunities, with no note loud enough to be heard that service for the state was a great trust, that public affairs were the study and lay within the province of the worthiest and the most competent class of citizens. All was sordid, clamorous quest for "jobs" and "plums" which the President was giving out to insistent senators, representatives and other politicians.[3] The more he sought to satisfy them the more impudently did they assail and persecute him.[4] He said of himself, with knowledge of his own character, that he was "wholly unfit for this sort of work." He found pleasure and exhibited capacity in dealing with "doctrines and events." But "contests of men about men" he disliked, and he could but indifferently distinguish individuals with reference to their motives and their merits.[5]

On Saturday, July 2nd, when he had been barely four months in office, a deranged eccentric named Guiteau, who conceived that he had a right to some office that was not given him, and who had haunted the White House approaches for weeks in his quest for preferment,[6] learning of the President's movements, transferred his position to a railway station in Washington and there lay in wait as Garfield came in to board a train for New York on his way to Williamstown to attend the Commencement exercises of the college of which he was a graduate. The

[1] Called so by MacVeagh.—House Mis. Doc., 48th Cong. 1st sess., pt. 2, p. 20.
[2] Smith, Life of Garfield, pp. 1160, 1162.
[3] W. H. Crook, Through Five Administrations, p. 257.
[4] He was, says his biographer, "driven nearly to desperation in trying to operate the spoils system." (Smith, Life of Garfield, p. 1146. See the descriptions of an employee at the White House at this time in Crook, Through Five Administrations, p. 257. Cf. App. Ann. Cyclop. for 1881, p. 846.) The President was likened to "a big, confused Newfoundland dog."— Smith, Life of Garfield, p. 1147.
[5] Smith, Life of Garfield, pp. 1147–8.
[6] Crook, Through Five Administrations, pp. 266–9.

fellow's opportunity was now at hand. He fired at and shot the President twice, once in the shoulder and the second time in the back. After capture he muttered something about being a Stalwart and about Arthur who would now be President, evidently thinking that, with Garfield dead, a better day for office hunters would dawn.[1] It was a shocking event and, if the result should be fatal, might lead to very dire consequences for the republic. The Vice-President, in the case of Garfield's death, must succeed to the Presidency.

Arthur could not but be viewed with misgivings. He was Vice-President simply because he would not conduct, in the public interest, a minor Federal office, which he held by grace of Conkling. Since his election he had been noted for nothing but his activity in presiding at dinners, attending meetings, lobbying at Washington and in Albany—all in the service of Conkling, criticizing, as he could, Garfield and the administration of which he might be considered to be a part. This man, if Garfield should die of his wounds, would be President of the United States.

Grant and Conkling found the occasion to reassure the country, as Garfield lay on his bed of pain, surrounded by the most eminent surgeons whom the medical science could provide. There need be no public apprehension. The Constitution prescribed the method of succession, the government would survive. However, men did not cease to feel unconcealed solicitude. Though hope rose and confidence was soon in large measure restored, as Garfield's robust physical strength asserted itself, there was a relapse. He was conveyed, to escape the heat of Washington, to the seaside at Long Branch, N. J., and there he died on September 19, 1881. As the tragic news was borne away by the electric current, to awaken the sympathy of North and South, and, indeed, of all the world, which was manifested in messages warm in feeling, Arthur took the oath of office to complete a term scarcely yet begun.

[1] Cf. Harper's Weekly, special ed., July 8, 1881.

CHAPTER XXVII

ARTHUR'S ADMINISTRATION AND THE ELECTION OF 1884

GARFIELD's death, which was not unexpected, found Vice-President Arthur at his home in New York City. He immediately, at about two o'clock in the morning of September 20, 1881, appeared before a judge of the Supreme Court of New York state for qualification for the assumption of duty as President, and set out for Long Branch to accompany the corse to Washington where, on the 22nd, he was more formally sworn by Chief Justice Waite of the Supreme Court of the United States.

After lying in state in the Capitol the body was borne to a railway station in Washington and the funeral train proceeded to Cleveland, where, on the 26th of September, amid memorable scenes, it was committed to a tomb, on which day, in accordance with the terms of a proclamation of the new President, services were held in the churches in all parts of the country and business was generally suspended. There were yet to follow criticism of the attending surgeons—which, indeed, had been in progress for some time before the distinguished patient's death, though they, without the facilities later afforded by science for locating the position of bullets in the human frame, had done, it appears, as well as conditions would allow,—and the punishment of the assassin. The trial engaged the attention of a court in the District of Columbia without delay and proceeded amid much vindictive excitement. The plea was insanity which the fellow attempted to confirm in the minds of the court, the jury and the public by every means in his power, including outbreaks in prison and in the court room which, if they were not the result of design, might have been taken to be proof of a disordered intellect. They, in any case, added to the public zest for the scene and drew a crowd around him. The trial was a "Roman

holiday"—women stormed the doors to laugh and applaud
as the trial progressed. Guiteau was a "spectacle." Notice
pleased his vanity. Experts were called. One declared the
man to be a "moral imbecile, a moral monstrosity." Other
alienists, in rebuttal, held a different view. The trial dragged
through weeks and it was January 25, 1882, before the jury
was charged and retired to form a verdict, which was agreed
upon unanimously almost at once. The prisoner, amid his
shrieks of disapproval, was found guilty, and he was sentenced
to be hanged on June 30th following.[1] Appeals tediously argued
failed and on the date set Guiteau was executed in the jail
yard at Washington.

Arthur followed his first official act on the 22nd of September,
which was the naming of a day of mourning for Garfield, accompanied by a little "inaugural address," chiefly expressive
of his own and the nation's grief,[2] on the next day, the 23rd,
with a proclamation convening the Senate in extra session on
October 10th, for the purpose, in particular, as was generally
understood, of electing a presiding officer who, in the event
of Arthur's death, might be President.[3] So much, owing to
a party deadlock, had been prevented in the special session
of the Senate which Garfield had assembled in March, 1881,
and the issue now must be faced at once.

It was another time of test and trial for the government.
The very shock of the assassination was sobering. Men sub-
merged their fears and patriotically hoped for a better outcome
than their knowledge of Arthur gave them reason to antici-
pate. His name had been added to the ticket by "a jaded and
half disgusted mob of delegates" in the convention at Chicago
on the eve of boarding their railway trains in hot weather for
their respective homes.[4] He was "chosen by the rules of blind
man's buff." [5] The exact truth is that Dennison and the whole
Ohio delegation, a majority of whose members had been vot-

[1] Cf. article on Guiteau in App. Ann. Cyclop. for 1881.
[2] Richardson, vol. viii, pp. 33–4.
[3] Ibid.
[4] Harper's Weekly, July 23, 1881.
[5] N. Y. Nation, July 7, 1881.

ing for Sherman, were so excited by the nomination of Garfield, one of their number, after wearisome days of fruitless balloting, that they literally ran to the New York men, and in order to placate them and gain the support of Conkling in the canvass soon to follow, declared that they would give their votes for the Vice-Presidency as the friends of Grant should direct.[1] They had no idea, they said innocently afterward, that the name of any "but an acceptable man would be presented"; when it was presented they "had to submit." [2] They were "very much annoyed." [3] The Massachusetts delegates remonstrated. "For Heaven's sake do not nominate that man Arthur!" Whitelaw Reid exclaimed.[4] Many of the Ohio men, indeed, withheld their favor, though most of them soon yielded in the belief that their action was "a political necessity," [5] still declaring such a choice "ill-advised" and "a mistake." [6] No one of proper perceptions would have consented, upon reflection, to the putting forward of such a figure as a candidate for Vice-President; but Arthur had been nominated and elected and now he was President—barring his death he would be this for almost the entire constitutional term of the office.

Even after his election to the Vice-Presidency, his bearing had been "most justly and generally condemned," said Harper's Weekly. In the office no prediction concerning his unfitness had been disappointed. It was clear that he "must abandon all his recent estimates of official duty and dignity for behavior worthy of the chief magistrate of a great people." [7] His familiars exclaimed—"Chet Arthur! President of the United States! Good God!" [8] Hayes, at his home in Ohio, when Garfield was shot, had said, as he viewed the prospect of Arthur's

---

[1] Dennison to Sherman, June 8, 1880, in Sherman Papers.
[2] Dennison to Sherman, June 15, 1880, in ibid.
[3] Ibid.
[4] N. Y. Nation, Sep. 15, 1881.
[5] J. M. Harris to Sherman, June 12, 1880, in Sherman Papers; cf. General Tichenor to Sherman, June 9, 1880, in ibid.
[6] Bateman to Sherman, June 12, 1880, in ibid.
[7] Harper's Weekly, July 23, 1881.
[8] Autobiography of A. D. White, vol. i, p. 193; cf. A. K. McClure, Recollections of Half a Century, p. 120.

succession, that it was a "national calamity"; it would be an administration of and for Conkling, "without the moral support of any of the best elements of the country." [1] "May Heaven avert the contingency of Arthur's promotion," Thomas F. Bayard wrote to Carl Schurz. [2] Surely the man must have been "appalled by the prospect of a position and duties" to which he, as well as others, could but feel that he was "unequal." [3]

A fine creature physically, in the prime of life, genial, courteous in contacts with other men, impeccably attired, Arthur was in some measure a *bon vivant*. He would sit in urbane and leisurely conversation for two hours at dinner. He moved to tasks rather sluggishly. What was to be done, one of his secretaries has said, could wait until to-morrow. He had entered politics to make a living which he was not industrious enough to gain in other fields and, though he had held lucrative posts, the income from them was not large enough for his support, as was made clear by the fact that his friends held his promissory notes, which now in due time could be paid. [4]

But there was in him something to respond to the vast responsibilities suddenly laid upon him. He had another side which he had not revealed. There were character under his well-tailored coat and some truth in the eyes that looked out over his carefully barbered "burnsides." It was noted that his father was an Irish clergyman, a Baptist in faith, who, at the time of the President's birth, had resided in Vermont. The son's heredity and upbringing which had included, besides parental instruction, a course at Union College, where his intelligence was high enough to qualify him as a Phi Beta Kappa man, were now not to be lost upon him. He had studied law; he had practiced it to the advantage of the slave, and the anti-slavery cause, as the country had been told when he was

[1] Diary and Letters of Hayes, vol. iv, pp. 23–4.
[2] Writings of Schurz, July 23, 1881.
[3] Harper's Weekly, July 23, 1881.
[4] Arthur Papers in Library of Congress; C. M. Depew, Memories of 80 Years, p. 116; T. C. Platt, Autobiography, pp. 182–3; W. H. Crook, Through Five Administrations, pp. 277, 278.

a candidate for the Vice-Presidency. Later, during the war, he had performed some services of importance in gentlemanly fields as an inspector of the New York troops and in the quartermaster's department, by appointment of Governor Morgan, for which he was rewarded with a brigadier-generalcy. Since that time his bread had been politics and, "appalled" by the outlook, as he may have been, when the assassin's bullet felled Garfield, it was fortunate for the republic that there had been in youth a background for the man who was to come to a place which no one, barring a few partisans, desired him to hold.

It was reasonable to expect, and the expectation was generally entertained, that he would boot the "Half Breeds" out of the cabinet and bestow the offices upon the "Stalwarts." But from the time that Garfield was shot Arthur, it was noted with satisfaction, had left off his dalliances with his friends at Albany. The "Stalwarts," indeed, were checked on all sides and prevented from executing their designs. Platt already recognized the hopelessness of his position as a candidate for reëlection and, after 31 ballots in the New York state legislature, withdrew his name.[1] On July 16th, Warner Miller, a man of a commercial turn of mind,[2] was elected to one of the vacancies and, on July 22nd, Conkling's "Spartan band," amid his praise of their "heroic constancy" in behalf of "principle and truth,"[3] capitulated and Elbridge G. Lapham, a lawyer venerable in years, who had served in Congress for several terms, was elected to the other place.

Arthur let it be known that he would like the members of the cabinet to remain at their posts until the meeting of Congress in December, but no one believed that many, if any of Garfield's appointees, could find it pleasant or useful to continue their official relationships with a government which would certainly seek and follow other advice. Wayne MacVeagh clearly foresaw that no Independent would be needed in Arthur's

---

[1] T. C. Platt, Autobiography, pp. 160–61; N. Y. Nation, July 7, 1881.
[2] A paper manufacturer. N. Y. Nation, July 21 and Aug. 4, 1881.
[3] Ibid., July 28, 1881.

entourage and he resigned at once. He was in the midst of the prosecution of the men involved in the Star Route frauds and, as others must take up this task, he would give over the Attorney-General's office without a day's delay to one of the President's choice. Arthur demurred and, to his credit, urged MacVeagh to remain.[1] It was clear that Blaine could not continue to serve as Secretary of State and he arranged his departure. All went, indeed, except Robert T. Lincoln who had been a "Grant man" and, therefore, a "Stalwart" ally in 1880, and to whom, as another assassinated President's son, the national heart was affectionately turned. Benjamin Harris Brewster of Philadelphia, who had just become associated with MacVeagh in the Star Route cases, was appropriately chosen to be Attorney-General. Windom left the Treasury to return to the Senate. Arthur was not fearful of the effect upon the party fortunes of the ogre of Wall Street as Garfield had been. Grant wrote urging the appointment of one of his rich patrons, John Jacob Astor, as Secretary of the Treasury.[2] Arthur himself determined to give the place to Edwin D. Morgan, the "War Governor" of New York, to whom he personally owed so much for his early advancement in politics. This nomination would have made an excellent public impression.[3] But Morgan would not listen to the proposal. Thurlow Weed was sent to see him and that old patriarch of Republicanism was nearly shown out of the house for daring to bear the message.[4] Judge Charles J. Folger, an adherent of Conkling who had come near receiving a place in the Garfield cabinet, was finally chosen, also a not unacceptable appointment.[5] Blaine was succeeded by Frederick T. Frelinghuysen, for two periods a United States senator from New Jersey, who was reckoned to be " Stalwart " in his sympathies, though a man of

[1] House Mis. Doc., 48th Cong. 1st sess., no. 38, pt. 2, pp. 23–4; N. Y. Nation, Nov. 24, 1881.
[2] Under date of Oct. 8, 1881.—Arthur Papers in Library of Congress.
[3] Harper's Weekly, Nov. 5, 1881.
[4] Weed to Arthur, Oct. 25, 1881, in Arthur Papers; cf. House Mis. Doc., 48th Cong. 1st sess., no. 38, pt. 2, p. 24.
[5] N. Y. Nation, Nov. 3, 1881.

pure character and conceded abilities. Bancroft Davis became his assistant. James, the Postmaster-General, after reducing the cost on the "Star Routes" to the extent of about $1,575,000 per annum[1] and performing other useful services, retired, and was succeeded by ex-Senator Timothy O. Howe of Wisconsin, an active "third term" partisan in 1880, occupying no high place in public estimation,[2] who, however, soon died, to be followed by Walter Q. Gresham of Indiana. William H. Hunt, the Secretary of the Navy, and Governor Kirkwood of Iowa, Secretary of the Interior, remained until April, 1882, when William E. Chandler, out of a place, since the Senate had refused to confirm his appointment by Garfield to be Solicitor-General, was made Secretary of the Navy and Senator Henry M. Teller of Colorado became Secretary of the Interior. Hunt as a *solatium* received the mission to Russia.[3]

The new cabinet, if "Stalwart" in its complexion, was this but mildly. It was a compromise. Its composition was proof that Arthur wished to follow a middle way. He was being visited with a sense of his high duty. Except for Chandler it is likely that the group, man for man, possessed as much character and ability for the discharge of their duties as those who had preceded them in their positions. The tradition which Hayes had established of putting a representative of the South in the cabinet was adjudged, it appears, to have no further value, and the recognition of the "Independents" ceased. If Conkling had had the expectation of being invited to become Secretary of State—not less was held before him as a peace offering by Garfield—he was disappointed. Nor did Arthur, so far as it appears, turn to the man to whom he had so long played flunky for counsel on any matter. There was a vacancy on the bench of the Supreme Court to which Conkling was named, though "Lord Roscoe" declined the compliment, thinking it, perhaps, beneath his notice,[4] and, with this gesture, a figure which had strutted the stage for so many years to cor-

[1] N. Y. Nation, Nov. 10, 1881.
[2] Ibid., Dec. 22 and 29, 1881.
[3] Thomas Hunt, Life of Wm. H. Hunt.
[4] Cf. N. Y. Nation, March 2, 1882; Conkling, Life of Conkling, pp. 676–7.

rupt the moral character of our institutions, practically passed from public sight and attention.

Arthur's refusal to displace Robertson, the "Half Breed" leader, who, by Garfield's appointment, was safely established as collector of customs in New York, was the clearest demonstration to the "Stalwarts," as it was to the country, that he was now President of the United States and not a factionist who would use the great office to which he had so accidentally come to even his friends' scores and to punish their foes. Conkling, Platt and the President's recent associates, to whom Arthur entirely owed his eminence, as they and every one else knew, were made to understand that they might not carry the methods of their "machine" into the White House to discredit him when the historian should appraise his administration. They might charge him with ingratitude, as they did,[1] but his was the responsibility; he had taken an oath to administer his office in accordance with his lights, and the duties which he faced, and which he was to fulfill, were his own.

Anyhow the knell of "Stalwartism" had been sounded when Guiteau's shots rang through the railway station at Washington,[2] and he would have been an unnatural man who could have wished to defend or prolong the squabble and feud which had produced assassination. An effort to do so would have repelled the country, as any politician could not fail to perceive. It was particularly incumbent upon Arthur, whose name the assassin had used in explaining his deed, to lean to the other side and make it plain that he would be no agent to undo what Garfield had done, or give over the government to those, who, it was generally believed, as well as feared, would profit by the succession. The Baltimore American, a Republican paper, had said a few hours after the assassination that Guiteau had been "inspired with the same motives" which, "from the very beginning," had "actuated the third term conspirators." The monomania of Guiteau was identical, "except as to its practical result, with that of Conkling and

[1] Platt, Autobiography, pp. 180, 183.
[2] Cf. ibid., pp. 63-4.

Cameron and Logan and Grant." The "Stalwarts" had "destroyed the President at last." [1] They were "the intrigues of Conkling and the slanders of Grant," said the Charleston News and Courier, a Democratic paper, which had "wrought up the miserable assassin to the pitch of regarding the death of the President as a political necessity." [2]

Harper's Weekly and other papers said, or intimated, as much in similar terms. Men who before were indulgent now could see and comprehend, and they did not fail to condemn those who fanned "the fire of party," which deliberately stimulated wild brains to take the life of one magistrate that another could have the place.[3] It would have been action of an unusual kind for Arthur to proclaim his "Stalwartism," as Guiteau had done, at such an hour.[4]

The President's grace was displayed principally in his social relationships. He was not gifted as an orator, nor did he exhibit art in literary expression. His first message to Congress in December, 1880, nevertheless, contained declarations which were honorable to him. Even on the subject of the civil service his position was not hostile, as it could have been expected to be. The way of the "reformer," which had seemed full of obstructions, was made the easier by Garfield's death. "Is there no method by which to divide the responsibility for the selection of competent officers and for maintaining them in their positions against the covetous practise of office hunters?" a writer asked passionately. "Must this generation die without any return to the traditions of the Fathers, without any knowledge of a condition of public affairs where party management for the mere advantage of partisans shall not predominate?" [5] It was, said Harper's Weekly, "the ferocity and insanity of party spirit, bred by the spoils system of office patronage, which had been the moving cause" of the assassina-

---

[1] Quoted in Harper's Weekly, July 8, 1881; cf. N. Y. Nation, July 7, 1881.
[2] Quoted in Harper's Weekly, July 8, 1881.
[3] Ibid., July 23, 1881.
[4] Cf. ibid., Sep. 3, 1881.
[5] App. Ann. Cyclop. for 1881, p. 847.

tion of the President. Throwing into every election a hundred thousand places as "the prize of success" was "directly to foster such crimes" as Garfield's death. If restraint could not be put on such a wrong "the republic is impracticable," Mr. Curtis continued. "Abolition of the spoils system is now the most essential and important public duty." [1]

Throughout the country men, without regard to party, were impressed by the need of a new system of distributing the offices so that seekers after them might no longer plague the President, and the administration of government could be made more honest and efficient. Even those who were so dense of intellect as scarcely to know what was meant by the words "civil service," and those who were so heedless of the public weal as to attach no importance to the demands for reform in this field had now had an object lesson that they could understand, and politicians, whose very existence depended upon patronage which they could distribute to the "workers," were for once on the point of being overborne. [2]

Arthur, in his first message to Congress, gave the principle, as well as definite proposals affecting the reform, his indorsement, though he expressed some doubt as to the value of any system of selection after competitive examination. [3] Hope of early action was strengthened [4] and, before the stimulation given to the reform should be withdrawn and the effect should be lost, its friends and promoters pressed it upon the attention of the Senate and the House. [5] The best thought regarding the question was spent upon, and given expression in, a bill which received sponsorship from Senator George H. Pendleton of Ohio. The various reform organizations had held a conference at Newport in the summer of 1881 and formed a national

[1] Harper's Weekly, July 23, 1881.
[2] "Guiteau's shot did much for civil service reform." (New York Nation, July 7, 1881.) The crime "acted on public opinion very like a spark on a powder magazine." It had "fallen on a mass of popular indignation all ready to explode."—Ibid., July 14, 1881.
[3] Richardson, vol. viii, pp. 60–63.
[4] Harper's Weekly, Dec. 17, 1881.
[5] Cf. ibid., Sep. 10, 1881.

league;[1] they had concentrated their efforts upon the draft of this measure.[2] Pendleton, like Arthur, was a strange instrument of reform, but none which presented itself could be too narrowly regarded. It was pointed out that it had been Marcy, a Democrat, under Jackson, a Democrat, who first had formulated the doctrine that "to the victors belong the spoils"; it was a Democrat now, Pendleton, who fifty years later would give his name to a project designed to overthrow this corrupting principle.[3]

The new Congress was oddly constituted. The House, since 1875, as a result of the elections of 1874, had been Democratic by varying majorities. It had been won back by the Republicans in 1880, so that in the Forty-seventh Congress they would have a narrow majority over the Democrats, Greenbackers and other opposition. The Senate, however, was an unmanageable body. In the Forty-fifth Congress, in 1877–8, the membership had been about equally divided between the parties and David Davis, who declared himself to be an Independent, though he had been elected to his place by the Democrats, with the help of the Greenbackers, in the legislature of Illinois, achieved prominence by reason of his power to turn from side to side. Now again he could sit upon the fulcrum of the seesaw, a distinction which he might share with a "rebel brigadier," William Mahone, of Virginia who had come to Washington as a result of a contest of the "Liberals" with the "Bourbons" about the state debt, which Mahone would repudiate. This adventurer, when the mood seized him, would act with the Republicans, who were coöperating with him in Virginia. With the party in such a position in the Senate it was held to have been the more inconsiderate for Conkling and Platt to have left the scene when their votes were absolutely necessary to make up a majority. Though they could not have foreseen Garfield's death and Arthur's succession it was plainly no matter to them what happened, if their own interests were

---

[1] Harper's Weekly, Aug. 27, 1881.
[2] Ibid., Aug. 20 and Dec. 24, 1881.
[3] Ibid., July 30, 1881.

not served, and the special session in March, April and May,
1881, had ended without action on a matter which, in a few
weeks, assumed much gravity, namely the choice of a presiding
officer of the Senate who would be President if Arthur should
die. Indeed, after the departure of Conkling and Platt, only
a Democrat could have been elected.[1] Now, in the special
session, convened in October, 1881, by proclamation of the
new President, the Republicans, knowing not what to do,
resolved to take advantage of Davis's vanity and make him
the president *pro tem.* and acting Vice-President. Seldom has
our public life sunk to so low a position—a customs collector,
dismissed from that office for conduct unbecoming an honest
man, was President; if he should die a lumbering giant, distinguished for naught but his physical proportions, who was
neither Republican nor Democrat, nor yet "Independent,"
in any but his own personal sense, would be the head of the
government.

Solicitude concerning civil service reform was closely pressed
by anxiety as to the course which the new President might
pursue in reference to the "Star Route frauds." MacVeagh's
retirement from the Attorney-Generalship, in the midst of
the investigation into these scandals and the pursuit of the
guilty men, led to criticism of his course.[2] But there was no
alternative for one who felt that he could not be a welcome
adviser of the President.[3] His resignation might better be
tendered at once so that his successor could be speedily chosen
to follow a policy which should have the unquestioned approval
of the administration. Benjamin Harris Brewster was a prominent and an able lawyer in Philadelphia already associated
with the prosecution, at MacVeagh's invitation, not without
a view to the succession,[4] and, therefore, familiar with the
subject in hand. His appointment was a signal that no favors
would be extended to the men, who, up to the end, had been

[1] Cf. Harper's Weekly, July 23, 1881. Bayard would have been chosen.—
N. Y. Nation, July 14, 1881.
[2] Cf. House Mis. Doc., 48th Cong. 1st sess., no. 38, pt. 2, p. 30.
[3] Ibid., pp. 31, 50-51.
[4] Ibid., pp. 22-3.

begging Garfield to believe them the objects of political persecution and to withhold pursuit on this account, or because
of their contributions in money to, or their services in behalf
of, the Republican party.[1]

In Arthur's first message he drew attention to the fact that
he had enjoined upon the officers of the Department of Justice,
engaged in the conduct of the cases, "the duty of prosecuting
with the utmost vigor of the law all persons" who might be
found "chargeable with frauds upon the postal service." [2] He
had done more than this—he had promptly ousted the Assistant Postmaster-General, though a "Stalwart" and of his own
household, because this officer had clearly known of, and had
winked at, the frauds which had now been brought to light.[3]

The facts in the conspiracy involving Dorsey as a United
States senator, Brady in the Post Office Department, Dorsey's
brother and brother-in-law and others were laid before the
grand jury of the District of Columbia in January, 1882. It
appeared that on nineteen of the routes in which this combination was interested the compensation allowed them by the government had been increased from $41,135 to nearly $450,000
per annum. On one route, in Dakota and Montana, which was
originally let at $2,350, the contractors, through increase
granted within a year by corrupt administrative officers in
the Post Office Department, received $70,000 annually. On
another, in Oregon, the increase within a twelvemonth was from
$8,288 to $60,000 annually; on another, in Nevada, from $2,982
to $49,000, and so on.[4] In one case the contractor carried over
the mountains the entire mail in the leg of his boot and the
government was made to pay $50,000 a year for the service.[5]

The indictments which had been prepared in the Department of Justice were agreed to by the grand jury and in March
the case appeared in the criminal court in Washington, the
mail contractors and their confederates, who had been arrested

[1] Cf. House Mis. Doc., 48th Cong. 1st sess., no. 38, pt. 2, pp. 618–9.
[2] Richardson, vol. viii, p. 53.
[3] N. Y. Nation, Oct. 20 and 27, 1881.
[4] House Reports, 48th Cong. 1st sess., no. 2165, p. 4.
[5] Ibid., p. 5.

and were at large only under bail, being represented by a
notable and numerous body of counsel,[1] which included the
famous atheist orator, Robert G. Ingersoll. All of the artifices
suggested by the minds of clever, if not scrupulous attorneys,
familiar with the trickery by which criminals may escape
their just deserts, were tediously employed to hinder the trial.
A jury made up of grocers, barbers, livery stable clerks and
their like, two of the men blacks, was finally in the box ready
to judge the case. The accused were no more candid when
put upon their trial than Babcock and the Whiskey Ring thieves
had been in the Grant administration. They used the same
political avenues to becloud the issue and procure immunity
from detection and punishment. The object was not to reveal
.the truth but to conceal it.[2] It was such a struggle of legal
talent that the lawyers, at the end of the trial in August, each
made addresses covering two or three days. In September
Attorney-General Brewster himself appeared in a closing argument extending over two days, and the case went to the jurymen,
who, it was openly charged, and generally believed, had been
bribed. They went out on the 8th of September and, after
repeatedly returning for instruction and with requests that
they might be allowed to state their agreement as to the guilt
or innocence of some of the defendants and disagreement as
to the culpability of the others, they, on the 11th, with the
permission of the court, brought in their verdict. Two men,
one of them dead, they acquitted. Two who were minor characters, mere employees of the principals in the conspiracy, they
found guilty. As to Dorsey, Brady, Dorsey's brother and another the jury disagreed. It appeared that as many as three
men had held out against the conviction of Stephen Dorsey
and two were friends of his brother and of Brady. It was a
preposterous verdict.[3] Those who had been convicted were
granted a new trial. The Attorney-General declared that he
would again seek to compass the conviction and punishment

[1] Cf. Senate Ex. Doc., 48th Cong. 1st sess., no. 156, p. 2.
[2] Cf. N. Y. Nation, Aug. 17, 1882.
[3] Cf. ibid., Sep. 14, 1882.

of those concerning whose guilt the jury could not agree. Proceedings were commenced against the corrupt jurymen.

From the beginning it was quite plain that obstacles of many kinds were being put in the way of the prosecution—persistently, maliciously and with a view to defeating the ends of justice. A number of newspapers were defending the thieves, and heaping abuse upon witnesses who dared to testify for the state and upon lawyers who were laboring to punish the offenders.[1] Such activity on the part of men in the service of, and receiving pay from, the government was intolerable. A number of them were named by Attorney-General Brewster. Dorsey and those who had been indicted with him, Mr. Brewster said, were "guilty men and merited the extreme punishment of the law." They had "projected, under cover of official power and under cover of official authority, a systematic plan of deliberate robbery of the public treasury." Millions of dollars had been perverted to private use. But, "from the first," those who had been aiding the Attorney-General in the discharge of his duty had been "encircled with snares, pitfalls and every species of vile device that could be invented to harm them, hinder their usefulness and prevent the administration of justice." Minor officials of the government surrounding the offenders knew no allegiance but to this "band of robbers"—they were "saturated with affinities for these bad men" and, "at the bidding of their masters," were obstructing public justice and defaming its officers, "with the hope of securing the acquittal and escape of the worst band of organized scoundrels that ever existed since the commencement of the government."[2]

Such words were plain enough. They were directed particularly at the marshal of the District of Columbia, the post-

[1] Cf. House Mis. Doc., 48th Cong. 1st sess., no. 38, pt. 2, pp. 29, 32, 50–51.

[2] App. Ann. Cyclop. for 1882, p. 766. The "Star Routers" were a "body of scoundrels," said the Attorney-General, who defied "the whole judicial power of the government," after they had " abused great public trusts, brought the public service into shame and scandal and robbed the public treasury of millions of money collected from the people and dedicated by law to a function of government of the greatest general necessity."—House Mis. Doc., 48th Cong. 1st sess., no. 38, pt. 2, pp. 863–4.

master and assistant postmaster in Washington, the foreman
of the Government Printing Office and ex-Senator Spencer of
Alabama, a carpetbagger, like Dorsey, now a resident of Nevada
and a commissioner of the Pacific Railroad,[1] who, if not a partner in the frauds, was a confidant of the conspirators.[2]

The Attorney-General's letter to the President was dated
November 24, 1882. The next day all the Federal officers of
whom complaint was made were removed, and here Arthur's
support of the prosecution was honest and vigorous,[3] although
some other men involved in the scandal were allowed to retain
their posts and, indeed, were promoted to higher positions.[4]

In December, 1882, Dorsey and his confederates came to
their second trial in the same court in which they had been
under unhappy treatment during the summer. He himself
issued a public statement reiterating the accounts of his friendly
and useful relations with Garfield and other leaders of the Republican party. He had been unfortunate, he said, in running
athwart the way of Postmaster-General James and Attorney-
General MacVeagh, whose elevation to places in the Garfield
cabinet he had opposed,[5] and much more in a like vein. Dorsey
in the second trial pleaded sore eyes as an excuse for not coming
into the court, but his attendance was enforced, and this time
he and the others took the stand in their own behalf, after a
clerk of Dorsey's, who had earlier made admissions damaging
to his employers, but had returned to their companionship before he could be utilized by the government, had pleaded guilty
and became a witness for the prosecution. The arguments of

[1] Cf. N. Y. Nation, June 22, 1882.

[2] A confidant also of William E. Chandler, to whom Spencer, on March
7, 1881, wrote that they could bring certain men to terms in a business
matter by threatening public investigation of their Star Service routes.
Spencer wished to be appointed minister to Brazil, where he could, he said,
make a fortune in the mines for himself and Chandler. Chandler recommended him to the President for this mission. See Chandler Papers in
which there are many references to the close connection of the two men in
business and politics.

[3] Cf. Brewster's testimony in House Mis. Doc., 48th Cong. 1st sess.,
no. 38, pt. 2, pp. 847, 879–80.

[4] Cf. ibid., pp. 11 and 538.

[5] Cf. James's testimony in ibid., p. 1.

counsel and the speeches to the jury, a repository of uncommon ignorance,[1] were again elaborate and protracted. It was one of the longest trials on record. In June, 1883, all of the prisoners, after a period of legal tergiversation covering six months, were acquitted and released.[2] Cheers rang through the court room. Mrs. Dorsey clapped her hands and cried. Dorsey was surrounded by his friends, whom, while the trial continued, he had been entertaining in a handsome manner to bind them to him and his cause, making of the trial altogether "a spectacle not often equalled off the comic stage."[3] To a crowd of negroes who serenaded him at Colonel Ingersoll's house in the evening he said that his trial had been one of those great struggles of innocence with power, such as had been described by Macaulay in the case of Warren Hastings.[4]

Fortunately other men held other views. The trial had ended for the culprits not with immunity from disgrace in public sight. They had appeared before a larger tribunal, "the people of the United States," said Attorney-General Brewster, "and they were convicted by the common judgment of the whole country. They are not punished by imprisonment," he continued, "but they had better be in prison than now at large, objects of scorn and aversion."[5] Dorsey left his place as secretary of the Republican National Committee and departed for the Western plains. The trials cleared Washington of the adventurers and jobbers who for so long had thronged the Federal offices, in particular the halls of the Post Office Department.[6]

Men found a variety of reasons for the result, disconnected with the character of the grand juries, which made the presentments, and the low intelligence and morality of the trial juries.[7] There were many corruptions in the Star Route service; one of the most intricate of the conspiracies had been chosen for

[1] Cf. James's testimony in House Mis. Doc., 48th Cong. 1st sess., no. 38, pt. 2, p. 615.
[2] App. Ann. Cyclop. for 1883, p. 777.
[3] N. Y. Nation, June 21, 1883.
[4] Ibid.
[5] Senate Ex. Doc., 48th Cong. 1st sess., no. 156, p. 2.
[6] Ibid., p. 3.
[7] Cf. N. Y. Nation, June 21, 1883.

prosecution. Simpler frauds, which could have been brought
more clearly within the range of the understanding of jurymen,
were passed over in order that Dorsey might be pursued. At
least two of these, the Salisbury and Parker combinations,
were more powerful than Dorsey's,[1] which, it was said, controlled
15 per cent of the contracts, while they each held as many as
30 per cent. But their cases never reached the grand jury.[2]
It was said that settlement with them would be made out of
court, illegal though this procedure would have been, and such
indictments as had been prepared were torn up.[3] Dorsey on
his side was a conspicuous politician. It was necessary to
prosecute him. Public opinion demanded it. Arthur had appeared at a dinner at Delmonico's in honor of this base man,
who not long ago had stood so high in the regard of the Republican party, though he was, as the senior counsel for the
government, Richard T. Merrick, said, "the originator and
center of the scheme, its inspiring genius and its master and
teacher."[4] If he were allowed to escape without pursuit, in
view of the extraordinary exertions which were being made
to secure his immunity, the scandal would have laid a heavy
hand on the President, the "Stalwarts," already in great disrepute, and the Republican party in general.

Moreover, it was charged that the case which had been chosen
was mismanaged in its preparation and during the trial, in
particular by a "Stalwart" named Bliss from New York,
who was appointed to the service at the turn of the administration from Garfield to Arthur with the object of propitiating
Arthur with reference to a subject in which MacVeagh and
others feared that the new President would exhibit weakness.
He, too, had attended the renowned Dorsey dinner and was
known to have relationships in politics with that man.[5] The
lawyers were quarreling [6] among themselves and with the Attor-

[1] House Reports, 48th Cong. 1st sess., no. 2165, p. 8.
[2] House Mis. Doc., 48th Cong. 1st sess., no. 38, pt. 2, pp. 543–4.
[3] Ibid., pp. 382–7, 555–7, 560, 648, 868–9.
[4] Ibid., p. 652.
[5] Ibid., pp. 650–51.
[6] Cf. N. Y. Nation, June 26, 1884.

ney-General about their fees, which were held to be extortionate.
The newspapers raised the cry of extravagance and the Attorney-
General, who was undergoing inquiry by Congress,[1] was in
doubt, since the public mind was so deeply wrought up by
the discussion, as to how he might proceed. Influences to
confuse and entangle righteous men and blacken their character, while procuring safety for the foul, were active on
every side.

Kellogg, the carpetbagger from Louisiana, was as guilty
as Dorsey. He did not escape indictment and pursuit for his
part in the scandal, although he followed Dorsey's example and
made much ado about "persecution." He cried and begged
for mercy with so much eloquence that no one could doubt
his culpability.[2] Indeed he admitted it. He had accepted the
money and used it for "political purposes in Louisiana." [3]
But, as he was still in the United States Senate where his
vote was needed by the Republicans, and where it was conceived that he could be more useful to them than in a jail cell,
prosecution was delayed.[4] His case did not receive attention
until 1884 when he, too, gained his release.[5] With these exceptions the indictments covered the crimes of only inconspicuous offenders and figureheads, and, when the proceedings
advanced even so far as this, the cases were "allowed to slumber
untouched." [6]

The civil suits for the recovery of the stolen money, estimated
to amount to $4,000,000 at least,[7] of which so much had been
heard, also came to nothing,[8] and a piece of rottenness which
reached far and deep into the vitals of the Republican party
passed into history. Only one man, insignificant in position
and unimportant in his relationship to the scandal, and he

[1] Cf. Senate Ex. Doc., 48th Cong. 1st sess., nos. 140, 150 and 156.
[2] House Mis. Doc., 48th Cong. 1st sess., no. 38, pt. 2, pp. 880–82.
[3] Ibid., pp. 573, 641–2.
[4] Ibid., pp. 32, 525–6, 564–5, 633.
[5] N. Y. Nation, May 8, 1884.
[6] House Mis. Doc., 48th Cong. 1st sess., no. 38, pt. 2, pp. 105, 538.
[7] House Reports, 48th Cong. 1st sess., no. 2165, p. 3.
[8] Ibid., pp. 17–20; House Mis. Doc., 48th Cong. 1st sess., no. 38, pt. 2,
pp. 869 et seq.

had confessed for the purposes of the prosecution under promise of immunity, which was violated, was convicted and did penance in connection with these "glaring and stupendous frauds." [1]

Arthur's appointments of collectors and other Federal officers were in many cases unhappy, and in the interest of factional dominance in neighborhoods and states, principally to the advantage of the "Stalwart" wing of the party. The "Pendleton bill" to reform the civil service made no definite progress toward early enactment by Congress and the elections of 1882 would ensue before anything should be achieved in this direction. Officeholders were being assessed in the most brazen ways. [2] Hubbell, who had made the collections during the Garfield campaign, led the assaults upon all classes of salaried men in the Federal service, and, while the President said that refusal to pay would lead to no one's dismissal from place, confidence was not restored in anxious minds and the money, blackmailed from ill-paid men in the customhouses, internal revenue offices, navy yards and in all departments of government employment, flowed into the hands of the Republican politicians, who were intrusted with the business of achieving party success in the election near at hand.

It was seen by the discerning that a revulsion of sentiment unfavorable to the men in control of public affairs, and their measures, was in active progress. The storm had been gathering. An interval was supplied by the Hayes administration. The Republican party had been given the opportunity for a thorough internal reform. It had proven itself unequal to the task, for it had disclaimed Hayes and chosen a policy of

[1] Majority report of Springer investigating committee in House Reports, 48th Cong. 1st sess., no. 2165, p. 3; cf. ibid., p. 9; House Mis. Doc., 48th Cong. 1st sess., no. 38, pt. 2, pp. 348–9; N. Y. Nation, Oct. 2, 1884; N. Y. Times, Sep. 30, 1884. It was a scandal reminiscent of the days of Grant, of which it was an outgrowth belatedly exposed, "when corruption ran rampant at Washington," to use the words of Thomas F. Bayard, "when Boss Shepherd had full swing, and honesty and honor were laughed at."— Bayard to Cleveland, Oct. 17, 1885, in Cleveland Papers in Library of Congress.

[2] Cf. N. Y. Nation, June 22 and 29, 1882.

compromise which was leading straightway to belief in, and search for, a more violent remedy.

The leaders of the revolution were competent. In 1881, an excellent old newspaper in New York being for sale, Henry Villard, a German of high intelligence and a fine feeling of moral responsibility, who had married a daughter of William Lloyd Garrison, having acquired a fortune in America, expressed a willingness to use it for the good of his adopted land. He purchased a controlling interest in the Evening Post from the heirs of William Cullen Bryant and established Carl Schurz, Edwin L. Godkin, owner and founder of the influential New York Nation, and Horace White as its editors.[1] In a short time, his talents being forensic rather than journalistic, Schurz retired and Godkin took chief direction of the paper in connection with his continued editorship of the Nation, which henceforward became, in a measure, a weekly edition of the Evening Post.[2] Godkin's power was immensely increased now that he could address an audience daily instead of but once a week, and an audience of newspaper readers rather than college professors and private literati, who composed the constituency of the Nation. It would be difficult to appraise too highly the services of this able and fearless monitor of the American republic in the two decades which were to follow. The penetration of his mind, his scorn of wrong, the withering satire which he aimed at the evildoers who infested our politics, his supreme journalistic talents were in tireless service. The "Boss," the "Machine," the "Boys" who to him, as in their own circles, were "Mikes," "Jakes" and "Barneys," the spoils system and all that appertained to it were under constant review and were set forth as the menace of our political institutions. And his influence did not end with the readers of the Post. His writing was provocative. He used the speech and employed the methods which the wayfaring man could understand. Other newspapers noticed his articles to express their

[1] Memoirs of Henry Villard, vol. ii, pp. 338–9; Rollo Ogden, Life of Godkin, vol. ii, pp. 119–21.
[2] Cf. Reminiscences of Carl Schurz, vol. iii, pp. 400–02.

favor or dissent. He guided the pens of many other writers, who may not have owed the debt, and thus became a force against corruption and for honesty, to be of the greatest value and meaning at once in the campaign of 1882.

Arthur made one gesture which definitely improved his own position in the public mind, if it did not reveal his party in a favorable light.[1] For many years there was increasing belief that the so-called "River and Harbor Bills" were covers for thievery. Members of Congress secured appropriations for expenditures in their districts under the cover of "internal improvements." There were trading and log rolling. The votes of a member and his friends interested in getting money for one neighborhood would be exchanged for the votes of other members with other objects in view. Thus were jumbled into a bill projects and enterprises which called for large expenditures, but were patently unjustified in any national sense. Arthur, when this appropriation bill reached him, in the summer of 1882, vetoed it. Provision was made in certain cases, he said, for works "not for the common defense or general welfare and which do not promote commerce among the states." These grants were "entirely for the benefit of particular localities," and, therefore, "beyond the powers given by the Constitution to Congress and the President." Attention was directed to the fact that, while in 1870 the entire sum voted for "river and harbor improvement" had been $3,975,000, in 1875, $6,648,000, and in 1880, $8,976,500, it had risen for 1881 to $11,451,000 and in this act, for 1882, to $18,743,000. The President remarked that the "extravagant expenditure of public money" was "an evil not to be measured by the value of that money to the people," who were "taxed for it." The country sustained "a greater injury in the demoralizing effect" which was produced by such expenditure upon those who, intrusted with official duty, misused their powers in this way.[2] But the President's reproof and admonition went for naught, for Congress almost immediately repassed the bill over his

---

[1] N. Y. Nation, Aug. 3 and 10, 1882.
[2] Richardson, vol. viii, pp. 120–22.

veto. Republicans and Democrats joined their forces to gain the ends dear to themselves and the voters of their districts.[1]

The corruption and favoritism which lurked in the protective duties on imports also came in for notice and condemnation. In the last hours of the canvass in 1880 the Republicans had tried to utilize the tariff as a party issue.[2] "Republican protection," they said, means plenty of work with good wages and empty poorhouses. "Democratic free trade" means closed factories and workshops, starvation wages and crowded poorhouses. The campaign orators developed the theory about the "pauper labor" of Europe and filled the mechanic and factory hand with visions of the unhappy lot which would be theirs also, if our customs barriers were removed.

Philadelphia continued to be conspicuous as headquarters for the activity of that class of economists and politicians who were prone to treat the opponents of their views as foreign emissaries and public enemies. Here were the offices of the American Iron and Steel Association, in charge of James M. Swank, to which Joseph Wharton, an indomitable man, largely interested in the metal industries, gave his support. With this organization was allied a so-called Industrial League, which in political campaigns distributed leaflets and tracts. Sums of money were collected from manufacturers and sent to protectionist candidates for Congress in all parts of the country who were contesting seats with candidates held to be revenue reformers and free traders. Mr. Wharton was untiring in the work of writing to, and advising with, public men. His nephew, Wharton Barker, a banker, founded a weekly newspaper, which he called the American, for the propagation of protectionist opinion, putting the periodical in charge of Robert Ellis Thompson, an Irish Presbyterian clergyman, a professor in the University of Pennsylvania. Thompson wrote

---

[1] N. Y. Nation, Aug. 10, 1882. The bill found a defender in Hoar, Autobiography of 70 Years, vol. ii, chap. viii.

[2] "This tariff," Senator Morrill wrote to an editor in Vermont, "helped us largely in 1880 and I hope it may do so in 1884."—Letter of Nov. 7. 1883, in Morrill Papers.

textbooks on political economy, engaged Sumner, Perry and
the "free traders" in the New England colleges in debate and
kept up an active fire upon the enemy. Members of the family
of Henry C. Carey were loyally devoted to their kinsman's
principles and made certain that the city's reputation as a
center for the radiation of protectionist doctrine should suffer
no decline. The textile manufacturers in Philadelphia were
also organized for their own defense, and had spokesmen and
writers who were never in repose.[1]

The "surplus" and the demand that customs duties should
be reduced for the equalization of taxation and expenditure
disturbed the protectionists. They held meetings in Chicago [2]
and New York.[3] If there must be change in the revenue system of the country they would do away with the internal
taxes so that the tariff need not be touched.[4] The free traders,
intelligently led by David A. Wells,[5] also had conferences and
made their voices heard in the land. They formed leagues and
associations and put printed material into circulation. The
"surplus" gave present force to their arguments and in their
activity they displayed determined strength.

Watterson had told Hancock and the Democrats in their
platform that they were in favor of "a tariff for revenue only." [6]
But it meant little enough to the masses in either great party,
who were yet to be educated to the vitality of the question as
it affected their own tables and hearthstones. "Who is Tariff
and why is he for revenue only?" [7] a humorous inquiry of the
day in Harper's Weekly, was not inexpressive of the sum of
knowledge in public possession on this subject.

There were protectionists, such as Samuel J. Randall, in
the Democratic party. Some interests in the South, as, for
example, the sugar planters in Louisiana, the coal and iron

---

[1] Cf. Morrill Papers; A. T. Volwiler, Am. Hist. Rev., Oct., 1930.
[2] N. Y. Nation, Nov. 24, 1881.
[3] Ibid., Dec. 1 and 8, 1881.
[4] Morrill Papers; cf. N. Y. Nation, Dec. 8, 1881.
[5] President of the "American Free-Trade League."
[6] N. Y. Nation, Sep. 22, 1882.
[7] Cf. ibid., Nov. 3, 1881.

men in Alabama, the cotton mill owners in Georgia, the wool growers in Texas,[1] were protectionists, at least with regard to what they produced and wished to sell. On the other hand there were tariff reformers in the Republican party. They were not silent, particularly in the West. But in the main it was understood that the Republicans were in favor of maintaining the existing tariff law and of obtaining, if possible, higher duties, while the Democrats were the advocates of more liberality in the treatment of imports, with a view to reducing prices in the interest of the poor and cutting down the large incomes which were founded on features in tariff schedules of benefit to particular trades.

It was accepted as a fact, however, now and on all sides, that a "substantial reduction of tariff duties" was "demanded, not by a mere indiscriminate popular clamor, but by the best conservative opinion of the country, including that which, in former times, had been most strenuous for the preservation of our national industrial defenses."[2]   President Arthur in his first message to Congress cautiously recommended "revision."[3] The "excess revenue" which was productive of a surplus, Senator Morrill said, "must somehow be cut off."[4]

Congress, on May 15, 1882, authorized the appointment by the President of nine men who were to be drawn from "civil life," which was taken to mean that they were to be men outside of Congress. Senator Morrill said that he was clear on several points—the majority should be politically Republican and should be "well known" to favor the principle of a protective tariff. No political or economic cranks should have membership in the body. Three Democrats should be named, and if one of these should be a protectionist in his sympathies no harm would be done. Though the revenue reformers were held in low esteem it was assumed that, in

[1] Cf. N. Y. Nation, May 4, 1882.
[2] Report of Tariff Commission of 1882, House Ex. Doc., 47th Cong. 2nd sess., no. 6, p. 5.
[3] Richardson, Messages and Papers, vol. viii, p. 49.
[4] Letter to a political friend in Vermont, Nov. 7, 1883, in Morrill Papers.

the interest of fairness, they should have representation on the commission, and Morrill suggested the name of Edward Atkinson of Boston.[1]

But, so much honor should not be accorded the free traders if the protectionists in Pennsylvania could prevent it. Atkinson was not to be thought of for appointment to the board. General Francis A. Walker should not be chosen—he was "an embryo David A. Wells."[2] Cyrus Elder's name was offered; he was a resolute supporter of the "Philadelphia political economy" and the secretary of Wharton's Industrial League.[3]

As a result of the maneuvering only rather inconspicuous men were selected. At their head, as the president of the commission, would be John L. Hayes of Cambridge, Mass., the secretary of the National Association of Wool Manufacturers, who was familiar with all branches of the textile industry— cotton, linen and silk as well as wool—and who, Senator Morrill said, "more thoroughly understood the present tariff laws than any man outside of Congress."[4] A. M. Garland of Illinois, president of the National Wool Growers' Association, which, like the manufacturers' association, had been expressing its anxiety about the composition of the commission, was named to represent sheep husbandry. These two men could somehow arbitrate the antagonistic interests of their respective followings. The other members of the board were Jacob A. Ambler of Ohio, one time a member of Congress; Robert P. Porter, a statistician in Washington; John W. H. Underwood of Georgia; Alexander R. Boteler of West Virginia; Duncan F. Kenner, a sugar planter of Louisiana, and William H. McMahon, an officer in the New York customhouse, who died before the commission made its report.[5] These "experts,"[6] throughout the summer and autumn of 1882, visited and held sessions in

---

[1] Morrill to Arthur, May 13, 1882, in Morrill Papers.
[2] Joseph Wharton to W. E. Chandler, May 23, 1882, in Chandler Papers in Library of Congress.
[3] Chandler Papers.
[4] Morrill Papers.
[5] Cf. Ida Tarbell, The Tariff in Our Times, pp. 101–2.
[6] Cf. N. Y. Nation, May 11, June 15 and 22, 1882.

thirty cities, going as far west as St. Louis and Des Moines, as far south as Charleston and Savannah, traveling altogether a distance of 7,000 miles. Manufacturers and other witnesses were heard. Wise men and cranks submitted essays on political economy in general and the tariff in particular. All must be printed in a report.[1] For this was the commission appointed, said Representative Carlisle of Kentucky—to gather and send to Congress "three or four thousand printed pages of testimony which not a half dozen members would read," [2] an anticipation which was fully met.

And other things were seen. A rising against political corruption had occurred in Philadelphia. There the government was not better than it had been in New York in Tweed's time. A prize was at hand in "gas works" which were owned by the city. This manufactory of a fluid which had come to displace "coal oil" for lighting the streets, mills, offices and the homes of the people, enriched a gang headed by a dexterous Irish politician, James McManes. Other men, with like objects in view, flocked about him and assisted him, in return for shares of the common plunder. They carried elections, put themselves and their friends on the public pay rolls and robbed the city at every point at which they could lay their hands upon public treasure and resources, until the people were aroused to the necessity of organizing a campaign for the overthrow of the wretched system. For some years now citizens' and taxpayers' associations, guided by Henry C. Lea and other Philadelphians of spirit, honor and intelligence, had drawn public attention to the evils and abuses of the "ring." A young man, a Democrat, Robert E. Pattison, was somehow elected in 1877 to be city controller, and reëlected in 1880. He was "a lion in the pathway" of the "bosses" and their henchmen.[3] In 1880 a "Committee of One Hundred," composed of about that number of leading citizens, was formed and, from its activities, supported by influential newspapers, came a revolt

[1] Cf. N. Y. Nation, Aug. 10, 17 and 24, 1882.
[2] Ibid., Aug. 24, 1882; cf. ibid., Jan. 5, 1882.
[3] George Vickers, The Fall of Bossism, p. 38.

which, in 1881, brought new influences to bear upon the municipal government of Philadelphia.[1]

In the state of Pennsylvania generally a like spirit filled the air, as was exemplified by the large vote polled in 1881 for an independent candidate for state treasurer,[2] and in 1882 a full independent ticket, headed by a candidate for governor, was nominated in a convention, held in Philadelphia, of Republicans, who would "not surrender their political rights," and who declared their enmity to the "spoils system," "bossism" and "machine rule." It was a revolution, and an ominous one, aimed at the Camerons.[3] The Democrats were wise enough, in this emergency, to make Pattison, the redoubtable young reform leader in Philadelphia, their nominee for governor. They, with the aid of virtuous Republicans, elected him and he assumed office in January, 1883.[4]

What was seen in New York had still wider meaning. There the breach in the Republican party created by the resignations from the United States Senate of Conkling and Platt, and their failure to secure a reëlection by the state legislature, could not be immediately closed. "Stalwarts" and "Half Breeds," Conkling's and Blaine's friends, continued their feud into the year 1882. The Independents displayed energy and were arousing the people to an understanding of the evils of the "spoils system" and the inefficiency and corruption of government administered by the "bosses." In 1881, Seth Low, a young college graduate, of an excellent family, with high political ideals, was elected mayor of Brooklyn, where he routed an evil gang. Theodore Roosevelt, scion of respected stock in New York City, had just come out of Harvard. He had been elected in 1881 to a seat in the legislature

---

[1] Out of this rising came a most amusing and illuminating satire on American politics by a Philadelphia lawyer, Rufus E. Shapley—"Solid for Mulhooly, I'm fur 'im, a Sketch of Municipal Politics under the Leaders, the Ring and the Boss." For a succinct account of this incident in the history of municipal government in the United States see Bryce, American Commonwealth, 1st ed., chap. 89.

[2] App. Ann. Cyclop. for 1881, p. 730.

[3] N. Y. Nation, June 1 and 22, 1882.

[4] App. Ann. Cyclop. for 1882, pp. 678–9.

at Albany where his voice was heard in new and resonant tones.

A governor of New York state was to be elected in 1882 to succeed Cornell, who had abandoned Conkling in that man's adversity, and was denied a renomination. The "Stalwarts" presented the name of the Secretary of the Treasury, Charles J. Folger, which seemed to carry with it the support of Arthur and the national administration. Folger came from Washington to lead the canvass. The proceedings in the state convention served but to increase the bitterness existing between the leaders and their factions, and the opportunity of the Democrats was at hand.

They maintained their numbers, were well organized and, for the most part, except in New York City where the Tammany Ring prevailed, were soundly led. In the person of a young man who, for more than twenty years, had practiced law in Buffalo and had just been elected by the Democrats to be mayor of that city, to reform its government, which had fallen into a disrepute common to American municipalities, hope appeared. Grover Cleveland was known and esteemed for independence of judgment, uprightness of character and rugged common sense. These he had manifested in the management of the mayor's office, as he had displayed them to his friends and neighbors as a lawyer and a citizen.[1] He would be presented, though he had the opposition of Tammany, which in the sight of better men was a good omen, for the suffrages of the people as the Democratic candidate for governor of New York.[2] David B. Hill, mayor of Elmira, eager for the honor,[3] was nominated for lieutenant-governor.

Mr. Cleveland in his letter of acceptance, in plain language, without resort to rhetoric, vigorously advocated reform in the civil service and the abolition of the system of blackmailing,

[1] Cf. Buffalo corr. N. Y. Herald, Sep. 25, 1882.
[2] "An able and highly respectable lawyer of Buffalo—not a man of national reputation, but he has just that kind of standing before the people which is apt to tell in a campaign like this."—N. Y. Nation, Sep. 28, 1882.
[3] Hill to Lamont, Sep. 2, 1882, in Cleveland Papers; Bigelow, Letters and Memorials of Tilden, vol. ii, p. 624.

and extorting campaign moneys from officeholders. He denounced the invasions of the workingman's rights by "aggregated capital" and all encroachments by corporations upon the interests of the individual citizen,[1] and otherwise spoke in terms so clear and electrifying that many Republicans at once offered him their support. His election seemed to be assured. And so it was, for in November his plurality over Folger was found to be nearly 193,000. A new and welcome figure, it was seen, had come forward to take his place in our public life.

The nomination and election of Cleveland in New York and Pattison in Pennsylvania were, in high degree, significant of the trend of political feeling, not merely in those states, but also as presaging an awakening of the popular conscience in regard to public affairs in the nation at large.

In Ohio, Indiana, Connecticut and New Jersey, as well as in New York and Pennsylvania, the Republicans were defeated. They had seen the oncoming storm. W. E. Chandler wrote to Blaine saying that "every personal sacrifice and subjugation of personal feeling and endurance of disagreeable incidentals that any Republican is capable of should be practised," to keep control of the House of Representatives, which had been regained two years ago.[2] It was all without avail. The "so called tidal wave of 1874," said the New York Nation, was "only a lively ripple compared with this overwhelming flood."[3] In disgust at the political situation, as it was so generally revealed to them, Republicans everywhere absented themselves from the polls, or voted opposition tickets in protest against conditions which had become too intolerable to be any longer borne. In the Congressional districts many Republican members lost their seats. The Democrats would have a majority of 80 in the next House. All of New York's delegation of 34, except 13, would be Democrats. In Illinois the Democrats gained three, in Pennsylvania five, in Indiana five,

[1] App. Ann. Cyclop. for 1882, pp. 608–9.
[2] Chandler Papers.
[3] Issue of Nov. 9, 1882.

in Ohio ten seats. Michigan, which had had no Democratic representatives in the Forty-seventh Congress, would have six in the Forty-eighth. Iowa which had had none in the last Congress would now have four.[1] In 1874 the Republicans lost their seats through the Whiskey frauds and the "Salary Grab"; in 1882 through the raid on the Treasury "by way of the sandy creeks and the mountain rivulets of the interior," [2] in the River and Harbor bill, and by the Star Route exposures.

Such results clearly betokened public unrest which could be taken by political leaders as a mandate for activity in directions where there had been none. It was also a threat and indicated, so it must be supposed, a determination on the part of substantial and numerous elements in the body of voters to punish that man who, and that party which, should appear to be heedless of popular feeling. The signs were read aright by the Congress. Under the spur of the elections that body upon assembling gave its attention to the business of the session "with a vigor and an alertness not seen in many years." [3] The members forewent their Christmas holidays in a burst of jealous attention to the public weal.

Nothing had yet been achieved in reference to the "Pendleton bill " to reform the civil service. In his first message Arthur, on this subject, had exceeded all the expectations which were earlier formed regarding him. But during the campaign in 1882 he had dismissed and appointed men in the factional "Stalwart" interest.[4] The offices were being used to bolster up candidacies and serve the ends of groups and parties in cities and states without regard for, and often in defiance of, the demands of good and proper public administration. Hubbell, the Congressman who had "passed the hat" before, was openly assessing Federal officeholders, from the highest to the

---

[1] McPherson's Handbook for 1884, pp. 2, 3, 129–31.
[2] N. Y. Nation, Dec. 7, 1882.
[3] Ibid., Dec. 14, 1882.
[4] R. C. McCormick wrote to W. E. Chandler, July 22, 1882, marveling that they were "so successful in finding an appropriate Stalwart for every vacancy." Why, he asked, "dismiss or appoint men upon an issue that is as dead as Julius Caesar?"—Chandler Papers.

lowest and, when taken to task for it by George William Curtis and the Civil Service Reform League, justified his course. All must contribute to combat the villainy of the Democrats who were suppressing Republican votes in the South.[1] Other Republican leaders, in and out of Congress, came to Hubbell's defense, calling the civil service reformers "visionaries," "dudes," "noodles" and like names.

Republican "rings" and "machines" in the states made similar calls upon the employees of the state governments and, while Arthur publicly informed Federal officeholders that they were not compelled to respond to such demands upon them [2] and the begging letters of the collectors spoke of "voluntary contributions," it was again clearly understood by the employee that he held his place and received his salary only at the pleasure of the "boss," and that, if he did not regard the request for money as a percentage assessment upon his wage, it would be the worse for him. Party platforms, indeed, contained declarations denouncing such methods and advocating reform, but this reform still awaited the action of Congress in the "Pendleton bill." Plainly sentiment on the subject of the civil service was aroused and it was angry. Cleveland had been frank and bold in pressing the issue as one of the prerequisites of good government, and his campaign in New York was won on this and other declarations expressive of discontent with an old and corrupt political order. Pattison had gained his victory over the Camerons in Pennsylvania on a similar statement of principles and, breathing the air around him, Arthur, in his message to Congress in December, 1882, gathered courage. He had said in his first message that he would sign a bill to reform the civil service. But he had expressed his doubts as to the practicability of the system which the "reformers" proposed.[3] Now he found that "the people of the country, apparently without distinction of party," had an "earnest wish for prompt and definite action," and "such action," he said,

---

[1] N. Y. Nation, June 29, July 6, 13, 27, Aug. 31, 1882.
[2] Richardson, vol. viii, p. 147.
[3] Ibid., pp. 60–63.

"should no longer be postponed." [1] He desired that the practice of assessing officeholders should be "effectively suppressed" by law. Such legislation would receive his "cordial approval." [2]

No longer was the issue to be evaded by Congress. The "Pendleton bill" was reported and, with comparatively little discussion or amendment, was passed by the Senate on December 27, 1882, with only five dissenting votes. The House followed on January 5, disposing of the matter in thirty minutes by a vote of 155 to 47,[3] and Arthur signed the measure on January 16, 1883.

The opposition came principally from Democrats, since it began to seem possible that they might gain the Presidency in 1884. A civil service law enacted at this time might be a device of the Republicans to establish their partisans in places from which they could not be dismissed upon a change in the government.[4] But not much was heard even on this point. Voices which had thundered about the "un-American," the "Prussian," the "doctrinaire," the "schoolmasterly" system of George William Curtis and the reformers, upon whose heads ridicule and contumely had been heaped by the office mongers and their press for year following year, now were silent or muffled. Hereafter there would be three civil service commissioners, to be appointed by the President. There would be competitive examinations to test the fitness of applicants for the public service. Grades would be established. Promotions would be from the lower to the higher grades on a basis of merit. Contributions to political funds would be forbidden and no occupant of office should be removed, or molested in his position, for failure to pay assessments levied upon him by agents of political parties. The provisions of the law would apply to clerks and other employees in the departments at Washington and to such employees as served, under the Secretary

---

[1] Richardson, vol. viii, p. 145.
[2] Ibid., p. 147.
[3] The passage of the bill was due to "two very different events," said Curtis in Harper's Weekly, "the murder of Garfield and the assessments of Hubbell."—Harper's Weekly, January 6, 1883.
[4] N. Y. Nation, Jan. 4, 1883.

of the Treasury, in the various customs districts and, under the Postmaster-General, in the larger post offices of the country, though only if the number of persons engaged in the Federal service at any one place should be as many as fifty. Exceptions were made for "old soldiers," "mere workmen" and those whose nominations for office were subject to confirmation by the Senate. A good deal too much was left to executive discretion, and hostility to the enforcement of the law in such a quarter might defeat its purpose. A foolish provision, in deference to the spoilsmen, limited the opportunities for the selection of employees—the several states and territories, under the new system, would be entitled to representation on the list of persons chosen on the basis of population.

But in some degree at least we should do away with what Josiah Quincy had likened to the fighting of a pack of hogs for access to the feeding trough.[1] Indeed the passage of the bill was, as the New York Nation said, "one of the most remarkable phenomena of recent times." Until lately such a result had not seemed possible for years to come.[2] President Arthur appointed the commission, with Dorman B. Eaton at its head, and the work was auspiciously begun.[3]

Soon the hands of the excited Congressmen were on the tariff. The issue had been stated in general terms in the New York campaign which resulted in the election of Cleveland, though specific references there to protection or free trade were avoided. The people were "overtaxed" and the money taken from them was used to deprave and corrupt the government. Laws which laid "unnecessary burdens upon the people" and which enabled "the powerful to oppress the weak" should be repealed.[4] The "rich were getting richer and the poor poorer" was a phrase which rang up and down the country.[5]

[1] N. Y. Nation, Dec. 14, 1882.
[2] Ibid., Jan. 11, 1883.
[3] Ibid., Feb. 22, 1883.
[4] New York Democratic platform in App. Ann. Cyclop. for 1882, p. 607.
[5] Cf. N. Y. Nation, Sep. 28, 1882. Chairman Faulkner, as he appeared before the New York Democratic convention in 1882, denounced a policy by which "the riches and privileges of the few" were "augmented" and the "poverty of the many made more miserable."—N. Y. Herald, Sep. 23, 1882.

The party in other states had spoken more definitely. It demanded, in Massachusetts, "thorough and immediate reform of the tariff." The "necessaries of life" and "raw materials" should be put upon the free list.[1] In Illinois the Democrats said that the tariff was framed in the interest of capital and that it fostered monopoly. It bore hard on the laboring man. The Constitution gave power to Congress to levy taxes to gain revenue, but not for anyone's "protection." [2] Democratic leaders in Congress denounced the corruption which lurked in the tariff schedules and advocated free trade.[3]

The Tariff Commission made its report when Congress met. Its sessions had drawn but few witnesses to them and it was the butt of a good deal of slighting allusion and ridicule. Though nearly all the members were looked upon as representatives of the protected trades [4] they actually recommended reductions in duties amounting, on an average, to 20 or 25 per cent; in many cases they had suggested cuts of from 40 to 50 per cent. If there were any truth in the theory that a lower tariff would lower prices the bill which they proposed, the commissioners said, would "benefit consumers to the extent of hundreds of millions of dollars." [5] The tariff reformers were surprised and elated. That there were incongruities and inconsistencies in the schedules was to be expected. These were remarked and complained of.[6] All of it was a small matter, however, for the commission was without any but recommendatory authority and the subject was soon entirely within the purview and jurisdiction of the Committee on Ways and Means, where it had been before, and where it would be again. This, that and the other prejudiced and selfish interest, concerned with the industries advantageously or disadvantageously affected by the proposed changes in the law, knew well where the power in

[1] App. Ann. Cyclop. for 1882, p. 518.
[2] Ibid., p. 385.
[3] See, e.g., Mayes, Life of Lamar, pp. 748–73.
[4] "Nine protectionists and not one tariff reformer."—Thos. F. Bayard, to Cleveland, Nov. 25, 1885, in Cleveland Papers.
[5] Report of Tariff Commission of 1882, p. 6; N. Y. Nation, Dec. 7, 1882; App. Ann. Cyclop. for 1883, p. 193.
[6] See, e.g., N. Y. Nation, Dec. 14, 1882.

the case rested, and brought their various influences to bear upon the politicians in this committee, and the forces in the party which might perhaps control the minds and hands of the committeemen.[1] The House was unable to come to any agreement, on which account the Committee on Finance in the Senate became the center of interest. It presented schedules of duties. These were attached to a House bill for reducing the internal revenue taxes on tobacco and other charges of our excise men and, after a parliamentary maneuver, came in due time before a conference committee,[2] led by "Pig Iron" Kelley of Pennsylvania and William McKinley of Ohio for the House and by Morrill, Sherman and Aldrich for the Senate. The product of their hands on the eve of the adjournment, on March 3, 1883, was approved in the Senate by a vote of 32 to 31 and in the House by a vote of 152 to 116, to be signed by the President.[3]

The two chambers had quarreled about their respective tights and privileges under the Constitution with regard to originating revenue legislation and, as a result of the conference, had raised a duty here and lowered a duty there without any distinct achievement in either direction. The duty on iron ore was increased to 75 cents a ton. The rates on pig and bar iron were lowered a little—so little as to make a change that was quite insignificant. Steel rails upon which the importer had been paying $28 a ton would now bear a rate of only $17, but this was held to be a matter of no importance to our manufacturers, since they had become so expert in this branch of production that the new duty was as prohibitory as the old one had been. The rate on copper was reduced from five to four cents a pound, on nickel from 30 cents to 15 cents a pound.

The *ad valorem* rates over and above the pound rates on wool were removed, but these, it was said, were still sufficiently high to bar foreign material except some of the better grades

[1] See letters from such men addressed to Wm. E. Chandler in Chandler Papers in Library of Congress.
[2] Cf. Taussig, History of the Tariff, pp. 231–3; App. Ann. Cyclop. for 1883, pp. 193–4.
[3] McPherson's Handbook for 1884, pp. 57–8.

of fleeces. There were reductions in the duties on woolen and cotton manufactures of the cheaper classes; on finer goods the rates were increased.[1] The sugar duties were revised and the levies hereafter would be made according to polariscopic test.[2]

Though the law was generally considered to be in the interest of the "reformers" it contributed but little to their content. What was achieved was mainly in connection with the internal revenue—the taxes upon luxuries rather than the necessaries of life.[3] In view of the "surplus," of which every one knew, and the "overtaxation" which this "surplus" was held to evidence, there seemed to be necessity, said the New York Nation, of passing some bill to save the Republican party in 1884 from charges of incompetency and a "summary reckoning at the polls." [4] But barring the reduction in the sugar tax the changes were "piddling trivialities." It was a "blundering" bill and quite clearly it was not a "finality"; the lobby which was assembled to follow its course through Congress was a promise of what would grow and fruit in other years with reference to such legislation.[5] The tariff question was rising rapidly to serve the uses of the Republican party, which, the Nation continued, could "no longer subsist on Ku Klux outrages and Southern wickedness." [6]

On the other side there was rumbling also. Though the wool manufacturers congratulated Morrill on the enactment of the measure, which had effected "a substantial reduction of duties, together with a substantial preservation of the protective features of our national economical system," they were, it appeared, not heartily pleased with what had been done. They did not want the tariff changed, said John L. Hayes, the president of the Tariff Commission, who had represented

---

[1] Taussig, History of the Tariff, chap. iv.
[2] Report of Tariff Commission of 1882, p. 22.
[3] A. D. Noyes, Forty Years of Am. Finance, p. 95; Stanwood, Am. Tariff Controversies, vol. ii, p. 218.
[4] N. Y. Nation, March 8, 1883.
[5] Ibid.; cf. Ida Tarbell, The Tariff in Our Times, pp. 131–2.
[6] N. Y. Nation, March 8, 1883.

them on that board.[1] The bill was a "concession to public
sentiment, a bending of the top and branches to the wind of
public opinion to save the trunk of the protective system." [2]
The iron and steel manufacturers in Pittsburgh were not satisfied with what had come to them.[3] With the duty at only $17
a ton the steel rail men were in a "position of danger." [4] The
coterie of high protectionists in Philadelphia viewed the bill as
a "surrender." [5] Joseph Wharton found the duty on nickel, a
matter of interest to him, reduced one-half,[6] and protested
vehemently. [7] "All concessions" made in the bill "to the free
trade sentiment," Wharton wrote to William E. Chandler,
were "mistakes in party policy and injurious to the country." [8]
The Finance Committee should have invited representatives
of leading manufacturers into conference before passing a bill
which, having been passed, had "sensibly weakened the hold
of the Republican party upon many thousands of working
men." [9] Columbus Delano and the "triumvirate" in Ohio,
persistent in their pursuit of every man at Washington who
spoke of "free" or reduced duties on wool, were profoundly
disturbed, as it was foreseen that they would be. They had
prevented much by their energetic exertions, but they had not
gained all and were preparing for new contests.[10]

No remedy seemed to be at hand. Ills, if there were such on
either side, must be suffered for a time. The next Congress,
the Forty-eighth, found the House and its Committee on Ways
and Means, as a result of the elections of 1882, under the direction of the Democrats, who, in the main, had been the advocates of lower duties, when the issue was drawn between the
parties as the voting had proceeded in the Forty-seventh,—

[1] Under date of March 20, 1883, in Morrill Papers.
[2] Bull. of Nat. Assoc. of Wool Mfrs., vol. xiii, p. 94.
[3] N. Y. Nation, March 8, 1883.
[4] Am. Hist. Review for Oct., 1930, p. 92.
[5] N. Y. Nation, March 8, 1883.
[6] Am. Hist. Review for Oct., 1930, p. 94.
[7] Morrill Papers.
[8] Nov. 23, 1883, in Chandler Papers.
[9] Swank to Morrill, Nov. 23, 1883, in Morrill Papers.
[10] Cf. Morrill Papers; Ida Tarbell, The Tariff in Our Times, pp. 130–31.

and of the tariff reform wing of that party, since John G. Carlisle had been preferred over Randall, the Pennsylvania protectionist, for the speakership.[1] No legislation on the subject could be expected; the Senate, by recent changes in its complexion, had become definitely Republican and would presumably prevent it, but the majority in the House could present its bill through William R. Morrison, who was now the chairman of the Committee on Ways and Means, on which account it was called the "Morrison bill." The measure was completed and reported out of the committee in March, 1884. It would "reduce import duties and war tariff taxes" by a general cut of 20 per cent. In addition to this "horizontal" reduction iron ore, coal, lumber and some other articles would be put upon the "free list." Randall and the protectionist Democrats prevented its passage even in the House, and it, therefore, became a mere "campaign document."[2]

The Presidential campaign of 1884 was to be, in many respects, one of the most memorable in the course of our political history. The Independents were a growing force in many communities. The colleges were being reorganized. Young men who had studied history and politics in them were gaining worthy ideals. Book and periodical spoke of better government. Men and women were learning to know good from evil in public conduct and were leavening the mass of apathy under which thievery throve. In the autumn of 1883 the people of Brooklyn, under the leadership of a body of young men, re-elected Seth Low mayor. Theodore Roosevelt had been re-elected to the New York Assembly in 1882 and again in 1883, and he was in the midst of a useful campaign in behalf of reform measures applicable to New York City which were loosening the grasp of Tammany. Grover Cleveland was approving the bills which Roosevelt drove through the legislature.[3] The

[1] N. Y. Nation, Dec. 6, 1883.

[2] McPherson's Handbook for 1884, pp. 135-7; N. Y. Nation, March 13, 20, May 8, 1884; Stanwood, Am. Tariff Controversies, vol. ii, pp. 220-21; Taussig, Tariff Hist. of the U. S., pp. 251-2; O. H. Perry in Quart. Jour. of Economics, Oct., 1887. Four Republicans voted for the bill; forty-one Democrats against it.

[3] N. Y. Nation, July 24, 1884.

Independents had had their part in making George Hoadly, Democratic candidate, governor of Ohio, and in an interesting event in Massachusetts. In 1882, at the time when party ties were loose, "Ben" Butler had seen his opportunity. Some years had elapsed since he had ceased to be a Republican. He had failed repeatedly to gain the nomination for governor as a Democrat, as he had failed of reaching that goal while he had been a member of the other party, though his turbulence and the lowering of the character of the electorate in the state by immigration had nearly secured him the prize. His declarations on the money question marked him for a Greenbacker and he found himself in an appropriate place in 1882 as a candidate of the paper money party. When to this was added the indorsement of the rabble in the Democratic party, which had gained control of the convention of that political organization, the old mountebank, after a stormy campaign, had been enabled to win the coveted distinction. But he was to enjoy his honors for only a year [1] for now, in 1883, though renominated, the Republican candidate, aided by an aroused Independent vote, defeated him, and his evil figure was finally eliminated from the public life of the state. [2]

The election for officers on the state ticket in New York in 1883 indicated a distinct loss for the Democrats, as compared with the vote for Cleveland in the preceding year, a number of the Independents, lacking reason for further protest, having returned to their usual affiliations. Many, however, were not firmly attached to the party and it were folly to suppose that their feelings and opinions could be lightly regarded. They had organizations. Meetings and resolutions expressive of their wishes and intentions with reference to the Presidency allowed no one opportunity to doubt that they would make themselves a potential force in the ensuing campaign. [3]

As early as December, 1883, a number of Republicans in Boston, fresh from their successful campaign for the overthrow

---

[1] And without the degree of LL.D. from Harvard hitherto always bestowed upon the governors of Massachusetts. See Butler's Book, p. 976.

[2] Hoar, Autobiography of 70 Years, vol. i, chap. xxiv.

[3] N. Y. Nation, April 10, 1884.

of Butler instituted a movement in favor of the nomination of
a fit man for President. A committee was formed and correspondence was opened with men of similar views in other parts
of the country, with the result that a conference of Independents was held in New York on February 23, 1884, preceded,
in the Brooklyn Academy of Music, on the evening of Washington's Birthday, by a large dinner which was addressed by
Carl Schurz, President Seelye of Amherst College and others.[1]
It was a warning. An executive committee was appointed to
further the organization, auxiliary bodies were formed in
Chicago, Cincinnati and other cities in the West,[2] and, as soon
as the delegates to the Republican convention were chosen in
the various states, letters were sent to them reminding them
of their responsibilities and soliciting their coöperation and support.[3]

That Arthur could be a formidable candidate for election to a
place into which he, upon the death of Garfield, had so accidentally fallen seemed difficult to imagine.[4] It was held to be
a point in his favor as a candidate, that in his administration
letter postage had been reduced from three to two cents. Every
citizen, when he stuck a stamp upon a letter, must think of the
President gratefully.[5] He had not been unmindful of the possibility of his nomination and had been making appointments not
without regard for the upbuilding of an organization which
would advance his personal plans. He yielded, indeed, to the
reformers to gain their applause, but he, at the same time, distributed places to practical politicians who, in his opinion,
would be useful to him in attaining his own ends. He would
match a good appointment with a bad one, and often claimed
the right, after bringing one acceptable man into office, of
naming two or three men who should, on no account, have
been introduced to, or kept in, the public service. It was agreed
that in all that related to measures Mr. Arthur had been "gen-

[1] N. Y. Tribune, Feb. 23, 1884.
[2] Ibid., March 27 and April 1, 1884.
[3] Ibid., April 30, 1884; App. Ann. Cyclop. for 1884, p. 767.
[4] Cf. A. D. White, Autobiography, vol. i, p. 193.
[5] See a leaflet, "The Great Postal Triumph," in Chandler Papers.

erally discreet, conservative and just." [1] That he had displayed
so much, or in fact any, wisdom in the administration of his
office was a subject of surprise, if not of astonishment. [2] But
his recognition of the right of the "bosses" in the states to
receive valuable posts for their henchmen made his approval
of the Pendleton civil service reform bill in considerable degree
a mockery. He could better have been true to his character as
a Conkling man, when he might have retained the support
of "Tom" Platt who now, not having had a large part in guiding Arthur's hand, in proof of the want of principle in his kind,
joined the "Half Breeds" and advocated the nomination of
Blaine. [3]

Arthur had fallen between two stools. [4] That his strategy as
an office monger met with approval on no side, though he had
made the attempt to satisfy every one, was proven when, in
1882, he entered the canvass for the governorship in New York
and gave the support of the administration to Judge Folger,
only to compass the election of Cleveland by a majority of
nearly 200,000. Arthur's prospects of choice as the candidate
of the party for President in 1884, however favorable they may
have seemed to be prior to this event, were henceforward
small, though, as the time came for the national convention
to meet in Chicago, the Federal officeholders who controlled
the party organization in the Southern states instructed their
delegations for him. Concerned only for the money which
they would draw from the Treasury of the United States, and
profoundly solicitous lest a new President should put them
out of their places, they were "Arthur men." [5] With this
"mercenary brigade," representing the "custom houses, post-
offices and other government positions in the South," [6] made
up of white parasites and some negroes as a nucleus of his

[1] N. Y. Nation, April 17, 1884; cf. ibid., May 22, 1884.
[2] "Mr. Arthur has shown us that a man may make quite a reputation by
simply doing less mischief than he is expected to do."—Editor of a Buffalo
paper to Cleveland, Dec. 2, 1884, in Cleveland Papers.
[3] Autobiography of Platt, pp. 180–81.
[4] Ibid.
[5] Cf. N. Y. Nation, April 24, 1884.
[6] Ibid., Feb. 28, 1884.

strength, the President gained friends now and again in the North. Many business men in New York, whose support it had been thought might have been better given to Sherman, were induced to hold a meeting and declare themselves favorable to Arthur's nomination. They had come to know him and satisfied themselves that he would not disturb the course of their lives.[1]

Blaine had been disengaged since he had left his post as Secretary of State shortly following the death of Garfield. His administration of that office had been interrupted in the midst of the formulation of a militant Pan-American program. His schemes echoed hoof beats and sounding brass. They were set before the country with a theatrical jingoism which was a part of the man and which he calculated would please and keep him near to the hearts of those whose admiration of him approached a kind of idolatry.[2]

His occupancy of the office at the State Department had covered only a few months but such had been his activity in this brief period that he was, at the time of his leaving it, deeply involved in the internal affairs of Chile, Peru and some other Latin American countries,[3] and he was proposing a congress in Washington [4] of delegates from the various American governments from the Rio Grande to Cape Horn with veiled, if not spoken, defiance to Europe on the subject of her supposed designs upon the liberties of the Western continent.[5]

His rather truculent air was emphasized by the unfortunate character of the instruments chosen for the work in hand.[6] The

[1] Arthur should be nominated "as a reward for faithful service," General Sherman wrote to W. Q. Gresham. (July 1, 1884, in Gresham Papers.) On the other hand it was said that he would display no strength as a candidate. People would speak well of him but would not vote for him.—W. A. Richardson to W. E. Chandler in Chandler Papers.

[2] The name "premier" was imported and applied to him because he seemed too dazzling a person to be reduced to the level of other members of the cabinet.—Mr. Blaine and his Foreign Policy, a pamphlet published by H. W. Hall, Boston, 1884.

[3] Cf. N. Y. Herald, Sep. 25, 1884.

[4] A great confederation of all the American republics, "a grand Amphictyonic Council."—N. Y. Nation, Feb. 9, 1882; cf. Harper's Weekly, Feb. 18, 1882.

[5] N. Y. Nation, Feb. 9, 1882.　　　　[6] Ibid., June 5, 1884.

ministers through whom he was acting in South America, and they seem to have been men of his own choice, were even less creditable to the nation than most of the members of our diplomatic service assigned at this time to inconsequent courts and capitals, and the gravest misunderstandings were averted only by Mr. Frelinghuysen's coming to the office with the announcement of more pacific policies.[1] Blaine's explanation of his course in South America was that he had a desire to save a "sister republic" from the "heavy hand of England" which she "felt upon her at every turn." The end, he said, would have been "an absolute domination of English influence in both Peru and Chile," which it had been his hope, through mediation of the United States, to prevent.[2] That his foreign policy rested, in some degree at least, upon a wish to appear to the people, before whom he remained a candidate for the Presidency, as anti-British in his sympathies (with particular regard for the large Irish vote) was confirmed on every side. Still more disquieting was it to realize that various speculators and adventurers interested in concessions and claims were being served, as it seemed, by the strong arm of the American State Department.[3]

In the Congressional investigation into this "spirited foreign policy" in South America, which ensued in 1882, Mr. Blaine spoke in his own defense,[4] attacking other men, one of whom, Perry Belmont, a member of the committee, who was pursuing the inquiry relentlessly, the ex-Secretary of State likened to "a garbage boy on the streets." Belmont retorted by calling Blaine "a bully and a coward" and the scene sank to the level of a barroom brawl.[5]

[1] Harper's Weekly, Feb. 4 and 11, 1882.
[2] N. Y. Nation, Feb. 2, 9, 16, 23, April 27, May 4, 1882, July 24 and Aug. 28, 1884.
[3] Cf. ibid., Oct. 2, 1884; Mr. Blaine and His Foreign Policy, earlier cited; Senate Ex. Doc., 47th Cong. 1st sess., no. 79; House Reports, 47th Cong. 1st sess., no. 1790.
[4] N. Y. Nation, April 27, 1882.
[5] House Reports, 47th Cong. 1st sess., no. 1790, pp. 223, 239, 243; N. Y. Nation, May 4, 1882. In Blaine's defense see N. Y. Tribune for corresponding dates.

However undignified the admixture of the administration of our foreign policy with the commercial speculations of private persons, without respect to the jingoism of this policy, may have seemed to be, the exceptional dexterity of Blaine in extricating himself from any corner into which he might be pressed continued to win for him the love of many classes of the people. He was heard from in the newspapers. Members of his family, who were industrious writers like himself, William Walter Phelps, Whitelaw Reid and the New York Tribune [1] and many others heralded his movements, advertised his merits and broadcast his views. He heard the call for civil service reform, but he would build up no "system" belonging to "royalty." He would make peace with both sides in this matter in his usual way and appoint men to office for seven years.[2] In 1883 some one proposed to distribute among the states the "surplus" which was being created by redundant Federal revenues. Instead of reducing taxation, it was said, let the taxes be gathered and returned to the people through their local governments. Blaine could not go so far. He would return only the whiskey tax since—his mind on the temperance vote—this should continue to be levied to discourage the use of intoxicating drink.[3] It was announced that he was giving his mind to historical letters which would result in nothing of greater importance than a work to be called "Twenty Years of Congress." The progress upon it was the subject of frequent allusions in the press; extracts were published with the design of fixing attention upon his person and his name.[4]

None could have reason to doubt his wish to gain the nomination and his candidacy was seen to be a formidable thing. He had failed in 1880 only through the opposition of Conkling and the "Stalwarts." This enemy had laid down the leadership when he had resigned from the Senate, and those at his heels had scattered, after his power was seen to be at an

[1] Cortissoz, Life of Reid, vol. ii, pp. 90–93.
[2] N. Y. Nation, Sep. 14, 1882.
[3] Ibid., Dec. 6, 1883, and Sep. 4, 1882.
[4] Cf. ibid., Feb. 7, 28, Apr. 3 and May 29, 1884; N. Y. Tribune, Apr. 28, 1884.

end, to follow more propitious banners. The faction had been
dispersed, to be incorporated for the most part in the retinue
of Arthur, despite the fact that many of Conkling's friends
considered the President to be faithless to the great traditions
of the Republican party, as they interpreted its purposes
and aims.

Grant, who in 1880 had been used as a mask by the "Stalwarts" for the seduction of the nation that they might return
to places where they could strut and filch as before, was now
in dire extremity. The hero to whom the "306," failing in
1880, swore a fealty in 1884 and for the rest of their lives, had
been tumbled from his pedestal. In 1882 General Logan had
prominently employed himself in trying to place Grant on
the retired list that he could enjoy the use of the money which
this act on the part of Congress would put at his disposition.
The project was not improperly resisted. So far as the public
could perceive Grant was not a poor man. It was pointed out
that in his last term as President he had been paid, under provision of the unrepealed sections of the "Salary Grab" law,
twice as much as any President had ever received before.
Wealthy capitalists, as a result of their latest activity in his
behalf, had given him a quarter of a million dollars.[1] He drove
spanking teams of horses. He hired a pew in a fashionable
church for $1,000.[2] In summer he lived luxuriously at Long
Branch,[3] and his name was written among the affluent rich of
New York City.[4]

Again and again commercial opportunities were offered to
him by friends, as well as strangers, who had schemes which
were to prosper on the strength of his reputation, could he be
persuaded to identify his name with them. "Exceedingly
eager to make money," as Whitelaw Reid said, he had become
interested, "body and soul," in railway enterprises in Mexico.
He had never had common acumen in any private business
matter, as his record in the Presidency would deny him claim
for talent in the management of public affairs. The magnitude

[1] Cf. N. Y. Nation, Feb. 23, 1882.   [3] N. Y. World, July 17, 1884.
[2] Ibid.   [4] Cf. N.Y. Sun, May 17, 1884.

of the Mexican projects "dazed" him, and it was predicted by those who knew his failings that he was headed for disaster.[1] But the crash came through an adventure which he and his sons had made in a great Wall Street business. He had been ensnared by some New York rogues, whose speculations, with his name as a figurehead, to lend them respectability, collapsed in a period of economic depression in which the country was now again involved. There were wide losses in the prices of stocks in Wall Street and, in May, 1884, Grant and Ward, as the firm was called, fell with two or more millions of liabilities, so it appeared, and no assets. The managers of the business had been telling innocent men and women that they had "government contracts," gained, presumably, through Grant's political influence, which were a complete myth. "The failure," said the New York Nation, was "the most colossal that ever took place among merely private firms in the United States, and one of the most disgraceful."[2]

Grant, who had been receiving large sums of money from the concern, for no given service and without the slightest knowledge of the means by which they had been won,[3] was again a candidate for the nation's pity. Once more he was absolved from share of culpability because of the debt which the country owed him as a military commander, though some of his associates, it was agreed, should be in jail and they were promptly put under arrest.[4] A trustful disposition and unfortunate alliances were somehow taken to be excuse, and explanation as well, for his plight, to solace him and pacify, if possible, the firm's many victims and dupes.

The bill placing him on the retired list with full pay as "General of the Army," advocated by General Logan,[5] was now

---

[1] He is "sure to be used in these schemes until he is only a squeezed orange."—Reid to Morrill, May 18, 1883, in Morrill Papers; cf. Morrill to Reid, May 15, 1883, in ibid.

[2] Issues of May 15 and 29, 1884.

[3] "Neither of the Grants is believed to have paid closer attention to details than the regular drawing of his allowance."—N. Y. Tribune, May 9, 1884.

[4] N. Y. Nation, May 22 and 29, 1884.

[5] Cf. Cong. Record, 47th Cong. 1st sess., p. 1285.

hurriedly passed. He was *"primus inter illustres* in the history
of this country," said Senator Edmunds,[1] who wished to have
the bill receive a unanimous vote. Only nine men, all Democrats, were found in the Senate to oppose the measure.[2] President Arthur in a message urged the House to action,[3] which
came on March 3, 1885, the last day of the session, when 78
members recorded their votes in the negative.[4] Arthur signed
the bill, the fact being announced in Congress amid "great
applause" on the floor and in the galleries, and henceforth
Grant would receive $13,500 a year from the Treasury of the
United States.[5]

That Grant, after the wreck of his Wall Street firm, could
be supported by 306 or any other number of delegates in the
Republican convention, which would meet in Chicago on the
third day of June, was not to be believed and, indeed, there
had been no sign at any time, after Conkling's explosion as a
public character, of an organized following for the famous
man whose "boom" had turned Blaine aside in 1880. The
"Half Breeds" were now the Republican party and, in spite
of some opposition not difficult to overcome, they would
give their leader the distinction which he so dearly desired to
enjoy.

The increase of certainty that this would be the result of
the convention increased the zest of Blaine's enemies in the
ranks of the Independents. He had been held before the nation
as a candidate who should not be chosen—by the forces in the
Republican party which had organized the Liberal movement

[1] Cong. Record, 48th Cong. 2nd sess., p. 684.
[2] Ibid., p. 685.
[3] App. Ann. Cyclop. for 1885, p. 226.
[4] Including General Rosecrans who found that Grant's military services
were "exaggerated and misrepresented" because "it was the interest of
a great political party" to do this and use him as their "servant and tool
to secure power." When "true history" should be written, General Rosecrans continued, Grant's reputation would be "pared down to very different dimensions."—App. Ann. Cyclop. for 1885, p. 226. See Cong. Record,
48th Cong. 2nd sess., p. 1758.
[5] N. Y. Tribune, March 5, 1885; McPherson's Handbook for 1886,
pp. 45–6; cf. ibid. for 1884, p. 189; Cong. Record, 48th Cong. 2nd sess.,
p. 2503; N. Y. Nation, Jan. 22 and March 12, 1885.

in 1872; which had supported Hayes in 1876; which had "scratched" Cornell for governor of New York in 1879 but had voted for Garfield in 1880; which had forwarded the election of Cleveland as governor in 1882, and which, on all occasions, had been defending ideals at variance with the corrupting practices that were dissociable from government in America in this era. No one could or did state and restate the reasons why Blaine should not be nominated so cogently and candidly as Mr. Godkin in the New York Evening Post and, by reprint, in the New York Nation. George William Curtis said, in Harper's Weekly, that, if Blaine were nominated, the campaign would be "a prolonged explanation"; it would be a "practical abdication of Republican character and purpose."[1]

Service of another kind in the interest of Blaine's undoing was performed by Puck, a New York satirical weekly, illustrated in colors. In a cartoon called "The National Dime Museum" the various candidates for the Presidency were shown as curiosities for public view. Blaine's plump figure, in a loin cloth made of the starry blue field of an American flag, his skin intricately tattooed like a sailor's in India ink, displaying the words "Mulligan Letters," "Northern Pacific Bonds," "Bribery," "Bluster," "Anti-Chinese Demagogism" and like inscriptions, met instant and nation-wide notice. At once for the purposes of the campaign he was the "Tattooed Man."[2] It was the work of a caricaturist named Gillam who combined with an unusual gift for draftsmanship the most intimate knowledge of our politics. With his aid, and that of others of like, if somewhat inferior, talents, Puck became a power during the campaign.[3]

It was plain that, if Blaine were nominated at Chicago, it would be without the coöperation and aid of the Independents. He had their complete reprobation. He stood for nothing but

[1] Issue of June 14, 1884.
[2] Issue of April 16, 1884. Logan was portrayed as a "Wild Zulu on the Warpath."
[3] At one time its circulation exceeded three million copies. (Issue of June 11, 1884.) Gillam was an Englishman and was dismissed as such by the Blaine press.—N. Y. Tribune, June 14, 1884.

"Jim Blaine." [1] His interest in the government of his country was interest in himself. But he was so quick to deny any charge affecting his own honor, so skillful in the art of finding a *tu quoque* to throw the pursuer off his own and upon another trail, so ready and forward in playing for notoriety and effect [2] in the sight of those who are prone to extend their admiring favor to men who are dashing and smart that he escaped his deserts, and, indeed, by his geniality of address and his amiable ways, increased the circle of his friends. [3]

Young Theodore Roosevelt, fresh from his adventures at Albany, was a figure among a group of men who would be sent to the convention from New York, which would include George William Curtis and Andrew D. White. They would not support Blaine and were turning hopefully to Senator Edmunds. [4] Edmunds would have the favor, too, of Henry Cabot Lodge, ex-Governor Long, Senator Hoar and other men in the delegation from Massachusetts. [5] The opposition was formidable, but those who held the management of the convention in their hands pretended, as always before, to think but little of its influence or strength. Blaine's enemies were a "squad of men," said the New York Tribune, "who were attempting to bully the party," threatening, if they could not have their own way, to elect a Democrat. [6]

William Walter Phelps, who, next to Whitelaw Reid, was Blaine's most eloquent advocate, had framed an elaborate

---

[1] N. Y. Nation, June 12, 1884.

[2] Cf. Writings of Schurz, vol. iv, pp. 154–5; N. Y. Nation, April 10, 17, 24, May 1 and 8, 1884.

[3] For ex-President Hayes's estimate of Blaine at this time (April 19, 1884) see his Diary and Letters, vol. iv, p. 146: "He fails in two points as a candidate. He lacks the confidence of thoughtful, high-minded and patriotic people. They doubt his personal integrity; they think he is a demagogue. . . . He does not belong to the class of leaders of whom Hamilton, Jefferson, Clay, Calhoun, Seward, Lincoln and Webster are types. He is of the Butler and Douglas type—more like Douglas in character and position than any other of the great leaders of the past. Clay would rather be right than be President. Blaine would gladly be wrong to be President."

[4] N. Y. Nation, April 24 and May 1, 1884.

[5] Ibid., May 8, 1884.

[6] N. Y. Tribune, May 5, 1884.

reply to the charges preferred against their friend and favorite and had sent it to the New York Evening Post.[1] It was held by them to be, and was referred to throughout the campaign as, a complete confutation of the "stale slanders" affecting Blaine's position as a public man. Incidentally Mr. Phelps had paused to cast reflections upon the honor of Edmunds, the candidate of the "reformers," who, it was alleged, had been as guilty as Blaine on the subject of railroads, a charge which Edmunds indignantly denied.[2]

The opposition which was organized against Blaine was, in fact, of little moment to his eager adherents, for one state after another instructed its delegates for him—Pennsylvania, Maryland, Kansas, West Virginia, California and Iowa.[3] Illinois found a "favorite son" in General Logan who was to have the vote of its delegation.[4] Sherman still had his friends in Ohio, but it was recognized that he had had his opportunity in 1880, when, fresh from his triumph in connection with resumption, and eloquently recommended by Garfield, the convention, after many fruitless ballots, failed to rally to his support. He would now be brought forward by Foraker. Mark Hanna, a rich business man rising to influence and power in the politics of Ohio, a member of the delegation, was a sincere friend, but McKinley and others sent to Chicago from that state would vote for Blaine.[5]

When the third day of June came the convention met in the painted wooden pavilion, the same Exhibition Hall, in which

[1] Issue of April 26, 1884; N. Y. Nation, May 1, 1884; N. Y. Tribune, April 27 and 28, 1884.
[2] N. Y. Tribune, May 1, 1884. For want of other argument the Tribune disposed of the Edmunds men by branding them as "conspicuous and noisy free traders."
[3] Ibid., April 28 and May 3, 1884.
[4] Logan wrote Schurz, seeking support, and got adequate reply.—Writings of Schurz, vol. iv, pp. 194–5.
[5] C. L. Kurtz to Sherman, June 8, 1884, in Sherman Papers. Cf. John Sherman's Recollections, pp. 885–6. Some of the Germans were friendly to Sherman in 1884, as they had been in 1880, though they called him an "iceberg." They liked his "methodical" habit, greatly preferring him to his brother, the General, whom they regarded as "a little eccentric and sometimes off his base."—A German editor to Chandler, May 27, 1884, in Chandler Papers.

the "306" had made their stand in 1880.[1] Excitement was at white heat. Blaine's friends controlled the national committee, as was evidenced when that body presented for temporary chairman the name of Powell Clayton, of Arkansas, who now, in return for the distinction, led his delegation away from Arthur for the advantage of the "Plumed Knight." This choice awakened the indignation of the Independents, but without influencing the course of the Blaine managers. There were 820 delegates in the hall. Those who were opposed to Clayton's election, led by Roosevelt[2] and Lodge, who in this matter were coöperating with Arthur's adherents, brought forward the name of John R. Lynch, a negro from Mississippi, and elected him, an indication that the anti-Blaine forces were strong enough, if they could be kept together, to prevent his nomination. It was in answer to good advice that ex-Senator John B. Henderson of Missouri was elected to the permanent chairmanship. But the reformers gained no more victories. There were only 93 votes for Edmunds on the first ballot and 30 for John Sherman;[3] while Blaine received 334½ and Arthur 278. The Independents were at a loss to know how to proceed. There were no bargains which could be made for the salvation of their cause. Alliances with Arthur were impossible, since his support, being almost entirely that of officeholders, was founded on no principle which was worthy of indorsement. Logan had proven himself an even more disturbing figure in politics than Blaine. He was entirely without proper appreciation or understanding of public service. Anyhow he was a candidate only that he and his delegation could "trade."[4] Those who saw in Robert T. Lincoln a chance to use an honored name were disappointed,

[1] N. Y. Tribune, June 4, 1884.

[2] At this convention Roosevelt, seated by the side of George William Curtis, was seen by the "Western people" for the first time. "His square head, matted with short, dry, sandy hair, and his eye glass, and nervously forcible gestures were remarked."—Chicago corr. N. Y. Tribune, June 4, 1884.

[3] Twenty-five of these from Ohio—there were 21 votes in that state's delegation for Blaine.

[4] N. Y. Nation, April 3, 1884. At the right time, when Blaine's star was seen to be rising, Logan made an "easy surrender."—C. L. Kurtz, to Sherman, June 8, 1884, in Sherman Papers.

as were some others who would raise the oriflamme of General Sherman's reputation [1] and march the enfranchised citizenry up to the polls as he had marched an army through Georgia, "from Atlanta to the sea." For General Sherman told inquirers, one and all, that "in no event and under no circumstances" would he permit the use of his name as a Presidential candidate.[2] He was still more definite in private correspondence. In a letter to Blaine he said that he would account himself "a fool, a madman, an ass" to embark, at 65 years of age, on a political career.[3]

There was to be no turning aside of Blaine's friends and no candidacy could withstand such force as had been organized behind his name. The delegates who were to make the decision as to the nominee were surrounded by ten thousand men, women and boys, stimulated to excitement by every artificial device which the fertile minds of persons practiced in such arts could suggest.[4] There were times when this great mob, encircling the seats of the relatively small body of delegates, with the purpose of sweeping the convention "in the direction of its own whims and fancies," absolutely controlled it.[5] On earlier occasions the convention system had earned reprobation at the hands of competent observers but never before 1884, in Chicago, had such a claque appeared to rob a body of men of their deliberative power.[6] Whenever Blaine's name was men-

[1] In spite of his Romanist connections. The Protestant church papers were hoisting the banner—"No Roman Catholic for President." See, e.g., Northwestern Christian Advocate, quoted in N. Y. Tribune, Feb. 25, 1884. Cf. Writings of Schurz, vol. iv, p. 203; Hoar, Autobiography of 70 Years, vol. i, pp. 407–8.

[2] Sherman Letters, pp. 357–62; A. D. White, Autobiography, vol. i, p. 203.

[3] Stanwood, Life of Blaine, p. 272. Some friends, however, still favored his nomination. "The more he kicks," they said, "the better"; the people would elect a man who did not want the office "with a whirl."—John Sherman Papers.

[4] N. Y. Nation, June 19, 1884.

[5] A. D. White, Autobiography, vol. i, p. 204.

[6] "From time to time the convention ceased entirely to be a deliberative body." Women jumped "up and down, disheveled and hysterical." Some men acted in the same way. The whole performance was "absolutely unworthy of a convention of any party, a disgrace to decency and a blot upon the reputation of our country."—A. D. White, Autobiography, vol. i, pp. 204–6.

tioned the crowd roared its approval. Logan also had his pack
in the galleries. By penny whistles, rattles, stamping, dancing,
yelling, hooting, "hi-hi" ing, the waving of hats, coats, handkerchiefs and open umbrellas, and disturbances of many other
kinds men who were not to the crowd's mind were cried down
and their voices were drowned in demands for those whose interests this army of outlaws had come to advance. Barnyard
cocks and black eagles, a helmet surmounted by a white plume
at the top of a flagstaff were paraded up and down the aisles,
state shields and banners were torn from the walls and the
platform.[1] The telegraphic dispatches from the convention
hall, said the New York Nation, read like accounts of "a mass
meeting of maniacs." [2]

The ticket was Blaine and Logan, chosen against the advice and amid the opposition of a respected and powerful
minority in the party who, so it appeared, would give it their
support reluctantly and half-heartedly, if they should vote for,
and exert themselves to elect, it at all. Over such the Blaine
enthusiasts had trampled roughshod, and what was at once
seen in the country at large was deserving of their notice. None
of the newspapers in New York, except the Tribune, promised
to give the ticket cordial and unquestioning support. Most of
them would actively oppose it. The New York Times was now
ready for service as an Independent journal,[3] and it would
stand beside the New York Evening Post, though its recent
conversion put its editors in a difficult place. The Boston
Advertiser declared its "inability to support the nomination."
The Springfield Republican said that what the Chicago conven-

[1] Witness the following in the New York Tribune's description of the
scene when Blaine's name was mentioned, in response to the call for nominations: "Whole delegations mounted their chairs and led the cheering,
which instantly spread to the stage and deepened into a roar fully as deep
and deafening as the voice of Niagara. The scene was indescribable. The
air quivered, the gaslights trembled and the walls fairly shook. The flags
were stripped from the gallery and stage and frantically waved, while
hats, umbrellas, handkerchiefs and other personal belongings were tossed
to and fro like bubbles over the great dancing sea of human heads."—
Chicago corr. N. Y. Tribune, June 6, 1884.
[2] Issue of June 12, 1884.
[3] Elmer Davis, History of the N. Y. Times, pp. 150–54.

tion had done was "revolutionary." The nominations would
"carry dismay and alarm to thousands of men" who had regarded the Republican party "as the party of safety, of integrity, of principle and of high moral ends." Such a choice of
candidates "deserved disaster and defeat." The Boston Tran-
script said that, for the first time in its history, the party had
nominated "a really vulnerable candidate for President." Boisterous crowds had overawed the convention and robbed it of
its judgment.[1] So it was throughout the country. Prominent
journals, whose favor was valuable, if they gave promise of
supporting the ticket, only reservedly stated their confidence
in the wisdom of the nomination and in party success.[2]

"Black Jack" Logan's name on the ticket for Vice-President
compounded the convention's offense. He had been named
in the Crédit Mobilier scandal. He had been Blaine's associate in the House of Representatives in connection with the
business of befriending the Little Rock and Fort Smith Railroad.[3] A hearty, jovial wire-puller, of small mental equipment, and on all occasions a "neck or nothing partisan,"
his nomination was no more acceptable to judicious men than
Blaine's.[4]

The Independents were never so active or clear in their
declarations.[5] The Massachusetts Reform Club repudiated
the nomination; Charles Francis Adams, Jr., was made chairman
of the committee to carry its will into effect.[6] Fifteen hundred
prominent citizens of Boston who had voted for Garfield in 1880
signed a call for a meeting in that city.[7] Colonel Charles R.
Codman, who had presided over the convention of the Republican party to nominate the ticket which had beaten Butler
in Massachusetts, took the chair. An executive committee
of one hundred was appointed. Another body of anti-Blaine

[1] Quoted in N. Y. Tribune, June 9, 1884.
[2] N. Y. Nation, June 12, 1884.
[3] Blaine's letter to Fisher of Oct. 4, 1869; N. Y. Nation, June 3, 1884;
N. Y. Sun, June 19, 1884.
[4] Cf. N. Y. Nation, April 3, 1884.
[5] Ibid., June 12 and 19, 1884; N. Y. Tribune, June 18, 1884.
[6] N. Y. Nation, June 12, 1884.
[7] Ibid., June 19, 1884; cf. ibid., July 10, 1884; N. Y. Sun, June 14, 1884.

Republicans crowded a hall in New Haven.[1] A national conference was called to meet in New York on June 17th. The Independents claimed such names as President Eliot of Harvard, Carl Schurz, James Freeman Clarke, Thomas Wentworth Higginson, Henry L. Pierce, President Seelye of Amherst, President Carter of Williams, President Capen of Tufts, George William Curtis, Moorfield Storey, Josiah Quincy, Richard Henry Dana, William Everett, Francis C. Lowell, Thomas Bailey Aldrich, Edward Atkinson, William T. Endicott, Jr., Henry L. Higginson, Francis G. Peabody, F. J. Stimson, ex-Governor D. H. Chamberlain, A. A. Pope, Henry Ward Beecher, Samuel Hoar, General Francis C. Barlow, Henry C. Lea, Franklin MacVeagh of Chicago, Simeon E. Baldwin and Charles J. Bonaparte.[2]

The Democrats were now plainly put upon their honor. A recitation of various kinds of almost divinely inspired service to the country had been adopted as a "platform" by the Republican convention. The Democrats responded, with some truth, that, so far as "principle" went, the Republican party was a "reminiscence." [3] Their opportunity had come, if they would but rid themselves of controlling forces which had so often led the party to disaster and present a candidate for the support of worthy and intelligent citizens. Butler's downfall in 1883 in Massachusetts had been complete. He, nevertheless, regarded himself as a suitable leader of the Democratic party in the national campaign. That he might be the choice of the convention he emphasized his well known views on the merit of paper money as a cure for the ills of the downtrodden masses of mankind, and he secured the nomination for President at the hands of the Greenback party.[4] Other Labor and Socialist factions, consolidated into an "Anti-Monopoly" party, who would make their appeal to the man who earned his bread "by the sweat of his face," [5] likewise chose Butler as their

[1] N. Y. Nation, June 26, 1884.
[2] Cf. N. Y. Sun, June 14, 1884.
[3] Cf. Democratic platform of 1884 in McPherson's Handbook of Politics, for that year, p. 211.
[4] McPherson's Handbook for 1884, pp. 215–8.
[5] Ibid., p. 219.

candidate, and the Democracy, had it wished to seek by such a door an entrance into the hearts of the voting population, might have done so. Fortunately it would escape the snare which was prepared for it. State conventions were being held, platforms were being adopted, delegates were being chosen. Men still spoke of Tilden and urged him to accept the nomination.[1] Though he had been set aside without too much mark of regret in 1880, his name in the sight of most Democrats was still synonymous with the victory in 1876, of which the party had been deprived only by a great fraud.[2] His health had been precarious four years ago; it was still such as to preclude active leadership in a Presidential campaign, if other reasons had not presented themselves to make his nomination appear inexpedient and, on June 10th, just before the meeting of the convention of the party in New York, he wrote a letter to his friend, Daniel Manning, chairman of the Democratic state committee, definitely withdrawing his name from consideration.[3]

The Tammany organization in New York City, led by John Kelly, made a demonstration in behalf of Roswell P. Flower in the hope of leading a movement away from Grover Cleveland, whose career as governor, for simplicity and frankness, for scorn of partisanship and demagogy, for honesty in the making of appointments to office, for courage in the use of the veto power and in the performance of his duties of whatever kind, had marked him as a man apart from them. He had been a thorn in the side of this gang ever since he had entered the governor's office at Albany and his elevation to leadership in the party could not be expected to advance their peculiar fortunes,[4] but they achieved no success in turning attention in other directions. Grover Cleveland was asked if he would accept the nomination, should it come to him. He finally

---

[1] Bigelow, Letters and Literary Memorials of Tilden, vol. ii, pp. 633–42; Bigelow, Life of Tilden, vol. ii, pp. 279–80, 404–10.
[2] Cf. N. Y. Nation, Feb. 28, 1884.
[3] Bigelow, Letters and Literary Memorials, vol. ii, pp. 647–52; Bigelow, Life of Tilden, vol. ii, pp. 281–4; N. Y. Nation, June 19, 1884.
[4] N. Y. Nation, June 19 and July 3, 1884.

told Manning, the party manager in New York, in writing, what he had repeatedly said to his friends in conversation, that he would be "entirely content to remain at the post of duty" which had been assigned him by the people of his state and that he had not "a particle of ambition to be President of the United States." However, if he were nominated, "my sense of duty to the people and my party," he continued, "would dictate my submission to the will of the convention." He made it clear that he should not, "in any condition of affairs or under any imaginable pressure," deem it his duty "to relinquish the trust," which he held for the people of his state, "to assume the duties of the Vice-Presidency"—the nomination for that office he could and would not accept "under any consideration whatever." [1]

While the New York convention had made no declaration of its preferences it was clear that Cleveland would have a majority of the delegates and, by the "unit rule," he would, therefore, receive the support of his own state. The drift was distinctly toward him in other states until, on the eve of the convention, it was plain that he would have nearly the necessary number of votes—two-thirds of all the delegates.

The Democratic national convention met on July 8th in the same "Wigwam" in Chicago in which Blaine had been shouted into a nomination, and Colonel W. F. Vilas of Wisconsin was placed in the chair. The anti-Cleveland men, of whom the Tammany "braves" and Butler and his following were prominent figures, had not yet given up hope of stemming the current which was moving inexorably in one direction. Cleveland, they said, could not carry New York.[2] His administration of the governor's office had antagonized the workingman. He had made enemies on all sides. It would be "suicidal," Kelly averred, to nominate him.[3] The Tammany men would have any one rather than Cleveland, and, though they must

[1] Cleveland to Manning, June 30, 1884, in Cleveland Papers; cf. N. Y. Nation, July 3, 1884.

[2] N. Y. Tribune, July 12, 1884.

[3] Ibid., July 6, 1884.

vote for him, under the unit rule,[1] failing to make progress with evil candidates, they tried to create a diversion by swinging their support to Mr. Bayard. It was of no avail. Cleveland was loved, said General Bragg of Wisconsin, in seconding the nomination, "for the enemies he has made," plainly an allusion to the Tammany gang and Ben Butler. The party had followed old leaders to its death—it needed new and young men at its head.[2] The first ballot resulted in 392 votes for Cleveland and 170 for Bayard, with smaller groups supporting Thurman, Randall, McDonald of Indiana, whom Hendricks favored, and Carlisle. An effort by the anti-Cleveland men to stampede the convention to Hendricks, who had been Tilden's associate in the ill-fated campaign of 1876, failed.[3] Pennsylvania which had been voting for Randall turned to Cleveland; smaller gains were made, and at the end of the second ballot his vote was 475. His nomination was assured. Two-thirds of the 820 delegates in the convention were 547; changes followed fast and, amid cheering, the blasts of horns in the brass bands and the reverberation of cannon, the ballot, after revision, gave Cleveland 683 votes, and he was declared to be the candidate of the party. Hendricks said again, as in 1876, that he would not accept second place on the ticket,[4] but, in his despite, now as then, he was nominated for Vice-President. Cleveland received the congratulations of his friends at Albany. He declared that the people were entitled to "pure, just and economical rule," which they had not enjoyed at the hands of the party which for nearly twenty-four years had directed the affairs of the country. He pledged every effort "to reach the sober thought of the nation and to dislodge an enemy entrenched behind spoils and patronage."[5]

The Republicans made pretense of being pleased with the

---

[1] Kelly shouted himself hoarse in his frantic effort to stay the hand of the Cleveland men.—A. K. McClure, Recollections of Half a Century, p. 126.

[2] N. Y. Nation, July 17, 1884.

[3] Cf. Doolittle to Manning, March 25, 1885, in Cleveland Papers.

[4] N. Y. Tribune and N. Y. Herald, July 12, 1884.

[5] N. Y. Nation, July 17, 1884.

nomination. Cleveland was "a small man everywhere except on the hay scales," said the New York Tribune.[1] He weighed 236 pounds and measured six inches "across the back of the neck."[2] He had had no experience in national affairs and would be "used by tricksters." If elected he would be "the mere dummy of his party" and a "tool of corrupt rings." "All the organs of British interests and of free trade" would support him and fix his status. Once more the Republican party could thank the Democrats for "undesigned favors."[3] The nomination, said the Baltimore American, was adding but another "to the long list of blunders" which had closed the doors of the White House to the Democratic party.[4] Cleveland would be the easiest man to defeat, said the Boston Journal; it was the nomination which Republicans desired.[5] He was "utterly unfit by education or practical training," said the Pittsburgh Commercial-Gazette, for the high duties of the office for which he had been named.[6] The Democratic platform, said the Chicago Journal, stood "on the dizzy edge of the fathomless abyss of nonsense."[7] "A more grotesque travesty on serious politics, there could not be," said the Worcester Spy, than was furnished by the nomination of such a candidate.[8]

Others were of a different opinion. The Massachusetts Reform Club offered Cleveland its hearty support. The Independent Republicans would hold a national conference in New York City on July 22nd. Delegates from many states came to the meeting, which was called to order by George William Curtis, and addressed by Carl Schurz, in behalf of the committee on resolutions. Blaine was declared to be "an unfit leader," who had proven himself "unworthy of respect and confidence." In his person he was "a representative of men, methods and conduct which the public conscience condemns and which illustrate the very evils which honest men would

[1] Issue of July 12, 1884.

[2] N. Y. Tribune, Aug. 22, 1884.

[3] Ibid., July 12, 1884; cf. ibid., Aug. 11, 1884, when the Tribune said that Cleveland was "too small and weak to be anything but a tool."

[4] Quoted in N. Y. Tribune, July 14, 1884.

[5] Ibid.   [6] Ibid.   [7] Ibid.   [8] Ibid.

reform." Cleveland was of a precisely opposite character. His name was "a synonym of political courage and honesty and of administrative reform." All Republicans who were in sympathy with the principles which they could not find in their own candidate were recommended to vote for Mr. Cleveland. Plans were laid and agencies were created to forward the end in view in New York, New Jersey, Connecticut, Massachusetts, Pennsylvania, Ohio, Illinois and other states.[1]

Young Mr. Roosevelt said that he would vote the Republican ticket. He would abide by the decision of the majority in the convention, but he would seek sanctuary on his Western ranch and take no part in the canvass, though he emerged near its end for some active service.[2] Henry Cabot Lodge in Massachusetts came to the support of the candidates.[3] Both men, in whom hope of a fine leadership had been reposed, thus nullified the influence for good government of which their recent activities had given promise. Their protests were of no moment to the party, if they continued to act with it and indorse its mistakes.[4] The only correction which might be applied to the conditions they complained of must be administered by citizens of more courage and sincerity, and with a different view of their relations to public life.[5] Ex-President Hayes said, on June 8, 1884, after Blaine's nomination, that he was "a scheming

[1] N. Y. Sun, July 23, 1884; N. Y. Nation, July 24 and 31, 1884; cf. Letters and Recollections of J. M. Forbes, vol. ii, pp. 206–9.

[2] W. R. Thayer, Theodore Roosevelt, pp. 52–5; N. Y. Nation, Oct. 30, 1884.

[3] Against Schurz's admonition—see his Writings, vol. iv, pp. 215 et seq.

[4] For A. D. White's reasons for voting against the dictates of his conscience see his Autobiography, vol. i, p. 208. The disappointment of those who had put their faith in young Roosevelt as a reformer was not easily expressed. His friends likened him to Webster (W. R. Thayer, Theodore Roosevelt, p. 52), who had betrayed another generation on an historic seventh day of March, and quoted Whittier's "Ichabod"·

> "Oh, dumb be passion's stormy rage,
> When he who might
> Have lighted up and led his age
> Falls back in night."

Senator Edmunds was not to be coerced. He made but a single speech during the canvass, and that a brief and perfunctory one, in which he did not commend Blaine.—N. Y. Nation, Nov. 25 and Dec. 2, 1886.

[5] Cf. N. Y. Nation, July 24, 1884.

demagogue, selfish and reckless." But he had been "fairly
nominated." Therefore Hayes would vote for the Republican
in preference to the Democratic candidate.[1] Similarly other
men and a number of newspapers were brought to order by the
fetich of party and the necessity of "regularity." It were
poor sportsmanship to leave the party just because its candidate was not one of your own choosing. Only some super-
elegant, "holier-than-thou" person would hold his own opinion
to be so much more valuable than the opinion of the majority as to decline to do that which he would have asked
and expected of others had he been successful in making his
will prevail.[2]

Much of the organized power which propelled the Blaine
movement before the convention had met, and in the convention, continued to be of avail now that this body had adjourned. Campaign biographies were ready to be hawked
about the country. One publisher said that each of his agents
was selling 50 copies daily. They were making fortunes.
The book would "outsell every book ever published in this
world."[3] Campaign song books, leaflets, tracts, posters issued from the presses, to be broadcast by every Republican
committee. By the sheer force of the agencies set up to effect
the nomination the reluctant and refractory were being ridiculed, intimidated and by various means whipped into line.
For the Tribune in New York, during months, no praise of
Blaine and the Republican party was too fulsome, no calumny
aimed at the enemy[4] too silly or false, no innuendo too malicious, no suppression and perversion of facts and opinions
about any matter at issue in the campaign too shameful for

[1] Diary and Letters of Hayes, vol. iv, p. 152.
[2] Cf. N. Y. Tribune, July 1, 1884.
[3] Advertisement in N. Y. Nation, July 10, 1884.
[4] For example the Tribune said on March 27, 1884: "The name of Democracy is a stench in the nostrils. It is associated with all that is meanest
and most infamous in American history. A man of sense might well give
five years of his life to get rid of a name that smells of defeat and dishonor,
of slave pens and Andersonville prison, of organized assassination and vote
stealing. . . . Such Democrats as have any desires higher than a beast's
hunger for something to eat would better get out into free air as soon as
they can," etc., etc. Cf. ibid., April 11, 1884.

it to spread before its readers and the little journalists who
followed such leadership.

Stephen B. Elkins, representing wealth taken from the
earth in Ohio and West Virginia, though he had lived for many
years in New Mexico, where he was engaged in mining, stock
raising and land jobbery on the public domain,[1] and enjoyed
some of the advantages arising from the Star Route contracts,[2]
became Blaine's "chief of staff," [3] though B. F. Jones, a rich
iron manufacturer in Pittsburgh, was nominally the chairman
of the Republican National Committee.[4] All signs pointed
to a campaign for and by the interests which had identified,
and which hoped in the future to identify, the Republican
party with material prosperity.[5]

There had been some expression of interest in a lower tariff
in the Republican national convention, especially from Western
delegates.[6] They may have remembered that the Tariff Commission of 1882 had made a report in favor of a liberal reduction of duties.[7] But the manufacturers, and the protectionist
interests generally, were alert and the leaders of the party
clearly foresaw the value of the tariff as an issue. "If, in the
next Presidential contest, we are to conquer," Senator Morrill
wrote to Reid in 1883, "it must be under this sign." [8] Duties
would be not "for revenue only." They must afford, the platform said, "security to our diversified industries and protec-

---

[1] N. Y. Herald, Sep. 17, 1884, quoting Denver Daily News.
[2] N. Y. Nation, July 3, 1884; N. Y. Sun, June 25, 1884; N. Y. Times,
Oct. 31, 1884. Still accredited in politics to New Mexico he resided now in
New York. He was a friend and associate of Blaine in business speculations.
(Life of H. G. Davis, pp. 58, 97, 140 and 141; N. Y. World, Oct. 8, 1884;
N. Y. Nation, Oct. 9, 1884.) Like Logan Elkins had been a rabid Democrat
in the early years of the war and had remained so until 1870.—N. Y.
Herald, Sep. 17, 1884, quoting Denver Daily News.
[3] It was with Elkins that Blaine communicated throughout the campaign.
(Cf. Stanwood, Life of Blaine, pp. 284–5, 287–8.) Chandler, as a member of
the cabinet, had supported Arthur and played a minor part in directing the
campaign.—Cf. Papers of W. E. Chandler for the period.
[4] N. Y. Nation, July 31, 1884.
[5] Cf. N. Y. Tribune, June 27, 1884.
[6] N. Y. Nation, June 26, 1884; cf. Republican platform in Mass. which
spoke for lower duties.—Ibid., May 8, 1884.
[7] Ibid., July 24, 1884.
[8] Under date of May 15, 1883, in Morrill Papers.

tion to the rights and wages of the laborer." The workingman,
as well as the capitalist, should have his "just reward." The
Republican party entered its protest "against the so-called
economic system of the Democratic party which would
degrade our labor to the foreign standard." The importance
of sheep husbandry, which was in a "serious depression,"
called for a "readjustment" of the duties on foreign wool and
"full and adequate protection of the industry." [1]

The Democrats, on their side, now said nothing about
"a tariff for revenue only." This was a demand which Henry
Watterson had written into their platform in 1880. Their
declarations were extremely cautious. They spoke of the need
of being "regardful of the labor and capital involved." There
was "an existing surplus" of more than $100,000,000 which
had "yearly been collected from a suffering people." Taxation
should be "limited to the requirements of economical government"; customhouse taxes should bear "heaviest on articles of luxury" and "lightest on articles of necessity." The
party pledged itself "to revise the tariff in a spirit of fairness to all interests," and without "wish to injure any
domestic industries, but rather to promote their healthy
growth." [2]

In spite of the conservatism of these declarations Blaine
and his managers determined to fasten "free trade" upon
their opponents, and make this the issue of the campaign.[3]
They would, if they could, assess the manufacturers of the
country in order to finance the campaign, offering them in
return favorable tariff rates which, it was said and believed,
would stimulate their various commercial activities; and would,
at the same time, seek the votes of the workingman by pictur-
ing to him the poverty and misery which would be his, if he
were to be degraded under "free trade" to the wage levels of
Europe. Thus both the men with the money and the men
with the votes could be taken in one trap. It was an old scheme.

[1] McPherson's Handbook for 1884, pp. 199–200; cf. ibid., p. 137.
[2] Ibid., pp. 211–4; cf. N. Y. Nation, July 17, 1884.
[3] Cf. Gail Hamilton, Biography of Blaine, pp. 574–5; N. Y. Tribune,
July 2, 1884.

But its possibilities were greater than anyone had yet imagined, so it appeared to astute men in charge of the campaign, and Blaine, sensing advantage, could be relied upon to embrace the opportunity which lay before him. In his letter of accept-ance he took occasion to develop the Republican platform in this direction. No reference was made to the recommenda-tions for a lower tariff which were contained in the report of the Republican commission of but two years ago. To the high war tariff all the prosperity and wealth of the country, if not the principal civic virtues of the people, were generously as-cribed. It was a simple matter then to argue that another policy would lead to national ruin and disaster, and, *ergo*, if the op-posite party were a "free trade" party, as Blaine determined and announced it to be, without too close a reference to its latest declarations, it were a patriotic obligation to bring about its defeat in the pending election. Trade must be extended with that land which, for some time, had held so large a place in Blaine's imagination, South America. The "sister republics" should buy from us rather than from England, and he would ap-peal to some all-American sentiment for an opening of lines of commercial interchange north and south, instead of east and west across the Atlantic Ocean. That the suggestion, as it stood, was claptrap for the campaign was taken for granted by men wanting in prejudice and old enough to be familiar with our electioneering methods. It was plain that the cam-paign was to be a "tariff battle," if so much could be brought about, and so, in large degree, by resort to oratory and the printing press, helped forward by ample supplies of money, it came to be.[1]

Comparative tables of wages to show that bricklayers who received $7.10 a week in England were paid $15 in the United States, that carpenters who received $12.64 in England were paid $17.50 in this country, and so on through the list, stared workingmen in the face on factory walls and telegraph poles. They were printed and reprinted in the Blaine newspapers and shouted from the stump. A vote for the Democratic candi-

[1] N. Y. Nation, July 24, 1884.

date meant "free trade and reduction of wages." A vote for Blaine and Logan and for the Republican protective tariff would be a vote "to maintain present wages" as against the "ill paid and pauper labor" of Europe, living in "pestilential human rookeries," amid "horrors" which recalled "the middle passage of the slave ship." The "British system" meant a "laboring class"—"suffering millions" doomed to serve an "aristocratic class." England had robbed and deprived us of manufacturing industry and commerce before the Revolution—she would do this again if we did not keep up our defenses. Farmers, no less than manufacturers, needed protection. The "home market" was the valuable market; foreign trade was a snare and a myth. Men said that the tariff was a "tax." It was not a "tax." Though it was laid in the interest of high prices and to hold up the rates of wages the Republican "economists" at the same time stood ready to prove that the foreigner, and not the American consumer, paid the duty.[1]

When Mr. Cleveland's letter of acceptance was ready in August he asked his secretary to show it, if possible, to Tilden and Hendricks. "I want the thing to suit them who are wiser than I," he said.[2] To the discomfiture of the opposition there was nothing in it about the tariff.[3] The candidate confined himself to a brief and simple declaration of the officeholder's obligation in a "government by the people" to represent the people, not to control them. When a citizen was chosen to manage the common affairs it was his duty "to assume for a time a public trust" instead of dedicating himself to the "profession of politics." The people paid the wages of public employees and they were "entitled to fair and honest work" which the money thus paid should command. The public departments would not then be filled with those whose first concern was to aid the party to which they owed their places, and the "unseemly scramble" for office, "with the consequent importunity which embitters official life," would cease.[4] It was a

[1] Cf. various pamphlets and tracts issued during the campaign.
[2] Cleveland to Lamont, Aug. 11, 1884, in Cleveland Papers.
[3] N. Y. Nation, Aug. 28, 1884.
[4] App. Ann. Cyclop. for 1884, p. 148.

fine call to civic duty by a competent leader, such as the nation had needed for many years.

The Independents found in Hendricks one who, of course, repelled them. His had been an unacceptable nomination to men of discernment who voted the Democratic ticket in 1876. His merit now was not greater. Nothing that he since had done had increased the confidence in his intelligence or candor. But he represented Indiana and elements in the party which had strength in the West and he must be taken, as he generally would be, as a negligible part of a better whole.[1]

The temperance sentiment which had been disturbing the calculations of politicians of the West, especially in the Republican party, again resulted in the nomination of candidates by a separate Prohibition party, which had held a convention in July in Pittsburgh. John P. St. John, who had been governor of Kansas, would stump the country and become President, if he could, on this issue.[2] Ben Butler who had gone to the Democratic convention as the nominee for President of some paper money and labor groups, having found himself with few friends in that meeting, entered into negotiations with the Republican campaign managers and that old harlequin announced his determination to run as a "Greenbacker."[3] He held the admiration of the editor of the New York Sun, for whom Cleveland had insufficient merit,[4] and some Tammany politicians in New York, who were spreading the story, with Republican aid, that the Democratic candidate was an enemy of the workingman,[5] and proceeded with his campaign among the ignorant and mischievous elements in Massachusetts, New York and other states in the hope of making inroads upon the

[1] N. Y. Nation, Aug. 7, 1884.
[2] McPherson's Handbook for 1884, pp. 220–22; N. Y. Nation, July 31, 1884.
[3] N. Y. Times, Oct. 19, 20 and 21, 1884; T. P. Rhynder to Cleveland, Feb. 23, 1887, in Cleveland Papers.
[4] Cf. J. H. Wilson, Life of Dana, p. 461.
[5] Cf. N. Y. Tribune, Aug. 14, 1884. The Tribune gave all possible encouragement and assistance to Butler throughout the campaign in the hope of taking the votes of laborers and farmers from Cleveland. Cf. issue of Aug. 30, 1884.

Democratic vote which, if it should not be large, might, in some places, turn the tide to the Republicans.[1]

So was the stage set for the proceedings of the summer and the autumn. The charges against Blaine in reference to his speculations with the land grant railroads were distinct and well established in the judgment of those who found wrong in such transactions. The truth of the matter was, however, that a vast number of the voters of the country saw no great evil in conduct of this kind in a public man.[2] Political leaders in both parties had been so careless of their reputations in this particular that to cry out against a confusion of private and public interest insured no one a hearing. There were exhibitions of remorse at the time of the exposures concerning the Crédit Mobilier, the "Salary Grab," the Whiskey Ring frauds and the Star Route trials, but they were not sincere. Too many men, in their hearts, had condoned such rascalities. Public leaders would do the same or a like thing again, if the situation called for it and it promised to be sufficiently profitable. To make money out of the government was held to be canny or smart, and, although general and specific denials were again entered by Blaine and his friends as to all the charges affecting his honor, the fact was that comparatively few persons very much cared what he had done in this regard. He was a "brilliant" party leader who had been twice denied the nomination for President, largely through the influence of Conkling and discredited factions in the party, no longer powerful in its direction. If he had faults, as some men averred, there were others to say at every political meeting and in recurring issues of a host of newspapers, supported by several pamphletary refutations, that the evil spoken of him was wholly false.

These principal points were positively made, however, and kept before the people—

[1] N. Y. Nation, Aug. 14 and 21 and Oct. 23, 1884; N. Y. Tribune, Aug. 20, 1884; cf. F. E. Haynes, Third Party Movements, p. 203. Butler truly states his object in his "Book," pp. 983–4. He had such an understanding he alleges with John Kelly. His cover, like Blaine's, was the tariff.

[2] Cf. N. Y. Nation, Sep. 18, 1884, article on "The Standard of Official Morality."

(1) That Blaine had, in 1869, and later, acted as an agent of the Little Rock and Fort Smith Railroad in the sale of bonds for which he had received commissions from some Boston capitalists; a connection which he had urgently sought and which he succeeded in establishing because of his having befriended this railroad, as he had reminded these gentlemen, when, while he had been Speaker of the House of Representatives, it required a renewal of its land grant, and on the promise not to be a "deadhead" in the future in the same relationship.

(2) That a portion of the bonds which came to him as his reward for activity of this nature at this time, or which he found himself possessed of in the course of trade, were taken over by the officers of the Union Pacific Railroad at a high price, to Blaine's advantage, because of his influential public position.

(3) That in 1870 he had received and sold an interest in Jay Cooke's Northern Pacific Railroad "pool" which had come to him, probably, as a gift, or, at any rate, because of his public connections at Washington.

(4) That he openly, categorically and in some noteworthy particulars falsely denied his parts in these transactions, especially in the case, and at the time, of the threatened confirmation of them by one James Mulligan,[1] who held letters in substantiation of the transactions in question, which, in some instances, were marked "private" and "confidential," which he had asked the receiver to "burn," and which Blaine, after frantic efforts to secure their suppression, knowing that they were about to be made public, seized in a hotel room in Washington. When Congress had the subject under investigation in the summer of 1876, on the eve of the Republican national convention, before which Blaine was a prominent candidate for the nomination for President, his explanations were interrupted by sunstroke, and he had never found the opportunity to resume them for the clearing of his name.[2]

[1] Bookkeeper and confidential agent of Warren Fisher, Jr., the Boston capitalist to whom the letters were addressed.
[2] N. Y. Nation, April 10, May 1, June 26, July 3, 17, 24, Aug. 28, Sep. 4, 1884. These articles in the Nation had appeared in issues of the New York Evening Post for prior dates. Many of them were reprinted in pamphlet

The reiteration of these charges, which converted Blaine from a "Plumed Knight" into a "Tattooed Man," and of proving him to be, and denouncing him as, a corruptionist, who had lied to cover his errancies, were the principal exercise of the Democrats and the Independents. With a candidate bearing a stained name at the head of the ticket the entire recent history of the party was recalled and brought under review.

To the newspapers in New York, which were to make themselves an active force on Cleveland's side during the canvass, was to be added the World, which had enjoyed a striking change of ownership.[1] Jay Gould had sold that journal, in May, 1883, to an eccentric Hungarian Jew, Joseph Pulitzer,[2] who had come from St. Louis, and who entered the lists to outdo Bennett of the Herald in the emphasis put upon crime and private scandal and the dissemination of impertinent triviality as a means of winning attention and of gaining readers for his gazette, a commercial adventure in which he achieved immediate success.[3] The World's services in behalf of Cleveland were sincere and valuable, as any reference to its columns will disclose. Its "Turn the Rascals Out" became the cry of the campaign.[4]

---

form for distribution in the campaign. See, too, "Facts for the People," leaflets issued by the Independent Republicans of Connecticut; Mr Blaine's Record, The Investigation of 1876 and the Mulligan Letters, published by the Boston Committee of One Hundred; Mr. Blaine and the Mulligan Letters, The Whole Story as Told in the House of Reps., published by J. S. Cushing & Co., Boston. The testimony before the Judiciary Com. of the House of Reps. in 1876 is in House Mis. Doc., 44th Cong. 1st sess., no. 176.

[1] See issues of the World for May 10 and 11, 1883.

[2] Don C. Seitz, Joseph Pulitzer; Alleyne Ireland, Joseph Pulitzer.

[3] Pulitzer made such advances that his rivals were soon compelled to reduce their prices. The Herald lowered its price from three to two cents. The Times from four to two cents and the Tribune from four to three cents a copy, when the World could no longer boast that it was the only newspaper of eight pages in the United States which was sold for two cents.—Cf. N. Y. World, Sep. 28, 1883.

[4] This slogan, which was probably the invention of the Sun (Cf. issues of June 23 and 24, 1884.) became the property of the World, which, for many consecutive days, concluded each of its editorial articles with the familiar line. Near the end of the campaign the World substituted for these words, "Save the Republic." (Cf. N. Y. World, Aug. 12, 1884, and subsequently.) To the Democratic cry the Tribune believed that it made effective answer with its "Keep the Rascals Out." When asked by a cor-

To what was being said about Blaine there was answer and it was not long in coming to utterance. It was asserted that Cleveland, the darling of the "reformers," was a libertine.[1] Ten or twelve years since this paragon and exemplar of all the excellencies had had irregular relations with a widow of some attraction of person. She was given to intrigue. She held that he, or one of his friends, was the father of a child whom she had borne. To save the reputation of one who seemed to be particularly involved, and whose name had been given to the infant to make the identification more certain (a married man with a daughter whom he idolized), Cleveland had assumed the responsibility.[2] There was no opportunity for denial of the charge, nor did he attempt to offer any; the fact was admitted.[3] His friends were asked to "tell the truth." The disclosure was a shock to the candidate's admirers,[4] and increased the difficulty many fold of winning him new adherents among citizens of "independent" mind.[5] Here was an issue between one man, who may or may not have had some more or less corrupt dealings with railroad companies (the candidate and his friends repelled every suggestion

respondent to give some reasons for supporting Cleveland the World replied: "(1) He is an honest man. (2) He is an honest man. (3) He is an honest man. (4) He is an honest man and he is, therefore, preferable to James G. Blaine, who does not possess this essential and Jeffersonian requirement."—Issue of Sep. 22, 1884.

[1] This episode in Cleveland's life was a fortunate discovery for the Republicans. On June 27, 1884, the New York Tribune could denounce him only because he was a "bachelor," like Buchanan and Tilden—a man "who had never had a home and never found any woman to put confidence in him" might befit "a party without principles," etc., etc. Cf. N. Y. Sun, Aug. 30, 1884.

[2] For what seems to be a correct account of the facts in the case see General King's statement in N. Y. World, Aug. 8, 1884; also Dr. Twining's statement in N. Y. Independent, Aug. 14, 1884; N. Y. Nation, Aug. 7, 1884.

[3] The New York Tribune found a preacher in Buffalo to say that Cleveland's "immorality" was continuing and that it extended down to date.—N. Y. Tribune, Oct. 31, 1884; cf. Writings of Schurz, vol. iv, p. 222.

[4] See, e.g., Writings of Schurz, vol. iv, pp. 223–4, 275.

[5] See, e.g., allusions in Diary and Letters of Hayes, vol. iv, pp. 175–6. "The Independents proclaimed Governor Cleveland to be pure and precious; the people have discovered that he is cheap and nasty."—N. Y. Tribune, Nov. 3, 1884.

of evil action or interest) and another man who confessed
that his career had been marred by sexual immorality.   It
was idle in farmhouses and country churches to attempt to
draw a distinction between a public corruption and impure
personal life.

It was one thing to be "independent" in a local or state
election, another, in a national election, when the Presidency
was at stake, and, to many voters, excuses for not doing that
which they, at first, had been impelled to do would be welcome.
The story had been started by some preachers, notably by
one in Buffalo, and was diligently circulated by them.   Religious
journals were turned from Cleveland to Blaine.[1]   Men who
might have supported Cleveland were looking with favor upon
the Prohibition candidate, John P. St. John of Kansas.[2]   The
Republican press, the pamphleteers, at the expense of the
party campaign committees,[3] the stump orators spread the
account of the scandal, adding many a touch which made
Cleveland appear as a coarse boor.[4]   The picture of him which
was drawn for use in this campaign, with an allusion to him,
now and again as "the hangman of Buffalo," suggested by
his having been at one time sheriff of Erie county,[5] in which
office, as a further tidbit for the newspapers, it was alleged
that he had stolen or squandered public money,[6] was never
quite obliterated from the minds of women, if it were forgotten
by their husbands and sons, though evidence accumulated of
the complete uprightness, sterling integrity and high value
of his life.   When a new parcel of Mulligan letters were injected into the canvass, in September,[7] the Republicans, with
fresh energy, prosecuted the attack upon the Democratic can-

[1] Cf. N. Y. Tribune, Aug. 29, 1884.   Henry Ward Beecher, very jealous
of his moral reputation because of recent events in his own life, was in panic
and wrote to Schurz.—Writings of Schurz, vol. iv, p. 222.

[2] Ibid., Sep. 1, 1884.

[3] N. Y. Nation, Oct. 23, 1884.

[4] Cf. N. Y. Herald, Oct. 24, 1884.

[5] Cf. N. Y. Sun, Sep. 15, 1884.

[6] N. Y. Tribune, Sep. 25 and Oct. 4, 1884.

[7] N. Y. Nation, Sep. 18 and 25, 1884; N. Y. Tribune, Sep. 16 and 17,
1884.

didate's moral character.[1] It is safe to say that no Presidential campaign has ever revealed in the American people such bitterness of heart and ugliness of spirit.[2]

Little else on either side was of particular use. Cleveland had hired a "substitute" during the war, but so had Blaine; neither had fought and bled that the Union might live.[3] Cleveland's, it was revealed, was a "criminal,"[4] a bad kind of a soldier, while Blaine's was an "office chair" man who never took the field and was sent to jail, indeed, for selling fraudulent exemption papers.[5] But it could not be said of Cleveland, as it had been of Tilden, that he had displayed sympathy for the rebellion, though it was alleged on every platform and in every journal, on the Republican side, that his election would put the "Confederate brigadiers" in the saddle at Washington, and give us a government, for the first time since Buchanan's, or, perhaps, Andrew Johnson's, administration, by and for the South.

As for Logan, he, before the war, had made speeches hostile to the negro. He had advocated measures which indicated his liking for the Southern cause,[6] and was on the point of recruiting, if he had not actually raised troops in "Egypt" for the Confederacy.[7] He had been the "Black Eagle" for

---

[1] N. Y. Nation, Oct. 23, 1884; N. Y. Tribune, Oct. 31, 1884.

[2] "On both sides the vilest political campaign ever waged." (A. D. White, Autobiography, vol. i, p. 209.) If confirmation be needed it may be found in the New York Tribune and the New York Sun which led the press of the country in the assault upon Cleveland. The Tribune called him a "rake," a "libertine," a man of "loose morals," the "father of a bastard," a man "stained with disgusting infamy" (Issues of Sep. 4 and 19, 1884), while the Sun, not to be outdone, demanded his withdrawal as a candidate. (Issues of Aug. 21 and Sep. 25, 1884.) He was "a gross and licentious man" (Issue of Aug. 21, 1884), a man of "gross and degraded tastes and habits." (Sep. 8, 1884.) His "personal character," the Sun said again, "flouts morality and defies religion." (Sep. 12.) He was a "moral leper." (Ibid.) He was "worse in moral quality than a pickpocket, a sneak thief or a Cherry Street debauchee, a wretch unworthy of respect or confidence." (Nov. 1, 1884.) His election would be a "public disgrace."—Oct. 28, 1884.

[3] N. Y. Nation, Aug. 21, 1884; N. Y. Tribune, Aug. 14, 1884.

[4] N. Y. Nation, Aug. 21, 1884.

[5] Ibid.; N. Y. Sun, Aug. 11 and 15, 1884.

[6] Cf. ibid., July 1 and 23, 1884.

[7] N. Y. World, Oct. 10, 1884.

the Democrats. After he had espoused the cause of the Union and Republicanism he was the "Black Eagle" for the party which now would make him Vice-President. The New York Nation disclaimed particular unfriendliness to him. It contented itself by setting him before the country from time to time as "a ranter and an ignoramus." [1] About Hendricks there was nothing new to say. He had been a "rank Copperhead" and an "inflationist" in 1876—he was these things in 1884. [2]

The activity of the Independent press, led by the New York Evening Post under Godkin's direction, with possibly too much virulence to gain the largest results, [3] the accomplished speaking of Schurz in English and German, which proceeded in many states as he traveled from place to place, [4] the cartoons of Nast in Harper's Weekly and of Gillam, Keppler and Opper in Puck, the announcement day by day of the names of men prominent in business and in the professions who would vote for Cleveland and not for Blaine, [5] the organization of these men into groups, as in the case of members of the Produce and Maritime Exchanges in New York, [6] were ominous. A large

[1] N. Y. Nation, July 31, 1884.
[2] Cf. Hendricks as a Public Man, by W. R. Hollaway, a pamphlet issued by the Mass. Rep. State Committee, 1884; N. Y. Nation, Aug. 7, 1884; N. Y. Tribune, Aug. 11 and 14, 1884. "Thomas A. Hendricks was their [the Solid South's] friend and ally during the Rebellion. He would be their pliant tool the moment they got power again." (N. Y. Tribune, Oct. 31, 1884.) General J. H. Wilson said that he was a "nincompoop" and a "rebel sympathizer." The only time Wilson had ever seen Hendricks was "in the cars with one arm over Jeff Davis's shoulder."—Wilson to Gresham, July 27, 1884, in Gresham Papers.
[3] It must be noted, however, that Godkin was dealing with an extraordinary situation. He was talking to the American voter in the midst of a campaign in which reasoning had been abandoned by most men. He was meeting the New York Tribune and the New York Sun on their own ground, and an opposition whose only answer to argument was deliberate misjudgment of the motives, and systematic excoriation, of citizens who had the highest objects in view, and the courage to state and defend their principles.
[4] Cf. Reminiscences of Carl Schurz, vol. iii, p. 407; N. Y. Nation, Aug. 14, 1884.
[5] In the clubs in New York Whitelaw Reid said that it was difficult to find anyone who expressed the intention of voting for Blaine.—Cortissoz, Life of Reid, vol. ii, p. 96.
[6] N. Y. Herald, Sep. 18, 1884.

body of members of the Young Republican Club in Brooklyn, Mayor Low's adherents, would vote for Cleveland.[1]

Ridicule is a powerful weapon and it was directed, with as much force as could be put into it, against the Independents. The New York Tribune, whose owner had been a reformer and now chose not to be, who, as rapidly as he could, after acquiring control of the principal organ of public opinion in America, had converted it into the most servile of partisan gazettes, led the van in its abuse of men who dared to hold their own views. They were called "saints," "gentle hermits," "doctrinaires," "aristocrats from the Back Bay and Beacon Hill," "anglomaniacs," "visionaries" and "dudes," in implication of their overfastidiousness of feeling and impracticability of mind. But this was not enough. They were "Pharisees," they "raved and frothed at the mouth." [2] They were "soreheads," "blackguards," "bolters," "apostates," "holy willies," "dependents" (in distinction to Independents; they were dependents of the Democratic party), "Democrats at heart, if Republicans in name," "hypocrites," "mutineers," "conspirators," "snakes," "nasty particulars," [3] "hired assassins," and so on.[4] Now and again they were called "mugwumps," but that name wanted the offensive meaning which, for the uses of this campaign, most of the Blaine organs sought to put into denunciation.[5]

---

[1] Cf. N. Y. Herald, Oct. 17, 1884.

[2] N. Y. Tribune, June 10, 1884.

[3] Ibid., Aug. 11, 1884.

[4] The Chicago Tribune, a paper which had once had a pleasant history, as the campaign neared its end, spoke of the Independents as "brawling pharisees and canting, sleek-faced hypocrites." Schurz it called a "malicious renegade." Issue of Oct. 31, 1884.

[5] The application of the name "mugwump" to the Independents is usually and erroneously credited to the New York Sun. That paper, on July 12, 1884, published an article headed "Dudes and Mugwumps," attributing the origin of the name to the Republicans. The New York Evening Post of June 20, 1884, said: "We have yet to see a Blaine organ which speaks of the Independent Republicans otherwise than as Pharisees, hypocrites, dudes, mugwumps, transcendentalists or something of that sort." The first use of the name which I find in the N. Y. Tribune, during the campaign, is in a communication from Rufus Choate, on July 14. It is used again in the issues of September 8 and October 25—both times in "headlines" and not in editorial articles. The only mention of the name which I have found in the Nation during the campaign is in the issue of July 24, 1884. On No-

There was no warrant, except in desperation, for such abuse of a body of citizens of the most valuable and useful type.[1] They had again and again warned Blaine and his managers that his running in 1884 would bring from them the opposition which they had offered to his "boom" on earlier occasions.[2] The fault had been Blaine's and those who were determined, in spite of all obstruction, to make him President.

On one account or another the movement of the prodigals back to the "Grand Old Party," which had started upon the adjournment of the convention, grew as the campaign advanced. Many men who, on June 1st, had found Blaine to be a most unsuitable leader were in August and September extolling him and advocating his election for the party's sake.[3] The whip was strong, the lash stung and it was wielded with effect, as the Democrats were arraigned for their past delinquencies and the prospect of their coming into power cast a shadow over thresholds which had always been Republican. The motto now was, Schurz said, "Hang moral ideas, we are for the party." [4] Its candidate might be unfit, but his election

vember 27 it is accepted, apparently, as a convenient and not too unpleasant designation. (N. Y. Nation of that date.) George William Curtis at a mass meeting in Brooklyn, on October 30, said: "All sorts of opprobious epithets have been hurled upon us. We have been called soreheads, assistant Democrats, renegades, fools, idiots and then, the English language giving out, mugwumps." Colonel T. W. Higginson, at the same meeting declared that he, for one, was not ashamed of being called a mugwump "for in the Indian language the word means a chief with a large following." (N. Y. World, Oct. 31, 1884.) The word, taken from the Algonquin Indians, had had occasional earlier usage in allusion to a man who thought himself of consequence, e.g., as late as March 23, 1884, in the New York Sun. It was so employed by the New York Tribune in 1877 when it said: "John A. Logan is the Head Centre, the Hub, the King Pin, the Main Spring, Mogul and Mugwump of the final plot by which partisanship was installed in the Commission. [The Electoral Commission to which the Tilden-Hayes contest was referred.]"—Issue of Feb. 16, 1877.

[1] What was found to be so reprehensible in "bolting" the Republican ticket became a mark of the highest virtue, intelligence and patriotism if it were a defection in the opposite party to Republican advantage.—Cf. N. Y. Tribune, July 19 and Aug. 26, 1884.

[2] Cf. Stanwood, Life of Blaine, p. 265.

[3] N. Y. Nation, Sep. 18 and 25 and Oct. 2, 1884; Writings of Schurz, vol. iv, p. 281.

[4] Schurz's speech in Brooklyn, Aug. 5, 1884. "The pernicious doctrine that the act of a convention, if it nominate Beelzebub, binds the con-

could not be so great a blight upon the country as the direction
of affairs by a Democrat, with all that this would imply,
since he could not be chosen without putting himself under
obligation and pledge to that body of enemies of the republic,
the "rebels," who were acting through the Democratic party
in the "Solid South." There was no Republican youngster
on farm or in hamlet who would not outshout his elders for
"Jim Blaine" on the "war issue," which was far from dead
in Northern hearts.[1]

When it was feared that old party and sectional differences
might not serve his end Blaine would importune his managers
"to agonize more and more on the tariff."[2] If his foes were
not "rebels" they could be called "free traders." The Democrats, one and all, were "free traders," the hated Independents,
when "dudes and Pharisees" and other names failed, were
denounced as such, as "importers and their hired men," as
"agents of foreign interests" and as "Englishmen," subsidized
by the Cobden Club.[3] Being what they were the Mugwumps
belonged within the Democratic party. They had been sapping
and mining in the Republican party when they were in that
organization, for the destruction of "American principles," and
the party were well rid of such traitors, who would close the
mills, throw men out of work and starve women and children.[4]

sciences and votes of the party is the issue in this campaign," said the
Illinois committee of Republicans and Independents of which Franklin
MacVeagh of Chicago was chairman.—Leaflet No. 1, issued on Sep. 20,
1884.
    [1] Cf. Bryce, American Commonwealth, 1st ed., vol. ii, p. 181.
    [2] Blaine to Whitelaw Reid, Cortissoz, Life of Reid, vol. ii, p. 83.
    [3] Cf. Bryce, American Commonwealth, 1st ed., vol. ii, p. 171; N. Y. Trib
une, June 10, 1884, and in many places prior and subsequent to this date.
Under one of Nast's inimitable drawings in Harper's Weekly of William
Walter Phelps and Whitelaw Reid, two exquisites in evening dress, toying
with their opera hats, were these lines—
    Phelps—"I say, my dear boy, is there anything more to be done after
that letter of mine in Blaine's defense?"
    Reid—"O yes, my dear Bangtry [Phelps was the "Jersey Lily"] we must
call those who do not protect Mr. Blaine's record free-traders and Britishers
and dudes and all that sort of thing, you know."—Issue of July 26, 1884.
    [4] Cortissoz, Life of Reid, vol. ii, p. 94. The New York Tribune in opening
the campaign dismissed the charges against Blaine as "calumnies which
had been exploded"; it would conduct "an aggressive campaign for

The September elections in Vermont and Maine yielded no
proof of gains or losses in party majorities, in comparison with
previous years, which could be taken to be prophetic of the
final determination of the issue. Elections would be held in
Ohio and West Virginia in October and these states, particularly Ohio, were the subjects of the gravest anxiety on the part
of the Republican managers. They had been told, George F.
Hoar wrote John Sherman, that, if Blaine were nominated,
he would "set the prairies on fire." [1] It was not so—the Republican managers viewed the scene anxiously. Blaine, with the approval of his friends, determined to take the stump. No nominee
for the Presidency had ever gone before the people, frankly
asking them for votes, except Stephen A. Douglas in 1860 and
Horace Greeley in 1872.[2] But Blaine's fluency was of a rare
order and his "magnetism" was well known. During the summer he had been trying to content himself at his home in Maine.
Now he packed his bags for his trip. He reached Boston on
September 17th. He had an enthusiastic popular reception
in that city and the next day he was welcomed in New York
by a number of campaign clubs which escorted him to the
Fifth Avenue Hotel where he remained for a week, with excursions for meetings, attended by parades, in New Jersey
and Philadelphia. On September 24th he left for the West
over a route which carried him through New York state and
into Ohio, where the managers had made appointments for
him, requiring speeches day and night. Several appearances
before crowds in West Virginia invigorated the party campaign
in that state. Because of German and other defections on the
temperance question, because of Schurz's hard blows,[3] and

Republican principles and American industry." (Issue of April 30, 1884.)
However, such methods were rather too crude, since leaders like Blaine
and Reid were intelligent men, for it to be quite certain that the people
were as foolish as it was hoped that they might be. "The 'protection of
American industry' as a fig leaf to cover the nakedness of his [Blaine's]
own disgraceful record is a dead failure."—N. Y. Times, Sep. 25, 1884.

[1] Under date of Aug. 26, 1884, in Sherman Papers.

[2] N. Y. Sun, July 3, 1884.

[3] N. Y. Times, Oct. 16, 1884; Writings of Schurz, vol. iv, p. 286; G. P.
Putnam, Memoirs of a Publisher, p. 83.

for other reasons, the result in Ohio, on October 14th, was clouded in great uncertainty. The Democrats had elected their candidate for governor in the preceding year.[1] But the Republicans now were more fortunate. As a result of stupendous effort, involving the expenditure of large amounts of money, the activity of Federal employees who left their posts at Washington for the service,[2] the "colonization" of voters, so it was said, "repeating" and other desperate measures, with which the Democrats, with few resources, could not cope, the Republicans elected their state ticket by a margin of about 11,000 votes, which they accounted a great victory. West Virginia, in spite of Elkins's activities, remained Democratic. Blaine was now released for Indiana, Michigan and Illinois.

Meanwhile Logan was touring the country and was making the welkin ring in his own and Blaine's behalf.

Cleveland, on his side, quietly pursued his way as governor at Albany.[3] The little which he said in conversation or letter endeared his friends to him. He wrote his secretary, Colonel Lamont—"I had rather be beaten in this race than to buckle to Butler or Kelly. I don't want any pledge made for me that will violate my professions or betray and deceive the good people that believe in me."[4] He visited Elmira to attend an agricultural fair in September.[5] Early in October he went to Buffalo, but asked that there be no "demonstration" in his honor. Nevertheless the Democratic clubs paraded before him and he made a speech in which he said that "the character of the government can hardly rise higher than the source from which it springs," and expressed other sentiments calculated to increase the public confidence reposed in him.[6] On October 15th he came to New York where his welcome was enthusiastic. Crowds surrounded his carriage in the streets. At a

[1] The Democratic plurality in 1883 had been more than 12,000.
[2] Notably Colonel Dudley, the Commissioner of Pensions, who later acted in the same way in Indiana. Cf. N. Y. Times, Sep. 26 and Oct. 11, 1884; N. Y. Nation, Oct. 2, 1884.
[3] Cf. N. Y. Nation, Oct. 9, 1884.
[4] Under date of Aug. 11, 1884, in Cleveland Papers.
[5] N. Y. Herald, Sep. 9, 1884.
[6] Ibid.

meeting in the Academy of Music, organized by the Cleveland clubs in the Stock Exchange and other exchanges and boards in the New York financial and commercial district, when Henry Ward Beecher spoke, the candidate said a few words in the interest of government "conducted on business principles." Thousands of torches in the hands of shouting adherents passed before him at the Fifth Avenue Hotel. The next day he attended a barbecue and other demonstrations arranged in his behalf in Brooklyn. On October 27th he again left Albany to receive the greetings of a crowd at Newark, N. J., where he denounced a system of taxation that took from the pockets of the people millions of dollars which were not needed by the government, and which tended to the "inauguration of corrupt schemes and extravagant expenditures." A few days later he found the occasion to visit Connecticut.

The canvass was now drawing to an end. The last strokes were to be laid on in New York where, as was well known, the need was greatest. The press was preponderantly for Cleveland.[1] The Tribune was the Blaine organ,[2] but the Sun, in another way, was acting as effectively in the same interest. That journal in professing to support Butler was merely aiming to accomplish Cleveland's defeat. Dana's attacks upon Blaine early in the campaign were designed to establish his paper's position as Democratic. Then he sought to create a diversion by leading a "bolt" in the Democratic party from Cleveland to Butler, which he likened to the Republican "bolt" to Cleveland. Thus it was supposed that the lower classes of working people and many Tammanyites, whose leaders secretly desired, though they could not openly labor, to effect the defeat of Cleveland, might be ensnared for the damage of the Democratic nominee.[3]

[1] Cf. N. Y. World, July 18, 1884.
[2] Which in spite of its frantic devotion to Republican principles could not conceal the fact that it was riding to prosperity and making money for its owner at the expense of George Jones and the Times.—Cf. N. Y. Tribune, Sep. 8 and 17, 1884.
[3] Meanwhile Butler, the "workingman's candidate," was touring the country in a new private car, painted in bright colors, hired at a cost of $150 a day for his use, with a pantry furnished with champagne, brandy, port wine and the finest liquors.—N. Y. Times, Oct. 15, 1884.

As the campaign progressed the Sun's purposes were clear. Its editor's abuse of Cleveland was more violent than the Tribune's. He openly expressed a preference for Blaine as between the two leading candidates.[1] His object, he declared, was "to save the country from Grover Cleveland," [2] who day by day was painted in the colors of the lowest criminal. The Sun's malignity was covered in each word and line by writing as incisive and dexterous as any that ever adorned the pages of an American newspaper and its seductive influence upon its readers, as well as the writers for other journals who turned to it for cynical amusement, was more for Blaine's advantage than for Butler's.[3] Two evening papers, the Commercial Advertiser and the Mail and Express, nearly completed the number of gazettes which served Blaine in New York City. The Evening Post, answering to Godkin's hand, the Times, now under the excellent direction of Charles R. Miller,[4] the World, the Journal of Commerce which spoke with effect to business men, the Staats-Zeitung, holding authority over the Germans, the influential Brooklyn Eagle, Harper's Weekly, the Nation, and the comic, as well as nearly all the rest of the periodical publications which admitted political discussion to their columns, advocated the election of the Democratic candidate. The Herald, with as much gravity as it was ever able to assume, spoke for him, as did its evening edition, the Telegram. No less than seven journals in New York City, with a circulation of about 500,000, which had favored Garfield's election in 1880, now supported Mr. Cleveland.[5]

The last word had been said in 1876 and 1880, so it had seemed, in the organization of the political meeting and the use of the torchlight procession. Now more was seen—more powder was burned, more drums were rattled and pounded, more horns snorted and blared, more fifes played "Marching Through Georgia," more men in finer regalia marched to music,

---

[1] Cf. issue of Oct. 20, 1884.
[2] Issue of Nov. 3, 1884.
[3] Cf. N. Y. World, July 15, 1884.
[4] Cf. Harper's Weekly, June 2, 1883.
[5] N. Y. World, Oct. 7, 1884.

more coal oil was burned to shed light in dingy lanes and dark streets, more flags were unfurled, more muslin transparencies announced the candidate's merits and his opponent's sins, more horses pranced and curvetted in the struggle to make Blaine President. "Plumed knights," helmeted and feathered, with battle axes, were on every side. The Democrats acted with what power they could command in like manner in the same field. But they were wanting in the resources of the Republicans, who still assessed the officeholders, all of whom were adherents of their party, and who controlled the wealth of the country. Through a Republican administration of the government much of this wealth had been amassed; through it more, it was hoped and predicted, would come to mine owners, manufacturers and the sponsors of all kinds of speculative enterprises. Every town and city had had its mass meeting, parade and celebration in the strife to get votes for one or the other candidate. But the outbursts of party enthusiasm reached their climax in New York City as the election day in November approached.

Blaine returned from the West with another dramatic progress through New York state. He arrived in New York City on October 28th. He had spoken more than twenty times on a single day; on one occasion he had made 29 speeches within 10 hours,[1] to crowds assembled to greet him. On the afternoon of the next day, October 29th, the Wednesday preceding the election, the Republican leaders organized a day parade of "Blaine business men." Brokers from the various exchanges, manufacturers, merchants, lawyers, doctors, insurance men, in silk hats, bearing walking sticks, were marshaled by vocations and trades, keeping step to the cries, uttered in unison, as they swung along, of "Blaine, Blaine, James G. Blaine," varied now and again with "O-O-O-hi-O," a reference to the victory at the state election in Ohio, and "No-no-no-free-trade."[2]

Whether there were 25,000, as the Tribune said, or only 13,000, as the World said, may be a matter of little importance. It was an impressive outpouring of men who declared, by their

[1] N. Y. Tribune, Oct. 29, 1884.   [2] Ibid., Oct. 30, 1884.

public appearance, that they would cast their votes on the following Tuesday for the Republican nominee. They swept from Bowling Green up Broadway to Madison Square where they were reviewed by Blaine. In the evening some 200 rich men, including Jay Gould, Russell Sage, Cyrus W. Field, John Jacob Astor, H. M. Flagler, Washington Connor, Levi P. Morton, D. O. Mills, John Roach and Andrew Carnegie, tendered him an elaborate dinner at Delmonico's. Canvasback ducks, terrapin, champagne, which were on the menu, widely copied in the newspapers,[1] laid the foundation for a cartoon in the New York World called "The Royal Feast of Belshazzar." Blaine and the "money kings" were shown at the groaning board, while a poor man, his ragged wife and a starving child were begging for the crumbs which might fall from it.[2] Nothing could have been so ill-timed as this "Boodle Banquet," but Elkins required more money for the campaign and the dinner was necessary, it was alleged, as the means of bringing the "millionaires and monopolists" together for the purpose of getting additional funds.[3]

In the same position as that which he had held while reviewing the day parade Blaine, on Friday night, October 31st, watched pass him a torchlight procession of probably 30,000 men.[4] Neighboring cities sent their clubs to the great Republican jubilee. The Democrats had arranged a parade of "business men" on Saturday, October 25th, which assumed large proportions, but their chief demonstration was reserved for the following Saturday, November 1st. It was a more numerous and a more impressive body of marching men,[5] many of them of the highest position in mercantile and commercial life, than had appeared in the Blaine parade on the preceding Wednesday. A considerable number of them had formerly

[1] N. Y. Tribune, Oct. 30, 1884.
[2] N. Y. World, Oct. 30, 1884.
[3] Ibid.; N. Y. Herald, Nov. 9, 1884.
[4] The New York Tribune said 60,000, the World 25,000.
[5] The New York Herald said that there were 40,000 men in line; on the preceding Saturday the number was given as 17,000.—Issue of November 2, 1884.

acted, as it was explained and as all well-informed persons
knew, with the Republican party. Cleveland reviewed the
procession from a flag-covered stand. In the evening thousands
of torches passed before him, the legions tramping to their
rallying cries of "Soap, soap, Blaine's only hope," "Scalp,
scalp, scalp, Jim Blaine," "Blaine, Blaine, Jay Gould Blaine,
continental liar from the state of Maine."

Blaine's friends had organized and attended "Belshazzar's
Feast." They made another misstep, which has been considered to have been still more stupid and costly. Throughout
the campaign a studied effort was put forth to secure the Irish
vote. In New York nearly all Irishmen were Democrats, to
which allegiance they were held by the Tammany organization. They were to be won to Blaine, so he had long believed,
by baiting England, in shrewd, as he thought, and often covert
ways.[1] His "spirited foreign policy" was directed particularly at Great Britain. Irish dynamiters would be taken from
British dungeons, the American flag would fly from the State
Department as well as the White House when he became President.[2] The declaration that "free trade" was English and,
conversely, that protection by a tariff was American, which
was reiterated constantly in the Blaine press and on the Republican stump, was for the hearing of the Irish as well as
other men to whom it might be an interesting communication.[3]
Irish leagues and Hibernian associations throughout the country, it was announced, as the campaign progressed, had come
over to Blaine. Irish-American clubs appeared in the parades.[4]
A number of newspapers in England were expressing disfavor
for the Republican candidate. Nothing could have better

[1] N. Y. Nation, Aug. 7, 1884.
[2] Gail Hamilton, Biography of Blaine, p. 584. "He always flies the American flag and the American eagle perches on his shoulder."—N. Y. Sun,
June 13, 1884.
[3] "A distinctly American policy of determined industrial antagonism to
British influence will arouse intense enthusiasm among Irish-Americans.
Nor will there be wanting other citizens who will remember how Great
Britain behaved during the Rebellion and how American commerce was
chased from the seas by British cruisers," etc., etc.—N. Y. Tribune,
June 10, 1884.
[4] Gail Hamilton, Biography of Blaine, p. 577.

served the purposes of such organs as the New York Tribune. Opposition from British sources proved that Blaine was an American for Americans (and Irishmen) whom Americans (and Irishmen) should support.[1]

The Irish, who were to be converted to Republican principles, were, for the most part, Catholics. Blaine's mother had been a Catholic, as were some of his relations,[2] though he, and his immediate family, attended the Congregationalist church. Here was peril even for a politician so adroit. The "pastors" could not be overlooked in a campaign like this one in which their interest was eager. Their tongues could not be still. Were Blaine of Catholic stock it would be well with the Irish, but it augured ill indeed in other quarters. Clergymen appeared to say that as much Catholicism as Blaine had known in his youth would do him no particular injury. One, a Reverend Ecob, remarked—"If, as a little child, he took his mother's hand and walked with her to church, why there is a good Protestant day of judgment coming which will, no doubt, purify, as by fire, the touch of that mother's hand."[3] But, however untoward such a speech by such a friend may have been, a worse day arrived in the midst of the final celebrations in Blaine's honor in New York. One morning, as a "last card," a delegation of a thousand preachers of various denominations, black and white, Jew and Gentile,[4] visited him in the Fifth Avenue Hotel. One called Cleveland "a self-confessed adulterer." The "pastors" would vote so that the White House would "never be changed into a bachelor's hall." Blaine addressed the "reverend gentlemen" and recalled the services of the Republican party in abolishing slavery, since which time, so he alleged, it had not been identified with a "single measure" which could not "challenge the approbation of Christian ministers and the approval of God." Now, he continued, the tariff was the great issue and through it the Republican party said to the people, "Here is bread for the hungry, here is clothing for the naked," and so on.

[1] N. Y. Tribune, July 2, 1884.
[2] Cf. N. Y. Sun, July 24, 1884.
[3] N. Y. Nation, July 10, 1884.
[4] N. Y. Tribune, Oct. 30, 1884.

All might have been well but for a fervid spokesman, a Rev. Dr. Burchard, who on Sundays occupied a prominent Presbyterian pulpit in New York,[1] and who, in addressing the candidate, to assure him of the assembled company's complete Republicanism, had said that they could not "bolt" the ticket, as some other men had done, and act "with the party whose antecedents have been Rum, Romanism and Rebellion." The campaign had several days yet to run. Blaine had not rebuked the indiscreet cleric, though he later tried to broadcast an expression of his disapproval of such a sentiment,[2] and the Democratic press, from one end of the country to the other, rang the changes on this alliterative trinity, "Rum, Romanism and Rebellion." [3]   Placards were displayed near the doors of Catholic churches [4] with no gain for Blaine in Irish circles in New York, however the witty sally may have swollen the enthusiasm for the Republican ticket in the Mississippi Valley. The "last card" became a "roorbach." [5] The invention and "nailing" of "campaign lies" completely occupied the attention of the political press.

The end of the canvass was reached in a welter of defamation and angry mistrust, and with confidence of no kind in the issue. Men went to the polls with more tense and bitter resolution, perhaps, than in any campaign since the war.[6]

There was real doubt in the minds of the Republican managers as to their prospects in New York state.   There might

[1] "A Silurian or early Palezoic bigot."—N. Y. Sun, Nov. 7, 1884.

[2] Philadelphia Press, Nov. 3, 1884.

[3] N. Y. World, Oct. 30, 1884; N. Y. Nation, Nov. 6, 1884. This speech was not reported in the Tribune and the Sun.

[4] Platt, Autobiography, p. 184; cf. Stanwood, Life of Blaine, p. 289.

[5] N. Y. World and N. Y. Herald, Oct, 31, Nov. 1, 2, 3 and 4, 1884. For "roorbach" see N. Y. Times, Nov. 4, 1884.

[6] Blaine who had lingered in New York until the last moment started for his home in Maine to vote and await the returns. The New York Tribune was singing,

> "See the rockets looming 'Blaine!'
> Hear the cannon booming 'Blaine!'
> Men and women praying 'Blaine!'
> And the stars are saying 'Blaine!'"—
> N. Y. Tribune, Nov. 4, 1884.

well have been. If they should also lose New Jersey Cleveland would need but three electoral votes to gain the Presidency, and the result in Indiana and Connecticut was concededly uncertain. Nevada and California might be carried for Cleveland.[1] The morning after the polling day, Tuesday, November 4th, found the issue still unsettled. The South was "solid," [2] with the possible exception of Virginia, where the demagogue, Mahone, and his faction were acting with the Republicans. So much was known, and New Jersey and Connecticut seemed to be Democratic, while West Virginia, Michigan, Illinois, Wisconsin, Indiana and, greater than all these, New York, with her thirty-six electoral votes, remained in doubt. Wisconsin and Illinois were soon seen to be Republican, while Indiana was clearly Democratic. Michigan was claimed by both parties until Friday, when it was declared to have given a majority for Blaine. The determination of the result depended upon the count in New York where the vote was close. The Blaine press, supported by the Associated Press [3] and the Western Union Telegraph Company, now controlled by Jay Gould,[4] confidently affirmed that the Republican electors had been chosen, and the campaign clubs throughout the country, which had been marching and countermarching, with the help of much drinking, throughout Tuesday night and Wednesday, were still celebrating the victory. Republicans of more years, with calmer vision, were congratulating themselves and one another less confidently, though it was not within the range of their imagination that Providence would give the country for four years into the care of such unfit custodians as the Democrats.[5]

---

[1] N. Y. Nation, Oct. 30, 1884.
[2] It is impossible to convey a correct idea of the evil meaning which a Republican could put into the seemingly harmless words "Solid South." There was in them sinfulness near the head of the catalogue. "This Presidential contest closes," said the New York Tribune on November 4, 1884, where the contest of 1880 closed, "with a Solid South desperately fighting for mastery of the nation."
[3] For its course at this time see N. Y. Times, Nov. 12, 1884.
[4] Cf. N. Y. Herald, Nov. 6, 7, 8, 1884; N. Y. Nation, Nov. 13, 1884.
[5] Cf. W. B. Parker, Life of J. S. Morrill, p. 313.

The Democrats, on their side, unaccustomed to success, even when it was within their grasp, as in 1876, were slow to believe that the count could bring them victory.[1]   In any case cheating would again, as before, deprive them of the prize. On Friday, as the day advanced, though the Tribune in the morning had claimed New York for Blaine, with much "crowing" over the result, the Associated Press announced [2] that Cleveland had received a plurality of about 1,500 votes.[3] It was clear that there would be 219 electoral votes for Cleveland and 182 for Blaine. A salute of 219 guns was fired in the New York City Hall park.[4] Blaine said that, after carrying the country, he and his friends did not propose to have New York taken from them by "fraud," and his organs did not concede his defeat until Sunday, and then with reservations, awaiting the official tabulation of the returns.[5]

Cleveland, in writing to his friend Wilson S. Bissell in Buffalo on November 13th, was ready to subscribe himself "the President-elect." He was "busy all day long" receiving the congratulations of his friends in person; thousands more sent him their felicitations "through the mail and by telegraph." [6] The Democrats throughout the country, assured of their success, were celebrating the happy event. Business was forgotten by the cheering crowds which filled the streets. Republican manufacturers met by Democrats were told the news and were asked when they would "shut down" their mills. Men marched along with brooms upon their shoulders shouting, "Blaine, Blaine, biggest thief in Maine," and, "Burn, burn, burn this letter," as matches were put to paper held aloft. Bands played the "Dead March," and campaign clubs stopped and groaned

---

[1] Cf. Mayes, Life of Lamar, p. 460.

[2] Cf. N. Y. Herald, Nov. 8, 1884.

[3] Later reduced to about 1,100.

[4] On Friday, when the man at the gun was told by some one who had come from the Tribune office that such jubilation was premature he answered, "Sure and thin we are firin' for the fun of the thing an' becuz it's a foine day."—N. Y. World, Nov. 8, 1884.

[5] Boutelle on November 15, 1884, in a letter to W. E. Chandler said, "the Greys [i.e., the rebels] are on deck."—Chandler Papers.

[6] Cleveland Papers.

in front of Republican newspaper offices. Other wits shouted
"Grover, Grover had a walkover" and

> "Blaine! Blaine!
> We gave him a pain,
> The con-ti-nent-al liar
> From the state of Maine,"

and sang, "We'll hang Jay Gould on a sour apple tree," or, perhaps, "We'll hang Jim Blaine on a sour apple tree," with a
chorus of "Glory, Glory, Grover Cleveland."

The Republican clubs had been tramping the streets to "Ma,
Ma, Where's my Pa?" The Democrats could now retort,

> "Ma, Ma,
> Where's my Pa?
> Gone to the White House,
> Ha, Ha, Ha." [1]

Salutes of cannon and smaller guns, fired 100 and sometimes
219 times, in parks and on hill slopes, the ringing of fire bells,
the passage through the streets of catafalques in mock funeral
processions, the sale by hawkers in the streets of roosters,
flags and tickets for presentation to Republicans for a sail
up "Salt River" continued for many days and nights. The
negroes in the South were told that they would be returned to
slavery.[2]

Suggestions by Blaine and his staff officers of an investiga-

---

[1] Phila. Press, Nov. 7, 1884; N. Y. World, Nov. 8, 1884.

[2] The N. Y. World (Nov. 8, 1884) adapted verses which the N. Y. Sun
had printed in 1876:

> "Wha-at-Jim?
> Jim Blaine!
> Beat him?
> Great Cain!
> Jim Blaine,
> Of the state of Maine,
> Smartest cuss in out of the rain.
> Beat him?
> Our Jim?
> Cheeky Jim,
> Full to the brim
> Of brass and sass and pluck and vim,
> Beat Jim?
> Why he's the festive little pill
> That went through catawampus Hill
> And made the chivalry so ill," etc., etc.

tion and a contest met with no favor.[1] Experience with such methods in 1876 was not calculated to encourage their use again. Cleveland was a more definite and vigorous leader than Tilden,[2] and he had the support of too large and important a body of the people, while Blaine's campaign had rested, throughout, upon uncertain ground.[3]

Men discussed the reasons for the result, and with much of the acrimony which had distinguished the canvass. It was easy to see that Burchard had been the main offender with his "Rum, Romanism and Rebellion,"—a poor preacher's words were used as a convenient and dramatic explanation of the want of less than a thousand votes which, if they had been transferred from Cleveland to Blaine, would have elected the "Plumed Knight." [4] But there were other reasons. Tammany had been false. Notwithstanding the large Independent vote Cleveland's plurality in New York City was not much more than equal to Hancock's [5] four years before.[6] Conkling and some of his friends had found satisfaction in "knifing" the candidate.[7] Blaine accused Arthur of having been unfriendly.[8] Butler, as was intended, drew votes from Cleveland in answer

[1] Except possibly in the heart of Senator Hoar.—Cf. Autobiog. of 70 Years, vol. i, p. 408.

[2] He said, "Nothing but the grossest fraud can keep me out of it [the Presidency] and that we will not permit."—N. Y. Herald, Nov. 7, 1884; cf. W. C. Hudson, Random Recollections, p. 227.

[3] Cf. N. Y. Times, Nov. 8, 9, 10, 11 and 12, 1876.

[4] Cf. Cortissoz, Life of Reid, vol. ii, pp. 97–9; Gail Hamilton, Biography of Blaine, pp. 587–8.

[5] To whom Tammany had also been unfaithful.—A. K. McClure, Recollections of Half a Century, p. 111; N. Y. World, Nov. 3, 1884.

[6] N. Y. Nation, Nov. 6, 1886. It was estimated that Cleveland had been betrayed by Tammany to the extent of about 40,000 votes.—N. Y. Herald, Nov. 6, 1884.

[7] Cf. Cortissoz, Life of Reid, vol. ii, p. 96. Conkling announced as early as in April, 1883, that the Republican candidate for President would be defeated in 1884. (Harper's Weekly, May 19, 1883.) Oneida County, where Conkling lived, which had given Garfield a plurality of 1,946, gave Cleveland a plurality of 69. (N. Y. Herald, Nov. 11, 1884; cf. N. Y. Times, Oct. 24, 1884.) Conkling's equivocal denial of interest in the result is in Conkling, Life of Conkling, p. 693; cf. Autobiography of Platt, pp. 181, 183, 184; A. K. McClure, Recollections of Half a Century, p. 122; W. C. Hudson, Random Recollections, pp. 199–204.

[8] Ketcham to Gresham, Dec. 28, 1884, in Gresham Papers.

to Dana's savage assaults upon the Democratic candidate, and on other accounts, though only 17,000 men were found in all New York state to give him their direct support. The Prohibitionists, nearly all Republicans, who had voted for St. John certainly had contributed to the result. There were 25,000 such in New York state. There had been only 1,500 in 1880. But for the Independents, who came out against Blaine and denounced him without ceasing, and who influenced many thousands of votes, he would have been elected. This was, indeed, the cause of his misfortune and the vindictive allusions of the Blaine press to the Mugwumps and their leaders, during and after the canvass, was proof, if it were needed, of a full understanding of the responsibility for what had occurred.[1] Their moral and intellectual campaign, because of the cross currents which the contest developed, had nearly come to naught, but, assuredly, it was their victory and they were justified in taking credit to themselves for it.[2] Their services for Cleveland were not confined to New York. With their aid he carried New Jersey by more than 4,000, Indiana by nearly 7,000, Connecticut by 1,200. The Republican plurality in Illinois in 1880 was 40,000; it was reduced to 25,000 in 1884. The Republican plurality in Massachusetts, which in 1880 had been 53,000, was now only 24,000, and, but for Butler's candidacy,[3] the state very probably would have chosen Cleveland electors. Wisconsin's Republican plurality in 1880 had been 29,000, now it was 14,000. Iowa's, which had been 78,000 in 1880, now was 19,000. Michigan's, which had been 53,000 was now 3,000.[4]

Blaine was defeated because he did not get enough votes, and he did not get these because he was not unanimously supported by his own party. The packing of the nominating convention hall in Chicago to override the candidacies of rivals

---

[1] Cf. Stanwood, Life of Blaine, p. 293.
[2] Cf. Ogden, Life of Godkin, vol. ii, pp. 123–5.
[3] Butler polled 24,000 votes and St. John 10,000 in Massachusetts.
[4] The Democrats and Greenbackers had formed fusion tickets in Iowa and Michigan. Cf. N. Y. Times, Nov. 14, 1884; N. Y. Nation, Nov. 27, 1884.

was covered by a legend of personal "magnetism." [1] The Republican campaign, as it affected the Democrats, was one long attempt, under a cloak of superior intelligence and respectability, to overwhelm, with vilification and scurrility, their nominee, while the Independents were dismissed as traitors, nearly fit to be hanged as such. The truth is that Blaine was a weak candidate imposed upon his party by his own ambition and the ambitions, little concealed by professions of admiration for him, of a knot of industrious and influential adherents,[2] and, if he narrowly missed seizing the prize which he so much coveted, the country as narrowly missed what must have been an administration of the government distinguished by personal advertisement and intrigue more than by useful and patriotic deeds.

[1] They were "now done with the magnetic craze and the plumed knight idiocy," a friend wrote John Sherman. It was a defeat of the candidate and not of the party. Hereafter they must put no man in nomination whom "a large and responsible minority cannot support."—Under date of November 16, 1884, in Sherman Papers.

[2] William Walter Phelps was to be Blaine's Secretary of State (A. D. White, Autobiography, vol. i, p. 214), while Whitelaw Reid could have had any reward for his valuable allegiance.

CHAPTER XXVIII

THE CHINESE

The curiosity commonly felt for strange peoples residing in little known lands, the mystery and romance founded on some casual knowledge gained from travelers, missionaries and through reading as to the odd aspect as well as the antiquity of the civilization of China had led to a feeling very sympathetic to that country and its inhabitants. The reluctance of the government to open the ports to trade having been at least partially overcome with regard to five of them, by the persuasions of Caleb Cushing, who visited Peking in this behalf,[1] which gave us the treaty of July 3, 1844, extended by provisions in another treaty on June 18, 1858,[2] we came to have a pleasant interest in the gradual unfolding of the nation from the chrysalis in which it so long had rested. This interest was deepened when a citizen who had been our minister at Peking, Mr. Burlingame, an eloquent speaker and for many years an attractive figure in American public life,[3] arrived in this country in the summer of 1868 with a new treaty recognizing the mutual rights of emigration and immigration,[4] which contained proof of a further widening of outlook among the Chinese people, and their wish, which at last seemed to be genuine, to take a part in the movements of the world. The conclusion of such an agreement, following the joyful celebrations which had recently attended the establishment of the Pacific Mail company's steamship line to the Orient, subsidized by Con-

[1] Haswell, Treaties and Conventions, pp. 145–54; J. W. Foster, American Diplomacy in the Orient, pp. 79–95.
[2] Haswell, Treaties and Conventions, pp. 159–68; Foster, op. cit., pp. 231–44.
[3] Representative W. W. Rice, of Massachusetts, described his eloquence as "marvelous." He had "the brain of a statesman, the heart of a philanthropist and the port of a prince."—Cong. Record, 47th Cong. 1st sess., p. 1939; cf. Foster, op. cit., p. 257.
[4] Foster, op. cit., p. 283.

gress, in confirmation of the national belief in the value of a better understanding and a larger commerce, was rather properly accounted an important achievement in diplomacy. It was a gain for the cause of international good fellowship.[1]

A spirit of brotherhood for all men which possessed large bodies of the people at the end of the war, and which expressed itself in friendship for the negro and the Indian, opened the national heart also to the Chinaman.[2] The theory that the republic was an asylum for every people of every land, whatever their race, color or previous condition, was strongly held and the problems connected with immigration gave us little concern. The railroad promoters wanted settlers along their lines, so that they might have passengers and freights. Eagerness to make conquest of the country's great natural resources and to explore and develop its wealth caused us to welcome hands that were willing to work. Employers everywhere desired that labor should be abundant and cheap, and in this factor was found the key to our national prosperity and growth. The black man in the South, the European peasantry in the North and in the Mississippi Valley, the Chinese from Asia on the Pacific coast were all agencies relied upon in the effort to gain the ends in view. "John Chinaman," as he was playfully and a little indulgently called by those among whom he lived, had many excellent qualities, as every one of observation and experience well understood. He was as indispensable to the employer of labor in California as the negro was, or ever had been, in Alabama and South Carolina.

The immigration had begun in sailing ships long before the Civil War. When the rest of the world was flocking to California during the mining excitement so, too, had the Chinese come to the "Gold Hills,"[3] or "Golden Mountains,"[4] as they called our El Dorado. The statisticians gave varying accounts

[1] Cf. vol. ii of this work, pp. 507–12.
[2] Cf. Cong. Record, 44th Cong. 1st sess., pp. 2851, 3099, 4419; ibid., 43rd Cong. 1st sess., p. 4535; Hoar, Autobiography of 70 Years, vol. ii, pp. 120–21.
[3] Senate Reports, 44th Cong. 2nd sess., no. 689, p. 1246.
[4] Otis Gibson, The Chinese in America, p. 223; Wm. Speer, The Oldest and the Newest Empire, p. 486.

of the arrivals and departures, and of the Chinese population of California and of the Pacific coast. It was supposed that 10,000 had reached our shores prior to 1852, and that 20,000 came in that year,[1] more than had ever since, in any one year, entered the country. One who had made some study of the subject calculated that in twenty years, from 1853 to 1873, 135,399 Chinese had arrived in the United States. The same authority, making estimates for 1874, 1875 and 1876 thought that the whole immigration from the beginning might have amounted to 233,000 souls. But it was an ebbing and flowing tide. It reached its high point in March, April and May in each year.[2] Every ship to China returned with some Chinamen, but in the autumn and early winter, at the approach of the rainy season and their New Year, a moving festival determined by a lunar calculation, coming as a rule in February,[3] which they wished to enjoy at home,[4] they were likely to crowd the outgoing ships.[5] In some years it was believed that more left the country than came to it.[6] Perhaps 93,000 in all had returned home which, after account was taken of the deaths and the migration inland to other states and territories, would leave approximately 90,000 Chinese in California in 1876,[7] probably less, it was said, than twenty years ago,[8] less it was said, too, than at one time during the Civil War.[9] The greatest number to arrive in any one year since the war had been 19,368 in 1872–3.[10]

By the official census of 1880 the total was as low as 75,000 for California which had, in all, 864,000 inhabitants. The Chinese, therefore, made up less than nine per cent of the entire

[1] Senate Reports, 44th Cong. 2nd sess., no. 689, pp. 75–6.
[2] Ibid., pp. 102, 177.
[3] Ibid., pp. 156, 515, 860.
[4] Especially as one-half the immigrants were married men who, on coming, had left wives and families behind them.—Coolidge, Chinese Immigration, pp. 18–20.
[5] Senate Reports, 44th Cong. 2nd sess., no. 689, pp. 177, 449, 619.
[6] Ibid., p. 513.
[7] Ibid., pp. 513, 795–6; ibid., App. Q; cf. ibid., p. 632.
[8] Ibid., p. 449.
[9] Ibid., pp. 670, 685.
[10] App. Ann. Cyclop. for 1875, p. 98.

population of the state.   There were 5,400 in Nevada where
they comprised not quite nine, and 9,500, in Oregon where
they were about six per cent of the population.[1]   The wildest
guesses were indulged in by those who wished to make statistics
serve their particular ends.   Some said that there were 130,000
Chinese in California in 1876;[2] others 150,000, and 200,000 on
the coast,[3] of whom 3,000 or 4,000 it was supposed were women.[4]
Quite a third of the immigrants were under 21 years of age;
a considerable number were boys of about 14.[5]   There were
25,000 or 30,000 Chinese in San Francisco who lived in a quarter
of their own called "Chinatown."[6]

A movement eastwardly beyond the Rocky Mountains went
forward only slowly, although efforts had been made to locate
the Chinese as laborers in other parts of the country.   Koop-
manschap, the Dutch trader, had brought a number of them
into the South.   Two ships laden with young Chinamen left
Hong Kong for New Orleans in the spring of 1870.[7] Altogether
possibly 1,500 came to the Southern states to build levees and
railroads and take the place of negroes on cotton and sugar
plantations.   But many of them were treated cruelly, some, it
was said, having been turned into the swamps to subsist upon
roots and berries until they could be rescued by one of their
own countrymen.[8]   A notable experiment with them as factory
hands brought 50 or 75 into shoe manufacturing in North Adams,
Mass., to break a strike.   They came in 1870, and, in spite
of the frantic excitement of the white workingmen which their
presence induced, they were successfully employed for several
years.[9]   One hundred and fifty Chinese were at work in a steam

[1] Census of the U. S. for 1880, p. 3.

[2] Senate Reports, 44th Cong. 2nd sess., no. 689, p. 1242.

[3] Ibid., p. 12.

[4] Cf. ibid., pp. 405, 638. By the Census of 1880 there were held to be
105,465 Chinese of both sexes in the U. S.; nearly 3,900 of these were women.
Cf. Gibson, The Chinese in America, pp. 17–21.

[5] Senate Reports, 44th Cong. 2nd sess., no. 689, p. 489.

[6] Ibid., p. 10; cf. Gibson, The Chinese in America, pp. 16–7.

[7] Senate Ex. Doc., 41st Cong. 2nd sess., no. 116.

[8] Senate Reports, 44th Cong. 2nd sess., no. 689, pp. 550–51, 1116.

[9] Ibid., pp. 550–51, 979, 982; Cong. Record, 44th Cong. 1st sess., p. 2853;
ibid., 47th Cong. 1st sess., pp. 1549, 1975–6, 2215–6, 2219, 3359.

laundry in Belleville, N. J.[1] Individual Chinamen opened "wash houses" in the Eastern cities and even in the smaller towns where, with their flowing garments, their shaven crowns, their queues and pattened feet, the odd names on their windows and the mysterious characters which they employed in marking the linen intrusted to them to be laundered and glossed, they became objects of great interest.[2] "Chinatowns" sprang up in New York, Boston, Philadelphia and other centers of population which, though smaller, partook of the character of that one in San Francisco.[3]

At first the Chinese had been viewed with favor, their coming was welcomed.[4] They pressed into the mining gulches; very few remained in San Francisco, and it was among the white miners, with their cry, "California for the Americans," that the antipathy earliest found expression.[5] Race animosity at the mines had spent itself in the beginning upon the "greasers" from Mexico, who were the object, in 1850, of a tax laid on "foreign miners," come "to steal the gold" of the United States. All persons not citizens of the United States (California Indians excepted) must obtain a license for mining at a cost of $20 a month.[6] The sum was too high, it could not be collected, the law was not effective and it was repealed at the next session of the legislature.[7] In 1852 a tax of $3 a month was imposed upon "foreign miners."[8] The charge was increased on March 30, 1853, to $4 a month.[9] The tax was now aimed at the Chinese, and they felt the force of the law.

[1] Senate Reports, 44th Cong. 2nd sess., no. 689, p. 550; Stewart Culin, China in America, p. 8.
[2] Cf. Culin, op. cit., pp. 8–10.
[3] Cf. ibid., pp. 10–12. Senate Reports, 44th Cong. 2nd sess., no. 689, p. 330. In 1880 Chinatown in New York was said to contain 2,000 people. —J. A. Whitney, The Chinese and the Chinese Question, p. 57.
[4] Gibson, The Chinese in America, pp. 224–5; Coolidge, Chinese Immigration, pp. 21–5.
[5] Coolidge, Chinese Immigration, pp. 255–7; Gibson, The Chinese in America, p. 241.
[6] Sess. Laws. of Cal. for 1850, pp. 221–3; Coolidge, Chinese Immigration, pp. 29, 30.
[7] Sess. Laws of Cal. for 1851, p. 424.
[8] Ibid. for 1852, pp. 84–7.
[9] Ibid. for 1853, pp. 62–5. Amended May 13, 1854—ibid. for 1854, p. 55.

A Democrat from Pennsylvania, John Bigler, who had been
elected to the governorship of California in 1851, for what he
thought would be his advantage in the mining towns, immediately put himself in a position of antagonism to the Chinese.
In 1852 he sent the legislature a special message on the subject
of immigration.[1] He repeated his recommendations several
times—in emphatic terms in 1855, when he was a candidate for
election for a third term—and, in answer to his urgency, on
April 28, 1855, the legislature passed "an act to discourage
the immigration to this state of persons who cannot become
citizens thereof." This restriction took the form of a "passenger
tax" of $50 a head on every Chinaman, collectible before
landing.[2] Two days later, on April 30, 1855, the legislature
amended the foreign miners' license law. The tax of $4 a
month to be paid by all aliens should, in the case of every one
"ineligible to become a citizen of the United States," be augmented $12 a month from and after October 1st in and for every
successive year progressively.[3]

A committee of Chinese merchants in San Francisco made
a public response to Governor Bigler, as they had in 1852.
They cited the treatment which their countrymen, though at
first made welcome, had lately received. If the "rabble" were
to "harass" the Chinese they would return to their "former
homes." The committee asked for a definite statement as
to the policy which was likely to be pursued.[4] The governor
defended his legislation. The laws had been adopted "in
response to the almost unanimous wishes expressed in the
most unmistakable manner" in the mining towns and had
effectually checked immigration. Chinese could come to Cali-

[1] Coolidge, Chinese Immigration, pp. 31, 56; McNeill, The Labor Movement, p. 443.

[2] Sess. Laws of Cal. for 1855, pp. 194–5; Wm. Speer, An Humble Plea
Addressed to the Leg. of Cal., a pamphlet, 1856, pp. 34–7; Coolidge, Chinese Immigration, p. 71.

[3] Sess. Laws of Cal. for 1855, pp. 216–7; Gibson, The Chinese in America,
pp. 227–8.

[4] Remarks of the Chinese Merchants of San Francisco upon Governor
Bigler's Message, San Francisco, 1855; Wm. Speer, The Oldest and the
Newest Empire, pp. 578–81.

fornia from Asia much more cheaply (for less than one-sixth) and in much less time, than immigrants from the Atlantic seaboard, or from Europe. There were 40,000 of them already in California. Existing statutes should not be changed. If so, "a new invitation" would be given, and "the tide of immigration" would "again roll in upon us."[1] The $50 head tax, following a belated attempt at its collection, was declared "invalid and void" by the supreme court of the state in 1857.[2] The foreign miners' tax law in its cumulative form was repealed, in spite of Bigler's plea in its behalf.[3] But the tax of $4 a month remained. As the Chinamen were practically the only foreigners who might not be naturalized and, as there was no wish to make the law apply to other men, they bore its burdens until 1870, when, in the first "Enforcement Act," passed for the advantage of the negroes, in amplification of the new guarantees in the Fourteenth and Fifteenth Amendments, the Chinese also found protection from unequal laws.[4] The foreign miners' tax, from 1850 to 1870, provided California with $5,000,-000, or one-half its total income.[5] Not less than 95 per cent of the whole amount was paid by the Chinese.[6] The local governments derived a large part of their revenues from the same source. The Chinese mining taxes saved several counties from bankruptcy.[7]

In the collection of the tax, as at all points of contact with the white man, the Chinese were cheated and robbed. If a mining claim proved to be valuable some one "jumped" it.[8] Many Chinamen were slain, frequently by the tax officers,

[1] Bigler's message to the legislature in 1856.
[2] People v. Downer, 7 Cal., p. 169; Coolidge, Chinese Immigration, p. 71.
[3] Sess. Laws of Cal. for 1856, p. 141; Gibson, The Chinese in America, pp. 228-40; Coolidge, Chinese Immigration, pp. 34-5.
[4] Act of May 31, 1870, U. S. Statutes at Large for 1870, chap. 114, sec. 16; Coolidge, Chinese Immigration, pp. 36, 70; Senate Reports, 44th Cong. 2nd sess., no. 689, pp. 62, 477-8, 974-6; 1 Fed. Reporter, p. 497; U. S. v. Jackson, 3 Sawyer, p. 59; McNeill, Labor Movement, p. 444.
[5] Coolidge, Chinese Immigration, pp. 36-7; Senate Reports, 44th Cong. 2nd sess., no. 689, p. 62; Gibson, The Chinese in America, pp. 37-50.
[6] Coolidge, Chinese Immigration, p. 70.
[7] Ibid., p. 343.
[8] Cf. Samuel Bowles, Our New West, p. 402; Coolidge, Chinese Immigration, p. 255.

who, when payment was delayed, or, in their judgment, was being evaded, shot the delinquents. The collectors then seized the "dust" of the murdered men and got their own fees,[1] though nothing might reach the treasury of the state. No one knew the number of Chinese who had been killed in the mountains.[2]

In 1852 a tax of from $5 to $10 a head was laid on immigrants, who were not citizens of the United States, for the benefit of the state hospitals.[3] For nearly twenty years, or until 1870, when this procedure was held to be in conflict with the provisions of the act to enforce the Federal constitutional amendments, the Chinese paid a head tax of $5.[4]

A law of April 26, 1858, prohibited all Chinese and other Mongolians from landing at any port in the state unless the vessel on which they might be passengers should be "driven ashore by storm or distress, or other unavoidable accident," in which case they should be immediately reshipped. They might not enter the state overland.[5] Though the act was not repealed no effort, following an opinion of the supreme court,[6] was ever made to execute it. An act of April 26, 1862, "to protect free white labor against competition with Chinese coolie labor, and discourage the immigration of the Chinese into the state of California," provided that every Chinaman, over 18 years of age, should pay a monthly capitation tax of $2.50 to be known as the "Chinese police tax," with exception for

[1] By the law of 1861, 20 per cent of the collections. (Sess. Laws of Cal. for 1861, p. 449.) The collection of the tax was without question an irritating task. Facially one Chinaman resembled another—to distinguish them was impossible. They passed rapidly from place to place, exchanging their tax receipts, knowing that the law was unfair and that they were not unjustified in their attempts to evade it.—Cf. Bret Harte, Stories in Light and Shadow, pp. 101–2.

[2] Senate Reports, 44th Cong. 2nd sess., no. 689, pp. 166, 1192, 1251; cf. Wm. Speer, An Humble Plea, etc., pp. 34–7; ibid., The Oldest and the Newest Empire, chap. xx, also, pp. 594, 598–9; Coolidge, Chinese Immigration, pp. 255–8.

[3] Sess. Laws of Cal. for 1852, pp. 78–83; Coolidge, Chinese Immigration, p. 70.

[4] Cf. Gibson, The Chinese in America, p. 270.

[5] Sess. Laws of Cal. for 1858, pp. 295–6.

[6] This case was not reported; cf. 20 Cal., p. 538.

those engaged in the production of sugar, rice, coffee and tea.[1] It was declared unconstitutional by the state supreme court in July, 1862.[2]

No Indian or negro could give evidence against a white man in any court of law in California.[3] In 1854 the chief justice of the state supreme court decided that the Chinese were Indians.[4]

No matter how grievously they were wronged the Chinese were legally defenseless. So long as such a system continued "any white ruffian might plunder and murder any half dozen decent and honest Chinese laborers." Unless the crime were witnessed by other white men he could not be convicted in a court of justice and punished, and such outrages were disgracefully frequent throughout the state.[5] All efforts to change the law to the advantage of the Chinese failed.[6] On March 18, 1863, during the war, negroes were excepted from this provision, but it was at the same time stated in the statute, and assurance was given, that Chinamen might not testify "in favor or against any white person."[7] The law was held to be not repugnant to provisions of the Fourteenth Amendment.[8] It was not until the codes were revised and a clause could be

[1] Sess. Laws of Cal. for 1862, pp. 462-5.

[2] Ling Sing v. Washburn, 20 Cal., p. 534; Coolidge, Chinese Immigration, p. 72.

[3] Sess. Laws of Cal. for 1850, p. 455.

[4] People v. Hall, 4 Cal., p. 399. It can "hardly be supposed," said the chief justice, " that any legislature" would attempt to exclude domestic negroes and Indians, " who not unfrequently have correct notions of their obligations to society," and, at the same time, "turn loose upon the community the more degraded tribes of the same species, who have nothing in common with us in language, country or laws."—Cf. Speer v. See Yup Co., 13 Cal., p. 73; People v. Elyea, 14 Cal., p. 144.

[5] C. L. Brace, The New West, pp. 221-3; cf. Wm. Speer, Answer to the Objections to Chinese Testimony, a pamphlet, 1857; Speer, The Oldest and the Newest Empire, pp. 595-6; Remarks of the Chinese Merchants upon Bigler's Message, 1855, p. 5; Senate Reports, 44th Cong. 2nd sess., no. 689, p. 478.

[6] Cf. Speer, Answer to the Objections, etc., pamphlet just cited; Speer, The Oldest and the Newest Empire, pp. 627-30; C. L. Brace, op. cit., pp. 221-3; N. Y. Tribune, May 1, 1869.

[7] Sess. Laws of Cal. for 1863, p. 69; cf. People v. Washington, 36 Cal., p. 658; People v. Brady, 40 Cal., p. 198.

[8] People v. McGuire, 45 Cal., p. 56.

inserted, of which the people knew nothing until after its adoption,[1] that this elementary human right was won.[2]

In 1860 a tax of $4 a month was laid on each Chinaman who desired to fish in the waters of California, the collector taking 40 per cent for his compensation.[3] The law was repealed in 1864.[4] On March 31, 1866, an act was passed declaring all Chinese houses of ill fame "public nuisances" and discriminations, with drastic penalties, were to be enforced against landlords, with large rewards to informers.[5] The county governments laid poll taxes upon the Chinese for the construction and repair of the roads.[6]

So, too, was it in Oregon, Nevada, Idaho and Washington, into which the Chinese came, and, were the course of legislation directed against them in those states and territories to be traced, many laws similar to those in California would be revealed. A provision was inserted in the constitution of Oregon of 1857 prohibiting all Chinese not residents of the state at the time of the adoption of the constitution from holding any real estate or mining claim, or from working any such claim.[7] This restriction was regarded as a "dead letter," not worthy of enforcement, or as much as an appeal to the courts.[8]

Now and again the question reached Congress. Thaddeus Stevens denounced the miners' tax in the House of Representatives. Such laws he said were "wholly in conflict with the generous spirit of our free institutions." They were "a mockery of the boast that this land is the asylum of the oppressed of all climes." Representative Sargent of California defended

---

[1] J. S. Hittell, Resources of Cal., ed. of 1874, p. 43.

[2] Beginning with the year 1873, Cal. Code of Civil Procedure, p. 493.

[3] Sess. Laws of Cal. for 1860, pp. 307–8.

[4] Ibid. for 1864, p. 492.

[5] Ibid. for 1866, pp. 641–2; cf. Senate Reports, 44th Cong. 2nd sess., no. 689, pp. 144, 479.

[6] N. Y. Tribune, May 1, 1869.

[7] Art. xv, sec. 8.

[8] Chapman v. Toy Long, 4 Sawyer, p. 36. For allusions to this subject outside of California see vol. i of this work, p. 296; Coolidge, Chinese Immigration, p. vii; Gibson, The Chinese in America, p. 285; Lucile Eaves, Labor Legislation in Cal., chap. iii.

the tax as a restrictive measure and in 1862 he advocated an increased tariff on rice still further to discourage Chinese from coming to, and living in, America. They were "a people of strange tongue, vile habits, impossible of assimilation and with customs difficult to penetrate" and they swarmed "by thousands to our shores like the frogs of Egypt." "In morals and in every other respect," Sargent continued, they were "obnoxious" to California. The race was so "deeply sunk in barbarism" that mere contact with it was "demoralization." [1]

To such a point beyond the range of honor and international justice, and, indeed, of common humanity, had the persecution proceeded that a joint select committee of the legislature of California in 1862 registered its protest. Burdens imposed upon the Chinese were too heavy to bear. No more laws should be enacted to "oppress and degrade" them. This "scourged race" had been of the greatest value to California. The money that they paid out annually to support the state and energize business reached an impressive total; what wealth they had brought to the country, what they yet might do for the development of agriculture and industry were intelligently described. Instead of driving them away bounties might well be offered them for their labor. Anyhow treaty obligations were to be observed. Reciprocity was required—but, on our side, there were only discrimination and insult. "Lamentably" was California falling short of "mutuality" in its conduct toward the Chinese. If there were those who should wish to exclude them, and there were such, appeal for remedy must be made to Congress. There was no power in California to bar this people from the privileges accorded other men and solemnly guaranteed to them, if it were accounted expedient, indeed, "to shut ourselves out from one of the most magnificent openings of the age," which commerce with China offered us. Californians should conduct themselves "as becomes a great, liberal, magnanimous people," manifesting "superiority

[1] Cong. Globe, 37th Cong. 2nd sess., pp. 2938–9; Cong. Record, 44th Cong. 1st sess., p. 2856.

by kindness" to "this industrious, numerous and cultivated family of mankind." [1]

The visit of Burlingame with his new treaty in 1868 was welcomed on the Pacific coast no less than in other parts of the country, as the establishment of a regular steamer line to Hong Kong had been. For a time outrages upon Chinamen ceased.[2] If the lower classes muttered they were overborne by what was a veritable outburst of popular enthusiasm. But within a year, in December, 1869, workingmen, both native and of European birth, were petitioning Congress for present relief and future security from competition with Asiatic wage-earners. By this time the Chinese were scattered over the state. The mining taxes had led to their leaving the gulches to find other employment. From a few hundreds in 1856,[3] the number had grown to many thousands in San Francisco,[4] where they were huddled together as closely as "eleme figs in a box." [5] "Chinatown" had come to hold a place as the principal spectacle of the city. Parts of it were maintained expressly for exhibition to tourists who viewed it with curious delight. The anti-Chinese party invited Mr. Seward, when he came to San Francisco in 1869, on his way around the world, to visit "Chinatown" to see its villainies, and the Chinese themselves, in answer, also bade him come for observation. He declined to involve himself in the controversy, though he was stoutly on the side of free immigration.[6] The very governor of the state, a Democrat, who was in office when Burlingame came bearing the olive branch, had been elected on a platform hostile to the Chinese.[7] The Democrats in their state convention in 1869 registered their complete opposition to immigration. The adoption of the Fifteenth Amendment filled

[1] Senate Reports, 44th Cong. 2nd sess., no. 689, App. P; App. to Opening Statement and Brief of B. S. Brooks, 1877, pp. 73–84.

[2] Gibson, The Chinese in America, p. 243.

[3] Ibid., p. 231, quoting Speer.

[4] Coolidge, Chinese Immigration, p. 38.

[5] Senate Reports, 44th Cong. 2nd sess., no. 689, pp. 12, 156, 514, 1188.

[6] Seward's Travels Around the World, p. 28; Coolidge, Chinese Immigration, p. 148; Gibson, The Chinese in America, pp. 3–4.

[7] Lippincott's Magazine, July, 1868, p. 38.

them with fear that the Chinaman would be naturalized, and that he, like the negro, would soon be voting and holding office. The Republicans still supported immigration,—to restrict it would be contrary to the spirit of the age, but they expressed hostility to the enfranchisement of the Chinese.[1]

The next year, 1870, the Republicans were complaining about the violation of the Federal anti-coolie laws. The State Department was asked to admonish American consuls at Chinese ports who, by their liberality in the interpretation of their duties, were making possible so great an inpouring at San Francisco,[2] and, in 1871, an anti-Chinese plank was inserted in the Republican party platform in order, if possible, to win enough votes to displace the Democrats who were in power, and who were outspoken in their declarations on this subject.[3] The Republican candidate for governor, Newton Booth, took a similar stand. In his first message, after assuming office, he denounced Chinese cheap labor, and called for the stoppage of immigration.[4] In Oregon, in 1870, a politician named Grover, a Democrat, procured his election as governor by abuse of the Chinese.[5]

In the same year, in 1870, the California legislature discovered that, in the past year, 1,156 females had been imported for immoral purposes, and had been added to the Chinese population of the state. These women, it was said, had been "kidnapped." This fact was communicated to Congress.[6] It had been asserted freely, by the newspapers and in political speech, that any state might protect itself from unwelcome immigrants, without regard to its Federal connections. The legislature of California, in 1870, conferred the power upon a state commissioner of immigration, appointed by the governor and stationed at San Francisco, to determine when and whether passengers on ships should be landed, and to issue permits.

[1] App. Ann. Cyclop. for 1869, pp. 79–80.
[2] Ibid., for 1870, p. 79.
[3] Ibid. for 1871, pp. 90–92.
[4] Ibid. for 1872, p. 87.
[5] Cong. Record, 47th Cong. 1st sess., p. 1545; App. Ann. Cyclop. for 1870, p. 606.
[6] Sess. Laws of Cal. for 1870, pp. 931–2.

All Mongolian, Chinese or Japanese females were prohibited from entering unless this commissioner should satisfy himself that they came "voluntarily" and were "persons of correct habits and good character." [1] At the same time, by another act, with a purpose of excluding "criminals and malefactors," and abolishing "a species of slavery" which was "at war with the spirit of the age," all male Chinese or Mongolian immigration was made subject to the arbitrary control of the same officer of the state,[2] a principle incorporated in more guarded language in the "Political Code" of California, adopted on March 12, 1872,[3] and amended in 1874.[4] In assertion of the state's rights in this matter the commissioner of immigration in San Francisco, in the summer of 1874, boarded the *Japan*, a Pacific Mail steamer, and arbitrarily picked out 22 women who were declared to be "lewd and debauched" within the meaning of the law. They were detained on the steamer, but on a writ of *habeas corpus* were brought before a judge in the City Hall, who remanded them to the ship. Again they were rescued by their friends for appearance in the supreme court. The case was heard in the name of Ah Fong, one of the little almond-eyed belles, and the ruling of the local court was sustained,[5] but, upon appeal to the United States Circuit Court, Justice Field ordered the release of the women.[6] By this time the steamer had sailed and they were confined in the county jail. That there might be a definite statement as to the constitutionality or unconstitutionality of the principle which California was endeavoring to establish, the matter, in the name of another of the young women, Chy Lung, was taken to the Supreme Court of the United States. Attorney-General Pierrepont appeared in person to argue the case, and the state of California offered no argument in defense of its unusual course.

---

[1] Sess. Laws of Cal. for 1870, p. 331.
[2] Ibid., p. 332.
[3] Political Code of Cal. of 1872, secs. 2949–68.
[4] Amendments to Code of Cal., 1873–4, pp. 241–3.
[5] Ex parte Ah Fook, 49 Cal., p. 402; cf. Report of Committee of Cal. State Senate, pp. 91–2; Gibson, The Chinese in America, pp. 146–55.
[6] In re Ah Fong, 3 Sawyer, p. 144.

The highest Federal court in October, 1875, severely condemned the whole proceeding and the state law was declared null and void.[1]

In 1873 the Board of Supervisors of San Francisco made so many orders bearing upon the Chinese, and the tone of speech and newspaper article was so acrimonious that a group of intelligent Chinese merchants issued an address to the people of the United States, repeating the offer of some years since to ask their government to abrogate the treaty and to cease mutual trade. They reiterated their wish to return to their homes, if international stipulations, solemnly agreed to and promulgated, were not to be respected.[2]

Memorials, resolutions of public meetings and petitions continued to be received from year to year in Congress.[3] It was seen to be largely a labor question and the commotion on the Pacific coast had aroused some sympathetic response in the breasts of leaders of labor organizations in other parts of the country.[4] Nevertheless, popular sentiment was not yet generally angry. The public mind had been pleasantly occupied with the prospect of the completion of the transcontinental railroad, which strongly appealed to the national imagination. The Chinese had been industriously engaged in its construction. Prosperity continued unbroken, even after the panic of 1873, which had laid so hard a hand upon business of all kinds in the East. Californians, behind their mountains, facing another sea, led their own lives as if they were scarce a part of the republic to which they were bound by political ties.

But now the railroad had been built and thousands of unemployed Chinamen were pitched into the labor market.[5] Feeling was undergoing a deep change. Those who had been commended for their vision, energy and enterprise in promoting

---

[1] U. S. Reports, vol. 92, p. 1275.
[2] Gibson, The Chinese in America, pp. 285–92.
[3] House Reports, 45th Cong. 3rd sess., no. 62, pp. 3, 4.
[4] See platform of National Labor Reform Convention of 1872, McPherson's Handbook, p. 211.
[5] Coolidge, Chinese Immigration, p. 350.

the material interests of the country were no longer looked upon as benefactors, and, in fact, were doing little enough to earn public respect, since they were confusing private and public rights in a manner which was characteristic of the period in the nation at large. Men, made suddenly wealthy [1] by mining, railway building and other speculation, had gained control of local and state governments, which were being administered for their own profit and advantage. Protest there must and would be, and the enmity for the rich man, and the Chinese who had helped with cheap labor to make him rich, would go forward hand in hand.

Agitators passed from house to house and from shop to shop in San Francisco in the winter of 1873–4 and over 16,000 signatures were obtained on a petition asking for an abrogation of the treaty with China. The names were bound in two large volumes and sent to Sargent, champion of the American workingman, now in the United States Senate, who, on February 13, 1874, with some explanatory remarks, laid them before that body, to be referred to the Committee on Foreign Relations,[2] where they were to slumber, he afterward complained, "as if inured with the Capulets." [3]

The zealots in California, when Justice Field, in September, 1874, set free the "lewd and debauched" women who had been seized in the harbor on a Pacific Mail steamship, pretended to be frantic.[4] They carried their case to President Grant and he had noticed it in his message to Congress in December, 1874. Following the information given him by his advisers

[1] One of these, Leland Stanford, at his golden wedding celebration said: "I can remember the time when a tent to cook in and a tent to sleep in constituted my sole earthly possessions and my wife and I had to lie very still when it rained, because there was a tin pan between us to catch the drippings from the canvas." At the death of his son, a lad of 16, he paid a New York pulpit orator $10,000 to go out to preach the funeral sermon and buried the boy amid "floral decorations" which cost $20,000.—N. Y. Nation, Jan. 8, 1885.
[2] Cong. Record, 43rd Cong. 1st sess., pp. 1463–4; ibid., 44th Cong. 1st sess., pp. 2856; Senate Reports, 44th Cong. 2nd sess., no. 689, pp. 324, 679, 927.
[3] Cong. Record, 44th Cong. 1st sess., p. 4418.
[4] Senate Reports, 44th Cong. 2nd sess., no. 689, p. 15.

he said that the Chinese, for the most part, did not come here voluntarily, but were "under contracts with headmen" who owned them "almost absolutely." Their women were prostitutes, who demoralized any community in which they settled.[1]

Horace F. Page, a representative in Congress from San Francisco, aimed to stand in that relation to the anti-Chinese movement in the House which Sargent held in the Senate. He exploded his bomb on June 3, 1874.

> "They came as the winds come when forests are rended
> They came as the waves come when navies are stranded."

He declared Chinese immigration to be "the greatest evil of the day." "American labor," which had made "all the actual wealth of the nation," was "humiliated before this insidious, far-reaching and dangerous foe to our institutions."[2] Out of this Congress, following Grant's suggestions, came the "Page Law" of March 3, 1875, supplementing earlier legislation. In addition to consular permits for immigrants from China, certifying that those who were embarking for the United States were coming voluntarily and were not bound to service, either for labor or prostitution, there was to be inspection of passenger ships upon their arrival by the collector of the port to determine if any obnoxious persons were on board.[3]

This law, which had been carefully framed by the Committee on Foreign Affairs of the House, should have mollified the Sinophobists. It was the regulation which they had pretended to want in California and had tried to express by local statute. But it had little influence in conciliating them. Justice Field's decision, they declared, had left them naked to their enemies. Obeying the injunction of Hercules to help themselves they had failed, said Sargent. Deprived of "all power" by the United States Constitution more than ever before was there need for the aid of Congress and the President.[4]

[1] Richardson, Messages and Papers, vol. vii, p. 288.
[2] Cong. Record, 43rd Cong. 1st sess., pp. 4534-7.
[3] Ibid., 43rd Cong. 2nd sess., pp. 19, 32, 1454, 1599, 2161, 2275; Senate Reports, 44th Cong. 2nd sess., no. 689, pp. 387-95.
[4] Cong. Record, 44th Cong. 1st sess., p. 2856.

It was the failure in the summer of 1875 of the Bank of
California, the death of Ralston, its president, and the shock
of business curtailment and unemployment, following that
disaster, which brought everything to a final issue.[1]   Over
the Pacific Railroad new fortune seekers, including many Irishmen, had arrived. The distress in the East, as a result of the
panic of 1873, had induced a large migration to the West, where
prosperous conditions were unimpaired. But now hard times
were at hand. Idlers congregated in the streets of San Francisco.
They looked around them for reasons for their unhappy situation and found it in the millionaires and the Chinese. How
had the rich made the money to build their "grand palaces
on all the prominent hills" of the city? [2] By the use of cheap
labor. Such work as was now to be had was being performed
by Chinamen; they must be driven out of the country so that
white men could have bread. Democratic platforms adopted
at county and state conventions denounced the Chinese in un-
measured terms of hatred and opprobrium. The Republicans,
the party of the more favored classes, who needed and employed labor, had been guarded in their attitude toward the
subject, though, now and again, their platforms had breathed
hostility to further immigration. Because of the defection
of Booth and his friends, who formed an independent party,
the Republicans suffered complete defeat in the election of
1875, an event which further served to frighten capital and
depress trade. To add to the commotion, early in 1876, a
number of ships laden with Chinese, the spring being the
season for them to enter the country, arrived in the harbor of
San Francisco. It was said that 6,000 came in a single month.[3]
Public meetings were called. Folly was in men's minds and they
were soon lost to any kind of rational reflection or argument.[4]

Several newspapers, which cared nothing for the favor of

[1] Coolidge, Chinese Immigration, pp. 351, 380.

[2] Senate Reports, 44th Cong. 2nd sess., no. 689, p. 79.

[3] Ibid., pp. 856, 924; cf. Cong. Record, 44th Cong. 1st sess., p. 3100;
Gibson, The Chinese in America, p. 294.

[4] Cf. Senate Reports, 44th Cong. 2nd sess., no. 689, p. 856; Gibson, The
Chinese in America, p. 294.

the Chinese, who could bring them no readers or advertisers, vied with one another in pandering to popular prejudice.[1] Their blatancy and much street corner oratory increased the urgency of the politicians, who, by more pandering, would gain votes from the ranks of the lower orders of white men. The Democrats, who had begun the crusade, were closely followed by the Republicans, lest they should lag behind a rival in a business which promised so much gain. The governor and the legislature of the state, the mayor and the city authorities in San Francisco, were soon in full cry after the Chinese. Secret societies were formed under various names—the "Order of Caucasians,"[2] the "Anti-Chinese Union"[3] and "Anti-Coolie Clubs." The members were drilling and, under military organization,[4] were marching through the streets with muslin transparencies, which exhibited skulls and crossbones and Mongolian heads caricatured into hideous forms.

Much abuse was directed at the steamship owners and agents, who brought the Chinese to our shores, and at the Six Companies. The steamship men were within their fair rights, as were the captains of the sailing vessels by which the immigrants still sometimes arrived.[5] They carried passengers for fares, they obeyed the laws of China and the United States governing their use of the ports. The movement proceeded under the protection and guarantee of international treaty.

The Six Chinese Companies (earlier and at first four companies or societies) were as useful to the unfortunate immigrants as they were to the white people, among whom these immigrants came. The Sam Yup, Kong Chow, Ning Wung, Hop Wo, Yung Wo and Yan Wo Companies—there are variant spellings[6]—were geographically sectional relief and benevolent as-

---

[1] Cf. Senate Reports, 44th Cong. 2nd sess., no. 689, pp. 704, 923.
[2] Ibid., pp. 1088–9.
[3] Ibid., pp. 1169–72.
[4] Ibid., pp. 926–7.
[5] Cf. ibid., pp. 102–3.
[6] Ibid., pp. 46–7; cf. Cal. State Senate Report, p. 44; Gibson, The Chinese in America, p. 21.

sociations.[1] They were voluntary organizations and each had under its surveillance the immigrants who had come out of a contiguous area in China. Each had in San Francisco a company house which, like the caravansaries of the East, were general meeting places. Often the halls were connected with temples or altars, dedicated to local divinities.[2] The organizations received the men upon their arrival and lodged them for a time in their houses [3] which such an enemy as Senator Sargent, likening the immigration to the slave trade, called "barracoons"; [4] informed them about the strange land to which they were to be introduced, aided them in securing homes and, if necessary, food and raiment, cared for them when they were sick, made compacts with them now, or before they had embarked, for the return of their bones to China in case of death,[5] arbitrated their disputes and, within limits, seem to have given advice concerning employment,[6] although there were agencies to which white contractors went to engage laborers.[7] The Chinese made contributions in fees and "bone money" to their respective companies [8] to cover the service rendered and, either directly or indirectly, funds were at times advanced to those who were in need. The managers were amply protected through an understanding with the steamship lines [9] that no one could embark upon their vessels and go home until he had secured a "permit," for which he must pay his company about $5, certifying that he was free of debt.[10] The companies, taken together, had a government of "Chinatown" and, indeed, of almost the entire Chinese population of the United States,

[1] Senate Reports, 44th Cong. 2nd sess., no. 689, pp. 405–6.
[2] Gibson, The Chinese in America, pp. 72–3. For a description of one of these company houses see Wm. Speer, Harper's Magazine, November, 1868.
[3] Senate Reports, 44th Cong. 2nd sess., no. 689, p. 647.
[4] Cong. Record, 44th Cong. 1st sess., p. 2854.
[5] Cf. Senate Reports, 44th Cong. 2nd sess., p. 447.
[6] Cf. ibid., pp. 176, 420–21.
[7] Cf. Gibson, The Chinese in America, pp. 60–61.
[8] Senate Reports, 44th Cong. 2nd sess., no. 689, p. 448.
[9] Ibid., pp. 176, 420, 447.
[10] Ibid., pp. 82–3, 446–7; Gibson, The Chinese in America, p. 340; California State Senate Report, p. 45.

since about 80 per cent of the immigrants came out under their
auspices, or were in some way commended to their care.[1] It
was believed that all but about one thousand of the Chinese
in California stood under the jurisdiction of the Six Companies.[2]

Because of the helplessness of the people who came here,
without knowledge of our language or customs, and their
extreme poverty, this control was of the first importance to
San Francisco, California, and the Pacific states and territories.
When misunderstandings arose, when conditions needed correction, when, on any account, communication between the
Chinese and the white inhabitants was esteemed to be an advantage individual citizens, organizations of citizens and local
governments could address the heads of the companies with
the certainty of reasonable action.[3] The attempt to spread
misrepresentation, with a view to raising prejudice and public
resentment on the subject of these associations, was, perhaps,
more reprehensible than anything which was undertaken by
the fanatics and demagogues who directed the anti-Chinese
tirade.[4]

The companies, indeed, regulated the immigration. The
embarkation of only the healthy and sound in body and mind
was encouraged, since it was not the part of wisdom to bring
out those who might become a charge upon those already
here.[5] If demand for labor declined and work was hard to
obtain the Six Companies asked that no more men take passage for America. When sentiment waxed too hostile, as during

---

[1] Senate Reports, 44th Cong. 2nd sess., no. 689, p. 175.

[2] Ibid., p. 200; cf. B. S. Brooks, App. to Opening Statement and Brief,
pp. 141–57.

[3] Senate Reports, 44th Cong. 2nd sess., no. 689, p. 173.

[4] Cf. ibid., pp. 23–5; Remarks of the Chinese Merchants of San Francisco
upon Governor Bigler's Message, 1855; Lippincott's Magazine, July, 1868,
pp. 36–7. Scribner's Magazine, May, 1871, p. 68; Gibson, The Chinese in
America, chap. xiv. Wm. Speer said of these companies that they were
institutions which had "no parallel for utility and philanthropy among the
emigrants from any other nation or people to our wide shores."—Harper's
Magazine, November, 1868; cf. Speer's The Oldest and the Newest Empire, chap. xix.

[5] Senate Reports, 44th Cong. 2nd sess., no. 689, p. 178.

political campaigns, they urged that the movement be suspended.[1] Now, early in 1876, seeing the rise of intemperate
feeling, they were telegraphing to China to effect, if possible,
an immediate arrest of immigration.

The situation, in truth, was rapidly becoming threatening,
if not dangerous. Street orators addressed crowds inciting
them to violence. The cry was "Organize! Organize! Organize!"
Anti-Coolie Clubs sprang up on every side.[2] They would
"drive every greasy-faced coolie from the land." They would
"take this insidious monster by the throat and throttle it,"
until its heart should cease to beat, and then hurl it into the
sea. Chinamen who passed by were knocked down and kicked
and cuffed in the most brutal manner.[3] There was such intimidation that men were afraid to rent or buy a building
in the erection of which Chinese had been engaged. Ruffians
might set it on fire,[4] and actually did so.[5] Incendiaries destroyed
bridges and other property of the Central Pacific Railroad
because its officers employed Chinamen.[6] Manufacturers received letters telling them that their mills would be burned,
if they did not discharge their Chinese workmen.[7] They must
hire additional watchmen for the protection of their property.[8]
Some factories, as well as quartz mills, wheat stacks and dwelling houses were burned.[9] Shopkeepers displayed placards,
"We employ no Chinese labor here," [10] in order to hold
their trade, since the members of the Anti-Coolie Clubs had
resolved not to buy of merchants who employed Chinamen,
and not to purchase goods which Chinamen had made, or
vegetables which they had grown.[11] The leaders prepared
"blacklists" on which appeared the names of dealers and manu-

[1] Senate Reports, 44th Cong. 2nd sess., no. 689, pp. 25, 38–9, 64.
[2] Gibson, The Chinese in America, p. 297.
[3] Ibid., pp. 304–5.
[4] Senate Reports, 44th Cong. 2nd sess., no. 689, pp. 588–9.
[5] Ibid., p. 171.
[6] Ibid., p. 672.
[7] Ibid., pp. 271, 1186.
[8] Ibid., p. 927.
[9] J. S. Hittell, Resources of Cal., ed. of 1874, p. 44.
[10] Senate Reports, 44th Cong. 2nd sess., no. 689, pp. 258, 319–20.
[11] Ibid., pp. 263, 927.

facturers who were contemptuous of popular sentiment on this subject.[1]

Congress was notified, through the newspapers, that, unless it should act, the question would be violently disposed of by a "Vigilance Committee." The Chinese in San Francisco were "sleeping upon a volcano." The Pacific coast would see a massacre rivaling that of St. Bartholomew.[2] The day seemed near at hand in April, 1876, when excitement ran so high that not a Chinaman dared to appear in the streets.[3] The Six Companies appealed to the mayor and the chief of police.[4] The Chinese issued a manifesto addressed to the American people explaining their side of the case.[5]

The state government fanned the flames. The legislature passed resolutions to be forwarded to Washington. "The low standard of living" of the Chinese deprived our own people of employment in which they had gained proficiency only after long apprenticeship. "Pauper wages" were driving our working classes and their families to the poorhouses. Congress must change the Burlingame treaty, so that "the immigration of a servile laboring element" should immediately cease.[6] The state senate appointed a committee of five, afterward increased to seven, members to institute and conduct an investigation, at the end of which it should make a report with recommendations for action, and prepare a memorial

[1] Senate Reports, 44th Cong. 2nd sess., no. 689, pp. 263, 265, 932, 1089. "The Tenth Ward Cigar Depot" in San Francisco advertised:

> "Cigars by all White Labor made;
> Workingmen, the place to trade
> Is at Isaac's. Yes, indeed,
> Use no nasty Chinese weed
> But smoke a real White Man's cigar,
> Isaac sells them near and far."—The Workingmen's
> Party of California, San Francisco, 1878, p. 110.

[2] San Francisco Commercial Herald and Market Review, March 30, 1876, quoted in Senate Reports, 44th Cong. 2nd sess., no. 689, p. 1184.
[3] Gibson, The Chinese in America, pp. 309–10.
[4] Ibid., pp. 303, 306–7; Senate Reports, 44th Cong. 2nd sess., no. 689, pp. 46–7.
[5] Gibson, The Chinese in America, pp. 300–03.
[6] App. Ann. Cyclop. for 1876, pp. 84–5.

to be sent to the governor for transmission to both houses of Congress.[1]

That the committee should have no misunderstanding of their duties a "grand anti-Chinese mass meeting" was held in San Francisco on April 5, 1876. The excitement was intense. Two hundred special policemen were sworn in for duty lest there be a sanguinary riot.[2] The governor, the lieutenant-governor and the mayor of the city, a particularly offensive enemy of the Chinese, appeared.[3] The governor spoke. Our civilization was being subverted. American labor was being degraded. An address was adopted by the meeting. The Chinese were as "formidable as the locusts of Egypt or the grasshoppers of Kansas," and they were as "destructive." They were crowded into houses unfit for human habitation where they were "a startling menace to public health." They had laws, and were controlled by officials, of their own. The immigration was "pure and simple peonage." They were "coolies," coming here and working under a system which was "immoral and brutalizing—worse than African slavery." They would not learn the English language. There were 10,000 Chinese criminals in San Francisco—gamblers, opium eaters, prostitutes—a terror to their own people and to the police. Properly they were looked upon "with fear and alarm." Congress was asked to give the subject its "immediate and earnest attention." Five "commissioners" were appointed to carry the address to Washington.[4] Five thousand dollars were appropriated to cover the cost of their journey.[5]

Sargent was taken by surprise. In his place, as the preëminent anti-Chinese leader at the nation's capital, he was teetering, but prior to the arrival of the "commissioners" he executed

---

[1] By resolution of April 3, 1875. Senate Reports, 44th Cong. 2nd sess., no. 689, p. 9; Coolidge, Chinese Immigration, chap. vi.

[2] Senate Reports, 44th Cong. 2nd sess., no. 689, p. 180; Gibson, The Chinese in America, pp. 311–3; Coolidge, Chinese Immigration, pp. 111–20.

[3] Gibson, The Chinese in America, p. 299.

[4] App. Ann. Cyclop. for 1876, p. 85; cf. Senate Reports, 44th Cong. 2nd sess., no. 689, p. 64; Gibson, The Chinese in America, p. 295.

[5] Sess. Laws of Cal. for 1876, p. 906; Senate Reports, 44th Cong. 2nd sess., no. 689, p. 478; Eaves, Labor Legislation in California, p. 148.

a skillful maneuver.[1] On April 20, 1876, he offered a resolution in the Senate urging the President to begin negotiations for a change in the treaty "to permit the application of restrictions upon the great influx of Chinese subjects to this country," [2] and he found the opportunity, on May 1st, to speak at length upon the topic.[3]

The California senate committee, which had attacked the task in hand without delay, was a "star chamber" committee.[4] Practically all the testimony was on one side, that little which was favorable to the Chinese was perverted by transcription.[5] But Sargent freely used this report. Though the importation of coolies was forbidden by statute, he said, it was the "almost universal conviction of Californians" that nine-tenths of the immigration was in violation of the law, that, though the importation of women for immoral purposes was prohibited, ninety-nine hundredths of the female immigration from China was of this character.[6] Sargent did not spare the enemy. He spoke of the inordinate influx of "corrupt humanity." [7] It was "peopling America with slaves." Our tolerance was "encouraging the darkest crimes against humanity, rather than opening our portals to the distressed of the earth." [8] The country was being converted into a "mere slop pail." Such conditions were "unendurable" to California and were "a near calamity to the whole nation." [9] The future would see San Francisco "a purely Asiatic city." [10] All America in the end would be compelled "to seek some other land to gain a subsistence." [11]

Senator Mitchell of Oregon also spoke. "The golden shores

[1] Gibson, Chinese in America, pp. 313-4.
[2] Cong. Record, 44th Cong. 1st sess., p. 2639.
[3] Ibid., pp. 2850-58.
[4] Senate Reports, 44th Cong. 2nd sess., no. 689, p. 212.
[5] Cf. Gibson, Chinese in America, pp. 325-6; Coolidge, Chinese Immigration, chap. vi; Eaves, op. cit., pp. 148-9.
[6] Cong. Record, 44th Cong. 1st sess., pp. 2850, 4418.
[7] Ibid., p. 2856.
[8] Ibid., p. 2854.
[9] Ibid., p. 2856.
[10] Ibid., p. 2851.
[11] Ibid., p. 2853.

of the Pacific," he said, were being "flooded with the serfs, the criminals, the mendicants, the opium-eating gamblers, the leprous prostitutes, the most debased in every sense of the word of the Chinese Empire." This "viper" must be crushed out "in its infancy"; should it live and grow it would "gnaw with deadening effect at the very vitals of the civilization of this country."[1] The Six Companies, in return, forwarded a memorial to Grant to controvert in some degree, if they could, the savage animadversions of their enemies.[2]

It was the year of a Presidential election when party managers were unusually sensitive to drafts of "public opinion." The national Republican convention, which, in June, 1876, nominated Hayes, declared it to be the "immediate duty of Congress to fully investigate the effect of the immigration of Mongolians upon the moral and material interests of the country." [3] The Democrats, when choosing Tilden as their candidate, denounced a policy which had "exposed our brethren of the Pacific coast to the incursions of a race not sprung from the same great parent stock." They demanded "such modification of the treaty with the Chinese Empire, or such legislation, within constitutional limitations," as would "prevent further importation or immigration of the Mongolian race." [4]

It was plain that some measures should be taken looking to the mollification of men clothed with the franchise who used such language in such heat. Page, who was a Republican, pressed a resolution to adoption in the House, requesting the President to open negotiations with China with a view to modifying the Burlingame treaty, so that its provisions might be restricted to "commercial purposes." [5] Piper, a Democratic member from San Francisco, secured the passage in the House of a joint resolution (the Senate not concurring), asking the President to submit to the Chinese government a proposal to add to the treaty an article which should expressly reserve

---

[1] Cong. Record, 44th Cong. 1st sess., pp. 3099, 3102.
[2] Gibson, op. cit., pp. 315–23.
[3] McPherson's Handbook for 1876, p. 211.
[4] Ibid., p. 216.
[5] Cong. Record, 44th Cong. 1st sess., p. 2158.

the right "to regulate, restrict or prevent the immigration of Chinese subjects into the United States, except for commercial pursuits." [1]   Nothing ensued; but the suggestion in the Republican national platform was adopted, and Congress authorized the appointment of a joint committee of the Senate and House of Representatives to proceed to California and to examine into, to consider and to report upon, the whole Chinese question.   Seven thousand dollars were set aside for its use. [2] The three senators on the committee were Morton of Indiana, who came to the subject with the liberality of feeling with which he viewed the negro, and who became the chairman, Cooper of Tennessee and Sargent.   The Speaker of the House appointed Piper, Meade of New York and James Wilson of Iowa, which left Page sputtering with such rage that the clerks were directed to exclude his remarks from the Record. [3]   The committee, barring Wilson, who declined to serve and did not attend any of the sessions, [4] reached San Francisco in October, while the Presidential campaign was at the height of its bitterness, and established their headquarters in a suite in the Palace Hotel.

Attorneys appeared for the interests concerned.   One represented the senate of the state of California, whose committee, under the goad of popular feeling had so quickly completed its task.   No one, except those who had been swept away by the prevailing excitement, attached value to its report, though the pamphlet was put into the hands of the members of the Federal committee with the purpose of coloring their views. [5] Sargent and Piper were demagogues of so high a rank that nothing more, it would seem, could have been required in this direction, but other talent of the same kind was provided, lest some opportunity for making a point against the China-

[1] June 10, 1876, Cong. Record, 44th Cong. 1st sess., p. 3763.

[2] Cong. Record, 44th Cong. 1st sess., pp. 4418–21, 4507, 4605, 4671–2, 4678, 4705, 4772, 4910, 5060, 5697.

[3] Ibid., p. 5697.

[4] Ibid., 45th Cong. 2nd sess., p. 1553.

[5] The pamphlet bears the title, "Chinese Immigration: the Social, Moral and Political Effect of Chinese Immigration," and covers 173 pages. As to its want of value see G. F. Seward, Chinese Immigration, pp. 226–7.

man should escape the intelligence of those two indomitable
defenders of our Aryan civilization. A notorious lawyer
and politician, named Pixley, who believed that the Chinese
were "the inferiors of any race God ever made," [1] and had
shouted one time that he would like to stand on Telegraph
Hill and see all of them hanged from the yardarms, and the
ships bearing them burned as they came into the harbor,[2]
represented the municipality of San Francisco. Still another
man voiced the same aversions and antipathies in behalf of
the Anti-Coolie Clubs. The Chinese, on their side, were
defended by two very capable and intelligent men, one, Colonel
F. A. Bee, who had come around the Horn with the pioneers,
and was employed by the Six Companies, and the other, B. S.
Brooks, who, like Bee, had arrived with the '49ers and had
seen San Francisco grow from a camp of a few tents and adobe
houses to a great city, and who purported to be a volunteer
in the service of an injured people.

The hearings were largely conducted, on the one side, by Pixley and Sargent, and, on the other side, by Bee and Brooks, with
Senator Morton acting as an intercessor. Among the witnesses
were vessel owners, shipping line agents and ship captains;
merchants and farmers, including Colonel Hollister, one of
the largest proprietors of land devoted to agricultural uses
in California; [3] physicians and lawyers; insurance men; health,
police, immigration and consular officers; tax collectors and
fire marshals; owners of property leased to the Chinese; judges
and ex-judges; the mayor and ex-mayors of San Francisco;
ex-Governors Low and Haight; Charles Crocker, the contractor
for the Central Pacific Railroad, and other builders of railways
and employers of the Chinese; heads of employment bureaus;
labor leaders and officers of the anti-Chinese associations;
Henry George, and, more interesting than all the rest, several

---

[1] Senate Reports, 44th Cong. 2nd sess., no. 689, p. 370; cf. Gibson, Chinese in America, pp. 244, 268–9.

[2] Senate Reports, 44th Cong. 2nd sess., no. 689, pp. 370, 876.

[3] House Mis. Doc., 45th Cong. 2nd sess., no. 36, p. 34; C. Nordhoff,
California for Health, Pleasure and Residence, p. 125; C. H. Dall, My First
Holiday, pp. 266–70.

missionaries, with the Rev. Otis Gibson at their head.[1] These religious leaders, who had lived in China and were closely associated with the Chinese in San Francisco, who spoke to them in their own tongue, who understood their ambitions, who shared their sufferings and felt their wrongs, proved to be ugly men for Pixley, Sargent and the examiners. In short the committee heard from all classes of people who could be persuaded to come before it, from all parts of the state, and holding the most various views, except the Chinese themselves, not one of whom was called in for the enlightenment of the Congressional inquisitors.[2]

The case against the Chinese included statements of fact and expressions of prejudice and feeling which followed these lines—

There were in China about four hundred million people. They lived cheek by jowl in a country which was too small for their use. They lay but four weeks away from San Francisco, and the price of passage hither was only $40 on a steamer and but $25 or $30 on a sailing ship. The fare was at times as low as $12.[3] It was an "inexhaustible hive." [4] Soon the Pacific states would be "overrun by this pagan horde," unless bars were raised and they were prevented from coming into our ports.[5]

Unlike other immigrants the Chinese acquired none of our national traits. They purchased little or no land or real property, and contributed almost nothing in taxes to the support of the state, though they were a burden and a charge in many directions upon its treasury.[6] They had no children to send to the public schools. They made no homes here and took no steps toward acquiring citizenship, nor did they desire to do so.[7] They

---

[1] The worthy successor of the Rev. William Speer, the missionary in San Francisco who so long had pleaded for justice and humanity in our dealings with the race.—Cf. Gibson, Chinese in America, pp. 161–2.

[2] A number of Chinese appeared, not very successfully, as witnesses before the committee of the California state senate.

[3] Cf. Gibson, Chinese in America, pp. 341–2.

[4] Senate Reports, 44th Cong. 2nd sess., no. 689, p. 31.

[5] Ibid., p. 10.

[6] Ibid., pp. 10, 16.

[7] They would say, "Me no likee Melican man; me no sabe Melican government."—Cong. Record, 44th Cong. 1st sess., p. 3101.

escaped jury service and military duty   They contributed
nothing to the support of the charitable and other communal
institutions of the land to which they came.[1] At first, it had
been said that they would introduce the culture of tea and
rice and the manufacture of silks. But not one acre of land
was yet planted with rice; not one tea shrub was set in the
ground; not a single industry peculiar to them and to their
country had been established in America [2] for the increase
of the national wealth. They gave their allegiance to the Six
Companies rather than to the city or the state in which they
dwelt. It was through their own organizations that they were
taxed, punished and governed. Their object in coming to America was to secure and lay by money—this done, it was, in
most cases, their aim to return to China. A few hundred dollars was a fortune upon which they could be happy at home
for the rest of their lives.[3] They traded among themselves, not
with white men.[4] They saved their money and took it or sent it
back to China, thus draining the country of its precious metals.
No women came out with them except one or two thousand
prostitutes who were bought and transferred by bills of sale like
cattle, at a price ranging from $300 to $900 each,[5] and who
were held in "the most degrading and abominable slavery." [6]
When a Chinaman died his remains were taken through the
streets amid burning joss paper and other odd ceremonies to
a cemetery to be held there until a cargo of bones should ac-
cumulate, when they would be carried to China for final sepul-
ture.[7] He would not even trust his dead body to the country
in which he made his money.[8] While some went home alive
and some in the "bone ships," most of the immigrants re-

[1] Senate Reports, 44th Cong. 2nd sess., no. 689, p. 33.
[2] Ibid., p. 17.
[3] Ibid., p. 16.
[4] Ibid., p. 33.
[5] Ibid., p. 22.
[6] Ibid., p. 16; cf. ibid., pp. 14 and 15; cf. Gibson, The Chinese in America,
chap. vii.
[7] Senate Reports, 44th Cong. 2nd sess., no. 689, pp. 16, 93.
[8] Cf. corr. N. Y. Nation, May 4, 1882.—The Chinese came "only on an
industrial predatory tour."

mained, burdening San Francisco, California, and the whole Pacific coast with an "indigestible mob of barbarians." [1]

Their competition in the labor market comprehended every field. In domestic service as cooks, butlers, waiters at table and "handy men" in the house, even, in tending children, they had their value, proof of this being found in the great numbers of them who were thus employed. [2] At least 7,000 held such positions, excluding as many white women from lucrative labor. [3] The "China boys" performed practically all kinds of "light labor," being particularly expert in work calling for the dexterous use of the fingers. They had nearly monopolized laundering—their washhouses were set about in all parts of San Francisco—cigar making, the manufacture of carpet slippers, overalls, shoes and sewing machine labor generally. They were largely engaged in assorting and re-packing teas, in silk and woolen manufacture, in picking, dry-ing and canning berries and fruits, in gardening, in cutting and harvesting grain crops, in hop-picking and vine-growing, in building levees for the reclamation of swamp and tule lands, in railroad construction, in placer mining and in fishing, in which employments, it was said, they had nearly driven out white labor. They peddled vegetables and fruits upon the streets. [4]

At home their wages were from $3 to $10 a month; [5] in Cali-fornia, working as domestic servants, from $3 to $8 a week. Laborers generally got from fifty cents to a dollar a day, board-ing themselves. [6] It was another "irrepressible conflict." [7] The Chinaman in the labor market undersold the Caucasian because his wants were small. His diet was rice, dried fish, dessicated vegetables, costing a few cents a day. [8] Labor of this kind was driving out of the field men with wives and children who were trying to live like civilized beings.

Furthermore the Chinese paid almost no rent. A white

[1] Senate Reports, 44th Cong. 2nd sess., no. 689, p. 31.
[2] G. F. Seward, Chinese Immigration, pp. 124–6, 133–5.
[3] Senate Reports, 44th Cong. 2nd sess., no. 689, pp. 33, 247.
[4] Ibid., pp. 17, 18.
[5] Ibid., p. 15.
[6] Ibid., p. 18.
[7] Ibid., p. 81.
[8] Ibid., pp. 19, 220.

man must have separate bedrooms for himself and his children. The Chinaman slept on a mat on the floor, or on a shelf packed against another one. One hundred Chinese occupied a space in which the poorest American family would think itself crowded. "Chinatown" in San Francisco was found at times in winter, during the rainy season, when work was slack, to contain as many as 75,000 souls. It was "heart, hive and home" of all the Chinese on the Pacific coast, and they left it for employment in smaller cities, where they formed smaller "Chinatowns," [1] or for the farms and mines of the interior, with the intention of return. Sixty thousand or 75,000 people, whatever the population of the quarter might be, practically all laborers without family relationships, lived in six or seven city blocks, in rookeries filled with decks and partitions, on balconies, in garrets, on roofs, in caves and tunnels underground,[2] "as thick as maggots in cheese." [3] Soon they would have possession of ten blocks.[4] "Chinatown" lay as "a black desert" athwart the way leading from one of the handsomest residential portions of the city to its business district.[5] It was "such a spectacle of squalor, filth, disease, wretchedness and crime," the anti-Chinese attorneys told the Congressional committee, as had never elsewhere been witnessed.[6] Without ventilation, drainage or sunlight it was "a seething mass of corruption." [7] It menaced the rest of the city with fire.[8]

The quarter might be raided in the interest of public health, but its inhabitants went back as fast as the police could take them out.[9] If they were gone and their places were occupied

[1] Cf. Senate Reports, 44th Cong. 2nd sess., no. 689, pp. 36, 309, 1109; cf. S. Bowles, Our New West, p. 394.

[2] Senate Reports, 44th Cong. 2nd sess., no. 689, pp. 129–30, 220–21.

[3] Cong. Record, 44th Cong. 1st sess., p. 2851.

[4] Senate Reports, 44th Cong. 2nd sess., no. 689, p. 160.

[5] Cf. Cong. Record, 44th Cong. 1st sess., p. 2852.

[6] Senate Reports, 44th Cong. 2nd sess., no. 689, p. 21.

[7] Ibid., p. 1188.

[8] Cf. Cong. Record, 44th Cong. 1st sess., p. 2852. See Report of Committee of Cal. State Senate, p. 53, and, in the same sense, a report of a subcommittee of the California state senate which visited the Chinese quarter in ibid., pp. 43–6.

[9] Senate Reports, 44th Cong. 2nd sess., no. 689, p. 1144.

by 60,000 white workingmen, each the head of a family of five,[1] it was easy to see, said the anti-Chinese agitators, that there would be 300,000 additional white people "to build over our peninsula." It were better to leave the gold in the earth, the tule lands unreclaimed, railroads unbuilt. Manufactures could await development with white labor. If capitalists and employers must seize for themselves the percentage of profit which they could "pinch from American laborers" by the use of these aliens, who could "live on the smell of a greasy rag," [2] California might better rely for its growth upon "less exacting and grasping men." [3]

That the Chinese came out voluntarily would be admitted,[4] while again they would be spoken of as "coolies" (which it was explained, though vainly, was only a name borrowed from India for laborers generally), "peons" and a "servile" people, brought here under contract.[5]

They were under indenture, if they were not actually servile. They were engaged to go out to America for three or five years for as many dollars a month. Money for passage hither was advanced to them in this country. There were laws against bringing in coolies or contract laborers, dating from 1862 and 1867,[6] but it was impossible for consuls at foreign ports to investigate all those to whom they gave certificates as "free passengers," [7] and it was said and believed that such men as we at the time placed in consular posts were unfit for, when they were honest in, the performance of their tasks.[8] Coolies came as before. They worked in gangs like slaves under headmen and they were kept at work through intimidation. Woe betide them if they should attempt to go

[1] Senate Reports, 44th Cong. 2nd sess., no. 689, p. 19.
[2] Ibid., p. 260.
[3] Ibid., p. 31.
[4] Ibid., p. 15.
[5] Cf. Wm. Speer, The Oldest and the Newest Empire, p. 478.
[6] U. S. Statutes at Large, vol. 12, pp. 340–41; ibid., vol. 15, p. 269; cf. Wm. Speer, The Oldest and the Newest Empire, pp. 479–85; Harper's Magazine, June, 1864; J. W. Foster, Am. Diplomacy in the Orient, pp. 280 et seq.
[7] Senate Reports, 44th Cong. 2nd sess., no. 689, p. 85.
[8] Cf. G. F. Seward, Chinese Immigration, pp. 265–8.

home or make other effort to escape the toils of the usurers who had brought them here. There were "highbinders," hired assassins, to see that the contracts were kept, which gave rise to violence and crime in Chinatown, whereof accounts now and again filled the newspapers.[1]

The moral condition of the immigrants was pronounced very ill. They were of the poorest and lowest classes from in and about Canton and were shipped out, usually, through the British port of Hong Kong.[2] Some who had come were declared to be pirates and river thieves. At least one such cargo had reached San Francisco a while ago and, since Justice Field's decision, there was no power at hand to turn them back. The "Page law," like the anti-coolie law, was of no value. Permits continued to be issued by the consuls in China without investigation.[3] If ships laden with criminals and prostitutes, it was observed, should freely enter the harbors of Boston and New York the whole East would be aroused; the country then would know the meaning of California's complaint.[4]

In religion the Chinese were idolatrous, they were "atheists and heathens." Their "joss-houses" were full of horrible painted deities which they worshiped instead of God.[5] They burned incense and made prostrations before the "tablets" of their ancestors,—pieces of wood bearing the names of their fathers and grandfathers,[6] which they set up on every side. They fed their dead on roast pork, chicken and tea. If they were Confucians it was not allowed that they followed the precepts of Confucius. They disregarded, if they had knowledge of the value or meaning of oaths, so that the truth could not be got out of them.[7] It was impossible to deal with them in the accustomed manner in the courts.

The efforts of the various churches to Christianize the Chinese were as nothing at all. No sympathy need be spent

---

[1] Cf. Senate Reports, 44th Cong. 2nd sess., no. 689, p. 94; cf. Gibson, The Chinese in America, p. 137.
[2] Senate Reports, 44th Cong. 2nd sess., no. 689, pp. 66, 85, 97.
[3] Ibid., pp. 986-7.
[4] Ibid., pp. 25-6.
[5] Ibid., p. 494.
[6] Ibid., p. 502.
[7] Ibid., pp. 13-5.

on "well-fed, well-salaried and comfortable missionaries" who, enjoined by Scriptural authority "to go forth from Boston to teach the Gospel in heathen lands," stopped in San Francisco where they were pleased to find California, for their convenience, importing the heathen.[1] Instead of "Christianizing the heathen" the process in California might better be called "heathenizing the Christian."[2]

The Chinese had no appreciation of the decencies of life. They lived like animals. Their sleeping rooms were closed at night; no air entered; filth and stench were on every side. They played tan, drew lotteries, smoked and ate opium, enticed young boys into their houses of ill fame. There were leprosy and small pox among them. Recently fourteen or fifteen lepers had been assembled and deported.[3] In 1876 the most alarming accounts of sanitary and health conditions in "Chinatown" were put in circulation. A small pox epidemic was imminent, if not at hand.[4] Disease, it was said, was concealed in the slippers and overalls coming from the factories in which Chinese were employed,[5] in the cigars which they had dampened with their saliva and rolled.[6] Since there were no white servants to be had the daughters of good families were working at the washboard to avoid infection in laundered clothes which the Chinese spattered with spittle in their washhouses.[7] Some prostitutes, as well as lepers, with the assistance of the Chinese merchants, had been sent away,[8] but without material improvement in conditions. "Chinatown" was a plague spot. It was to this evil and unsanitary quarter that laborers, even domestic servants employed in household service, returned each night, from it that they issued the next morning. A dreadful picture was drawn for all to see. The

---

[1] Senate Reports. 44th Cong. 2nd sess., no. 689, pp. 31, 584.
[2] Ibid., p. 259.
[3] Ibid., pp. 131-2, 182, 199-201.
[4] Ibid., pp. 128-9.
[5] Ibid., p. 139.
[6] Cf. Gibson, Chinese in America, p. 103.
[7] Ibid., p. 102; Senate Reports, 44th Cong. 2nd sess., no. 689, p. 245.
[8] Senate Reports, 44th Cong. 2nd sess., no. 689, p. 397; cf. Gibson, op. cit., p. 145.

Chinese were "filthy, vicious, ignorant, depraved and criminal"—they were "a standing menace to our free institutions and an ever threatening danger to our republican form of government." [1]

Anyhow the Chinese did not want the Burlingame treaty. It was not of their seeking. They disapproved of the emigration of their people—it was a movement in contravention of all their traditions. Burlingame had made the treaty on his own account and there was doubt whether it had ever been ratified by any competent authority representing the Chinese government. [2] Only 5,000 Americans resided in all China, and they enjoyed no such privileges as were accorded the Chinese in this country. The balance of trade was against us in our exchanges. Commerce with China was not worth a thousandth part of what it cost in damage to California and the Pacific coast.

On the other side men of intelligence, substance and influence appeared to say that they valued the Chinaman. He was a "labor machine" and the best in the country. California had needed him. [3] It still needed him. The early inhabitants of the state were adventurers drawn from all parts of the world, interested in gaining their fortunes quickly by speculation, particularly in the mines. White immigrants now still would say that they had not come to work—they came to make money. [4] There was no class of white men or women which could be drawn upon for labor involving steady and responsible application. Every householder, every man with capital who wished to make it active, every employer knew too well that this was true. Only the presence of the Chinese had rendered possible the development of California from the position of a mining camp to a substantial commonwealth. [5]

They were mild, pacific, docile, [6] respectful and subordinate.

---

[1] Senate Reports, 44th Cong. 2nd sess., no. 689, p. 34.

[2] Ibid., p. 28.

[3] Ibid., pp. 35, 440.

[4] Ibid., p. 440; cf. ibid., p. 623.

[5] Cf. Scribner's Magazine, May, 1871, pp. 66–7.

[6] One observer from the Eastern states called their rather indifferent attitude to what lay about them a "sluggish decorum"; even when taking their pleasure, as in gambling, they acted like "a crowd of blacksnakes on

They were the "most industrious people in the world" [1] and could be seen in all parts of the state working like bees. A woolen manufacturer said that they were "the most powerful imitators" of whom he had knowledge. [2] Show them once and they could perform any operation. An employer of white men was never certain until Monday morning whether his workmen would arrive for the labor of the following week. But there were no strikes among the Chinese. [3]

Four-fifths of the grading on the Central Pacific Railroad had been done by Chinamen; [4] 10,000 of them had been employed in completing that work. [5] They were building the new Southern Pacific [6] and lateral railways in California. Though in general it was true that the Chinese were seldom used in underground mining, in foundries, in operating machinery, in heavy stone work, in the forests or in any capacity involving the management of horses, [7] they had been given successful trial by the Central Pacific Railroad contractors in work of this kind. Even in blasting and rock cutting in the tunnels Crocker said that they were better than Cornish miners who were put beside them. [8] In no other way could the line have been built. The wild assertions of the demagogues that it were better had the road never been constructed it were folly to discuss. [9]

In 1876 there were 800,000 tons of wheat in California to be harvested and sent to market. The growth of this crop had become one of the state's most important commercial interests. It was founded on Chinese labor. There was no other field

a rather cold day in May." (C. Nordhoff, California for Health, Pleasure and Residence, pp. 85–6.) They were no more disturbed by what went on before them than "slugs on a garden wall." (C. H. Dall, My First Holiday, p. 106.) " Always busy yet never hurried," their faces wore an appearance of "half contempt" for our haste and barbarism.—C. L. Brace, The New West, p. 208.

[1] Rev. Otis Gibson, in Senate Reports, 44th Cong. 2nd sess., no. 689, p. 432. Ex-Governor Low said, "they are the most industrious people I ever saw."—Ibid., p. 70.

[2] Ibid., p. 554.
[3] Ibid., p. 608; cf. ibid., p. 669.
[4] Ibid., pp. 77–8.
[5] Ibid., pp. 669, 724.

[6] Ibid., pp. 504, 600.
[7] Ibid., pp. 303, 604.
[8] Ibid., pp. 78, 667, 691.
[9] Ibid., pp. 522–3.

hand so good, not even the Swede, and he was the best white man.[1] No Irish hoodlum who was stoning Mongolians in San Francisco would go out to a farm at harvest time, though he were to receive two dollars and a half a day, the wages which white men asked and commanded. Anyhow, if white labor were to be had, the farmers could not pay for it. At such prices they could not move their crops to the seaports and ship their wheat to Europe to compete with grain from the shores of the Mediterranean.[2]

Some of this wheat was grown on tule lands in the deltas and on the margins of rivers.[3] No less than a million acres, on which from 50 to 90 bushels of wheat to the acre could be gleaned, the richest in the state, had been reclaimed by the Chinese. Standing in water to their waists, stung by mosquitoes, they patiently labored day by day, digging ditches and raising dikes. In no other manner could work of this kind have been performed.[4] Labor Leagues, Eight Hour Clubs, Anti-Coolie Clubs were challenged to produce evidence in another sense. Irrigating canals for farming purposes, dams, canals for supplying mines with water, wagon roads—all were the products of Chinese industry and toil.

Ten years since California had sent $40,000,000 a year to the Eastern states for manufactured goods. But, with the aid of Chinese labor, there had been such a development of manufactures that barely one-half of that amount was now paid to the East for its products.[5] Cordage which came from New Bedford, boots and shoes imported from New England and Philadelphia were now made at home. Two-thirds of all the cigars used on the Pacific coast were made in San Francisco.[6]

Men borrowing money for commercial operations must pay as much as one or one and a half per cent a month for its use.

[1] C. L. Brace, The New West, p. 440.
[2] Ibid., p. 40; cf. G. F. Seward, Chinese Immigration, p. 55.
[3] Cf. G. F. Seward, Chinese Immigration, pp. 30–31, 165–6; C. Nordhoff, Northern California, pp. 127 et seq.
[4] Senate Reports, 44th Cong. 2nd sess., no. 689, pp. 40, 78, 438, 442.
[5] Ibid., pp. 44, 516.
[6] Ibid., p. 618.

Without cheap labor they could not compete with the East where the prevailing rate was six per cent a year.[1] Indeed without the Chinese there could have been no manufacturing in California.[2] Manufacturers of many and very various articles appeared before the committee of Congress to attest to the value of the Chinese as workmen and to the important, if not indispensable, part which they had had in the industrial development of the state.

The Chinese instead of hampering the development of the Pacific slope had vastly stimulated it. While before the Burlingame treaty San Francisco had had only a few clippers engaged in the Oriental trade there were now more than 400,000 tons of shipping which was employed in carrying Chinese merchandise to the United States and flour and other goods to China.[3] The government had been obliged to coin a "trade dollar" to supply the needs of, and to facilitate, our growing commerce with the Orient. Silver was a leading product of the Pacific coast where dwelt the very people who were now so unreasoningly engaged in jeopardizing treaty relations with one of the greatest silver-using nations of the world.[4]

Many thousands of families had come to California for the simple purpose of getting free of the tyranny of white servants and of enjoying the cheap fruits and vegetables which the Chinese produced.[5] More farming land to till, more railroads to cheapen and quicken communication, more factories, more industries, if they were furnishing work to the Chinese, also widened the opportunities and extended employment for white men. New avenues were opened for the display of enterprise, new labor was provided in fields which the Chinese could not enter, new facilities were at hand for the accumulation of wealth.[6] All southern California at and around Los Angeles had been started on the way to its future importance by the

---

[1] Senate Reports, 44th Cong. 2nd sess., no. 689, pp. 41, 818.
[2] Ibid., p. 90.
[3] Ibid., pp. 41, 618.
[4] Cong. Record, 47th Cong. 1st sess., p. 2136.
[5] Senate Reports, 44th Cong. 2nd sess., no. 689, pp. 451, 458.
[6] Ibid., pp. 400, 435, 515.

construction of the Southern Pacific down the San Joaquin valley from San Francisco. This railroad could not have been built without Chinese labor. Towns, whole counties, containing land which a little while ago had been rentable only at ten cents an acre, had become populous as by the wave of a wand.[1]

Without the Chinese, a well known employer of labor said, California would not have had one-half of its present material wealth. The value of what the Chinese had produced, said another, was equal to what had come out of the mines, not only of that state, but of Nevada and Dakota as well.[2] Laborers had raised a clamor against the cradle when it replaced the sickle and, in turn, against the reaper which followed the cradle. Railroads were cried down by the breeders of horses and the stagecoach drivers. The descendants of these men were complaining about the Chinese.[3]

It was agreed that "Chinatown" was filthy. But so were the "Barbary Coast," "Tar Flat," "Ragtown" and other parts of San Francisco, in which poor white men dwelt.[4] So were the "Five Points" in New York[5] and the tenement house districts of all great cities throughout the world. One reason why "Chinatown" was so dirty was that the municipal authorities excepted the quarter from public cleaning, and compelled the Chinese to make provision for the removal of their own offal.[6] If the city should clean "Chinatown" and furnish the poor with water, at a price which would bring it within their reach, it would be clean.[7] If the public health officers were to perform their duties in a proper and effective manner there need be little fear of disease appearing in, and

---

[1] Senate Reports, 44th Cong. 2nd sess., no. 689, pp. 776–7.

[2] Ibid., p. 438.

[3] Ibid., pp. 692–3.

[4] Ibid., p. 648.

[5] Henry Ward Beecher said that there were 290,000 people living on one square mile of ground in New York which would gain 50 per cent if she could exchange her tenement quarters for San Francisco's "Chinatown."— Phila. Inquirer, March 4, 1879.

[6] Senate Reports, 44th Cong. 2nd sess., no. 689, pp. 217–9, 649.

[7] Ibid., pp. 59, 170–71, 648.

spreading out of, such a center.[1] Reputable physicians said that the panic which the agitators were trying to raise on this subject was a "farce." [2] The Chinese washed their bodies from head to foot daily. Their clothes were clean.[3] Their most fanatical foes must admit that they were sober. Many witnesses appeared to declare that they had never seen a drunken Chinaman.[4]

It was plain enough, too, that very few used opium; none smoked it while at work,[5] in spite of the emphasis which the anti-Chinese spokesmen put upon the prevalence and demoralizing effect of this vice. Anyhow that indulgence stupefied and never led to violence.[6] There were Chinese prostitutes, but they were not so numerous, nor were they so active in plying their seductions and wiles for the unsettlement of the morals of the community as the French.[7] Physicians, to the horrification of many good persons, told the committee that there were too few for the Chinese male population—they said that there should be more women rather than less.[8] There were few fires in "Chinatown." Insurance men disproved the charge that the Chinese were a menace in this regard.[9]

In Bret Harte's despite, when he attached to the "heathen Chinee" a reputation "for ways that are dark and tricks that are vain," they were, it was said, honest. There were few thieves among them and no beggars.[10] Laborers kept their contracts conscientiously.[11] They were truthful.[12] The Chinese mer-

---

[1] Senate Reports, 44th Cong. 2nd sess., no. 689, pp. 187–8; cf. ibid., pp. 130, 644.

[2] Ibid., pp. 645–6.

[3] Ibid., pp. 59, 581, 644–5, 715, 819; cf. Cong. Record, 44th Cong. 3rd sess., p. 1387; C. L. Brace, The New West, p. 211.

[4] Senate Reports, 44th Cong. 2nd sess., no. 689, pp. 45, 60, 581, 603, 608, 644, 653, 669, 820; cf. Cong. Record, 47th Cong. 1st sess., p. 1520; S. Bowles, Across the Continent, p. 241.

[5] Senate Reports, 44th Cong. 2nd sess., no. 689, p. 772.

[6] Ibid., pp. 221–2, 772.

[7] Cf. ibid., p. 653.

[8] Ibid., pp. 141, 143, 652, 655–6.

[9] Ibid., p. 661.

[10] Ibid., pp. 582, 820; Cong. Record, 47th Cong. 1st sess., p. 1520.

[11] Senate Reports, 44th Cong. 2nd sess., no. 689, pp. 18, 43, 509, 544, 667.

[12] Ibid., p. 821.

chants were shrewd but high-minded and correct in their dealings with other business men.[1] As a class their credit was good,
and their mercantile houses were "unsurpassed" in San Francisco.[2] A Chinaman's word would be taken for a cargo of
goods, while a bond would be demanded of a white man.[3]

Though the Chinese reaching the United States were drawn
from the least educated classes it was denied that the immigrants were illiterate. Nearly all could read and write in their
own language.[4] The teachers in the mission schools in San
Francisco testified that the boys who came to them were apt
in study and eager for knowledge. No other class of foreigners
in America "with so little encouragement," said the Rev. Otis
Gibson, made "equal efforts to learn our language, laws and
customs."[5] Between 100 and 200 Chinese students were enrolled at colleges in the Eastern states.[6]

That the Chinese were a people of criminal instincts, who·
unduly taxed the correctional and penal systems of the city
and state, was an allegation palpably false. For the year ending June, 1876, 17,991 arrests were reported for the white
population of San Francisco and 2,117 for the Chinese. Therefore about ten per cent of all the arrests were of Chinese,[7] who,
however, were often taken into custody in answer to discriminative and special laws, and on flimsy pretexts.[8]

Anyone who would have had it appear that for one hundred
Chinese inhabitants of the city more arrests were made than
for one hundred whites must remember, said the defense,
that the Chinese were almost entirely an adult male population. For the purpose of the calculation, if comparisons were

[1] Senate Reports, 44th Cong. 2nd sess., no. 689, pp. 490, 510, 530–31,
542, 550, 558, 719, 763–4.
[2] Ibid., p. 619.
[3] Ibid., p. 543. For a picture of the Chinese Merchants' Exchange in
San Francisco see Harper's Weekly, March 18, 1882. "No greater contrast
can be imagined than that presented by a concourse of Chinese merchants
in this elegant structure and a gathering of 'hoodlums' in a grog shop to
rave and howl against these 'barbarians.'"—Ibid.
[4] Senate Reports, 44th Cong. 2nd sess., no. 689, pp. 491, 716–7; cf.
Report of Com. of California Senate, p. 84.
[5] Senate Reports, 44th Cong. 2nd sess., no. 689, p. 401.
[6] Ibid.   [7] Ibid., pp. 156–7.   [8] Ibid., pp. 164–5.

to be indulged in, women and children, who were not anywhere, as a rule, given, in great numbers, to violation of law, should be disregarded,[1] when the advantage would be seen to be largely on the side of the Chinese. Furthermore the comparison should be made with an adult foreign-born population, as, for instance, with the Irish.[2] There were in San Francisco 3,000 whiskey shops with which the "pagan Chinese" had nothing to do.[3] Much crime in the city grew out of the improper and excessive use of intoxicating liquor. More than one-third of the arrests were for drunkenness. Not one charge of this kind was lodged against a Chinaman.[4] There were comparatively few Chinese in the jails for any just reason, or in the almshouses, or in the hospitals.[5] That they were an onerous charge upon the white taxpayers, therefore, was a statement unsupported by the facts.[6] That they were really regarded by anyone of candor and intelligence as a disproportionately dangerous and criminal element was disproved by the circumstance that the chief of police of San Francisco assigned only seven or eight officers to "Chinatown," even during the winter when the population was so much increased.[7] The Chinese, or their Six Companies, were left to make their own police arrangements, just as they were given the task of cleaning their streets of garbage and filth.[8] To this end they hired, voluntarily or under blackmail, special policemen or watchmen to patrol their quarter of the city.[9] If the same ardor and diligence

[1] Cf. Senate Reports, 44th Cong. 2nd sess., no. 689, pp. 163–4, 167.

[2] Ibid., p. 402.

[3] Ibid., p. 402; cf. Gibson, The Chinese in America, pp. 357–8.

[4] Senate Reports, 44th Cong. 2nd sess., no. 689, p. 60.

[5] Ibid.; cf. Gibson, op. cit., pp. 364–5.

[6] Joaquin Miller wrote to the New York Tribune on February 23, 1879: "I sat on the bench as judge of this county [Grant County, Oregon] for four years and I will state, on the honor of a magistrate, that the calendar, both criminal and civil, showed the names of at least ten white men to one Chinaman, although the Chinese population during the most of this time outnumbered the white."—Quoted in Cong. Record, 47th Cong. 1st sess., p. 1520.

[7] Senate Reports, 44th Cong. 2nd sess., no. 689, p. 167.

[8] Ibid., pp. 217–9, 649.

[9] A "regular policeman" was asked during the hearings before the California state senate how "local" or "special" policemen were paid. "By

were used in ferreting out the faults of character of 30,000 immigrants from Europe of the common laboring classes the result, said Otis Gibson, could not fail to be "a chapter of crime, vices and misery quite equal to that presented against the Chinese." [1]

As for the country being covered ere long by Chinese the fear was born of foolishness and hysteria. The anti-Chinese leaders, the New York Tribune said, were "chasing a phantom." [2] Men saw a great many in San Francisco. They guessed that there must be 100,000, and then they imagined that 400,000,000 might cross the Pacific which would be the end of white civilization in America. But these hot spirits could be reminded that, if, after 25 years of immigration, only about 100,000 remained to tincture and adulterate our population 250 years would pass before we should have as many as a million. [3] There was a demand for Chinese labor else it would not have been attracted to California, nor would it have remained on the coast. The remedy was with the white people, resident in this part of the United States; when they should cease to employ Chinamen the immigration would cease.

It might be true that "Chinatown" was extending its boundaries, [4] that churches, hotels and other buildings were being abandoned when they stood in the path of the tide, and that surrounding property was losing its value for the purposes to which, up to this time, it had been devoted. [5] But owners of

residents on their beats," he answered. "In the Chinese quarter they are paid by Chinese. They have no regular price but get all they can." (Report of Cal. State Senate Committee, p. 61; cf. ibid., pp. 62, 75.) Some are said to have had an income of $1,000 a month.—Coolidge, Chinese Immigration, p. 417; cf. Gibson, The Chinese in America, p. 89.

[1] Senate Reports, 44th Cong. 2nd sess., no. 689, p. 402.

[2] Quoted in Gibson, The Chinese in America, pp. 22–3. But, said Henry George, "the wild mustard can crowd wheat from the field, sheep may drive from the pasture the stronger ox, the locust may put the buffalo to flight."— N. Y. Tribune, May 1, 1869.

[3] It was clear to him, said George F. Seward, the American secretary of legation at Peking, to Secretary Fish, under date of March 22, 1876, that no great immigration would take place. China was not so densely over-populated as some said and apparently believed, nor were the people so poor.—App. Ann. Cyclop. for 1876, pp. 231–2.

[4] Boundaries in 1876 defined in Gibson, The Chinese in America, p. 13.

[5] Senate Reports, 44th Cong. 2nd sess., no. 689, pp. 136, 160–61.

such property found their new tenants profitable,—they obtained, perhaps, twice as much from it as when it had been occupied by white men.[1] The Chinese paid their high rents punctually,[2] and the sum of the toll levied on them by white landlords in San Francisco was not less than a million dollars a year.[3] If "Chinatown" were growing in size so was the city of which it was a little part.[4]

The anti-Chinese agitation had not been started and it was not directed by old Californians who had labored for, and assisted in, the growth of the state. It did not represent California, or the feeling of her people, said Charles Crocker.[5] Others corroborated this view.[6] The ruction about the Chinese was begun and carried on by foreigners, and particularly by the Irish.[7] Their genius for making pother by talk and their quickness in putting their wits to work for their advantage in our politics was undeniably the principal force behind this piece of popular turbulence.[8] Men with capital, employers of labor, were for the Chinese.[9] The complaint about the want of employment, said ex-Governor Low, came from those who would not work under any circumstances.[10] Gentlemen of unquestioned integrity testified that, again and again, they had advertised for, and sought, labor. When responses were received at all they were from fellows who would not go to the places where the work was to be done, or do that kind of work which it was desired should be done.[11] Those who desired em-

[1] Senate Reports, 44th Cong. 2nd sess., no. 689, pp. 220, 255.
[2] Ibid., pp. 398, 648.
[3] Cf. Gibson, The Chinese in America, p. 347.
[4] Senate Reports, 44th Cong. 2nd sess., no. 689, p. 620.
[5] Ibid., p. 687.
[6] E.g., Joaquin Miller, Cong. Record, 47th Cong. 1st sess., p. 1520; C. Nordhoff, California for Health, Pleasure and Residence, p. 139.
[7] Senate Reports, 44th Cong. 2nd sess., no. 689, p. 49. They would punctuate street harangues with cries of "Immeriky fur Immerikans, bejabers."—Congregationalist, Dec. 21, 1881.
[8] Senate Reports, 44th Cong. 2nd sess., no. 689; cf. Gibson, The Chinese in America, p. 52.
[9] Senate Reports, 44th Cong. 2nd sess., no. 689, p. 399.
[10] Ibid., pp. 83-4.
[11] Cf. ibid., pp. 40, 721-31; cf. C. Nordhoff, Northern California, p. 143.

ployment would have it in the city. All lads wished to be clerks or to engage in light labor for short hours. Farmers and others settled in the interior would have been without cooks or servants of any kind but for the Chinese.[1] Opposition to them did not come, except in the unusual case, from business men or from native Americans.[2] It was confined to the white laboring class, and particularly the lazy oafs and blatherskites in that class, of alien nativity, with the favór and aid of demagogues who were seeking political preferment, and who wrote for the newspapers that were groveling for a larger circulation among the lower orders of mankind.

Though the contractors of the Central Pacific Railroad had sent circulars to every post office in the state, inviting white labor, they had failed to get more than 800 men for the work. It was in desperation, and as a last resort, that they had turned to the Chinese, with what result every one knew.[3] Of the white men who were employed on the road, Superintendent Strobridge said that seven-tenths got drunk as soon as they were paid.[4] If the Chinese, "instead of keeping themselves in their peculiar dress were to drink whiskey and patronize the barrooms," as the white laboring man did, observed one of the leading manufacturers of San Francisco, sardonically but sagely, the prejudice against them would "disappear immediately."[5]

Idleness there was, undoubtedly. The "Arabs" and "Mohawks" who gained the name of "hoodlums" in San Francisco, and children six and seven years old who were running through the city until two o'clock in the morning[6] were proof of depravity in youth, as well as of idleness. One reason for the hoodlum might be found in the fact that boys were excluded from learning trades, since the labor organizations, to keep up wages, limited the number of apprentices.[7]

[1] Senate Reports, 44th Cong. 2nd sess., no. 689, p. 745.
[2] Ibid., pp. 658, 721.
[3] Ibid., pp. 666–7.
[4] Ibid., pp. 726, 728.
[5] Ibid., p. 538.
[6] Ibid., pp. 495, 498.
[7] Ibid., pp. 81, 172, 190; cf. Gibson, Chinese Immigration, pp. 397–8.

That the Chinese did not buy real estate, or bring out their wives and children, or make homes, or interest themselves in our government to the point of expressing a desire to be naturalized and to vote, or of learning the English language and reading our newspapers and books, or of "assimilating" with the dominant white population of the country, as other new elements from Europe, and even the negroes, were wont to do, were facts susceptible of something akin to satisfactory explanation. Sufficient reason was found in the treatment which the Chinese had received in the Pacific coast states. They were the objects of insult, persecution and actual physical violence from the day of their setting foot upon our shores. Loaded on the wharves into open express wagons, to be conveyed behind scrawny mustangs to the company houses in "Chinatown," they would be stoned all the way to Kearny street. They virtually ran the gauntlet. Their scalps were cut, blood streamed down their faces leaving a red trail along the way.[1] At times when hostile and cruel men were in control of the customhouse the immigrants were sent forth from it nearly naked. The simple clothes on their backs being held to be dutiable, these would be seized and they would be discharged into the street without enough covering to protect them from the weather. Their later experiences in the country, to which they had innocently come, were not calculated to improve their impressions. Night after night, as they returned to their poor homes with their peddlers' baskets, it was with wounded heads and bloody garments. White hoodlums who infested the streets ready to commit any crime in the calendar,[2] catching a Chinaman in the city, would shower him with wet mortar from the beds around unfinished buildings, pelt him with rocks or any convenient missiles, lasso him with ropes, pursue him with dogs or, perhaps, deliberately strike him— if at close range—in the face.[3] He was subjected to insults

[1] Senate Reports, 44th Cong. 2nd sess., no. 689, pp. 37, 472, 602, 821, 912; cf. Gibson, The Chinese in America, pp. 50–52.
[2] Senate Reports, 44th Cong. 2nd sess., no. 689, p. 169.
[3] Ibid., pp. 472, 635; cf. C. L. Brace, The New West, pp. 211–3, and articles from newspapers quoted there.

"in every conceivable shape," which were "uncalled for even to a dog."[1] In the best cases young blackguards would hoot at him, pull his queue, knock off his hat, bespatter with mud the clothes which he had just laundered, jostle his baskets and overturn the contents into the gutter.[2] The chief of police of San Francisco, while under examination by the committee, said that the Chinese were "treated most outrageously." They were "stoned, beaten and abused in the most shameful manner." If a Chinaman were found alone he was "very fortunate" when he "escaped with his life," or a maiming.[3] Chasing "pigtails" was the sport of the youth of San Francisco. One hoodlum could drive fifty Chinamen before him.[4] Members of a political club going home from a meeting would destroy all the Chinese "washhouses" on the route, young ruffians hurled stones through the windows of mission schools which struck boys while they sat at their books,[5] and into hospitals containing the sick.[6] Even girls in the Methodist Mission, when they went abroad, were rudely assailed, though it be in the daytime and in sight of the City Hall.[7]

While it was said that the Chinese were less likely to be annoyed and attacked in the interior than in San Francisco they had active enemies in the "Pikes," the wandering gypsy-like "poor whites," who, in the country districts, were what the hoodlums were in the towns.[8] There had been atrocious outrages in Los Angeles, San Diego, Truckee and Antioch. In Los Angeles more than twenty were shot and hanged by a mob.[9]

---

[1] Senate Reports, 44th Cong. 2nd sess., no. 689, p. 820.

[2] Cf. Nordhoff, Northern California, p. 141; E. E. Baldwin, The Chinese Question, p. 6.

[3] Senate Reports, 44th Cong. 2nd sess., no. 689, p. 169.

[4] Cf. ibid., pp. 37, 169, 687; Gibson, The Chinese in America, pp. 327–9. "The slaves in the South were never treated like the Chinese are now being treated in California."—Interview with a New York Chinaman in N. Y. Tribune, Feb. 27, 1879.

[5] Senate Reports, 44th Cong. 2nd sess., no. 689, p. 501.

[6] Ibid., pp. 647, 650.

[7] Gibson, The Chinese in America, p. 298.

[8] C. Nordhoff, California for Health, Pleasure and Residence, pp. 137–9, 196, 232.

[9] Senate Reports, 44th Cong. 2nd sess., no. 689, p. 1007; App. Ann. Cyclop. for 1871, pp. 92–3.

In Truckee the cabins of the Chinese were set on fire and the inmates shot, as they ran from the blazing buildings.[1] In Antioch, at the end of April, 1876, all the Chinese in the place were driven out of the town and their houses burned to the ground.[2]

The entire police force of San Francisco numbered only 150 men,[3] who were fellows appointed as a reward for low party service. They usually stood by and laughed at the attacks on the Chinese; such incidents were treated humorously in the newspapers.[4] Very few offenders were ever arrested, practically none was ever convicted or punished for crimes committed upon Chinamen. Even for the most dastardly murders men went free. So far as appears no slayer of a Chinaman in twenty years had been hanged.[5] If one of the least of such outrages had been committed upon an American citizen in the Celestial Empire we should have risen with united resolution "to wipe China from the face of the earth."[6] So little resentful were the Chinese that, though the whites had cheated, robbed, beaten and killed them, they "returned it all with docility and faithful service," which seemed the more to enrage their persecutors.[7]

Authorized taxgatherers, or swindlers in their guise,[8] were met with on every hand. The Chinese were in the presence of the tax collector at the steamer landings, when they arrived, at the docks and the railway stations when they went away.[9]

---

[1] Senate Reports, 44th Cong. 2nd sess., no. 689, p. 912; Gibson, The Chinese in America, pp. 326–7.

[2] Senate Reports, 44th Cong. 2nd sess., no. 689, p. 1186; Cong. Record, 44th Cong. 1st sess., p. 3101; Gibson, The Chinese in America, p. 327. For a list of outrages upon the Chinese see D. O. Brooks, App. to Opening Statement and Brief on the Chinese Question, San Francisco, 1877.

[3] Senate Reports, 44th Cong. 2nd sess., no. 689, p. 60.

[4] Cf. San Francisco Examiner, March 6, 1882; cf. Gibson, The Chinese in America, pp. 51–2, 328–9.

[5] Senate Reports, 44th Cong. 2nd sess., no. 689, pp. 170, 912, 1007–8.

[6] Ibid., pp. 602, 660.

[7] C. L. Brace, The New West, pp. 209–10.

[8] N. Y. Tribune, May 1, 1869.

[9] Senate Reports, 44th Cong. 2nd sess., no. 689, pp. 215, 256, 481, 484, 995–7. The Chinese are the "first that the tax collector 'goes for' and the last he leaves in peace."—N. Y. Tribune, May 1, 1869.

Often they were made to pay two or three times over.[1] They paid school taxes, though their children were never received or taught in the white schools and no separate schools were provided for them;[2] poll taxes, though they could not vote;[3] hospital taxes, though they were not welcomed in the hospitals when they were sick, but were sent to the "Pest House";[4] road taxes though they had no horses or vehicles and did not use the roads.[5] They were prohibited from engaging in labor on any public work,—municipal, county or state.[6] When contractors employed them for private enterprises they were often cheated out of their wages[7] which, in any case, were always much lower than the white man's for equal or better service. They paid higher rents to their white landlords, by whom they were robbed by such a system, said Colonel Bee, as was "never before laid before the world."[8]

Under the recent excitement onerous and discriminative regulations were multiplied and more oppressive agents appeared to administer the laws. An act had been passed by the legislature in 1876 prohibiting the use by fishermen of nets with fine meshes. It was said that nearly a million dollars worth of shrimp and other small denizens of California's waters had been dried and exported to China in 1875. In 1880 the value of these exports was supposed to be $3,000,000. Only Chinamen were aimed at by those who had devised this law. Italians, Greeks and Dalmatians, who had votes, wanted the business for themselves.[9]

[1] Coolidge, Chinese Immigration, p. 81; How the U. S. Treaty with China is Observed, By Friends of International Right and Justice, San Francisco, 1877, p. 3.

[2] Gibson, The Chinese in America, pp. 270, 376; Coolidge, Chinese Immigration, p. 78.

[3] Senate Reports, 44th Cong. 2nd sess., no. 689, pp. 480–81; cf. House Mis. Doc., 45th Cong. 1st sess., no. 36, pp. 16, 18.

[4] Coolidge, Chinese Immigration, pp. 267–8; Gibson, The Chinese in America, pp. 70–71.

[5] Senate Reports, 44th Cong. 2nd sess., no. 689, p. 452.

[6] Ibid., p. 435.

[7] Ibid., p. 45.

[8] Ibid., p. 45.

[9] Ibid., p. 478; Coolidge, Chinese Immigration, p. 73; Alta California, Jan. 2, 1876, quoted in Coolidge, op. cit., p. 73; cf. App. Ann. Cyclop. for

The Chinese were prohibited by the Board of Supervisors of San Francisco in 1870 from carrying on the sidewalks of the city the baskets which it was their custom to suspend from poles fitted to their shoulders.[1] A tax of $10 a quarter was imposed upon the peddler who sold his wares from baskets. Only the Chinese did so. The white man who brought his vegetables, fruit and fish in a wagon, drawn by a horse, paid but $2.[2] The Chinaman who delivered the laundry in a basket must pay a license of $15 a quarter, while the white man, riding behind a horse, paid only $2, if he drove two horses, $4.[3] Enacted at first in 1873,[4] to be vetoed by the mayor,[5] the order was reënacted in 1876 and the poor Chinamen were put to the trouble and cost of going to court to have it set aside.[6] The legislature of California, on April 3, 1876, following earlier enactments of the same kind in San Francisco, dating back to 1870,[7] passed a law making it a misdemeanor, punishable by fine or imprisonment, for anyone to sleep in a room in which there were less than 500 cubic feet of air for each person occupying it.[8] It was enforced vindictively.[9] Chinamen, insufficiently clad, without regard to the weather, were dragged out of their sleeping quarters, tied together by their queues, hauled away and crammed into a filthy hole called a prison under the City Hall,[10] where there may have been eight cubic feet of air for each occupant. In 1873 as many as 75 or 100

1878, p. 71. This law, if passed, as it is declared to have been, is not included in the published statutes of the legislature for 1876.

[1] Eaves, Labor Leg. in Cal., p. 143; Gibson, op. cit., pp. 58–9.

[2] Senate Reports, 44th Cong. 2nd sess., no. 689, pp. 34, 38; cf. ibid., p. 894; Gibson, op. cit., pp. 58–9.

[3] Ordinance of June, 1873, no. 1098; Eaves, Labor Leg. in Cal., p. 144.

[4] Gibson, op. cit., pp. 282–3.

[5] Ibid., p. 284; Eaves, op. cit., pp. 144–5.

[6] Senate Reports, 44th Cong. 2nd sess., no. 689, p. 479.

[7] Eaves, op. cit., pp. 142–3, 143–4; Coolidge, Chinese Immigration, p. 261; cf. Report of Cal. State Senate, p. 75; Senate Reports, 44th Cong. 2nd sess., no. 689, p. 235; C. Nordhoff, Northern California, p. 142.

[8] Sess. Laws of Cal. for 1875–6, p. 759; App. Ann. Cyclop. for 1879, p. 120; Senate Reports, 44th Cong. 2nd sess., no. 689, pp. 154, 477; How the U. S. Treaty with China is Observed, 1877, pp. 4–7, 149.

[9] Ibid., p. 234; cf. Ho Ah Kow v. Nunan, 5 Sawyer, p. 552.

[10] Senate Reports, 44th Cong. 2nd sess., no. 689, pp. 62, 155, 191 655, 659–60.

would be brought in nightly. One police officer, who boasted of having arrested 1,100 Chinamen under the terms of an ordinance of this kind, while it was being enforced in San Francisco, crowded the jail and the court rooms with his prisoners and blocked the regular course of legal procedure.[1] The law was enacted and applied "simply and entirely to molest and drive out the Chinese."[2] If it had been enforced impartially and generally nearly every block of houses in the city, it was said, would have been found to be defective in this regard.[3]

The Chinese in San Francisco were taxed for taking up their dead for return to China. Efforts were made to prohibit disinterment absolutely. As it was it was made so expensive and so many regulations attended the exhumation and shipment of bones that it became nearly impossible for the Chinese to gratify a sentiment which had something like the force of a religious rite.[4] The restrictions were later incorporated in a state law.[5]

In ways other than by the basket laws the Chinese were persecuted and restrained in the conduct of the laundry business in which they were generally engaged. Ordinances were adopted in San Francisco prohibiting washing and ironing by hand,[6] confining "washhouses" to specified districts, forbidding work at night or on Sundays, requiring for this purpose the use of buildings of brick or stone, though nine-tenths of all the houses in the city were of wood, except by special permit which was given to the Irish but withheld from Chinamen.[7] The Chinese in San Francisco were arrested for exploding fire-

[1] Report of Committee of Cal. State Senate, p. 75; Senate Reports, 44th Cong. 2nd sess., no. 689, p. 234; Coolidge, Chinese Immigration, p. 261; cf. Ho Ah Kow v. Nunan, 5 Sawyer, p. 552.

[2] Senate Reports, 44th Cong. 2nd sess., no. 689, p. 655.

[3] Ibid., p. 659.

[4] Coolidge, Chinese Immigration, p. 264; Wm. Speer, The Oldest and the Newest Empire, pp. 615–6.

[5] Act of April 1, 1878, Sess. Laws of Cal. for 1877–8, p. 1050; cf. Coolidge, p. 261; House Mis. Doc., 46th Cong. 2nd sess., no. 5, p. 342; In re Wong Yung Quy, 2 Fed. Reporter, p. 624.

[6] Coolidge, Chinese Immigration, pp. 261, 269.

[7] Cf. Soon Hing v. Crowley, 113 U. S., p. 703; Yick Wo v. Hopkins, 118 U. S., p. 356; In re Quong Woo, 13 Fed. Reporter, p. 229; In re Wo Lee, 26 Fed. Reporter, p. 471; How the U. S. Treaty with China is Observed, pp. 8 et seq.; Eaves, op. cit., pp. 320–21.

crackers and for beating gongs in front of their theaters. Hours were set for their theatrical performances.[1]

It was said that the basket laws were passed because baskets were a nuisance on the sidewalks, that the regulations as to the exhumation of bones and the cubic air laws were in the interest of public health, that the laundry ordinances were designed as a protection against fire, but these were excuses, except, possibly, with reference to the disinterment of the dead, which little concealed the ends in view.

White men gambled day and night,[2] but Chinamen, for playing tan, or looking on, indeed, while it was being played, would be seized in a purely inquisitorial and malicious spirit. In 1878 seventy Chinamen were arrested as spectators in a gambling house, tried and sentenced to imprisonment for fifty days. They were kept in jail without fires, though it was cold weather, for twenty days before their friends could secure their release.[3] But control was spasmodic and confined to periods of public excitement, when crusades against "Chinese vice" were instituted for political effect. The dens in which gambling was carried on were a principal source of profit in bribes to white politicians connected with the city government.[4] The ordinances aimed at the use of opium also brought many Chinamen to arrest and punishment,[5] and now and again enriched the police.

Prostitution proceeded with little interference except when it involved the Chinese.[6] But, as in gambling, control, even of the Chinese women and of the landlords who leased real estate for such uses, was intermittent and in answer to public outcry—at other times corrupt white men identified with the government in San Francisco viewed it indulgently, so that they could levy blackmail and enjoy the graft.[7] White

---

[1] Coolidge, Chinese Immigration, p. 264.
[2] Ibid., pp. 451–2.
[3] House Mis. Doc., 45th Cong. 2nd sess., no. 36, p. 11.
[4] Gibson, The Chinese in America, pp. 89–90, 282, 329.
[5] Senate Reports, 44th Cong. 2nd sess., no. 689, p. 221.
[6] Cf. ibid., p. 144.
[7] Ibid., p. 450; cf. App. Ann. Cyclop. for 1878, p. 71; Gibson, The Chinese in America, pp. 155–7, 282; E. E. Baldwin, The Chinese Question, pp. 8–9.

men were concerned, in the first place, with the importation
of Chinese girls for immoral uses, and they profited from the
traffic from beginning to end.[1]

The queue was a characterizing mark of each Chinaman. It
was a prized possession and proof of position and caste. It
indicated loyalty to country and king. By losing it a man de-
nationalized himself and became "a waif in the world without a people and without a country."[2] Nor could he go
back to China without this long braid.[3] Yet to cut off
"pigtails" was the ambition of every hoodlum on the Pacific
coast.[4]

In June, 1873, the Board of Supervisors of San Francisco
decreed that any male incarcerated in the county jail should
have the hair of his head cut to a uniform length of one inch
from the scalp.[5] It met the veto of the mayor.[6] On June 14,
1876, the Board of Supervisors reënacted this law.[7] Each
Chinaman, therefore, after sentence, for no matter how short
a time, for no matter how trifling an offense, was put "under
the scissors" and lost his queue.[8] In April, 1878, a Chinaman,
Ho Ah Kow, who had been arrested for sleeping in a room containing too little air for his welfare, failed to pay his fine and
went to the county jail, where his "pigtail" was clipped.
He took his case to court, asking for $10,000 in damages from
the Irish sheriff who had done the deed. Reviewing the facts
and circumstances Justice Field in the Circuit Court said that

---

[1] Cf. Gibson, The Chinese in America, pp. 137–8.

[2] Ibid., pp. 118–20.

[3] Lippincott's Magazine, July, 1868, p. 38; Gibson, op. cit., pp. 76–7.

[4] In the hearings before the Congressional committee in San Francisco
in 1876, when reference was made to a scholarly Chinaman who had just
received the degree of LL.D. at Yale, Pixley said, "We will cut off his
queue." (House Reports, 44th Cong. 2nd sess., no. 689, p. 461.) Senator
Stewart of Nevada said that he had known Chinamen to commit suicide
after they had lost their queues. By this act they believed that they had
become outcasts.—Cong. Globe, 41st Cong. 2nd sess., p. 5125.

[5] Gibson, The Chinese in America, p. 282.

[6] Ibid., p. 283. Eaves, Labor Leg. in Cal., pp. 144–5.

[7] Gibson, op. cit., p. 299.

[8] Text of ordinance in Senate Reports, 44th Cong. 2nd sess., no. 689,
App. D; see ibid., pp. 48, 154, 201, 208, 479; How the U. S. Treaty with
China is Observed, pp. 7 et seq.

such a law was legislation "unworthy of a brave and manly people." He declared it invalid.[1]

Constantly facing inhospitalities which reached the grossest proportions, and in complete violation of the national faith, how could the Chinese be expected to "assimilate?" Could it be anticipated that they would send for their families?[2] Their wives would have fared little better than they—those that were here were mistaken for prostitutes.[3] Their children would not be received in the public schools,[4] but must go to the missions to learn English, or for educational training of any kind, and there systematic assault was made on their religious beliefs. They did not buy real estate and establish homes because they feared that their houses would be burned by ruffians, or that they, by chicanery, would be dispossessed of their property.[5]

It was complained that the immigration brought only the lower classes to America. How, under prevailing circumstances, could there be hope of drawing hither Chinese better educated and of a more desirable character?[6] And what propriety was there in the observation that they did not seek citizenship? Though the Burlingame treaty expressly excepted naturalization as a right to be exchanged by the nations, which were parties to the compact,[7] individuals had been naturalized now and again by local courts in New York, Boston and elsewhere. By a Federal statute of July 14, 1870, when the naturalization laws applicable to "free white persons" were extended to "aliens of African nativity and to persons of African descent," it was distinctly determined by Congress, though a minority

[1] Ho Ah Kow v. Nunan, 5 Sawyer, p. 552; App. Ann. Cyclop. for 1879, pp. 120–21.

[2] Senate Reports, 44th Cong. 2nd sess., no. 689, pp. 63, 405; cf. Congregationalist, Dec. 21, 1881.

[3] Cf. interview with a New York Chinaman in N. Y. Tribune, Feb. 27, 1879.

[4] Senate Reports, 44th Cong. 2nd sess., no. 689, pp. 401, 432–3, 452; Coolidge, Chinese Immigration, pp. 77–8.

[5] Ibid., p. 454; cf. Gibson, The Chinese in America, p. 320; J. S. Hittell, Resources of Cal., ed. of 1874, p. 45.

[6] Senate Reports, 44th Cong. 2nd sess., no. 689, p. 1194.

[7] Art. vi of the Treaty.—Haswell, Treaties and Conventions, p. 181.

headed by Sumner advocated an opposite course, that the Chinese should not be eligible to citizenship.[1] Upon a revision of the statutes in 1875 the committee in Congress in charge of the subject, inadvertently or otherwise, had omitted the words "white persons" which made a great ado in California, although no Chinese seem to have presented themselves for naturalization, and seven or eight months later, on February 18, 1875, the words were restored to their place.[2]

This was conclusive. Reviewing the subject competently, Judge Sawyer, in 1878, in the United States Circuit Court in San Francisco, said that a Mongolian was not a "white person,"[3] though the Chinese might vote, it was believed, as intelligently as the negroes who had so lately been intrusted with the privilege.[4] It was maintained, indeed, that they were better qualified to exercise the franchise than the blacks in the South.[5] In any event it was quite certain that the politicians who were so loudly proclaiming the unfitness of the Chinese for citizenship, had counted the heads of this people when they had wished to obtain for California another Congressman at Washington.[6]

That the Chinese were "pagans" was no matter. The fervid defenders of Christian civilization, in order to make a point against the Chinese, were the same men who ridiculed the whole missionary movement and insulted the men who were devoting their lives to the work of giving the "heathen" the "Jesus religion."[7]

[1] Cong. Globe, 41st Cong. 2nd sess., pp. 5121–77 passim; U. S. Statutes at Large, vol. 16, p. 256; cf. N. Y. Tribune, March 11, 1882; vol. ii of this work, pp. 206–7.

[2] Revised Statutes of the U. S., sec. 2165; Statutes at Large of the U. S., vol. 18, p. 318; Cong. Record, 43rd Cong. 2nd sess., pp. 1080–82; In re Ah Chong, 2 Fed. Reporter, p. 739.

[3] In re Ah Yup, 5 Sawyer, p. 155; cf. Senate Reports, 44th Cong. 2nd sess., no. 689, pp. 288, 290; App. Ann. Cyclop. for 1878, p. 76; Cong. Record, 47th Cong. 1st sess., p. 1747.

[4] "The first one that got naturalized," a witness said to the Federal committee, "would be hanged to a lamp post as soon as he left the court room."—Senate Reports, 44th Cong. 2nd sess., no. 689, p. 954.

[5] Ibid., p. 602.

[6] Ibid., p. 171.

[7] Gibson, The Chinese in America, p. 286.

As any fair-minded person might see the entire argument about "assimilation" was a farce, since it was precisely this that the anti-Chinese organizations were formed to oppose and would do everything in their power to prevent.[1]

The committee adjourned, on November 18th, for further meetings in Washington, though not before new demonstrations of popular feeling which were meant to impress it with the need of prompt and drastic action. On November 16th another great mass meeting, attended, it was said, by 7,000 people, was held in San Francisco. The mayor, who was completely at the service of the Anti-Coolie Clubs, presided. A street parade of these organizations had again brought out transparencies full of dire threat and ugly promise. The Rev. Otis Gibson, the devoted missionary, who had so unflinchingly given his testimony as a witness, was singled out for particular insult. His effigy was hung from a gallows tree. When the mob entered the hall the figure was taken down and burned at the stake.[2] The missionaries were told to go back to China where they had "bummed a living for twenty years."

Throughout the hearings any witness who dared to speak favorably of the Chinese had been most insolently dealt with by Sargent, Pixley,[3] Piper and other demagogues.[4] Whatever was said was perverted by the newspapers. The intimidation through the Anti-Coolie Clubs and the press was such that it was extremely difficult to find men who were willing to come forward to speak for the Chinese. Fear of damage to be suffered in business or politics, if not physical violence, deterred all but the boldest from answering the summons to appear and make public their views.[5]

[1] "Are we prepared to legislate," inquired the New York Nation, "that no race which is not likely to amalgamate completely with the bulk of the existing population shall be allowed to remain here? If so, how should we deal with the negroes?" N. Y. Nation, August 15, 1878; cf. N. Y. World, June 5, 1876.

[2] Senate Reports, 44th Cong. 2nd sess., no. 689, p. 849; Gibson, The Chinese in America, pp. 381-7.

[3] Pixley on one occasion took a clergyman by the beard and struck him in the face.—Gibson, The Chinese in America, pp. 385-6.

[4] Cf. ibid., p. 380.

[5] Cf. Senate Reports, 44th Cong. 2nd sess., pp. 922-3. In California at

The report reached Congress in 1877 and was ordered to be printed.[1] Sargent had dominated the committee and the paper was distinctly unfavorable to the Chinese. Undoubtedly they had contributed much to the material progress of California. Otherwise nothing indulgent of their immigration, settlement or continued residence in the country was contained in the argument. The fear in California that the Asiatic races would in no long time overrun the Pacific coast found plain expression. The movement was across the mountains and toward the East—the problem, which now was California's, in twenty-five years more must be met on the banks of the Mississippi and, perhaps, of the Ohio and the Hudson. Congress should act at once "to restrain the great influx of Asiatics to the country." The Executive should aim to bring about a modification of the existing treaty with China, confining its grant of privileges to commercial relationships. Whether such action on our side were or were not acceptable to the Chinese government it was a duty to the Pacific states and territories now "suffering under a terrible scourge." [2]

The chairman, Senator Morton, held very different views. After release from his close occupation with the dispute over the Presidential election and after Hayes was seated, he prepared a minority report, but his gathering infirmities prevented his completing or presenting it.[3] He found the animosity to the Chinese to be not unlike that manifested for the negro— it belonged "to the family of antipathies springing from race and religion." It was a theory of the Declaration of Independence, the Articles of Confederation and the Constitution that the country was "open to immigrants from all parts of the world," that it should be "the asylum of the oppressed and unfortunate." Few now could wish to "resurrect and reëstablish those odious distinctions of race which brought upon us the late Civil War and from which we fondly hoped that God,

this time "nobody who ever expected to hold office dared to say a word in favor of the Chinese."—Coolidge, Chinese Immigration, p. 95.

[1] Cong. Record, 44th Cong. 2nd sess., pp. 1961, 2004–5.
[2] Senate Reports, 44th Cong. 2nd sess., no. 689, pp. iii–viii.
[3] W. D. Foulke, Life of O. P. Morton, vol. ii, pp. 427–8.

in his providence, had delivered us forever." Morton found
that Chinese labor had been indispensable to California's
growth. But for the presence of this people the state could
not have had more than one-half or two-thirds of her present
white population. It was through their agencies that California
had become so inviting a field for white immigration, offering
"ample employment," at high wages, to all who had the will
to work. The Chinese came here as freemen and remained
such. Their intelligence was high. Their vices were not greater
than other men's. A price for labor could not be fixed by law
and there was no proper support for a contention that "men
who live cheaply and can work for lower wages shall, for that
reason, be kept out of the country." [1]

In 1877 feeling grew wilder and more bitter. In March of
that year a secret society, sworn to obey the orders of a "Council of Nine," made its appearance in Chico. Its objects were
to expel all Chinamen from the town. Threats to burn the
property of those who employed Chinese labor were heard.
Five Chinamen were murdered. There were virtue enough
in popular opinion and sufficient strength in the government
to condemn and punish such affronts to good order. The officers
of the club were arrested and the association was dissolved. [2]

As the summer of 1877 wore on and the railway strikes in
the East spread their infection into the Mississippi Valley,
and over the mountains to the Pacific coast, the excitement
increased. The times grew worse. The collapse of mining speculation, which had involved all classes of the people, from "railroad kings" down to store clerks and maidservants, [3] brought
from the mountains new idlers, many of them desperate characters. Drought, crop failures and the fall in land prices added
to public distress and political discord. [4]

---

[1] Senate Mis. Doc., 45th Cong. 2nd sess., no. 20; cf. Cong. Record, 44th
Cong. 2nd sess., p. 1961; ibid., 44th Cong. 3rd sess., p. 1383; ibid., 45th
Cong. 2nd sess., p. 1553; Coolidge, Chinese Immigration, chap. vii.
[2] App. Ann. Cyclop. for 1877, p. 80.
[3] Coolidge, Chinese Immigration, p. 113; Bryce, American Commonwealth, 1st ed., vol. ii, p. 376.
[4] Cf. Eaves, Hist. of Cal. Labor Legislation, pp. 27-8.

San Francisco in July, 1877, was the prey of mobs which wreaked vengeance on the Chinese in their washhouses, scattered over the city, now for some time barricaded against hoodlums with iron bars and wire netting to keep out cobblestones and other missiles, until they looked like prisons,[1] and invaded "Chinatown." Fires were lighted—all the lawless elements were astir. The governor, leading citizens, clergymen, the archbishop of San Francisco, counseled an observance of law. A Committee of Public Safety, made up of business and professional men of substance and character, came to the support of the city authorities. Within twenty-four hours, 5,000 volunteers put themselves at the disposal of William T. Coleman, the president of the old Vigilance Committee of 1851. They were supplied with hickory pick handles, and, as the "Pickhandle Brigade," patrolled the city day and night until danger had passed.[2] The blame was laid at the door of the Burlingame treaty and the failure of Congress to modify and abrogate it. The governor improved the opportunity to say that the Chinese had "encroached on the white laborers in all branches of industry" and, knowing this, "the hoodlums, thieves and internationalists" had started a rising in the hope of being joined by laboring men generally. They had been disappointed this time, but would the workingmen always "exhibit the same forbearance and splendid self-control?"[3] The archbishop made similar observations. He deplored anarchy, but he pointed out the cause. The government at Washington moved slowly, it would yet afford relief.[4]

A sinister and picturesque figure was now coming into prominence, Denis[5] Kearney. He was born in County Cork in 1847. He went to sea as a cabin boy and reached San Francisco on a clipper ship in 1868 where, after 1872, he remained as a

[1] Cf. Coolidge, Chinese Immigration, pp. 268–9; J. S. Hittell, Resources of Cal., ed. of 1874, p. 43.
[2] M. F. Williams, History of the San Francisco Vigilance Committee, pp. 407–8.
[3] App. Ann. Cyclop. for 1878, p. 80.
[4] Ibid.
[5] His name was spelled both Denis and Dennis, but Denis is the form usually given in the contemporary press.

driver of carts.[1] He was not naturalized, it was said, until the summer of 1876 and, therefore, he had but lately gained his citizenship.[2] At first displaying sympathy with "capital" his dough had been soured by unsuccessful speculation in stocks and he was now ready for service on another side.[3] It was discovered that he had a talent for fluent and abusive speech which, with the aid of some newspaper reporters, who arranged his phrase so that his meaning might be plain, brought him notoriety and a following promising him political rewards. He was the leading spirit in a campaign club called the "Working-men's Trade and Labor Union" which exerted some influence in the election of 1877. He harangued the crowds in the streets and particularly on a barren open space, or common, called the "Sand Lot," upon which an unfinished city hall stood. Here he formed what came generally to be known as the "Sand Lot party" and in it, through his fiery eloquence and the sympathy which the masses felt for the measures which he advocated, and the hatred which they had for what he so effectively denounced, won wide attention. His men were rowdies and he was an ignorant blackguard.[4] But he was a symptom of a condition which was responsible for great social unrest on the Pacific coast and he was welcomed as a brother of the radicals and communists who, in nests in this country and in Europe, advocated a general popular upheaval for improvement of the lot of the common man.

Two newspapers in San Francisco which were using the Chinese question to win a circulation, each at the expense of the other, the Chronicle and the Call, in keeping with the worst of their kind, took up the cause of the "Sand Lot men." The Chronicle improved and gave attractive form to Kearney's speeches and followed his movements, in return for which

---

[1] The Workingmen's Party of Cal., pp. 95–6.

[2] Coolidge, Chinese Immigration, p. 115.

[3] Henry George, in Popular Science Monthly, August, 1880, p. 438.

[4] William Lloyd Garrison spoke of him as a "most ignorant, profane, strife-engendering and besotted declaimer," who was "much more entitled to be in a lunatic asylum than running at large." (N. Y. Tribune, Feb. 17, 1879.) The N. Y. Tribune called Kearney "a ranting knave."—March 14, 1880.

service he commended the journal to the workingmen of San
Francisco. The Call was not far behind its rival and thus,
with journalism debauched and at the beck of revolution,
whipping up a "maelstrom of blind rage and fury," [1] clerks,
mechanics and classes of the people somewhat higher in social
rank were brought into the movement. [2]   Kearney knew his
game and played it artfully   He dressed as a workingman.
While he instituted no disorder which reached the proportions
of a serious breach of law and order he denounced politicians
and capitalists alike, threatening them with hemp and brim-
stone.   Instead of loading ships with wheat he would pile
them full of Mongolian slaves and send them back to China.
If it became necessary every freeman, who had a clear right
"to keep a musket in his house," would do so, and he would
use it.   Kearney spoke of the "whetted sabre," of "lozenges
of cold steel followed by pills of lead."   Every verbal extravagance which his reportorial mentors could invent was put into
his mouth, while they stood aside and laughed at the denota-
tions of the guns which they had packed for his discharge. [3]

If we should not settle this Chinese question in the next two
years, Kearney said, "the system will have settled us."   If there
were resistance by any committee of safety he would drive
out the "white pigtails" and deal with "John Chinaman"
afterward, and so on, sentiments which he would utter amid
"uproarious applause." [4]   When the "Ruffian King of the
Sand Lots" was arrested, in front of the home of one of the
Central Pacific Railroad's magnates on Nob Hill, for incendiary
speech, which was "delivered right into the teeth of a class to
whom the workingmen attributed, in a great measure, their
suffering condition," [5] his ambition was nearly fulfilled.   Other
noisy street orators shared his fate and were thrown into
prison.   They formed the "Workingmen's Party of California,"

---

[1] Cong. Record, 44th Cong. 3rd sess., p. 1387; cf. Henry George in Pop.
Sci. Monthly, August, 1880.
[2] Cf. Bryce, American Commonwealth, 1st ed., vol. ii, pp. 378-9.
[3] San Francisco corr. Boston Advertiser, July 12 and 13, 1878.
[4] Cf. The Workingmen's Party of Cal., pp. 19-20.
[5] Ibid., pp. 24, 26-7; Henry George, loc. cit.

the "W.P.C.," as it was generally called, and, as its president, Kearney became a state, if not a national, figure in his own time and for history.

The railroads who robbed the people, the steamship companies which brought in the Chinese, all the corporations which sucked the blood of the poor would be dealt with in due time by the militia, when his party should gain control of the state government. His followers wreathed his head with chaplets of flowers, they drew him through the streets in his own dray, when he issued from jail, reporters of the press gathered around him and hung upon his words, politicians who feared his power sought him out, paid their respects to him and begged his favors. The communists and "internationalists" would have had it appear to be a movement for the destruction of rights in property. It rested essentially, however, on prejudice against the Chinese and determination to be rid of them as competitors in the labor market.

The committee of the California state senate, intrusted with the preparation of the memorial which the governor was to forward to Washington, performed its duty. The paper reached Congress at the special session in October, 1877. It was couched in familiar terms. The abrogation of the Burlingame treaty would be well enough, but the movement of Chinese to America, as to Australia, where they were likewise unwelcome, came through Hong Kong, a British colony. The British government should be requested to coöperate with the United States in checking a traffic "resembling the slave trade." If any Chinese should be permitted to land the number ought to be restricted to not more than ten from each vessel.[1] The state senate committee maintained its organization and continued to pursue the subject. At a meeting in San Francisco, on August 13, 1877, it adopted "an address to the people of the United States upon the social, moral and political effect of Chinese immigration." This was a formidable document— an abstract of the report of the committee with extracts from the book of testimony. It appeared in the House of Representa-

[1] App. Ann. Cyclop. for 1877, pp. 81–2.

tives and, on November 7, 1877, was referred to the Committee on Education and Labor.[1] Though not one new idea was contributed to the discussion it was widely distributed among newpaper editors in all parts of the country in the hope of winning sympathy for the cause where yet there was none.

A counter memorial was sent to Congress by the officers of the Six Chinese Companies. When the legislature met in December, 1877,[2] Governor Irwin, in his message, reiterated his well known views. Should the civilization of this country be Christian or Chinese? he asked. One or the other must go. The handwriting was on the wall. If the situation underwent no improvement, if no redress were given the people of California there would be conflict, violation of the provisions of the Burlingame treaty and, he added gravely, of the laws of humanity.[3] The legislature of California again adopted resolutions in which the case was restated and commended to the attention of Congress and the President. The state's senators were "instructed" and its representatives at Washington were "requested" to use "every exertion," to the end that the flow of Chinese immigration should cease.[4]

The legislature did what was of more value—it reorganized the police system of San Francisco, abolishing the "special" officers who battened on vice in "Chinatown" and other thickly populated quarters in the city. It was plain enough that much of that which was complained of was supported by, and throve under the protection of, corrupt white men who directed the municipal government.[5]

The year 1878 offered no happier signs. Thousands of unemployed laboring men roamed the streets of San Francisco. These out-of-works held meetings, listened to inflammatory speeches, besieged the mayor's office and petitioned the legis-

---

[1] House Mis. Doc., 45th Cong. 1st sess., no. 9.
[2] App. Ann. Cyclop. for 1877, p. 82.
[3] Ibid., p. 82.
[4] Ibid., pp. 82-3; House Mis. Doc., 45th Cong. 2nd sess., no. 20.
[5] Sess. Laws of Cal. for 1878, p. 879; G. F. Seward, Chinese Immigration, p. 288; App. Ann. Cyclop. for 1878, p. 71.

lature for labor or doles. If they could not get bread honestly they said that they would steal, so that they might be fed in the public prisons.[1] Kearney was at the head of the "revolution" for "work, bread or a place in the county jail." He would take from his pocket a noose to illustrate his speech. Oaths, obscenity, epithets punctuated his boisterous declamation. He began to call himself the "Little Napoleon" and the "Cæsar" of his time.[2] The threats of him and other tramp orators, who shared the platform with him, to blow up the docks and ships of the Pacific Mail Company, to precipitate dynamite from balloons into "Chinatown," to make infernal machines for the destruction of the obnoxious rich, with advice to the masses to fetch guns and bludgeons to public meetings, seemed too much for public indulgence.[3] There was substantial opposition to conduct which manifestly gave incitement to the gravest disorder. Troops were called out, a United States warship took the Mail Company's docks under its care. The legislature put $20,000 at the disposal of the governor for use, at his discretion, "for the conservation of the public peace."[4] It passed a "gag law," as Kearney and his men called it,[5] which, they said, was in denial of "free speech," and they made such an ado that the measure, though it was soon repealed,[6] was probably of more advantage to them than to their foes. The "Workingmen" protested their innocence of a wish to plunder and burn the city and to kill the people: the ballot box, they said, would now be their battlefield. They would wage war on "the capitalist, the land grabber and the Chinese Six Companies" until the "Chinese pest" should be abated.[7]

And in truth they did give their minds actively to politics.

---

[1] App. Ann. Cyclop. for 1878, p. 69.
[2] San Francisco corr. Boston Advertiser, July 12 and 13, 1878.
[3] Nat. Cyclop. of Am. Biography, vol. 14, p. 111.
[4] Sess. Laws of Cal. for 1878, p. 879.
[5] Amendments to the Codes of Cal. for 1878, pp. 117-8; Coolidge, Chinese Immigration, pp. 117-8; App. Ann. Cyclop. for 1878, p. 73; The Workingmen's Party of Cal., 1878, pp. 46, 50.
[6] Ex-parte Kearney, 55 Cal., p. 226.
[7] Kearney's address to the legislature in App. Ann. Cyclop. for 1878, p. 73.

They raised the cry, "The Chinese must go!" and would exert themselves to give effect to that laconic sentiment.[1]

An agitation, covering a considerable period, in behalf of a revision of the constitution of the state by a convention had had successful issue in September, 1877, when the people, by a substantial majority, gave the project their approval. If the legislature could or would not act it might be directed to do so. New ways might be opened for a settlement of the Chinese question by a refreshment of the government at the source of its life, the sovereign people. Such a hope, and the outburst of antagonism to the railroads, and "monopoly" generally, were the strength of the movement. Delegates to the convention were elected in June, 1878. Kearney improved the season of his victory to visit the East, the country, as he characterized it, of "Cæsarism, corruption and insanity."[2] The Eastern newspapers chronicled the "rake's progress."[3] He brought himself and his doctrines as far as Massachusetts where he found sympathy and companionship in "Ben" Butler who was still running for governor.[4] Butler said that the Chinese were "a curse," and as such could be expelled from the country No state, he declared, could, against its will, so long as it was "independent and sovereign, be made the lazar house of the world."[5] Beyond being generally denounced in the newspapers, which dignified Kearney, to his gratification, with serious attention as an example in communism and a menace to society, he went home without profit to himself or his cause.[6]

---

[1] "America" appeared in a new form,
> "Californians awake!
> All you cherish is at stake!
> China's fetters you must break;
>   Strike yourselves the blow.
> Oust the pagans, far and near,
> From your fields and homes so dear,
> Falter not, your duty's clear;
>   They or you must go."
>   —Waldon Shearer, Which Shall It Be?

[2] N. Y. Nation, August 22, 1878.
[3] Boston Advertiser, July 23, 1878.
[4] N. Y. Nation, August 8, 1878.
[5] Ibid., August 15, 1878.
[6] Ibid., August 22, 1878.

At the election for delegates to the constitutional convention Kearney and his party secured 49 of the 152 members. Nineteen out of 31 who were chosen for San Francisco were foreign-born; 15 were not taxpayers; 12, it was said, had been registered for voting only a few weeks or months since. Cooks, barbers and a horse thief were numbered among those whom Kearney had put forward to give a new constitution to California.[1]

The convention assembled in September, 1878, in Sacramento, and for 157 days it wrangled over the Chinese and other questions, presenting, at the end of that time, a paper marked by much radicalism as well as idiosyncrasy. It was proposed that the Chinese should be dealt with as vagrants, paupers and criminals, or as persons who might become such, in spite of the fact, as the Sacramento Record observed, that they were numbered among the most industrious races in the world.[2] Many measures hostile to this people were gravely, often angrily discussed. "Foreigners ineligible to become citizens of the United States" were to be barred from license to carry on trade. They might not catch fish in the waters of the state. They might not sue and be sued; or own, purchase or lease real property. Corporations should not employ such persons for any kind of labor. Foreigners ineligible to citizenship should be excluded "from residence or settlement." They should be turned back at the borders of the state. They were "dangerous to the well being" of the commonwealth and measures were taken to make it certain that, if by any turn of fortune they were ever naturalized, they should not vote. "No native of China, no idiot, insane person or person convicted

[1] San Francisco corr. Boston Advertiser, July 12 and 13, 1878.

[2] "It is their industry that renders them so dangerous to our civilization. . . . No race was ever so hated unless it was feared. . . . The Chinaman is formidable because he is industrious, temperate, frugal, patient, tractable and, above all, cheap. . . . He has found his way into every industry on the Pacific coast because those who want labor find that his labor pays. . . . That is the reason we are all trying to get rid of him. . . . We wish to get rid of him because we fear that he will drive us to the wall. That is a perfectly good reason for excluding him and we believe that it will prove far less difficult to solve the problem on that line than by attacking his morals and talking about his diet."—Sacramento Record quoted in App. Ann. Cyclop. for 1878, pp. 77, 79–80.

of any infamous crime" should ever exercise the privileges of an elector. Those who should introduce such immigrants "within forbidden limits" should receive appropriate punishment. Public officers should not hire Chinese on penalty of dismissal from public service. No one who had employed a Chinaman within three months prior to his election to office should be qualified for the place for which he was a candidate. Even the right of suffrage was to be denied to those who employed Chinamen.[1] Much of this statement and declaration was adopted by the convention and sent out to the people.[2]

The constitution was looked upon as Kearney's. He and his kind had exerted a large influence upon the convention and conservative interests were arrayed against him in a demand for the defeat of its work. For a few weeks no other subject was discussed. One hundred and fifty newspapers opposed the adoption of the constitution, while only 47 favored it. A Republican mass meeting at Sacramento declared that it was "lacking in the essential qualities of a constitution"— if it were ratified it would work "irreparable damage to California." The people were asked to vote against it, thus defeating it and Kearney "at one and the same time." Kearney, on his side, made support of the constitution a test which all must pass if they were to continue to be members of his party.[3] He was aided in the country districts by the Grangers who were in a fury about railroads and "monopolies."[4] The whole state was aroused. In some counties at the election, in May, 1879, more men voted than had done so at the Presidential election in 1876, a violation of every precedent and rule for referenda in the United States. The campaign waged upon Kearney was, probably, too vehement for gaining the object in view. At any rate the constitution was adopted by a majority of about 10,000. Demonstrations by the "Workingmen,"

[1] App. Ann. Cyclop. for 1878, pp. 77–8; Eaves, Labor Leg. in Cal., pp. 150–60.
[2] App. Ann. Cyclop. for 1879, p. 107. See art. xix of the Constitution.
[3] App. Ann. Cyclop. for 1879, p. 108.
[4] Bryce, American Commonwealth, vol. ii, pp. 382, 386; N. Y. Nation, Aug. 28, 1878; Coolidge, op. cit., p. 122; Henry George, Pop. Science Monthly, August, 1880. p. 446.

in celebration of the event, carried their leader to the very
pinnacle of his enjoyment and glory. He was acclaimed as
he had never been before. Socialists and Internationalists
in Chicago, New York, London, Paris and over all the world
spoke his name and saw in his success hope for them and
their particular cause.

Wiser men knew that many provisions in the constitution
were unrealizable and that in the end these provisions would
fall under review, and would be rendered nugatory by the Federal courts.

The election for governor and other state officers and representatives in Congress would soon follow, and political agitation was continued acrimoniously for months. The "W.P.C."
held a nominating convention over which Kearney presided.
A long platform, filled with suggestions, demands and statements of belief, was adopted for the guidance of the candidates
and as an invitation for popular support. Many of the declarations now seem less dangerously revolutionary than they
did at the time of their promulgation, when the public mind
was unduly disturbed. The most radical sentiments of Kearney
and his men, to which they gave expression in this paper, ex-
cepting the familiar references to the Chinese, concerned rates
of passenger fares and freights on the railroads, the administration of the public domain in the interest of the "landless"
instead of the corporations, to which so much had been granted
by Congress, the eight hour day, equal pay for women for work
equal to man's, the election of President and Vice-President
and United States senators by direct vote of the people, the
compulsory attendance of children at free public schools with
free school books, laws to prohibit lobbying, bribery, mal-
feasance in office and the corruption of the ballot, a maximum
rate of six per cent for interest on lendable money, and the
establishment of postal savings banks.

Kearney and his "Workingmen" were determined, so they
said, that "the government of our country shall be so administered as to secure equal rights to all our people, be they high
or low, rich or poor, black or white" (not yellow). Thus would

the Union be "perpetuated forever."[1] The other parties were goaded into some expressions indicative of their interest in reform, especially with reference to the railroads. A very strong minority in the Republican convention would have had it make declarations denouncing the Central Pacific company for its treatment of the people of California. As many as five parties entered the field with candidates and confused the issue in such a way that the outcome was in much doubt. But the Republicans won by considerable pluralities, where there was not fusion of interests against them.[2]

After the dispute concerning the Hayes-Tilden election had ceased to engage popular attention the Chinese question, in the winter of 1877-8, was again pressed upon the President and Congress. The proposals which Sargent had to make on this subject were merely referred to the Committee on Foreign Relations. He was not quieted, however, until after he had had his day with an argument in behalf of the Chinese by Joseph C. G. Kennedy, which had been printed by the Senate,[3] and which he described as the "production" of a "lobbyist in the interest of the grand slave masters of the Pacific coast, called the Chinese Six Companies."[4] Proposals in the House reached the Committee on Education and Labor which, at the session of the Forty-fifth Congress, ending in the summer of 1878, was willing to make a report in favor of restriction, and to recommend that "immediate correspondence be opened upon this subject" with China and Great Britain.[5] Nothing came of it all but a concurrent resolution, framed in the Committee on Foreign Relations of the Senate,[6] drawn in fact by its chairman, Hannibal Hamlin,[7] and adopted by both houses, expressive of the opinion that

[1] App. Ann. Cyclop. for 1879, pp. 109-11.
[2] Ibid., pp. 111-5.
[3] Senate Mis. Doc., 45th Cong. 2nd sess., no. 36; cf. Cong. Record, 45th Cong. 2nd sess., p. 1544.
[4] Cong. Record, 45th Cong. 2nd sess., p. 1544; cf. ibid., 47th Cong. 1st sess., p. 2225.
[5] House Reports, 45th Cong. 2nd sess., no. 240.
[6] Senate Mis. Doc., 45th Cong. 2nd sess., no. 62.
[7] Cong. Record, 45th Cong. 3rd sess., p. 1384.

the provisions of the Burlingame treaty, allowing "unrestricted" immigration, "might wisely be modified so as to subserve the best interests of both governments." The "attention of the Executive" was "respectfully invited to the subject." [1]

In the next session more was seen. None of those who shouted "The Chinese must go!" on the streets of San Francisco dared to go farther than say that "The Chinese shall not come!" when they tried to make themselves articulate at Washington. A memorial from the legislature of Oregon was presented in January, 1879.[2] The constitutional convention of California had forwarded to Congress a paper of the same kind.[3] Several bills also appeared, responsive to sentiment which Sargent said was unanimously held, in answer to the conviction of the people of the Pacific coast, by every senator and by every representative from that part of the United States.[4] One of these came to the House from the Committee on Education and Labor. "The general welfare, justice, domestic tranquillity and the blessings of liberty" being of "supreme importance," and over and beyond the Constitution of the United States, these boons could not be "taken from the people by any treaty, however solemnly ratified." The Executive department of the government was affording the Pacific slope no relief; a duty abided in Congress. The "character, source and extent of immigration," generally and of all kinds, without regard to the Chinese, should be "regulated and controlled with reference to our own wants and welfare." In these terms did the committee recommend the passage of the bill.[5] After the date on which it should become effective no ship should carry to, and deliver at, any port in the United States more than fifteen Chinese passengers on any one voyage. Penalties were prescribed.

The debate included a reading of Bret Harte's "Plain Lan-

[1] Cong. Record, 45th Cong. 2nd sess., pp. 3226, 4782; ibid., 45th Cong. 3rd sess., p. 1384.
[2] Ibid., 45th Cong. 3rd sess., pp. 361, 367, 1072.
[3] App. Ann. Cyclop. for 1878, pp. 78–9.
[4] Cong. Record, 45th Cong. 3rd sess., p. 1072.
[5] House Reports, 45th Cong. 3rd sess., no. 62.

guage from Truthful James" and another characteristic outburst by Mr. Page, who brought forward the old petition,
signed by 16,000 persons in 1874. Representatives from the
Pacific slope, supported by members who were moved by the
demands of Eastern labor organizations, which were acting
in sympathy with Kearney and his element, passed the bill
in summary fashion on January 28, 1879, by a vote of 155 to
72.[1] Reaching the Senate it was referred to the Committee
on Foreign Relations, which reported it back, without recommendation, for place on the calendar,[2] from which it was
taken on February 12th by Sargent.[3] It was discussed on
three or four days.[4] Those who, like Sargent, advocated its
passage advanced no new arguments. Stanley Matthews of
Ohio, who was taken to express the views of President Hayes,
said that he would vote against the bill. We had "forced the
treaty out of" the Chinese; he would not bring upon us "the reproach of covenant breakers." He made an impassioned plea
for a display of reason, for liberality of opinion, for justice, for
caution and delay.[5] Blaine, with the vote of the Pacific coast
in view, as a support for his aspirations for the Presidency,
was unable to resist the temptation which the occasion afforded
and, of course, revealed himself as anti-Chinese.[6] His jaunty
speech met challenge from Matthews, Dawes, Morrill and from
his colleague, the senior senator from Maine, Hannibal Hamlin,
the chairman of the Committee on Foreign Affairs, who took

[1] Cong. Record, 45th Cong. 3rd sess., pp. 791–801.

[2] Ibid., pp. 813, 816, 1072.

[3] Ibid., pp. 1235–6.

[4] As against Sargent's assertion as to unanimity of sentiment in California
is Joaquin Miller's testimony, "I venture to assert that not half of the
solid wealth and worth of the far West, outside of the politicians, favor this
bill."—Cong. Record, 47th Cong. 1st sess., p. 1520.

[5] Ibid., 45th Cong. 3rd sess., pp. 1274–6.

[6] Cf. N. Y. Nation, Feb. 20, 1879. Blaine was willing to "barter his manhood for a prospective mess of pottage," said William Lloyd Garrison.
(N. Y. Tribune, Feb. 17, 1879.) Blaine responded to Garrison at great
length, proving himself as artful in his discussion of the subject in a newspaper as he had been in the Senate. He was "pleading the cause of the free
American laborer," etc., etc. (Ibid., Feb. 24, 1879.) Blaine's explanations,
Garrison returned, were "simply a repetition of the irrelevant allegations
and empty fallacies contained in his Senatorial rodomontade." Garrison
restated his "plea for human brotherhood."—Ibid., Feb. 27, 1879.

the younger man to task [1] with all the authority of high ability, enforced by nearly fifty years of continuous public service.

Mr. Hamlin entered his "solemn protest" against legislation "that caters to your Denis Kearneys and to your unnaturalized Englishmen" [Irishmen]. It was a mere "counterpart of that wild craze that ran over this land known as Native Americanism." [2] There were "great and fundamental principles coeval with the formation of this government." Ours was "established as 'the home of the free,' where the outcast of every nation, where the child of every creed and of every clime could breathe our free air and participate in our free institutions." When the treaty with China was negotiated no section of the country had been "so earnest, so forward" in securing it "as that which lies upon the Pacific coast." A remedy for wrongs and evils might be needed. But it must be a "proper remedy." Mr. Hamlin would not apply that "remedy of might which subverts the remedy of right." He would vote against the measure, and leave that vote "the last legacy" to his children, to be esteemed by them as "the brightest act "of his life. [3]

Hoar opposed the bill because it involved a breach "without necessity" of "the public faith," because it overthrew "guaranteed rights" of so large a portion of his fellow citizens on which "so much of their wealth and their commerce depends," because it violated "the fundamental principle announced in the Declaration of Independence" and to which, "by our whole history, the American people are pledged." [4]

Edmunds, as the discussion closed, briefly expressed his "utter abhorrence" of the principle underlying the bill, namely that, "without negotiation, without motive, without any step that the fair and honest comity which should exist among nations would require to be taken," a provision of a treaty with a friendly power could be abrogated by legislation. [5] In spite of such admonition the Senate passed the measure by a vote of 39 to 27. [6]

[1] Blaine's remarks, with the attending colloquy, in Cong. Record, 45th Cong. 3rd sess., pp. 1299, 1303.
[2] Ibid., p. 1315.
[3] Ibid., pp. 1383–7.
[4] Ibid., p. 1312.
[5] Ibid., p. 1400.
[6] Ibid.

President Hayes had been not inattentive to the debate in Congress. He believed that the record of our relations with the negroes and the Indians proved us ill fitted for dealing with "weaker races." We should "oppress" the Chinamen; their presence here would make "hoodlums or vagabonds" of their oppressors.[1] Moreover the bill was a distinct violation of the treaty the negotiation of which, only ten years since, the whole country had "applauded." Therefore he must veto it.[2] Not one of his friends and advisers in the cabinet gave him other counsel.[3] The New York Chamber of Commerce called a meeting. Many of the leading merchants of the city attended and uttered vigorous protest.[4] "This bill must not become a law," said Joaquin Miller; "every one of the great names advocating it ought to be condemned to everlasting infamy."[5] Thurlow Weed characterized it as a reversal and an abandonment of the "principles" of the Declaration of Independence. We were seeking to "wantonly violate" a treaty, which we had wrung from the Chinese.[6]

On the other side there was activity also. Delegations from California appeared and pressed their views upon the President.[7] In memorials and petitions, resolutions of mass meetings, letters and telegrams from San Francisco, Portland and other places on the Pacific coast, and from labor organizations everywhere he was besought to sign the bill.[8]

The message, when it appeared, was worthy of the President and in keeping with the responsibility inhering in his high office. "Up to this time," he said, "our uncovenanted hospitality to immigration, our fearless liberality of citizenship, our equal and comprehensive justice to all inhabitants, whether they abjured their foreign nationality or not, our civil freedom and our religious toleration had made all comers welcome." He

---

[1] Diary and Letters of Hayes, vol. iii, p. 522; cf. ibid., p. 524.
[2] Ibid., pp. 523–4.
[3] N. Y. Tribune, Feb. 24, 1879.
[4] Ibid., Feb. 28, 1879.
[5] Ibid., Feb. 25, 1879.
[6] Ibid.
[7] Ibid., Feb. 26 and 27, 1879.
[8] Ibid., Feb. 25, 26, 27 and 28, 1879.

noted a change of feeling on this subject. The Chinese entering our ports seemed to be "strangers and sojourners" and were not becoming "incorporated elements of our national life and growth," presenting, therefore, an unexpected political and social problem. Discontent on the Pacific coast there was and there had been, and the situation of the people was deserving of the solicitous attention of the President and Congress. But the immigration of the Chinese had lately shown signs of declining. Patience might well be displayed. It must be remembered that, while we should employ ourselves in withdrawing guaranteed protections from the Chinese in the United States, American citizens, enjoying reciprocal protections in China, were exposed to reprisals. It was a sword with two edges. Remedy in any case must follow negotiation, through the regularly established channels with the government with which the agreements had been contracted. With these negotiations Congress was told courteously but plainly that it had nothing to do. The law-making branch of the government could not usurp the functions of the treaty-making power.[1]

The House of Representatives made an attempt to pass the bill over the veto, but only 110 members approved of this course, while there were 96 against it, and the scheme failed.[2]

Viewing the question entirely as a breach of treaty rights, the bill, the New York Nation said, was "absolutely indefensible."[3] The President was correct in holding the matter to be "beyond Congressional competence."[4] He voiced the "best opinion of the country," said the New York Tribune.[5] He had "saved the character of the country from humiliation among the family of nations," said the Public Ledger of Philadelphia.[6] His message was "wise and manly," said the Philadelphia Inquirer. Here was proof that he had "courage to do right

---

[1] Cong. Record, 45th Cong. 3rd sess., pp. 2275–6; Richardson, Messages and Papers, vol. vii, pp. 514–20.
[2] Cong. Record, 45th Cong. 3rd sess., pp. 2276–7.
[3] N. Y. Nation, Feb. 20, 1879.
[4] Ibid., March 6, 1879.
[5] Issue of March 3, 1879.
[6] Ibid.

against all force, blandishment or pleading to make him do wrong." [1]

The anger of the Californians was not concealed, though Hayes had the support of a valuable portion of public opinion even in that state, as was plain when such men as D. O. Mills, president of the Bank of California, General Beale, lately American minister to Austria, who had a ranch of 200,000 acres in the southern part of the state [2] and Colonel Hollister were numbered among his counselors. [3] He had not been misled by them or by anyone, however, as to the earnestness of a popular desire on the Pacific coast for a change in our relations with China. [4] The denunciation which he now suffered west of the Rocky Mountains could but serve to confirm his judgment. He was spoken of contemptuously as "Missey" Hayes. [5] The "fraud President" had disgraced his high office and ruined the Republican party. A coward and a craven he had yielded to the clamor of a few New York merchants and the missionaries, while the West would suffer as before. [6] Flags were at half-mast, the President was burned in effigy [7] while he was writing in his Diary with great sympathy for his detractors. Such a population as the Chinese must be "hateful," he said. That the invasion might not "permanently override our people" should be "made certain"; it could not "safely be admitted into the bosom of our American society." [8]

The Democrats of California took the opportunity in 1880 to name and condemn the President in their party platform. They declared that there could be "no relief from the scourge except through a Democratic adminstration." [9]

---

[1] Issue of March 3, 1879.

[2] C. Nordhoff, California for Health, Pleasure and Residence, pp. 234–7.

[3] House Mis. Doc., 45th Cong. 2nd sess., no. 36, pp. 33–4.

[4] Diary and Letters of Hayes, vol. iii, p. 524.

[5] "Pigeon English" for Mister.—N. Y. Tribune, March 4, 1879, quoting San Francisco corr. of Cincinnati Enquirer.

[6] San Francisco Call, March 2, 3 and 4, 1880; San Francisco corr. Phila. Inquirer, March 4, 1879.

[7] San Francisco corr. Phila. Inquirer, March 4, 1879.

[8] Diary and Letters of Hayes, vol. iii, pp. 525–6.

[9] App. Ann. Cyclop. for 1880, p. 78.

The hoodlum element now became particularly demonstrative. President Hayes's veto, together with the coming into effect of the radical constitution, led to an arrogance of posture on the part of Kearney and his friends which was very menacing to good order. In the winter and spring of 1880 violent and incendiary speech again filled the air. Blood-curdling placards appeared on walls and hoardings. Citizens were threatened with death and the community with fire and sword.[1] The police were armed, the militia were made ready for emergencies, weapons, powder and ball which had been accumulated in the armories were put under Federal protection and removed to places of greater safety. The "Workingmen," on their side, again engaged in military drill. At any moment the whole country was led to expect an outburst of pillage and massacre.[2]

Threats to condemn and destroy "Chinatown" were repeated. The government of San Francisco was in control of the Kearneyites. The Board of Health declared the quarter a public nuisance. Thirty days were allowed for a general "clean up" at the end of which time the officers of the law would be compelled "to empty this reservoir of moral, social and physical pollution, which is constantly extending its area and threatens to engulf, with its filthiness, the fairest portion of our city." It was predicted that the prisons which yawned for Chinamen would be taxed for space to hold those who should be carried up to the jail doors, but long before the month had expired the entire district, except for some houses which were owned by white landlords, was put in order through the competent influence of the Six Companies.[3]

The efforts of the legislature to give effect to the provisions of the new constitution were watched with curiosity and solicitude. Laws aimed at the Chinese who were described, to escape the inhibitions regarding class legislation, as "aliens incapable of becoming electors," were numerous. Municipal governments were authorized, at their pleasure, to remove

[1] N. Y. Nation, March 18, 1880.
[2] Ibid.
[3] App. Ann. Cyclop. for 1880, p. 78.

Chinese residents beyond the city limits.[1] Corporations and their officers were prohibited from employing Chinamen,[2] who were, in other bills, rendered incapable of receiving licenses to carry on trade,[3] or to fish in the waters of the state.[4] It was even proposed to brand Chinese prisoners on the forehead with the letter "C," whereupon they should be transported from the state, and 19 members of the assembly were found to cast their votes for this scheme.[5] As intelligent men had anticipated the United States courts, when the subject reached them on appeal, promptly declared most of these measures unconstitutional.[6]

The new constitution now, rather than the Chinese, was regarded, on many sides, as the cause of unemployment and hard times. The burdens which it laid upon capital had so restricted business that leading and representative merchants, manufacturers, lawyers and other gentlemen in San Francisco formed a "Citizens' Protective Union" with an "Executive Council of 200" to give battle to Kearney and the "Sand Lotters."[7] The incendiary utterances of the hoodlum leaders were also an influence to alienate many of the clerks, mechanics and other men in the middle class who had been coöperating with them. The English language by this time, the limits having been so often reached by declamatory ruffians, seemed to be entirely too small and poor to satisfy the forensic energies of Kearney and his men. Denis himself was arrested for profane and threatening speech, calculated to create a breach of the peace, directed at Claus Spreckels, a rich German sugar manufacturer in San Francisco, and was convicted and sentenced to pay a fine of $1,000, or suffer six months' imprisonment in the House of Correction, though he escaped his punish-

---

[1] Sess. Laws of Cal. for 1880, p. 22.

[2] Amendments to the Penal Code of Cal., 1880, pp. 1–2.

[3] Sess. Laws of Cal., p. 39.

[4] Ibid., p. 123.

[5] San Francisco Examiner, March 17, 1880.

[6] See, e.g., In re Parrott, Fed. Reporter, vol. i, p. 481; In re Ah Chong, ibid., vol. ii, p. 733; App. Ann. Cyclop. for 1880, p. 73; Cong. Record, 47th Cong. 1st sess., p. 2135; N. Y. Nation, March 11, 1880.

[7] N. Y. Nation, March 18, 1880.

ment through an appeal to a higher court.[1] A clerical demagogue, Isaac S. Kalloch, was the Kearneyite candidate for
mayor of San Francisco. He was a glib orator who had mixed
his religion and his politics to gain considerable notoriety. He
had had a Chinese Sunday School but he had shut it up when he
saw his way to preferment in politics.[2] The "Reverend Doctor"
had had a picturesque and chequered past in Boston and New
York, as well as in the West, which, in the tumult accompany-
ing the adoption of the new constitution, the Chronicle, edited
by the brothers Michael and Charles De Young, had exposed
and ornamented to their liking. That newspaper, which had
got all it could from Kearney, now opposed him and led a
party of "Independent" politicians, whom the "Sand Lotters"
had nicknamed the "Honorable Bilks."[3] Kalloch took exception
to the Chronicle's vivid account of his career and, in return,
described the lives of the brothers De Young from the ros-
trum of his church. More than could get inside of the "Metropolitan Temple" assembled to hear him. "Charley and Mike".
the preacher said, were a "delectable pair of social pariahs,"
who were vainly struggling for the recognition which decent
society had denied them, and who, "by a persistent and damnable system of blackmailing," had built up a newspaper whose
every issue filled "the surrounding atmosphere with poison."
The Chronicle was "the most infamous paper ever produced·
this side of the infernal regions." Kalloch had heard of the
wickedest man in New York; Charles De Young was "the
wickedest man in the world" and he would be "without a
rival in hell"—he was "the embodiment of all baseness, pol-
troonery, sensuality, effrontery, mendacity, barbarity," and
more that was worse affecting his and his brother's line of
parentage.

The next morning Charles De Young armed himself with
a pistol and a long knife, entered a hackney coach and, when
the driver came to a point in front of Kalloch's "study,"

[1] Ex parte Kearney, 55 Cal., p. 212; App. Ann. Cyclop. for 1880, p. 77;
N. Y. Tribune, March 16 and 17, 1880.
[2] Henry George, Pop. Sci. Monthly, loc. cit., p. 447.
[3] Because many of them were "ex-Honorables," i.e., ex-officeholders.

dispatched a boy to call out the cleric, whom the editor, from behind a curtain in the cab, shot. De Young then asked that he be taken into custody by the police. Before this result could be attained the carriage was overturned by a mob which shouted, "Let's hang him," and more to like purpose, though they contented themselves by going to the Sand Lot and leveling resolutions at "that ulcerous, journalistic running sore, the San Francisco Chronicle" and pledging themselves, with a change of metaphor, to stamp out, as "the seed of a viper," this "vile and venomous organ." [1] Kearney said it was not De Young who had done the deed; he had been but a tool of "the land robbers and the Chinese Six Companies and other wealthy villains"; while Wellock, another religious exhorter, whose tongue was now serving the "Workingmen," an unnaturalized Englishman who had recently called the brothers who owned and edited the Chronicle "the lineal descendants of Pontius Pilate," [2] declared that, if these men did not "die by another hand, they should die by that of William Wellock." [3]

Kalloch's wounds it appeared were not mortal. The preacher lived for martyrdom. The "Workingmen" rallied to his support and he was elected mayor. Eight months later, in 1880, the mayor's son, also a pulpiteer, in revenge, entered the business office of the Chronicle and shot and killed De Young, [4] whose liberty had been not long restrained in punishment for his crime, though trial, which it was fairly believed would prove a farce, impended. [5] Young Kalloch when he, in turn, came to trial was acquitted and the Sand Lotters, overjoyed, took the horses from the carriage in which he drove away from the courthouse and drew it, with him in it, receiving the plaudits of the populace, for a distance of three miles. [6] Steps were taken looking to the impeachment of the mayor. These measures failed.

[1] San Francisco Call, August 24 and 25, 1879.
[2] Ibid., Aug. 23, 1879.
[3] Ibid., August 25, 1879.
[4] Ibid., April 24, 1880.
[5] N. Y. Nation, April 29, 1880.
[6] Ibid., March 31, 1881.

The Citizens' Union by this time had organized a political party in opposition to the "Workingmen" and was ready to assert its power at the municipal election in April, 1880.[1] Kearney was defeated in this trial of strength with the aroused citizens, and his reign was at an end.[2] Feuds arose in the ranks of his followers and his party split asunder in the Presidential compaign of 1880, a portion under his leadership acting with the Greenbackers, while Kalloch and his friends supported the regular Democratic ticket.

To those who had set store by the new state constitution as a remedy for the Chinese "evil" the fruits were disappointing. It was clearer than ever that redress must be sought at Washington. Petitions, memorials and bills were still being referred in the Senate to the Committee on Foreign Relations, in the House to the Committee on Education and Labor. It was not very feasible longer to question the practical unanimity of feeling on the part of the people of the Pacific coast concerning the Chinese.[3] At the time of the submission of the constitution the question of the prohibition of immigration was also referred to popular vote, though in a peculiar manner. As a result of trickery in printing the ballots [4] 154,638 votes were cast for exclusion, only 883 against it.[5] In 1880 the same question was taken to the people of Nevada, where there were 18,397 for and 183 against restrictive measures. The governors of both states, as they were enjoined to do, transmitted the facts to the President and to Congress.[6]

A Select Committee of the House had been authorized in 1878 to conduct an investigation into the causes of industrial depression in the United States, and these men had visited

[1] If the time ever comes when it must be settled whether the city should "belong to the men who built it or to Kearney and his tramps," said one of the newspapers, "God help Denis, that's all."—N. Y. Nation, March 11, 1880.

[2] Ibid., April 8, 1880.

[3] Cf. House Reports, 46th Cong. 2nd sess., no. 572, pp. 2, 36.

[4] Coolidge, Chinese Immigration, pp. 123–4.

[5] McPherson's Handbook for 1880, p. 87; App. Ann. Cyclop. for 1878, p. 115.

[6] Cong. Record, 46th Cong. 2nd sess., p. 151; ibid., 46th Cong. 3rd sess., p. 709; ibid., 47th Cong. 1st sess., p. 1482.

the Pacific coast in the summer of 1879 to hear witnesses on the Chinese question. The revival of business made their mission useless and their reports of little public interest,[1] though that one upon the Chinese, covering the testimony of a few voluntary witnesses given in a period of less than four days, was so hostile as possibly to bring the matter home to new groups of men in the East,[2] in spite of a vigorous dissenting minority opinion.[3] While it was true that immigration had been checked by the outbursts so unfavorable to the Chinese and by conditions in business which greatly restricted the opportunities for employment,[4] the popular fury was too mad to be quelled by any fact or argument. Nothing else during the Hayes administration, after the veto of the "Fifteen Passenger Bill," promising to avail the Sinophobists, they must content themselves with a request of the President, in a resolution of the House, adopted on February 12, 1880, for a statement of what he had done with respect to their urgency expressed in a former resolution.[5] Had he engaged in correspondence with China and Great Britain in the interest of the abrogation and annulment of obnoxious clauses in the Burlingame treaty?[6]

Common sagacity required that the managers of the Republican party, before entering upon the Presidential campaign, should take some definite steps toward a satisfaction of the people of the Pacific coast on the Chinese question. In 1876 a commission had been sent to California to study the situation; now, in 1880, the State Department, which had been earnestly endeavoring for some time, in conferences with the officers of the Chinese legation at Washington[7] and, through George F. Seward, our minister at Peking, to open negotiations

---

[1] Cong. Record, 46th Cong. 2nd sess., p. 2030; House Mis. Doc., 46th Cong. 2nd sess., no. 5.

[2] House Reports, 46th Cong. 2nd sess., no. 572.

[3] Ibid., pp. 31-9.

[4] House Mis. Doc., 46th Cong. 2nd sess., no. 5, p. 243.

[5] Of February 25, 1878.

[6] Cong. Record, 46th Cong. 2nd sess., pp. 678, 846; House Ex. Doc., 46th Cong. 2nd sess., no. 70.

[7] Cong. Record, 45th Cong. 3rd sess., p. 1384.

for a revision of the treaty,[1] suggested a commission which should proceed to China to discuss with commissioners of the Chinese government the points at issue.

All the parties, Republican, Democratic and Greenback, in their national platforms in 1880 condemned the unrestricted immigration of the Chinese. The Republicans had the advantage of their opponents because they had been in a position to initiate the project for a modification of the treaty, and Garfield made use of his opportunity in extended references to the subject in his letter accepting the nomination.[2] It availed him little, however, for he lost the electoral votes of Nevada and five of the six votes in California, in some degree, as it seemed, because of the circulation by his enemies, in the last days of the campaign, of a forged letter. This paper, called the "Morey letter," since it purported to be addressed to one H. L. Morey, officer of an "Employers' Union" at Lynn, Mass., expressed the Republican candidate's sympathy for "our great manufacturing and corporate interests," which required cheap labor, on which account it was stated that he would not now favor the abrogation of the Burlingame treaty. The effect of this disclosure was instantaneous. The letter was reproduced in *facsimile* in the newspapers. Garfield said that he had never written it and his friends knew that he had not done so. It was the work of a cunning penman who had the design of injuring the chances of Republican success. An investigation was begun, a newspaper man and the publishers of the sheet which employed his talents, were arrested, witnesses who perjured themselves were sentenced to prison. The trick was laid at or near the doors of leading Democratic campaign managers. But all of this came too late to check the influence of the publication, which was undeniably potential in drawing votes away from the Republican candidate.[3]

Our envoys to China for the modification of the treaty were

[1] House Ex. Doc., 46th Cong. 2nd sess., no. 70; Senate Ex. Doc., 47th Cong. 1st sess., no. 175.

[2] Cf. Cong. Record, 47th Cong. 1st sess., p. 1482.

[3] John I. Davenport, History of the Morey Letter, New York, 1884; cf. App. Ann. Cyclop. for 1880, p. 576.

James B. Angell, president of the University of Michigan, who was appointed minister to China in Seward's room and became chairman of the commission; [1] John F. Swift of California, a lawyer and politician, an intractable Chinese hater, [2] who would have prohibited immigration entirely, [3] and William Henry Trescot of South Carolina, skilled in international law and diplomacy, and they, without any particular instructions from Washington for their guidance, continued negotiations which for two or three years had been in progress between our State Department and the Chinese government. [4]

China on her side was complaining, with reason, of the rough and unmannerly usage of her subjects in California, while we could have answered, had we wished to do so, that no privileges were accorded our citizens in China, in the extent of the opportunities or the freedom of movement allowed them (in spite of Kearney and the hoodlums) in any way comparable to the liberties enjoyed by the Chinese in the United States. [5] Our three commissioners had a number of meetings with the Chinese Emperor's representatives, who were two members of his Privy Council [6] and, on November 17, 1880, approved and signed two new treaties, one covering the question of immigration and the other relating to commercial intercourse. The important point gained was that the government of the United States, whenever "the coming of Chinese laborers," or their residence in the country, in its opinion, "affects or threatens to affect the interests" of the United States, or to "endanger" its "good order," might "regulate, limit or suspend such coming or residence." The limitation or suspension, it was specified, should be "reasonable," and it should never reach absolute prohibition. Such restrictive measures should apply only to

[1] J. B. Angell, Reminiscences, p. 131.
[2] See his testimony in Senate Reports, 44th Cong. 2nd sess., no. 689, pp. 951–68.
[3] J. B. Angell, Reminiscences, p. 142.
[4] Cf. Coolidge, Chinese Immigration, pp. 151–2; Chester Holcombe in N. Y. Outlook, April 23, 1904.
[5] See Seward to Evarts, March 22, 1878, in Senate Ex. Doc., 47th Cong. 1st sess., no. 175; R. Mayo-Smith, Emigration and Immigration, pp. 234–5.
[6] J. B. Angell, Reminiscences, pp. 139, 141, 142–6.

"laborers," and, with reference to them, no rule should be made leading to their "personal maltreatment or abuse."

It was specified, too, that teachers, students, merchants, tourists, together with their servants, and that "laborers" already in the United States, should come and go, "of their own free will and accord," enjoying the rights, privileges and immunities of subjects of "the most favored nation."

The nature of the legislative measures which should be adopted in accordance with the concessions made to the government of the United States in the new treaty should be communicated to the government of China. If such measures should "work hardships" upon the subjects of China the matters in question were to receive consideration at Washington by the Chinese minister to the United States and by our Secretary of State, and at Peking by the Chinese Foreign Office and the American minister to China.[1] President Hayes in his fourth and last message to Congress, in December, 1880, was able to report that Mr. Trescot was on his way home, bringing the treaties,[2] which were laid before the Senate to encounter the opposition of Hoar and a few other advocates of human brotherhood,[3] but to be ratified on May 5, 1881, and to be proclaimed in the following October.

The way was now open and it could have been hoped, if not expected, that Congress would keep faith with China, as it had been pledged to her representatives by our commissioners when she had made the concessions which we sought, all duly accepted, confirmed and ratified by the President and the Senate of the United States. On the contrary the fanatics of the Pacific coast and those who were coöperating with them set out, in full face of the definite statements in the articles modifying the treaty, to enact a very harsh law. Petitions on both sides of the question appeared in Congress. Men on the Pacific coast and labor unions everywhere contributed their importunities in favor of exclusion. The Board of Trade in

[1] Foreign Relations, 47th Cong. 1st sess., pp. 168–98; Haswell, Treaties and Conventions, pp. 182–5; App. Ann. Cyclop. for 1880, pp. 105–6.
[2] Richardson, Messages and Papers, vol. vii, p. 609.
[3] Hoar, Autobiography of 70 Years, vol. ii, p. 122.

New York, including many men prominently engaged in the China trade, and merchants and mercantile firms in the East acting for themselves,[1] remonstrated against the proposed legislation. Senator Lapham in presenting the petition of the Board of Trade quoted lines from a song, "Jefferson and Liberty," which had been ringing in his head since his youth,

> "Here strangers from a thousand shores,
>   Compelled by tyranny to roam,
> Shall find, amid abundant stores,
>   A freer and a happier home." [2]

Presbyteries, conferences of the Methodist church protested. Missionary interests were imperiled. Treaty relations with China should be continued undisturbed "that the Gospel may be preached to Chinamen in China and to Chinamen in America." [3]

Though Sargent by this time had been left at home through the whirl of local party politics, [4] to be succeeded in the Senate by a Democratic "Sand Lotter" named Farley, who joined General John F. Miller, a rich Republican ranch owner and business man,[5] little loss was suffered by California in the practice by its representatives in Congress of the vituperative arts. The scheme, the outgrowth of a variety of suggested measures, developed and took its final form in the hands of Miller, who began the debate on the last day of February, 1882.[6] For his convenience immigration had somewhat revived—18,561 Chinamen had "poured through the Golden Gate" in 1881. In the first two months of 1882 about 4,000 more had arrived.[7] He concluded his oration with soaring periods. The land which was being "overrun by the Oriental invader" was the "fairest portion of our heritage." Its winter was "perpetual spring," its summer "a golden harvest." Miller would see "its fertile plains, its sequestered vales, its vine-

---

[1] Cong. Record, 47th Cong. 1st sess., pp. 2229, 2933.
[2] Ibid., p. 2878.
[3] Ibid., p. 2933.
[4] Cf. N. Y. Nation, March 2, 1882.
[5] N. Y. Tribune, March 9, 1886.
[6] Cong. Record, 47th Cong. 1st sess., p. 1481.
[7] Ibid., p. 1482.

clad hills, its deep blue cañons, its furrowed mountain sides dotted all over with American homes . . . like the homes of New England," and "yet brighter and better far" than these homes they should be "in that wonderland by the sunset sea, the homes of a race from which shall spring

'—the flower of men,
To serve as model for the mighty world,
And be the fair beginning of a time.' " [1]

Senator Hoar spoke on March 1st, making the most spirited opposition to the bill. While the debate was at its height the governor of California proclaimed March 4th a holiday on which the people of the state were to close the doors of their stores and their workshops, and assemble in San Francisco and in every town and hamlet in "solemn mass meeting." [2] Resolutions were adopted, scores of telegrams were sent to Washington to be read into the Congressional Record. [3]

By the bill, as it was passed by the Senate, where the legislation originated, immigration of "Chinese" laborers was to be suspended for twenty years. It was provided furthermore that every Chinaman already in the country should, before departing from it, if he wished to reënter it, register himself at the United States customhouse and secure a certificate; also that every Chinaman, of whatever interest or occupation, whose entrance was not prohibited, must, before coming, provide himself with a passport in the English language, describing his person and his intentions, obtained from the Chinese government and countersigned by the diplomatic representative or a consular representative of the United States in China. Upon arrival he must put his name in a book, provided for the use at the customhouse, and state divers facts about himself for the information of the authorities. He would then be given a certificate by the collector of customs. Perjury, forgery or fraud in registration would mean imprisonment in a penitentiary for ten years. Penalties were prescribed for masters of vessels

[1] Cong. Record, 47th Cong. 1st sess., p. 1488.
[2] Ibid., p. 2034.
[3] Ibid., pp. 1667–9; San Francisco Examiner, March 6, 1882.

violating the law as to the landing of Chinese passengers, and for those aiding in any way to procure the entry of Chinese immigrants of the prohibited class. Amendments were added forbidding state and Federal courts from admitting Chinese to citizenship, and making it clear that "Chinese laborers" meant both skilled and unskilled men and those employed in mining. The vote, taken on March 9th, was 29 to 15, Aldrich, Allison, Dawes, Edmunds, Hoar and Morrill being included among those who opposed the measure, as they earlier had contended for change in its form.[1]

The House began consideration of the bill on March 14th,[2] and continued the discussion along familiar lines which developed opposition such as had been encountered in the Senate from men who were grounded in the historical traditions of the government and who denounced its proposed policy as "un-Democratic, un-Republican and un-American." [3]   The measure was passed on March 23rd by a vote of 167 to 66,[4] and it was sent to the President. It bore the dignified title, "An act to execute certain treaty stipulations relating to Chinese," but Arthur, like Hayes, was not to be thrown into a panic. He read the bill, esteemed it to be open to grave objections and, on April 4, 1882, vetoed it. To aid him in an interpretation of the treaty, he had before him the papers outlining the progress of the negotiations between the commissioners at Peking and a memorandum of the Chinese minister at Washington, who, immediately upon the passage of the bill, had entered protest against it under five heads.[5] The new treaty of 1880, the President observed, was "unilateral, not reciprocal," and it was left to us to define the limitations which China had courteously allowed us to apply to the immigration of her subjects. It was her right to expect that we would not "overstep the grant and take more than has been conceded to

[1] Cong. Record, 47th Cong. 1st sess., p. 1753; McPherson's Handbook for 1882, pp. 92–5.
[2] Cong. Record, 47th Cong. 1st sess., p. 1899.
[3] Ibid., p. 2184.
[4] Ibid., pp. 2227–8.
[5] McPherson's Handbook for 1882, pp. 99, 102.

us." The Congress had fixed the term for which immigration would be suspended at twenty years. Gentlemen in the Senate and others in the House had sought to make the period ten years, but their motions were disagreed to. Twenty years were "nearly a generation," said the President; such a provision in the bill was an "unreasonable" restriction within the meaning of the treaty.[1] It was in his view "a breach of our national faith." The "honor of the country" constrained him, therefore, to return the bill with this objection to its passage. He further pointed out that we were bound under the new treaty to continue to extend to such Chinese as resided in the country all the privileges and immunities accorded to citizens of the most favored nation. The provisions in the act as to personal registration and passports the President found to be unusual. Such requirements he declared to be "undemocratic and hostile to the spirit of our institutions." A nation like the United States, he said, might well hesitate before it should incorporate into its policy "a system which is fast disappearing in Europe before the progress of liberal institutions."

It was only after the establishment of "a great seat of commerce on the Pacific," the President continued, that we had broken down the barriers which so long had fenced in the ancient Chinese nation. Those immigrants who had come to the United States had performed the most useful services in the construction of railways. The Pacific states were filled with "evidences of their industry"; enterprises which had proven highly valuable would have "lain dormant" but for the Chinese laborer. No part of the country had benefited so largely from the opening of China to the commerce of the world as the people settled on our Pacific slope. It were well to remember, the President said, that the policy which it was now proposed that we should adopt would, in all probability,

[1] One of the commissioners, Swift of California, inimical to the Chinese, was cited as witness that twenty years was a "reasonable" restriction within the meaning of the treaty. (House Reports, 47th Cong. 1st sess., no. 1017, pt. 2, pp. 3, 6; N. Y. Tribune, April 6, 1882.) Angell was of a different opinion.—Cf. Coolidge, op. cit., pp. 164, 175.

"repel Oriental nations from us" and drive their trade into friendlier hands.[1]

The Union League Club of New York,[2] and many other respectable and influential organizations, as well as individuals, commended the President for his course. The intelligent press in the East approved his action. It was "sound, prudent and patriotic," said the New York Herald.[3] Harper's Weekly said that the bill was "founded on race hatred and panic." It was panic, since, after thirty years, there were only about 100,000 Chinese in the United States, while, during the same time, some five or eight millions of persons had come here from other countries.[4] So had the Irish once, not a long time ago, opposed the great movement, to free the "naygurs," who, they declared, would overrun the North and take bread from the mouths of white men.[5] The message was "temperate and excellent," the writer in Harper's Weekly continued.[6] The New York Nation said that the bill, instead of executing the treaty, violated it. It shut out the only class of Chinese who ever had, or ever would, come here,—Chinese travelers, students and scientific men would not fill a "small omnibus." Turning to the bill, in its relation to our national doctrines and policies, the Nation concluded that it was "one of the most extraordinary pieces of tergiversation in political history."[7]

On the other hand the Pacific coast was in a blaze of indignant resentment. The San Francisco newspapers voiced the temper of the people. The veto "appalls every Republican in the state and proves that the President is the slave and not the master of the Eastern bigots and scared New York merchants," said the Alta California. It was "the most arbitrary act" of

[1] Cong. Record, 47th Cong. 1st sess., pp. 2551–62; Richardson, Messages and Papers, vol. viii, pp. 112–8; McPherson's Handbook for 1882, pp. 96–8.
[2] Cong. Record, 47th Cong. 1st sess., p. 3207; N. Y. Times, April 14, 1882.
[3] April 5, 1882; cf. N. Y. Tribune and Times of the same date.
[4] Ibid., April 22, 1882.
[5] Harper's Weekly, April 1, 1882.
[6] Ibid., April 15, 1882.
[7] N. Y. Nation, March 16, 1882; cf. ibid., April 6, 1882.

any American President, said the Call. "Anger and despondency" filled every heart, said the Chronicle. The state must
be abandoned to the Chinese, said the Examiner, until relief
should come.[1] As the son of a clergyman Arthur had done
what he had done because of the pressure brought upon him
by the denominational ministry.[2] The message was the work
of the Chinese ambassador at Washington, said the Bulletin;
the President had acted as his clerk.[3] Flags were hung at
half-mast in San Francisco; some merchants "draped their
stores in deep mourning." The streets were filled with excited
and angry people.[4] It was "another echo" from the "bulldog
pistol of Charles J. Guiteau," said the Chicago Tribune.[5] In
some towns in the interior the President was burned in
effigy.[6]

Threats to drive the Chinese out of California by main
strength and, if possible, to the East, where their friends resided,
were renewed.[7] The people "must move in a determined and
heroic manner," shouted Kearney to 1,000 of his hoodlums
on the "Sand Lot." The veto was "an insult to the workingmen of the country." They had received "a slap in the face."
The "man made President by the bullet of an assassin's pistol
was now making an attempt to assassinate the people of the
Pacific slope."[8]

The labor organizations in the East were heard from. Many
of them coöperating in Philadelphia held a mass meeting,
preceded by a parade which was participated in by some 8,000
persons. They threatened Arthur with the "Nemesis of out-
raged labor." The meeting expressed "emphatic condemnation"
of his action taken "at the dictation of the capitalists and
corporations, who curse the country," and "contempt" for
the President himself and his "aristocratic and time serving

---

[1] Cited in N. Y. Herald, April 6, 1882.
[2] San Francisco Examiner, March 29 and April 3, 1882.
[3] Cf. ibid., April 7, 1882.
[4] Ibid., April 5, 1882.
[5] Quoted in ibid., April 6, 1887.
[6] Ibid., April 6, 1882; San Francisco Call, April 5 and 6, 1882.
[7] Cf. San Francisco Call, April 7, 1882.
[8] Ibid., April 6, 1882.

advisers." [1] Similar meetings were held in New York, Chicago and St. Louis,[2] all speaking in the most emphatic terms in a like sense.

An attempt on the part of the Senate to pass the bill over the veto failed,[3] and the anti-Chinese leaders immediately brought forward another, containing features which they believed would meet the objections of the Executive. In the first place the term of exclusion was fixed at ten years. The principle, which Arthur had unfavorably remarked, and which required Chinese already in the country, if they should wish, after leaving, to reënter it, and those not "laborers," still inclined to come hither, to be registered and certificated, was retained. Indeed the system was developed in even more inhospitable ways. The House received this measure from the Committee on Education and Labor on April 17th,[4] and, amid much commotion, under suspension of the rules, it was immediately passed by a vote of 201 to 37.[5] In the Senate there were a number of amendments; some of importance became the subject of stirring debate. The anti-Chinese majority was small. For example, the section construing the words "Chinese laborers" to mean both skilled and unskilled workmen and miners which, in committee of the whole, it had been agreed by a majority of one vote to strike out,[6] the Senate adopted by a vote of 25 to 20;[7] 25 favored while 16 opposed the clause prohibiting naturalization.[8] The bill was passed in the Senate by a vote of 32 to 15,[9] Hoar, Dawes, Edmunds, Morrill, Hawley and other men of similar intellectual rank continuing to express their distinct opposition to treatment of China which was so harsh. Hawley said that the whole bill read as if it had come from the "dark ages." It sounded like the old fugitive slave law. If, in the middle of the 19th

---

[1] Phila. Public Ledger, Phila., April 16 and 17, 1882.
[2] San Francisco Call, May 8, 1882.
[3] Cong. Record, 47th Cong. 1st sess., p. 2617.
[4] Ibid., p. 2967; House Reports, 47th Cong. 1st sess., no. 1017, pts. 1 and 2.
[5] Cong. Record, 47th Cong. 1st sess., pp. 2973–4.
[6] Ibid., p. 3264.
[7] Ibid., p. 3411.
[8] Ibid., pp. 3411–2.
[9] Ibid., p. 3412.

century, such a measure were to be put upon the statute books of the country let it be done "in silence and mourning." [1] In the sight of the world China had been the particular exemplar of such benightedness, said John Sherman; we had persuaded and led her out of it. Now we were putting ourselves in her old place. [2]

The President approved the bill, [3] with reluctance, perhaps, at any rate with not too much consistency, in view of his recent words, [4] but with the conviction, generally entertained, that the issue must be met to quiet a clamor which, by much reiteration and long continuance, had by this time become a common nuisance.

At last California could rejoice. Half a loaf was better than no bread. [5] A hundred guns were fired from a hill in San Francisco and that their reverberation might be more eloquent they were "turned over Chinatown." Fifty guns proclaimed the news at Stockton, 38 in Bodie. [6] Flags were flung out. [7]

It was, in truth, a departure in national policy. The liberal principles and traditions actuating the founders of the government, reborn in the soul of, and restated by, a group of powerful men who had made their voices heard and their will to prevail in the movement for the abolition of slavery and the enfranchisement of the negro, were strongly held. [8] On ground

[1] Cong. Record, 47th Cong. 1st sess., p. 3264.
[2] Ibid., p. 2608; cf. N. Y. Nation, March 16, 1882.
[3] Cong. Record, 47th Cong. 1st sess., p. 3777.
[4] Cf. N. Y. Tribune, May 9, 1882.
[5] San Francisco Examiner, May 9, 1882.
[6] San Francisco Call, May 9, 1882.
[7] Ibid., May 10, 1882.
[8] The confession that a hundred thousand peaceful men endangered the welfare of fifty million Americans came strangely from the Republican party, said Harper's Weekly. Congress had adopted the principle of Stephen Douglas, "I am for the white man against the negro and for the negro against the alligator." They were the "first to renounce the claim that America welcomes every honest comer and offers a home to the honest victim of the oppression of kings and of cruel laws." (Harper's Weekly, May 20, 1882.) Holding the doctrine "that neither race nor ignorance in any way disqualifies a man for citizenship" with reference to a race "far inferior to the Chinese in constructive power and far below them in culture," the old leaders of the Republican party, said the New York Nation, were in an uncomfortable position. (N. Y. Nation, Jan. 23, 1879.) "The discourse

somewhere between that occupied by such an one as Senator Hoar, and that on which the Californians stood, moved as they were by race prejudices and the purely selfish motives of their labor leaders, lay the way the nation would hereafter take. The United States, to use the picturesque phrase of a member of Congress, introduced in the debate on the exclusion bill, was not to be "a sort of continental menagerie of nationalities," "a sort of ethnological animal show," "a zoological paradise." [1] The "rights of asylum and of migration and expatriation," [2] the duty to receive and assimilate, if not to naturalize and enfranchise, all manner of men in the name of "democracy," or "republicanism," or the still larger one of "humanity," might be "the brightest jewels in our coronet of glory," [3] but we were now launched on a new course. It had been determined, though liberal minds said that we should live to regret the day of our decision, [4] and would turn back to the oiden way, that the republic should not offer a refuge to, and become a home for, all who presented themselves at its portals, if to receive them affronted the racial sentiments, or did not suit the practical convenience of a majority of those already domiciled here and incorporated in the body politic. [5]

Having tasted success the labor leaders increased their de-

in Congress of some of its new leaders was calculated to make Thaddeus Stevens or Joshua R. Giddings, e.g., turn in his grave."—Ibid., March 16, 1882.

[1] Cong. Record, 47th Cong. 1st. sess., p. 2126.

[2] Hoar stated this to be "the right [of everyone in whose frame God had placed "a human soul"] to go everywhere on this globe that he shall see fit to go and to seek and enjoy the blessings of life, liberty and the pursuit of happiness, at his will." (Cong. Record, 45th Cong. 3rd sess., p. 1312). Congress had recently defined the "right of expatriation" to be "a natural and inherent right of all people, indispensable to the enjoyment of the rights of life, liberty and the pursuit of happiness." (Act of July 27, 1868, 15 U. S. Statutes at Large, pp. 223–4.) It was described in the Burlingame treaty as "the inherent and inalienable right of man to change his home and allegiance," and to enjoy "the advantage of free migration."— Art. v, Burlingame Treaty, Haswell, Treaties and Conventions, p. 181; cf. R. Mayo-Smith, Emigration and Immigration, pp. 228–9; Senate Ex. Doc., 47th Cong. 1st sess., no. 175, p. 3.

[3] Cong. Record, 47th Cong. 1st sess., p. 2189.

[4] Ibid., p. 3265.

[5] Cf. R. Mayo-Smith, Emigration and Immigration, p. 229; G. F. Seward, in North American Review for June, 1882.

mands. In the period following the passage of the exclusion act 17,000 Chinese had gone home and only 3,415 had arrived, these being, for the most part, men who had once been in the United States and were entitled to return.[1] The number of arrivals had been reduced, the San Francisco Chronicle said, from 1,500 to 66 a month.[2] Not more than 500 or 600 new immigrants had found their way into the country. But the anti-Chinese outcry was so useful to the politicians of the Pacific coast, and the salaried officers of workingmen's associations in all parts of the country, that it must go on. The daily newspapers of San Francisco, except the Alta, would not let the subject rest. There was, said the Argonaut, a sage weekly observer of life in California, "no depth of absurdity nor height of wickedness" to which they would not "crawl or climb" to secure the good will of the "ignorant and demagogue element of the labor class." [3]

Instead of honoring passports presented by returning Chinese such papers were presumed to be fraudulent. The holders were arrested and their cases were thrown into court.[4] The exclusion law was being evaded, it was said. Twenty thousand Chinamen were in British Columbia eager to cross our borders. So much immigration was surreptitious that the official statistics gave no correct measure of its magnitude. The United States Circuit Court in Massachusetts had admitted a Chinaman who had been born on the British island of Hong Kong. Native "English Chinamen" in that colony, as well as in Singapore, would fall upon us as a plague, if the law were not amended at once.[5] A mass of petitions appeared in the Congress which met in December, 1883.[6] The senators and representatives from the Pacific coast conferred and agreed upon a supplementary bill to make the law more effective. Several men in the House, notably Rice of Massachusetts and Hitt of Illinois,[7]

[1] Cong. Record, 48th Cong. 1st sess., p. 3754.
[2] Ibid.
[3] Ibid., p. 3755.
[4] Ibid., p. 3754.
[5] Cf. N. Y. Times, April 15, 1882.
[6] See Index to Cong. Record, 48th Cong. 1st sess., p. 72.
[7] Cf. N. Y. Nation, July 3, 1884.

interposed objections to the "continual hectoring" of the Chinese.[1] The bill was "clap-trap and surplusage," said Mr. Rice.[2] Vainly it was argued that to interfere with the movements of "English Chinamen" might lead to difficulty with other governments as well as with China, which induced one of the California labor leaders to shout, amid applause,—"If amity with Great Britain is only to be purchased and obtained at the price of the degradation of the laboring people of this country, then, Mr. Chairman, I say the price is too high."[3]

In the House only 13 voted against the supplementary bill,[4] and, at the very end of the session, in the Senate, where Hoar, hopelessly overborne, simply said that to him the bill and the law which it was to amend rested on "sheer barbarism,"[5] only 12 votes were mustered against it. President Arthur's approval followed.

[1] Cong. Record, 48th Cong. 1st sess., p. 3757.
[2] Ibid., p. 3754.
[3] Ibid., p. 3752.
[4] Ibid., p. 3777.
[5] Ibid., p. 5938.

CHAPTER XXIX

PRESIDENT CLEVELAND

THE assurance, finally given by the "official count" in New York state, that Cleveland was to be President of the United States after March 4, 1885, left the average Republican party man in a state of stupefaction. His amazement that a Democrat was about to occupy such an office was mingled with a sullen contempt not only for Democracy generally, because of its alliances with slavery and rebellion, but for him under whose leadership it had been able to achieve its triumph. Men not unintelligent and uncandid dimly realized that it was a deserved defeat, that rebuke for the arrogances, excesses and corruptions which had characterized the Grant administration, if long delayed, was some day due, and that the surrender of the party to such a man as Blaine and his friends was an error, which invited precisely what had come to pass. Yet it is consciousness of doing wrong which often makes reproof the more bitter, and it was with something of this inner spirit, as well as outward manner, that Republicans, who had followed Whitelaw Reid and the New York Tribune, revealed themselves in this conjuncture. Reid, the "reformer," who had abandoned his olden friends honestly interested in the improvement of the government, and who had spoken about them throughout the campaign in language which he could have applied with more propriety to some of his new associates, for many days said nothing of the President-elect. On November 17th, a fortnight after the poll was taken, the Tribune conceded Cleveland's election, "by suppression of the right of suffrage at the South, and by dishonest misrepresentations in four Northern states."[1] Consolation was found in the fact that the Senate would be Republican and could block the "free trade Copperheads," who

[1] Issue of Nov. 17, 1884.

would control the House, and the President.[1] On Thanksgiving Day the Tribune intimated that the Democrats would eat their dinner "with a relish" which they had not known "since they elected their last old bachelor President, James Buchanan."[2] It was November 29th before the Tribune grew magnanimous. It was "right," it then said, "to hope for the best, right to assure the President-elect that his political opponents will not be indisposed to give him credit for whatever sound judgment or patriotic purposes he may display."[3]

Mr. Cleveland viewed the scene with clear sight and a full sense of his great responsibilities. "I intend," he wrote to his friend Bissell in Buffalo, "to cultivate the Christian virtue of charity toward all men, except the dirty class that defiled themselves with filthy scandal. I don't believe God will ever forgive them and I am determined not to do so."

"I look upon the four years next to come," he said, "as a dreadful self-inflicted penance for the good of my country. I can see no pleasure in it, no satisfaction, only a hope that I may be of service to my people."

"As I look over the field," he continued, "I see some people lying dead whose demise will not harm the country, some whose wounds will, perhaps, serve to teach them that honesty and decency are worth possessing and some whose valor, fidelity and staunch devotion are rewarded with victory and who have gripped themselves to me with hooks of steel."[4]

The President-elect was on his guard; he was no neophyte in the world into which he had been precipitated. If Buffalo were but a small city and the law, as it was practiced there, no important school for the profession of statecraft it was soon made clear that he would be able to take care of himself and the great office into which he would shortly be inducted. The concern of the Republican newspapers lest he should reveal his incapacities, and the solicitude of those who had done all things to keep him from the Presidency on the subject of his ability

[1] Cf. N. Y. Tribune, Nov. 18 and 21, 1884.
[2] Ibid., Nov. 27, 1884.
[3] Ibid., Nov. 29, 1884.
[4] November 13, 1884, in Cleveland Papers.

to form an administration without their aid, were as droll as they were needless examples of editorial surveillance.[1] Even the congratulatory messages which poured in upon him were received not without suspicion. Many of them he observed came from those who had held aloof during the canvass and now, in the hour of success, desired to take some of the credit for it. He almost thought, he wrote his friend Bissell, that the "professions" of most of his "pretended friends" were "but the means they employed to accomplish personal and selfish ends." [2]

Men bearing gifts also excited his distrust. Many sought to direct attention to themselves by this avenue. The limit of patience was reached when an admirer in Brooklyn sent a Newfoundland dog. Mr. Cleveland replied and gave his letter to the press. "I am very averse to the receipt of gifts, especially in the situation of strangers which you and I sustain to each other," he wrote. "The acceptance of gifts of value which could involve an obligation I should deem, in my present position, entirely inadmissible, and I confess I should feel better if all gifts of any description were discontinued. I shall please myself, and I hope not offend you, by sending the dog by express to your address tomorrow at my expense." [3]

There was reason for suspicion. The President-elect, in the governor's office at Albany, was almost immediately under siege by men who wanted offices and jobs. They were a "hungry horde"; the triumph of their party after an administration of the government for nearly 25 years by the Republicans meant the opportunity of seizing the honors and rewards which an enemy had enjoyed, and the sweet revenge of driving that enemy from place and power.

[1] The New York Tribune suggested a guardianship for so inexperienced a man and recalled the words of the old ballad in which the complacent lover sang,

"When I go out to serenade
I always look so gay
I have to take my dog along
To keep the girls away."—

Issue of Dec. 6, 1884.

[2] To Bissell, Christmas Day, 1884, in Cleveland Papers.
[3] Nov. 27, 1884, in Cleveland Papers.

"Now in the hour of victory," one wrote to Cleveland, "we cannot and will not sit down and fold our hands and close our eyes and let the devil come in the shape and size of the Honorable George William Curtis as a ministering angel of a defeated party." The Republicans must be made to understand that they have been "dethroned," that their "past rotten record" will be "dug up and exposed by an honest and judicious Democratic administration." [1]

A letter from Mr. Curtis to the President-elect inquiring in behalf of the National Civil Service Reform League as to his attitude toward the great matter which had led so many Republicans to give him their support in the recent campaign was forwarded to Albany on December 20, 1884, and the reply was dated on Christmas Day. It was a direct, courageous and commendable statement. Mr. Cleveland said that he was pledged to the enforcement of the civil service law; his faith he would keep. The "spoils system" was "deeply rooted." He was not certain, he sagely and fittingly observed, that even those who professed to favor the reform would firmly advocate it when they found that it obstructed "their way to patronâge and place." As for government positions without the purview of the civil service statute, removals would not be made "solely on partisan grounds." But it must be remembered that many now holding such offices had used their places "for party purposes in disregard of their duty to the people"; instead of being "decent public servants" they had proven themselves "offensive partisans and unscrupulous manipulators" in local political contests.

In conclusion Mr. Cleveland said that, while Democrats "may expect all proper consideration" from the new administration, there would, nevertheless, be "sufficient inquiry as to fitness"

[1] Cleveland Papers. An editor in Indiana said in a letter to the President-elect, "Remember the motto 'To the victors belong the spoils' will make our party strong in 1888. The Western people desire a change in the offices. What are we here for? Surely not to keep Republicans in office. Turn the rascals out." He wanted to know the size of Cleveland's boots; he had the hide and would make and send the President a pair to wear on March 4th to kick the Republicans out of office.—In Nov., 1884, in ibid.

in making appointments, and that such examination would have more weight than "persistent importunity or self-solicited recommendations on behalf of candidates." [1]

Such clear promise of a determination to bring about improved conditions in politics created a feeling of deep satisfaction in the minds of men holding correct views of public life. In newspaper and by letter the President-elect was warmly congratulated on his bravery of purpose.[2] He made no other statement of importance as the weeks advanced toward the day of his induction into office except the significant one in response to an inquiry by Congressman A. J. Warner and other members of the House of Representatives as to his views on the silver question. The mints were "still turning into the vaults [of the United States Treasury] each month two million light weight dollars to be added to the tons of superfluous coin already idle there." [3] A provision of the law of 1878 committing us to this folly had authorized a further pursuit of the phantom agreement with other nations, particularly of the so-called Latin Union, too obviously in order to make a market for our Rocky Mountain miners and to justify the theories of our bimetallists. The conference in Paris in 1878 having ended in failure, agitation was continued until France was persuaded to join us in the convocation, in 1881, of another. Sixteen states, together with Canada and British India, were represented. Evarts, who had just retired from the Hayes cabinet, led the delegation from the United States, which included two United States senators recently relieved of their offices, Timothy O. Howe of Wisconsin and Allen G. Thurman of Ohio. In Paris all found the opportunity to deliver resounding discourses, Howe's being a Western "stump speech." After sessions for a few days in May the conference declared a recess for six weeks, during which time our delegates enjoyed the, to them, unfamiliar "sights" of Europe, returning to their useless discussions in July. It could well have been confessed, as one said, that the entire movement,

[1] N. Y. Tribune, Dec. 31, 1884; McPherson's Handbook for 1886, p. 116.
[2] Cleveland Papers.
[3] N. Y. Tribune, Feb. 11, 1885.

which the meeting was called to promote, had collapsed, failing the adhesion of certain states, notably England and Germany.[1] Such a result all intelligent men had foreseen, but the bimetallists were unwilling to adjourn—they would prorogue the conference until the following year.[2] When that time came, the futility of reassembling being obvious, the French government asked for delay until there should seem to be some basis for new discussions.[3]

No rebuffing fact quieted our inflationists. Now again, in the last days of the Forty-eighth Congress, with a change of party government near at hand, a group of Democrats were moved to ask the man, whose election to the Presidency made him the leader of the party, for his views about the currency question. He gave it in terms which staggered them.[4] The withdrawals from the Treasury for the purchase of silver to be coined into dollars under the act of 1878 were so great, he said, that soon there would not be a sum of gold large enough to redeem the "greenbacks." A "financial crisis" was "close at hand." These were facts, he declared, that "do not admit of difference of opinion," they "call for no argument." The further purchase of silver should be stopped. "I am, gentlemen," he concluded, "with sincere respect, your fellow citizen, Grover Cleveland." [5] It was plain enough that a man with understanding, devoted to the public interest, would soon occupy a position at the head of the government.[6] Partisans, like the writers in the Tribune, could still dilate upon "tallow candles" which would not shine in proximity to "suns," thereby inferring that Cleveland would choose mediocrities for his cabinet;[7] upon the

[1] House Mis. Doc., 49th Cong. 1st sess., no. 396, pt. 3, p. 505.

[2] Ibid., pp. 506, 519; cf. Senate Ex. Doc., 49th Cong. 1st sess., no. 29, p. 19; N. Y. Nation, July 14, 1881.

[3] House Ex. Doc., 47th Cong. 1st sess., no. 221.

[4] As to the authorship of this letter cf. McElroy, Grover Cleveland, vol. i, pp. 107–10.

[5] N. Y. Tribune, Feb. 28, 1885; McPherson's Handbook for 1886, p. 117; cf. Letters and Memorials of Tilden, pp. 671–2; N. Y. Nation, March 5, 1885.

[6] "Your silver letter," Tilden wrote, "is absolutely perfect. It is the only silver thing I know that transmutes itself into gold."—To Cleveland on Feb. 28, 1885, in Cleveland Papers.

[7] N. Y. Tribune, Jan. 3, 1885.

fact that he had had "no experience," that he was wanting in "brilliant qualities" and was in possesson of "little knowledge of public men or affairs." [1] It amused readers of the Republican press, it is to be presumed, to hear him called "the political what-is-it," [2] "a conundrum in the flesh," "a man who may be or do almost anything, or almost nothing," [3] a creature of the "New York gang," [4] a man without ideas, and without thoughts. [5]

If, by this time, the President-elect was regarded as a "conundrum" it meant that his career as governor of New York had not been observed or studied. Men attached to the Tammany and Albany gangs were not in much doubt about his character. Those who gave their minds to public affairs in all parts of the country understood Cleveland's point of view and measured his intellect; if they were men of rectitude they loved him, as had been said in the nominating convention, "for the enemies he had made." It is very true that some, without any degree of perspicuity, the small politicians in the party ranks, were not without hope, or, perhaps, expectation, of reaping personal benefits. And leaders of higher position, whose business it was to exploit the electorate that they might stay in office and use the government for the material advantage of themselves and their friends, tried to think that the President-elect would now have softer moods. To this extent he was a "conundrum"; he was being "explored" [6] as a new and somewhat unknown, if not really strange, figure injected into our public life.

The weeks passed. Mr. Cleveland, on January 5, 1885, wrote a brief message to the legislature—"I hereby resign the office of governor of the state of New York," action which automatically brought the lieutenant-governor, David B. Hill, into the place, and the President-elect was free for the tasks which confronted him—the formation of a cabinet and the preparation of his inaugural address.

Tilden's name continued to be prominently associated with

[1] N. Y. Tribune, Jan. 3, 1885.
[2] Ibid., Jan. 14, 1885.
[3] Ibid., Jan. 9, 1885.
[4] Ibid., Feb. 13, 1885.
[5] Cf. ibid., Feb. 12, 1885.
[6] Ibid., Jan. 27, 1885.

the Democratic party. His friends were of opinion—and the
egotistical and disappointed old man shared the view—that
scant honor had been done him at the nominating convention
and during the campaign. They still controlled the party
organization in New York The chairman of the state committee was Daniel Manning who owned a newspaper in
Albany, and had other business interests, including the presidency of a bank. He was a practical politican, nourishing few
ideals with reference to government, though he had had a
leading part in naming Cleveland for the governorship in 1882
and labored loyally for his nomination and election to the
greater office in 1884. It was Manning who had visited Tilden
and had persuaded him to make a definite withdrawal from
the field, thus clearing the way for another candidate.[1] In
August, during the excitement attending the canvass, Manning accompanied Cleveland to "Graystone," Tilden's seat at
Yonkers. On this account, and for other reasons, it was declared that, if Cleveland were elected, he would give the country "a thoroughly Tilden administration." [2]

The time was at hand when the truth of this statement
would be put to the test. Men were writing to Tilden begging
the favor of his influence in giving them places of honor and
power in the new government. Governor George Hoadly of
Ohio, Governor Robert M. McLane of Maryland, Senator
Garland of Arkansas and others wished to be remembered
in the organization of the administration, though the "martyr"
of 1876 truly replied that he did not know "to what extent,
or in what cases, if any," he might be consulted by the President-
elect.[3] To the old Nestor of the party the younger man, in
the moment of victory, should turn for counsel and leadership. But Cleveland's eyes were fixed on other objects.[4] It

[1] Bigelow, Life of Tilden, vol. ii, pp. 280–81.
[2] Letters and Memorials of Tilden, p. 646; cf. ibid., pp. 675–6.
[3] Ibid., p. 661; cf. ibid., pp. 659–60, 663–4, 669–71; Bigelow, Life of
Tilden, vol. ii, pp. 289–91. Hoadly said that it would be "a sad day" for
Cleveland if he ignored Tilden, and did not seek wisdom where it abounded,
etc. (Letters and Memorials of Tilden, p. 662.) Samuel J. Randall and
others expressed similar views.—Ibid., pp. 662–3.
[4] Cf. McElroy, Grover Cleveland, vol. i, pp. 107–10.

was not his wish to bring his administration under the control of reactionaries who, with grudges to nurse and scores to even, would have only a secondary interest in the proper conduct of the country's affairs. Nevertheless, for taking himself out of the way, Tilden and his friends pretended to think that they should have important recognition in the cabinet. They even declared that they had had definite assurances that they could have what they liked, and it was a rude awakening when they were brought to understand that the fruits would be spare.

If some of our Presidents have had freedom in the selection of their counselors it was not to be Cleveland's experience with the office. The claim of the Tilden faction to recognition, if not to complete control of the new President's movements, was but one of many impudent advances. Indeed only a man with "a head of his own"—and it was soon discovered that Cleveland was such an one—could withstand the attacks that were made upon him from every side for appointment to places in the cabinet. Letters, resolutions, petitions, visits from individuals and delegations announced the candidacy of two or three score party leaders in all portions of the country— flattery, demand and scarcely veiled threat accompanied the applications for preferment. Persistent agitation was begun and was continued in behalf of General McClellan who, it was held by the writers of many letters to Mr. Cleveland, had suffered so much indignity at the hands of the Republicans; John P. Stockton of New Jersey, Judge Vanderpoel of New York who should be the Attorney-General; Senator McDonald of Indiana, Senator Thurman of Ohio, Senator Jonas of Louisiana, Governor Hubbard of Texas and Senator Garland of Arkansas. George H. Pendleton of Ohio, William M. Springer of Illinois, Governor Hoadly of Ohio, Governor Pattison of Pennsylvania, Samuel J. Randall, Abram S. Hewitt, ex-Senator Doolittle, Lyman Trumbull, General C. W. Blair and Governor Glick of Kansas, Governor Colquitt and General Gordon of Georgia, General Hancock, General Rosecrans, General Walthall of Mississippi, General Reagan of Texas, John G.

Carlisle, and a host more, were strongly pressed upon the President-elect's notice.

He quietly kept to his course. It was early predicted that his choice for Secretary of State would be Thomas F. Bayard of Delaware,[1] though some said that Bayard would be invited to the Treasury.[2] This would be so fitting an appointment that the most irrational of critics [3] could say little in disparagement of him who tendered the office, or of him who might accept it. But when a little later it was surmised that Senator Garland would be chosen for Attorney-General,[4] an office which he greatly desired, the Republicans expressed, as could have been foreseen, mad dissent. He had been a member of the convention which had taken his state out of the Union and of the "Rebel" Congress. He might shoot negroes in Arkansas, said the New York Tribune, but, if he should import such methods into the North, where crimes of this kind were regarded as "acts of rebellion," he would be made to understand things that he doubtless did not yet know. It was the part of the Attorney-General to "instruct and control all district attorneys and deputy marshals of the United States in the enforcement of the election and other laws." Garland was a "leader of the lawbreakers," yet it was proposed that he be designated "to enforce the laws." [5] Even men in his own party viewed the suggestion of his appointment doubtfully, in some degree, perhaps, because of his very active solicitude in his own behalf. They said that he was a "Hamiltonian," and not a "true blue Democrat." He had voted for the "Blair bill." [6] Northern Democrats,

---

[1] Cf. N. Y. Tribune, Dec. 11, 1884; Writings of Schurz, vol. iv, p. 296.

[2] Cf. Writings of Schurz, vol. iv, pp. 296, 349; Letters and Memorials of Tilden, pp. 662-3, 670; McElroy, Grover Cleveland, vol. i, p. 102. Bayard wrote to Schurz on November 17, 1884, soon after the election, "I know but little personally of the President-elect. Heaven grant that he may comprehend and fulfil the needs of the hour."—Writings of Schurz, vol. iv, p. 291.

[3] One of these was Washington McLean.—Letters and Memorials of Tilden, pp. 669-70.

[4] N. Y. Tribune, Dec. 31, 1884.

[5] Ibid., Dec. 3, 1884.

[6] Garland to Lamont, Dec. 29, 1884, in Cleveland Papers.

like the Republicans, were not clear as to the propriety of having a Southerner in the office. Anyhow such an appointment would invite criticism, which it would be well to avoid.

It became clear, too, in no long time, that Cleveland would ask William C. Whitney, son-in-law of Henry B. Payne who had just been elected a United States senator from Ohio, one of the few wealthy men of business who were attached to the Democratic party, himself a man of large means, to accept a place in the cabinet. Tilden had been reducing his claims, founded on the understanding, which, it was alleged, that he had had with the President-elect. Now, he would, it seemed, consider himself fortunate if he could name one member of the group of advisers standing at Cleveland's side and, presumably, this one would come from New York. But Whitney was not allied to the Tilden organization, he was not Tilden's choice. Chairman Manning and Smith M. Weed were acting as the "old man's" lieutenants and were tirelessly engaged in trying to mold Cleveland's mind. He had "some queer ideas" which must be "talked out of him"; he was "very set on Whitney" and could not be "changed" in that design, they wrote their chieftain. It had done no hurt "to let him alone for a couple of weeks."[1] Manning would fetch Cleveland to see Tilden at "Graystone" where, as early as on January 2nd, the President-elect had been invited to be a guest for "a few days' repose."[2] On a Thursday, February 4th, Cleveland came down from Albany and remained until Saturday at a hotel in New York where he was immediately besieged by "leaders," coming singly and in delegations from all parts of the country, who gained nothing for their pains except confirmation of what had been earlier known that the man whom they had elected to the Presidency was "a good listener but a poor talker."[3] Having completed his visit in the city he proceeded to Yonkers, where he remained with Tilden throughout Sunday and Monday morning,[4] but

---

[1] Letters and Memorials of Tilden, pp. 666-7.
[2] Ibid., p. 665. Letter of invitation in Cleveland Papers.
[3] N. Y. Tribune, Feb. 6, 1885.
[4] Ibid., Feb. 9 and 10, 1885.

the meeting was not productive of any increase of assurance on Tilden's side that he would play a considerable part in guiding the course of the new President. If Whitney were chosen, and if Tilden were to have one of the appointments, New York would have two members of the cabinet. This was clear. Either Manning or John Bigelow would meet Tilden's views, with Manning leading in favor, and he should be Secretary of the Treasury to keep Whitney out of a place which controlled so much patronage.[1]

No account had yet been taken of Schurz and the Mugwumps. They had rendered the President-elect a distinctly valuable service, and they were not loath to remind him of his indebtedness to them, which they would have discharged by high-minded appointments as a guarantee of better government. Schurz wrote to, and conferred with, Cleveland in the interest of the civil service question.[2] The part which the Mugwumps had taken in the election was explained, if not emphasized, and the redoubtable reformer found himself in a friendly presence when he visited the President-elect, who freely recognized the value of Schurz's exertions in the campaign, expressing the sincere wish "to merit the good opinion of the men" who had "trusted him," and confessing himself, with a modesty which placed him in a highly attractive light, to be one who knew "little" of what awaited him "in his new sphere of duty." [3]

The Mugwumps, or those who owned Schurz as their leader, and he was *facile princeps* in their circles,[4] opposed the claims of both Manning [5] and Whitney.[6] Manning was a skillful

[1] Hewitt wrote to Cleveland. Manning, he said, was better known to the country as a man of capacity than Whitney, but he was not able enough "to deal successfully with the financial problem." A Secretary of the Treasury should know the law. "I think I know why Mr. Manning has been so earnestly pressed upon you. It is a dangerous quarter from which to take advice." Every "appearance of rewarding personal political services" should be avoided. "If the impression once gets abroad that you have debts to pay and are paying them your administration will be wrecked."— Feb. 17, 1885, in Cleveland Papers.

[2] Cf. Writings of Schurz, vol. iv, pp. 288–90, 297–308.

[3] Ibid., p. 297.

[4] Horace White to Cleveland, Feb. 2, 1885, in Cleveland Papers.

[5] Writings of Schurz, vol. iv, pp. 351–4.

[6] Ibid., pp. 348–51, 355–60; Letters and Memorials of Tilden, p. 668.

party manager and nothing more. E. L. Godkin and Horace
White of the New York Evening Post said that they and
George Jones of the New York Times could not explain such
action to the readers of their newspapers should these appointments be made.[1] They knew the force of the demand
and the difficulty of resisting it but bade the President stand
firm at any cost. Whitney's only reputation, said Schurz, was
"as Senator Payne's son-in-law, the brother-in-law of the
Standard Oil Company, worth several millions," and as a
contributor of $25,000 to the Cleveland campaign fund.[2]

At the right time, in spite of all protest, Manning was offered
the Secretaryship of the Treasury. He said that he had "no
heart for it." The thought of taking up such tasks had made
him ill for two days.[3] But no excuse availed. Tilden told him
that it was his duty to accept; unless he should do so "the
veterans" would have "no true and reliable friend" at the
new President's side. It would "chill the masses"—those
who gave the party its strength and who were on the point
of being entirely ignored, though they had served well and
made the victory possible, would insist that Manning assume
"the trust which sacrifice, duty and honor" demanded at his
hands. With this great charge upon him Manning entered

[1] Letters of Godkin and White in Cleveland Papers.
[2] Writings of Schurz, vol. iv, p. 356. Up to Feb. 5, 1885, it is stated in
a memorandum in the Cleveland Papers that $453,000 had been contributed
to the Democratic National Committee. The principal subscribers were

Wm. H. Barnum, chairman of the committee	$27,500
Wm. L. Scott of Erie, Pa.	24,000
Wm. C. Whitney (approximately)	20,000
Cooper and Hewitt	20,000
Abram S. Hewitt (personally)	5,300
Oswald Ottendorfer	18,000
D. Willis James	16,000
Roswell P. Flower	16,000
A. P. Gorman	15,000
Daniel Manning	14,000
Addison Cammack	11,000
George Gray	10,000

Tilden gave $6,000, L. Z. Leiter of Chicago $6,000, James J. Hill $5,000
and Joseph Pulitzer $1,000.

[3] Letters and Memorials of Tilden, p. 678. If he knew the "enormous
responsibilities" of the place Abram S. Hewitt felt certain that he would
not take it.—Hewitt to Cleveland, Feb. 17, 1885, in Cleveland papers.

the cabinet,[1] though, as Tilden's friends complained, "never welcomed to it, nor in it." [2] Whitney, like Manning, had made no motion in his own behalf.[3] He would be Secretary of the Navy. You would "vainly look" Schurz wrote to Lamar, "for just such a couple of appointments from the President's own state in the history of cabinets." [4]

If there were among the Independents those who had expected Schurz himself, or another representative, to be intrusted with a portfolio,[5] there was disappointment for such an one was not named, unless the selection of Judge William C. Endicott, descended from old, socially-distinguished Massachusetts families, an overseer of Harvard College, as Secretary of War could be taken to be in answer to this feeling.[6] But he had been steadfast, if quiet and inactive, in his attachment to the Democratic party, and it was pointed out by Republican journals that, since he was not a "turncoat," the Independents could not regard him as a disciple of their principles in public life.

Garland was finally, on February 25th, invited to become

[1] Letters and Memorials of Tilden, pp. 675-8.

[2] Bigelow, Life of Tilden, vol. ii, p. 291.

[3] "I should feel really hurt," he wrote Cleveland, "if I thought you would have any feeling of obligation to me. What I have done was from a sense of duty to our party and country." And he added, "If, for reasons personal and sound, you should desire me that's one thing, but I hope you believe this of me—that, if you should not, it would not make the slightest difference in our relations, nor in my feelings, nor in what I would do for you." (Whitney to Cleveland about Jan. 1, 1885, in Cleveland Papers.) Men wrote to John Sherman asking that Manning, Lamar and Garland be not confirmed. Manning had enriched himself through the Tweed Ring. Prior to 1872 he had been "a common legislative reporter." He got public printing for the Albany Argus. Thus had he become a wealthy man. Lamar's and Garland's appointments were an insult to all living soldiers and sailors of the United States and to the children of those who had died in the war in defense of its flag. One of Sherman's correspondents held a small Federal office. He would leave it—he would not serve under "traitors"; he would rather "break stone" on the roads, etc.—Sherman Papers.

[4] Cf. Writings of Schurz, vol. iv, p. 357.

[5] Cf. ibid., pp. 293-5, 358.

[6] "He is the idol of the Massachusetts bar, a man of great learning and practical wisdom and a gentleman of the very first type." (A Massachusetts Independent to Cleveland, Feb. 25, 1885, in Cleveland Papers.) Endicott telegraphed his acceptance of Cleveland's proffer of the office on Feb. 26th, after considering the suggestion for two or three days.

Attorney-General and he, of course, accepted at once. Another
Southern man was called upon for service in the new cabinet,
Lucius Quintus Cincinnatus Lamar of Mississippi, who, instead of one of a number of men in the West who had been
pressed for appointment to the office, became Secretary of
the Interior. He had been asked to use his influences in behalf of General Walthall, a choice which he said that he would
cordially approve, though he observed that he had "no talent
whatever for getting up influences and agencies to subserve
the advancement of any man." He had devoted his abilities
"to operating on masses and not on single individuals." Anyhow he was not "in connection with the lines of communication
with the President-elect." He would wait to be asked for
advice before giving it.[1] The suggestion that he himself should
receive an appointment came to Lamar, therefore, as a surprise. Men called him a "dreamer." [2] He would be the "literary
man" of the cabinet.[3] It was bitter to Republican tastes that
he rose so often in the Senate to deny that Jefferson Davis
was a "traitor"; but his remembered eulogy of Sumner, his
intelligence and courage, as, for example, on the currency
question, and his recognized abilities as a thinker and in argument went far to reconcile the Republican North to his
choice. The West would have for its representative Colonel
William F. Vilas of Wisconsin. He had been chairman of
the Democratic national convention and had led the delegation to Albany to notify the candidate of his nomination.
He would be Postmaster-General.[4]

The new President's understanding of the Constitution of
the United States, and the form of government which had
been established under it, was simple enough. He stripped
the political system to its fundamentals. He would rid it of
tendencies toward a submergence of the states, and of the

[1] Letter of Dec. 18, 1884, in Cleveland Papers.
[2] N. Y. Tribune, Feb. 19, 1885.
[3] Mayes, Life of Lamar, p. 490.
[4] When it became clear that McDonald of Indiana would have no place
in the group 21 Democratic senators put their signatures upon a letter
urging the President to take notice of his claims.—Cleveland Papers.

individual citizen. Socializing and centralizing enterprises had gone forward without his sympathy. Since the war only Andrew Johnson had represented such a school of political opinion in the Presidential office. To this fund of principles and views Cleveland added hatred of sham and humbug, of the arts of the demagogue as well as the wiles of the corruptionist and the thief.[1] He bade fair to make an indelible mark on the course of political history in his time, with or without the approval of elements in his own old party, or in the other party which for so long had too arrogantly directed the destinies of the country.

Cleveland was now 48 years of age. He came of excellent New England stock which for several generations had produced Congregational or Presbyterian ministers in Connecticut. His father was a minister. An elder brother was a minister. His youngest sister, Miss Rose Elizabeth Cleveland, a teacher, lecturer and writer, had presided hospitably at the governor's mansion in Albany and would become the "lady of the White House." His parents, when Grover, or Stephen Grover, as he was christened, was born, lived in northern New Jersey,[2] but they soon removed to Oneida county, N. Y. His education, if it had come to an end at an early age, was not mean. His associations as a boy were with men and women of cultivation and high principles.[3] On his way to Cleveland, O., where he had determined to seek his fortune, he had visited an uncle in Buffalo, where he settled, and in a short time commenced the study of the law, which led to the accumulation of some means and a reputation for talent and integrity at the bar, and in politics, which came to interest him. From the first his words, whenever he touched public life, rang with a sense of duty and responsibility and a striving for the reali-

[1] He was mentally honest, a man, said a friend, "who loves truth, justice and fair play, who says what he means and means what he says." (J. R. Doolittle to Manning, March 25, 1885, in Cleveland Papers.) "The only way to do," he said, "is to find out what is right, and then do it without any regard to the result."—N. Y. World, July 22, 1885.

[2] At Caldwell. The name of an old and respected former pastor of the church at that place was Stephen Grover.

[3] Cf. McElroy, Grover Cleveland, vol. i, pp. 5–6.

zation of a rule of action expressed in the phrase—"public office is a public trust," which, if he had never uttered it in that compact form, was the governing principle of his political career.[1]

Life had brought him hard experience. He was one of nine children; his father, who had never earned more than $1,000 a year, died when he was but 16 years old and he must provide, as he could, for his mother and sisters. He had not expended any considerable portion of his days in dreaming dreams and uttering airy nothings. In social contacts he exhibited a reticence and a dignity which, at first, were regarded as bashfulness if not gruffness. His friend and partner in the practice of law in Buffalo, Wilson Bissell, had had to do with "plain men, the active, hard-fisted, busy men, earnestly engaged in the struggles of life." [2] So had Cleveland. He was not quite comfortable in situations in which others found pleasure, and he eschewed relationships with those in Buffalo who gladly would have welcomed him to their homes.[3] Any inhospitable atmosphere with which he at times seemed to surround himself disappeared in the presence of companions whose hearts lay open before him, and whose purposes were seen to be good, as his partners and those who met him from day to day in Buffalo learned to understand. He was simple and frank in his intercourse with them; they knew him to be true and kind. They were loyal to him; he was the soul of loyalty in thought and deed with reference to them. They called him "Cleve"; he wrote them often, even after he became President, in the flowing and not readily decipherable hand which they called "copper plate," enjoying in retrospect the days of "simple, honest, hearty friendship" to which there had come to be "few bonds," [4] and wished himself among them again.[5] Of a

[1] R. W. Gilder, Grover Cleveland, pp. 38–9; W. C. Hudson, Random Recollections, pp. 175–83.

[2] Cleveland Papers.

[3] Cf. N. Y. Independent, Aug. 14, 1884.

[4] To Bissell, Nov. 23, 1884, in Cleveland Papers.

[5] "I must go to dinner," Cleveland concluded a letter to Bissell, from the White House, on December 14, 1885. "I wish it was to eat a pickled herring, Swiss cheese and a chop at Lew's instead of the French stuff I shall find."—Cleveland Papers.

visit to the White House from his old partner, Lyman K. Bass, he wrote to Bissell, "It seemed so like old times and he appeared so really glad to see me, and I was so boyishly glad to see him, that, when I was obliged to bid him good-bye to go and make postmasters, I felt like giving up the Presidency, and going with him." [1]

To the new friends with whom he sought recreation and solace in fishing and shooting, as to those who knew him best in Buffalo, he exhibited no trace of the austerity which many read into his nature. They found even tenderness and sweetness in him, an unpretentiousness of spirit, reaching self-depreciation.[2] He was "honest and manly and simple and brave."[3]

Opponents, eager to discover and celebrate his faults, attributed a certain ponderosity to his thought and expression. It is undeniable that his accustomed gait was slow. He had, said Lucius B. Swift, "the calm and steady demeanor of a judge." [4] His demand for facts was "almost insatiable." [5] He sought and mastered them, and reasoned from them patiently, with a feeling of the most conscientious responsibility. But when stirred by what has been called "moral fury" he could coin "hot and memorable phrases," [6] and competent examination of the subject will give him high position in the use of clear and precise language in framing his public statements. His resistance to selfish counsel, which was, now and again, called stubbornness of temper, was, in truth, the finest courage. Men who sought to mold his views, to shape his policies for their own ends, the very men who complained of his reserve and awkwardness of utterance, found him fluent enough when they pressed him for undeserved favors. Provoked to it he could swear as roundly as George Washington.

Mr. Cleveland was described as not unhandsome in appear-

[1] Under date of July 16, 1885, in Cleveland Papers.
[2] Cf. McElroy, Grover Cleveland, vol. i, p. 100; G. F. Parker, Recollections of Grover Cleveland, pp. 11–2; Buffalo corr. N. Y. Herald, Sep. 23 and 26, 1882.
[3] Charles R. Codman to Schurz in Writings of Schurz, vol. iv, p. 473.
[4] N. Y. World, July 22, 1885.
[5] Ibid.
[6] R. W. Gilder, Grover Cleveland, p. 42.

ance. His hair and mustache bore no traces of silver and his bearing was youthful and strong. He had a large frame which had filled out until he weighed more than 200 pounds. That he was a bachelor few readers of newspapers were allowed to forget. It was said that he had never traveled widely even in his own country—he had never been as far west as Chicago.[1] But from boyhood he had been an industrious reader with a view to extending the boundaries of his knowledge in useful fields. The problems which had faced him as governor of New York and which would demand his attention at Washington employed him far into many nights.

With the inauguration as a text much was said about "Jeffersonian simplicity." It pleased many to picture Mr. Cleveland as one who would make some marked and bizarre protest against the display and luxury attendant upon induction into the Presidential office. Arthur sent a secretary to Albany bearing him an invitation to come to the White House upon his arrival in Washington, which was declined. As his political opponents had said so much during the campaign, and afterward, which was meant to fill the negroes with fear of a Democratic administration Abram S. Hewitt suggested that, to allay their apprehension, Mr. Cleveland take lodgings at Wormley's which was kept by a colored man.[2] But this suggestion was repelled. No dramatic affectation of any kind characterized his departure from Albany. On the evening of March 2nd he boarded a special train with members of his family—his brother, sisters, nieces and a few friends. None witnessed him leave and none was at hand to welcome him in Washington the next morning when his journey had ended, though two or three members of a reception committee soon appeared, and he was quietly driven to his apartments at the Arlington Hotel.

He called at the White House. Mr. Arthur returned the visit and on the following day they together proceeded through the streets to the United States Senate to see Vice-President

[1] N. Y. Tribune, Dec. 4, 1884; McElroy, Grover Cleveland, vol. i, p. 163; letter of June 1, 1885, from Mrs. Drury in Cleveland Papers.
[2] To Cleveland, Dec. 1, 1884, in Cleveland Papers.

Hendricks installed in office, and then to the platform on the west side of the Capitol, overlooking many thousands of persons, who had assembled from all parts of the country, in a soft sunlight, unusual at such a season in the latitude of Washington, to witness the Chief Justice administer the oath of office to the new President and to hear the inaugural address.

All observers agreed that Mr. Cleveland made an impressive appearance on this occasion and spoke with emphasis and power. Fidelity to the Constitution, economy in the administration of the government, a safe and sound financial system, revenue laws which, while relieving the people of needless taxation, should have "due regard to the interests of capital invested and working men employed in American industries," with no accumulation of a "surplus" in the Treasury "to tempt extravagance and waste," the application of business principles to public affairs, the extirpation of vicious methods in the civil service, the enforcement of the amendments with reference to the freedmen—these were his themes. The speaker's voice was clear—its tones rang far into the air as he made his simple exposition, without the use of manuscript, of the principles of the Constitution and uttered his promises of faithful and honest service.[1] Though, in print, the speech filled little more than a column of a newspaper it was spoken with such deliberation and earnestness that it occupied a half hour.[2]

Many states sent military bodies for the procession which, it was said, comprised no less than 25,000 men, who were three hours in passing the reviewing platform at the White House. Mr. Cleveland stood throughout this time receiving and acknowledging the salutes of companies of militia, campaign clubs, civic societies which moved in the street before him. He was "fitly guarded," said the New York Tribune, by a former chief of the "rebel secret service." This "Confederate bloodhound" at the head of a corps of detectives stood by while Cleveland took the oath of office.[3] Republicans saw hated gray

[1] Cf. G. F. Parker, Recollections of Grover Cleveland, p. 74; S. M. Cullom, Fifty Years of Public Service, p. 225.

[2] Cf. Washington corr. N. Y. Tribune, March 5, 1885.

[3] N. Y. Tribune, March 5, 1885.

uniforms from the South and heard the "rebel yell." [1] But in the main it was a time for expressions of good will and for generous celebration. A striking exhibition of fireworks at night, a parade by a "Flambeau Club" and a ball in the Pension Building, to the music of Sousa's Marine Band, which was continued far beyond midnight, completed the festivities. No "Jeffersonian simplicity" was seen on any side. It was a normal, an interesting and a pleasant commencement of an administration which held new promise for the republic.

The last Congress had spent its time fruitlessly. It had displayed little wisdom or purpose. "Politics" had engaged the attention of both parties, the leaders of which were united in opinion regarding few of the important issues coming before them for determination. It was generally held, however, that Arthur had been a fairly satisfactory President. His succession to the office, at Garfield's death, had been accompanied by expressions of doubt and not misplaced fear, in view of the manner in which he had been nominated for Vice-President, and his complete want of experience in the management of any public office greater than a customhouse. But he had dissociated himself from small friends and unworthy sponsors. He had approved some good measures and vetoed evil ones. His administration, the New York Tribune said, had been "a pleasurable disappointment to the country." He went out of office "in the enjoyment of a more general good will than at any previous period of his life." [2]

The names of the gentlemen selected for posts in the cabinet were sent to the Senate. Two, Bayard and Lamar, were statesmen. Both, like Cleveland, held views concerning the fundamental character of the government at variance with those entertained by the Republican leaders, and one had openly and unashamedly espoused the cause of those who in the South had abandoned the Union and had waged war to create another government. Garland, Vilas and Endicott, if not preeminent national figures, were highly respected ones in the communities in which they dwelt; one of these, Garland, had

[1] N. Y. Tribune, March 5, 1885.   [2] Ibid., March 4, 1885.

been a "rebel." Mr. Whitney was a friend of the new President and had been influential in preparing the way for his nomination. He was rich, to be sure, as the Mugwumps and others had observed, and he had not had experience in statecraft, but he was a man of intelligence and honor, who was entirely worthy of trust as a Presidential adviser and as the head of an important department in the new government.[1] Only of Daniel Manning, at the head of the Treasury, was there criticism deserving to be remembered. All men knew why he had been appointed; the reasons made the selection seem no more admirable.[2] But the giving away of one place in the cabinet, if this were to be all, was a small price to pay Tilden for heirship on the one side and abdication on the other.

The new government was fairly launched. The Republican New York Tribune wished Mr. Cleveland "a successful and honorable administration." As President of the United States he was to be "fairly judged." [3] But it was from this side still less than from that portion of the Democratic party of which Manning was a spokesman and a representative, to say naught of the Tammany "gang," that understanding of Mr. Cleveland's aims would be evidenced, and sympathy with his purposes would be expressed. The rancors of the campaign persisted and in the state of party feeling bitterness was not to be allayed.[4]

The first few months of the administration, until the new Congress should assemble in December, 1885, were occupied with appointments to office and the reorganization of departments, bureaus and Federal agencies generally. These proceedings were witnessed both anxiously and curiously. A Democratic President in action furnished the country an unusual spectacle.

---

[1] "Mr. Whitney is one of the ablest and more promising of the younger generation of Democrats. He is high, and deservedly high, in Mr. Cleveland's confidence" (N. Y. Nation, Feb. 12, 1885), a rather generous estimate in view of Mr. Godkin's attitude as it was reflected in correspondence in the Cleveland Papers.

[2] Cf. N. Y. Nation, March 12, 1885. It must be regarded as a surrender to the enemy; Manning was "a terrible load to carry " said Carl Schurz.—Writings of Schurz, vol. iv, p. 355.

[3] N. Y. Tribune, March 5, 1885.

[4] N. Y. Nation, March 12, 1885.

Not since the war had such a sight been seen; a new generation had, meanwhile, come forward to take its part in public affairs. Those who had been 45 when James Buchanan left office were now 70. Men who then had been children were now in middle life. Many not then born had cast their votes for Cleveland, or against him, in 1884. And the Democracy of Buchanan stood in small relation to that which would be put to trial under direction of the present expositors of party principles. Questions and issues were new. In what manner would they be approached and met?

The President and his associates at the head of the departments proceeded on their way quietly, but with obstinate energy. The problem of the civil service was of first importance; by his course in reference to this matter, which had come to have so prominent a place in political discussion, particularly at the hands of the Mugwumps, would he be judged, and he was face to face with the difficult and ungrateful task of determining, under what circumstances, Republican officeholders should be retained and what manner of men should be invited to occupy the places which should be vacated to make way for the adherents of his own party.

The Pendleton law had put Federal employees to the number of about 14,000 [1] above the reach of change for political reasons. This measure it would be the new President's pleasure to enforce under the direction of the Civil Service Commission. But many classes of officials had not yet been brought under civil service rules and were, for the most part, mere creatures of Congressmen and other leaders and "bosses" who had procured them their "jobs." It was believed and stated by Secretary Lamar that not less than 3,000,000 persons in the United States voted entirely with reference to Federal patronage in the hope of being benefited, either directly or through friends, by appointments to office. [2] The pressure upon Mr. Cleveland

[1] The civil service list comprised 100,000 persons in all.—Message of President Arthur of 1882 in Richardson, vol. viii, p. 145.

[2] Mayes, Life of Lamar, p. 486. Elections in the United States since Jackson's time had been "pitched battles for the spoils."—N. Y. Nation, March 10, 1887.

which had commenced with the announcement of his election
was unremitting. "The thirst for a general 'turn out' all over
the country," Lamar said, was "almost fearful." [1] It was a
"pernicious" system, said Wade Hampton. He was "utterly
disgusted at the pertinacity, the deceit and the greed" seen on
all sides. He, for one, would not "enter the scramble." He
could not regard it "as a duty of a senator to become an attorney
for office-seekers." He would bring in a bill making it an
offense for any member of Congress to recommend an appointment unless he should be asked for it in writing by the President,
or one of the heads of the departments. [2]

Cleveland had made a declaration of his policy, but measures
were being taken every day to compel him to depart from it.
He had said that officeholders would not be disturbed merely
because they were Republicans. If they gave useful and faithful
service to the government they would be allowed to continue
in their places, unless they had shown themselves to be "offensive partisans." [3] Men who neglected their duties and subordinated their tasks to political maneuvering would be adjudged
unsuitable for public office, and might not expect any longer
to enjoy its rewards. That the entire body of civil servants
should be composed, at any time, of men who were adherents
of the Republican party was an indefensible contention. It was
especially inappropriate that this should be so when another
party was in power and had been made responsible for the conduct of the government. Much that was said on the Republican
side at this conjuncture was preposterous, and is unworthy of
record for remembrance. It could be pointed out that appointees
were "rebels," or "Copperheads," or "free traders," with a view
to creating in the minds of the people prejudices which might
be rendered active in ensuing party contests. It could be said
that a man who had been removed from office was not an
"offensive partisan," that such a charge lodged against him
was a mere pretext to take a place and a salary from an experi-

[1] Mayes, Life of Lamar, p. 485.
[2] June 12, 1885, in Cleveland Papers.
[3] Cf. Mayes, Life of Lamar, pp. 486–7.

enced person in order to make room for one of another political
faith. The Democrat would be as "offensive" to the Republican
in 1888, as the Republican had been to the Democrat in 1884.[1]
Raillery directed at such a reorganization of the civil service was
continued day by day until the public mind was utterly confused. Men but casually interested in the course of public affairs
wondered whether there was any merit in "reform," and grew
tired of hearing about it.

On the other side the Democratic politicians were swelling
with a kindred displeasure. For what purpose had they voted
for Cleveland and moved upon Washington, if not to "rescue"
the government from the hands of "a hungry official aristocracy"?[2] The patronage was theirs. It had been won and it
must be distributed. Tilden, retired in his small world, sought
to fan the flames of discontent. In "strictly confidential"
letters he addressed Manning, his only avenue of approach to
the new government.[3] He was a warm advocate of "turning the
rascals out" and repeatedly registered his impatience in reference
to Cleveland's course in failing to remove country postmasters
and other officials who ought to be active in serving the Democratic instead of the Republican party.[4] When he found that
Manning's influence was unavailing, even with reference to the
Treasury Department, he felt himself completely alienated
from the new President, and sought to put his impress upon
the government through his friends in Congress.

Cleveland was not without a becoming sympathy for the
Democratic leaders and their point of view. The Secretary of
State, Mr. Bayard, was asked why he had made certain consular
appointments. "I am prepared," he said, "to give no other than

[1] For example, Congressman Reed of Maine said that Cleveland's civil
service letter was "an assurance to all the sneaks in the party that they
are to be kept in office, if they are in office, while honest Republicans are
notified that they are to be turned out,"—"sneaks" being those who attended to their duties as civil servants, "honest Republicans," those who
had "worked" zealously for the ticket.—Cf. N. Y. Nation, Jan. 8, 1885,
and ibid., May 21, 1885.

[2] Cleveland Papers.

[3] Letters and Memorials of Tilden, pp. 680–81.

[4] Ibid., pp. 686–7.

the same reasons which have controlled the nominations of diplomatic officers—in order that the foreign service may be in more perfect political harmony of opinion and policies of action with the administration which is now responsible for their action." [1] Cleveland's "idea," he told Manning, was this— officials who had held their places for four years should "as a rule give way to good men of our party." Those who had been "guilty of offenses against our political code," he continued, "should go without regard to the time they have served," and "we should gladly receive all resignations offered us," filling the vacancies thus created "by our friends." [2]

Such a statement of principles should have satisfied reasonable men. But more was required. Tammany gangsters, state and county leaders—all trained in the school of low party politics— looked on with impatience and distrust. The President reproved his critics. "Removals, when they should be made, and the appointment of reputable and fit persons to fill vacancies would be much aided, and the Democrats of different localities might find reason to be better satisfied," he wrote a small Democratic chieftain in New York state, "if those having their interest in charge and acting as county committees, &c., would coöperate with us in furtherance of our plans, instead of breeding dissatisfaction by meeting for the purpose of grumbling and finding fault." [3]

Honest service was demanded of all alike, whatever their party affiliations. Vilas was asked to impress the fact upon employees in the Post Office Department that "no indulgence" would be granted by the Executive to those who "violate the law or neglect public duty." [4] That he made mistakes in his choice of men for office Mr. Cleveland was ready, at need, to acknowledge. Now and again he was imposed upon by those whom he trusted;—they were taken to task for the carelessness of their judgments. [5] Appointees who proved to be faithless

[1] April 2, 1885, in Cleveland Papers.
[2] June 20, 1885, in ibid.
[3] July 8, 1885, in ibid.
[4] April 4, 1885, in ibid.
[5] Cf. McElroy, Grover Cleveland, vol. i, pp. 132, 136, 164.

were removed and, though the most powerful influences would be used to arrest his hand and effect their reinstatement, he kept to his way with unshaken will.

The Mugwumps, the particular guardians of the reform, found that not all of their expectations were fulfilled and at times were sorely tried as they strove to make the President see through their eyes. Yet George William Curtis wrote on May 25, 1885, that he and other friends of the movement felt that already, in the few past weeks, "very much more" had been accomplished "than under previous administrations." [1] Schurz said a month later that the President, although he had made mistakes, was "constantly gaining friends." There was more trust in him than in the party.[2] And, after six months, in September, 1885, the New York Nation declared that no more removals of civil servants had been made than were usual in a change from one Republican to another Republican administration. The "check" which Cleveland had put upon the "spoils" system had been thus far his "chief merit." Sinecures in many departments had been abolished and expenditures reduced, while there was marked gain of efficiency in the running of the government.[3] The Republican press did not cease its efforts to estrange Cleveland's friends, the "reformers," by telling them that they had been betrayed, but with indifferent success. "Every one of us in this town [Hartford] who voted for you last fall," said Mark Twain in September, 1885, "would vote for you again today. And would be glad to do it, too,"[4]— a sentiment which was supported by the testimony of William Everett of Massachusetts, who said, in October, that he had yet to find a Mugwump "who regrets voting for you, or is anything but rejoiced that he did so." [5]

Even resolute men have spirits which are ruffled by detraction. Those who have a general sense of justice are resentful

[1] Cleveland Papers.
[2] To Cleveland, June 25, 1885, in ibid.
[3] N. Y. Nation, Sep. 10, 1885; cf. ibid., Aug. 13, 1885; Dorman B. Eaton, North Am. Review, July, 1885.
[4] Sep. 23, 1885, in Cleveland Papers.
[5] Oct. 5, 1885, in ibid.

of injustice done themselves. It is doubtful if anyone who ever occupied the office of President of the United States possessed a conscience more highly organized than Mr. Cleveland's. He was disturbed by the allegations of his hypocrisy uttered by the Republicans, of his inconsistency and insincerity, now and again the complaint of the Mugwumps, of his ingratitude and his pretense to being better and wiser than other men, the charge emanating from his own party. He took up his burden every morning, he said, and carried it as well as he could till night, and "frequently up hill." [1] He was "sick at heart and perplexed in brain" during the most of his "waking hours," he wrote his friend Bissell. [2] "For three months," he said in the summer of 1885, "I have stood here and battled with those of my party who deem party success but a means to personal advantage." They were "refused and disappointed," but they could not say that he had denied them the favors they craved in order to make places for his personal friends, and had "bestowed patronage in payment of personal political debts." He was told that his administration was "strong and popular"—if it were so it was for the very reason that he had thé courage to do what he believed to be right. [3]

"This cursed office filling," he one time called it. [4] Again it was "this dreadful, damnable office seeking" which hung over him like a "nightmare." [5] He would struggle on—the end would come, and, if on that day, he said, "I can retire with a sure consciousness that I have done my whole duty, according to my lights and my ability, there will be some corner for me where I can rest." [6]

In every department it was said that the President and the members of the cabinet were conducting public affairs upon business principles. [7] They had put the party's past behind them. Relaxing its hold upon old issues they would have it take a firm

[1] Writings of Schurz, vol. iv, p. 363.
[2] Christmas Day, 1884, in Cleveland Papers.
[3] June 25, 1885, in ibid.
[4] McElroy, Grover Cleveland, vol. i, p. 136.
[5] Ibid., p. 149.
[6] To Bissell, June 25, 1885, in Cleveland Papers.
[7] N. Y. Nation, Oct. 22, 1885.

grasp upon the new. They had introduced rules of action based upon adherence to law and regard for the public welfare, "rather than upon the consideration long shown to political favorites and powerful financial interests." [1]

Other classes of men, as well as the office mongers, early found Cleveland's honest and forthright policy an exasperation to them. No time was lost in investigating, and putting a check on, the spoliation of the public lands. From the first day of his administration the new President had exact information and correct views on this topic. In his inaugural address he said that "the public domain should be protected from purloining schemes and unlawful occupation," [2] and he and Secretary Lamar were not reluctant or sparing in their support of the new Commissioner of the General Land Office. [3] This man, W. A. J. Sparks, recently a militant Democratic Congressman from Illinois, [4] attacked with zeal the complicated system of fraud by which the government was robbed and the people cheated out of the benefits extended to them by the land laws. He was not long in confirming the "widespread belief" that the land department had been "very largely conducted to the advantage of speculation and monopoly, private and corporate, rather than in the public interest." [5]

Surveyors were paid at exorbitant rates; they gave the government dishonest service. Monuments were willfully destroyed in order to make resurveys necessary. The business was in the hands of "surveying rings," acting in connivance with speculators, who profited by early notice of the preparation of desirable lands for entry, which they would lay claim to and hold for a time for sale to others to the disadvantage of *bona fide* settlers. [6] The country was denuded of timber by lawless lumber companies which, without let or hindrance,

[1] N. Y. Nation, Sep. 10, 1885.
[2] Richardson, Messages and Papers, vol. viii, p. 302.
[3] Haynes, Life of J. B. Weaver, pp. 237-8.
[4] Cf. ibid., pp. 191-2.
[5] Report of Sec. of Int. for 1885, vol. i, p. 155; cf. Geo. W. Julian, North Am. Review for August, 1885.
[6] Report of Sec. of Int. for 1885, vol. i, pp. 167-8.

set up steam sawmills. Organized for trespass and robbery
they felled trees right and left and shipped away the product.
Their depredations were "universal, flagrant and limitless,"
said Mr. Sparks.[1] His predecessor in office had assembled proof
of thievery of this kind during the year 1884 amounting to
more than $7,000,000.[2] In the next year the cases investigated
and reported, looking to action for recovery, aggregated a
value of $3,000,000.[3] Valuable minerals were taken out of the
earth, regardless of title or right, by brazen men, often in
collusion with petty, if not higher, officials. Great herds of
cattle roamed over government and Indian lands, and the
owners, for their own profit and advantage, defied all restraint,
even fencing in the public domain so that they could monopo-
lize streams and water holes and bar small farmers and graziers
from settlement.[4]

Railroad companies made "overwithdrawals"—their claims
were approved by agents of the government in bulk without investigation, often, indeed, without surveys or maps.[5] In indecent
haste, on the eve of the change of party administration in
March, the grant having been forfeited if not extinguished,
patents were issued and title to three quarters of a million
acres in the South passed from the United States to a group
of railroad promoters.[6] Over 100,000,000 acres of land, which
had been donated by Congress to various railroad companies,
an area equal to the combined superficial extent of New York,
New Jersey, Pennsylvania, Delaware, Maryland and Virginia,
should be returned at once to the public domain. These companies were in default. Their rights had not been extended
by Congress. The land which they were actively exploiting
for the profit of stockholders, or, as was more often the case,
of officers, of corporations, was subject to declaration of for-

[1] Report of Sec. of Int. for 1885, vol. i, p. 233.
[2] Ibid. for 1884, vol. i, p. 15.
[3] Ibid. for 1885, vol. i, p. 233.
[4] For a further discussion of this subject see infra, chap. xxxii.
[5] Ibid., pp. 182–3.
[6] Ibid., pp. 90–91; Mayes, Life of Lamar, pp. 476–7; Cong. Record, 49th
Cong., special sess. of Senate, pp. 9–19.

feiture and was restorable to the United States for distribution to the people.[1]

Old Spanish and Mexican private grants were manipulated with amazing results. A square league of land in New Mexico was made to include more than a hundred square leagues. Another grant was extended from 96,000 to 1,700,000 acres. Still another of 48,000 acres became, in the hands of the surveyors, 594,000 acres, and patents for these great tracts were issued by the government, in spite of the pitiful appeals of settlers for protection against such fraud, which, for all the attention they received, might as well have been "consigned to a fiery furnace." [2]

Altogether, on the various accounts, Commissioner Sparks said that there were hundreds of millions of acres of land to be wrested from illegal control.

It is doubtful if such a system of fraud upon any government, under cover of involved, confusing and ill-contrived law, was ever seen as that which he described in his first annual report. Commissioners in Republican administrations had recommended reforms.[3] Sparks now asked for action at once "if the rapidly disappearing lands of the nation" were to be preserved "for actual settlement." [4] Those who had passed the vaunted homestead law had failed to repeal the preëmption law. The government might give every man a farm; it was never intended that, by double entry, he should receive two farms— one to live on and the other for speculation.[5] The preëmption law, the desert land law, the timber culture law and many features of other laws with reference to the administration of the public lands were incitements to men to trick and swindle the government. The way of the honest settler was beset with difficulty, while the sharper and the thief stripped the public domain of every valuable resource.

[1] Report of Sec. of Int. for 1885, vol. i, p. 196.
[2] Ibid., pp. 169–78.
[3] Cf. Mr. Sparks's immediate predecessor in Report of Sec. of Int. for 1884, vol. i, pp. 5–19.
[4] Ibid. for 1885, vol. i, p. 219.
[5] Ibid., p. 221.

The westward movement of the population was not yet spent. Settlers were eager and still pressed the borders of every tract of agricultural and pasture land of which they had favorable accounts, as men would rush to a gold field. A multitude of attorneys and land agents increased the confusion.[1] Home seekers, as well as speculators, were swarming around and entering the "Oklahoma country," [2] in the heart of the Indian Territory, a large part of which had been put to no use by the Indian department. Squatters, armed and under desperate leaders, defying repeated expulsions and arrests,[3] still dared the government to evict them. Cleveland, on March 13, 1885, little more than a week after taking office, in the most definite language, proclaimed the "Oklahoma lands" to be Indian lands and declared all and every person or persons in occupancy of them, or threatening to enter and settle on them, to be intruders who would be removed by the military power of the United States.[4] Troops were at hand and the invasion was turned back.[5]

A few days before relinquishing office President Arthur had added to the public domain the old Winnebago and Sioux, or Crow Creek, Indian reservations in Dakota territory. Complaints were made to Secretary Lamar in behalf of the Indians who were being displaced by white settlers, for Arthur's order had taken effect at once. President Cleveland, following the advice of his Attorney-General, who said that Arthur's action had been unwarranted under the treaty, issued a proclamation, on April 17th, announcing this fact, and ordered all who were on the ground to vacate it within 60 days, in order that the "solemn pledges and plighted faith of the government" should be maintained "inviolate."[6]

The leases or pretended leases obtained by the cattlemen

[1] Cf. Mr. Sparks's immediate predecessor in Report of Sec. of Int. for 1884, vol. i, p. 231.
[2] Cf. Haynes, Life of J. B. Weaver, pp. 234–5, 270.
[3] Ibid., p. 278.
[4] Richardson, vol. viii, pp. 303–4.
[5] App. Ann. Cyclop. for 1885, p. 762. For a full discussion of this subject see infra, chap. xxxii.
[6] Richardson, vol. viii, pp. 305–7; Report of Sec. of Int. for 1885, vol. i, pp. 30–32.

from the Indians were referred to the Attorney-General. Disturbances among the Cheyennes and Arapahoes alarmed the people of Kansas. General Sheridan was asked to visit the scene. He ascribed the trouble to the aggressions of ranchmen whose herds grazed on the reservation.[1] President Cleveland on July 23rd declared the leases void.[2] The protests of the cattle owners were of no avail; the lands were soon cleared and again in possession of the Indians.[3]

Those who pastured and watered their stock behind fences erected on public lands heard from the new President in a proclamation issued on August 7th. Following Secretary Lamar, who said that the public domain was held by the government "in trust for all," and that, therefore, no one could properly inclose it for his own uses and obstruct transit over it, or interfere with settlement upon it,[4] the President directed attention to the provisions of the law of Congress approved on February 25, 1885, and ordered every unlawful fence to be "immediately removed." He commanded officers of the United States to see that his will was obeyed.[5]

Conditions in the Navy Department invited the early attention of the new government. The navy, since the Civil War, when it was not regarded seriously, as it should have been, and denounced as a disgrace to the nation, was an object of jest. It consisted of only one "first rate" ship, the *Tennessee*,[6] used as a flagship, eleven "second-rates" and nineteen "third-rates," making in all thirty-one vessels ranging from 900 to 4,840 tons displacement.[7] Only three—all very small boats—had iron hulls; the rest were wooden ships, a legacy of the Civil War, and they were not worthy of repair,—indeed, by

[1] Report of Sec. of Int. for 1885, vol. i, pp. 14–9.
[2] Richardson, vol. viii, p. 307.
[3] App. Ann. Cyclop. for 1885, p. 762.
[4] Report of Sec. of Int. for 1885, vol. i, pp. 44–5.
[5] See infra, chap. xxxii.
[6] Said to be "so decayed" by the Secretary of the Navy in 1886 that she could be used only a few months longer.—Report of Sec. of Navy for 1886, p. 21.
[7] Ibid. for 1884, p. 14; cf. ibid. for 1882, pp. 5–8; cf. Thomas Hunt, Life of W. H. Hunt, pp. 220–22.

wise provision of Congress, they might not be reconditioned for service, if the expense involved should exceed twenty per cent of the original cost of construction.[1]

Robeson, against whom, during the Grant administration, so much criticism had been not unjustly aimed, had found a not unfitting successor in the Arthur administration in William E. ("Bill") Chandler. Robeson's amenability had made him incompetent to hold a great office of trust. Chandler, on the other hand, was a stirring, intelligent and cunning leader. He had directing power, as was shown in his management of several national Republican campaigns. He believed in the maxim that a political party, like an army, travels on its stomach, and he would put the principle into force. Government was to be seized by any convenient means and made useful to those who had been clever and energetic enough to get control of it. He particularly concerned himself with the negroes and the white men who composed the Republican party in the Southern states, and was the politician in the North to whom they principally turned for patronage and money to assist them in the maintenance of their organizations. Manufacturers and powerful men in all parts of the country looked to him as a manager and lobbyist from whom aid might be had. He had been a "Blaine man"; he would be for other men if it promised him gain.

One of his friends was John Roach, an illiterate Irishman, who had come, by some obstinate, native business talent, to be the owner of large shipyards at Chester on the Delaware River. Men around him wrote speeches for him to deliver and articles on economic subjects which appeared over his name in the North American Review. He had reached the

---

[1] One old wooden boat, the Shenandoah, built in 1862 at a cost of $463,-000, was charged with repairs amounting to $906,000. Upon the Ossipee, built in 1861, at a cost of $407,000, had been lavished, since that time, no less than $1,197,000. To keep the historic Kearsarge afloat had cost $1,123,-000, though she had been built originally for $286,000. (Report of Sec. of Navy for 1884, pp. 15–6.) In a period of four years $572,000 had been invested in the old wooden Omaha, the price of a new steel ship. In the event of war, said Secretary Whitney, she could "neither fight nor run away."— Ibid. for 1885, p. xxxix.

belief that his prosperity was synonymous with the welfare of the country. If the government would authorize him to build a new navy and grant subsidies to merchant ships, which he, too, might build, so that the American flag would be seen again on every sea, all would be well with the republic.

Roach was a kindly, open-handed old man. Chandler did not call upon him in vain during political campaigns and, indeed, was personally befriended when need arose.[1] Chandler was eager to get into the Arthur cabinet, since the Senate had refused to confirm his nomination by Garfield to be Solicitor-General, and Roach seems to have had a hand in procuring him his appointment as Secretary of the Navy.[2]

The construction of three new steel war vessels and an armed dispatch steamer had been authorized by acts of Congress of August 5, 1882, and March 3, 1883. Chandler, now in office, awarded the contracts to Roach under circumstances which resulted in expressions of dissatisfaction by other shipbuilders and a suspicion of favoritism.[3] The Cramps who had large yards for the building of ships, also on the Delaware, and were experienced in the business, expected at least a part of the work to be given to them. They declared that Chandler had "put the old man up to going in for all of it." They were so irate that they would have, they said, no further interest in the rebuilding of the navy.[4]

Roach, on the other hand, was elated. Competitors were jealous of his success. They were Democrats who did not like the awards being given to so conspicuous a friend of the Ameri-

[1] See, e.g., Roach's letter of Nov. 12, 1879, transmitting $1,000 to his "Dear Friend" at a time when it was known that his "expences now must Be large."—Chandler Papers.

[2] Roach to Chandler from New York, Jan. 1, 1882: "I saw the President while he was here and Talked with him about your mater. I said I need not tell him the kind of man you were. He must Have Known you him Selfe, that the kind of Men he wanted Round him ware Bright Cleer Headed Positive men with no halfe way Polisies about them, that you ware agoahead Positive man true to your friends, and a Better selection could not Be made from the Estern states for a Position in His Cabinet," etc., etc.—Chandler Papers.

[3] N. Y. Sun, July 26, 1883, and Baltimore American, July 18, 1883.

[4] Chandler Papers.

can merchant marine.[1] Chandler also covered his movements with bluster about the American flag. Subsidies must be paid American shipbuilders and shipowners to reduce the power of Great Britain on the seas, and the best shipbuilders, he would have the country infer, if he did not say so much, were those who made large contributions to the Republican party treasury. The cruisers, the *Chicago*, the *Boston* and the *Atlanta*, would be completed, it was expected, in January or February, 1885, and the dispatch boat, the *Dolphin*, in the summer of 1884.

At the same time work was resumed on four double-turreted monitors of an antiquated type which had been authorized, and had been brought under construction, during the Grant administration. The hulls had been resting uncompleted in the yards of the contractors since 1877.[2] Three of these ironclads, the *Puritan*, the *Amphitrite* and the *Terror*, were in the hands of shipbuilders on the Delaware, one having fallen to Roach, while the fourth, the *Monadnock*, lay at Mare Island in San Francisco.

The cruisers and the *Dolphin* were to cost $2,440,000, excluding work which was to be done upon them at the navy yards, the ironclads $3,598,000. Mr. Chandler had asked Congress for authority to build seven more unarmored steel cruisers and some rams and torpedo boats. At least seven new ships, he said, should be built annually for the next ten

[1] "I stated it was a fact that you ware my friend Before you became Secretary of the Navy, but after that there was no friendship between you & I so Far as the Business of the Department was conserned. . . . for years those men has been Ploting and full of Jalosie . . . Before I Bid for the Crusers I steady the whole Mater and am entirely Satisfyed with what I have done it gives me an Excellent oppertunitie to explain my whole Busenes with the Navy Department if there is any day of My Life that I will feel happy it is to Be Brought Before a Democratic Congres to explain all . . . there Can Be Know Ring now the contracts are awarded to me and anuff is savd to the Goverment to Build Another Cruser. I Pledge my Selfe to you that the work shall Enqual to the Best in the World of its class I also Pledge my Selfe to you that every Precaution in my Power to see that there is no Extra Bills and that you can Proudly say when this work is done that no Private Endevidual Garded His own interest with more vigilence and care than you Have in this instance garded the Interest of your Department," etc., etc.—Roach to Chandler in Chandler Papers.

[2] Report of Sec. of Navy for 1882, p. 23.

years that we might come as soon as possible to have a "new
steel navy." War was not expected, it was not desired. But
to be prepared to maintain "safety and honor" was the first
rule of independent nations. We must be able "to assert at all
times our natural, justifiable and necessary ascendancy in
the affairs of the American hemisphere." [1]

The Navy Department was acting under the advice of an
advisory board, organized by Secretary Hunt during his brief
administration of the office, while Garfield lived,[2] and composed of men esteemed to be competent in marine engineering.
It had the advantage of counsel from another commission as
to the policy to be pursued with reference to the navy yards,
which were no more than nests to hold lazy heelers and political lieutenants of the Republican party in the regions in which
the yards were placed. At the approach of elections hundreds
of men would be put on the pay roll in return for their support
of the Republican ticket. Thomas B. Reed would appeal for
the Kittery yard, Henry Cabot Lodge for Charlestown, "Bill"
Leeds, the Republican "boss" in Philadelphia, for that city,
General Mahone for Norfolk.[3] Some of these yards, it had
been recommended, should be reorganized and others closed,[4]
though no progress was made in this direction, and, without
a policy, valuable government property was being abandoned
to "waste and ruin." [5]

Mr. Whitney was projected into this situation. He was
intent upon giving the department a business-like administration and he immediately applied himself to his tasks to
the alarm of those who "made a living" out of the navy. In
May he told the commandant of the Mare Island navy yard
to stop making "repairs" on the *Mohican*, a small wooden
ship of about 1,900 tons. Since 1872, when she should have
been sold and broken up, $900,000 had been expended on
the boat, two-thirds of which had been squandered in three

[1] Report of Sec. of Navy for 1883, pp. 3-9.
[2] Thos. Hunt, Life of W. H. Hunt, p. 222.
[3] Chandler Papers.
[4] Report of Sec. of Navy for 1883, pp. 15-9; ibid. for 1884, pp. 16-9.
[5] Ibid. for 1885, pp. iv-v.

years under Chandler's administration of the department to give work to Republicans in California. Secretary Whitney ordered the officers in charge to take the navy yards out of politics and confine themselves to their proper duties.[1]

The prospect of a change of party control, assured by the election of Cleveland, had painfully disturbed Roach and Chandler. A violent discussion had raged around the "New Navy." The types of ships chosen were in no manner equal to modern requirements. They compared very unfavorably with the recent output of foreign, and particularly British, yards. Unarmored cruisers were useless unless they possessed speed, when they could be employed as commerce destroyers. The ships under construction by Roach were not designed for rapid movement. The new merchantmen could run away from them.[2] The money put into the new ships was sunk, as the vessels themselves would be on the first good occasion in case of encounter with the fleet of any one of several European naval powers. Size, speed, armament, machinery, every feature and quality of the boats fell under expert review and debate in the press and among the people. Chandler was hard pressed for a defense of his department, and, while his attitude was jaunty and secure behind the names of the members of his advisory board, the fact seemed to be that the "New Navy" had made a false start.[3]

Mr. Whitney confirmed the impression by his earliest official acts. The *Dolphin* he held to be no more than a "pleasure boat."[4] For this vessel, as well as the cruisers, plans had not been ready until the approach of the day set for the submission of bids. Even then the contractor, and, indeed, the department heads themselves, were uncertain about the details of the work to be performed, on which account misunderstanding and delay attended the prosecution of it.[5] Roach had bent all

[1] N. Y. Nation, May 28, 1885.
[2] Report of Sec. of Navy for 1886, pp. 5–6.
[3] Cf. ibid. for 1884, pp. 4–8; N. Y. Nation, Aug. 6, 1885.
[4] Report of Sec. of Navy for 1885, p. xix.
[5] Ibid.

his efforts to complete the vessels before the Cleveland administration should commence, but ill fortune attended him. He was in distress in the summer of 1884 and regretted that he had ever taken the contract.[1] He was paying out over $30,000 a week in wages, and working overtime. He had used 14 million pounds of steel in the hulls and machinery of the vessels. Large quantities of material were on hand for which he had advanced money to the manufacturers six months since.[2]

In a preliminary trial in November, 1884, to test the mechanical capacities of the *Dolphin* she fully met the expectations of the government, Mr. Chandler said, but she fractured a shaft because of the inexperience of our American steel makers who, it was specified, must provide the material, and formal acceptance of the ship from the contractor was delayed.[3] As the weeks passed Roach was in a state of mind not far from panic. Though he had contributed $3,500 to the Democratic campaign fund,[4] but a small part of what had been taken from him in the interest of Blaine, he was naturally without assurances as to the future. Chandler was only little less comfortable. He was an agile politician but it would require skill for him to escape exposure for what had been very stupid management of a great government office, to say no more of his administration of it. Though he might successfully guide his own steps there was no knowing what to expect of Roach, who was an open, forthright man, and "hard to manage." The old shipbuilder was talking freely and bitterly. Chandler told him to be "cool and sensible" and not to get "rattled."[5]

The question of accepting the ships was still pending when Mr. Whitney became Secretary of the Navy, and one of

[1] Letter to Chandler, July 3, 1884, in Chandler Papers.
[2] Chandler Papers.
[3] Report of Sec. of Navy for 1884, p. 3. Some of the iron had been purchased by Roach from a small manufactory in New Hampshire in order to propitiate Chandler's neighbors and friends.—Chandler Papers.
[4] Cleveland Papers.
[5] Chandler Papers.

the first tasks confronting him was to write his name on a paper which was put before him, signalizing the transfer of the *Dolphin* to the government. This he refused to do. He found, upon inquiry, that the boat, during trial, had not developed sufficient horse power, though the advisory board held that, with better coal and under more skillful navigators, she would satisfy this provision in the contract. Mr. Whitney demanded another trial. Roach, after a time, complied. A board of examiners was appointed to attend and issue a report. In their judgment, after four trips to display the powers of the ship, the tests still revealed deficiencies, although some alterations had been made to meet criticisms as to structural strength as well as speed. Mr. Whitney also discovered that the department, under his predecessor, had dealt so generously by Roach that money not rightfully due on the various contracts had been paid the shipbuilder so that the government was without remedy.[1]

Meanwhile Attorney-General Garland, to whom the subject had been referred, was examining the contracts and he found and declared them to be invalid. The ships had been built "without authority of law." Roach made an assignment for the benefit of his creditors. His men, 2,400 in number, were discharged and the plant was closed. His "dear friend" Chandler, to whom he wrote long maundering letters, reminiscent, explanatory and regretful, gave him but little comfort in the day of his downfall. "Mr. Roach must not humiliate me," was the sum of the ex-Secretary of the Navy's interest in the poor old man.[2] Chandler was free to state the reason for the trouble into which Roach had been plunged. It had been brought about by the Democratic party. The immediate causes aside—Garland, Whitney and the *Dolphin*—the Republicans, who favored the restoration of the American mercantile marine and the promotion of foreign trade under the "Stars and Stripes," had lost the election. The Democrats, who were

---

[1] These payments were made to Roach, Chandler explained, to save his credit, so that he would not be prevented from finishing the vessels.—Chandler Papers.

[2] March 27, 1885, in ibid.

the advocates of "free ships," coming into power had frightened the country and there was no business in sight for the American shipbuilder.[1]

Roach's failure, as well as his death, which soon ensued,[2] gave him a kind of martyrdom in circles in which he was looked upon as a public benefactor. It was, indeed, a pathetic scene, though the fact was generally overlooked that he had been a weak vessel in which to put the hopes of the nation for a new navy. He had been magnified for the Secretary of the Navy's purposes into a greater man than nature had ever meant him to be. The irregularities in the department's dealings with him found defense from the ready pen of Chandler, and generally in the Republican party.[3] It was simply political persecution. The Democrats were trying to discredit a patriotic Republican administration. Men were asked to remember Whitney's record in connection with public transit in New York City.[4] Scandalous disclosures which would make the Roach business seem like the merest peccadillo were imminent.[5] Battalions would tramp the streets in political campaigns to the beating shouts of "Who killed John Roach," as eloquent as their "No-no-no-free-trade." Nothing remained but for the government to take over the work on the three cruisers, as

[1] Roach had failed said the New York Nation, voicing another view because of his "neglect of business principles," and the mixing of politics with his business "in undue proportions."—N. Y. Nation, July 23, 1885; cf. ibid., July 30 and Aug. 6, 1885; N. Y. Tribune, July 20 and 21, 1885.

[2] N. Y. Nation, Jan. 13, 1887.

[3] Ibid., Aug. 6, 1885; cf. ibid., July 30, 1885, and sources there cited.

[4] He was associated with Elkins and "Pete" Widener, a "sheep butcher" of Philadelphia, in speculation in franchises which gave them the use of city streets.—Chandler Papers.

[5] Whitney, Chandler said, as he settled to his task, "would say anything, do anything, take responsibilities, use government moneys illegally, coax, threaten, lie, cheat and steal in order to excuse and vindicate himself for his atrocious conduct towards his predecessor in office, the advisory board, the four cruisers and Mr. Roach." (To Weed, May 11, 1886.) The total sum of Whitney's "infamy" was that he was a rich man who used his money ostentatiously. He was the first example of the New York "millionaire" in Washington, the first to introduce "metropolitan splendor" into social life in the national capital.—Writings of Schurz, vol. iv, p. 467; Thos. Hunt, Life of W. H. Hunt, p. 213.

well as on the *Dolphin,* and complete them along the lines on which they had been designed.[1]

Congress at its last session, under the Arthur administration, had authorized the construction of two more cruisers and two gunboats at an aggregate cost of about $3,000,000.[2] An act approved August 3, 1886, increased the number of new cruisers to three and added two ironclads and a torpedo boat. Secretary Whitney gave early attention to the preparation of models and plans for these ships in the hope of making them valuable units in the new fleet.[3] Cruising vessels we must have, the new Secretary said, unless we were to continue to repair "worthless" wooden ships and abandon all pretense of "affording the security and protection of our presence and power throughout the world, wherever our people sojourn."[4] We had "nothing," he said, deserving to be called a navy,[5] though the country had expended, since July 1, 1868, more than 75 millions in construction and repair work, which had been "substantially thrown away."[6] Every one admitted our impotency as a nation at sea; every one deprecated such weakness, particularly in the case of a country of so great an area, with so long a coast line and with such important commercial interests. Naval vessels had become products of science. A nation could as well have no navy as one that failed to give the highest expression to recent progress and achievement.[7]

The last Congress had inserted a provision in the Post Office Appropriation bill granting $400,000 to American steamship owners for the carriage of the mails to foreign countries. It had been the subject of bitter party discussion. In effect it was a postal subsidy for the encouragement of the American

[1] Report of Sec. of Navy for 1885, pp. xx–xxv; cf. App. Ann. Cyclop. for 1885, pp. 760–61; N. Y. Nation, Aug. 13, 1885.

[2] Act of March 3, 1885.

[3] Report of Sec. of Navy for 1885, pp. xvii, xviii; N. Y. Nation, Aug. 6, 1885.

[4] Report of Sec. of Navy for 1885, p. xxv.

[5] Ibid., p. xxxiii.

[6] Ibid.; cf. ibid., p. xxxvii.

[7] Ibid., p. xxxiv.

mercantile marine, like the navy, reduced, since the Civil War, to a pitiable position.[1] The Postmaster-General was authorized to execute contracts, after competitive bidding, at a rate not exceeding fifty cents a nautical mile. There were but a few companies, owning but a few ships, with which such arrangements could be made and they were not competitors, on which account Mr. Vilas refused to make a distribution of the grant. The existing rate of compensation for carrying the mails, he said, was adequate. The vessel owners, who considered themselves aggrieved, operating lines to the West Indies, Central and South America, New Zealand and Australia, led by the Pacific Mail Steamship Company, which was to be principally benefited by the subsidy, declined, after August 1, 1885, to serve the Post Office Department and, amid party commotion, contracts were signed with ships sailing under foreign flags, though this measure involved the forwarding of the Australian mails, made up at San Francisco as well as at New York, by way of Great Britain.[2]

The aspirations of the nation for a canal to join the Atlantic and Pacific oceans at or near the Isthmus, so long held, were quickened by the sight of work proceeding under the direction of de Lesseps and a French company at Panama, which will have description elsewhere. A movement taken to be speculative, under cover of patriotic, if not jingoist, feeling, was inaugurated in behalf of a rival canal in Nicaragua to be American in its management and ownership. In President Arthur's administration a treaty had been negotiated with that little Central American state authorizing the work to proceed.

A vote had been taken indicating a violent difference of opinion among the senators,[3] to whom it was sent for ratification, and there the matter rested when Arthur's term came to an end and Mr. Frelinghuysen retired as Secretary of State.

[1] McPherson's Handbook for 1884, pp. 49–51.
[2] App. Ann. Cyclop. for 1885, p. 763; Report of Postmaster-General for 1885, pp. 35–47; N. Y. Nation, June 18, and Aug. 6, 1885.
[3] N. Y. Nation, Feb. 5, 1885; Senate Ex. Journal, vol. 24, pp. 377–80, 409, 421, 423, 426, 444, 447–53.

Mr. Cleveland withdrew the treaty from the Senate [1] and announced his determination not to resubmit it. Following salutary counsel "from Washington's day" we had avoided "entangling alliances with foreign states." The new President could not favor "a policy of acquisition of new and distant territory." There was enough to be done in the "cultivation of the arts of peace within our own borders." What was wanted was a neutral route. This was not to be such. Mr. Cleveland would not recommend schemes "involving paramount privileges of ownership or right outside of our own territory, when coupled with absolute and unlimited engagements to defend the territorial integrity of the state where such interests lie." [2]

The new Attorney-General, supported by the President, gave his attention to delays in litigation in overburdened Federal courts, and particularly directed his criticism at the method of compensating United States marshals and district attorneys by fees. Thus were they encouraged to institute arrests on petty charges, to transport offenders and witnesses to distant places for trial in order to earn mileage, and to devise other schemes to swell their accounts and mulct the government. [3]

Ever since the enactment of the "Arrears of Pensions" scheme, during the Hayes administration in 1879, [4] dating the payments from the time of allowance back to the time of death, or of discharge, or the development of disability, [5] complaint had been rising on the subject of the management of the Pension Bureau. This law which had been passed in an outburst of generosity, if not of indifference, since the proposal received little attention either in Congress or in the press, gave immediate impulse to deception and fraud. The prize to be gained was large enough, by reason of the added arrears, to encourage the manufacture of claims by those who otherwise would have made no movement to have their names placed upon the pension

[1] Senate Ex. Journal, vol. 25, p. 8.
[2] Richardson, vol. viii, pp. 327–8. See infra, chap. xxxii.
[3] Cf. ibid., p. 354.
[4] Act of Jan. 25, 1879, modified on March 3, 1879. W. H. Glasson, Hist. of Military Pension Leg. in the U. S., chap. v.
[5] Cf. House Reports, 46th Cong. 3rd sess., no. 387, p. 7; N. Y. Tribune, Dec. 5, 1881.

rolls. Before the act was passed less than 1,600 cases in a month had reached the bureau, but the number rose at once to more than 10,000 monthly.[1] Washington was aswarm with attorneys and other middle men attracted by the prospect of substantial fees.[2] Secretary of the Interior Teller said that in the whole country there were 16,000 of them.[3] They widely and greedily advertised for clients, prepared claims and pressed their demands upon the government. Some built up immense businesses. Agents in Washington, it was said, represented two-thirds of all the cases before the department, and a dozen firms in that city had a preponderating part of this "practice."[4] One, named Lemon, employed 70 clerks and had no less than 150,000 claims in hand for prosecution, about half of all the claims on file in the Pension Office.[5]

Since 1878 these agents had been allowed to make a charge of $10, payable in advance. Frequently, when they got their fee from a claimant they dropped the case, and the poor dupe must pay $10 to another attorney, perhaps no more trustworthy.[6] Enormous sums were collected by the tricky rascals who found authority for their operations in this provision of the law.[7] A better system was needed—some measure directed at the horde of small swindlers and thieves who preyed upon the "old soldier" must be devised. Whether or not it was to be found in a return to the arrangements which had prevailed before 1878, such a "fee law" was reënacted in 1884, after some jugglery in the conference committee, to which the bill went, involving the activities of lobbyists acting for Lemon, who had quietly and shrewdly acquired the business of a leading rival in

---

[1] "I do not say that none of this money [made available by the Arrears of Pensions act] would be worthily bestowed," wrote a "Veteran" to the editor of the New York Nation, "but I do affirm that, for the most part, it will go to a worthless set of shirks and bummers."—N. Y. Nation, Feb. 20, 1879; cf. ibid., Feb. 27, 1879.

[2] House Mis. Doc., 48th Cong. 1st sess., no. 43, p. 27.

[3] House Reports, 48th Cong. 2nd sess., no. 2683, pt. 1, pp. 108, 109; House Reports, 46th Cong. 3rd sess., no. 387, p. 189.

[4] House Reports, 46th Cong. 3rd sess., no. 387, p. 191.

[5] House Reports, 48th Cong. 2nd sess., no. 2683, pt. 1, p. 108.

[6] House Reports, 46th Cong. 3rd sess., no. 387, p. 194.

[7] Ibid., p. 9.

the trade, even while the bill was pending, knowing, it was complained, that he had the power to secure its approval. Instead of a fee of $10 in advance, the agent would, in the future, be entitled to $25, contingent upon a successful issue, and collectible through the government. Lemon's fees would have aggregated $1,500,000 on his 150,000 claims under the law of 1878. It was easy to see that now, at $25, if 60 per cent of all applications were allowed (the anticipated return), his income would be $2,250,000.[1]

The operations of the pension agents, as well as the officers of the government with whom they came in contact, were under constant and well founded suspicion. The smaller agents, those who had one, or three, or five cases each, whatever might be said of the leading attorneys, took no note of the terms of the "fee laws" anyhow. They were seeking the poor and ignorant soldier to whom a large sum was due in arrears, and whom, after it was procured, they would cruelly fleece.[2] Frequently they acted in the interest of, and procured pensions for, very undeserving persons. Records were falsified. Men who had performed no military service, or none of value, were pensioned. Infirmities not traceable to such service were made the basis of claims and awards. It was freely said, even by those who could not be accused of a want of sympathy for the Union soldier, that the Treasury was raided. Ingenious rogues [3] hoodwinked department officers who themselves, now and again, were agents for these rogues.[4] Although various persons were at times disbarred, and the House of Representatives on one occasion demanded the papers from the Interior Department in proof of irregular practices, the material, when it was printed, filling more than 1,600 pages in small type,[5] the whole pension system continued to be a national scandal.

The war was now drawing into the distance. Twenty years

[1] House Reports, 48th Cong. 2nd sess., no. 2683, pt. 1, pp. 24–5, 39, 71, 73, 131–2, 136–7; cf. House Mis. Doc., 48th Cong. 1st sess., no. 43, pp. 26–30.
[2] House Reports, 46th Cong. 3rd sess., no. 387, p. 192.
[3] Report of Sec. of Int. for 1885, vol. i, p. 111.
[4] Ibid., p. 110.
[5] House Ex. Doc., 48th Cong. 1st sess., no. 172; cf. House Reports, 46th Cong. 3rd sess., no. 387, p. 190.

had passed since Appomattox. Time was frosting the hair, dimming the eye and impeding the step of the "boys in blue." Commanders were writing their memoirs, soldiers were indulging in reminiscence in the soft haze which surrounds deeds successfully done. Historians were describing the campaigns in book and magazine. Grateful sentiment was rising in the people of the North and West, and, under its cover, payments were made for the advantage of the political party which had fought and won the war, and which had so long enjoyed uninterrupted power.[1]

Conditions had grown materially worse while the bureau was under the direction of Colonel Dudley, the man whom Garfield had put at its head as a reward for his political services in Indiana in the campaign of 1880. In three years Dudley had increased the running expenses of the office from $5,000,000 to nearly $30,000,000 annually. It employed 1,680 persons.[2] It was virtually an annex of Congress. In one year over 75,000 letters from senators and representatives in regard to claims reached the commissioner, and to this epistolary avalanche were added personal calls in the interest of constituents, and friends of constituents, of the gentlemen gathered at Washington to make the nation's laws.[3] Dudley's political activities were continued in the campaign of 1884. Then he actually left his office for several months, though continuing to draw his salary of $5,000 a year, and by bribe of promise to hear and grant claims to Republicans and threats to withhold money from Democrats, and by like maneuvers involving the administration of his office, organized the "soldier vote" in Ohio and other parts of the West for Blaine.[4]

---

[1] The Pension Bureau was administered entirely by Republicans and almost wholly for their benefit. "The vast machinery of a professed governmental office became a party power."—Report of Sec. of Int. for 1885, p. 111; cf. N. Y. Nation, Dec. 3, 1885.

[2] House Reports, 48th Cong. 2nd sess., no. 2683, pt. 2, pp. 87, 242.

[3] Ibid., pt. 1, pp. 9–10.

[4] Ibid.—See pt. 1, pp. 1–2 and Testimony in pt. 2, especially that of Colonel Dudley himself. Also N. Y. Nation, Feb. 26, and March 5, 1885. For this subject cf. W. H. Glasson, Fed. Military Pensions in the U. S. and his earlier Hist. of Fed. Military Pensions Legislation in the U. S.

It was no enviable task to expose and combat forces entrenched
in such a position, and the new administration, which was under
so much suspicion of unfaithfulness to Northern interests, and
indifference to Northern opinion,[1] would move cautiously in
this direction. Cleveland had sagaciously appointed a Northern
Democratic veteran of the Union Army, General John C. Black
of Illinois, as Commissioner of Pensions.[2] On June 30, 1885,
the government carried 345,125 persons—"invalids," widows
and minor children—on its war pension rolls, which meant an
expenditure of $38,000,000 annually, although to cover arrears
due new pensioners, over $64,000,000 had been paid out in the
fiscal year 1884-5.[3] General Black instantly, upon assuming
office, instituted inquiries looking to a general purging of the
rolls of names fraudulently placed there.[4] He was honestly engaged, with the sincere support of the Secretary of the Interior
and the President, in "purifying the public service."[5]

Such a conduct of the government induced active opposition
to the President at the elections held in 1885. The Republicans,
as a matter of course, were arrayed against him and the "rebel"
colonels and brigadiers, to whom they were pleased to say that
he had surrendered the government. The Democrats themselves in many quarters did little to conceal their antagonism;
when the baser elements could gain control of the party conventions they made articulate their disapprobation of his
course.[6] In New York, the President's own state, his party
expressed its want of sympathy with his high-minded policies.
John Kelly, leader of Tammany Hall, having exhausted his
resources to prevent Cleveland's nomination, then treacherously
serving the ticket on election day, had made advances toward
peace in the hope of securing valuable patronage.[7] This gesture
being without avail, the hostility of the New York City organi-

[1] Report of Sec. of Int. for 1885, vol. i, pp. 111-2.
[2] Cf. Mayes, Life of Lamar, p. 497.
[3] Report of Sec. of Int. for 1885, vol. i, p. 99.
[4] Ibid., pp. 107-8.
[5] Ibid., p. 112.
[6] Cf. N. Y. Nation, Aug. 13, 1885.
[7] McElroy, Grover Cleveland, vol. i, pp. 129-30.

zation was resumed. Kelly struck hands with Hill who, as
lieutenant-governor, had fallen heir to the governorship upon
Cleveland's leaving the office and who desired the nomination
for the next term. He was, as the New York Nation said, nearly
everything that Cleveland was not.[1] But the President without
any hesitation, though his party in New York was on the point
of falling completely into the hands of his enemies, on September 11, 1885, reaffirmed in the most explicit terms his resolution
to adhere to the policy of civil service reform and to enforce
the law.[2] In the Democratic convention, with the support of
Kelly and similar elements,[3] Hill defeated Abram S. Hewitt,
who was put forward as an opposition candidate.[4]

The Republican nominee for governor held views at variance
with Hill's on the civil service question, and he was, for this
reason, indorsed by the Independents.[5] The newspapers which
were foremost in praising the President were supporting the
Republican ticket.[6] Cleveland's position was a "cruel one."[7]
His enemies thought that they now had him in a corner from
which he could not extricate himself. The New York World,
which, for its own purposes, had become very antagonistic,
called upon him as a Democrat to come out for the ticket.
Where did he stand? Was he a Republican or a Democrat?
That is what many men in the party which had elected him to
office had long wished to find out. There was no alternative, if
the President were not to lay down his claim to leadership. He
finally said that he would go to Buffalo to vote. He forwarded

[1] N. Y. Nation, Oct. 1, 1885; W. C. Hudson, Random Recollections,
p. 256.
[2] McPherson's Handbook for 1886, pp. 117–8.
[3] McElroy, Grover Cleveland, vol. i, p. 155.
[4] The "temper" of the convention, Hewitt said, was "exceedingly hostile"
to Cleveland.—To Lamont, Oct. 5, 1885.
[5] Cf. Writings of Schurz, vol. iv, pp. 409–14.
[6] "Nothing could induce me to vote for Hill," Silas W. Burt wrote
Lamont. "I distrust the man and his warmest supporters are those who
opposed Mr. Cleveland's nomination and election and his administrative
policy." Two-thirds of the Independents would have voted for a worthy
candidate had the Democratic party presented his name, but they could
not eat "such a gamey-flavored crow as Hill."—Oct. 7, 1885, in Cleveland
Papers.
[7] Ibid.

$1,000 to Alton B. Parker of the Democratic state committee, but accompanied it with a letter containing some allusions to those who were "howling about the administration and claiming that it should speak out." He would tell them "that campaigns are successfully fought by pushing the merits of candidates and principles and not by a foolish attempt to discredit an administration, which is doing all that is possible to assist the canvass." The "greatest enemy to the success of your ticket today," he continued, "is the man or the paper which is constantly yelling to the administration to come to its rescue," and so on.[1]

In the election, if Hill lost the votes of the Mugwumps, he gained the support of the Irish, who had been Blaine's friends in 1884, and he was elected by a plurality of 11,000, which, though small, exceeded Cleveland's in the previous year.[2]

In Ohio the Democrats, who were also endeavoring to elect a governor, gave no hearty support to Cleveland. But they fared less well than their brethren in New York; they were beaten by the Republicans who, like the Democrats, cared nothing for honest government, and won the election by lampoon and harangue about the "bloody shirt" and the "treason-stained saddle" of Robert E. Lee. The victory insured the re-election of John Sherman to the United States Senate.[3]

Similarly the Democrats in Massachusetts started back at the thought of commending the civil service law and the President's endeavors to abide by its terms.[4] But everywhere it was noted that neither Republican nor Democratic officeholders, and for the first time, meddled with the elections. Lest they be suspected of "offensive partisanship" they left off political activity and tranquilly performed the tasks for which they were employed and paid.[5]

Before the meeting of the new Congress Vice-President Thomas A. Hendricks, suddenly, in November, 1885, died at

[1] Oct. 22, 1885, in Cleveland Papers.
[2] Cf. N. Y. Times, Sep. 26, 1885; N. Y. Nation, Oct. 1, 22 and Nov. 5, 1885.
[3] N. Y. Nation, Aug. 27, Oct. 15 and 22, 1885.
[4] Ibid., June 25 and Oct. 15, 1885.
[5] Ibid., Oct. 22 and Nov. 12, 1885.

his home in Indiana, and the administration was to go forward without the aid, whatever it might have been, of a leader, as the presiding officer of the Senate, who, if he were esteemed for his courtesy as a gentleman and his integrity in the public places which he held, was but little in sympathy with the elements in the party arrayed for action under Mr. Cleveland.[1] The President *pro tem* of the Republican Senate was now the next in succession to the Presidency, but that body had no such officer. Anxiety for Cleveland's safety in this conjuncture was so great that his friends, Tilden among the number, strongly objected to his facing the dangers which attendance at Mr. Hendricks's funeral might entail. Others urged him to go. He would be as "safe in the West as in the East." He listened to his various advisers. But, "in the present peculiar and delicate situation," he said that he should not "take even the remote chance of accidents incident to travel." "No stubborn idea of heroism" would justify it. He would not subject his countrymen "to any greater risk of disaster" than attended his performance of "strict duty" in Washington.[2]

On the subject of a president *pro tem* the Republicans in the Senate immediately commenced maneuvers looking to the election of Logan, their defeated candidate for Vice-President,[3] who had recently won so close and tedious a contest in the legislature of Illinois for a seat in the upper house of Congress.[4] He, with credit to himself, when the right day came, declined the place,[5] and John Sherman was chosen, who now, until the enactment of the Presidential succession bill, designed to assure control to the party, which, by popular mandate, had formed an administration, would, in case of Mr. Cleveland's death, become the President.[6] By the new law of January 19, 1886, which had been under long discussion, and was manifestly in the interest of order as well as justice and right,[7] the succession

[1] Cf. N. Y. Nation, Dec. 3, 1885.
[2] Cleveland Papers; N. Y. Times, Nov. 28 and 30, 1885.
[3] N. Y. Nation, Dec. 3 and 10, 1885.
[4] Cf. ibid., Jan. 1 and 29, Feb. 26 and March 12, 1885.
[5] He would have been "a bull in a china shop."—Ibid., Dec. 10, 1885.
[6] Cf. ibid., Dec. 24, 1885.
[7] Cf. ibid., Dec. 3, 1885, and Jan. 21, 1886.

would pass from the President and Vice-President to the Secretary of State, the Secretary of the Treasury, and on through the cabinet in a specified order.[1]

The death of Tilden in August, 1886, put an end to the uncongenial influences which radiated from the restless man who had led the Democratic party in 1876, and who had sought, through the Secretary of the Treasury, to get patronage from, and guide the policy of, the new administration.[2]

For eight years Horatio Seymour had been prostrated from a sunstroke. He had written Tilden from Utica in 1885 that he could never visit New York again.[3] He died in February, 1886, three days after General Hancock. The previous October had seen the end of George B. McClellan. Four of the party's Presidential candidates, therefore, were removed by death in the period of nine months.

The death of Grant occurred in July, 1885. He had been swept aside by the Republican party, but his end, because of its peculiar tragedy and the public gratitude which his name continued to evoke, deeply impressed the nation. The explosion of Grant and Ward, which so disgracefully involved him in the operations of Ferdinand Ward, a young "Napoleon of Finance," not above thirty years of age, who soon proved himself to be one of the most audacious as well as picturesque adventurers in the history of Wall Street, and James D. Fish who, from his vantage point as president of a fiduciary institution chartered under the National Banking law, the Marine Bank, furthered the firm's highly scandalous feats, reverberated through the land for many months. The firm had borrowed without security. Such collateral as they had was pledged three or four times over. Their affairs went into court and Ward and Fish were sentenced to long terms in prison.[4]

[1] McPherson's Handbook for 1886, pp. 89–92.
[2] Cf. Bigelow, Life of Tilden, vol. ii, pp. 304–20; Letters and Memorials of Tilden, pp. 692, 724, 729–30.
[3] Letters and Memorials of Tilden, p. 700; A. J. Wall, Life of Seymour, p. 74.
[4] Cf. N. Y. Nation, April 16, June 11, July 2 and November 5, 1885. Ward and Fish were a "pair of thieves who were working harmoniously together to cheat everybody who could be induced to trust them." (Ibid.,

U. S. Grant, Jr., had married a daughter of the wealthy Senator Chaffee of Colorado who, with the desire to find employment for his son-in-law, had provided a considerable sum of money for the firm's use. This was lost in the crash.[1] The blow to Grant was overwhelming. To find that he had committed his name and fame to such rascals, and that he was thrown, with them, into a maelstrom of civil and criminal litigation was nearly as mortifying to the nation as to the victim of so much misfortune.[2]

The subscribers to the fund of $250,000 collected for his advantage in 1880-81 met and put it in the hands of trustees, who would pay the income to his wife during her lifetime and afterward to the children; but the sum had been invested in railroad stocks, at the moment of little value, though Governor Morgan, while he lived, and then his estate, had guaranteed to the beneficiary an income of about $15,000 a year for a period of ten years.[3]

In his distress Grant had turned to William H. Vanderbilt, son of Commodore Vanderbilt, principal heir to that magnate's fortune and manager of his railroads. The $150,000 thus received on all the security which could be offered, including the trophies of war and peace of better days, were put into the vortex, and a movement was begun by General Sherman to secure from the wealthy men, who had befriended Grant before, a sum large enough to discharge the debt.[4]

To Grant's credit he, in a letter to Cyrus W. Field, declined to receive the assistance which seemed to be at hand. Mr. Vanderbilt having bought in all the property which had been transferred to him as the basis for the loan, proposed to present it to Mrs. Grant, with the proviso that the personal mementoes of any historical value included in the pledge should

July 2, 1885.) Fish made repeated efforts to gain his release from Sing Sing, naming Ward as the "wicked partner," to which Ward protested vigorously in letters to President Cleveland.—Cleveland Papers.

[1] N. Y. Times, May 7, 1884; N. Y. Nation, May 15, 1884.
[2] Cf. N. Y. Nation, May 22, 1884.
[3] Cong. Record, 48th Cong. 2nd sess., pp. 684-5; ibid., 47th Cong. 1st sess., p. 1289; N. Y. Nation, Oct. 29, 1885.
[4] Cf. N. Y. Nation, Jan. 1, 1885.

eventually pass to the national government. With like delicacy of sentiment she said that she could not receive the gift, though she acceded to the suggestion that the swords, medals and other decorations be placed in Washington. The plan was laid before Congress by President Arthur who asked that body to accept the trust and thank the donors.[1] Mr. Vanderbilt's further offer to create a fund for Mrs. Grant's benefit was declined.[2]

Before this turn in Grant's fortunes, he having, at the invitation of the editors, contributed a series of articles to the Century Magazine, a publisher formulated a plan for the issue of his Memoirs, if he would write them, and to this task he had set his hand. While that work, which was to meet praise and profitable sale, was still unfinished it was announced that he was suffering from a cancer of the mouth attributed to the excessive smoking of tobacco.[3] He retired under his distress to a cottage on Mount MacGregor, near Saratoga, N. Y. Several times his life seemed near its end, but diligently and determinedly he went on, and completed his writing only four days· before his death on July 23, 1885.

Nation and world-wide honors were done his name. President Cleveland issued a proclamation, framed in the warmest terms of appreciation. Bells were tolled throughout the land. Everywhere symbols of mourning were displayed. The President ordered the White House and all public buildings to be draped in black in token of respect. The cable bore the family messages of sympathy from all parts of the world. A memorial service, attended by a distinguished assembly of government ministers, peers and members of the House of Commons, was held in Westminster Abbey. A burial place was found in New York City overlooking the Hudson River and, on August 8th, after the body had been viewed by a quarter of a million people at the City Hall, where it lay in state for two or three days, the ceremonies were concluded by a military funeral. The President ordered a suspension of public business and caused appropriate

[1] App. Ann. Cyclop. for 1885, p. 226.
[2] N. Y. Tribune, Jan. 12, 1885.
[3] N. Y. Nation, March 5, 1885; G. W. Childs, Recollections, p. 113.

honors to be shown the dead hero of the war by the army and navy. It was a national holiday.[1]

The meeting of Congress in December, 1885, brought to Washington a Senate having a Republican majority of six to hold in check the Democratic majority in the House, which was more than 40.[2] John G. Carlisle of Kentucky was reëlected Speaker. It was a body from which too little support might be expected by the President—a Senate which was hostile and a House which, though of his own party, contained, in the majority, elements out of sympathy with his purposes.

He continued to be overwhelmed with applications for office. Dorman B. Eaton, though his name was prominently known in connection with civil service reform was declared by E. L. Godkin, to Cleveland's surprise, to be "a very impracticable and wrong-headed person." Other letter writers from the ranks of the Independents spoke of his indiscretions and found him to be incapable as an administrative officer. Eaton's resignation as president of the Civil Service Commission, to be followed by the retirement of the other two members, of Arthur's appointment, called for the reorganization of that body. Instantly scores of persons in all parts of the country, many of them obviously unsuitable, asked for the vacated posts, pressure which continued until a man named Edgerton of Fort Wayne, Ind., who had been a member of Congress thirty years ago and who, it was said, had not visited Washington from that day to this, was called from an affluent and studious retirement to head the new commission.[3]

The President complained that he could not write his message to Congress because of "the d——d everlasting clatter for office."[4] His friends feared that he would break down from overwork as he strove to get the facts concerning men to be appointed and men to be removed, and to enforce the rules which he had made for himself and his administration in relation to office holding.

[1] Richardson, Messages and Papers, vol. viii, p. 308.
[2] In the Forty-eighth Congress it had been nearly 80.
[3] Cleveland Papers; cf. N. Y. Nation, Nov. 12 and March 18, 1886.
[4] To Bissell, Nov. 25, 1885, in Cleveland Papers.

His first message was anticipated with uncommon interest since it would be the first extended statement of the policies of the administration. The paper, though its author was under close siege during the entire time of its preparation, was entirely statesmanlike. It was long and contained opinion, argument and recommendation covering the whole range of governmental activity. The work undertaken by the departments was reviewed. The new policies inaugurated by Secretary Lamar in the Interior Department, by the Postmaster-General, by the Secretary of the Navy, by the Attorney-General were explained and indorsed. The President advocated in not to be mistaken terms the putting of the nation in such a posture that it could defend itself, if need be, by war vessels. Efforts to revive our sea power had been "little better than blind gropings and expensive, aimless follies." The Navy Department recently had been simply "a shabby ornament to the government." It must be reorganized, in accordance with the suggestions of Secretary Whitney, to meet the hope, "shared by all patriotic citizens," that the day might be not far distant when our navy should be such as to befit "our standing among the nations of the earth." [1]

The interests of the people at the moment were economic. Conditions in business were a constant reminder that no question could transcend this one in importance, and the words of the President on these points were awaited with lively anticipation, though with too little wish to heed them and accept his leadership. During the campaign so much had been said, on the Republican side, in emphasis of the relation of a high tariff to work, wages, the scale of living, general employment and national prosperity, so much intended to fill the country with distrust of Cleveland and his administration in his dealing with this topic, that there must have been disappointment in Republican circles when his message was read. It was difficult, on the face of it, to pillory him and set him before the country for bombardment as one who would close the mills and deluge the land with British manufactures. He spoke of the "surplus," the excess of public revenues over necessary and proper ex-

[1] Richardson, vol. viii, p. 351.

penditures, which had been noted for some time, and recommended the bringing about of a balance by a reduction in customs collections. The question of "free trade" was not involved, nor was there at the moment any occasion "for the general discussion of the wisdom or expediency of a protective system." "Industries and interests" built up by tariff laws should not be "ruthlessly injured or destroyed." "American labor" should be safeguarded.

But, in the public interest, a "certain reduction" was necessary, and Mr. Cleveland said, modestly enough, that he thought this remission of revenue should be in the taxes upon "imported necessaries of life," which would "directly lessen the cost of living in every family of the land and release to the people in every humble home a larger measure of the rewards of frugal industry." [1]

He then passed to the coinage and the currency system, than which nothing was "more important" to the public welfare. This subject had been treated repeatedly in Presidential messages. No one who knew aught about the correct principles of national finance had any other opinion than that, when John Sherman had met the silver miners and the cheap money fanatics halfway in 1878, and Congress had pledged the government to the purchase of $2,000,000 worth of silver bullion each month for coinage into silver dollars,[2] they had done vast injury to the business interests of the country. It is true that the new compromise with evil was not different from other adventures with the currency which were undertaken to gain the votes of the ignorant by men who must periodically run the gauntlet of popular reëlection. The "silver men," "bimetalists," as they liked to be called, if they were glib enough to speak and write about their subject, were not worse than the "Greenbackers." But to make peace with any corruption or heresy, as President Hayes well knew, when he vetoed the first

[1] Lamar had told the President that, at the moment, there was not much interest in the tariff, and he need say little about it in his message.—Cleveland Papers.

[2] This was approximately one-half of all the silver mined in the United States.—Report of Sec. of Treas. for 1884, p. xxxv.

silver bill, and understood again, it must be supposed, when, overborne by Sherman, he had signed the second one, is the public man's gravest mistake.

President Arthur in his first message to Congress had asked that the silver purchase law be repealed and that, henceforth, only so much silver should be coined as might be needed to meet the demand.[1] He repeated this counsel,[2] his last message, following the urgent advice of Hugh McCulloch, who had lately become Secretary of the Treasury, having contained the most distinct statements on the subject. The country, he said on that occasion, was approaching the point when silver was likely to be "our sole metallic standard." [3]

President Cleveland now stated the case still more plainly. Since silver had been bought for coinage over 215,000,000 silver dollars had left the mints of the United States. Only about 50,000,000 of these had found their way into circulation; the rest remained in possession of the government. Congress had appropriated $100,000 in 1883 to increase the storage space by new construction and by the rental of vaults and safes at the subtreasuries, and to transport silver from places where it could not be taken care of to other places. In 1885 Secretary McCulloch informed Congress that the sum had been spent. The subtreasurer at San Francisco must have "relief." He had three new vaults—all had been filled with "buzzard" dollars. The mint could hold no more. The branch at Carson in Nevada was "crowded." Money was required to hire storage facilities, or to convey the useless coin to the East, which involved the payment of high carrying charges. And in the East like conditions prevailed. The assistant treasurer at Cincinnati said that he had no more room. The officers in that city and Boston had been relieved by shipments to Washington. In Philadelphia, the mint being full, $20,000,000 were hauled in canvas bags to the post office.[4]

[1] Cf. his first message to Congress in 1881 in Richardson, Messages and Papers, vol. viii, p. 46.
[2] Cf. ibid., p. 133.
[3] Ibid., pp. 243–4; cf. Report of Sec. of Treas. for 1884, pp. xxix–xxxiv.
[4] N. Y. Times, May 8, 1886.

A new vault had been completed in the office of the Treasurer of the United States at Washington. Only $40,000,000 more could be put in this space, and there was some room still available in New Orleans. McCulloch asked for $500,000 "immediately" that he might safeguard the coin which the mints poured upon him.[1] Still on and on two millions a month were added to the idle mass. McCulloch's request falling upon deaf ears, the department, in 1886, renewed the request for an appropriation. At that time it was said that no space remained anywhere except at New Orleans, and this should be held for the output of the mint in that city.

President Cleveland in his first message to Congress declared that before long all the gold which the government could obtain would be used for purchases of silver. The two coins would "part company," as paper and gold had gone their separate ways before the resumption of specie payments. Gold was now being hoarded; it was, for safety and gain, being withdrawn from circulation. Soon we should have silver money only, since it would be impossible for the government to keep a gold dollar, worth one hundred cents, and a silver dollar, worth but eighty cents, in use at the same time. There would be another standard of value. Confidence shaken, trade disturbed, credit withdrawn from business and speculative enterprise the country was, and would continue to be, barring remedial action, in a state of apprehension, destructive of orderly economic development.

The President turned also to the international situation. Upon coming to office he had delegated one in whom he recognized "especial competency in the practical monetary and economic sciences," Manton Marble,[2] to proceed to Europe on "a special confidential mission" and, in coöperation with our ministers to England, France and Germany, obtain full knowledge and make report as to the attitude of those governments toward silver coinage. Marble's inquiries were exhaustive.

[1] House Ex. Doc., 48th Cong. 2nd sess., no. 146; Report of Sec. of Treas. for 1884, p. xxxviii; cf. Washington corr. N. Y. Tribune, Jan. 29, 1885.
[2] On May 13, 1885. Senate Ex. Doc., 49th Cong. 1st sess., no. 29, pp. 3–4.

He met many men in Great Britain and enjoyed confidential communication with them.[1] He talked with high officials in Paris[2] and Berlin.[3] The consul-general in Paris had been charged to acquaint himself with the proceedings of the conference of the Latin Union to be held in that city in the summer of 1885.[4] Through these and other informants it was made clear to the President, and to intelligent men generally, that no coöperation was to be expected in other countries.[5] "Without an ally or friend," the President said, "we battle upon the silver field in an illogical and losing contest." He recommended the suspension of the compulsory coinage of silver dollars.[6]

All this was well. But Congress made a not unexpected answer, clearly reflecting party feeling. At the moment the Republican leaders in the Senate were engaged in warfare upon the President on the subject of his appointments and removals, and were approaching the limit of their authority in calling for documents and in putting other obstacles in his way in the performance of his duties. In a message on March 1, 1886, he reviewed, in the clearest way, the entire subject of the relations between the President and the Senate under the Constitution, as well as of such parts of the "Tenure of Office acts," which were passed to embarrass Andrew Johnson in 1867, as had not been repealed for the advantage of Grant in 1869,[7] and concluded with the statement that nothing would "discourage or deter" him from "following in the way" which he was convinced led to "better government for the people." In the course of the paper, in allusion to the old laws, he had used the words "innocuous desuetude," which

---

[1] Senate Ex. Doc., 49th Cong. 1st sess., no. 29, p. 5.

[2] Ibid., pp. 6–8.

[3] Ibid., pp. 8–9; cf. Manning Papers in Library of Congress.

[4] Senate Ex. Doc., 49th Cong. 1st sess., no. 29, p. 11.

[5] Tilden wrote to Hugh McCulloch, then Secretary of the Treasury (February 11, 1885): "After looking over the discussions of the last two international conferences, I cannot avoid the conclusion that it is hopeless to make any further attempt to obtain the coöperation of the leading commercial powers in fixing a ratio between gold and silver coins."—Letters and Memorials of Tilden, p. 674.

[6] Richardson, vol. viii, pp. 342–6.   [7] Cf. N. Y. Nation, Aug. 13, 1885.

were extracted by the editors of Republican gazettes who, by much ridicule of the phrase, seemed to believe that they might confound the indomitable man who had written it.[1] His admirers called the message a "second Declaration of Independence." "Thank God we have a President!" they exclaimed; he had displayed the "spirit of Jackson."[2] The Republican leaders sat uncomfortably under their rebuke, the more so since they were made aware that they were dealing with one who could well defend himself and exhibit the triviality and shallowness of their stratagems. They made a demonstration on the subject of their prerogatives. Removals, like appointments, should have their assent.[3] The controversy, for a time, fed the popular love for tirade and battle, but shortly the Senate itself would move to free the statute books of the final vestiges of restriction upon the President's powers in relation to removals from office, and we should return to the system of undivided executive responsibility which had prevailed from the foundation of the government.[4]

Throughout the Arthur administration the Republican party had been distinctly divided on the silver question. Its leaders were timid, even some of those who had the most wisdom drew back before the threatful outbursts of the aggressive Western miners, and the "money cranks," who were constantly working on that most extraordinary of superstitions prevalent among the ignorant masses that much money, in quantity, and cheap money, in price, will somehow confer benefits on the poor.[5] Delegates from a half dozen states and territories

[1] Richardson, vol. viii, pp. 375–83.

[2] Cleveland Papers.

[3] They were supported by Schurz who saw in the law, so long as it continued to be in force, a check upon the Executive in imminent and prospective assaults upon the civil service. Writings of Schurz, vol. iv, pp. 414–20, 421–8.

[4] Act of March 3, 1887. See Hoar, Autobiography of 70 years, vol. ii, chap. xi; McPherson's Handbook for 1888, pp. 46–7; N. Y. Nation, March 10, 1887.

[5] "They [Bland and his following] are not bimetallists at all. . . . What they want is the poorest money attainable. This happens to be silver; consequently they are silver monometallists. If anything less valuable could be found which public opinion would tolerate, they would be for that," etc.—N. Y. Nation, Jan. 15, 1885.

to a National Silver Convention held in Denver in January, 1885, had passed resolutions in favor of "free and unlimited" silver coinage, condemning Secretary of the Treasury Hugh McCulloch for his course in relation to silver, and calling upon President-elect Cleveland to place some one in this office who would not act in the interest of "national banks," "Eastern brokers" and the "magnates of Wall Street." They appointed a committee whose business it would be to organize a "National Bimetallic Association." [1]

As for the Democratic party, which was essentially the poor man's party, it was, in the West and South, largely in the control of leaders who knew no better, or, if they had insight and sagacity on such a topic, played the demagogue and sold their consciences to gain and retain political power. The Republican Senate should have come to the President's support on a matter which was high above party. The Committee on Finance, Senator Morrill chairman, was made up, as in the preceding Congress, with a bare majority in favor of bringing to an end, sooner or later, the compulsory coinage of silver.[2] In the last Congress it had reported a bill, though at too late a day, authorizing suspension of purchases of bullion at the end of eighteen months, if no international agreement should be reached meanwhile.[3]

The House, with its Democratic majority, on the other hand, as had been anticipated, and as soon was proven, was entirely out of accord with the President's views. Certainly the Treasury Department had not been surrendered to the silver men. Manning, if unsympathetic with the President, as Tilden and Tilden's friends declared, unflinchingly supported the administration in the management of the subjects which came under his care. He asked the Attorney-General for an opinion as to whether the act of 1878, requiring the expenditure of $24,-000,000 annually in the purchase of silver was "properly a permanent appropriation." [4] He won and held the confidence

[1] Denver corr. N. Y. Times, Jan. 31, 1885; N. Y. Nation, Feb. 5, 1885.
[2] N. Y. Nation, March 19, 1885.
[3] Ibid., Jan. 14, 1886.
[4] Nov. 16, 1885, in Manning Papers in Library of Congress.

of bankers and men acquainted with correct principles of finance, both at home and abroad. As the months passed the Mugwumps and those who had been doubtful of his sincerity, no less than of his capacity, expressed very different views. He had "surprised everyone by his administrative ability and the statesmanlike papers which he had submitted to Congress," said Silas W. Burt.[1] He was doing more than anyone else, in the opinion of Horace White, "to root the administration in the confidence of the thinking people of the United States."[2]

Speaker Carlisle who had appointed Bland to the chairmanship of the House Committee on Coinage in the last Congress had found it necessary to continue that "financial lunatic"[3] in the place. But from the composition of the committee it was guessed that the vote might be seven to six in favor of some modification of the silver purchase law.[4]

The fury of the silverites increased as they rose in their places in Congress in defense of their favorite money, and in denunciation of those who held it in smaller regard. They spoke and acted on an assumption that they were under persecution. They had the fiat money man's view of the question. For the government to say that 75 or 85 cents[5] were a dollar would, they said, make it worth so much. Hope centered around the Latin Union, though the countries composing it were closing their mints to silver;[6] it was very doubtful whether the compact would be extended, but they had patched up a truce, and, for self-protection in a failing cause, would

---

[1] To Cleveland, March 25, 1886, in Cleveland Papers.

[2] White to Lamont, May 17, 1886, in ibid.

[3] N. Y. Nation, Dec. 31, 1885.

[4] Ibid., Jan. 14, 1886.

[5] In September, 1885, because of the fall in the price of silver the Bland dollar was worth only 79 cents. (N. Y. Nation, Sep. 24, 1885.) So much was being taken out of the mines that the price in August, 1886, was as low as 40 pence per ounce. This made the bullion price of a Bland dollar less than 72 cents. (Richardson, vol. viii, p. 512.) The mines in Montana were being closed until such time as the ore could be worked at a profit.—N. Y. Times, Aug. 5, 1886; N. Y. Nation, Aug. 12, 1886.

[6] N. Y. Nation, March 19, 1885.

endeavor to maintain their agreement for five more years with no additional coinage.[1]

There would be, it was said, general and larger international combinations in behalf of silver money—always only a few months or a year away. But for the "gold bugs" in America and the "perfidy" of England the world long since would have enjoyed the blessings of bimetallism. Bismarck was a convert; the silver zealots remembered that he had said so to William D. Kelley of Philadelphia in 1879, though they had forgotten that in the last Monetary Conference in 1881, in Paris, the German delegates, under instruction, distinctly declined to experiment with the double standard.[2] Samuel Smith, a member of Parliament in England, H. H. Gibbs, one time a governor of the Bank of England, M. Cernuschi, a French "savant,"[3] other men in Europe were bimetallists and presented their views, to be advertised by our silver men as leaders of immense consequence, who would soon· bring their governments into another conference, if it were but possible to put a quietus on the gold monometallists in America.[4] Did not Professor Thorold Rogers, Robert Giffen and others in England admit that there had been "a rise in the value of gold" which would produce "an overwhelming mass of human sorrow?"[5]

It was plain, said the "silver maniacs"[6] in the House, that the administration was organized in the interest of wealth and privilege; it was formed to serve the bondholders, the monometallists and those who grew rich by creating a monopoly in money. To argue with men who held such opinions and

[1] Senate Ex. Doc., 49th Cong. 1st sess., no. 48; N. Y. Nation, Nov. 19, 1885.

[2] House Mis. Doc., 49th Cong. 1st sess., no. 396, pt. 3, p. 29; N. Y. Nation, March 12, 1885.

[3] "The recognized and preëminent leader of the bimetallists" in France. —Manton Marble in Manning Papers.

[4] Cf. N. Y. Nation, Aug. 13, 1885.

[5] Cf. House Mis. Doc., 49th Cong. 1st sess., no. 396, pt. 3, p. 349. "I do not see how any reasonable being can ask or wish this government to continue coining in opposition to the Latin Union."—Bayard to Manning in Manning Papers, Nov. 9, 1885.

[6] N. Y. Nation, Feb. 26, 1886.

harbored such prejudices, in order that they might gain votes
every second year in the Congressional elections, was futile,
and the few leaders of the President's party in the House
who appeared in his support, in his rôle of "champion and
defender of an honest dollar," [1] were as voices in the wilderness.

In the Senate even worse conditions prevailed. Beck, a
Democratic senator from Kentucky, found that silver, which
the banks would not take because they believed that it could
not be kept at par with gold and which was held at par now, in
fact, only because it could be used to pay customs dues, the
equivalent of its redemption in gold by the government,[2] was
being locked up in the Treasury through some foul deal with
the "gold bugs." It were better he said, if a thief should steal
it or that it should be squandered than that it should be hoarded
by the government.[3] The "most powerful body of capitalists"
in the country was organized against silver coinage.[4] Another
Democrat in the Senate, Vance of North Carolina, declared
that the campaign which was being conducted for the "degradation" of silver was "one of the grandest conspiracies against
the rights of the people ever inaugurated by human greed." [5]
The "repudiation of the silver dollar" was making the rich
man richer and the poor man poorer.[6] Brown of Georgia,
Maxey of Texas, Pugh of Alabama and other senators of the
President's political party were heard in similar language.
Wild allusions to "Wall Street gamblers," "Wall Street with
its congeners," "plutocratic rule," villains who "cornered"
markets and made victims of the poor punctuated the debate,
the text of which was a revival of the old scheme to pay the
government debt, principal and interest, in silver money.[7]

Eustis, a senator from Louisiana, would have Secretary
Manning redeem $10,000,000 of bonds, which he had called,

[1] N. Y. Nation, Feb. 26, 1885.
[2] Ibid., Jan. 14, Feb. 11 and March 4, 1886.
[3] Cong. Record, 49th Cong. 1st sess., p. 355.
[4] Ibid.
[5] Ibid., p. 605.
[6] Ibid., p. 606.
[7] Cf. W. B. Parker, Life of J. S. Morrill, pp. 317–8.

in silver dollars, though it was perfectly clear that this silver would almost at once make its way back to the Treasury with loss of transportation charges in both directions.[1] If the Bland law were to be changed and coinage suspended, Ingalls of Kansas said that this should be done only after the aggregate amount of silver dollars outstanding had reached $500,000,000.[2] John Sherman would discontinue the coinage of silver, but continue to purchase it, and issue a new kind of paper money founded on bullion. The government would then save the expense of coinage.[3]

The Senate's intelligent men from New England, together with Evarts, recently elected from New York, remained silent, lest they be suspected of sympathy for a President belonging to another party and lest, by their coöperation with him, they might increase his repute and make him a greater figure than they would like him to be. Only Morrill of Vermont came forward in the "silver standard blizzard" then raging.[4] Though Teller, the new Republican senator from Colorado, representing the miners, vigorously supported Beck and the Democratic demagogues,[5] Morrill chose to call it a "family quarrel."[6] Regretting that men of the President's own party should "represent the Secretary of the Treasury as being little better than a common thief," and allege that the President and the Secretary together had been "bought up by the bondholders,"[7] he had the manliness to raise a voice in defense of the common welfare, though it were, at the same time, in defense of a political foe.[8]

Bland was not able to buttress his free coinage scheme with a favorable report of his committee. He wanted one vote to gain the end which he so persistently pursued.[9] But he could

[1] N. Y. Nation, Jan. 14, 1886.
[2] Ibid., Jan. 21, 1886.
[3] Ibid., Feb. 4, 1886.
[4] Cong. Record, 49th Cong. 1st sess., p. 773.
[5] Ibid., pp. 747–56.
[6] Ibid., p. 773.
[7] Ibid., p. 357.
[8] Cf. W. B. Parker, Life of J. S. Morrill, pp. 316–7.
[9] N. Y. Nation, Feb. 18 and 25, April 1, 1886.

muster a majority in the House for a resolution inquiring of the Secretary of the Treasury whether he would or would not pay out silver in operations having to do with the reduction of the public debt, and asking like questions designed to set that officer before the people of the West and South as an advocate of the "gold standard," though his views had been competently explained in his annual report.[1] At the same time, further to embarrass Mr. Manning, the Committee on Ways and Means, in which, on the currency question, the President seemed to have only one friend, Abram S. Hewitt, in an interval when it was not engaged in the work of devising a tariff bill, demanded to know how the Secretary regarded the project to redeem government bonds with the "surplus" or "balance" in the Treasury in excess of $100,000,000, which must be held to support the issue of greenbacks.[2]

Bland brought his free coinage bill before the House without the support of a recommendation from the Coinage Committee, and on April 8, 1886, the scheme was defeated by a vote of 163 to 126.[3] At the same time the House refused to suspend the purchase of bullion at the rate of $2,000,000 a month, as authorized by the act of 1878—an amendment to the free coinage bill, fixing July 1, 1889, as the date upon which the folly should cease, unless, by concurrent action, the nations of Europe should meanwhile remonetize silver, being rejected by a vote of 201 to 84.[4] It was an unhappy outlook. But responsible men viewed the scene not unhopefully. The decisive vote against free coinage, from which it was feared at times that there might be no escape, under a form of government which intrusted such a question as the determination of the character of its currency to the ignorant masses, was full of encouragement. The issue had been brought prominently be-

---

[1] See resolution of Feb. 3, 1886. Manning's reply in House Ex. Doc., 49th Cong. 1st sess., no. 100; cf. McPherson's Handbook for 1886, pp. 93-8.
[2] N. Y. Nation, Feb. 18 and 25, 1886; McPherson's Handbook for 1886, p. 226.
[3] Seventy Democrats and 93 Republicans voted against free coinage; 97 Democrats and 29 Republicans for it.
[4] N. Y. Nation, April 15, 1886.

fore the people, and there were signs, the New York Nation believed, of a turn in the tide of opinion, though it was plain that the "campaign of education" must continue until a majority of the voters in the West and South should grow tired of paying taxes to hold up the price of silver, or rather until they could be made to see that it was taxation.[1]

The session was prolonged far into the summer, with each party seeking to gain advantage over the other in the people's sight in preparation for the Congressional elections in the autumn. Some disposition must be made of the "surplus" which, however, as times grew worse, displayed a tendency to disappear, ere the problem which it presented could be solved.[2] The sum, whatever it was, must not be allowed to rest in the Treasury. In mid-July the House passed a resolution directing Secretary Manning to disburse the amount in hand above $100,000,000 at the rate of $10,000,000 a month, and apply it to the payment of the interest-bearing indebtedness of the United States. Two hundred and seven members (143 of them Democrats) voted for this resolution and 67 (14 Democrats) voted against it, and it went to the Senate.[3] The wiser men in that body had the discretion to amend it and take from it a mischievous feature. The reserve to be held in the Treasury was given a maximum limit of $130,000,000 a minimum of $110,000,000, and the Secretary, in cases of emergency, might, at will and on his judgment, in order to maintain the public credit, entirely suspend bond purchases. Thirty-six senators voted for this amendment and 27 (14 Democrats and 13 Republicans) against it.

Having done so much of value the Senate, lest it be suspected of some treason to silver, agreed to another amendment authorizing the redemption at their face value of 75 cent trade dollars, which were now held almost entirely by speculators who, in many cases, had acquired them for merely the price

[1] N. Y. Nation, April 15, 1886.
[2] Ibid., Feb. 18, 1886.
[3] McPherson's Handbook for 1886, pp. 225-6; N. Y. Nation, July 2 1886.

of the metal.[1] In conference between the houses in the last days of the session the resolution was freed of this piece of buffoonery and the original text, with the safeguard thrown about it by the Senate, went to the President, who refused to sign it within the specified period, and it failed to become a law.[2] He believed the measure to be "unnecessary," he said in a memorandum which he filed with the State Department, and would not approve it, lest it "endanger and embarrass the successful and useful operations" of the Treasury and "impair the confidence which the people should have in the management of the finances of the government."[3] The resolution under a seductive covering was taken to be, as it was, the last device of the "bimetallists" to impose the silver standard upon the country, and it had failed.[4] Thus the entire session, continuing through eight months, had been unproductive of any legislative measure bearing upon the money question.

Meantime the Ways and Means Committee employed itself with the tariff, both with a view to attacking the "surplus," which arose from too ample a revenue, and with the purpose of improving the lot of the poor. Morrison who had been chairman of the committee in the last Congress was again at its head, and he presented another bill, which, in Republican circles, fell under the suspicion, as had its predecessor, of being in the interest of England, and the importers of foreign merchandise, and would, in short, fasten "free trade" upon the American states. He was "Bill" Morrison to the young humorists who wrote for the newspapers, and his bill was the "Morrison bill"; he had been, and was still, "Horizontal Bill" because of his proposal in the last Congress for a "horizontal" reduction of the tariff. It was February, 1886, when he was ready to present his measure to the House. It would, said he, reduce the income of the government to the extent of about

---

[1] N. Y. Nation, Aug. 5, 1886; cf. ibid., May 6, 1886. For a defense of this measure see N. Y. Tribune, April 19, 1886. Cf. Report of Sec. of Treas. for 1884, p. xxxvii.

[2] McPherson's Handbook for 1886, pp. 225–9.

[3] Richardson, vol. viii, p. 488; cf. N. Y. Nation, Aug. 5 and 12, 1886.

[4] N. Y. Nation, Aug. 5, 1886.

twenty millions a year. One-half of this amount would come
from sugar and nearly all of the remainder from raw or only
partly manufactured materials, a number of which were to
be put upon the free list. Some lowering of the rates on pig
iron, steel rails and window glass was calculated to stir interests in Pennsylvania engaged in the production of these
articles.[1]

The bill went to the Committee on Ways and Means which,
in the usual manner, invited hearings.[2] Farmers, manufacturers,
importers, labor leaders, the agents and attorneys of these,
and other men, who felt that their material welfare was imperiled and who, on this account, wanted one duty raised
and another reduced, again swarmed into Washington. If
it were a sordid spectacle the system which produced it was
in some way bound up with our democracy. The Congressman
must have votes to compass his reëlection, else he would be
retired to private life and, in the Eastern states at least, the
manufacturers were the most likely to assist him in paying
his campaign expenses. A time was coming, if it were not
already at hand, when, in very many instances, Republican
Congressmen felt that they were the agents of manufacturers;
and the mill owners and the politicians together, assisted by
the local newspapers, told the workingmen that factories would
close and wages could be paid no longer, if tariff rates were
disturbed. A few Democrats received their support at home
from similar interests, among them Randall in Philadelphia,
who still led a faction in his party, which, on this subject,
coöperated with the Republicans.[3]

It is true that some manufacturers wanted free raw materials—free wool, free hemp, free coal, free ores, free lumber—
so that they might produce more cheaply. But the farmers
were made to believe, by a diligent preaching of the doctrine,

---

[1] N. Y. Nation, Feb. 18 and March 4, 1880.

[2] Ibid., March 11, 1886.

[3] "In Randall's case it was simply the performance of the slavish work
for which he is retained by the Republicans of Pennsylvania, the payment
of the service for which he is permitted to hold his seat."—N. Y. Times,
June 18, 1886.

that their interests would be jeopardized by such a policy, and attempts were made to balance the hostile forces, amid a withering fire of spoken and printed raillery about free trade. Only in parts of the Northwest—in Minnesota and, perhaps, in neighboring states—were there tangible evidences of sentiment among Republicans which might give pause to the peculiarly ardent politicians who were making a high tariff the test of party fealty.[1] Such a waste of time on the part of manufacturing executives, of money for railway fares, food and lodging in Washington and fees to glib lawyers to present cases, while a committee of Congress listened to expositions about imports, exports, wages and producing costs on every salable article from lead pencils to locomotive engines, concerning which no member of it had valuable knowledge, would be difficult to celebrate in comedy or burlesque. But the drama gravely proceeded, while the New York Tribune and the Republican press generally hurled "free trade" at anyone who dared to say aught that was complimentary of Mr. Morrison, Abram S. Hewitt, the President, or of Democrats generally, barring Mr. Randall and his friends.

It was plain in June that nothing would come of the rhetorical fanfare. The danger, from the standpoint of the high tariff men, had been warded off; the inequalities and injustices noted and emphasized by the tariff reformers would receive no correction. The House by a vote of 140 to 157 declined even to consider the matter of tariff revision, since 35 Democrats, under Randall's lead, were found to join 122 Republicans and to vote against it.[2] The President was vouchsafed no support for his recommendations on this topic, even in that branch of Congress which was under the control of his own party.

If Mr. Cleveland were not able to remove the cause of the "surplus" he could protect it from raids which would have absorbed it, and which, possibly, would have made inroads

[1] Four of the five Republican representatives from Minnesota had joined the Democrats in test votes on tariff questions in 1884.—McPherson's Handbook for 1884, pp. 136–8; cf. N. Y. Nation, Sep. 30, 1886.

[2] Cong. Record, 49th Cong. 1st sess., pp. 5829–30; N. Y. Nation, June 24, 1886.

upon the reserve. Congress was busily engaged in forwarding plans of all kinds for the expenditure of public money. A senator from New Hampshire, Blair, desired that funds be taken from the Treasury of the United States to advance popular education, particularly in benighted parts of the South.[1]

Others saw outlets for the public money in the scheme of James B. Eads to take up ships, put them on a railway and transport them from the Atlantic to the Pacific oceans over the isthmus of Tehuantepec in Mexico;[2] and in the Hennepin Canal, an old project to connect the Mississippi at or near Rock Island, Ill., with the Illinois River at Hennepin in the same state, a distance of 65 miles at a cost of six or seven millions, thus opening a route from New Orleans and St. Louis to Chicago and Lake Erie.[3] A River and Harbor bill to disperse large sums for local uses in Congressional districts underwent some changes in the interest of economy, and was sent to the President who reluctantly signed it, since he could not reach its separate items, and must approve or disapprove it as a whole.[4] New schemes for increasing soldiers' pensions appeared. All the measures which were devised in Congress to gain the "soldier vote," and to invite the opposition of the President, so that he might be seen as the "rebel" sympathizer which he was alleged to be, had they been passed and approved, would have scattered an enormous sum of public money.[5] As it was the session yielded an act increasing, from $8 to $12 a month, the rate of pay for widows of soldiers and making other changes in the pension system for the advantage of minor children and dependent relations of men who had lost their lives in their country's service;[6] and a law making some increases in the sums allowed to soldiers whose disabili-

---

[1] Infra, chap. xxxi.
[2] House Mis. Doc., 46th Cong. 3rd sess., no. 13; Senate Reports, 47th Cong. 1st sess., no. 213; House Reports, 46th Cong. 3rd sess., no. 322.
[3] Senate Ex. Doc., 47th Cong. 2nd sess., no. 78; House Ex. Doc., 49th Cong. 1st sess., no. 117; Senate Reports, 49th Cong. 1st sess., no. 46, app., pp. 200–10; N. Y. Nation, July 15, 1886; N. Y. Times, Jan. 30, 1885.
[4] N. Y. Nation, Aug. 12, 1886.
[5] Cf. ibid., May 27, 1886.
[6] App. Ann. Cyclop. for 1886, pp. 255–8.

ties arose from the loss of arms or legs in wars of the United States.[1]

But interest was principally centered in the private pension bills. Instead of relying upon the regular machinery of the Pension Bureau Congress continued to pass a multitude of measures which were direct drafts upon the Treasury. Every Congressman was applied to for salaried offices for inhabitants of his district—his constituents also bore down upon him for money to relieve some man, woman or child whose condition it was believed might be made ascribable to the war. Other Presidents had been signing such bills without carefully looking at them. Mr. Cleveland gave them responsible attention and intrepidly, without regard for the criticism which he knew would be leveled at him, vetoed many of them as steals.

On a single day 240 special bills were put in his hands for his signature. He referred them to the Pension Bureau for examination. A few of them, upon their return, he signed. The others, though he thought that many of them should be vetoed, he allowed to become operative without his approval.[2]

On June 21 he said that he had already received 493 pension bills, while 111 more would reach him in a day or two, making more than 600 in all since the beginning of the session, nearly three times the number passed at any entire previous session since 1861. He was "thoroughly tired of disapproving gifts of public money" to individuals, who, in his view, had "no right or claim" to it. The grants were "promiscuous and ill-advised." [3] Could it be supposed that a committee of Congress had a better opportunity to judge of the merits of claims than the bureau which was specifically organized and administered for such a service? When Congress did interpose, the President said, the occasion should be "rare and exceptional." [4] The bills were passed without consideration or discussion, and sent to him, in the knowledge, as well as the hope, that he would veto them, when an ado could be made about his unfriendliness to the Union soldier, and the relations and friends

[1] App. Ann. Cyclop. for 1886, p. 259.
[2] Richardson, vol. viii, pp. 416-7.
[3] Ibid., pp. 437-8.
[4] Ibid., p. 416.

of the suppliants for relief could be converted into active and vindictive workers against the Democratic party.[1] The President's first veto came on May 8, 1886, and before the Congress adjourned, in August, he had forwarded messages in disapproval of more than a hundred such bills.

As he patiently reviewed the cases presented to him of men with sore eyes, rheumatism and "chronic diarrhea," whom Congress had voted to befriend, of the widows of such men who were made the objects of public sympathy, his eyes were not closed to wounds that had never been received, but were simulated, wounds which came in brawls and while plundering the neighborhood, often, indeed, before enlistment or after discharge from service. Women whose husbands had fallen from ladders and into canals or open cellars while drunk, had crossed streams in buggies which overturned and then drowned because they could not swim by reason of rheumatism resulting, as was declared, from exposure during the war, lay down on railway tracks, or deliberately hanged themselves in despondency while waiting for their cases to come through the Pension Bureau, did not escape the President's careful study. He remarked grants for men, or for their widows, when not a single day's service had been rendered the nation, even when the name of the claimant was not to be found upon the muster rolls.

When he discovered fraud his comment was often caustic. Nowhere else in the messages and papers of our Presidents is to be found so much ironical writing as in the memoranda of this grave and unflinching man as he returned these pension bills to the Senate and the House of Representatives. Not unmerited ridicule came to one who said that he had been wounded in the leg in a certain skirmish, though at the time he was absent on sick leave, and who now, twenty years later, induced Congress to vote him a pension because he had recently broken that leg in stepping across a ditch while gathering dandelions;[2] to another who had contracted rheumatism in the "inhospitable climate of Port Tobacco within the state

---

[1] Cf. N. Y. Nation, July 15, 1886.
[2] Richardson, vol. viii, p. 432.

of Maryland"; [1] to another who had made an "attempt to include sore eyes among the results of diarrhea"; [2] to many who, while riding, sustained injuries from the horns of army saddles. The number of such instances led the President to conclude that "those saddles were very dangerous contrivances." [3] One, William Bishop, who had been in a post hospital with the measles may also have considered himself roughly used when it was revealed that his military record had covered but one month and seventeen days, and "as a substitute at a time when high bounties were paid." Fifteen years "after this brilliant service and this terrific encounter with the measles" the claimant had discovered that the disease had "settled in his eyes." [4] But Bishop may be held to have fared as well as Andrew Wilson who joined the army a few weeks before the surrender at Appomattox, and came out of the service with a dozen diseases which were carefully enumerated. "Whatever else may be said of this claimant's achievements during his short military career," the President observed, "it must be conceded that he accumulated a great deal of disability"; if there were ailments to which he might "honestly lay claim," the President continued, it was certain that "his title to the same was complete before he entered the army." [5]

In refusing to sign another bill for the relief of a widow, while her application was still pending in the Pension Bureau, he said he was certain that she would at the right time "receive ample justice through the instrumentality organized for the purpose of dispersing the nation's grateful acknowledgment of military service in its defense." [6]

Many of these bills, when he returned them to the Senate or the House, were presented for repassage, but, although the discussion was frequently angry, in only one instance were enough votes obtained to secure the two-thirds majority necessary to override the veto. [7]

[1] Richardson, vol. viii. p. 435.
[2] Ibid., p. 436.
[3] Ibid., p. 439.
[4] Ibid., p. 443.
[5] Ibid., p. 450.
[6] Ibid., p. 447.
[7] App. Ann. Cyclop. for 1886, p. 260; cf. McElroy, Grover Cleveland, vol. i, pp. 192–9.

The state of the public mind in reference to leading economic questions, such as the currency, betokened and revealed a disturbance of judgment with many classes of the people on the subject of property generally. A disposition to question the rich man's right to his gains and to invent devices for checking his advances, in the interest of those who could make less progress, had been developing for a number of years. The attitude toward the silver purchase law of large elements in the two parties, particularly in the Democratic party, was the poor man's. To be "for silver" was to be for the "common people" as against the "gold bugs" and the "bloated bond-holders." To be a friend of "cheap money" was indigenous with ignorant men, and a pose with the politician who would lead groups of such men.

In persons entertaining such sentiments it was easy to implant other ideas; their philosophy became in some measure communist, socialist and even anarchist. It must be confessed that those made powerful by money had not mended their ways; they still did little enough to reduce the force of the hostile feeling which was being marshaled for their discomfiture, and much of it was the outgrowth of the peculiarly and entirely lawless management of the railroads. Rate "wars" continued. One company would offer to carry passengers or goods at an amazingly low price; other companies in reprisal followed. In June, 1886, a man could travel from Chicago to St. Paul for $3.[1] In January, 1885, a ticket from Chattanooga to Memphis cost $2; the usual rate was $9.30.[2] The new West Shore road in 1884 reduced the fare from New York to Albany to $1.55, and to Buffalo to $4.65.[3] A few months later it issued a round trip ticket from New York to Niagara Falls for $6.[4] A ticket from Chicago to St. Louis was sold for a dollar.[5] At one time in 1881, a passenger was carried from New York to Chicago for $5—he paid $15 and got a rebate of $10 upon arrival at his destination.[6] Tickets from New York to the Pacific coast were,

[1] N. Y. Times, June 15, 1886.   [4] N. Y. Times, Jan. 31, 1885.
[2] N. Y. Tribune, Jan. 26, 1885.   [5] N. Y. Tribune, Oct. 17, 1884.
[3] N. Y. Herald, Oct. 18, 1884.
[6] Report of Senate Com. on Ed. and Labor, 1885, vol. i, p. 609.

in March, 1886, as cheap as $49.50, with a rebate of $5 at the
end of the trip.[1] The rate from Chicago to San Francisco at
the same time was $14.05 out and $29 for a round trip ticket,
good for 30 days.[2] In April, 1886, the price of a ticket from
New York to San Francisco was $29.50. Travel was so actively
stimulated by these low rates that it exhausted the facilities
of the Pullman company, and there were not enough sleeping
cars to accommodate those who would take advantage of such
unusual opportunities to cross the continent. A Western railway official said that the companies had transported all who
had any need of going to, or wanted to see, California and,
in consequence, they were now carrying "tramps."[3] At one
time immigrants were taken from New York to Chicago by
the Pennsylvania Railroad in competition with the West Shore,
for one dollar a head.[4]

Brokers or "scalpers," as they were called, bought unused
and partially used tickets, and sold them again at prices much
below the scheduled rates. These men, often very shabby
characters, stood in and around the railway stations, and
frequently hired offices in proximity to terminals so that they
might the better ply their trade.

Still more was involved in the "wars" when the reductions
affected freight rates. In 1878 the freight from New York to
Chicago, on certain kinds of goods, was one dollar per hundred
pounds. It was only 75 cents over the same lines from Boston
to Chicago, via New York, in spite of the expense of trans-
shipment in the latter city.[5] Nevada paid the same rate as
San Francisco, with extra charges for local delivery. For example a carload of candles would be carried to the coast for
$300, but, if left in Elko, 619 miles east of San Francisco, the
railroad company collected $800, the through rate plus the
local rate from San Francisco back to Elko.[6] A farmer in

[1] N. Y. Tribune, March 20, 1886.
[2] Ibid., April 1, 1886.
[3] Ibid., April 10 and 13, 1886.
[4] Ibid., Jan. 27, 1885.
[5] House Mis. Doc., 47th Cong. 1st sess., no. 55, pp. 22–3.
[6] Ibid., p. 28.

New York state paid $26 a carload for cattle coming to him
from Buffalo, a distance of 150 miles; the same railroad company carried cattle from Buffalo to New York City, through
the same village, 350 miles farther east, for $16.[1] A shipper
50 miles west of Chicago might pay 15 cents per hundred pounds
to get his grain into that city and only 10 cents, during a "war"
of rates, to take it on to New York.[2] Freight from New York
to New Orleans at times paid a rate of 50 cents per hundred
pounds. It passed through Atlanta. Merchandise on the same
train taken off at that city was charged for at the rate of one
dollar per hundred pounds.[3]

A barrel of flour would be transported from Chicago to
Richmond, 1,100 miles, for 28 cents, while a miller in Virginia,
only 175 miles away from the city, paid 57 cents a barrel to
get his product to the same market.[4] A manufacturer in Chicago bought wire in Cleveland. It was shipped to him at 15
cents per hundred. He wished to reship it to a village 12 miles
away and the rate for this service was 25 cents per hundred.
There it was worked into another shape, and the rate to the
factory in Chicago over the 12 miles was 75 cents per hundred.[5]

The New York Chamber of Commerce found that at one
time, in 1879, the rate for grain from Chicago to New York
was 18 cents per hundred pounds. Citizens of interior towns
of New York state saw this freight passing their railway stations, where they would be asked to pay five or six times as
much by rule of distance for carriage of their wheat, oats
or barley to the seaboard,[6] and a few months since the rates
from Chicago to New York had been as low as 11 cents per
hundred.[7] Freight in Liverpool would be given a cheaper
rate to Chicago than if it were laid down upon the wharf in
New York.[8] A rate of 18 cents per hundred from Chicago to

[1] House Mis. Doc., 47th Cong. 1st sess., no. 55, p. 44.
[2] Ibid., p. 177.
[3] Ibid., p. 178.
[4] Senate Reports, 49th Cong. 1st sess., no. 46, app., p. 100.
[5] Ibid., p. 197.
[6] Report of Hepburn Committee, p. 6.
[7] Ibid., p. 27.
[8] Ibid., p. 6.

the East was met by a 40 cent rate in the opposite direction, though most of the cars were returning empty.[1]

Vanderbilt had opened an attack upon his rivals in the summer of 1881, which continued to strike at railway company earnings and derange stock market values and commodity prices, and was "unexampled in point of severity and duration in the history of such contests."[2] Again in 1885 business was done at a loss. There had come to be four Pacific railroads instead of one; there were six lines from New York to Chicago instead of four.[3] The carrying charges from New York to San Francisco were from 50 to 75 cents per hundred pounds, and even these "ruinous" prices were "shaded" by the competing lines in order to get business.[4] They fell as low as 25 cents.[5]

When the rates westwardly out of Chicago were only 30 cents a hundred pounds, dealers in that city could ship apples, potatoes and onions to California. Apples were taken across the Rocky Mountains to San Francisco for less than it cost the Californians to bring them down from Oregon.[6] But the rule did not work both ways. California would raise fruit for the rest of the country; the railroads were charging $400 to carry a carload to Chicago, $600, if the car were attached to a passenger train, to insure speedier delivery.[7]

During the "war" in 1881 the New York Central carried freight from Chicago to New York for 10 cents per hundred pounds.[8] There were times, said Chauncey M. Depew, president of that company, when they had hauled cattle from Chicago for a dollar a car and paid back the dollar in New York.[9] Dividends ceased, the prices of railway shares fell.[10]

[1] Report of Hepburn Committee, p. 6; cf. ibid., pp. 271, 289–90.
[2] N. Y. Nation, Aug. 18 and Dec. 29, 1881.
[3] Cf. App. Ann. Cyclop. for 1883, p. 336.
[4] N. Y. Tribune, March 20, 1886.
[5] Ibid., Apr. 22, 1886.
[6] N. Y. Tribune, March 23, 1886.
[7] N. Y. Nation, Nov. 26, 1885.
[8] House Mis. Doc., 47th Cong. 1st sess., no. 55, pp. 114, 177, 178.
[9] Ibid., p. 205; cf. Report of Hepburn Committee, p. 1659.
[10] "So much money had been lost by the war of rates," said the New York Nation in October, 1885, "and so thoroughly are the combatants exhausted,

The refrigerator cars enabled packers to kill beef in Chicago and send it to New York in a merchantable condition in competition with the product of the Eastern slaughterhouses. The "trunk lines" juggled the rates so that the prices on locally killed and "Chicago beef" would be equalized, which amounted to fixing a high price for butcher meat on the Atlantic seaboard. The dressed beef rate was 75 per cent higher than the live cattle rate.[1] Other railways equalized freights on silver ore of different assay value, though of the same weight,[2] on rough timber and sawed lumber, so that they might not be deprived of revenue by processes devised to leave the refuse on the ground and reduce the cost of living.[3]

The "war" at an end the companies would form combinations, "pool" their interests and exact unjustly high tariffs. They would charge "all that the traffic would bear," not what the service was really worth.[4] Greater charges for "short hauls" than for long ones,[5] rates favorable to one city and unfavorable to another, special rates, or rebates and drawbacks for individual shippers, to the disadvantage of other shippers,[6] were wrongs which awakened attention on every

that they must needs get their second wind before they can renew the fight," etc.—Issue of Oct. 8, 1885; cf. App. Ann. Cyclop. for 1884, p. 328.

[1] Senate Reports, 49th Cong. 1st sess., no. 46, app., p. 160; Report of Senate Com. on Ed. and Labor, 1885, vol. i, p. 607; N. Y. Nation, March 4, 1886; Joseph Nimmo, The Community Interest Method of Regulating Railroad Traffic, pp. 155–6; J. F. Hudson, Railways and the Republic, pp. 33–6.

[2] Cf. Report of Senate Com. on Ed. and Labor, 1885, vol. i, pp. 605–6.

[3] N. Y. Nation, March 4, 1886.

[4] Cf. Senate Reports, 49th Cong. 1st sess., no. 46, pp. 184–5; Report of Senate Com. on Ed. and Labor, 1885, vol. i, pp. 605, 608; ibid., vol. ii, pp. 463 et seq., 520–21, 965–6; ibid., vol. iv, pp. 546–9; A. T. Hadley, Railroad Transportation, chap. vi.

[5] "Frequently shippers are required to pay higher freights for a half or a third of the length of haul than for the whole distance. This ought not be so," etc.—Reagan in 1878 in House Reports, 45th Cong. 2nd sess., no. 245, p. 5.

[6] "Each of these corporations, when not restrained by legislative authority, can discriminate in freight rates and charges in favor of and against whom they please and may in this way benefit some persons and places, while they injure relatively other persons and places, as may suit their interests and inclinations."—Reagan in 1878 in House Reports, 45th Cong. 2nd sess., no. 245, pp. 3–4.

side. Scheduled or published rates were no guidance to a shipper, since they were not adhered to. No man knew from day to day what he must pay for the transportation of his merchandise.[1]

Five grocery firms at Syracuse received a special rate of 10 cents when the tariffs given out to the freight agents of the railroad company called for charges of from 18 to 37 cents. These special rates at times were less than one-fifth of the authorized and published prices for carriage. An officer of the New York Central said that 50 per cent of the freight business out of New York and 90 per cent of the business at Syracuse were done at rates fixed after private negotiation with the shipper.[2]

One or two firms in such cities as Baltimore, Philadelphia, New York and Boston, by connivance with the railroad companies, got the major part of the trade in grain and provisions exported from each of those cities.[3] Previous to advancing rates agents at railway stations would contract for future shipments at the prevailing prices, thereby putting at a disadvantage those who were not advised of the impending increase.[4] Large shippers said that they knew nothing of tariffs— by conference with the officers of the railway companies they

[1] Wm. H. Vanderbilt was called before the Hepburn Committee at Saratoga Springs on August 21, 1879. The following questions and answers are recorded in the report of the hearing:

"Q. Do you believe publishing your rates is a useful thing so that the world may know what they are?

"A. Yes; providing they can all be equal; if you can get to the point where you have not got to change them every day I believe in publishing them.

"Q. Why couldn't you publish them even if you have to change them every day?

"A. We might have to publish them a dozen times a day.

"Q. What harm would there be in that?

"A. We don't keep printing presses. That is not our line of business; we would have to hire a printing press; that belongs to other people to do.

"Q. There are printing presses engaged by the newspapers which would be very glad to publish that information.

"A. We don't publish newspapers, we run a railroad."

—Hepburn Committee Report, p. 1261.

[2] Cf. A. N. Merritt, Federal Regulation of Railway Rates, pp. 92–3.

[3] House Mis. Doc., 47th Cong. 1st sess., no. 55, p. 34. For conditions on the Pacific coast with reference to sugar see N. Y. Nation, Dec. 8, 1881.

[4] Hepburn Report, vol. i, p. 28.

made their own rates.[1] A merchant in Evansville, Ind., boasted that, while the regular rate from that place to Boston in the summer of 1877 was 90 cents a hundred, he was paying but 45 cents.[2] It was a system, an observer said, more commonly associated with the horse jockey than with business conducted according to, and resting on, sound principles.[3] It was suspected, and often proven, that railroad officials were interested in mining, manufacturing and other industrial enterprises operating along their lines.[4] These were favored, as were businesses conducted by acquaintances and friends. There were men in authority in the management of transportation companies who would grant advantages to shippers in return for secret payments for these advantages. The Standard Oil Company bulldozed the railroad men. It cost the company less to carry crude oil to Cleveland for refining and then from that city to tidewater for sale or export than another producer must pay for the shipment of crude oil to Philadelphia.[5] It is certain that, for a time, the railroads involved hauled petroleum for one-third or one-fourth of the actual cost of transportation at the dictation of the Standard Oil Company to serve the purposes of that company, which was engaged in the destruction of the credit and in breaking down the business of its competitors.[6]

In a case cited in Ohio that corporation had a rate of only 10 cents a barrel, while small independent shippers were paying 35 cents. Not satisfied with this discrimination in their favor the officers of the company exacted that the sum in difference, or 25 cents, collected from other shippers should be given to them as a rebate.[7] In a period of 18 months four

---

[1] Simon Sterne in address at 10th meeting of National Board of Trade, 1880, p. 11.

[2] Cong. Record, 47th Cong. 1st sess., p. 3399.

[3] Has Congress the Power to Regulate Interstate Commerce?, a pamphlet, 1877, p. 2.

[4] Cf. Senate Reports, 49th Cong. 1st sess., no. 46, pt. 2, p. 456.

[5] F. B. Gowen's argument before Committee on Commerce, Jan. 27, 1880, a pamphlet, p. 27.

[6] Ibid., pp. 14–7, 19–20, 25.

[7] Senate Reports, 49th Cong. 1st sess., no. 46, p. 199; Report of Senate Com. on Ed. and Labor, 1885, vol. i, p. 605 and vol. ii, pp. 1021–4.

railroad companies paid in drawbacks to the Standard Oil Company $10,151,000. Other private arrangements not more extraordinary in their terms were in force between this group of men and the "common carriers."[1] Thus did the company drive out of the trade, and ruin, all competitors. By the hard bargains which it imposed upon the railroads it was enabled to build up one of the most notorious of American monopolies.[2]

Officers and managers of railroad companies were growing rich by the "watering" of stock and the creation of fictitious capitalization;[3] by speculation in Wall Street based on knowledge in their sole possession; by timely purchases of real estate in territory which lines were soon to be built to serve; by "side companies"—"Blue Lines," "White Lines," "Star Lines," "Fast Lines," "Dispatch Lines," parcel and baggage companies, bridges, ferries, stockyards, grain elevators, wharves and what not else—which absorbed profits rightfully belonging to the stockholders.[4]

Annual "passes" issued to business men, to newspaper owners and editors and to politicians, private Pullman cars, even special trains put at the disposal of large shippers, lobbying in city halls, state capitols and at Washington, the exchange of stocks and bonds for business received or expected, and

[1] House Mis. Doc., 47th Cong. 1st sess., no. 55, p. 34; cf. Senate Reports, 49th Cong. 1st sess., no. 46, app., p. 108; N. Y. Times, July 11, 1887; Ida M. Tarbell, Hist. of Stand. Oil Co., vol. i, chaps. iii, iv, v and vii and vol. ii, chap. xi; J. F. Hudson, Railways and the Republic, chap. iii. "It became apparent to us gradually that this clandestine arrangement was being made; it crept over us; we felt it in our business after a while that there was some untoward influence, some illegitimate influence, operating, and gradually they became stronger and we became weaker . . . we were gobbled up and there was no help for us."—An independent oil man in Hepburn Report, pp. 2532–4.

[2] Wm. H. Vanderbilt said in his testimony before the Hepburn Committee: "They are very shrewd men. I don't believe that by any legislative enactment, or anything else, through any of the states or all of the states, you can keep such men as them down; you can't do it; they will be on top all the time; you see if they're not." "You think they get on top of the railways?" "Yes and on top of everybody that comes in contact with them; too smart for me."—Hepburn Report, p. 1669.

[3] Cf. Senate Reports, 49th Cong. 1st sess., no. 46, p. 512.

[4] Cf. N. Y. Times, July 11, 1887; Hepburn Report, pp. 8–9.

the acceptance of shares in companies which were being favored as shippers, as e.g., the Standard Oil Company, made a railway president and his associates into figures little respected by those who held correct views regarding the relations which should exist between the people and their transportation agencies. It was probably not going far beyond the bounds of truth to say that American railway management in this period exhibited "the most shameless perversion of the duties of a common carrier to private ends that has taken place in the history of the world." [1]

It was plain to most men that the system of free competition which was much advocated as being in the public interest had failed in this field and was now intolerable. There were those, indeed, who would have the government take over the railroads and give them public management such as met with praise in the postal service. Anyhow remedy must be found for some of the most notorious abuses. State laws, which often were administered under the eyes of commissions, had borne little fruit. [2] Legislatures, governors, even courts of justice of the highest rank had fallen under the control of the corporations whose affairs were to be regulated. The railroad companies themselves were "at theirs wits' ends." The presidents of the principal lines conferred. Their meetings ended simply in new disorder. [3] In the interest of a stabler system and to disarm their critics they formed "joint traffic associations," [4] appointed "eveners," to enforce rules which would "even" or equalize the returns to the trunk lines from traffic, [5] and commissions and "umpires" to hold up "agreements," adjust differences, prevent squabbles and "wars" and in this service had enlisted, at high salaries, a number

---

[1] Hepburn Report, p. 3970.

[2] For the progress in this field up to 1886 see Senate Reports, 49th Cong. 1st sess., no. 46, pp. 64–137; cf. A. T. Hadley, Railroad Transportation, chap. vii; Frank H. Dixon, State Railroad Control.

[3] Joseph Nimmo, The Community of Interest Method of Regulating Railroad Traffic, pp. 10, 16–7.

[4] Ibid., p. 22; A. Fink, Argument before Com. on Commerce, Jan. 14, 1880, a pamphlet, New York, 1880, pp. 18–21, 41–8.

[5] Cong. Record, 47th Cong. 1st sess., p. 3399.

of very able men.[1] But such commissioners had no police power; they must rely on moral suasion.[2] The old system of managing and directing the railways, since they had gained such importance and extent, had failed, and the officers of the companies themselves knew that they must submit to some kind of Federal control.[3] It was "simply competition run mad" and, as such, must come under restraint.[4]

The Federal government was intrusted by the Constitution with power to "regulate" commerce "among the several states,"[5] and for several years a bill had been pending in Congress looking to the creation of a commission which should make a beginning, at least, in the work of curbing and disciplining executive officers of American railroad companies. Judge Reagan, a representative in Congress, had long since attached his name to the movement,[6] but he seemed to distrust the appointing power—the commission, like the state commissions, he feared, would fall into the hands of the railroad companies,[7] and he refused to follow his colleagues on the committee who would put the matter in the hands of specifically named officers. He, for his part, would incorporate regulations and inhibitions, which are now commonplaces, in a penal statute which should, as one of his critics said, "execute itself in rare spasms."[8] A part of the picture had

[1] For one of them, Albert Fink, see Report of Hepburn Com., pp. 481 et seq.

[2] House Mis. Doc., 47th Cong. 1st sess., no. 55, pp. 192–4, 248; Report of Senate Com. on Ed. and Labor for 1885, vol. i, p. 606; ibid., vol. ii, pp. 463 et seq.

[3] House Mis. Doc., 47th Cong. 1st sess., no. 55, p. 248; A. T. Hadley in N. Y. Independent, quoted in N. Y. Nation, June 23, 1887.

[4] Cf. Nimmo, loc. cit.

[5] For a discussion of the clause in the Constitution see House Reports, 45th Cong. 2nd sess., no. 245, pp. 5–16; cf. ibid., 43rd Cong. 1st sess., no. 28, pp. 1–10; also House Mis. Doc., 47th Cong. 1st sess., no. 55, pp. 237–45; Senate Reports, 49th Cong. 1st sess., no. 46, pp. 28–39; also, of course, many legal and quasi legal works.

[6] House Reports, 45th Cong. 2nd sess., no. 245; House Mis. Doc., 47th Cong. 1st sess., no. 55, p. 1; cf. N. Y. Nation, March 18, 1886; McPherson's Handbook for 1880, pp. 70–72; ibid. for 1882, pp. 125–9.

[7] Cf. House Reports, 47th Cong. 1st sess., no. 1399, pt. 2, p. 2; App. Ann. Cyclop. for 1885, p. 21.

[8] App. Ann. Cyclop. for 1886, p. 212; cf. N. Y. Nation, May 28, 1885.

been seen by the farmers when they were conducting their attacks upon the railroads through the "Grange." But their outlook had been narrow and they discerned only that little which lay at their doors on the agricultural frontier. Now importers and exporters on the Atlantic seaboard, manufacturers, men identified with domestic and foreign trade of all kinds were compelled to take notice of the irregularities and hazards in which they were involved in the simplest operation when the railroad was brought into the equation. Some had had personal experience of business in Europe where transportation was under control. Others visited foreign countries and, by observation, came to know conditions there. Students of the problem were writing of it and pointing the way to a different order in the United States.

The most certain evidence of public understanding of the wrongs of the system and a determination to apply remedies and corrections was found in statements of such bodies as the Chamber of Commerce, the Board of Trade and the Produce Exchange of New York City.[1] The head of the Chamber of Commerce was ready to show that thousands of men had been ruined financially by the policies which were being pursued by the railroads.[2] The New York Board of Trade found that the city was at their complete mercy; they could determine whether it should be prosperous or unprosperous and fix the degree of its prosperity.[3] The present commercial and financial distress and the continuing depreciation in the value of real estate could be laid at the door of the "great transportation routes,"[4] which, though public enterprises, were subjected to as little supervision as the business of selling dry goods or boots and shoes.[5] In 1879 the New York legislature appointed a committee to investigate the question and make a report. This committee came under the chairmanship of A. B. Hepburn and its labors were prolonged and stupendous. No such body of testimony had ever been assembled on such

[1] Report of Hepburn Committee, pp. 1–35.   [4] Ibid., p. 16.
[2] Ibid., p. 20.   [5] Ibid., p. 19.
[3] Ibid., p. 19.

a topic. The hearings were transcribed for the newspapers to arrest public attention and start discussion. The proceedings when printed filled several volumes, comprising no less than 4,000 pages of useful information.[1]

The people were at last aroused. Meetings were held, committees were formed; resolutions, memorials and petitions from state legislatures, chambers of commerce and other business men's organizations, manufacturers, farmers, poured into Congress, which was compelled to note the rise of a determined public sentiment.[2] At every session bills proposing various remedies for the evils at hand appeared. Opposition was powerful and it was expected. Washington had been filled with "railroad men" and their skillful attorneys,[3] whenever, during ten years past, this subject had come forward for discussion. They trod the corridors and invaded the committee rooms of the Capitol, even pressing in upon the floors of the Senate and the House, with the patent object of preventing legislation calculated to restrain them in the exercise of their accustomed activities.[4] Public control was denounced as communism; the movement in its behalf was directed against those who had capital invested in railroads.[5]

Nevertheless, in January, 1885, in the Forty-eighth Congress, Reagan's bill aimed at the "monopoly powers" of railroad corporations, "to protect the people against unreasonable charges and extortionate exactions,"[6] passed the House. The

---

[1] Cf. House Mis. Doc., 47th Cong. 1st sess., no. 55, pp. 196, 199.
[2] Ibid., pp. 163, 263.
[3] "We are as one against a thousand," said a representative of the New York Chamber of Commerce who had come before the House Committee on Commerce to advocate the passage of an interstate commerce law. "You have had before you, and will have before you, the ablest legal talent in the country to present the views of the railroad companies."—House Mis. Doc., 47th Cong. 1st sess., no. 55, p. 21.
[4] For the reasoning offered by the railway men see argument of Wayne MacVeagh, speaking for the Pennsylvania Railroad Company (House Mis. Doc., 47th Cong. 1st sess., no. 55, pp. 1–21; Report of Senate Com. on Ed. and Labor, vol. ii, pp. 510–12; App. Ann. Cyclop. for 1886, p. 210), and of George R. Blanchard for the New York Central.—Published in a pamphlet, New York, 1882.
[5] Cf. Report of Hepburn Committee, p. 5.
[6] House Reports, 49th Cong. 1st sess., no. 902.

Senate, under the leadership of Shelby M. Cullom of Illinois, who, though he had but lately come to a seat in that body, in succession to David Davis, doggedly pursued the subject until he had overcome the apathy, if not avowed hostility, of his colleagues,[1] approved another bill in relation to the same subject, which would create an interstate commerce commission of nine members. But the pressure of business in the concluding hours of the session, the division of sentiment in the two chambers and the active exertions of the "lobby" prevented agreement as to either plan.[2]

Cullom, like Reagan, was not to be put down. It was one of the "most important" questions "now before the country," he said,[3] and, on March 17, 1885, at the session of the Senate of the new Forty-ninth Congress, called to receive Cleveland's nominations, he offered a resolution authorizing the appointment of a select committee of five to sit during the recess and to "investigate and report upon the subject of the regulation of commerce among the several states."[4] He became the chairman of the committee,[5] which held hearings in a number of cities and, at the end of the year, presented an exhaustive report, the testimony filling a book of more than 1,500 pages.[6]

When Congress assembled in December, with this report as a basis for the discussions, the contest was renewed. The two houses again passed their separate bills and again failed to agree before the day of adjournment.[7] The debates forcibly directed attention to the very singular and improper relations existing between the railroads and the public, and served to increase public dissatisfaction and social unrest.

The growth of the "labor" movement had been slow but certain and it now, under astute leaders, was gaining a momen-

[1] Cf. Washington corr. N. Y. Tribune, Feb. 5, 1885.
[2] McPherson's Handbook for 1884, pp. 10–26; Cong. Record, 49th Cong. special sess. of Senate, p. 64.
[3] Cong. Record, 49th Cong. special sess. of Senate, p. 61.
[4] Ibid., pp. 54, 61–8.
[5] The other members were Warner Miller, Orville H. Platt, Arthur P. Gorman and Isham G. Harris.
[6] Senate Reports, 49th Cong. 1st sess., no. 46; N. Y. Nation, Jan. 21, 1886.
[7] McPherson's Handbook for 1884, pp. 136–46, 233–4.

tum and power which politicians, as well as employers, were unable to disregard. "Organized labor" were words heard on every side. In these circles there was a rising sentiment unfavorable to immigration on the ground that those who came in from foreign countries were taking employment away from, and reducing the wages of, those already here, albeit they themselves were, in most cases, but recent arrivals at our ports, if, indeed, they were yet naturalized for citizenship. The inpouring tide was in truth mighty. In the year ending June 30, 1881, the number of immigrants was 669,431; in the next year it reached the unprecedented total of 788,992, a number in excess of the combined population of the states of Oregon, Nevada, Delaware, Rhode Island and Colorado. There were 603,322 in 1883; 518,592 in 1884 and but few less than 400,000 in 1885, in all nearly three millions in the past five years, more than for the entire ten years from 1870 to 1880, and the number in that period had been the largest for any decade in our national history.[1]

The antipathy of the older immigrant for the new one, based on the dislike of his competition as a laborer, was enforced by a growing concern about social conditions in our great cities. This solicitude was particularly active in New York, and, in the rest of the country, for New York. The tenement house, the slum, the insanitary and squalid state of the ghettos and other foreign settlements into which the poor, who were newly come in upon steamships, were packed, appealing to sympathy on humanitarian grounds, as well as affording problems to health officers not yet well acquainted with their tasks or armed with power to perform these tasks, alarmed social investigators who, in turn, alarmed larger groups of men and women with philanthropic minds. The poor must live under better housing conditions. They must have fresh air and clean surroundings. They must have pure water. There must be parks and playgrounds for their use. They should have

[1] N. Y. Nation, July 30, 1885; cf. Report of Comm'r of Labor for 1885 in House Ex. Doc., 49th Cong. 1st sess., no. 1, pt. 5, p. 245; App. Ann. Cyclop. for 1881, pp. 412–3; Prescott F. Hall, Immigration and Emigration, pp. 10–11.

half holidays on Saturday, more time as well as opportunity
for recreation.[1] It was observed, too, that these immigrants
would soon have votes; they could be controlled for low and
sinister ends by designing politicians. They might become,
if they were not now, a menace to our republican institutions, which had been established by the Anglo-Saxon and
the control of which it would be well to keep in his
hands.[2]

A beginning had been successfully made with the Chinese
and there was bitterness enough still remaining in workingmen of other races to demand further legislation directed at
Asiatic immigration. It was not enough that no more Chinese
might come to our shores, that degrading conditions, not imposed upon other nationals, should attend the departure and
return of those domiciled here and guaranteed by treaty the
right of continued residence in the United States. Nothing
short of summary expulsion and deportation of the race would
satisfy the prejudices and serve the ends of the elements which
were arrayed against the Chinaman in the Western states
and territories.[3]

In the interest of such a movement it was given out that
the Chinese population on the Pacific coast was actually increasing since the going into effect of the exclusion law. Coolies
were impersonating merchants, students and other excepted
classes of immigrants. Certificates illegally issued were sold
in "Chinatown" and in Canton and Hong Kong. Corrupt
immigration officers at San Francisco were getting rich out
of the traffic in "tags." All Chinese looked alike; thumb marks
must be taken and used for identification. They were being
smuggled over the border from British Columbia.[4] A Treas-

[1] Cf. N. Y. Times, May 18 and 20, 1886; N. Y. Herald, May 2 and 9,
1886.

[2] Cf. Report of Senate Com. on Ed. and Labor, 1885, vol. i, pp. 93–101,
343–4; ibid., vol. ii, pp. 621–6, 646–72.

[3] N. Y. Nation, Sep. 24 and Nov. 19, 1885; N. Y. Times, Nov. 27, 1885;
cf. Report of Senate Com. on Ed. and Labor, 1885, vol. i, pp. 266–7, 282,
452.

[4] Senate Ex. Doc., 48th Cong. 1st sess., no. 62, pp. 74–5; Report of Sec.
of Int. for 1886, vol. ii, p. 886; ibid. for 1885, vol. ii, pp. 1118–9.

ury agent was sent to the Pacific coast to investigate the situation and said that the Chinese population of the country had decreased in three years by fully 20,000. He found that the movement was to, and not from, China. Departures greatly exceeded arrivals. Chinese labor was scarce, as was proven by the advance in its price.[1] It was to no effect. The officers of the Treasury Department were wholly unable to satisfy the Pacific coast in their interpretation of the law and the making of regulations for its enforcement.[2]

The imagination of the anti-Chinese fanatics was excited beyond control. Proof of this was soon given in impressive terms. At Rock Springs, in Wyoming, the Union Pacific Railroad Company owned coal pits. Both Chinese and white men were employed as miners. One day early in September, 1885, the whites, "all of foreign birth and mostly aliens,"[3] armed themselves and drove the Chinese, to the number of 700 or 800, from the camp. Their houses were burned and a score or more were roasted, shot and otherwise brutually killed, while the rest were driven into the mountains. Similar massacres were threatened in other parts of Wyoming, and were prevented only by the urgent call of the governor of the territory for United States troops, which shortly arrived upon the scene.[4] When some of the survivors returned to Rock Springs and resumed work, under military protection, the whites threw down their tools and started a strike against the railroad company.[5] The cry, "The Chinese must go!" was raised in all parts of Wyoming. Employers of Chinamen were "boycotted."

The excitement spread. An "Anti-Chinese Congress" was

[1] Senate Ex. Doc., 49th Cong. 1st sess., no. 103; cf. House Reports, 48th Cong. 1st sess., no. 614.

[2] House Ex. Doc., 48th Cong. 2nd sess., no. 214; Senate Ex. Doc., 48th Cong. 1st sess., no. 62; Senate Ex. Doc., 49th Cong. 1st sess., no. 118; App. Ann. Cyclop. for 1882, pp. 387–92.

[3] Governor Warren's report in House Ex. Doc., 49th Cong. 1st sess., no. 1, pt. 5, p. 1228; cf. Col. Bee's report in House Ex. Doc., 49th Cong. 1st sess., no. 102, p. 12.

[4] House Ex. Doc., 49th Cong. 1st sess., no. 1, pt. 5, pp. 1230–2, 1234; Report of Sec. of Int. for 1885, vol. ii, pp. 1218–20, 1225–34.

[5] N. Y. Nation, Sep. 24, 1885.

convened in Seattle. A new national organization of working-men, the "Knights of Labor," would drive such competitors in the "labor market" out of the country. In coal mines in Washington territory, a mob attacked and burned barracks occupied by the Chinese, who took to the woods.[1] At Tacoma they were dragged from their homes and driven out of the town in a cold storm.[2] In Montana, at Butte City, they were told to leave—they would be lynched if they remained.[3] In Seattle committees of leading citizens united in the interest of law and order, but were powerless to cope with the madness without the presence of troops. The situation in the territory of Washington was so alarming that President Cleveland, on November 7, 1885, issued a proclamation warning "evil dis-posed persons" to disperse on or before noon of the following day, and threatening them with an assertion of military power.[4] The quieting effect of such a measure was only temporary. In February, 1886, an "immense mob" assembled and 400 Chinese were forced to leave their abodes in Seattle. Some of them were put on a steamer for San Francisco and shipped, passage paid, to that city. Others moved back to their quarter under local military protection, and, when the white rabble attacked them, the "home guards" fired. The governor of the ter-ritory proclaimed martial law. The President was appealed to and he again issued a proclamation ordering the rioters to disperse. United States troops were again called to the scene.[5] In Olympia, Portland and other places feeling ran high and breaches of the peace, it was believed, would cer-tainly ensue.[6]

Wild orators still shouted their anathemas at the Chinese on the "sand lot" in San Francisco.[7] In February, 1886, the Chinese merchants in that city complained to the Chinese minister at Washington. Their countrymen were being driven

[1] N. Y. Nation, Sep. 17, 1885.
[2] Report of Sec. of Int. for 1886, vol. ii, pp. 906–9.
[3] N. Y. Nation, Sep. 24, 1885.
[4] Richardson, vol. viii, pp. 311–2; N. Y. Nation, Nov. 12, 1885.
[5] Richardson, vol. viii, p. 488; N. Y. Nation, Feb. 11, 1886.
[6] Report of Sec. of Int. for 1886, vol. i, pp. 866–915.
[7] N. Y. Nation, Jan. 7, 1886.

from pillar to post, threatened indeed with expulsion from "nearly all the towns and cities" in California. The merchants would be absolutely ruined, if their customers in the country were subjected to such persecution. "Property protection" was required at once.[1] The Chinese Six Companies also formulated protests. Their people throughout the state were "terrorized" and were flocking into San Francisco in a destitute condition. Societies existed with the purpose of driving all the Chinese from America. The governor, the sheriffs of the counties afforded them no hope of safety. Similar conditions prevailed in Oregon.[2] Many fled to the East where public sentiment was more friendly, and mobs did not hang at their heels.[3] The Chinese minister, on February 13, 1886, after the exchange of many notes and a number of personal interviews with Secretary Bayard, called upon him for an observance of treaty rights.[4]

As the time for the election of a governor in California approached, in 1886, meetings were held on every side. The Board of Supervisors in San Francisco restated the old charges against the Chinese and published them in a book. Fresh attacks were made upon the filth and disease in "Chinatown." [5] Local anti-coolie leagues appointed delegates to attend a state convention which was to meet at Sacramento on March 10, 1886, and propose "relief for the Pacific coast from the Chinese evil." This body adopted resolutions and appointed a committee to frame another "memorial." A "life and death struggle" was going on "for the possession of the Western shores of the American continent." The history of the ancient and

---

[1] House Ex. Doc., 49th Cong. 1st sess., no. 102, pp. 59–60.
[2] Ibid., p. 60.
[3] N. Y. Nation, March 25, 1886.
[4] House Ex. Doc., 49th Cong. 1st sess., no. 102, pp. 57–9.
[5] Report of the committee, with map of Chinatown, published in July, 1885. That nothing had been changed is made clear by the attack of the committee on the Chinese missionaries in San Francisco. The souls of the Chinese were not worth salvation. "The beasts of the field, the vagrant dogs that the pound-master gathers upon the streets to put to death by drowning are vastly better worthy of our commiseration than the whole Mongolian race, when they seek to overrun our country and blast American welfare and progress."—Ibid., p. 43; cf. Coolidge, Chinese Immigration, pp. 188, 191.

modern world was explored for analogies that would serve
the purposes of the excited writer or writers of the paper, to
which was appended the names of five men, led by John F.
Swift, who had been a member of the Angell commission to
China in 1880, and ex-Senator Sargent. Burlingame they
said had imposed an outrageous treaty upon the American
people for which service he had been paid 100,000 taels in
Chinese silver. It was "conceived in fraud and chicane" and
was "an international lie." The people of California demanded
speedy "relief" from a situation which had become "practically
insupportable." A general boycott of those who employed
Chinese labor, or used the products of that labor, was recommended to the local leagues, and a committee was named
to form a permanent association to be called the "California
Anti-Chinese Non-Partisan Association." [1]

To all of this hostile activity Colonel Bee, the friend and
attorney of the Chinese during the Federal investigation in
1876, who was acting as the Chinese consul in San Francisco,
made answer. He addressed a "memorial" to the people and
to the Congress of the United States pleading for a return to
sanity and the exhibition of a spirit of fair play,[2] but to no
purpose for the anti-Chinese politicians in the House, headed
by a member named Morrow of California, presented the
draft of a new and more drastic exclusion law, which, at the
first opportunity, they were determined to pass.[3]

The outrages committed upon the life, limb and property
of the Chinese in the West called for investigation. Their
minister at Washington sent the Chinese consuls at San Francisco and New York to Rock Springs to ascertain the facts
regarding that butchery. Was it quite true that the Chinaman
had no rights which a white man was bound to respect? Had
the American people no sense of honor with reference to a
treaty solemnly concluded with another power? Was there
no redress for that power when fiends plundered and slaugh-

[1] Senate Mis. Doc., 49th Cong. 1st sess., no. 107; cf. App. Ann. Cyclop.
for 1886, p. 126; Coolidge, Chinese Immigration, pp. 188–9.
[2] See Bee, The Other Side of the Chinese Question.
[3] Cf. N. Y. Nation, March 18, 1886.

tered its nationals, doing so, as it appeared, with the sympathy and support of too large a part of the people of that section of the country in which the barbarities were perpetrated?[1] Proof of connivance of the community with the murderers was at hand when, if arrests were made, as at Rock Springs, the bills of indictment were ignored by the grand jury and the guilty men, all of whom were easily and clearly identified,[2] were freed, to be welcomed home by their neighbors with congratulatory celebrations.[3]

The Chinese government demanded an indemnity for the massacre in Wyoming. The names of the victims of the mob who were killed and injured, the damages suffered by owners of property were carefully stated.[4] But Secretary Bayard, on February 18, 1886, wrote a polite letter to the Chinese minister disclaiming responsibility for the outrage. The subjects of the Emperor of China had gone to a "remote and unprotected region" at their own risk. Under our system of government it was the duty of local, not the Federal, authorities to suppress civil disturbance. These murders had been committed by aliens—assailants, like the assailed, were "strangers in our land." The President would address himself to the subject.

From Mr. Cleveland a message came in a few days, more authoritatively stating the position of the administration. The Chinese minister had suggested reparation for injuries done his countrymen in a riot in Denver in 1880, though Evarts first, and then Blaine, through the State Department, had found reasons for declining to make any offer of satisfaction. Now Mr. Cleveland, enforcing what Mr. Bayard had said, pursued a somewhat similar line of argument. Though condemning such lawlessness and expressing ample sympathy

[1] Cf. N. Y. Nation, Sep. 24, 1885.
[2] Colonel Bee in Alta-California, Oct. 10, 1885, cited in House Ex. Doc., 49th Cong. 1st sess., no. 102, pp. 27–8.
[3] Cf. Governor Warren's report, House Ex. Doc., 49th Cong. 1st sess., no. 1, pt. 5, pp. 1233, 1235.
[4] House Ex. Doc., 49th Cong. 1st sess., no. 102, pp. 4–57. The papers are also printed as House Report, 49th Cong. 1st sess., no. 2044.

for the victims of it, he could not admit a national duty to provide redress, though he denominated the proceedings looking toward the punishment of the offenders "a ghastly mockery of justice." He would merely commend the matter to "the benevolent consideration" of Congress which, if it should act, would do so "with the distinct understanding" that such action was "in no wise to be held as a precedent," but was "wholly gratuitous," and was resorted to "in a spirit of pure generosity." [1]

The message was calculated to gain the acclamation of the anti-Chinese party in the West as well as of the unthinking masses everywhere. The American people were uninstructed as to matters of foreign policy. Although extremely sensitive and irritable with reference to any affront offered the nation, its citizens or its flag in any part of the world they were too little disposed to take care of the feelings of others in a like case. [2]

The Senate knew enough about correct international procedure to vote on June 4, 1886, to the sufferers for the outbreak at Rock Springs,[3] $150,000, a small enough sum when compared with the indemnity of about three-quarters of a million dollars which China granted to the United States for mere property losses sustained by Americans in that empire during a rebellion there prior to our Civil War, a portion of which was still held by our Secretary of State as a reminder of the justice demanded by us of others, and withheld from them in a similar case.[4] The Committee on Foreign Affairs recommended payment,[5] but the members of the House were too timid, in the face of public sentiment on the Pacific coast and the rabid outgivings of the labor organizations, to follow the Senate, though, in the next session, the sum of

---

[1] Richardson, vol. viii, pp. 383–6; N. Y. Nation, March 4, 1886.
[2] N. Y. Nation, March 4 and 11, 1886.
[3] McPherson's Handbook for 1886, pp. 180–81.
[4] Senate Reports, 48th Cong. 2nd sess., nos. 934 and 1190; House Reports, 48th Cong. 1st sess., no. 970; App. Ann. Cyclop. for 1885, pp. 241–2; Coolidge, Chinese Immigration, p. 274.
[5] House Reports, 49th Cong. 1st sess., no. 2044.

$147,748.74 was appropriated and placed in the hands of the Chinese minister for distribution to the victims of the slaughter.[1]

If there were propriety and right in Chinese exclusion it might be regarded as certain that the labor unions, under active leaders, and the social reformers would soon move upon immigrants of other lands, and a beginning would be made with "contract labor." As much that was offensive was read into these words as could be made to reside, during a political campaign, in the "pauper labor of Europe." The agitation for a "contract labor" law was fairly aimed at the employment of Hungarians, Italians, Poles and other ignorant men who came in a body to be let for hire at low prices in mines, in railway building and in like employments. They were known by numbers rather than names and lived uncleanly in camps near the scene of their toil, doing offense to the better feelings of native workmen.[2] A bill to prohibit the importation of "contract laborers," with exceptions in the cases of professional actors, lecturers and singers, and skilled labor not obtainable in the United States, was adopted by the House, without a division, in 1884.[3] At the next session, in 1885, it was passed by the Senate and approved by President Arthur,[4] to be somewhat extended in meaning and effect in 1887.[5]

While the law was undoubtedly in answer to public sentiment, its enforcement led to complications which soon were furnishing amusement to the readers of newspapers. In the summer of 1885 ten Irish girls were detained at Castle Garden in New York. Some one had advanced their passage money.[6] Foreign silk weavers and zinc smelters were refused a landing.

[1] Act of Feb. 24, 1887, U. S. Stat. at Large, vol. 24, p. 418; N. Y. Nation, March 31, 1887.
[2] Cf. Carroll D. Wright's report for 1885 in House Ex. Doc., 49th Cong. 1st sess., no. 1, pt. 5, p. 246; Report of Senate Com. on Ed. and Labor, 1885, vol. i, pp. 334–8, 583; N. Y. Nation, March 24, 1887.
[3] McPherson's Handbook for 1884, p. 193.
[4] Ibid. for 1886, pp. 47–9; App. Ann. Cyclop. for 1885, pp. 231–4.
[5] N. Y. Nation, March 24, 1887.
[6] Ibid., June 25, 1885.

They were "under contract." Those who needed their labor said that it was not procurable in the United States—the labor unions held and proclaimed another view.[1] A North German Lloyd steamer was bringing in a band of 40 musicians from Austria to play at a summer amusement park in Philadelphia. American performers on "percussion" and "brass" asked that their competitors, upon arrival, be sent home.[2] It was a strange law for a "civilized people which owes a large part of its greatness to immigration," said the New York Nation, but, continued the sagacious writer in that journal, it was not different in principle from the protective tariff. One excluded foreign workmen, the other the product which he made, and more in a like sense.[3] "Whole shiploads" of unskilled laborers were received. They might come "under a contract for idleness," but not to work.[4] "A greater absurdity in legislation," said the New York Times, "was never perpetrated by an enlightened nation."[5]

Nor were criticism and protest withheld, if law was not invoked in the case, from the Canadian French who were immigrating with their large families into the New England factory towns. They lived so squalidly and worked at such low wages that they came to be called the "Chinese of the Eastern states," and were little more welcome than the Chinese in the sight of our native workingmen.[6]

The "organized labor" leaders were never so active. The wrongs of the workingman due to the oppression of employers were recited and emphasized. Capital was cried down and

[1] N. Y. Nation, July 7, 1887; N. Y. Times, June 30, 1887;
[2] N. Y. Times, May 1, 1886.
[3] N. Y. Nation, June 25, 1885; ibid., Feb. 26, 1885. Cf. Ingalls in the U. S. Senate: "We have for years past been declaring that the interests of American labor should be protected, and we are now to say whether the interests of the American laborer shall not be protected, not alone against the competition of the ill-paid labor of Europe, but against that most infamous free trade in labor itself which imports men here under servile contract."—App. Ann. Cyclop. for 1885, p. 233.
[4] N. Y. Nation, July 7, 1887; cf. Jenks and Lauck, The Immigration Problem, p. 338.
[5] N. Y. Times, June 30, 1887.
[6] Report of Senate Com. on Ed. and Labor, 1885, vol. i, pp. 66–9.

labor was wreathed in myrtle so systematically and effectively that something like a social revolution was seen, by clear observers, to be in progress.

The socialist preachment about the rewards which should come to the workingman was supplemented by an assault upon private ownership of land, which was inaugurated by Henry George. Born in Philadelphia in 1839 he had adventured at sea, in mines in British Columbia, and then in California as a printer and a journalist, always without success, which seems to have led him to apply his active mind to reading and speculation in behalf of the poor in the field of political economy. Out of his observations and meditations came a new economic system which, in 1879, he stated in a book called "Progress and Poverty." [1] This volume attracted widespread notice. It contained enough truth to awaken controversy and invite rejoinder in the ranks of economists. Many of the cranks who infest the borderland of this branch of knowledge instantly took up with George and his theories—writing, speaking, interrogating and disturbing other speakers, and organizing with the zeal of moral crusaders over all the country. Economic capital was no longer the cause of poverty and of social ails generally but economic rent. Land was the source of wealth, and this had become a monopoly; [2] the holder of it profited without making corresponding or just return to society. There was an "unearned increment," and it should be seized by the state. The "single tax" and the "nationalization of land" became phrases which fell from every tongue. The laboring man would hear this as willingly as doctrine which denied the right of the capitalist to a portion in the distribution of wealth. George put new ferment in the mass which was astir with a sense of value beyond its rewards, and a determination, by one or another means, to rise in the social scale and gain better standards of living.

Cleveland's election and induction into office had found

[1] H. George, Jr., Life of Henry George, pp. 315–37.
[2] Cf. George in Report of Senate Com. on Ed. and Labor, 1885, vol. i, pp. 466–501, 503–25.

the country in another period of "hard times." The effort of
the Republicans to synchronize Democratic control of the
government with industrial panic and depression, which was
to become a proverb, had its beginning in his administration, though nothing could be so completely unfounded as
the ascription of cause and effect to his coming to the
Presidency and the unhappy state of business in 1885. In
the Hayes, Garfield and Arthur administrations the country
had enjoyed two or three years of industrial activity and
material prosperity. Unfinished enterprises had been completed, new ones had been undertaken. Employment was
general at higher wages. Imports, exports, trade of all kinds,
immigration indicated a healthy and prosperous tone in business, and from 1878 to 1882 economic ills were in a measure
forgotten. But in 1882 and 1883 a reaction had set in
and new signs were seen. Failure followed failure, some of
them of large extent and far-reaching in their untoward
influences.[1]

The Northern Pacific Railroad Company which had ruined
Jay Cooke and brought on the troubles in 1873 again was a
wreck. Other railway and construction companies were insolvent. In 1884 37 companies, operating 11,000 miles of
railroad, went into the hands of receivers. In 15 months, ending in March, 1885, corporations with aggregate stock and
bond issues of a billion dollars were in bankruptcy.[2] Stocks
generally fell and brought ruin to many men. Early in May,
1884, a prominent Wall Street speculator, James R. Keene,
failed. The Grant and Ward and the Marine Bank explosion
was followed by the failure of the Second National Bank
in New York, an officer of which had stolen three millions of
dollars, and the failure of the Metropolitan Bank which was
carried down by the notorious speculations of its president.
The suspension of other banks and brokerage houses followed
so fast one upon another that the money markets for a few

---

[1] See Commercial and Financial Chronicle, Feb. 13, 1886, p. 200; Report
of Comm'r of Labor for 1885 in House Ex. Doc., 49th Cong. 1st sess., no. 1,
pt. 5, p. 67.
[2] Senate Reports, 49th Cong. 1st sess., no. 46, app., p. 71.

weeks were in a panic. A crisis such as the country had not known since 1873 was at hand.[1]

New York Central stock which had been selling at 126 in 1883 was quoted around January 1, 1885, at 86. Erie fell in the same time from 40 to 14; St. Paul from 108 to 69; Wabash from 36 to 4; Texas and Pacific from 43 to 12; Western Union from 88 to 53; Northern Pacific from 53 to 16; Denver and Rio Grande from 51 to 8; Chesapeake and Ohio from 23 to 5; Union Pacific from 104 to 44, and it had sold in 1884 at 28.[2]

Men with capital had taken note of the situation which was filling the Treasury with useless silver;[3] of the agitation regarding the tariff, looking toward changes of rates; of the rising discontent of labor and the prospect of finding it less amenable for use.[4] Money earlier held for investment was withdrawn and was no longer procurable at the banks.

How many men were idle it is difficult to determine. But those who recently had been employed and were not at work in 1885, Carroll D. Wright, head of the new Bureau of Labor,[5] said, numbered about one million.[6] As prior to the panic of 1873 so just before the period of depression beginning in 1882 the speculative building of railroads into unsettled regions had approached a craze. The new listings of railway securities in the New York Stock Exchange in the five years ending with 1883 had a par value of more than two and a half billions of

---

[1] N. Y. Times, May 15 and 16, 1884; N. Y. Nation, Feb. 7, May 22 and 29, 1884; cf. A. D. Noyes, Forty Years of Am. Finance, pp. 99–100.

[2] App. Ann. Cyclop. for 1884, p. 330.

[3] The purchase of silver bullion and its coinage was "a fraud upon the public," said Edward Atkinson, "and is one of the chief elements which prevent the restoration of activity and prosperity in almost all departments of business." (N. Y. Tribune, Jan. 27, 1885.) If "this dark cloud" were "removed from the financial horizon," said the New York Nation, relief would be extended to all business.—Issue of February 5, 1885.

[4] "Nothing is more certain than that people who have money will withdraw from business operations which are at the mercy of a lot of ignorant, irresponsible demagogues."—Corr. N. Y. Nation, April 22, 1886.

[5] Established by Congress by act of June 27, 1884. There were labor bureaus in fifteen states, beginning with Massachusetts in 1869, prior to the creation of the Federal office.—House Ex. Doc., 49th Cong. 1st sess., no. 1, pt. 5, p. 7.

[6] Report for 1885 in House Ex. Doc., 49th Cong. 1st sess., no. 1, pt. 5, p. 66.

dollars, and there were issues recorded also in Boston, Philadelphia and other cities, and some that were unrecorded.[1] In the five years, ending in 1885, the total railway mileage of the country had advanced from 86,497 to more than 125,000. The capital invested in railroads in the same time is believed to have increased from $4,800,000,000 to about $18,000,000,000. So remarkable an expansion, it was said, had never been seen in a like period in this or any other country.[2]

Borrowed money was prodigally spent; iron, steel and equipment were freely purchased; large bodies of laborers were leveling the ways and laying sleepers and rails. But over a half million men who had been employed in this work in 1882 were discharged in 1883. Two railway projects alone had cast upon the country 20,000 men, most of whom a short time before had been brought from southern Europe for the purpose in hand.[3]

Wages fell. In 1885 the average rate of pay for men for work during a ten hour day was as low as $1.25 in the cotton industries and little more than $2 in any employment, while women and children sometimes received but 60 and 80 cents a day.[4] Only a few skilled workmen in highly organized trades were paid as much as $3.50 or $4 a day.[5] The "consuming power" of the nation was reduced. The prices of commodities seeking a market moved to a lower level. In New York in September, 1885, wheat was sold at 70 to 97 cents a bushel, corn at 48 cents, oats at 27 to 30 cents. Cotton was quoted at 9 to 10 cents a pound, flour at $2.70 to $3.50 a barrel. The ruling price for dressed pork was 6 to 7 cents a pound, butter 14 to 20 cents a pound, cheese 5 to 8 cents a pound, coffee 8 to 10 cents a pound, sugar 5 to 6 cents a pound, eggs 15 to 21 cents a dozen, dressed chickens 7 to 16 cents a pound, turkeys

---

[1] H. V. Poor in Senate Reports, 49th Cong. 1st sess., no. 46, p. 14.
[2] Senate Reports, 49th Cong. 1st sess., no. 46, p. 49; App. Ann. Cyclop. for 1884, p. 677.
[3] House Ex. Doc., 49th Cong. 1st sess., no. 1, pt. 5, p. 243.
[4] Laws regarding child and female labor already in force in states are summarized in ibid., pp. 457–85.
[5] Cf. ibid., pp. 226, 295–410.

12 to 15 cents a pound, anthracite coal $5 to $5.25 a long ton. Prices in the retail markets in cities were enough higher than the sums named to give the dealers small profits; but in country towns and in the West, near the places of production, they were at an even lower level.

In the shops in New York and Philadelphia men's "finest calfskin shoes" were offered for sale by responsible merchants at $2.75 and $3 a pair, ladies' "kid boots" at $2 and $2.50 a pair. A man could buy a derby hat for $1.50 and a silk hat for $3. He could get a ready-made suit for $10 and an overcoat for $5 or $8. The newspapers were filled with advertisements of woolen blankets at $5 and $6 a pair and all kinds of dress goods and finished apparel for amounts which indicated plentiful supplies and but small demand.

Houses containing six rooms could be had in Philadelphia for a rental of $10 or $11 a month. Three story cottages in fashionable suburbs of the city were advertised at $22 and $25 a month. "First class boarding" at the seashore, or in the country, was offered at $8 and $10 a week. A competent girl could be hired for $2.50 or $3 a week.[1] Prices had been very low in 1878—now in 1884 and 1885 everything was nearly, if not quite, as cheap as in that year.[2]

Low wages, the arrogance of employers of labor and the spread of socialistic doctrines had led to a strike of telegraphers in 1883. Jay Gould, after Fisk's death and his dissociation from "Erie," had turned his attention to speculation in the stocks of railroads in the West, in a number of which he came to be a controlling force. It was in a deal with Thomas A. Scott, involving railway property, that he had acquired the New York World. Telegraphy was associated with railroading and he became the major factor in the ownership of the Western Union Company which, by a score or more of combinations and absorptions, had gained a monopoly of communication by the electric telegraph,[3] a power as menacing as it was vast

[1] From New York and Philadelphia papers in September, 1885.
[2] N. Y. Nation, Oct. 1, 1885.
[3] Cf. Report of Senate Com. of Ed. and Labor, 1885, vol. i, pp. 388–97, 447–8, 866, 909.

were it not correctly used.[1] In 1883 the company transmitted 40 million messages over more than 400,000 miles of wire.[2] Its stock had been "watered" until its nominal capital was $80,000,000. Gould and his friends were getting 28 per cent in dividends on a proper valuation of the property, as well as large stock dividends.[3] The average pay of "commercial operators" was $54; of "railroad operators" only $39 a month. They alleged that they worked every day in the year, including Sunday, for ten, twelve or even fourteen hours, and received less than common laborers. In 1870 wages had been 40 per cent higher. One day at noon, in the summer of 1883, 12,000 of them, men and women, in the great cities of the country left their instruments, and business which was dependent upon their activities was seriously disorganized.[4] Wires were cut and grave violence was threatened.[5] The strike continued for several weeks. A rival, the Postal Telegraph, which was too stubbornly directed to follow the way of other rivals into Gould's hands, appeared upon the scene.[6] The prejudice which his name excited awakened discussion in and out of Congress of the question of government management of telegraphs in connection with the postal administration.[7] The railroads might be under public ownership in the future—the telegraph should be in government control now. The charges were too high, they were unequal and discriminative, so much power over news and knowledge should not be confided to one man, even if he had public respect in much greater measure

[1] Senate Reports, 48th Cong. 1st sess., no. 577, pt. 1, p. 18; N. Y. Nation, Aug. 16, 1883.
[2] Report of Senate Com. of Ed. and Labor, 1885, vol. i, pp. 186, 868–9, 961.
[3] Ibid., vol. i, pp. 120, 121, 135, 171–2, 195–7, 400–02, 877–8.
[4] Ibid., pp. 103–6, 134; N. Y. Tribune, Aug. 14, 1883; N. Y. Nation, July 26 and Aug. 2, 1883.
[5] N. Y. Nation, Aug. 16, 1883.
[6] Ibid., Aug. 23, 1883; Report of Senate Com. of Ed. and Labor, 1885, vol. i, pp. 398–9.
[7] N. Y. Nation, Aug. 2, 1883, Feb. 14, 1884, and Dec. 17, 1885; N. Y. Herald, July 30 and Aug. 1, 6, 10, 14 and 23, 1883; Senate Reports, 48th Cong. 1st sess., no. 577, pt. 2, pp. 71–118. It was a scheme, John Hay wrote to John Sherman, "to steal the telegraph and throw it into politics."— Letter dated Feb. 9, 1884, in Sherman Papers.

than Jay Gould.[1] The president of the company, Dr. Norvin Green,[2] was busily employed in presenting proof of service more valuable to the people at lower prices than it was performed in the United Kingdom and in other countries of Europe, where there was public control, and in defending private ownership.[3]

Popular reprobation followed Gould also into the ownership and control of the elevated railroads on which 600,000 persons each day passed by the bedroom windows and chimney tops of the people of New York City. As owner of the New York World he could, so it was said, attack the companies, and depress the prices of their securities at his pleasure. In 1881 he consolidated the lines and "watered" the stock, a *coup* which he executed in association with Russell Sage and Cyrus W. Field, and which in no long time reduced Mr. Field to complete poverty and a sad old age.[4]

In the summer of 1885 a great strike paralyzed the iron and steel trade in and around Pittsburgh; 100,000 men were out of work, thereby stopping the mining of coal and iron ore. It had been ordered by the Amalgamated Association of Iron and Steel Workers because of a reduction in wages posted by the manufacturers and made necessary, these manufacturers said, by the state of the market for their products.[5] All work ceased until, after a conference with the masters, the representatives of the association signed the "scale."[6] A strike closed the iron mills in Cleveland. The Knights of Labor boycotted the Mallory steamship line because the company had discharged some men who were members of their

---

[1] Turnbull White, The Wizard of Wall Street, chap. xi.

[2] M. Halstead, Jay Gould, chap. xi; Report of Senate Com. on Ed. and Labor, 1885, vol. i, pp. 953 4.

[3] Cf. Senate Reports, 48th Cong. 1st sess., no. 577, pts. 1 and 2; Senate Mis. Doc., 50th Cong. 1st sess., no. 39; Report of Senate Com. on Ed. and Labor, vol. i, pp. 873–6, 888–91, 900; N. Am. Review, Nov., 1883.

[4] Cf. App. Ann. Cyclop. for 1881, p. 659; Turnbull White, op. cit., chap. xii; Murat Halstead, Jay Gould, chap. v; Warshow, Jay Gould, chaps. xvii and xviii.

[5] N. Y. Nation, June 4 and 25, 1885.

[6] This method of adjusting wages is described in Report of Senate Com. on Ed. and Labor, vol. i, pp. 1118 et seq., 1169 et seq.

organization. For several weeks no freight passed in or out of Galveston in Texas.[1]

In March, 1886, came railway strikes aimed at Jay Gould. One of his Western roads was the "Wabash." In the recent period of expansion this company had been refinanced by speculators and, when values had collapsed, he had stepped in and gained control of the property.[2] After a strike and boycott on lines of this system in Missouri and Kansas in 1885, followed by a peace, arranged by the governors and railway commissioners of those states in a conference with Gould and his managers,[3] which was favorable to the Knights of Labor, that body resumed its activities in 1886 on related and connecting roads. Wages on Gould's railways, it appeared, beginning on September 1, 1884, had been repeatedly reduced,[4] and "the last straw upon the camel's back," the Knights said in their own defense,[5] was the dismissal of a man named Hall, the foreman of a shop at Marshall, Texas, for having absented himself from his place of labor for three, or parts of three, days to attend a district meeting of their organization. With this action Gould had had nothing to do. The company by which Hall had been employed and which discharged him was the Texas and Pacific, at the time in the hands of a receiver. To procure this man's reinstatement the Knights instituted a strike on the road which had done one of their members such affront and extended it to the Missouri Pacific and its lines. Soon 6,000 miles of railway in the "Gould Southwestern System" were blockaded; neither passenger nor freight traffic could proceed. No locomotives or cars, except those engaged in bearing the United States mails, were allowed by the strikers to pass.[6]

Meetings were held, papers were printed, handbills were circulated. Men who were lukewarm in their support of the

[1] N. Y. Nation, Nov. 12, 1885; ibid., March 25, 1886.
[2] Ibid., April 16, 1885.
[3] N. Y. Tribune, March 13, 14, 15 and 16, 1885; N. J. Ware, The Labor Movement, pp. 140–45.
[4] House Reports, 49th Cong. 2nd sess., no. 4174, pp. i–ii.
[5] Ibid., pt. 2, p. 444.
[6] N. Y. Nation, March 11, 1886; cf. Carroll D. Wright, Industrial Evolution of the U. S., pp. 307–8.

Knights were intimidated. Gould and the managing vice-president of the Missouri Pacific, H. M. Hoxie, a resolute man, were vilified and threatened with assassination. Anyone would slay a mad dog—these "tyrants," "monsters," "Molochs" were worse than mad dogs.[1] Engines were "killed"— the water was let out of boilers, the fires were "dumped," essential parts of the machinery were detached and removed. Cars were uncoupled. Workmen who were engaged and dared to take the places of the strikers were brutally attacked and the trains which they manned were derailed. Rioting led in due time in several states to the mobilization of the militia. It was declared to be the greatest railroad strike in the history of the United States.[2]

Coke workers in January, 1886, were rioting in western Pennsylvania. They demanded higher wages.[3] This strike was scarcely composed when it was announced that 20,000 men in the bituminous coal mines in Pennsylvania, Maryland, West Virginia and Ohio had quit work. Ten thousand men in the textile and the boot and shoe industries were on strike in New England; 4,000 nail makers laid down their tools in mills west of the Alleghanies. Strikers stopped some of the horse railroads in the streets of New York City. From silk mills, bakeries, printing shops, wherever men were working for wages, came accounts of quarrels between employers and employed. Not an issue of a daily newspaper in the early months of 1886 that did not contain references to strikes, boycotts, "walkouts," "tie-ups," lockouts, blockades, some begun in protest against a reduction of wages, some for shorter hours, others to compel employers to recognize the orders and behests of labor organizations.[4]

To the trades unions and their militant methods capital had grown in some degree accustomed, if not reconciled. Men working in a trade in one city, forming a union, would ally themselves with those in the like trade in other cities. Thus

[1] House Reports, 49th Cong. 2nd sess., no. 4174, pp. 379–80.
[2] Ibid., p. xii.
[3] N. Y. Nation, Jan. 21 and 28, 1886.
[4] Cf. ibid., March 18, 1886.

they gained regional and national organization under paid executives, with subordinates in administrative posts, including the notorious "walking delegates," who passed from one place to another, haranguing, exhorting and "buttonholing" workingmen in behalf of the "union" cause. These executives received salaries, often quite liberal, which were paid from levies upon the individual members of the organization.

Such a union as the Brotherhood of Locomotive Engineers, directed by P. M. Arthur, the officers of railroads had been brought to respect.[1] Indeed there were advantages in the discipline of workers who in a mass could be kept to their contracts under more or less responsible leadership. But in the Knights of Labor something else was seen—a general enrollment of workingmen for controversy and combat, at need, with capital, a combination of "all the scattered battalions of labor's mighty host in one grand whole."[2] This organization had been formed by a few garment cutters in Philadelphia as long since as 1869.[3] But little had been heard of it until Terence V. Powderly came to its head. He was a machinist, though he had not followed his trade since 1877, after which time he had been occupied with "Labor politics," causing himself to be elected mayor of the city of Scranton in Pennsylvania, and having advanced so far as to think himself, in 1885, a suitable person to apply to President Cleveland for appointment as head of the new Federal Bureau of Labor.[4] Oaths and secret hocus pocus lent a mystery to the movements of the organization. The members were "brothers," the "local assemblies" met in "sanctuaries." The officers had sounding names— Powderly himself was called the "Grand" or "General Master Workman." For some time now manifestos and pronunciamentos from him and his underlings filled the newspapers. Demands and threats disturbed employers and excited the sensibilities of politicians. In some localities the Knights would

---

[1] Cf. N. Y. Tribune, April 28, 1886; N. Y. Nation, April 1 and 29, 1886; Report of Senate Com. on Ed. and Labor, vol. ii, p. 515.
[2] Powderly's words, see N. Y. Times, May 11, 1886.
[3] House Reports, 49th Cong. 2nd sess., no. 4174, p. 26.
[4] Cleveland Papers.

protest against the employment of workingmen not resident in those localities, especially if these men were not members of the organization. They would denounce child labor, very properly and effectively, convict labor and prison-made goods, which came into competition with the products of their hands,[1] and established coöperative stores in opposition to the "pluck me" and company stores in proximity to mines and in factory towns. Eight hours should constitute a day's work. The local and district "assemblies" were so militant as to presuppose a numerous membership with active units in all parts of the country, though the secretary said in 1883 that the enrollment did not exceed 67,000 persons,[2] and Powderly three years later, in 1886, made no claims to numbers beyond 600,000.[3]

Unfortunately the organization was under the direction of a none too admirable set of men. Its officers at Omaha had extended active sympathy to the murderers of the Chinese miners at Rock Springs. They had been on the point of ordering a general strike to aid these assassins,[4] and the Knights in the West at many places involved themselves in the outrages directed at the Chinese. A vulgar loafer, Martin Irons,[5] who had come to a position of authority in the organization in the Southwest, had ordered the strike on the Gould roads. Powderly, however menacing his own counsel and influence may have been,[6] perceived the impropriety of what Irons had done. But "the cause of one brother was the cause of all,"[7] and the "General Master Workman" was bound to support

[1] Cf. N. Y. Nation, July 7, 1887.
[2] Report of Senate Com. on Ed. and Labor, 1885, vol. i, p. 3.
[3] N. Y. Nation, April 29, 1886; cf. R. T. Ely, The Labor Movement, pp. 75–88; Carroll D. Wright, Industrial Evolution of the United States, pp. 246–52; Geo. E. McNeill, The Labor Movement, chap. xv; Report of Senate Com. on Ed. and Labor, vol. i, pp. 1–41; App. Ann. Cyclop. for 1882, pp. 453–4. Much that is interesting about Powderly and the organization is found in N. J. Ware, The Labor Movement.
[4] House Ex. Doc., 49th Cong. 1st sess., no. 102, p. 12; N. Y. Nation, Sep. 24, 1885.
[5] For his record see N. Y. Times, May 10, 1886. A Congressional committee called him "a dangerous, if not pernicious man."—House Reports, 49th Cong. 2nd sess., no. 4174, p. xiv.
[6] Cf. N. Y. Nation, July 22 and Aug. 5, 1886.
[7] House Reports, 49th Cong. 2nd sess., no. 4174, p. xxii.

his men in their war upon Gould, the "money monarch," Gould, the "giant fiend," Gould, the "human monster" and the "arch enemy of mankind," who was perpetuating "the most debasing form of white slavery." [1]

It was conceived that a man might decline to work for an employer, just as an employer might refuse to engage and hire. Groups of workingmen under one roof in one trade might strike, if they liked; at any rate they, for a long time, had done so. But the assertion of the right of a locomotive engineer in Missouri to strike because a stevedore had been discharged in Texas, or *vice versa;* or of a tinsmith in one place to strike because a carpenter, or a cigar maker, or a street car conductor in another place had fallen out with his employer was generally disputed. And the use of the boycott to enforce a strike, the conspiracy of one man with another and one organization of men with another, to interfere with and damage the business of a person who was, perhaps, in no way related to, or cognizant of, the issues originally in controversy was rightly held to be indefensible. [2]

Workingmen, if one in their ranks suffered affront, would attempt to injure employers generally. Owners of railroads and mills could not use their property until the demands of the employees of some other railroad or mill were satisfied. Contributions were exacted from men at work, and doles from this fund were distributed to the strikers, who were thus encouraged to hold out until the desired end was gained. When employers put forth an effort to raise the blockade on their railway lines and to start their mills by hiring those who were not bound by the rules of the organizations these would be denounced as "scabs," "rats" and "blacklegs." [3] Groups of "union" men stood at the gates of mills and railroad yards to prevent new men from entering for work. Violence was certain to ensue, as it had ensued in the Southwest and in other

---

[1] House Reports, 44th Cong. 2nd sess., no. 4174, p. 41; cf. N. Y. Tribune, April 16, 1886.

[2] N. Y. Nation, June 3, 1886. "In nearly all cases the boycott has taken the form of dragooning the public to side with the boycotters."—Ibid., Dec. 24, 1885; cf. ibid., April 15, 1886.

[3] Report of Senate Com. on Ed. and Labor, vol. i, p. 40.

places in 1886. The Knights of Labor sought the distinction of leading in this nation-wide war which was to be waged by labor generally upon capital. Martin Irons pretended to have the power to call out the Knights and to blockade every railroad in the country, and threatened to do so.[1] He took Denis Kearney's place as the hero of the sans-culottists. Employers were astounded by such an assertion of the right of some ignorant despot in a labor organization by the crook of a finger to bring to a standstill the wheels of industry over a large territory, and pointed out the impossibility of proceeding with business under conditions which were so preposterous. The strikers were so stubborn, however, that politicians, in the state of parties at the time, with the Congressional elections approaching, were disposed to temporize with the Knights, who invited arbitration. The governors of the states affected by the disturbance had attempted mediation.[2]

Though there seemed to be very little ground for dignifying their quarrel by the adoption of such a measure [3] the House of Representatives could not neglect the opportunity to appoint a committee on "Existing Labor Troubles," which, for two months or more, under the chairmanship of Andrew G. Curtin, the "War Governor" of Pennsylvania, who had entered the House of Representatives as a Democrat in 1881, carried on an investigation of conditions in the Southwest. Such action made matters worse. In it the strikers saw hope of a settlement to their advantage. Irons in a dirty shirt, a shining stone in its front, spitting the juice of tobacco, which he chewed vigorously, took the stand to present his side of the case.[4] Powderly, Jay Gould, Vice-President Hoxie, the man in Texas who had been dismissed for attending the meeting of the Knights of Labor, the ostensible cause of the

---

[1] N. Y. Tribune, March 23, 1886.
[2] N. Y. Nation, March 25, 1886.
[3] Cf. ibid., March 18, 1886.
[4] House Reports, 49th Cong. 1st sess., no. 4174, pt. 2, pp. 435–67; cf. N. Y. Nation, May 20 and 27, 1886. When Irons was asked what had been gained by the strike he said, "Right smart."—House Reports, 49th Cong. 1st sess., no. 4174, pt. 2, p. 460.

strike, and hundreds of persons—strikers, boycotters, railway superintendents, switchmen, train dispatchers, mayors of towns and cities and local politicians—added their testimony at hearings in Washington, St. Louis, Kansas City, Atchison, Fort Worth and other places, which appeared at the end in a great volume, with a report, which it was hoped might somehow gain votes for one party and take them away from the other.

President Cleveland also noted conditions. On April 22nd he sent a message to Congress in which he equally deplored "the threats and violent demonstrations" of labor and "the grasping and heedless exactions of employers," suggesting a law which would create a new Federal commission of three members to adjust differences "arising between laboring men and their employers." Perhaps two commissioners might suffice, if they would act in coöperation with Carroll D. Wright, the head of the new Bureau of Labor.[1]

The first of May found the railway and other strikes still unsettled. It was an ominous day. The "Internationalists" in Europe made it the time for labor risings, and socialists, who were recently come from Germany and other foreign countries would, here in America, in the same manner, on May Day, launch their threats against capital. The central demand of the labor leaders was for a working day of eight hours with pay for ten hours. So long since as in 1868 Congress had been induced to pass an "eight hour law" governing labor done for the government of the United States, and, with this as a rallying point, they pressed the question upon the attention of private employers. The worker needed more time for recreation and rest. It was argued with an appearance of scientific precision, that, with the relaxed muscles, the freshened spirit, the happy mind which would follow upon fewer hours at his occupation the return in service to the employer would be as great or greater than before. The tired, hard-driven, laboring man was of doubtful use to the railroad company, the shipbuilder, the manufacturer, the contractor who hired him—

---

[1] Richardson, vol. viii, pp. 394–7; cf. App. Ann. Cyclop. for 1884, pp. 192–5.

of little use to himself or to society. It was more than a movement in the interest of a class—it was an indispensable social
reform.[1] On the other side it was contended, also with scientific
precision, that in no manner could ten hours' labor be put
into eight,[2] that the man who had so few hours to work would,
from the beginning, have his mind on quitting. And when
he had gained the eight hour day he would want to work only
six, and then later for but four hours. Employers generally
looked upon the agitation with entire disfavor. They were
suffering sufficiently now from inefficiency and drunkenness
without allowing their men more time for dissipation.

The socialists called upon labor for a demonstration of its
power. The working people would never get the eight hour
law reform unless they rose *en masse* and, at the appointed time,
on the first of May, 1886, men in many industries "walked
out,"—they would not return if they were to be held to work
in the future under such oppressive conditions. In fright and
confusion, employers, in many cases, not knowing what else
to do, acceded to the demand. Temporarily at any rate, pending further discussion of the subject, eight hours would be
a day.

If the railroad riots in April had alienated public sentiment
and made labor seem to be in the wrong, vastly more that was
unfavorable to the workingman's cause resulted from the
demonstrations in May. In Chicago excitement rose higher
than anywhere else. Thither many foreign agitators had
recently gone and were assembled for mischievous activity.
It was said that there were 40,000 men who, at the demand
of the labor leaders, had stopped work on May 1st in that
city. All trades were affected by the strikes. With freight
handlers, lumber men, metal workers, packing house employees
and others idle and disaffected a mob of 7,000 or 8,000, led
by ruffians, many of them Germans, Bohemians and Poles, attacked the McCormick reaper works in the belief, which was

[1] Report of Senate Com. on Ed. and Labor, 1885, vol. i, pp. 293–301,
328–34, 361–2, 403–4, 582, 615, 620–22.
[2] Cf. N. Y. Nation, April 29, 1886.

mistaken, that the employers had refused to agree to an eight hour day. The police were called. Stone throwing was followed by the discharge of revolvers, when the officers charged and fired, wounding a number of the rioters. This affray provided the socialists and anarchists, who were incited to violence by a paper published in German called the Arbeiter Zeitung, and by other sheets, an excuse, on the night of May 4th, for a mass meeting at the old Haymarket, an open place capable of holding 20,000 men, at which one of the speakers, mounted on a wagon, uttered language so incendiary that he was interrupted by the police who, to the number of 170, had appeared upon the scene. The crowd was ordered to disperse. The anarchist on the wagon shouted, "To arms!" Suddenly there was a great explosion; a dynamite bomb had been hurled into the ranks of the policemen killing and wounding more than thirty of them. The surviving officers vigorously charged the murderous mob which returned the fire, but soon fled and scattered into the dark alleys surrounding the square, carrying their injured with them. Milwaukee also had a number of leaders of the "social revolution." There the governor called·out the militia and a mob was dispersed by a volley fired over their heads.[1] A few days later, in another mêlée in that city, the soldiers killed three men.[2]

"Infernal machines" were discovered in Chicago, Cincinnati and New York and were destroyed. A general hunt for anarchists was instituted. John Most, editor of a paper called Freiheit, who was regarded as the foremost promoter of such doctrine in the United States, and two or three others were arrested in New York. Most was sent to the penitentiary for a year. Soap box and cart tail orators were arrested in other cities and their papers were suppressed. The fomentors of the riots in Milwaukee were apprehended. Suits were begun against divers and sundry boycotters on charges of conspiracy. Irons, deserted by his followers, was sent to jail.[3]

[1] N. Y. Nation, May 6, 1886.
[2] Ibid., May 13, 1886; cf. N. Y. Times, May 14, 1886.
[3] N. Y. Tribune, Sep. 24, 1886.

The Haymarket anarchists merited and would receive their punishment. A score or more were caught and indicted and eight were arraigned for manufacturing, transporting and throwing dynamite and for other part in the massacre of the police in Chicago. Leading the number were August Spies, who edited the incendiary Arbeiter Zeitung, Michael Schwab, an associate editor of the paper, Parsons who edited another paper and Sam Fielden, at least three of whom had spoken on the fatal night, calling upon the mob to avenge the oppressions of capital and the use of the police and the militia to put down "workingmen," who, it was asserted, were risen merely to defend their plainest rights. Feeling ran high. No fewer than seven of the wretches, who assumed an impudent front during the period of the trial, which extended over a period of five or six weeks in July and August, 1886, and surrounded themselves with the air of martyrdom, were found guilty of murder and were sentenced to be hanged.[1]

Reprieves and other stays were sought and a vast amount of "liberal" sentiment on the subject of free thought and free speech was marshaled by the anarchists for the advantage, if possible, of their doomed leaders. Two escaped death by commutation of sentence to life imprisonment. When no hope remained one killed himself in his jail cell by exploding a cartridge in his mouth. On November 11, 1887, four met their not unmerited end on the scaffold.[2]

The Knights of Labor already, before the Haymarket riot, had taken the advice of the Congressional committee with reference to their quarrel with Gould. Strikers were reëmployed unless they were known to have committed depredations on the company's property.[3] Following the outbreak in Chicago the strikes everywhere collapsed. The men returned to work, either on the old terms or, after concessions on the part of employers, who, by reason of contracts in hand, could not afford to carry on a tedious contest with their employees.[4]

[1] App. Ann. Cyclop. for 1886, pp. 12–5; N. Y. Nation, Aug. 26, 1886.
[2] N. Y. Nation, Nov. 17, 1887.
[3] Ibid., May 6, 1886.
[4] Cf. N. Y. Times, May 12, 1886.

The Knights of Labor and the trades unions tried to dissociate themselves from the bombers, and disclaimed any desire or intent to effect their objects by such methods.[1] They were, nevertheless, in some degree discredited and the Knights, in particular, suffered in public estimation. Their influence from this time on waned,[2] and their faith and purpose were transmitted to a successor in a like field, the American Federation of Labor.[3]

While the President was in the midst of the grave responsibilities which he faced so earnestly, a report gained currency that, upon her return from Europe, whither, soon after she had been graduated from college, she had gone with her mother in the summer of 1885, with some inkling of her future estate, he would marry a beautiful and amiable young woman. The newspapers spread the interesting gossip, not without innuendo and impertinence.[4] Was it mother or daughter whom the President would marry? How had the courtship been conducted? Likely by "proxy" through his secretary, "Dan" Lamont, who was in New York ordering flowers and "capacious dress suits." The lady would arrive in a steamer soon, but in which one? Why was there so much secrecy about the whole matter? What had become of "Jeffersonian simplicity" when she must be brought into the country from an out of the way port "like a package of smuggled goods."[5] The bachelor President would hereafter have a wife to soften his social contacts.[6]

Frances Folsom was the daughter of Oscar Folsom, a deceased friend of Mr. Cleveland and his partner in legal practice in Buffalo. She reached New York in the last days of May, 1886, and the President met her there on Memorial Day.

[1] Cf. N. Y. Times, May 6, 11 and 12, 1886.
[2] Cf. N. Y. Nation, Dec. 9, 1886.
[3] Cf. C. D. Wright, Industrial Evolution of the United States, pp. 254, 256; Samuel Gompers, Seventy Years of Life and Labor, vol. i, chap. xiii; N. J. Ware, The Labor Movement, chap. xii.
[4] Cf. N. Y. Tribune, April 24, 1886.
[5] N. Y. World, May 29, 1886; cf. McElroy, Grover Cleveland, vol. i, pp. 184–5.
[6] N. Y. World, June 2, 1886.

The bands, as he reviewed a military parade, merrily struck up a reigning refrain, "He's going to marry Yum Yum, Yum Yum," and Mendelssohn's "Wedding March." The people in general were happy in the prospect of a "White House bride," especially after they became aware of her pleasant graces and unspoiled charms, and the event served, at least for a time, to still the tongues of most of those who had trafficked in partisan impudences in the campaign of two years since.

Once the public had been taken into the President's confidences as to his matrimonial plans no time was lost in the execution of them. The wedding was celebrated in the White House on June 2, 1886, in the presence of only a few relations and intimate friends,[1] and Mr. and Mrs. Cleveland sought seclusion from the prying eyes of newspaper reporters, with only partial success, in a cottage at Deer Park, a mountain resort in Maryland.[2] But the honeymoon was soon ended and they were again in Washington, he surrounded by pension bills to be vetoed and she ready to assume the arduous duties of social life imposed upon "the first lady of the land."

[1] Including the members of the cabinet. The President wrote Secretary of War Endicott on May 28, "hoping that in this grave crisis" he might have the "support" of his "official family."—Cleveland Papers.

[2] A patrol had been sent up from the White House to protect the "bride and groom" from "newspaper nuisances." Certain limits had been established, the President wrote Lamont, "within which such animals are not allowed to enter, and these limits are to be watched and guarded night and day. There are a number of newspaper men here, and I can see a group of them sitting on a bridge, which marks one of the limits, waiting for some movement to be made which will furnish an incident." The President asked Vilas, of whom he was very fond, and Mrs. Vilas, as well as Colonel and Mrs. Lamont, to make them a visit. "Frank"[Mrs. Cleveland] said that if it had not been for "poor Colonel Lamont" they could not have been married at all. The President sent "love from the new firm" to him and to Mrs. Lamont.—Cleveland to Lamont, June 3, 1886, in Cleveland Papers; cf. McElroy, Grover Cleveland, vol. i, pp. 187–8; N. Y. Times, June 10, 1886.

CHAPTER XXX

CONGRESS, having set the stage for the autumn elections as well as the respective party leaders could compass this end, adjourned on August 4, 1886, and the President and his bride shortly thereafter fled the heat of the far advanced summer for a few weeks' respite from its rigors in the Adirondacks.

To the curiosity with which Mr. Cleveland's comings and goings were regarded was now added an inquisitive interest concerning his wife. To the importunities which involved him were now added those that affected the free movements of the young woman at his side. Letters, gifts, requests for money and other favors were increased in volume. Babies were named for him, and now also for her. Books, boxes of oranges, barrels of oysters, roasting cuts, carcasses of mutton, neckties, goldheaded canes, paper weights from tin in the Black Hills, whiskey, wine, mineral water, salmon, trout, venison, domestic and wild turkeys, ducks, cigars, tea, coffee, cakes, watermelons, bait pails, trolling spoons, cures for obesity, the left hind feet of graveyard rabbits and what not else poured into the White House. Invitations to come here and go there arrived by every post.

No escape seemed possible even during the vacation days. "I am pestered almost to death with importunities from all parts of the country aimed at procuring my presence at all sorts of places and holding out all kinds of inducements," the President wrote his friend Dr. Samuel B. Ward of Albany, with whom he planned to spend the holidays in the Adirondacks. He "yearned" to be where he should be "let alone" and he vowed that he would "fly from any spot" where "the free privilege of bringing no trouble to any human being" was "denied" him.[1] His destination, he wrote Ward again, would be "pretty well known"—it could not be concealed. "I begin to fear," he said, "that the pestilence of newspaper correspondence will find its way to our retreat and Mrs. Cleveland's presence will, I suppose, increase this publicity. I am thinking a little of selecting some gentleman of the craft and inviting him to go and report to the Associated Press all that can, by any possibility, interest any decent citizen of the United States, and giving it out that all other reports are spurious. One thing is certain—if the newspaper men get there I shall leave; I will not have my vacation spoiled by being constantly watched and lied about, and I won't subject my wife to that treatment." [2]

The President's friends made the arrangements with care, the reporters were outwitted at nearly all points and the few weeks in the mountains were a fortification for the cares of the autumn and winter, to which he returned late in the month of September.

Even before the adjournment of Congress in August party conventions were assembling in the states, platforms were being adopted and candidates were being put in nomination for office. Many governors, legislatures which would elect United States senators and an entire new House of Representatives were to be chosen.

In the Democratic conventions there were in 1886, as in 1885, voices which indicated impatience with, and disapproval of, the President's course in regard to the distribution of offices. Indeed the dissatisfaction was increased and came now to fuller expression. Indorsement of "the wise, patriotic and statesmanlike administration" of the President [3] was generally considered a duty, though omission of, or cool, reference to civil service reform was noted in many quarters. It was a task, indeed, as George M. Stearns wrote Secretary Endicott, to bring the "untamed, hot-headed political brigadiers" of

[1] June 14, 1886, in Cleveland Papers.
[2] Aug. 9, 1886, in ibid.
[3] From resolutions of South Carolina Democrats; cf. N. Y. Nation, Aug. 12, 1886.

the party to the "high standard" which Mr. Cleveland endeavored to maintain.[1]

Most of the platforms mentioned the tariff and called more or less clearly for modification in the interest of lower taxes, though the California Democrats, following those of Ohio, denounced the wool duties, as they had been modified in 1883, and wished the rates to revert to those of the Wool and Woolens Act of 1867, for the benefit of those who raised sheep.[2] Some attacked the attempt to make gold the sole standard of value.[3] There were few expressions of interest in the President's recommendations in regard to the suspension of silver coinage. The Massachusetts Democrats asked for "honest money."[4] Other conventions demanded stricter exclusion of the Chinese and put honey in their traps to catch the Knights of Labor and the organizations which were arraigning capital for its oppression of the workingman.

The Republicans also sought the "labor vote" and would outdo their adversaries in seductive phrase, with plentiful abuse on the Pacific coast of the friendless Chinaman. They, too, made no frank or courageous statements on the silver or civil service questions. In Massachusetts, indeed, they demanded the suspension of the purchase of silver.[5] But in states in the West, where they could do so to advantage, they denounced the President for seeking to deprive the people of that metal as a circulating medium.[6]

Everywhere the Republicans were pleased to assail him for his insincerity and hypocrisy on the subject of appointments to, and removals from, office. His "reform" was no "reform";

---

[1] Oct. 23, 1885, in Cleveland Papers. Though he failed in the execution of his purpose Bourke Cockran, a Tammany leader, would have had the Democratic state convention of New York declare the reform a "humbug" and "an undemocratic and unwarrantable invasion of popular rights."—N. Y. Tribune, Sep. 30, 1886.

[2] App. Ann. Cyclop. for 1886, p. 127; Taussig, Some Aspects of the Tariff Question, pp. 323–5; N. Y. Tribune, Aug. 6, 1883.

[3] The Democrats of Ohio said that this would be "an act of monstrous injustice."—N. Y. Nation, Aug. 26, 1886.

[4] Ibid., Oct. 7, 1886.

[5] App. Ann. Cyclop. for 1886, p. 531; N. Y. Nation, Oct. 7, 1886.

[6] As in California, cf. N. Y. Nation, Sep. 2, 1886.

they must again be intrusted with power if it were to be gained, though they had earlier, and still now, manifested little enough interest in the matter and held to the belief, as it appeared, that the people were indifferent to the character of their public servants.[1] The issues which the Republicans brought forward were their old ones—the record of the Democrats with reference to the Civil War, and the tariff. The "bloody shirt" was waved again with general denunciation and abuse of the President for the evidences of his sympathy with the "rebels" contained in his vetoes of pension bills. The tariff must be preserved and, if changed at all, raised to protect the country from the cheap products of Great Britain, which would deluge the land and reduce the living standards of our working people.[2] Only in Minnesota [3] and, perhaps, in one or two other cases, did Republican leaders, sensing the feeling of the voters in their states, express a different view.

The crystallization of opinion on the liquor question recommended resolutions on this topic, especially in states in which the parties were evenly balanced, and a few thousand votes more or less would spell failure or success. Drinking was the curse of the poor man and of his wife and children. The employer found that his workmen were made inefficient, that their productive power was reduced. Moreover the business had become inextricably involved with politics. The distiller and the brewer contributed to campaign funds. The very polling places were in taverns and saloons, majorities were made and unmade in and around drinking houses and the corruption of the electorate was unmistakably promoted by what came to be called the "organized liquor power." Some states, as Kansas, Iowa and Rhode Island, had followed Maine in prohibiting the traffic in strong drink; others sought to do so and demands were frequent that the proposal should be submitted to popular vote. There was a general desire to

[1] The member of the Republican National Committee for Illinois, Littler by name, called the civil service law "an infernal, unrepublican and un-American measure."—N. Y. Nation, Aug. 12, 1886.

[2] Cf. Republican platform in Iowa.—App. Ann. Cyclop. for 1886, p. 448.

[3] N. Y. Nation, Sep. 30, 1886.

stop short of action so drastic, on which account the device of allowing counties and other local communities the "option" of determining, after a reference of the subject to the people, whether or not they would have prohibition was advocated. "High license" [1] was proposed as a restrictive measure, and in some quarters temporarily satisfied the demand for regulation. Great charges for the privilege of selling and manufacturing liquor would exclude from the trade those who most offended the public sense, and reduce the number of persons engaged in it. In this case "speakeasies," "blind tigers" and other unlicensed sales places flourished, but it was clear that they existed also in counties and states having prohibitory laws. In any event strife between the local authorities, who had little capacity, and, perhaps, less desire, to enforce the law, and the well-meaning citizens, who in every neighborhood were directing the temperance cause, was constant. The popular mind was profoundly disturbed. The sight of the corrupting alliances made by the party leaders with the liquor business had driven many into the separate Prohibition party, which in 1884 had cost the Republicans the loss of enough votes in New York, New Jersey, Connecticut and some other states to defeat their candidate for President. [2]

The politicians, both Republican and Democratic, were between Scylla and Charybdis. To say that they were prohibitionists was to alienate the liquor dealers, most of the drinkers of liquor and those who saw in restrictive laws a violation of personal rights. On the other hand an announcement of sympathy for the business, no matter how guarded, would certainly displease those voters, whatever their number, who had chosen to form a separate party, now actively engaged in the work of inducing others to follow their example and desert the politicial organizations to which they had formerly adhered.

It was clear that most of the prohibitionists were Republicans, who, by inheritance, were attracted to moral issues and who,

[1] Cf. N. Y. Nation, Jan. 21, 1886, and March 31, 1887.
[2] Ibid., Nov. 18, 1886.

in political feeling, were without scruples regarding what was called sumptuary legislation. The Democrats, therefore, had the least to lose by ignoring the question and oftentimes believed it to be to their advantage openly to espouse the liquor cause under the cover of a defense of personal liberty and right. The Democrats in Illinois in 1886 were certain enough of their position to declare that prohibition was "contrary to the fundamental principles of free government." [1] The temperance reformers on the farms and in small towns, therefore, would call the Democratic party the "whiskey party." The Republicans, who in the cities had to deal with elements holding views far from puritan, were in a difficult position. Losses which they could ill afford were to be prevented. The favorite device was to "straddle" the question. If definite statements of interest in the matter were included in the Republican platforms it was with a quiet understanding with the "liquor men" that it was for vote-getting purposes only. To keep the "bolters" in order groups of men in a number of states, under the guidance of the politicians, calling themselves "Anti-Saloon Republicans," held meetings and drew up resolutions. A national convention in this interest met in Chicago in September, 1886. It was attended by delegates from twenty states, some of whom had come with the purpose of reforming their party with reference to liquor, while others were merely intent upon making a spectacle which would beguile the prohibitionists. [2]

As usual the interest of the politicians in the elections of 1886 turned first to Maine, both because this was the "home state" of Blaine, who was on the stump defending his title to party leadership, and because, as usual, the polling would be made in September, nearly two months before the general elections in November. Blaine displayed his accustomed agility in charge, answer and controversy, and it was universally understood and acknowledged that his position, with reference to a renomination in 1888, depended upon the outcome of the campaign. Speakers from other states were called in, and the canvass was warm and intensive. A governor was to be

[1] N. Y. Nation, Sep. 2, 1886.   [2] Ibid., Sep. 23, 1886.

chosen and the Republican must be elected by a sweeping
majority in order that Cleveland and his party might be made
to comprehend how low they stood in popular regard. The
result was not sufficiently decisive to afford Blaine and his
friends reason for congratulation. The Republicans indeed
won, but by a considerably smaller plurality than in 1884,
and Blaine, who had been belaboring "British free trade"
among his neighbors, was released for speech in other
states, notably in Pennsylvania, "the home of the tariff,"
where he could procure the largest measure of sympathetic
hearing for that principle which it was his determination to
make the party issue in the national campaign two years
away.[1]

The struggles in the states over the governors and the members of Congress were not more provocative of interest and
comment than the contest for mayor in New York. Henry
George, rapidly advanced to fame by his "Progress and Poverty," had left San Francisco for the East, and in New York
City the labor and socialist organizations combined to present
his name to the people as one who would lead them out of
their world of work to some Elysian field. In the state of the
public mind the outlook was ominous.[2] If such a man were
elected to such an office in the greatest of American cities
no one could say what might not befall property and the
owners of property. Abram S. Hewitt was appealed to in
the emergency and he consented, at some personal sacrifice,
to set up his respected figure as a protest against communism.

He was an eminent man of affairs, a large employer of labor,
an authority upon economical questions and of proven character as well as experience. He had freely conferred with Cleveland during the campaign of 1884 and offered him counsel
after the election, to be treated, as he thought, rather incon-
siderately. Having been invited to no post in the cabinet
he, on March 28, 1885, was given the option of the missions

[1] Cf. N. Y. Nation, Oct. 21 and Nov. 4, 1886.
[2] Ibid., Sep. 30 and Oct. 7, 1886.

to Russia, Austria or Spain. The proffer did not please him,[1] but the real affront came when he reminded the President of a debt incurred during the campaign. It was a conspicuous service, Mr. Hewitt said, and conduced to Cleveland's success. The only return which could be made for it was a directorship of the Pacific Railroad. The President said the appointment which was suggested was improper; he would not yield and the relations between the two men, though the greatest kindness marked the correspondence on Cleveland's side, had practically come to an end.

Having been thus set aside, as he considered, Hewitt was the more ready to leave Washington. The Tammany organization which had defeated him for the nomination for governor, when, in the convention, he had opposed Hill in 1885, now, to every one's surprise, gave him its support.[2] Indeeed, for their own reasons, the leaders had originated the movement for his nomination.[3] He entered the contest actively and called upon the voters of the city to rally under his standard. The Henry George campaign was an attempt, Hewitt said, to array class against class and it was, therefore, at war with American political ideals.[4]

At this point the Republicans, whose managers had little more interest in the party than the use of the organization to "make trades" with Tammany (when they had aught to offer) wrote upon their banners the name of Theodore Roosevelt, still not yet twenty-eight years of age, and he, for the satisfaction of his avid love of activity, as well as of public notice, though he had repeatedly declared that partisan considerations should not be allowed to affect municipal elections,[5] accepted the nomination. The Republican politicians of the city no more wanted him than Tammany wanted Hewitt, but, being in the field, he would win votes on national issues from

[1] Cleveland Papers.

[2] N. Y. Nation, Oct. 14, 1886; N. Y. Tribune, Oct. 15, 1886; Writings of Schurz, vol. iv, pp. 461–2.

[3] Cf. L. F. Post, The George-Hewitt Campaign.

[4] N. Y. Nation, Oct. 21, 1886; H. George, Jr., Life of George, pp. 472–3, 475–6.

[5] N. Y. Nation, Oct. 25, 1888.

respectable elements attached to the party,[1] who otherwise, on this occasion, would have supported the Democratic candidate, thus converting what would have been a plain contest between socialism and the established economic order into a triangular struggle, which would be of manifest advantage to George.

The very fact of Roosevelt being put in nomination by such a body of men, said the New York Nation, was "a strong sign of unfitness for the place." He would not make "a good mayor" in any event—"even twenty years' longer experience of life and affairs than he has had would hardly make him a good administrator," which, the Nation observed, is not "the same thing as a good reformer." [2]

The influence of President Cleveland was exerted resolutely throughout the campaign to keep the officeholders at their public tasks. He issued an order in July to the heads of all departments asking them to warn their subordinates of the entire impropriety of their using their positions in attempts to control political movements in their localities. "Office-holders," he observed, "are the agents of the people, not their masters." [3] Assessments of money for party uses were not to be laid—if laid they were not to be paid. During the progress of the campaign wholesome examples were made of several who had not seen fit to respect the rules for civil servants, dictated by common sense as well as by law, and had followed a course which the President had said was "indecent and unfair." [4]

The election, in November, revealed tendencies which furnished the editors and other high pundits of the parties with much material for analysis and comment. The truth was that, if no considerable damage or loss was suffered by Mr. Cleveland, no very great advantage was reaped by the Repub-

[1] Elihu Root in his speech as chairman of the convention said, amid "loud and prolonged applause,"—"The Republican party is the party which has freed the slave, which has saved the nation's life. . . . the party of protection to American industries, the party of honest government," etc., etc.—N. Y. Tribune, Oct. 16, 1886.
[2] N. Y. Nation, Oct. 21, 1886; cf. ibid., Nov. 4 and Dec. 2, 1886.
[3] Ibid., July 22, 1886.
[4] Cf. ibid., Oct. 14, 28, Nov. 4 and Dec. 2, 1886.

licans. In New York the Democrats elected a judge on a general state ticket but the Republicans would control the new legislature. Much was made of the fact that the Republicans had carried Indiana by a plurality of about 3,000, though Cleveland had had the advantage of Blaine by more than 6,000 in 1884. Spoilsmen were pleased to see in this a rebuke for the President, who must "either prove himself a Democrat in the remaining years of his administration, or prepare to meet emphatic repudiation by his party." [1] On the other hand the Democrats had cut down a plurality of 43,000 in Minnesota to 2,600. They increased a plurality in Missouri of 33,-000 in 1884 to 50,000 in 1886. They elected a governor in New Jersey by a plurality of 8,000—Cleveland's two years ago had been barely 4,000. In Massachusetts, Connecticut, New Hampshire, Rhode Island, Colorado and California no sign of distrust of the President was seen. Both Colorado and California had elected Democratic governors and a Republican had won by the smallest margin in New Hampshire. The plurality in Massachusetts was reduced from 24,000 to about 10,000. Hewitt polled 90,000 votes and was elected mayor of New York City over George with 68,000 and Roosevelt with 60,000.[2]

It is true that the Democratic majority in the House, as a result of the poll, would be somewhat reduced. In the Forty-ninth Congress there had been 184 Democrats and 139 Republicans; in the Fiftieth there would be 160 Democrats and 152 Republicans, with 4 Laborites and Independents. The Senate would remain Republican, but by the meager majority of two; in the last Congress it was eight.[3] The Republicans made much of the fact that Colonel Morrison, the chairman of the Committee on Ways and Means, was defeated for re-election to a seat in the House for his district in Illinois, that

[1] N. Y. Nation, Nov. 11, 1886, quoting Indianapolis Sentinel.

[2] "It was a mistake ever to take him [Roosevelt] seriously as a politician, and the probabilities are that his drafts on public attention in this latter capacity will now steadily diminish."—N. Y. Nation, May 19, 1887.

[3] McPherson's Handbook for 1888, pp. 89–91; cf. N. Y. Nation, Jan. 20, 1887.

Frank Hurd, a well known "free trader," a lawyer in Toledo, Ohio, had lost his seat, that the Speaker, John G. Carlisle, in Kentucky, was returned by a majority which had dwindled to a few hundred votes.[1]

A tribute paid to the President a few days after the election was more satisfying to him and the friends of good government than any which might be found in the popular poll. It was on the occasion of the 250th anniversary of the foundation of Harvard College. Mr. Cleveland had been invited to attend the ceremonies and he said that he would do so, accompanied by Mrs. Cleveland, if he were not to receive the degree of LL.D.[2] With "high appreciation" of his "eminent ability," his "stanch integrity" and his "patriotic devotion to the welfare of the nation" the Republican governor of Massachusetts extended a welcome in behalf of the people of the state. James Russell Lowell in the commemorative address, before an assemblage of gentlemen as representative of intelligence, understanding and service as any which could be brought together in America, made references personal to Cleveland. At one point the orator gracefully put the President in the place of Seneca's pilot who uttered the immortal speech, "O! Neptune, save me if you will, or sink me if you will; but whatever you do, I will keep my rudder true." The house rang with applause at sight of his face and at every mention of his name.[3]

When the Forty-ninth Congress convened for its final session, in December, 1886, it received a message which was notable in few regards, except in respect of the silver purchase law and tax reduction. The President's suggestions on both of these topics were in accord with those which he had made in the previous year. Nearly 30,000,000 new silver dollars had been coined in the past fiscal year. "Every fair and legal effort" had been put forth to distribute this currency among the people, but it remained in the Treasury, and more vault room was

[1] N. Y. Tribune, Nov. 4 and 5, 1886; N. Y. Nation, Nov. 11, 1886.
[2] Cleveland to Endicott, Nov. 5, 1886, in Cleveland Papers.
[3] N. Y. Nation, November 11, 1886.

needed to store it. He again urged the suspension of the "compulsory coinage of silver under the act of 1878," since "the only pretense" for such action was "the necessity of its use by the people as a circulating medium." [1]

The revenues of the government were still in excess of the expenditures. The surplus in the Treasury at the end of the last fiscal year was nearly $94,000,000; it had been $63,000,000 on June 30, 1885. The President predicted a surplus of $90,-000,000 on June 30, 1887.[2] He reiterated his recommendations, which had not been taken by Congress at its last session. More plainly than before he asked for reductions in the tariff rates on imports. These charges were but little less, in some cases more, than during the war. "Large and important industries" should not be disturbed, but, if the people required relief from needless taxation, the owners and managing executives of these industries should coöperate with Congress for the "public good." The "leading strings useful to a nation in its infancy," the President observed, could be "discarded," to a great extent, "in the present stage of American ingenuity, courage and fearless self-reliance." [3] The revenues should be adjusted, too, with reference to the welfare of the workingman. While reducing "the expense of living" and bringing "within his domestic circle additional comforts and advantages" there should be no curtailment of "the opportunity for work," or lowering of the wages of American labor. No less, and furthermore, the farmers must be kept in view. They numbered nearly one-half of the population. The "unnatural profit" given to the manufacturer, favored by the government as the agriculturist was not, increased the price of many "necessaries and comforts of life," which "the most scrupulous economy" enabled our farmers to bring into their homes, and of "their implements of husbandry." [4]

The tariff laws should be amended, the President concluded, and the revenues be brought into balance with expenditures in such a way as to "cheapen the price of the necessaries of

---

[1] Richardson, vol. viii, p. 513.
[2] Ibid., pp. 507–8.
[3] Ibid., p. 510.
[4] Ibid., p. 511.

life and give free entrance to such imported materials as, by American labor, may be manufactured into marketable commodities." [1] He put his political philosophy into plain words. "Good government," he said, "and especially the government of which every American citizen boasts, has for its objects the protection of every person within its care in the greatest liberty consistent with the good order of society, and his perfect security in the enjoyment of his earnings with the least possible diminution for public needs." [2]

These were more definite statements than Mr. Cleveland had included in his first message. They were welcomed by the tariff reformers and the free traders, as they were by the Republicans who read the New York Tribune. It was the issue which Blaine and the politicians in his following wished to raise and take to the people again. They believed that, with "British free trade" on the one side and "protection for American labor" on the other, they could wage a successful contest and regain possession of the government.

The Congress was as indifferent to the question at its second session as it had been at its first. On June 17, 1886, it had declined to consider the tariff question; the House now again almost at once, before the holidays, on December 18, 1886, Randall and his group of Democrats supporting the Republicans, confirmed, by a vote of 154 to 148, its indisposition even to discuss the Morrison bill. [3]

As fruitless were the President's recommendations regarding the currency, for Congress rushed to the task of redeeming the "trade dollars" for the advantage of the speculators who held them. Again and again the scheme of taking up this circulation had been urged upon Congress. [4] It was at first provided that the exchange should be credited upon the two million monthly bullion purchase account. But the silverites, with their unremitting fanaticism, sensitive to every movement

[1] Richardson, vol. viii, p. 511.
[2] Ibid., p. 509.
[3] McPherson's Handbook for 1888, p. 52.
[4] N. Y. Nation, Feb. 24, 1887; J. L. Laughlin, Hist. of Bimetallism, pp. 208–10.

which they could regard as aimed at their favorite money, made it quite certain that the trade dollars, when they were received to be recoined, should not be counted as part of the bullion required to be taken from the miners by the act of 1878. Only five men in the Senate voted against this proposal and the House adopted it without a division. The President saw the uselessness of opposition and the bill became a law by lapse of time without his approval.[1]

Mr. Cleveland was deterred in no way from open statement and positive action, in proof of his principles, in reference to another measure. Politicians in both parties continued to attach importance to the "soldier vote." The professional "veteran" of the war, often no more than a blatherskite, who had never seen actual service but had pressed his way into some Grand Army post as a means of political preferment, had the power, which he did not fail to exercise, of intimidating party leaders. Few Republicans dared to put a low estimate upon the value of a policy of generous treatment of the Union soldier. Not many Democrats in the North cared to have it appear that they were wanting in consideration for him. Therefore it was that one pension bill followed another with nobody, until Cleveland had appeared, brave enough to set obstacles in the way of legislation which was now making large demands upon the Treasury. Already 365,000 persons were on the pension rolls of the United States involving an outlay of $75,-000,000 annually,[2] and a total sum, since 1861, of more than $800,000,000,[3] and Congress now, while the President was again, as during its last session, vetoing grants improperly and unworthily made to individuals who could not get attention at the Pension Office, approved and sent him the draft of another general law. The scheme would give $12 a month to any man who had ever been in the military or naval service of the United States and concerning whom it might be shown that he could not now earn his living, and was "dependent."

[1] McPherson's Handbook for 1888, pp. 48–9; N. Y. Nation, Feb. 17, 1887; A. B. Hepburn, Hist. of Coinage and Currency, pp. 308, 571.
[2] N. Y. Nation, Feb. 3, 1887.
[3] Richardson, vol. viii, p. 550.

Parents unable to support themselves, in case of his decease, could claim and would be paid the same amount. The New York Nation said that there were a million persons who might apply for this stipend, that a half of this number would get it. We should then have 500,000 more men on our pension rolls at a yearly added charge of $72,000,000.[1] And this estimate was not considered very exorbitant even by those who advocated the measure. William McKinley, a member of the House from Ohio, said that the bill, together with a Mexican War pension bill which was simultaneously making its way through Congress, might take from the Treasury $50,000,000 a year, and perhaps "a great deal more." [2] If the guess were as wide of the mark as it had been in the case of the Arrears of Pensions bill of 1879, of which it had been said that the government, in passing it, would not incur obligations in excess of $20,000,000, though up to date the outlay on this account had been more than $218,000,000, there was no telling how expensive an adventure this new one might prove to be.[3]

It was believed by most men holding such opinions as were commonly entertained about the correct functions of government with reference to the citizens, even when that citizen had given service to his country in war, that all of those who deserved public assistance were now receiving it. The new bill was the invention of the claim agents whose lobby was powerful. The removal of limitations about wounds and incurred disability, which were to be proven, and the placing of the case upon a basis of mere enlistment and alleged inability of the claimant to provide for himself by his own exertions, would greatly enliven the business of the pension agents. The New York Nation called it the "Pauper Pension bill." If it were to pass every slacker who had been brought into the army by the draft laws and by offers of bounties, who had been hired to fight and then had shirked service, would come forward for his $12 a month. It was "the rubbish of the army," said

[1] Richardson, vol. viii, p. 550.
[2] N. Y. Nation, Feb. 3, 1887; cf. ibid., Jan. 20, 1887.
[3] Ibid.; W. H. Glasson, Hist. of Military Pension Legislation, chap. v.

General Bragg of Wisconsin, which Congress now proposed to reward.[1]

In his message vetoing the measure the President expressed similar views. He said that this was a "service pension bill," the first of the kind with reference to soldiers of the Civil War; all others presupposed death or disablement while engaged in military duty. He had examined the provisions of the bill which were intended to define the conditions under which the benefit might be applied for and received. They were vague and would invite deception and fraud. The "race after the pensions" opened by this measure would "put a further premium on dishonesty and mendacity" on the part of claimants and their attorneys. The bill was so carelessly contrived that no man could certainly say how great an appropriation might be required to satisfy the demands made in answer to its grants. The expense might be "almost appalling." It had been called a "charity measure." The President did not believe that the soldiers still in the prime of life, who had gone out from their homes to serve their country for patriotic motives, wished to be regarded as objects of charity. In pay and bounty the soldiers in the Union army had been given such compensation as had "never been received by soldiers before, since mankind first went to war." Never before had there been, after a war, so many generous laws for their relief on account of injuries sustained in it; never before such preference in public employments, such ample provision in institutions for their comfort, if they were homeless. The people in time of peace were still paying war taxes. They demanded relief from these burdens. If this bill should become a law, "with its tremendous addition to our pension obligation," the President was "thoroughly convinced," he said, that efforts "to reduce the Federal revenue and restore some part of it to our people" would, of necessity, cease.

He had just approved the Mexican War pension bill which

[1] N. Y. Nation, Feb. 3 and 10, 1887. Henry Watterson, engaged in drawing attention to himself by picturesque speech, called the bill "a liniment to abolish vagabondage by pensioning a lot of tramps."—Foraker in N. Y. World, June 17, 1887.

was a "service pension bill." It offered every man who had
been enlisted in the war with Mexico, for a period of at least
60 days, regardless of his disability or his indigence, if he were
more than 62 years of age, $8 a month, and such as were under
62 a like sum, if they were dependent, and had not served in
the war against the Union during the "late rebellion." But
39 years had elapsed since that war had ended and there were
only a few survivors. These had reached an age when their
disability could be definitely distinguished and fixed. Mr. Cleveland approved that scheme, it is true. But he could not do
else, charged as he was with his great public responsibilities,
than disapprove the bill extending similar benefits to the soldiers of the Civil War—he would act in the case, he said, "regardless of all consequences," except such as appeared to him
"to be related to the best and highest interests of the country." [1]

Five days later the President had the opportunity further
to reveal his views as to the relations which under the Constitution should subsist between the government and the people.
Congress had passed a bill setting aside $10,000 which it author-
ized the Commissioner of Agriculture to expend in the distribution of seed grain in several counties in Texas, where the farmers were suffering from the effects of a drought. Their crops
had been ruined, they themselves would be if they were not
enabled to replant their fields. Mr. Cleveland said that charity
was a private function. "Paternal care" on the part of the
government "weakens the sturdiness of our national character."
He would veto the bill and enforce the lesson "that, though
the people support the government, the government should
not support the people." Since Congress appropriated $100,-
000 a year to meet the cost of seeds, which the members of
that body distributed to their friends in their respective electoral
districts, he pertinently enough observed that they might discover the means in this quarter, without damage to their political prospects, to assist the sufferers in Texas.[2]

---

[1] Richardson, vol. viii, pp. 549–57; McPherson's Handbook for 1888,
pp. 17–22,
[2] Richardson, vol. iii, pp: 557–8,

In this short and last session of the first Congress with which he had to deal during his administration the President vetoed 23 private pension bills in messages containing reasons for his action as trenchant as those which had awakened so much remark in 1886. He defeated the hopes of an old mail contractor to whom Congress had voted indemnity,[1] the heirs of a recreant Indian agent [2] and the populations of two or three towns which had asked for new public buildings and had been selected by the Senate and House of Representatives for "Federal decoration." [3] When Congress sent him the River and Harbor bill, which included an appropriation for the Hennepin Canal scheme in Illinois, he treated it to a "pocket veto." [4]

The courage needed for such an exercise of the executive prerogative was considerable, and again it was proof in the President of an independence of mind and of a responsible understanding of public duty which called for the admiration of right thinking men.[5] Many soldiers of the war, of intelligence and character, had urged Cleveland to veto the pension bill; when he had done so they addressed him congratulating him upon the event. Not a few newspapers, held to be representative of feeling and expressive of opinion in the Republican party, hastened to commend him for his bravery in withstanding such an onrush for public money, though it had been organized under cover of patriotism and "love of the flag." [6]

Those who had other views, and for personal and partisan reasons wished to assert them, were neither slow nor loath to do so. The New York Tribune said that Cleveland's veto of the pension bill was full of "insinuations" against the honesty of "loyal veterans." It ill became a President,

---

[1] Richardson, vol. viii, pp. 540–42.
[2] Ibid., pp. 564–5.
[3] Ibid., p. 565.
[4] N. Y. Nation, March 10, 1887.
[5] A rhymster (Cleveland Papers) brought this idea to expression—
  "Grover Cleveland's President
   And guides our ship of state,
   His backbone's stiff as his upper lip
   And he weighs three hundred-weight."
[6] Cf. N. Y. Nation, Feb. 17 and 24, 1887.

"elected by rebel votes," to "slur" the "defenders of the Union." [1] The chairman of the Committee on Invalid Pensions in the House was a Democrat, the majority was Democratic, yet they had presented the scheme and now issued a statement defending themselves against the President's objections. They made the point that from the day the Congress had met they had been beset with proposals for the distribution of public money to the old soldiers,—that many of these schemes, including a project for repealing the time limit set in the Arrears of Pensions bill of 1879,[2] another to give a pension of $8 a month to every one who had been enlisted in the military service on the Union side, had champions of great zeal and earnestness, and that, of the number, the plan to aid the indigent and dependent appeared to be the most just and economical. The President was rather roughly answered. The statement was plainly such as would reach the sympathies of entirely thoughtless people and it was unfortunately mixed with evidences of adherence to the doctrine of that extraordinary school of political economists, so numerous in our legislative assemblies, that to appropriate money and scatter it about was to increase the common welfare. The public revenues were excessive. There was a surplus in the Treasury, as the President knew and said. Under this pension bill the money, which was now an embarrassment to the government, would "go among the people in small amounts" and would be "spent in their midst."

The committee could not avoid references to Wall Street. It seemed to them that opposition to the bill came from "moneyed centers," which they would infer controlled Mr. Cleveland's mind—"moneyed centers in which all water which does not turn their mills is considered worse than wasted." They unanimously, "without a dissenting voice," recommended that the bill should pass, "notwithstanding the objections of the President." [3] It had received a vote in the House on January 17,

---

[1] Issue of Feb. 12, 1887.

[2] A promise that this would be done was contained in the National Republican platform of 1884; cf. N. Y. Nation, Feb. 10 and March 10, 1887.

[3] McPherson's Handbook for 1888, pp. 22–9; cf. N. Y. Nation, Feb. 24, 1887.

1887, of 180 to 76. A number of Democrats, after a reading of Mr. Cleveland's message, gained courage, and, on February 24th, it failed of enactment over his veto. The yeas were 175, the nays 125, and it wanted, therefore, the necessary two-thirds vote.[1]

The principal fruit of the session of Congress ending in March, 1887, was the passage of the Interstate Commerce bill. The houses which had disagreed at the first session, the Senate holding to the advantage of Cullom's bill providing for the appointment of a commission to superintend the railroads, and the House insisting upon Reagan's scheme for a mere penal statute, composed their differences through their conferees and one of the most notable, as well as imperative, movements in the direction of fair dealing and public right was happily begun. It was only an initial step, but to establish the principle and put the government on the way to more and better control of the companies which had been running riot as they grew in wealth and power, disturbing all business enterprise and corrupting our public life, was an inestimable gain. Provision was made for a commission of five members, acting in connection with the Interior Department, to be appointed by the President, not more than three of whom should be drawn "from the same political party." They should not engage in any other business while serving in their offices. The salary would be $7,500 a year.

The bill forbade discriminations in special rates, rebates or drawbacks, and greater compensation for the short haul than for the long haul, under like circumstances and conditions, subject to exceptions to be approved by the commission, an attempt at regulation in a very difficult field.[2] It specified that tariffs should be printed and be open to public inspection, that changes in these tariffs should not be made without due prior notice. Pooling in restraint of competition was declared to be unlawful. Companies should not combine to allocate

---

[1] McPherson's Handbook for 1888, p. 29.
[2] Cf. A. N. Merritt, Federal Regulation of Railway Rates, p. 165; N. Y. Nation, Jan. 13, 1887.

business and divide their earnings. Penalties were prescribed; enforcement would be secured with the aid of the Federal courts. The conference report was agreed to in the House by a vote of 219 to 41, the majority being made up without regard to party lines, and the bill was signed by the President.[1] The railway interests had continued their hostility. Those publicists whose political philosophy rested on a belief in competition unhampered by public control found little of value in the law, or the principle which it established, and called it "anti-railroad legislation," and "a piece of state socialism."[2]

But nothing could alter the fact that there were evils which justified complaint and the search for remedy, that it was a victory, after a long contest, for those who were honestly interesting themselves in the public welfare, and that popular opinion on the subject had been aroused to such a degree as to make regulatory action necessary. If defects in the law were discovered after experience, and in the light of interpretation by the courts in suits certain to ensue, amendment could be made, and legislation could be extended to cover the requirements of the case.

A lively contest for places on the new commission ensued. Mrs. Grant asked the President to appoint her son Jesse.[3] Nothing was further from his mind. Judge Gresham's name was proposed. The President, it was said, considered the law "very crude and of doubtful construction"; he would procure the best available men for the work in hand.[4] Don M. Dickinson, Cleveland's adviser in Michigan, was asked to "feel out" Judge Thomas M. Cooley, who expressed an interest in the subject.[5] With this as a beginning the President promptly announced his appointments. They were all of a high character—Judge Cooley, who was exceptionally familiar with the law affecting railroads through his management of receiverships and as a member of pooling committees, and

---

[1] McPherson's Handbook for 1888, pp. 7–13.

[2] N. Y. Nation, Feb. 3, 1887; cf. ibid., April 21, 1887.

[3] Cleveland Papers.

[4] Bristow to Gresham, Feb. 9, 1887, in Gresham Papers in Library of Congress.   [5] Cleveland Papers.

who was elected chairman; A. F. Walker of Vermont, a lawyer who had been at close quarters with a corrupt railroad ring in New England; Walter L. Bragg, who was at the head of the state railroad commission in Alabama; Judge Augustus Schoonmaker, a lawyer held in high esteem in New York, and William R. Morrison, the chairman of the Committee on Ways and Means in the House of Representatives, who had just been deprived of his seat by a reverse at the polls in Illinois.[1]

That element in the Republican party which was high protectionist and opposed to any reform of the tariff, and which, on every available occasion, denounced those who opposed their views as "British free traders" and for their own advantage fomented anti-British sentiment, together with the politicians seeking the Irish vote, sought to involve the President in international entanglements over our fishing rights in Canada. What lay behind the rancor which was spent upon him on this subject was very plain. A few men in New England who sent out boats from Gloucester, which was the "grand headquarters" of our fishing people,[2] and other towns to the waters bordering on the British provinces, together with the canners in Maine, were quite certain that they could carry on their trade more profitably if they had a monopoly of the American market. Under the Treaty of Washington fish, salted, pickled and otherwise cured, came into the United States from Canada free of duty. Fresh fish were on the free list in the general tariff law. Both advantages enjoyed by the Canadians our New England fishermen wished to convert into disadvantages. Since refrigerating processes had come to be developed and more rapid means of transportation on the railroads were employed fresh fish could be delivered over an extended area. Thus had the market for salt fish been invaded. The tariff law should be amended to tax fish intended for "immediate consumption."

But the issue at hand now was the want of a tariff on Canadian

[1] N. Y. Nation, March 24 and 31, 1887.
[2] Senator Edmunds in Senate Reports, 49th Cong. 2nd sess., no. 1683, p. 74; cf. F. H. North, Century Mag., Oct., 1886, p. 817.

salt fish, and this condition could be corrected by abrogating the fishing clauses in the Treaty of Washington of 1871. The award to Great Britain of $5,500,000 by the Halifax Commission had been loudly protested at the time. Whenever they thought of this transaction it had not ceased to roil the New Englanders.[1] The Belgian umpire had "betrayed" us and had served England. As early as in 1879, six years before any action could be taken under the terms of the treaty, the Senate angrily passed a resolution urging negotiations which would somehow correct an intolerable situation.[2] Incidents had increased the unpleasant feeling, notably at Fortune Bay, in 1878, when the crews of several American herring smacks ran afoul of a mob of Newfoundland fishermen and lost their nets, tackle and other equipment.[3]

The fishing people pursued the subject, and on the earliest feasible occasion, under the terms of the treaty, Congress, by joint resolution, on March 3, 1883, gave the required two years' notice of desire on our part to terminate, upon July 1, 1885, reciprocal relationships, when salt fish from Canada would immediately become subject to duty and the two governments, perforce, would revert to the rules laid down for their mutual guidance by the Treaty of 1818.[4] But Article I of that treaty required interpretation and definition. The British held that entry at Canadian ports, except within territorial limits, particularly specified in the convention, could be made only for shelter, repairing damages, purchases of wood, obtaining water and "for no other purpose whatever."[5]

---

[1] Senate Reports, 49th Cong. 2nd sess., no. 1683, p. xiii; N. Y. Nation, Feb. 17, 1887. Our representatives at Halifax had been "outmanœuvred and outwitted" by the Canadian agents.—N. Y. Tribune, Jan. 15, 1886.

[2] Senate Mis. Doc., 50th Cong. 1st sess., no. 109, p. 12.

[3] House Ex. Doc., 46th Cong. 2nd sess., no. 84; Senate Ex. Doc., 46th Cong. 2nd sess., no. 180; App. Ann. Cyclop. for 1880, p. 218; H. L. Keenleyside, Canada and the United States, p. 268.

[4] Cf. N. Y. Nation, May 26, 1887; Richardson, Messages and Papers, vol. viii, p. 499; House Reports, 49th Cong. 2nd sess., no. 3648; Senate Reports, 49th Cong. 2nd sess., no. 1683.

[5] House Ex. Doc., 49th Cong. 2nd sess., no. 153, p. 26; Senate Ex. Doc., 49th Cong. 1st sess., no. 217; House Ex. Doc., 49th Cong. 2nd sess., no. 19, pp. 39–41.

Earnest controversy, whenever this treaty had governed our relations with British North America, had prevailed and much irritation at different periods had arisen over the meaning of its language.[1] There was dispute as to whether the three mile limit within which fishing might not be carried on should follow the shore line, or whether it should be reckoned from headland to headland;[2] about entering ports to buy bait, salt, barrels and provisions; about the issue and recognition of fishing licenses and the distinction to be drawn between these licenses and permits for trading vessels; about going ashore to mend nets and dry the catch; about landing men to visit their friends, buy newspapers and for rest and diversion; about shipping men to increase the crews; about putting in with a cargo for transportation to the United States over the Canadian railroads; about report, when coming in, with no matter what object, to the harbor authorities, and the making of formal entry and clearance.[3]

Clear understanding of disputed points was now more than ever important because of the changes in seventy years in methods of fishing and in disposing of the catch, the growth of the population of British North America, as well as of the United States, the increase of the number of men engaged and of the capital invested in the fishing business on both sides of the boundary, and the quickening of intercourse between the two countries.[4]

When July, 1885, came, citizens of the United States were in their boats in British American waters. Were their operations to be interrupted in the midst of their ventures? Mr. Bayard entered into negotiations with the British minister in the United States, Sir Lionel Sackville Sackville-West, and an agreement was reached for a temporary extension of the rights

[1] It had been the cause of "unnumbered international differences and disputes."—House Reports, 49th Cong. 2nd sess., no. 3684, p. 4; cf. House Ex. Doc., 49th Cong. 2nd sess., no. 19, pp. 2, 52; Chas. Isham, The Fishery Question.

[2] Cf. House Ex. Doc., 49th Cong. 2nd sess., no. 19, p. 16.

[3] Cf. App. Ann. Cyclop. for 1885, p. 132; N. Y. Nation, Nov. 3, 1887.

[4] Cf. Chas. Isham, op. cit., pp. 76–7; J. W. Collins, Century Magazine, October, 1886.

guaranteed by the Treaty of Washington "in the interest of good neighborhood and of the commercial intercourse of adjacent communities," pending the submission of the matter to Congress which would, it was confidently supposed, authorize the appointment of a commission to consider and settle, upon a just basis, the questions at issue.[1] In his first message, in December, 1885, the President stated the case and recommended early and appropriate action.[2]

Congress for several months took no heed of the President's suggestion. Then the Senate, Frye of Maine and other members who were expert in the art of "twisting the lion's tail" leading the discussion, contemptuously dismissed the proposal for international parleys in which they well understood that they would not have a part. With a view to making a disturbance which would be unfavorable to the President they, on April 13, 1886, formally declined to authorize the creation of the only agency which could have brought about a settlement.[3] Another fishing season was at hand and Canada and Newfoundland, which did not desire to have their ports near the Banks made the basis of operations of competitors, who would, in turn, give them no market for their fish,[4] prepared to enforce the restrictions of the treaty. A fleet of swift cruisers was fitted out to patrol the fishing grounds, and the summer was marked by seizures and detentions, a notable case being that of the *David J. Adams*, a schooner from Gloucester, which had entered Digby Gut for bait.[5] Other boats were warned off and subjected to "rude surveillance"[6]—all to the intense indignation of the American captains and crews, many of whom were talking truculently and had been seeking occasion to bring about collisions;[7]

---

[1] House Ex. Doc., 49th Cong. 2nd sess., no. 19, pp. 5–6; 199–210.

[2] Richardson, vol. viii, pp. 331–2. President Arthur had made a similar recommendation in 1883.—Ibid., p. 170.

[3] McPherson's Handbook for 1886, p. 216; Richardson, Messages and Papers, vol. viii, p. 499.

[4] Statement of Chamberlain in N. Y. Herald, March 3, 1888.

[5] House Ex. Doc., 49th Cong. 2nd sess., no. 19, pp. 127–36.

[6] Senate Ex. Doc., 49th Cong. 2nd sess., no. 55; cf. Senate Mis. Doc., 49th Cong. 2nd sess., no. 54.

[7] House Ex. Doc., 49th Cong. 2nd sess., no. 19, p. 124.

of the owners, resident in various ports of New England; and of the anti-British readers of American newspapers.[1] Incidents which were of little importance induced jingoist demonstrations until they attained the proportions of *casi belli*.[2]

By telegram and letter Mr. Bayard heard from the fishermen and their attorneys. They assembled affidavits which, during the summer of 1886, were poured in upon him, and he was urged to instant and vigorous action. Nor was he slow or reluctant to proceed. Two accomplished lawyers, George W. Biddle of Philadelphia and William L. Putnam of Portland, Maine, were retained to study the cases as they arose and to give the fishermen legal protection.[3] Protests, remonstrances and demands for explanation and apology marked correspondence which was industriously carried on in this country between the Secretary of State and the British Minister at Washington, and in England between Minister Phelps and the British Foreign Office.[4] The communications were filled with references to Canada's "surly hostility," to her "churlish and inhospitable treatment" of our fishermen, to the "rude acts" of her petty authorities, even to the "inhospitable and inhuman conduct" of certain officials when the right of obtaining water, so it was alleged, had been refused an American crew. Those responsible for such misconduct should be "rebuked" and "reprimanded."[5]

The administration of the laws in the British provinces, Mr. Bayard said, should not be "conducted in a punitive and hostile spirit," which could "only tend to induce acts of a retaliatory nature"; he protested against the "arbitrary, unlawful, unwarranted and unfriendly action" of the Canadian government,[6] and their "flagrant violations of treaty rights."[7] Nor would we, said Minister Phelps in London to Lord Rose-

---

[1] Cf. House Ex. Doc., 49th Cong., 2nd sess., no. 153, pp. 9–22; Senate Ex. Doc., 49th Cong. 1st sess., nos. 217 and 221; App. Ann. Cyclop. for 1886, pp. 131–3, 614.

[2] Henry Cabot Lodge at a political dinner said that "whenever the American flag on an American fishing smack is touched by a foreigner the great American heart is touched."— N. Y. Nation, May 19, 1887.

[3] House Ex. Doc., 49th Cong. 2nd sess., no. 19, p. 177.

[4] Senate Ex. Doc., 49th Cong. 1st sess., no. 217, p. 2.

[5] Ibid., p. 46. [6] Ibid., p. 14. [7] Ibid., p. 27.

bery, be "coerced by wanton injury" into the making of a new
treaty, and admitting fish into the United States free of duty,
which was the object in view, it was suspected, of such Canadians as were engaged in "harassing and annoying" our fishermen.[1] Very certainly the British government would be held
responsible for pecuniary losses suffered by our citizens. Indemnity would be required for damage ruthlessly done unoffending men.

The dominant note in Great Britain's replies was that we did
not clearly comprehend her political relations with her American
provinces and that we seemed to be denying the Dominion
of Canada the right to take any steps for the protection of
its interests under the convention of 1818. If the rather me-
dieval provisions of that convention were inconvenient it was
through no fault of Great Britain or the British people. They
had "not ceased to express their anxiety to commence negotiations" with a view to arriving at a mutually agreeable
settlement.[2]

Such attention to the national honor, in tones which should
have satisfied even our most active jingoes, called for public
appreciation. Instead the New York Tribune, when Secretary
Bayard had made the *ad interim* arrangement, postponing
the clash of interests in 1885, though this arrangement in
no way touched the tariff rates on fish, declared that he had
been "entrapped by the British minister." Being a "free
trader" he became the "willing dupe" of Great Britain. The
Yankee fishermen could take care of themselves if one or
two United States vessels of war should be sent north to
guard their rights. All they asked for was "protection in their
calling, protection in home markets, protection against foreign
diplomacy."[3] Outrage was not resented, ships of war were
not dispatched to the north to protect our fishing boats. Instead efforts were still being made to surrender everything
to an "arbitration commission."[4] A "patriotic secretary"

[1] Senate Ex. Doc., 49th Cong. 1st sess., no. 217, p. 137; cf. ibid., pp. 173–4.
[2] Cf. House Ex. Doc., 49th Cong. 2nd sess., no. 19, pp. 29–39, 53.
[3] N. Y. Tribune, Jan. 15, 1886; cf. ibid., Aug. 10, 1886.
[4] Ibid.

would have sprung to the nation's defense. As a "free trader" Mr. Bayard was attending to the interests of British manufacturers, rather than to those of the American people. It was his first concern to "break down the protective tariff." [1]

The correspondence was called for by the Senate repeatedly, but without avail. At the end of the year the papers were submitted to Congress. Mr. Bayard, writing to the President, declared that he would look to Great Britain for compensation for the loss and damage suffered by our citizens as a result of the "unwarrantable action" of the local authorities in Canada in the fishing season of 1886; he suggested the appointment of a commission to take and record proofs of injuries of claimants for proper presentation to Her Majesty's government. [2] President Cleveland in alluding to the "unfriendly and unwarranted treatment" of our fishermen on their voyages in the north supported the Secretary of State in his request for preliminary action looking to pecuniary demands upon Great Britain. [3]

The New Englanders did not cease to tell the Republican politicians that they were in debt, that they had been ruined by the Treaty of Washington. The Canadians had prospered with "free fish." Their fleet had grown; their boats were bringing in larger and larger catches to glut the American market. [4] It was their aim to "bully" us until they should "wipe out" our Atlantic fisheries. [5] The Gloucestermen said that there should be a tariff on fish just as there were duties on beef, pork and potatoes. [6] The fishermen in the British provinces lived "coarse." Masters of boats in Nova Scotia and Newfoundland paid lower wages to their men; they built their vessels "cheaper" than similar craft could be built in New England. [7] Being in no degree an "infant industry," since fishing was one of the most ancient of the various pursuits by which men

---

[1] N. Y. Tribune, May 28, 1887.
[2] House Reports, 49th Cong. 2nd sess., no. 19, p. 2.
[3] Ibid., p. 1.
[4] Senate Reports, 49th Cong. 2nd sess., no. 1683, p. 51.
[5] House Ex. Doc., 49th Cong. 2nd sess., no. 19, p. 174.
[6] Senate Reports, 49th Cong. 2nd sess., no. 1684, p. 47.
[7] Ibid., p. 38; cf. ibid., pp. 52–3, 111, 123, 149.

on this continent strove to make a living,[1] it was necessary for those who now were so clamorous for government benefits to take refuge behind "pauper labor."

In answer to the insistencies of the fishing people the Republican Senate authorized its Committee on Foreign Relations to hear their views.[2] A subcommittee, dominated by Edmunds and Frye, during the summer of 1886, visited Boston, Portland, Provincetown and Gloucester to make inquiries and take testimony. What we had received under the treaty, it appeared, was no equivalent for the loss of the "home market" for fish. No one now needed to go ashore for bait; American boats carried clams with them, or caught squid on the Banks.[3] Inshore fishing was poor. Sometimes mackerel came within the three mile limit, but for a long time these had been caught in purse seines. It was dangerous to cast these expensive nets near the rocks, and it was never done.[4] There was, in fact, if our excited fishermen were to be believed, no occasion for any of them to visit the shore on their northern voyages. They asked no privileges and wanted none. The master of a boat at Provincetown, when questioned by Senator Frye as to what he would like Congress to do with Canada for his benefit, replied, "Blow it up with dynamite."[5]

But the facts seemed to belie the allegations of the Yankee boatmen that they did not need to go ashore, since no less than 117 American vessels had entered Canadian ports in the summer of 1886 to involve themselves in trouble with the local authorities (and this was far from a complete list),[6] while many more had put in, without bringing into question the provisions of the old treaty of 1818, or encountering official protest.[7]

---

[1] Mr. Bayard reminded Sackville-West in the course of the correspondence between them on the fishery question that when the northeastern coast of America was wrested from France for Great Britain that end was effected in large measure "by the valor and enterprise of New England fishermen." —Senate Reports, 49th Cong. 2nd sess., no. 1683, p. 52.

[2] Ibid., p. 1.

[3] Ibid., p. 45.

[4] Ibid., pp. xiii–xiv, 40, 42.

[5] Ibid., p. 55.

[6] House Reports, 49th Cong. 2nd sess., no. 4087, pp. 27–34.

[7] Cf. Senate Mis. Doc., 50th Cong. 1st sess., no. 109, p. 59.

Instead of conversation and correspondence in the interest
of neighborliness the protectionists and the jingoes were agreed
that we should retaliate. England, said Senator Ingalls of
Kansas, has always been "the ruffian, the coward and the
bully among the nations of the earth." Wherever there was
a helpless people she appeared for "rapacity, plunder and
conquest." Her history for years had been "a record of crimes
against the human race." Her conduct toward us had been
"characterized by jealousy and malevolence from the beginning of our national existence." [1]

The Republican Senate Committee on Foreign Relations presented its report. The President should have the power, and it
should be his duty, to make rejoinder in kind. When our vessels
were denied fair treatment Canada's should not be permitted
to enter our ports. When our rights were not respected we
should prohibit the entry into this country of Canadian fish. [2]
The Democratic House Committee on Foreign Affairs, not to
be beaten in the game, went farther, and said, on January 18,
1887, that the British crown had practically proclaimed nonintercourse, since in Canada, as the treaty of 1818 was being
interpreted, permits to "touch and trade" given to our fishing boats were not recognized. A vessel bearing an American
flag, if its business were fishing, might not go into a bay in
Canada to bury a dead man, though in life he had been a British
subject. It was "a policy of threat and coercion" which should
be "instantly and summarily dealt with." We, on our side,
should answer by proclaiming complete nonintercourse in our
ports against Canadian vessels, and we should exclude her
fish and other products from our markets. [3]

The two houses passed their respective bills, the Senate
on January 24 and the House of Representatives on Feb. 23,
1887. [4] In general the House proposed the absolute cessation
of commerce by water and land, including the passage of railway trains across the border, while the Senate, unwilling to

[1] App. Ann. Cyclop. for 1887, p. 179.
[2] Senate Reports, 49th Cong. 2nd sess., no. 1683, pp. xv–xvi.
[3] House Reports, 49th Cong. 2nd sess., no. 3648, pp. 18–9.
[4] McPherson's Handbook for 1888, pp. 38–42.

give the President such "enormous power," emphasized the
trade in fish, particularly espousing the cause of the littoral
population of New England.[1] The House, at length, receded
from its position as to the nature of the countervailing operation, the Republicans gaining enough Democratic votes to
pass the Senate bill,[2] and the President, at the end of the session, in March, 1887, was authorized by Congress, when our
fishing vessels were "unjustly vexed and harassed," a phrase
frequently repeated in the law, to retaliate by proclamation.[3]

A most unpleasant duty was imposed upon Mr. Cleveland,
which he promptly told the fishing men, who addressed him,
that he would exercise, not for their particular advantage,
but for the "general welfare." [4] The bill was contrived to
relieve the Congress, which had passed it, from further responsibility, and to lay the burden at Mr. Cleveland's door. However
he should use his new power the measure was calculated to
"vex and harass" him as much, or more, than any Gloucester-
man had ever been exacerbated on summer-time excursions
to the fishing banks.[5]

The President's struggles with the office hunters had not
always had entirely successful outcome in the view of the
civil service reformers. Schurz and the Mugwumps were un-
sparing critics. They found some of Cleveland's appointments
not such as they could approve.[6] From time to time men unworthy of high trust were brought into the public service and
were rather obstinately kept in it against good advice. Plainly
the appointees were very often not the superiors, if, indeed,

[1] Cf. N. Y. Nation, Feb. 17, 1887.
[2] The vote was 148 to 136.—McPherson's Handbook for 1888, p. 41;
Senate Reports, 49th Cong. 2nd sess., no. 1981; Senate Mis. Doc., 50th
Cong. 1st sess., no. 109, pp. 76–8.
[3] App. Ann. Cyclop. for 1887, pp. 181–2.
[4] McPherson's Handbook for 1888, p. 42.
[5] Cf. N. Y. Nation, Feb. 3 and March 10, 1887. Mr. Cleveland's failure
to retaliate, and to bring the two countries to the verge of war, led the
New York Tribune to speak on February 25, 1888, of the "disgraceful
sacrifice of American rights by a British administration," of the "unfaithful
administration" of Mr. Cleveland, etc., etc.
[6] Cf. report of committee of National Civil Service Reform League, ibid.,
Aug. 11, 1887; Writings of Schurz, vol. iv, pp. 402, 405, 407–8, 418–9,
429–30, 435–9, 447–51, 457, 464–70.

they were the equals, of those who had been displaced. It was difficult for a long time to shake the President's trust in Randall who, although in no wise representative of the Democratic party in Pennsylvania, presumed to act as the distributor of patronage in that state.[1] In Maryland and Indiana, where the Democratic "machines" were shamelessly sordid, the leaders had deceived the President, and their demands had been too freely met to the dishonor of the government.[2] But it was true, as all competent observers who had at heart the improvement of the civil service would agree, that the cause had been substantially advanced by Mr. Cleveland. When his term was half done it was stated that at least 30,000 and, perhaps, 40,000 of the 120,000 Federal offices were still occupied by Republicans. In two years he had removed only 23 out of every 100 Republican postmasters. A third of the foreign consuls who had been serving under Arthur were undisturbed and remained in the service. Large customhouses and post offices were being conducted upon business principles. The departments at Washington, in the main, were manned and administered efficiently by civil servants who were earning their salaries instead of taking their pay as a gift or bounty for something done at home around the polling places two years ago, or what it was hoped that they would do, in like ways, "to save the party" two years hence.[3] The President had yielded too often to the spoilsmen in his party, but the impression he had made upon the country, said the New York Nation, was that of an "honest man" who was "trying to do his duty." He retained the admiration of the Independents. They, in general, remained his friends. He had made mistakes. He had turned at times from the straight way but, "on the whole," he had held "pretty steadily to his course," and had made "decided progress." [4]

[1] See Cleveland Papers for many protests against appointments made at Randall's dictation.

[2] Cf. N. Y. Nation, July 28, 1887; Writings of Schurz, vol. iv, pp. 454–5, 471–2, 474–5. For Indiana see W. D. Foulke, Fighting the Spoilsmen, pp. 37–45.

[3] Cf. Writings of Schurz, vol. iv, p. 441.

[4] N. Y. Nation, March 10, July 28 and Aug. 25, 1887; cf. N. Y. Times, June 15, 1887.

Lamar assured Schurz in October, 1886, that the President would not "swerve one inch from his policy." The country could never get "a more sincere" civil service reformer, nor one who with deep-rooted convictions combined "such intrepidity of character."[1] Leaders in the party who came to him for benefits knew better than Schurz of his resisting powers. Abram S. Hewitt had made acquaintance with them. William M. Springer, of some influence in Congress, befriended a young man who had been appointed chief justice of New Mexico and who had been suspended for associating himself with Dorsey. To every appeal in this behalf the President was unyielding.[2] Governor Hoadly of Ohio was a friend. "Keep on as you are doing and concede to spoilsmen only what you really cannot avoid," he said. Pursuit of this policy would give him "a place in history as the best of Presidents."[3] Hoadly made a suggestion for an appointment which was definitely declined on the ground that it was one unfit to be made.

A cashier in the San Francisco subtreasury, an "old, experienced and safe official" was to be dismissed to make way for the brother-in-law of a Congressman. "I don't exactly see," the President wrote to Secretary Manning, "why my wishes in this matter, coupled as they are with a regard for the public welfare, should be put aside to gratify somebody belonging to the class of whom we so freely conversed last night."[4]

It was easy to stir the evil temper of the followers of Blaine in the Republican party, and the angry spoilsmen and silverites in the Democratic party.[5] Mr. Cleveland had suffered sorely from the newspapers and he was not one to submit quietly to unwarranted abuse. He deplored their want of respect for the truth, their disregard and neglect of their large responsibilities with reference to the formation of correct judg-

---

[1] Mayes, Life of Lamar, p. 488.
[2] Cleveland Papers.
[3] June 29, 1886, in ibid.
[4] Jan. 11, 1886, in ibid.
[5] They had much in common. "The working politicians are members of a guild that recognizes no differences in party and is bound together by the cohesive power of public plunder."—Silas W. Burt to Lamont, Jan. 14, 1887, in ibid.

ments in the people. He had now and again taken them to task for their ignorance and malevolence, as well as for policies which lifted their own commercial ends above the public welfare.

Of Keppler of Puck it had been alleged by a Republican newspaper that his support of the administration had been affected by failure to obtain political preferment for himself or his friends. He asked the President for a denial of the charge that he had sought office in return for whatever he may have done for the cause in 1884. "I don't think there ever was a time," Mr. Cleveland remarked on this occasion, "when newspaper lying was so general and so mean as at present, and there never was a country under the sun where it flourished as it does in this. The falsehoods daily spread before the people in our newspapers," he continued, "while they are proofs of the mental ingenuity of those engaged in newspaper work, are insults to the American love for decency and fair play of which we boast." He said that the publication of which Keppler complained was "entirely and utterly false," and he hoped that such a statement as he now made to this effect might be "sufficiently explicit." [1]

The President again found the opportunity to read a lesson to the press at Cambridge on the occasion of the celebration of the 250th anniversary of the founding of Harvard College.[2] He was in friendly surroundings, among men who thought as he. His allusions to "unjust and false accusations" and "malicious slanders invented for the purpose of undermining the popular trust in the administration of their government," to "the silly, mean and cowardly lies that are every day found in the columns of certain newspapers which violate every instinct of American manliness and in ghoulish glee desecrate every sacred relation of private life" met hearty and enthusiastic response.[3]

But the more he condemned their "lying" the more vio-

[1] McElroy, Grover Cleveland, vol. i, p. 148.
[2] N. Y. Nation, Nov. 18, 1886.
[3] N. Y. Tribune, Nov. 9, 1886; N. Y. Nation, Nov. 18, 1886.

lently did those editors who thought it to their advantage to
follow these tactics assail him.[1] Two journals in particular,
the New York Tribune, eager to speak for Blaine, and the
New York Sun, still the agent of Tammany and of other sinister
interests, both smartly edited, led the opposition press. They
had used every weapon of attack upon Mr. Cleveland during
the campaign in 1884, and had continued their abuse and
ridicule on every available occasion.[2] They set the fashion
for newspaper writing, consciously or unconsciously, in all
parts of the country. Another New York newspaper, the
World, in its active search for a field that it could profitably
occupy, usually esteemed it to be to its advantage to make
the President a butt for criticism.[3]

The truth was that the New York newspapers had got themselves into close quarters in a contest for "circulation," and,
if they were free in their allusions to individuals, they at the
same time, in the exchange of impertinencies, did not spare
their rivals of the craft. They excelled in calling one another
names. "Ananias," "Judas," "Flopover," and "the Bilk"[4]
were appellatives which disinterested observers would agree
were not inappropriately given to the "metropolitan dailies"
to which they were applied. They had reduced their prices
in 1883. By a return to higher prices in 1887—the Herald
would hereafter be three instead of two cents a copy—it was
believed, or at any rate hoped, that the chase for an enlarged

[1] McElroy, Grover Cleveland, vol. i, pp. 147–8.

[2] On a day in March, 1887, the Sun published on its editorial page
an alleged allusion of a United States senator to Mr. Cleveland as
"that d——d old hind quarter of beef up at the White House."—
(Quoted in N. Y. World, March 28, 1887.) Day after day its editorial
page was filled with impertinences concerning the private life of Mrs.
Cleveland.

[3] Cf. N. Y. World, March 29 and April 6, 1887. It may be said for the
World that its criticism was not personal. It was ingratiating itself in a
search for readers as the "people's friend," and pretended to knowledge of
policies (not socialistic) which would be good for the "people," in smashing
"trusts" and corporations, not in possession of the President. In the West
Henry Watterson, to whom happiness was impossible unless he was in the
public eye, used the Louisville Courier Journal in opposition to the administration.—Cf. McElroy, Grover Cleveland, vol. i, pp. 265–6.

[4] Cf. N. Y. Nation, Nov. 10, 1887.

reading class might end, and attention would again be given to "the graver concerns of the community," instead of "its foulnesses, and follies, and sillinesses." [1]

The personal relations of Mr. Manning and the President were not to be pleasant if the activity of mischief makers could bring so much about. The Secretary of the Treasury, the only "Tilden man" in the cabinet, Tilden's friends said that he was "the only Democrat in the cabinet," [2] had performed the duties of his office, it was agreed, in an intelligent way. His attitude toward the money question commended him to men of the best judgment, but it was clear that he continued to have views concerning the civil service which were at variance with the President's. In no way was this want of harmony so impressively shown as in relation to the collectorship of the port of New York, that office which had been a storm center for so many years. Manning and the faction which he represented in the state desired the appointment of Hubert O. Thompson.[3] Nothing would do but that this man should have a place controlling so much valuable patronage. The President quite positively refused to do as he was bidden, and chose a business man named Hedden who had hitherto lived apart from politics.[4] Though there had been reason to expect useful service from the appointee his conduct in the selection of subordinates, in disregard of the plain provisions of the Pendleton act, brought upon him and the President charges of bad faith.[5] He was "weak" and he had manifestly fallen under the influence of designing persons.[6] Cleveland addressed personal letters to him. "The ordinary recommendations which are presented by those seeking office," the President wrote him, "are but snares and delusions." [7] Kind

[1] N. Y. Nation, Dec. 1, 1887. A prophecy which, however, was not fulfilled.
[2] Bigelow, Letters and Memorials of Tilden, p. 719.
[3] Hudson, Random Recollections, pp. 257–8.
[4] Ibid., p. 270.
[5] McElroy, vol. i, pp. 149–54; Writings of Schurz, vol. iv, pp. 405, 407–8.
[6] Cf. Burt to Cleveland in Cleveland Papers, Aug. 12, 1886.
[7] Cleveland to Hedden, Oct. 14, 1885, in ibid.

and fatherly advice failing, the collector was, after a while, obliged to make way for a more suitable person.[1] When this time came Manning again insisted that Thompson be installed in the place. Cleveland remained obdurate on that point and Manning became so angry that he spoke of resigning and of making public a statement of his reasons for doing so, thus creating, in the state of feeling at the time, a dangerous rupture in the party in New York state. On his return to the Treasury Department, after a conversation on this subject with the President, he was stricken with apoplexy, brought on, it was believed, by his excitement of mind.[2] Retirement must follow now, it seemed, on the ground of broken health and incapacity for the performance of his duties. But, if he should go, his friends would hope to involve him in a controversy calculated to embarrass the administration. The President was on his guard, especially as Manning, after a time, gave signs of "going to pieces" mentally as well as physically.[3] It was a delicate situation. Smith Weed was deputed to procure a letter of resignation from the Secretary of the Treasury who, it appeared, was not willing to sign such a paper unless it should have the approval of Manton Marble, the influence which, it was on good ground suspected, had been at work in the case, and which would be exerted to discomfit the President and hurt his position in the party. After much parleying by Marble, Manning and Weed a letter was finally drafted with the omission of phrases which indicated the ill treatment of the Secretary of the Treasury. However, not enough of the offensive matter had been removed to satisfy Mr. Cleveland and further negotiation was necessary before the letter was ready for use.[4] Offered in May, 1886, the President, in generous and appreciative terms, asked that the resignation be withheld until August, and later he extended the

[1] Cf. Writings of Schurz, vol. iv, p. 452; Burt to Cleveland, Oct. 23, 1886, in Cleveland Papers.
[2] Hudson, pp. 270–71.
[3] Letter to Lamont, March 16, 1887, in Cleveland Papers.
[4] See memorandum of Smith Weed in Manning Papers. Various drafts of the letter, with interlineations in Cleveland's hand, are to be found in the Cleveland Papers.

day until October when, after a rest, Manning could determine whether he would be able to return to his duties. At that time, as a result of personal conferences, he was requested to remain a little longer, and he continued nominally to hold the post until March 4, 1887, upon the adjournment of Congress. For many months his assistant, Charles S. Fairchild, a "genuine" civil service reformer, well known as such, who in due time became the honored head of the department, performed the duties of the office,[1] Cleveland all the while writing the kindliest of letters to Manning telling him of the proceedings of cabinet meetings, of the movements of his old colleagues and treating him as one of the "official household." [2]

There had been signs of an improved spirit in the sections made hostile by the war and a degree of magnanimity was coming to be evidenced in many quarters. Now and again a group of Northern soldiers would address a Confederate regiment and tender it a flag which had been captured on some Southern field.[3] An Alabama regiment restored a flag to Connecticut.[4] In July, 1887, on the anniversary of the battle there would be a reunion at Gettysburg of the survivors of the body of men who had made the memorable charge with Pickett, and of the Pennsylvania troops who had turned back that thrust into the Northern line.[5] It was proposed in Philadelphia that three flags taken on that day now be, on the very ground, returned to the hands of those who had borne them so far into the heart of the North.[6]

A competitive "drill" of militia companies from many states would be held in Washington at the end of May, 1887. One day the assembled troops passed before President Cleveland and the governors of several Northern and Southern states. Negroes had entered the contest, on which account a white organization in Alabama had refused to come to Washington.[7]

[1] Cf. N. Y. Nation, April 7, 1887.
[2] Cleveland Papers.
[3] Cf. N. Y. Nation, June 23 and 30, 1887.
[4] Sep. 6, 1887, in Cleveland Papers.
[5] N. Y. Nation, June 23 and July 7, 1887.
[6] Ibid., June 23 and July 7, 1887.
[7] Ibid., April 7, 1887.

Companies from Vicksburg and Memphis, after coming, withdrew from the parade because "niggers" were in line.[1] The "drill," nevertheless, was held to be in the interest of better intersectional feeling, and indicative of growing good comradeship.

John Sherman, than whom few Republican leaders were more prone "to wave the bloody shirt,"[2] having been invited to speak at Nashville uttered some generous sentiments which were not forgotten, though to meet the necessities of the stump in the North, in his eagerness to distance Blaine, as the candidate for President in 1888, he soon again steeled his heart against kindly impulses.[3] Hoar in Massachusetts, usually as savage in mien as Sherman, welcomed a company of Confederate veterans from Richmond in Fanueil Hall in Boston with gracious tributes to their bravery in war and their virtues in peace.[4] The President had been invited to attend the unveiling of a statue of Calhoun at Charleston. He made his excuses.[5] Lamar, the orator on that occasion, in finding one of the war's fruits to be "the indissolubility of the Union and the universality of American freedom," drew forth expressions of warm approval in the North.[6] The President had been asked to attend the annual "Encampment" of the Grand Army of the Republic, which was to be held in St. Louis at the end of September, and he had accepted. As never before there was reason to suppose that wounds were healing, that at last a spirit of amity and good fellowship was spreading over the land.

But the disillusionment was near at hand and it was rude. That Cleveland himself had not fought in the war, but had

[1] The commander of the "Vicksburg Southrons" explained the action of his company. It was due to the "niggers" from Virginia who marched in front of his men. Being "Southern gentlemen" they could not be seen with those whom they considered below them in the "social scale." (N. Y. Times, May 26, 1887.) As a douceur, in the evening, President Cleveland shook hands with every member of the colored company which had been treated with so much disrespect.—N. Y. Nation, June 2, 1887.

[2] Often called the "bloody shirt senator."—Cleveland Papers.

[3] N. Y. Nation, June 9, 1887.

[4] Ibid., June 23, 1887.

[5] N. Y. Tribune, April 23, 1887.

[6] N. Y. Nation, June 23, 1887; Mayes, Life of Lamar, p. 784.

hired a "substitute" no reader of a gazette was permitted to forget. He had gone fishing on "Decoration Day."[1] That sooner or later he would pay the "rebel debt" and make some bargain with "Jeff" Davis to undo all that had been done in the war was, by the New York Tribune, put into as many silly and inflammable minds as could be reached by the innuendo of its industrious writers. The veto of the Dependent Pension bill reached the ugly side of the professional "old soldier." Resentment was expressed in speech and print. A man in Iowa who had come to the highest office in the direction of the affairs of the Grand Army in that state, who had been shown out of the service, it was said, for blackmailing a cotton planter and for similar conduct unbecoming a soldier,[2] declared that the posts over which he presided would insult the President, if he came to St. Louis.[3] Mr. Cleveland would certainly be made to understand in what disapprobation he was held by Union soldiers. His life might be in danger, if he should attend the "Encampment," the expression of a sentiment regarding the Commander-in-Chief of the Army and Navy of the United States which General Sherman took occasion to denounce as "monstrous."[4]

The Adjutant-General, in April, had made a proposal to Secretary of War Endicott who, in turn, addressed the President. In June the order was published. It authorized the return of flags to the states whose regiments had borne them. These flags, packed in boxes, were stored in attic and cellar rooms of the War Department, some of them of Northern military organizations, captured in battle and recovered at the fall of the Confederacy, others of the Southern armies, taken by the North during the conflict.[5] It was meant to be a graceful act. The Adjutant-General expressed the thought in mind in clear terms. In spite of the *impasse* induced by the presence

---

[1] N. Y. World, June 1 and 17, 1887. He was spending a vacation in the Adirondacks.
[2] N. Y. Nation, July 21 and Aug. 4, 1887.
[3] Ibid., July 14, 1887.
[4] Ibid., June 16, 1887; N. Y. Times, June 13, 1887.
[5] Cf. House Ex. Doc., 50th Cong. 1st sess., no. 163.

of the negroes, he had been encouraged by the fraternal spirit
recently exhibited at Washington on the occasion of the coming
together of Southern and Northern militia companies for the
"National Drill." [1] It had not been a war with foreign enemies;
anyhow it had ended twenty years ago, and South and North
were again in a common Union, "treading the broader road
to a glorious future." [2] Letters were prepared and sent to
the various governors, whereupon such an outcry arose as
had not been heard since the time of Andrew Johnson. In
the commotion directed by the press, with aid from every
Grand Army post room and Republican campaign club and
committee room in the North and West, even sane men lost
their reason. The tirade was led by General Lucius Fairchild
of Wisconsin. He was the guest of some Grand Army men in
New York City when the news reached him. He spoke plainly.
"May God palsy the hand that wrote the order," he exclaimed;
"may God palsy the brain that conceived it, and may God
palsy the tongue that dictated it!" [3] Foraker, the fire-eating
governor of Ohio, sprang into the breach. Words could not
express the indignation of the patriotic people of his state.
No flag captured by Ohio troops should be returned to rebel
hands. Legal action would be taken to prevent the carrying
out of such a scheme to extenuate "the crime of the age." [4]
The Republican governors of Kansas, Nebraska, Wisconsin
and other states forwarded their frantic protests. [5]

Indeed letters and telegrams came to the President from
all sides. "The bloody emblems of a treason that cost so many
precious lives" should be held—they were proof of "rebellion
conquered and Union triumphant." The proposal to surrender
them could be viewed only with "indignation and abhorrence."
An Iowa post wrote in "burning letters of red on blood red
paper" the resolutions which it had passed, inclosed them in

[1] Cf. Adjutant-General Drum in N. Y. World, June 17, 1887.
[2] McPherson's Handbook for 1888, p. 100.
[3] N. Y. World, June 16 and 17, 1887.
[4] Ibid., June 16 and 17, 1887; cf. McElroy, Grover Cleveland, vol. i,
pp. 206–8.
[5] Cleveland Papers.

a blood red envelope and tied them with a crimson ribbon.[1] The President was asked to recall his "infamous order." Adjutant-General Drum should be dismissed from the service; for him to continue in his office would be an "insult to all old soldiers." Others demanded the resignation of the Secretary of War.[2]

The New York Tribune filled its columns with articles headed, "The attempted rape of the flags"; "The nation ablaze with wrath"; "The old slave whip cracking again"; "Now pay the rebel debt"; "Slapping the veterans in the face," and so on.[3]

Under such a fire the President on June 16th revoked the order. The matter before had been presented to him orally. Upon further consideration he was convinced that such a disposition of the captured banners as had been proposed was not authorized by law or justified as an executive act. A measure of this kind should originate with Congress. The Adjutant-General, therefore, withdrew the offer to the governors [4] and the popular temper was allowed to cool, though not until the President, on July 4th, as an outcome of the excitement, had announced his reconsideration of his acceptance of the invitation to attend the "Encampment" in St. Louis. If he were to go, he should bear with him "the people's highest office," the "dignity" of which it was his duty to "protect." He knew that what had been recently said was not a general expression of the feeling of the membership of the Grand Army, but he must conclude that there were some in it who were determined on this occasion to denounce him and his official acts, and it was his wish that they should be at liberty to do so "unrestrained" by his presence.[5]

[1] Cleveland Papers.
[2] Ibid.
[3] Issue of June 17, 1887.
[4] McPherson's Handbook for 1888, pp. 100–01; McElroy, Grover Cleveland, vol. i, pp. 206–7.
[5] N. Y. Times, July 8, 1887; N. Y. Nation, July 14, 1887. The reunion of the "Blue and Gray" was held at Gettysburg in July, but the Union soldiers of kindly and forgiving hearts, who had proposed a return of flags on that occasion, were silent.—N. Y. Times, July 4 and 5, 1887; N. Y. Nation, July 7, 1887.

The motion had come from the wrong side. General Grant might have returned the standards. Republicans could do so, but Cleveland and the Democrats must choose their ways cautiously.[1] It was clear enough that a great case was being made out against the President and his party for presentation to the people in the following year.[2]

Late in August Pennsylvania, Ohio and West Virginia posts paraded at Wheeling. They came to a banner bearing a portrait of Cleveland and the words, "God bless our President, Commander-in-Chief of our Army and Navy." Most of them swerved into the gutter to avoid passing under it, and furled or trailed their colors in further exhibition of their state of mind.[3]

The citizens of St. Louis were instantly aroused. The "bigots" and "fanatics" of the Grand Army must be rebuked; the city would not be deprived of a visit from the President. A "monster mass meeting" was held on July 8th. The mayor, David R. Francis, presided and, amid enthusiastic demonstrations, a delegation of fifty was appointed to proceed to Washington to invite Mr. and Mrs. Cleveland to come to St. Louis early in October, after the old soldiers had made their departure, and to participate in the festivities which in the autumn annually directed attention to the city. Indeed invitations poured into the White House from all directions. Mayors, boards of trade, committees and individuals bade him visit their towns and cities. A number of persons who had climbed to the summit of Pike's Peak met and adopted resolutions inviting him to Colorado. Others urged him to extend his journey to the Pacific coast.[4] It was clear that some care must be given to the choice of a route. If the President were to go to St. Louis he must visit Chicago. If he should honor the St. Louis Fair by his presence he must visit the Piedmont Exposition at Atlanta. When his plans were made known he was the

[1] N. Y. Nation, July 7, 1887.
[2] Richardson, vol. viii, pp. 578–9; McPherson's Handbook for 1888, pp. 100–01.
[3] N. Y. Nation, Sep. 1, 1887; McElroy, Grover Cleveland, vol. i, pp. 215–6.
[4] Cleveland Papers.

subject of new importunities from places on the way, a little beyond his destination and north and south of his line of progress.

The old soldiers in the posts wanted pensions—so much was clear. The New York Tribune questioned them and, although they were advised not to reply to the inquiry they generally did so, with expressions of a "unanimous" desire, not only for the "Dependent," or "Subsequent Disability," bill which the President had vetoed, but for doles based on service, thus dispensing with the duty of furnishing with the application for "relief" proofs of any kind, except of enrollment in the army or navy of the United States.[1] Their leaders sought lucrative political offices, and they for some years had been looking upon preferment as almost a right. In every post room the air was astir with discussion of candidates for the shrievalty, the mayoralty, commissionerships, governorships, seats in Congress, the Presidency and Vice-Presidency of the United States. But the more intelligent elements in the "G.A.R." clearly saw that their spokesmen had put it in a bad light. Some of the partisan ardor of the organization was spent, some of its untempered hostility to the President had cooled before the host met for the annual business of social reunion and the passage of resolutions.

At this meeting they again called upon Congress to enact a Dependent bill so similar to, as to be indistinguishable from, the one which Cleveland had vetoed. But they did not approve the scheme for pensions based upon mere service, though a persistent minority organized a "National Service Pension Association" to push that scheme until it should become a law.[2] The delegates at St. Louis defeated a resolution, which some hotheads had offered, condemning the President for violating, by his veto, a "pledge made to the soldiers when they flocked to the standard of the country at the time of her greatest peril," for inflicting "irreparable cruelty upon those who should be the objects of the tenderest consideration,"

---

[1] Cf. N. Y. Nation, July 21, Aug. 11 and 18, Sep. 15, Oct. 6, 1887.
[2] Ibid., Oct. 6, 1887.

and more in a like sense.[1] They could have known, had they been minded to inform themselves, that Mr. Cleveland had been as warm and effective a friend of the "old soldier" as his Republican predecessors in the President's office, for in the first two years of his administration he had approved 77 more private pension bills than Grant and Hayes together in their twelve years in office, and 127 more than Garfield and Arthur had approved in four years. Finding 345,125 names on the pension rolls on July 1, 1885, there were, two years later, on July 1, 1887, 402,000, a gain of 56,875 as compared with 41,467 for the preceding two year period under "Republican rule."[2]

While the old soldiers were striking their tents at St. Louis the President and Mrs. Cleveland were speeding westward on their special train. They left Washington on the morning of September 30th and proceeded by way of Pittsburgh, taking part in informal receptions at their stopping places until after nightfall. Dawn the next day found them in western Ohio. Crowds again appeared at all the stations. At Indianapolis a halt was made for a parade through the streets, a reception and a luncheon. The President's arrival in St. Louis awakened much pride and enthusiasm. Banners bidding him welcome, muslin transparencies on which were printed "Public Office Is a Public Trust," portraits of himself on "cathedral glass," arches, colored lights were seen on every side. He and Mrs. Cleveland were driven amid acclaiming crowds to the residence of Mayor Francis, where they remained over Sunday in readiness for the pleasant experiences soon to follow.

On Monday they visited the fair grounds, attended receptions, viewed parades. Much of the same nature followed on Tuesday, and, just before leaving for Chicago, on the evening of that day, they witnessed the pageant and the ball of the Veiled Prophets. The following week-end found them at the home of Postmaster-General Vilas at Madison, Wis.[3] Through St.

[1] N. Y. Times, Oct. 1, 1887; N. Y. Nation, Oct. 6, 1887.
[2] From memoranda in Cleveland Papers, quoted in McElroy, Grover Cleveland, vol. i, pp. 200–01.
[3] The warmest of the friends of the President who wrote to Bissell on

Paul and Minneapolis they went to Sioux City to see a "corn palace," and on to St. Joseph and Kansas City, entering the South at Memphis, and stopping for the next Sunday at the stock farm, near Nashville, of ex-Senator Jackson of Tennessee. Their engagements now carried them, by way of Chattanooga, to Atlanta, where at the capital of the "New South," which was celebrating its rebirth of spirit by an exposition, they had a memorable reception.[1] After a short excursion farther south to visit Montgomery, in Alabama, Mr. and Mrs. Cleveland, weary of the crowding and handshaking, of banquets, receptions and parades, the train filled with trophies and mementos put into their hands along the way, reached Washington on Saturday, October 22nd, after an absence of three weeks, during which time they had passed through, or entered the limits of, nearly twenty states. The journey was properly held to be nonpartisan. The receiving committees were made up of Republicans as well as of Democrats. Those who had been Union men in the North, those who had been Confederates in the South united in acclaiming the President and his gracious young wife. Mr. Cleveland's many speeches had been creditable to him and worthy of the high office which he held. His bearing had been dignified, his tone patriotic, his counsel statesmanlike.[2]

The elections which soon followed were without great significance. The Democrats carried New York. Republican governors were reëlected in Ohio and Massachusetts. Neither party could reach any other conclusion than that the contest of the following year would be close and bitter. It was already clear that Cleveland and his advisers had the election of 1888 in view, and manifest attempts to propitiate influential groups of men in the party, who had expressed open dissatisfaction with the administration because it did not forward their mercenary designs, were disquieting to the Independents. What seemed to be necessary from the party standpoint gave little pleasure to many excellent citizens who had supported Cleveland

August 14, 1886, "He [Vilas] is one of the most complete men, mentally, morally and politically, I ever met."—Cleveland Papers.

[1] N. Y. Times, Oct. 19, 1887.
[2] Cf. N. Y. Nation, Oct. 27, 1887.

in 1884, and desired the opportunity of cordially doing so again. But whatever the Mugwumps and high-minded Democrats may have thought of his gestures in encouragement of such state machines as Hill's in New York and Gorman's in Maryland, few could do else than wonder whether he had real concern for his own or the party's future when he, in December, 1887, in his message to the new Congress took an irrevocable stand in reference to the tariff.

The silver question at the moment need not be disturbed. The President had given the country his advice about it, pointing to the dangers which resided in such a currency system. But both parties had declined, in spite of the counsel of the wisest of their leaders, to repeal the silver purchase law, and, because of a rising demand for silver certificates issued on the basis of coin deposits, and recently in smaller and more acceptable denominations, alarm about the immediate future was allayed.[1] The silver men, including the miners with bullion to sell and the bimetallic theorists—the "debtor class" at the moment cared little about the matter—still abated none of their faith in an international agreement. To convince them that the administration was not unmindful of the subject the President, in 1885, as we have seen, had sent Manton Marble abroad to survey the field; in 1887 he commissioned Edward Atkinson, who wrote industriously and with authority on economical subjects, to conduct a similar investigation in Europe. Mr. Atkinson stated conclusions which entirely agreed with Mr. Marble's, and which were so generally accepted by intelligent men everywhere as to make particular inquiry and report unnecessary. It was again clear enough that the countries of Europe had no intention whatever of returning to the silver standard. Mr. Atkinson furthermore declared that no one except a few theorists was giving any consideration to the subject, and that there was no group with which a similar body of men in America could coöperate to gain the end in view.[2]

[1] Cf. N. Y. Nation, Nov. 17, 1887, and April 12, 1888; A. D. Noyes, Forty Years of Am. Finance, pp. 106–8, 111–2.

[2] Senate Ex. Doc., 50th Cong. 1st sess., no. 34; N. Y. Nation, Dec. 29, 1887.

The currency having been put aside for a time the hour seemed to have come for the President to discuss the tariff. Thus far he had spoken cautiously. He had given little attention to the subject and had confessed to friends a good deal of ignorance of its intricacies.[1] His declarations had been rather casual and such as should have been satisfactory to the Republicans who had approved and subscribed to the findings of the Tariff Commission of 1882.[2] Indeed candid and well informed men of both parties, not so long since, were agreed that the "war taxes" of the Morrill tariff law should be revised. The platforms of both parties in 1884 called for reduction for the relief of the taxpayers.[3] But lately almost no Republicans, except a few in the Northwest, indorsed such sentiments.

The manufacturing industries were organized, and they were gaining strength. The owners and managers knew their power; their alliance with the Republican politicians in some states was so close that the two were inseparable in the public mind. A leader named Quay had become the Republican boss in Pennsylvania. A very adroit and canny man, without ideals for society or in government, to whom personal advancement and party success were the highest good, he rose, through corruption, to such a position that the legislature of his state had, in 1887, elected him to the United States Senate.[4] He took over the management of the Cameron "machine" and developed it to such a point that it came to have a new, albeit a quite sinister, influence in party matters in the nation at large. The power of this "organization" was founded on the tariff. So long as it served those who grew rich from manufacturing it could draw upon these men for the money which was needed for the conduct of successful campaigns. The more money the greater the majorities; the greater the majorities the bolder and the more arbitrary was Quay's leadership,

[1] McElroy, Grover Cleveland, vol. i, pp. 268–9.
[2] Cf. N. Y. Herald, Dec. 9, 1887.
[3] Cf. ibid., Dec. 10, 1887; Writings of Schurz, vol. iv, p. 515.
[4] Cf. N. Y. Nation, Jan. 13, 1887; cf. A. K. McClure, Old Time Notes of Pa., chaps. xcvi, cii, cv and cvi.

the more contemptuous was he of the feelings and opinion, of a minority who could view what went on before their eyes with distrust, if not with shame. In other states politicians had similarly struck hands with the wealthy to pollute the springs of free government.

The proprietors of industries favored by a high tariff·upon their products, and secure from foreign competition, were beginning to form combinations which were called "trusts." The Standard Oil Trust was an awful example which was allowed to escape no one's notice. It had grown and flourished not by reason of the tariff, but through surreptitious bargaining with the railroad companies. Thus, principally, had it crushed small producers and gained undisputed control of an entire industry. The day was near, if it were not at hand, it was said, when the production of lead, sugar, meat, rubber, steel, copper, oil cloth, whiskey, and it was not clear how many other articles necessary to daily human existence, would be concentrated in a few hands. All of these businesses would be monopolies. The "trusts," the combinations of manufacturers, like the individual manufacturers would make their own prices behind high tariff walls.[1]

The economists in the colleges had been free traders, teaching the subject from such English texts as Adam Smith and John Stuart Mill, whereat there was revolt by our protectionists who succeeded in creating a few centers for the indoctrination of young men with the theories of Henry C. Carey. But as we turned to Germany for higher learning and our Ph.D.'s came home ready to be installed in professorial posts we began to put protection upon the more satisfactory basis of the Germans, which was frankly socialist. It was a duty of the government to foster and promote business by tariffs, adjusted and fixed, presumably, by intelligent, disin-

[1] N. Y. Nation, Nov. 10, 1887; Writings of Schurz, vol. iv, p. 524; Ida M. Tarbell, The Tariff in Our Times, p. 151; W. Z. Ripley, Trusts, Pools and Corporations; J. W. Jenks, The Trust Problem; A. D. Noyes, Forty Years of American Finance, pp. 117–8. These "immoral" organizations were on the eve of an extended Congressional investigation—see House Reports, 50th Cong. 1st sess., no. 3112.

terested agencies. That was one thing and might win the acceptance of those who sought light in the colleges and universities; it was another to give tariffs to those who would pay for them through politicians and party machines on the principle of barter and sale, while they, all the while, were browbeating the poor with picture and description of the "pauper labor" of Europe to which level American workingmen would be reduced, if they should ever fail to vote the Republican ticket. The tariff did not raise prices. Anyhow who wanted commodities to be cheap? "Cheap and nasty" was a phrase uttered by the very boys in the street.[1] In essence this was what was called the "Philadelphia political economy"; it fell familiarly from the lips of James G. Blaine; it was propagated daily by the New York Tribune. The madness— for the manner in which it obsessed many men gave it this character—had practically made conquest of the entire organization of the party which acted in opposition to the Cleveland administration; it had been fastened on an active minority faction within the President's own party. The tariff had come to be sacrosanct. Even to presume to argue about it in a liberal spirit was to invite ridicule and proscription, and such a man as Cleveland, who had a hearty hatred of all attempts to put the government to private uses, seeing the intent behind the mask, would some day be tried to the breaking point.[2]

And he stood not alone. It seemed to be so patently a putting of the government to the selfish uses of a class that protection itself, root and branch, was coming to repel a larger and larger number of young, as well as older, men. Free trade and tariff reform leagues held meetings and passed resolutions. Influential citizens in New York and New England spoke with feeling and vehemence in condemnation of such an alliance as they found to exist between rich tariff beneficiaries and the government. Ably conducted newspapers were not silent, and the hour had probably come for such leadership as that

[1] Garfield discovered this phrase in his reading of Carlyle.—Cong. Record, 44th Cong. 1st sess., p. 4561.
[2] McElroy, Grover Cleveland, vol. i, pp. 270–71.

which Cleveland now promised to give to the cause. Nevertheless, on the eve of a Presidential election it was esteemed by many of his advisers to be a brash and daring adventure, which he might better not undertake.[1]

George Hoadly was in doubt. He was in favor of free raw materials and the imposition of duties on luxuries. But large bodies of workingmen would be alienated, he believed, if it were suspected that the party were choosing a course which would indicate a sympathy with the views of Henry Watterson and Frank Hurd.[2] The manufacturers, Secretary Lamar observed, would regard "with undisguised apprehension" a reduction in the tariff.[3] It was a "question of policy," said Whitney. The tariff ought to be lowered, but it was, he thought, not the right time to "push it."[4] Silas Burt saw danger in the money which would be raised by the "protected interests" and would be thrown into the canvass, if the tariff were made the issue of the campaign.[5]

Cleveland was not to be deterred. "Do you not think," he asked a friend who had endeavored to dissuade him, "that the people of the United States are entitled to some instruction on this subject?"[6] He would have stultified himself, if he had drawn back from any fear that what he was about to do might affect his candidacy for reëlection. "What is the use of being elected or reëlected," he said again, "unless you stand for something?"[7] So disquieting were conditions in business, that, in the summer of 1887, he had pondered the idea of an extra session, which he had relinquished in favor of an emphatic declaration when Congress should meet in December.[8]

The message, Mr. Cleveland's third, was entirely devoted to the surplus and the tariff. A hundred topics usually pass under review in such a state paper. It had been so in his

---

[1] N. Y. Times, Dec. 7, 1887.
[2] Nov. 22, 1887, in Cleveland Papers.
[3] Sep. 10, 1887, in ibid.
[4] Dec. 11, 1887, in ibid.
[5] To Lamont, Dec. 9, 1887, in ibid.
[6] R. W. Gilder, Grover Cleveland, p. 14.
[7] McElroy, Grover Cleveland, vol. i, pp. 271, 300–01.
[8] Cf. R. W. Gilder, Grover Cleveland, pp. 8–15.

messages in 1885 and 1886; now no other subject was allowed to intrude that he might make the deepest impression on the public mind. Thus would he the better display his earnest purpose to lay bare a humbug, hiding under a thickness of pother, which insulted his intelligence and challenged him to a battle for justice and right.

The President said that revenues were in excess of expenditures for the eleven months of the year ending on December 1st to the extent of $55,000,000. The surplus in the Treasury, it was estimated, would be, on June 30, 1888, not less than $140,-000,000. The government "idly" held money "uselessly subtracted from the channels of trade." Government bonds not yet due had been called and these operations of the Treasury Department had been continued by reason of "representations of distress in business circles," though, in some instances, a high premium was paid. This resource had been exhausted; there was no further outlet in that direction. Other plans for correcting a situation which involved "a withdrawal from use of the people's circulating medium," and restoring it to its place in the business community, "without waste or extravagance," were considered and discussed. The President briefly dismissed them and went to the source of the difficulty—the system of taxation which exacted sums "largely" in excess of the requirements of the government "from the industries and necessities of the people," and which was "crippling our national energies, suspending our country's development, preventing investment in productive enterprise, threatening financial disturbance and inviting schemes of public plunder." The Treasury should exist only as "a conduit, conveying the people's tribute to its legitimate objects of expenditure"—the taking of more than this from them, in deprivation of the fruits of their industry and enterprise, was "indefensible extortion and a culpable betrayal of American fairness and justice."

The condition of the Treasury presaged "financial convulsion and widespread disaster." The scheme of Federal taxation consisted of a tariff on imports and the internal revenue taxes on liquors and tobacco, which no one could regard as "necessaries." It was the tariff laws which were "the vicious, inequitable and illogical source" of the trouble, and they should be "at once revised and amended." They were raising the price to consumers of all imported articles, and, at the same time, of all similar articles made at home. Thus were the whole people taxed, those who bought foreign goods, paying the duty to the government, and those who bought goods of domestic manufacture, paying the added price to the manufacturer, which came to him under the name of "protection." The President would not entirely sweep this away. In the readjustment "the interests of American labor," as well as "the preservation of our manufacturers," should be "carefully considered." But there was suspicion, in view of the stubborn opposition to all suggestions of a lowering of the tariff by our manufacturers, who were acting as an "organized combination," that their "infant industries" were enjoying too great an "advantage." Instead of "moderately profitable returns" from their investment they were realizing "immense profits." They would have it thought, he observed, that the usufruct was not theirs but the workingmen's, expressed in higher wages in our mills and factories. The President said on this point—that of 17,000,-000 persons engaged in productive pursuits less than 3,000,000 had connection with manufacturing and they, while interested in the maintenance of a high wage scale, were consumers like other men. All together were concerned as to the price of the things they must buy with their earnings for the comfort of themselves and their families. The manufacturers and their spokesmen declared, too, that the price was often reduced behind the tariff wall by competition of one manufacturer with another, that the price was not that of the similar foreign article, plus the tax. If this were so it could only prove, the President said, that the duty was unnecessary; but it was "notorious" that competition was too often "strangled" by combinations called "trusts," whose object was to regulate supply and demand for the benefit of a few men without consideration of the interests and rights of the people.

The President found that more than 4,000 imported articles

were subject to duty. Many in no way competed with our products—these should be added to the free list. The taxation of luxuries should continue—it meant no hardship; but duties which increased the cost of living in every home should be greatly reduced. In a particular way the President named "raw materials" used in manufacturing; they should come into the country free, or with low duties. He directed his aim unerringly at the small group of woolgrowers in Ohio who were so insistent and voluble,[1] and he dared to name wool as a prominent example of an article which, when it was taxed, increased the cost of living in every household. With free materials manufacturers in this branch, and in nearly all other branches, of industry, could make their products more cheaply. The President gave them a vision of competition with the world and a foreign trade. He spoke of patriotism—it was no time for a spirit of partisanship in those "intrusted with the weal of a confiding people"—it was no time for "dwelling upon the theories of protection and free trade." The question of "free trade" was "absolutely irrelevant," and to describe as "free traders" those who earnestly desired "to relieve the people from unjust and unnecessary taxation," and to restore to the people money held in the Treasury, "through a perversion of governmental powers," was a mischievous device. "It is a condition which confronts us," said the President, "not a theory," and he sounded the call to duty.[2]

From the beginning the Republican leaders had been baiting him on this subject. To have him come out into the open as a "free trader" was their whole wish, so that they could denounce him more eloquently than ever. Now all was made plain. He was an enemy of his country—a friend of England, of pauper labor, of the New York importers. He would close the mills and starve the people. The surplus was no matter

---

[1] One of the "three musketeers" in Ohio, David Harpster, wrote Cleveland at the end of 1887 complaining of the "unfriendly" legislation of 1883 which had been enacted "at the dictation of New England." It had reduced the number of sheep in the United States more than 6,000,000 head, the clip of wool more than 35,000,000 pounds.—To Cleveland, Dec. 17, 1887, in Cleveland Papers.

[2] Richardson, vol. viii, pp. 580–91.

anyhow. It could be spent for rivers and harbors, or seacoast defenses, or new post offices, or pensions, or by Blair to educate the ignorant South. If taxes were to be reduced at all let it be on tobacco and whiskey. If it were believed that the prohibitionists would be estranged by the suggestion about making whiskey cheap, let that tax be continued and the money derived from it kept in a fund to be given to the states, according to the plan proposed by Blaine. He who would touch the tariff could beware—the people would rise to crush him under the weight of their condemnation and scorn.

Though this was said by the partisan editors and politicians, the President knew that there were intelligent men of the upper classes who would commend his views, as well as an understratum of the population gifted with common sense. He was not wrong in thinking that, with his leadership, a large body of the people would give some care to the consideration of their condition as to taxation, prices and the cost of living.[1] There were men too, he knew, Democrats and Republicans, whatever they might be called, who shared his opinion that the government was an agency to be seen and felt as little as possible, that it should levy no more taxes than would provide for its needs, that to take more led to waste and could be likened to robbery. Anyhow he was right—he knew full well that he was right and he would submit the case to the country, make the issue for the elections in 1888 and take the consequences.

His friends saw in the declaration another proof, and a decidedly eloquent one, of the President's "moral courage." It was "a coup d'état unequalled in our political annals," said Silas Burt. It was "a bold and admirable stroke of statesmanship to have infused a vital issue into the stagnant current of politics."[2] Though Whitney had used his influences to deter the President he, after the message was out, said that no one would rise from reading it "without understanding

[1] Cf. McElroy, vol. i, p. 271; Writings of Carl Schurz, vol. iv, p. 492.
[2] To Cleveland, Dec. 8, 1887, and to Lamont, Dec. 9, 1887, in Cleveland Papers.

the subject." The tariff would be "a winning issue." [1] A man told Richard Watson Gilder that "the bravery and honesty of the act" settled the personal question in the next campaign in so far as he was concerned. [2]

The press uttered similar views. The New York Evening Post declared the message to be "the most courageous document" sent from the Executive Mansion "since the close of the war." The gun that had been fired would be "heard in every corner and hamlet in the country." It would give the people "something to think about that bears relation to their daily life" and "supply parties with an issue that they have long needed." [3]

For the President to have taken such a position, said the New York Times, was "an act of statesmanship in the best sense." It was "unprecedented for any President to summon a Congress at the threshold of a session to consider one subject only," but in doing so he gave to the Democratic party a policy in the pursuit of which they might find "a sound and valid reason for existence." [4]

The New York World, which had been withholding its support from the administration, was gratified. The President had provided his party with that which it lacked—"an issue and a leader." His action was "bold, sagacious and statesmanlike." The Philadelphia Record praised the President's "Jacksonian backbone." The Philadelphia Inquirer said that the message was "the freshest, best argued and most important tariff paper" which had appeared in many years; [5] the Brooklyn Eagle, that it put the President "in the plane of the best public thought." [6] To him the people must look, said the Baltimore Sun, for the overthrow of trusts and other combinations which were raising the prices of the necessaries of life. He discussed the issue and brought it home, said the Boston Globe,

[1] Whitney to Cleveland, Dec. 11, 1887, in ibid.
[2] Gilder to Lamont, Dec. 12, 1887, in ibid.
[3] N. Y. Nation, Dec. 7, 1887.
[4] N. Y. Times, Dec. 7, 1887.
[5] Phila. Inquirer, Dec. 7, 1887.
[6] Brooklyn Eagle, Dec. 7, 1887.

"to everybody's apprehension." [1] Significant support, which was warmly welcomed, was tendered the President by the influential Providence Journal. [2]

The Republicans met every expectation and raised the "old free trade shout." It was a "free trade lecture," a "free trade tract," a "free trade essay." It was as good, said William McKinley of Ohio, "as if written by the Cobden Club," that fearsome citadel whose smoking embrasures would one day reduce the breastworks behind which American industry was pursuing its comfortable way. The message established the Democratic party's "complicity with the attack on the protection of American industries," said Thomas B. Reed of Maine. [3]

The country was deeply indebted to Cleveland, said the Philadelphia Press, for such an avowal of his "extreme free trade purposes." He had "plunged into the abyss"; the party must follow him. [4] The President's fame was secure in England, said the New York Tribune. [5] The "British Hallelujah Chorus" would be heard around the world. [6] The Blaine organs rang the changes on the phrase, "It is a condition which confronts us—not a theory," and made it as familiar to the man in the street as the President's "innocuous desuetude." Now, they said, and possibly believed, nothing could prevent their winning in 1888. Some pretended to think that Cleveland had gone so far that his party would not dare to nominate him for another term. The manufacturers in Pennsylvania, New England and other parts of the country were "interviewed" by the reporters of enterprising newspapers, and they were enabled to express their opinions of the President. They spoke of closing their mills. [7]

Whitelaw Reid found Blaine in Paris. The "Plumed Knight" had gone abroad for travel and recuperation. The Tribune had located him but a day or two ago and a cablegram an-

[1] Quoted in N. Y. Tribune, Dec. 8, 1887.
[2] Cf. N. Y. Nation, Dec. 22 and 29, 1887.
[3] N. Y. World, Dec. 7, 1887.
[4] Phila. Press, Dec. 7, 1887.
[5] N. Y. Tribune, Dec. 8, 1887.
[6] Ibid., Jan. 4, 1888.
[7] Cf. N. Y. Nation, Dec. 15 and 22, 1887.

nounced his improved state of health, all in the interest of his renomination for the office, which he had failed to capture in 1884, and which was soon again to be the subject of contest.[1] Reid caused his friend to be interviewed on the subject of Cleveland's message by George W. Smalley who was aided by a "short hand reporter," and the statement was clear. The "surplus" did not disturb Blaine—it was better than a deficit. The money should be spent—he cannily named the fortification of the Atlantic seaboard as a good object, citing views expressed by Tilden on this subject in 1885.[2] If the income of the government were too large, reduce the internal revenue taxes, but preserve and defend the tariff at any cost. Strike the tax from tobacco to help the grower as well as the consumer. To millions of men tobacco was a necessity. Blaine had watched them at work on the farm, in the coal mine and on the railroads—95 in 100 were chewing. He was bidding high, it was wittily observed, for the "quid vote."[3] But he was not to be caught in any counter fire from the prohibitionists. There was "a moral side" to the question of reducing or abolishing the internal revenue tax on whiskey. He would not do this. If, after freeing the quid, the pipe and the cigar, money still came too fast into the Treasury he would, rather than cheapen whiskey, lower the too high taxes on real estate and follow the plan, which he had earlier formulated, for a distribution of the surplus among the various states.

Cleveland's message, Blaine said, was a "free trade manifesto." There was joy when men read it in England; our import trade would be increased tenfold. The sheep men must be protected by a tariff on wool. Free coal, free iron ore, free raw material of any kind would mean a breaking down of the protective system, throw men out of work and bring wages to the low and demoralizing levels which prevailed in Europe. Foreign trade was of no value to Americans. What they must have was the "vast domestic trade between 38

[1] N. Y. Tribune, Dec. 7, 1887.
[2] Letters and Memorials of Tilden, vol. ii, pp. 714–8.
[3] N. Y. Times, Dec. 9, 1887.

states and 8 territories," with a population of 62 millions. This was "illimitable"—"our own great market for our own people" was "the heritage of the American people, of their children and of their children's children."

Blaine, like the others who had spoken before his voice was added to protection's benison, welcomed the "full and fair contest on the question" which the President's message invited. It must be "settled." The people must deal at once with the Democratic party, which so long as it remained in power was "a standing menace to the industrial prosperity of the country." [1]

Sherman, "the greatest of living American financiers," [2] like Blaine a candidate for the Republican nomination for the Presidency, made his reply to Cleveland in the United States Senate. While he avoided any reference to Blaine's scheme for dividing the whiskey tax among the states he made various Delphic references to the internal revenue system. His line of approach upon the surplus was a larger expenditure of public moneys. If Cleveland had not vetoed so many appropriation bills there would have been no problems growing out of an excess of public income. About the only tariff duty which Sherman would reduce was that one on sugar, and this he would restore to the producer in the form of a bounty. [3]

The New York Tribune found in the statement of Blaine "characteristic boldness." His suggestions, it said, were "full of originality and practical statesmanship." [4] Sherman's argument was "admirable," showing plainly as it did Cleveland's "subserviency to British interests." It ought to be "placed in the hands of voters by the millions." [5]

The "originality" of Blaine's message from Paris was in the Tribune writer's fancy. There was in fact nothing new, or original about the issue, or the statement of it, on either side. The New York World summarized it,

[1] N. Y. Tribune, Dec. 8, 1887.
[2] Ibid., Jan. 5, 1888.
[3] N. Y. World, Jan. 5, 1888; N. Y. Nation, Jan. 12, 1888.
[4] N. Y. Tribune, Dec. 8, 1887.
[5] Ibid., Jan. 6, 1888.

"The Democratic policy—Off with the needless taxes on clothing, fuel, shelter, food. Let alone the taxes on whiskey, beer, tobacco.

"The Republican policy—Off with taxes on whiskey, beer, tobacco, so as to keep the war taxes on clothing, fuel, shelter, food." [1]

The one new thing in the situation was Cleveland's presenting the case and accepting the challenge for himself and his party. A large body of Democrats would follow him, a large body of Republicans would oppose him. What remained to be discovered was the attitude of Randall and his protectionist faction in the Democratic party, and of the tariff reformers in the Northwest who had been acting with the Republicans.

Randall made no concealment of his disagreement with the President's views.[2] The newspaper which reflected his mind more nearly than any other, and whose owners he, in a measure served, the Public Ledger in Philadelphia, where nearly all men were protectionists, said the message was a "shortsighted, ill-advised lecture based upon defective information, reproducing hackneyed arguments, couched in overwrought phrases and vehemently partisan." [3] Plans were laid by W. L. Scott and others to unhand Randall and take his following away from him "one by one" until his detachment from the party should be made plain to him and to other men.[4] Signs of the development of industrialism in the South filled the Republicans with hope that they would find a joint in the Democratic armor in that part of the Union.[5] In the Northwest, on the other hand, the Democrats looked with confidence to defection for their advantage. Undoubtedly the farmers were feeling the burdens of a system, which they well enough understood might be beneficial to an Eastern manufacturer, but which brought them no happiness or ease. Quite a third of the members of the Republican state convention in Nebraska had voted

[1] N. Y. World, Dec. 9, 1887.
[2] Cf. N. Y. Herald, Dec. 2, 1887.
[3] Public Ledger, Dec. 7, 1887.
[4] Scott to Cleveland, Sep. 16, 1887, in Cleveland Papers.
[5] Cf. N. Y. Nation, Nov. 24, 1887.

for a declaration in favor of a general revision of the tariff. Members in Congress from that state and the Omaha Bee made articulate the complaints of the population settled west of the Missouri and on the banks of the Platte.[1] Republican leaders in Minnesota expressed opinions which indicated that dissent was still rife in that quarter.[2] Newspapers like the St. Paul Pioneer Press and the Minneapolis Journal reflected public feeling sympathetic to the reform which the President proposed.[3] More significant than any other utterance was that of the Chicago Tribune which now, for some time, had been engaged in the advocacy of tariff reduction. The Eastern Republicans could ill afford to call it a "free trade sheet." It was a powerful organ of opinion which had long since ceased to be Independent or Mugwump in its leanings. It had unquestioningly accepted Blaine and whatever bore the Republican name. But it had attributed the defeat of the party in New York in November, 1887, to the emphasis which had been put on the importance of a high tariff.[4] This newspaper gave whole-hearted approval to Cleveland's message. It was "moderate protection doctrine" which he preached, not free trade. The President had risen "above party lines" and presented a ground on which Republicans and Democrats, "by every consideration of the public welfare and of political expediency," should "stand together." The message was simply the report of the Tariff Commission of 1882. The Tribune sounded a warning. If relief were not granted now, a time would soon come, as the President had said, when "an abused and irritated people" might insist upon "a radical and sweeping rectification of their wrongs."[5]

After Blaine had spoken over the cable the same newspaper continued its advice to the party. Blaine in a word, it appeared, desired that the "war tariff" should be "perpetuated." In-

[1] N. Y. Nation, Dec. 1 and 29, 1887.
[2] Ibid., Dec. 15 and 29, 1887. For "free trade" sentiment in Minnesota see Hay to Wharton Barker, Jan. 11, 1887, in E. G. Hay Papers in Library of Congress.
[3] Cf. N. Y. Nation, April 5, 1888.
[4] Ibid., Dec. 1, 1887.
[5] Chicago Tribune, Dec. 7, 1887.

stead of reducing the taxes which bore "upon the producing
and consuming classes with crushing weight," Congress was
recommended to devise means for "squandering the surplus."
Such a proposal would not commend itself to the American
people. No national party could expect to go into a Presidential campaign on such an issue and win.[1] Senator Allison
of Iowa corroborated this view. He said that the people of
the West were in a determined mood; it would go hard with
the Republican party should it give no heed to the demand
for tariff reform.[2]

The reëlection of Carlisle as Speaker was an assurance to
the President that there would be sympathy with his views
on the tariff question in that quarter. Morrison had failed
to hold his seat in Illinois; another must be found for the chairmanship of the Committee on Ways and Means, which would
have the duty of preparing and presenting a bill. Roger Q.
Mills, a Confederate colonel, three times wounded during the
war, who had entered Congress from Texas in 1873, was
assigned this position; seven other Democrats and five Republicans, including Kelley of Pennsylvania, Reed of Maine,
McKinley of Ohio and Burrows of Michigan made up the
committee.[3]

The New York Tribune complained that six of the members
came from the South which presumably knew nothing of, and
cared nothing for, the tariff.[4]

The Democratic majority put their minds to the task before them and were ready in March with a schedule of duties
which they were willing to submit to public discussion. In
brief they would reduce the revenues by about $50,000,000
annually—$11,000,000 on sugar, $22,250,000 on raw materials,
including wool, $12,000,000 on woolen manufactures and $5,000,-
000 on various other articles. An internal revenue reduction

[1] Chicago Tribune, Dec. 9, 1887; cf. quotations from ibid. in N. Y.
Nation, Feb. 2, 1888.
[2] N. Y. Nation, Jan. 12, 1888; N. Y. World, Jan. 7, 1888.
[3] N. Y. World, Jan. 6, 1888.
[4] N. Y. Tribune, Jan. 6, 1888; cf. E. Stanwood, American Tariff Controversies, vol. ii, p. 231.

bill, chiefly affecting tobacco, would yield a further cut in the public income equal to $25,000,000 or $30,000,000 a year. It was said that the reductions were much less drastic than the Republican Tariff Commission had proposed in 1882. It was said, too, that never before in the history of the country had the average tariff charge on dutiable goods been so high— it was now 47 per cent. If it were oppressive before in the sight of Republicans, as well as Democrats, would a proposal to lower it now be so menacing to American industry as the public would be asked from the house tops to believe? [1]

The opposition was outspoken before the nature of the measure was yet known. The work of Mills and his associates was condemned unseen; it must be an assault upon the country's welfare if it came from such a source. If they were Democrats, if they were from the South, if they were compiling a measure which would satisfy the President, if they, in a word, were touching the tariff at all, with the purpose of lowering it they were public enemies. It was a "dark lantern" bill.[2] The Democratic majority had contrived it without taking Reed, McKinley and the Republicans into their confidences. But the truth now was out, and these men, as well as manufacturers, trade organizations, editors, politicians and citizens generally, could "try their teeth on it."[3]

Randall framed a bill,[4] which he put forward as an obstacle in the way of the "Mills bill." The Republican minority of the Ways and Means Committee was soon ready with a counter statement attacking the whole plan for a reduction of duties on the broad principle, said the New York Nation, that the producer was to have what he wanted and that the consumer had no rights.[5]

The "Mills bill," although it very partially expressed Mr.

---

[1] Cf. N. Y. Nation, Sep. 1, 1887, and March 8, 1888; Writings of Schurz, vol. iv, pp. 517–8.
[2] Cf. N. Y. Tribune, March 1, 1888.
[3] N. Y. Nation, March 8, 1888.
[4] Ibid., March 5 and 22, 1888.
[5] Ibid., April 5 and 12, 1888.

Cleveland's hopes and wishes,[1] became the administration measure. Mr. Mills made his opening speech in advocacy of it on April 17th, a fearless and able statement from the standpoint of the tariff reformers. He recited the history of the fiscal policy of the Republican party up to 1883, when they had finished their "magnificent shaft," which for years they had been erecting, and "crowned it with the last stone by repealing the internal revenue tax on playing cards and putting a 20 per cent tax on the Bible." [2] "Pig Iron" Kelley replied for Pennsylvania and the minority of the committee, and the parliamentary battle was on.[3]

The debate continued until late in July. The bill drew, in all, 151 speeches from members of the House in their efforts to convince their constituents of their economical learning, or, at any rate, of their diligence in so critical a conjuncture. Representative Springer of Illinois denominated it, and said that it would take its place in history, as the "Great Tariff Debate of 1888." [4] The final words were spoken by Mr. Mills,[5] by which time most of the Democrats who were numbered in opposition to the bill had been brought into line, and it was passed on July 21st, by a vote of 162 to 149, and sent to the Senate.[6]

The Presidential campaign was now well advanced and the Nestors of the Republican party resolved to present a tariff bill of their own. It had been said, very confidently, that the tariff should not be touched unless it were to be increased. But

[1] McElroy, Grover Cleveland, vol. i, p. 273. "The Mills bill, if enacted into a law, would still leave behind it one of the highest protective tariffs the world has ever seen—aye, a higher tariff than was designed under the stress of our civil war."—Carl Schurz to a correspondent in Writings of Schurz, vol. iv, p. 518.
[2] "Free poker and a taxed gospel." Cong. Record, 50th Cong. 1st sess., pp. 3057–63.
[3] Ibid., pp. 3064–71; cf. N. Y. Nation, April 26, 1888.
[4] App. Ann. Cyclop. for 1888, p. 194.
[5] Cong. Record, 50th Cong. 1st sess., pp. 6604–9.
[6] Only six Republicans voted for the bill, only four Democrats against it. Randall was ill and was "paired" against it, further proving his opposition by writing a letter to be read to the House.—Cong. Record, 50th Cong. 1st sess., p. 6660; McPherson's Handbook for 1888, pp. 165–6; E. Stanwood, American Tariff Controversies, vol. ii, pp. 232–9.

it came to be believed, as the summer passed, that it might not
be enough to cry "free trade" in protest against the "Mills
bill." There might be tariff reformers in the Northwest, and,
perhaps, in New England and the East also, with votes which
would be cast in November, who had been moved by Cleveland's arraignment of the rich manufacturers and the trusts,
and his plea for lower duties in the interest of lower living
costs. Another bill from Republican hands, with another
schedule of duties, distinguishing it somehow from the "Mills
bill," must be set before the people.[1]

The "Mills bill" upon reaching the Senate was referred to
the Finance Committee which held prolonged hearings. The
Democratic House had not sought the advice of the manufacturers who crowded Washington, since they were regarded
as interested parties and lobbyists.[2] Now they could say their
say. Clerks employed by the committee worked through the
summer upon a substitute measure. The Republicans would
lay a high duty on wool. Several articles were put upon the
free list, but not the product of our shepherds in Ohio. Taxes
on sugar[3] and iron of certain kinds were, in some degree,
reduced to satisfy what might prove to be a popular demand
for revenue reform, and Senator Allison, as a tariff reformer,
was put forward by his colleagues to present the committee's
scheme.[4] He spoke so eloquently for lower duties for the ears
of the West that his argument, the New York Nation said,
should have been printed as a Democratic campaign document.[5] What the Senate substitute bill really was it was left to
Nelson W. Aldrich of Rhode Island, who spoke to the audience
in the East, more truthfully to explain.[6]

[1] N. Y. Nation, Aug. 2, 1888.
[2] E. Stanwood, American Tariff Controversies, vol. ii, pp. 232, 239.
[3] The high duty on sugar had long been resented as in the interest of the
"Sugar Trust."—Cf. App. Ann. Cyclop. for 1883, pp. 219–20.
[4] Ida M. Tarbell, The Tariff in Our Times, pp. 165–73.
[5] N. Y. Nation, Oct. 11, 1888.
[6] Ida M. Tarbell, The Tariff in Our Times, pp. 168–73. For reports and
testimony taken by the committee see Senate Reports, 50th Cong. 1st sess.,
no. 2332. Cf. E. Stanwood, American Tariff Controversies, vol. ii, pp. 239–
40.

The Senate, having refused to accept the "Mills bill," made no effective motion to pass its own,[1] and Congress finally adjourned on October 20th, little more than a fortnight before election day, having met continuously throughout the campaign lest one side or the other might, at so critical a time, miss some opportunity to use an advantage or rectify a mistake. Stump speeches and parliamentary wrangling, born of party malice for party ends, had continued until the proceedings of the session filled ten volumes of more than 10,000 pages of that publication called the Congressional Record.

At least two other questions were made into party matters to serve the purposes of the campaign—the fisheries and the Chinese questions. Since nothing could be expected of Congress in the direction of a settlement of the irritating differences which had arisen between our New England and the Canadian fishermen, as to their mutual and respective rights, and that body had come to rest on the subject, after granting power to the President to retaliate, the responsibility for originating some plan of settlement remained with Secretary Bayard. The Gladstone ministry, disrupted by the proposal to extend "Home Rule" to Ireland, had given way in the summer of 1886 to the Conservative and Unionist government of Lord Salisbury. The fishing season had closed, leaving the memory of many vexatious incidents, and the marine police force in the waters of British North America had been withdrawn. Mr. Bayard, in November, directed our minister in London, Mr. Phelps, to invite the new British government to consider the adoption of measures which would, before the next year, prevent the repetition of conduct, on the part of the Canadian officials, likely to "endanger the peace of two kindred and friendly nations."[2] Our objections to port regulations, which were friendly to trading vessels but were hostile to fishing craft, were stated. "A treaty of friendship" was not to be "tortured into a means of such offense," and a memorandum of agreement, covering questions at issue, was inclosed to Mr. Phelps

[1] App. Ann. Cyclop. for 1888, p. 217.
[2] Senate Ex. Doc., 50th Cong. 1st sess., no. 113, p. 5.

for presentation to Her Majesty's Secretary of State for Foreign Affairs,[1] proposing a commission definitively to compose misunderstandings and a *modus vivendi* to govern the situation until final settlement could be made. It was March, 1887, since it was always necessary to consult the desires of the Dominion government, which exercised in some degree an autonomous sovereignty,[2] before a response making counter proposals was received,[3] by which time the chase, firing of shots and boarding of our fishing boats had recommenced off the coasts of Canada,[4] although operations of this kind were restricted and repressed because of knowledge that differences were in course of settlement.[5] Shortly, in May, 1887, Sir Charles Tupper, Minister of Finance in the Canadian government, visited Washington, and he had conferences with the President and Secretary Bayard, which promised more direct action than could be obtained by way of London. Mr. Bayard frankly said that the two countries had come to "the parting of the ways." If wise counsel were not taken there would be "a career of embittered rivalries staining our long frontier with the hues of hostility," a condition of affairs "which ought to be abhorrent to patriots on both sides."[6] It was July, 1887, when, after expression of favor for the plan had been received from Lord Salisbury, the appointment of a commission was agreed upon.

The President named, in behalf of the United States, the Secretary of State, Thomas F. Bayard; William L. Putnam, the Portland lawyer, who had been representing the government in fishery litigation, and James B. Angell, president of the University of Michigan.[7] The Queen appointed Joseph Chamberlain, at the moment very prominent in public life in England because of his recent desertion of Gladstone on the "Home Rule" question; her minister at Washington, the

[1] Senate Ex. Doc., 50th Cong. 1st sess., no. 113, pp. 7–8.
[2] Cf. ibid., p. 112.
[3] Ibid., pp. 46–54.
[4] N. Y. Nation, April 4, 1887.
[5] Senate Ex. Doc., 50th Cong. 1st sess., no. 265.
[6] Ibid., no. 113, p. 113.
[7] Ibid., p. 117; N. Y. Nation, Oct. 6, 1887.

Hon. Sir Lionel Sackville Sackville-West, and Sir Charles Tupper, the Canadian leader, who had interested himself in the subject of a settlement. Chamberlain, soon after his arrival in this country,[1] was a guest at the annual dinner of the New York Chamber of Commerce.[2] He and the other plenipotentiaries were formally presented to the President, and they held their first meeting on November 22, 1887. The character of the men chosen to consider the matters at issue should have insured for them more than the outwardly respectful reception which was accorded them in such social contacts as they made here, and in the press. But Chamberlain had won the displeasure of the Irish because of his attitude toward "Home Rule" and, in order to get their votes, it was a part of the program of the Republican party, under Blaine's leadership, to outreach the Democrats in attention to the feelings and prejudices of that people settled in America.

Anyhow there was no wish to deal frankly with the questions involved. The protectionist philosophy required that we should be at enmity with, rather than friendly to, a great industrial rival like Great Britain. Instead of reciprocity between this country and Canada we should be constantly on our guard lest we be somehow outwitted in a game which the British were supposed to be playing at our expense. From the beginning the whole idea of a commission had been decried by the Blaine press. A President, the Republicans said, might not engage in the negotiation of a treaty without the previous assent of Congress, regardless of the fact that so recently as in 1874, Secretary Fish, in the Grant administration, had done precisely this, and with reference to our Canadian relations.[3]

It was February 15, 1888, before the draft of the treaty was concluded and the conference adjourned, Chamberlain meanwhile having visited Canada where the subject was being booted about between the party in power and that one out of power,

---

[1] N. Y. Herald, Nov. 8, 1887.
[2] Ibid., Nov. 16, 1887.
[3] N. Y. Nation, Nov. 17, 1887.

as in this republic.[1] The bugaboo of annexation to the United States, which was constantly discussed on both sides of the border, as well as the tariff, complicated the case. In England the people cared practically nothing about the question, their whole interest in it consisting of a desire to avoid a quarrel.[2]

The treaty provided for the appointment of a "Mixed Commission" to delimit the territory, named in Article I of the convention of 1818, about which dispute had so long prevailed. In establishing the three mile line the sinuosities of the shore should be followed,—the claim to jurisdiction over waters within imaginary lines drawn from headland to headland, at any rate with reference to large estuaries, was abandoned and certain beginning points were fixed upon for the guidance of the commissioners, which promised us a fair result.[3] The privileges in entering harbors and the rights to be enjoyed while in port were defined. The free navigation of the Strait of Canso was for the first time affirmed and guaranteed our fishing boats.

Reciprocity would not be allowed to endanger the treaty, which had been framed to apply to existing tariff conditions. It was specified in Article XV, however, that, when the United States should remove the duty upon fish and fishery products, as well as upon barrels and other containers useful in the fishing industry, these articles should have free entry into Canada and Newfoundland from the United States. In that case our fishing vessels might receive licenses, free of charge, for entering ports, bays and harbors on the British North Atlantic coasts to purchase food, bait, ice, seines and other supplies, to transship the catch, and to hire men for crews.[4] Any proposal of change in the revenue laws of the country was left wholly subject to the action of Congress.

In view of the fact that some time must elapse before the ratifications could be exchanged the text of an *ad interim* arrangement, as Mr. Bayard had suggested, to cover a period of two years, was prepared by the British plenipotentiaries

[1] Cf. Keenleyside, Canada and the U. S., p. 270.
[2] N. Y. Nation, Feb. 23, 1888.
[3] Cf. map in N. Y. Herald, Feb. 25, 1888.
[4] Senate Ex. Doc., 50th Cong. 1st sess., no. 113, pp. 137-8.

and presented to our representatives, if, for temporary use, we should desire to avail ourselves of its terms.[1]

On February 20th Cleveland transmitted the treaty to the Senate with a statement of his approval. It had been framed, he said, "in a spirit of liberal equity and reciprocal benefits" and it provided "a satisfactory, practical and final adjustment upon a basis honorable and just to both parties" of a "long standing controversy." By its terms he believed that "a beneficial and satisfactory intercourse between the two countries" would be established "so as to secure perpetual peace and harmony." [2]

The Senate referred it to the Committee on Foreign Relations. A few days later, on March 5, 1888, a mass of papers relating to the negotiation were transmitted to Congress. They were accompanied by a letter from the Secretary of State. What had been done, Mr. Bayard said, had "transferred and elevated" the question of the interpretation and administration of the treaty of 1818 "from the obscurity with which it had been suffered to lapse," and "restored" it from the practical control of minor and local officials of the Canadian Maritime Provinces. Hereafter, and for the first time since 1818, "just and hospitable treatment" for United States fishermen while within the jurisdictional waters of Canada or Newfoundland, and the unmolested enjoyment of a "full measure of their rights" under that treaty would be guaranteed.[3]

Cleveland, Bayard, Chamberlain and the commissioners might have saved themselves the trouble to which they were put in giving their minds to the many small questions involved in the negotiation. They had worked industriously and intelligently and had presented a plan which deserved a fair hearing. Instead the response of the Republicans was wrath and dudgeon. The difficulty at ground was that the Democratic President might not amicably settle a matter which, while it remained unsettled, could be made available in the opposite

---

[1] Senate Ex. Doc., 50th Cong. 1st sess., no. 113, pp. 124–5, 141.
[2] Richardson, vol. viii, pp. 603–7.
[3] Senate Ex. Doc., 50th Cong. 1st sess., no. 113, p. 2.

party's avocation of heckling England and capturing Irish-American votes; [1] that, if there were credit to be had by settlement, it should accrue to the Republicans and not to the Democrats; and that the Yankee fishermen wanted, and must receive, protection against Canadian cod, mackerel and halibut. While this was not a reciprocity treaty "free fish" might very likely follow the Chamberlain-Bayard parleys. If an inch were given the enemy he would take an ell. [2]

No treaty was wanted. This one, therefore, was foredoomed. The State Department under Cleveland, the New York Tribune said, was a mere "center of British American diplomacy." [3] Bayard had never approached the subject from "the American point of view." He had displayed, in dealing with it, "the spirit of a pettifogging lawyer"; he had not acted "as the patriotic representative of a great nation under obligation to resent insults to the flag." [4] In a word he had been "duped" [5] by Mr. Chamberlain who had "served his government with astuteness and singular success," and who deserved a peerage at its hands. [6] The treaty marked "the lowest point of degradation which American diplomacy had ever reached." [7] It was "a monstrous proposition." [8] The Senate should "make short work of it." [9]

The extortionate sums exacted of us by the Halifax Commission were again brought forward to inflame, if possible, the popular mind. We had paid Canada, said William Henry Trescot, who had been counsel for the United States before the Halifax Commission and was now a lawyer in Washington, the "enormous amount" of $10,000,000—$5,000,000 in cash and the rest in twelve years' remitted duties on Canadian

---

[1] Cf. Keenleyside, Canada and the U. S., p. 271.
[2] Cf. N. Y. Nation, Dec. 1, 1887; House Ex. Doc., 49th Cong. 2nd sess., no. 19, p. 174.
[3] N. Y. Tribune, Feb. 17, 1888; cf. N. Y. Nation, March 1, 1888.
[4] N. Y. Tribune, Feb. 22, 1888.
[5] He had been "bamboozled" by Chamberlain "at every point."—Hoar, Autobiography of Seventy Years, vol. ii, p. 149.
[6] N. Y. Tribune, Feb. 24, 1888.
[7] Ibid., Feb. 23, 1888.
[8] Ibid., Feb. 24, 1888.
[9] Ibid., Feb. 23, 1888.

fish. What had we received in return? The privilege of catching $700,000 worth of fish in British American waters, about $58,000 annually.[1]

The report of the Committee on Foreign Relations was a party pronunciamento. The Republican leaders had said in the beginning, they said again, that the President had acted without authority in that he had not asked the Senate for permission to proceed with the negotiation, to the extent at least of submitting the names of the "plenipotentiaries" for confirmation. The Senate had convened soon after these public ministers were named. It was a course adjudged to be a particularly grave "usurpation of unconstitutional power,"[2] in view of the fact that barely two years had passed since Frye of Maine, and his fellow custodians of the interests of the New England fishermen, had put on record their disapproval of the whole idea of a commission which Arthur, and then Cleveland, had advanced.[3] "The existing matters of difficulty," they said, were not "subjects for treaty negotiation."[4] The committee, in effect, declared that the President had no duty in the premises except to follow Congress and to enforce the provisions of the "Retaliation act" of March 3, 1887.[5] To this statement, expressive of a preference for embroilment with the greatest naval power in the world, to orderly procedure by conversations, Senators Sherman, Edmunds, Frye, Evarts and Dolph appended their names.

Chamberlain, before leaving the country, was, on March 3rd, the guest at dinner of the Canadian Club of New York. He had seen and heard enough to know the temper of the opposition, and he entered upon an able defense of the treaty. It was submitted, he said, amid applause, "not to the impassioned prejudices of partisans, but to the calm and superior

---

[1] N. Y. Herald, Feb. 27, 1888; N. Y. Tribune, Feb. 24, 1888.
[2] Senate Mis. Doc., 50th Cong. 1st sess., no. 109, p. 17. For a statement of the many cases in the history of the country in which this had not been done with reference to diplomatic agents see ibid., pp. 103–4.
[3] Ibid., p. 15; cf. ibid., p. 75.
[4] Ibid., p. 34.
[5] N. Y. Nation, May 17, 24 and June 14, 1888.

judgment, to the common sense and reason, and, above all, to the friendly feeling of both countries." Surrender had been spoken of in Canada and also in the United States. But both had gained "substantially what they had contended for." There had been "no surrender at all, on either side, of national honor or national interest." Chamberlain expressed the hope and belief that the treaty would be ratified.[1]

It was not to be so. The treaty in a Presidential canvass was inseparable from the general tariff question. It was put in a class with the "Mills bill" and the Cobden Club. Some American fishing smacks caught about $55,000 worth of fish annually in Canadian waters and they must have "protection."

That the tirades of Frye and his fellow senators might carry far and sink deeply the treaty, contrary to usage, was discussed in "open executive session." Such words were spoken, such charges were made in the course of the debate as are seldom uttered in time of peace regarding another government. The men who fulminated "their idle bulls" against the President were recognized to be partisans, heated in the fires of a political campaign. But the assertions of the want of all civilized attributes in the British people generally and Canadians in particular, as Senator Morgan, who had made the minority report for the Committee on Foreign Relations, truly enough said, were of a kind which, if uttered and aimed at us in Parliament in Ottawa, or in London, would be regarded throughout the United States as "a challenge to war."[2]

The treaty was rejected by a definitely divided party vote, 27 Democrats being counted for it and 30 Republicans against it.[3] It would find application simply as a campaign document in parts of the country where men thought in terms of fish, as pig iron, sugar and wool in other places were used to beguile voters who, in a democracy, are too often and too easily persuaded to put their personal interests above the public good.[4]

[1] N. Y. Herald, March 3, 1888; N. Y. Nation, March 8, 1888.
[2] App. Ann. Cyclop. for 1888, p. 223.
[3] Cong. Record, 50th Cong. 1st sess., p. 7768; McPherson's Handbook for 1888, p. 223.
[4] Cf. N. Y. Nation, April 26, 1888. The relations of the United States and

The President was not to be left with the burden of a pro-English record at his door. He sent a message to Congress on August 23, 1888. He said that our citizens engaged in fishing enterprises had been treated by the Canadian authorities "in a manner inexcusably harsh and oppressive." The treaty which had been rejected would have promoted more friendly intimacy and the Senate, while disapproving, had exhibited no disposition to alter the provisions of the agreement or, indeed, to meet the situation in any manner whatever. He must turn to a "plan of retaliation." The act of 1887 remained unenforced; at need, on occasion, he would enforce it. But while he would dissociate himself from those suspected of friendliness to England he would be clear of alliance also with the New England fish men, who thought of no retaliation except a kind which would increase the price of what they had to sell. The President asked for new legislation. He asked for authority to suspend by proclamation the privilege which Canada enjoyed of transporting goods across the territory of the United States in bond. During the past six years this trade had reached a value of $270,000,000. He also alluded to the tolls and charges on Canadian canals, while canals which we maintained for the navigation of the Great Lakes remained free.[1] He would have Congress legislate so that there might be justice and equality on these points. "If we are generous and liberal to a neighboring country," the President said, we should "reap the advantage of it by a return of liberality and generosity."[2]

The Chinaman would, of course, fare worse than the Englishman during an angry party campaign. He had had few friends when he was the subject of earlier legislation and, so far as appeared, he now had none, at any rate none actively

Canada on the subject of the fisheries, although limited to two years, continued to be governed by the *modus vivendi* which Mr. Chamberlain and his fellow commissioners offered us until 1924, even after the matters in question were submitted for settlement to the Hague Tribunal.— Keenleyside, Canada and the United States, pp. 271, 289.

[1] Cf. Senate Ex. Doc., 50th Cong. 1st sess., no. 265; House Ex. Doc., 50th Cong. 1st sess., no. 406.

[2] Richardson, Messages and Papers, vol. viii, pp. 620–27; cf. ibid., pp. 628–30; House Ex. Doc., 50th Cong. 1st sess., no. 434.

identified with our "politics." The "hoodlum" and "sand lot" view of the Chinese question had come to govern the whole Pacific coast in so far as that region made declaration of its sentiments through political parties, and what Senator Sherman called a "race" was begun between the two houses of Congress, one Democratic and the other Republican, to determine which could most abase itself in order to gain favor in the West for its candidate for President.[1]

The anti-Chinese leaders in California did not cease to say that the provisions of the "Restriction act" were too liberal, that it was being evaded, that bread was being taken from the mouth of the American workingman by the hated intruder with a yellow skin from Asia. To the murders and riots in the Western states and territories were added, in the summer of 1886, brutal outrages in Alaska.[2] In the summer of 1887 ten Chinamen were horridly murdered on the Snake River in Idaho.[3] These events were notice to the Chinese government, were more needed, that further treaty arrangements would be desirable if its subjects here were to enjoy any measure of peace and security. The Chinese minister at Washington and Secretary Bayard gave their attention to the matter with a view to presenting a statement of relationships between the two countries on the subjects of immigration and residence to which the people of our Western states and territories might be willing to conform. To the treaty was joined the proposal on our side, to make a further payment to China, though still denying obligation to do so, to cover outstanding claims for losses suffered by her nationals at the hands of mobs, amounting to $276,619.75, which should be "full indemnity."[4] The Senate treated the subject as a party matter. Credit for the negotiation must not accrue to Cleveland and the Democratic administration. To prevent so undesirable an eventuality

[1] Cf. Coolidge, Chinese Immigration, p. 183.
[2] Senate Ex. Doc., 50th Cong. 1st sess., no. 272, pp. 6–8. Rep. of Sec. of Int. for 1886, vol. ii, pp. 972–80.
[3] Senate Ex. Doc., 50th Cong. 1st sess., no. 272, pp. 24–9.
[4] Correspondence regarding, and text of, treaty in Senate Ex. Doc., 50th Cong. 1st sess., no. 272.

and to capture the labor vote, the Senate, in confirming the treaty, added amendments, one of which provided that Chinese should be prohibited from entering the United States, whether holding "return certificates" or not.[1] The Chinese minister at Washington noted the changes in the text; in due time he would announce, he said, the ratification of his "august sovereign."[2]

But diplomacy was too slow for the needs of a political campaign. Though the treaty itself had gone to China only in March and the amendments in May, 1888, impatience was growing and some action, from the standpoint of the party managers, was imperative at once. Congress busied itself with a bill which had originated in the Senate "to prohibit the coming of Chinese laborers to the United States." This measure would be supplementary and would take effect when the treaty should be ratified. The bill passed the Senate, on the third reading without a division, on August 8th,[3] and the next day, pressed by a Californian, appeared in the House where it was passed on August 20th, also without a division, to be sent to the President.[4] Cleveland, unwilling to be made the victim of sharp practice, added his approval.[5]

But before he had affixed his signature to the measure news came through the press that the Chinese government had rejected the treaty, whereupon W. L. Scott of Pennsylvania, the President's friend and a leading manager of his campaign for reëlection, anxious to seize advantage for the party, brought a bill into the House to enforce immediate prohibition upon the entry of Chinese laborers, declaring that no more "return certificates" should be issued and making void such as were outstanding and had not yet been presented to our port authorities. It was passed by the House in a few minutes, without reference to, or report from, a committee, and was sent to

[1] McPherson's Handbook for 1888, pp. 193–4; N. Y. Nation, May 17, 1888.
[2] Senate Ex. Doc., 50th Cong. 1st sess., no. 272, p. 35.
[3] Cong. Record, 50th Cong. 1st sess., p. 7323.
[4] Ibid., p. 7759.
[5] On September 13, 1888.

the Senate.[1] Such high-handed playing of the "game of politics" met some protest in the Senate, and from men belonging to both parties. But after Democrat had tried to discredit Republican, and Republican reproached Democrat for the party record on the question, they hurried it to passage in spite of the fact that, on September 7th, the President submitted official information to the effect that China had not rejected the treaty as press dispatches had declared, but was holding it for further discussion and amendment.[2] All obstruction was in vain.[3] Legislation was to be substituted for international agreement. On October 1st the President signed the bill.[4] He labored in a message, as best he could, to justify his action, alluding to a want of sincerity, as indicated by delay, and the absence in the negotiations on China's part of a coöperative spirit,[5] putting blame upon the Chinese government which he must have felt unjustifiable. He did, indeed, note the unfairness of voiding the certificates of Chinese already at sea on their way back to America, and emphasized the expediency of paying the proposed indemnity.

Twenty thousand Chinese who had left the United States with certificates entitling them to return, 600 of whom were actually on steamships soon due to arrive, many of them having left their families and valuable property behind them when they, in good faith, started away on a visit to their homes, would be barred when they should reach San Francisco.[6] There was no redress for any of them. The customs and immigration authorities were unyielding, protests to the President, to the State Department and appeals to the courts were without avail, and the matter on our side had come to an end. The

[1] September 3rd.—Cong. Record, 50th Cong. 1st sess., p. 8226; cf. ibid., pp. 8254–5, 8332.

[2] Ibid., p. 8365; Senate Ex. Doc., 50th Cong. 1st sess., no. 271; cf. Senate Ex. Doc., 50th Cong. 2nd sess., no. 47.

[3] For attitude of N. Y. Chamber of Commerce and its protests see Chinese Exclusion Act, Report and Resolutions, Dec. 5, 1889.

[4] 25 U. S. Statutes at Large, p. 504.

[5] Senate Ex. Doc., 50th Cong. 1st sess., no. 273; Richardson, Messages and Papers, vol. viii, pp. 630–35.

[6] Coolidge, Chinese Immigration, pp. 203–4.

Chinese ministers at Washington, with that dry humor and eloquent sarcasm of which they had a peculiar command, stated their case, and restated it. "I was not prepared to learn," said one of them, "that there was a way recognized in the law and practice of this country whereby your country could release itself from treaty obligations without consultations, or the consent of the other party," and more to like effect.[1] Secretary Bayard had declared, during the negotiations, that, if Congress should enact a law in disregard of treaty stipulations, the President "would, of course, veto it."[2] Bayard responded now that the "Scott act" was passed with such "unanimity in both houses" that it "palpably rendered an interposition by a veto of the Executive wholly futile."[3]

The indemnity was paid in an offhand way by including the item in the deficiency appropriation bill, a few days before adjournment, with the familiar explanation that it was "out of humane consideration and without reference to the question of liability" for the deeds, which so darkly reflected upon the state of government and society in the republic.[4]

There were a few movements on the part of the President during the campaign which were more in keeping with his reputation for a statesmanlike mind, and which must have filled him with a feeling of greater satisfaction in the quiet of later life. The Dependent Pension bill, somewhat modified to answer Executive objections, again made its appearance in Congress with the support of the Grand Army organization[5] to be passed by the Senate,[6] but it made no progress in the House, and the President was not called upon for further statement of his views on this subject. He continued to veto private pension bills,[7] and a number of schemes to erect public

---

[1] Coolidge, Chinese Immigration, p. 203.
[2] Ibid., p. 202.
[3] Ibid., pp. 183, 202.
[4] 25 U. S. Statutes at Large, p. 566.
[5] N. Y. Tribune, March 1 and 10, 1888; N. Y. Nation, July 21, Aug. 11 and 18, Sep. 15 and Oct. 6, 1887, March 8, 1888.
[6] Cf. N. Y. Nation, March 15, 1888.
[7] Cf. ibid., April 19, May 3, 10 and 24, June 28, July 12, 1888; Richardson, vol. viii, pp. 638-740 passim.

buildings in small towns and cities, advocated in many cases, now as before, merely for the improvement of the position of individual Congressmen in the sight of the communities in which they dwelt. [1]

There was merited criticism of the President for his "serious lapses" in the matter of civil service reform.[2] These had multiplied under the demands of the party managers as the time of election approached. The New York Nation said that he had "fallen far short of his promises." [3] The Indian service was in a deplorable condition, worse, it was believed, than ever before, and though it seemed to be true that the President, under existing law, might have extended the classified system to cover the Western agencies, he had not done so.[4] His record in some particulars pained his admirers of four years ago, especially as he had preferred strong guarantees that he would follow other courses.[5]

It could be pointed out, nevertheless, that he had withstood the devices and stratagems of the spoils hunters with more blunt vigor than any of his predecessors. His surrenders were very likely small in view of the attempts which were made to unhand him and, through his agency, or in his despite, wring money and lucrative place from the government. The ordeal which he, or any other President, must daily pass through could be known to none, it was observed, but those who had held the same position and had been subjected to like experiences.[6] It must be noted and remembered that, upon assuming the Presidency, Mr. Cleveland had made no "clean sweep" of the offices; that he had kept Republicans in place, though some of them seized every opportunity to revile him, often publicly and in the most offensive ways; that now, near the end of his term, as before, such large busi-

---

[1] Richardson, vol. viii, pp. 658–9, 669–70, 672–4; N. Y. Nation, May 17, 1888.
[2] N. Y. Nation, June 21, 1888.
[3] Ibid., June 14, 1888; cf. Writings of Carl Schurz, vol. iv, pp. 511–2; 527–8.
[4] N. Y. Nation, Jan. 21, 1886, and March 15 and May 31, 1888.
[5] Ibid., June 7, 1888; Carl R. Fish, The Civil Service, pp. 222–3.
[6] Cf. N. Y. Nation, June 14, 1888.

ness establishments as the New York customhouse and the New York post office were undisturbed by politics; that Executive influence was distinctly on the side of an honest and efficient administration of the government, and, by precept, if not always by example, vigorously against the system of regarding public office as party spoil.[1]

New civil service rules were promulgated to take effect on March 1, 1888.[2] This was declared to be "a long step forward," and was an effective answer to those who said that the President had abandoned the reform.[3] On March 21, 1888, he urged the Civil Service Commission to revise its classifications in the various departments, in the interest of uniformity, and, with a view to the extension of the limits of the field of its activity, so that a greater number of offices should be put above the reach of partisan appointive authority. The commission complied.[4] The order was issued on July 1st. Its effect was to bring within the range of the reform every person in the government departments, except laborers and unskilled workmen in the lowest, and those specifically excepted from the operation of the rules in the higher, places, practically then the entire body of Federal employees at Washington.[5] It was a significant extension of "the application of the reform principle," said the New York Times. A man who, at "the very threshold" of a canvass for reëlection, "deliberately" reduced his own and his partisans' power of rewarding his friends for their labors in his behalf, could not be denied "the credit of the sincerity that goes with courage."[6]

[1] Cf. N. Y. Nation, June 14 and 21, 1888.
[2] Richardson, vol. viii, pp. 744–62; N. Y. Nation, Feb. 9, 1888.
[3] N. Y. Times, Feb. 4, 1888.
[4] Richardson, vol. viii, pp. 763–4; cf. ibid., pp. 616–9.
[5] N. Y. Nation, July 5, 1888.
[6] N. Y. Times, July 3, 1888; cf. R. W. Gilder, Grover Cleveland, pp. 19–23.

CHAPTER XXXI

THE withdrawal of the Federal troops, during the administration of President Hayes, the lifting of the corrupting hand of the Northern "carpetbag" politicians and such allies as they were able to find in the disreputable resident white elements in the population, who had gained and held their ascendancy by the manipulation of the new negro voters, left the people of the South free for such progress as they could make at their own pace. When Garfield was elected 15 years had passed since the war's end, when Cleveland became President 20 years were gone by, and it was beginning to be plain to intelligent observers that a ferment was at work in the states which had seceded from, and which had been brought back into, the Union. The people had been told that they might better give up recrimination and, by education and work, face the problems of human existence. The North had been counseled by such leaders as had a proper portion of sagacity to quiet its pæans of triumph, put forgiveness where vengeance had been and grant the late armed enemy the opportunity to live comfortably and contentedly in the Union to which they had been returned by military force. Politicians rose in Congress and on the hustings in electoral campaigns, editors fulminated in newspapers, but they met less and less encouragement from the people, who are the quiet strength of states which order their affairs in accordance with the principles of democracy. No man, except possibly the politician and the editor, could live by mouthing about a dead war.

Nowhere was advancement in business and the prosperity which is reflected by banking, manufacturing, transportation and commercial movements so much a subject of comment as in Georgia which came to be called the "Empire State of the South," [1] and particularly in the city of Atlanta. Burned by Sherman, left a desolate ruin by the Northern army which visited it in the last year of the war, it had risen with rapidity to a position, in point of population and wealth, scarcely dreamt of by its inhabitants before its day of calamity.[2]

Governor Colquitt, in 1880, found, "everywhere within the broad limits" of Georgia, "progress, order, thrift and contentment." Industries had thriven, resources had been "multiplied and developed," all sections of the state had "grown in wealth and population."[3] The governor of Louisiana, in 1881, directed attention to the "wonderful development" of his state's resources. No longer could men speak of "poor Louisiana and her impoverished people." She was "rich," and she would soon take her place in "the front rank of states."[4] Alabama was prospering, said the governor of that state in 1886; commercial and manufacturing enterprise was reaping large rewards. Her mineral resources had "challenged the attention of the world" and "eager capital from remote countries" was coming forward to hasten her industrial development.[5]

In Atlanta appeared daily a newspaper which came to be regarded as the herald of the "New South." While the Northern reader looked to several well known journals for expressions of Bourbonism, which it was, to many, a satisfaction, as it seemed, to discover in Southern places among Southern men, in support of a bitterness which still was found in Northern breasts, the Atlanta Constitution told of other things. Its editor, Henry W. Grady, had a gifted tongue. He could speak as well as write; he uttered words as an orator which electrified the country and made the North know that the South had been reborn. When, on the night of December 22, 1886, on Forefathers' Day, at the invitation of the New England So-

[1] App. Ann. Cyclop. for 1880, p. 303.
[2] Report of Senate Committee on Ed. and Labor on Relations between Labor and Capital, vol. iv, 1885, pp. 677–81.
[3] App. Ann. Cyclop. for 1880, p. 303.
[4] Ibid. for 1881, p. 515.
[5] Ibid. for 1886, p. 6.

ciety, he appeared before a distinguished audience at Delmonico's in New York, General Sherman, who was considered by some in Atlanta, as Grady said, "a kind of careless man about fire," and many others sat at the board. Grady's speech was the event of the night. Fact and common sense, interspersed with pleasantry, noble sentiment, humorous illustration, fine periods, true eloquence, kept his hearers laughing, applauding and cheering. More than once all, as of one accord, rose to their feet and at the end, as the band played "Dixie," they gave three ringing huzzas for Grady, and three more for the "Empire State of the South."

The very fact of a Southerner appearing at a New England Society dinner was an omen of new fellowship. As the orator spoke of Lincoln, who "comprehended within himself all the strength and gentleness, all the majesty and grace of this republic," the "sum of Puritan and Cavalier, in whose ardent nature were fused the virtues of both," in the depth of whose great soul "the faults of both were lost," men knew that Grady had approached his task, as he had declared, with "a sense of consecration." He was not silent on the subject of the "Old South," he loved it. But it was gone and in its place was a country made over by work. The people did not repine; somehow they had "caught the sunshine in the bricks and mortar of their homes," and had builded in them "not one single ignoble prejudice or memory." They had "sowed towns and cities in the place of theories and put business above politics." They had "challenged" the spinners of Massachusetts and the iron makers of Pennsylvania. The rate of interest on money had been reduced from 24 to 6 per cent and they were floating bonds at 4 per cent. They had learned that the free negro was better than the bondman. The shackles that had held them "in narrow limitations fell forever when the shackles of the negro slave were broken." They had learned that one immigrant from the North was worth 50 "foreigners," wherefore "we have smoothed the path to the southward," Grady said, "wiped out the place where Mason's and Dixon's line used to be and hung our latchstring out to you and yours."

The "Old South" had rested everything on slavery and agriculture; the "New South" spoke of another system, "less
splendid on the surface but stronger at the core—a hundred
farms for every plantation, fifty homes for every palace and
a diversified industry that meets the complex needs of this
complex age." The "New South" was "enamored of her
work." Her soul was "stirred with the breath of a new life."
The "light of a grander day" was "falling fair on her face."
She was "thrilling with the consciousness of growing power
and prosperity." [1]

"In all its four score years," said the New York Times,
"the society of Plymouth Rock worshippers never heard a
speech that was better worth its while to hear and think
about." [2] "It was wonderfully effective," said the New York
World, and "truly eloquent." [3] It was "infused with the vital
qualities of oratory," said the New York Nation, it was "the
perfect expression" of what was so difficult to understand in
the North—"the real attitude of the South towards the past
and future." [4] Even the New York Tribune, not omitting its
familiar allusions to outrages upon the negroes and election
day frauds, said that the speech had "reached a high plane
in contemporary oratory"—the nature that could "grudgingly,
or with strained courtesy, meet this frank and manly proffer
of brotherhood," it said, "must indeed be barren of all grace
and nobility." [5]

Upon Grady's return to Atlanta he was met at the railway
station by a brass band. Through streets filled with cheering
throngs he was escorted to the principal hotel of the place,
where prominent citizens tendered him a dinner in appreciation of his achievement in so clearly setting the South before
Northern eyes. [6]

Other men, other newspapers appeared upon the scene—
all acting in a similar spirit toward like ends; among them
notably, Daniel A. Tompkins, who controlled the Charlotte

[1] New York Tribune, Dec. 23, 1886.   [4] N. Y. Nation, Dec. 30, 1886.
[2] N. Y. Times, Dec. 23, 1886.   [5] N. Y. Tribune, Dec. 24, 1886.
[3] N. Y. World, Dec. 24, 1886.   [6] Ibid., Dec. 25, 1886.

Observer in North Carolina,[1] and Richard H. Edmonds, an indefatigable advocate and recorder of Southern progress, who published the Manufacturers' Record in Baltimore.

The South found the basis for its growth, principally, in two fine resources which, while she had restricted herself to agricultural interests, she had neglected, and these were her coal and iron and the water power with which to turn the wheels of mills engaged in cotton manufacture. Soft coal measures and iron ore lay side by side in Alabama, Tennessee, and northwestern Georgia. In 1880 men began to say that the supply was "inexhaustible." In 1872 only 10,000 tons of coal had been mined in Alabama; in 1880 the total production was 324,000 tons, valued at $2,000,000; in 1887, 1,900,000; in 1888, 2,900,000, and in 1889, 4,000,000 tons.[2] Nearly all of this came from a great field in the northwestern part of the state, two-thirds as large as the coal area of Great Britain, covering a region drained by the Black Warrior River. The state geologist said that the measure would produce one hundred billion tons, worth enough money to buy everything else of value in Alabama 200 times over.[3]

In 1880 the mines in the Cumberland plateau in Tennessee yielded nearly 500,000 tons;[4] in 1886 nearly 2,000,000 tons.[5] Shipments were being made to the Gulf ports where vessels were laden for the North and for foreign countries. Even in the little towns of the South, if they were reached by railway, wood was being abandoned as a fuel and coal, furnished at low prices, was burned in its stead.[6] Virginia's, West Virginia's and Kentucky's mines were at the same time greatly increasing their output.[7]

The iron industry found its principal centers in two new towns, called, appropriately enough, Birmingham and Sheffield,

[1] G. T. Winston, A Builder of the New South, chap. xiv.
[2] R. H. Edmonds, The South's Redemption, p. 25; cf. N. Y. Nation, Dec. 9, 1886; App. Ann. Cyclop. for 1881, p. 8; ibid., for 1882, p. 4.
[3] N. Y. Nation, Dec. 9, 1886.
[4] App. Ann. Cyclop. for 1881, p. 831.
[5] Ibid. for 1888, p. 763.
[6] Ibid. for 1884, p. 7.
[7] R. H. Edmonds, op. cit., p. 25.

and in Chattanooga. Before the war the ores had been worked in a small way by crude processes. Now men of vision and ability gave their attention to the construction of modern furnaces and iron and steel mills. The first coke furnace was erected in Tennessee in 1867, the second in 1872. One or two furnaces of improved construction were put in operation at about the same time in Alabama. In 1888, in the Birmingham district, there were 21 large coke furnaces; in and around Chattanooga, 15 coke and 13 charcoal furnaces. General Willard Warner, one of the pioneers in the industry, said that when he had visited the site of Birmingham in 1870 it was a cotton field; he could have purchased it for $10 an acre. In 1880 it had a population of 4,500; in 1886, 30,000; and in 1888, probably, 50,000. Property in the "Magic City" in 1887 had a taxable value of more than $33,000,000. Iron ore, coal, limestone abounded nearby. Pig iron could be made here for $10 or $12 a ton.[1] Six trunk lines of railway, 11 banks, 4 daily and 11 weekly newspapers, 66 miles of tramways certified to the commercial activity of the place.[2]

In 1870 a man had bought the site of Anniston and the land surrounding it for a song. Outcroppings of iron invited mining in "open cut." The ore could be shelved down and gathered up without excavation. A town was laid out in the midst of this plenty and it had rapid growth. In 1888 it had 12,000 inhabitants, twice its population in the preceding year.[3] A short while since the site of the town called Sheffield had been a cornfield. Bessemer had had no existence, nor had South Pittsburg which quickly spread over the fields at the "Great Bend" of the Tennessee River in the state of Tennessee.[4] Chattanooga had not been much more than a village when it

---

[1] Report of Senate Com. on Ed. and Labor, 1885, vol. iv, pp. 300, 384, 406, 445.

[2] App. Ann. Cyclop. for 1888, p. 159; N. Y. Tribune, Dec. 23, 1886; cf. ibid., Sep. 7, 1883; W. D. Kelley, The Old South and the New, pp. 7-8; Historical and Statistical Review of North Alabama, p. 29; J. W. DuBose, Mineral Wealth of Alabama; Report of Senate Com. on Ed. and Labor, 1885, vol. iv, pp. 280-81, 347-8, 349-50.

[3] App. Ann. Cyclop. for 1888, p. 158; W. D. Kelley, op. cit., pp. 9-13.

[4] App. Ann. Cyclop. for 1889, p. 160; W. D. Kelley, op. cit., pp. 68-89.

came into notice as a battle ground during the Civil War; now
it was a prosperous city of 50,000 people.[1]

The total production of pig iron in Alabama in 1880 was
77,000 tons; it was 190,000 tons in 1884 and 915,000 tons in
1890. Production in Tennessee increased from 70,000 tons in
1880 to 157,000 in 1884 and 300,000 in 1890.[2] The output of all
the Southern states in 1890 was nearly two million tons in
a total of ten million tons for the entire United States.[3] Steel
rails and other finished products were beginning to be made
in new mills by improved methods to take their places in the
markets of the country beside the best from Pittsburgh.[4] The
largest manufacturing enterprise in this field, the Tennessee
Coal, Iron and Railroad Company, had a capital of $10,000,-
000,[5] soon to be increased under the hand of John H. Inman,
a native of Tennessee who had become influential in the cotton
trade in New York. The capital invested in the iron and steel
business in Alabama, which had been $2,700,000 in 1880, was
nearly $18,000,000 in 1890.[6] New furnaces in Virginia were
rapidly increasing the output of iron in that state.[7]

Mr. Inman extended and improved the transportation system
of the South and made himself active in the management of
more than 12,000 miles of railway. He had sent, Grady said,
a hundred million dollars to the South for investment.[8]

The men who raised tobacco in Virginia and North Carolina
saw the opportunity which lay at their doors. Why should
they not make the leaf which they grew into snuff, smoking
tobacco, cigarettes, when these came into fashion, and chewing
plugs, instead of sending the crop away to give employment
and profit to the manufacturers of the North? Durham in

[1] Cf. R. H. Edmonds, The South's Redemption, pp. 10–11; W. D. Kelley,
op. cit., pp. 5–6, 47–67.
[2] J. M. Swank, The Manufacture of Iron in All Ages, p. 296.
[3] Ibid., pp. 296, 376; cf. R. H. Edmonds, The South's Redemption, p. 20.
[4] J. H. Dodd, A History of Production in the Iron and Steel Industry in
the Southern Appalachian States, p. 96.
[5] N. Y. Tribune, Dec. 20, 1880.
[6] J. H. Dodd, op. cit., p. 65.
[7] Cf. R. H. Edmonds, The South's Redemption, p. 13.
[8] Grady to Lamont, Aug. 2, 1887, in Cleveland Papers.

North Carolina prior to the Civil War had had but one small tobacco manufactory. In 1888 it contained the largest business of its kind in the world with a production of 10,000,000 pounds of smoking tobacco yearly. Already in 1886 a company in the same town made and shipped away over 250,000,000 cigarettes.[1] Lynchburg and other towns, set in the midst of a region where the tobacco plant throve, grew at an amazing pace.[2] Prosperity in this industry rested on a change from the "black" to "bright," or "yellow," tobacco, which required another soil and permitted a great extension of the area of culture.[3]

Cane from the brakes of Louisiana had been crushed for years for sugar and molasses, but the processes were rude. More could be done to make this industry thrifty. Already in 1878–9 the production was 208,000 hogsheads, surpassed by only a few crops in the history of the business in Louisiana.[4] In 1882 the yield from sugar was $25,000,000, from molasses $5,000,000.[5] Some of the planters by the adoption of new methods nearly doubled the product of their sugarhouses.[6]

The steaming wastes of Florida were full of prophecy. They could be planted with citrus fruits. In 1877 more than 20,000,-000 orange trees were standing in the groves. They would bear in seven years and reach their full yield in 20 years, when the average return for each tree would be in excess of 500 oranges. Enough trees were productive in 1877 to give the state a crop of 16,000,000 [7] which, in spite of unwelcome frosts, was increased in 1881 to about 80,000,000 individual pieces of fruit.[8] Many Northern people were fascinated by the prospect of a business about which they know but little, and it was estimated, in 1880, that more than $10,-000,000 were invested in it.[9] They had a sad awakening in January, 1886, when the temperature in Fernandina fell before a westerly gale to 15 degrees Fahrenheit, with readings

---

[1] App. Ann. Cyclop. for 1888, p. 163.
[2] Ibid. for 1887, p. 124.
[3] Ibid. for 1881, p. 668.
[4] Ibid. for 1879, p. 570; ibid. for 1880, p. 482.
[5] Ibid. for 1882, p. 485.
[6] Ibid. for 1888, p. 500.
[7] Ibid. for 1879, p. 377.
[8] Ibid. for 1881, p. 301.
[9] Ibid. for 1883, p. 342.

of the thermometer far below the freezing point for all northern
and central Florida. Such weather continued for three or four
days. It was the most severe cold experienced in this latitude,
it was said, since 1835. The groves, as well as the crop of the
year, were destroyed. Nearly 1,000,000 trees had been brought
into bearing condition in 1884, and, under such punishment,
a wide belt in the northern part of the state was permanently
abandoned by the orchardists.[1]

Georgia, as well as Florida, was raising large quantities of
melons.[2] In many Southern states berries, vegetables and
small fruits could be made ready for Northern markets several
weeks before they could be expected from any other source.[3]
The refrigerator car on the railroads conveyed the products
of the gardens and fields, planted on land that had been held
to be unprofitable, if not useless, to man, to cities in the North
which welcomed them. Mississippi was cultivating a valuable
trade with Chicago.[4]

Forests of pine were to be felled. Sawmills and planing
mills rose in the wilderness to prepare lumber for local use
and for export. Florida and North Carolina had immense
areas which invited the axe.[5] So had Mississippi in which
state it was said that twelve billion feet (board measure) of
long leaf, or "yellow," pine were standing. There were seven
billion feet of short leaf or "white" pine lumber in the state.[6]
In 1880 it was estimated that Alabama had fifteen billion feet of
long leaf pine timber within her borders, but it was being consumed so rapidly that in less than 25 years the supply, it
was predicted, would be exhausted.[7] Cypress abounded in
many states and the brakes were yielding vast quantities of
valuable wood.[8] Companies were formed in Wall Street to
purchase large tracts of Southern timberland, and to build rail-

[1] App. Ann. Cyclop. for 1886, p. 350.
[2] Ibid. for 1883, p. 388.
[3] Cf. ibid., p. 342.
[4] Ibid. for 1879, p. 635.
[5] Ibid. for 1881, p. 300; ibid. for 1883, p. 583.
[6] Ibid. for 1883, p. 545; cf. ibid. for 1882, p. 561.
[7] Ibid. for 1884, p. 8.
[8] Report of Senate Com. on Ed. and Labor, 1885, vol. ii, pp. 185–6.

roads across it in order to take out all that was of useful size in the briefest possible time at the greatest profit to themselves. This business, while it spoke of activity and wealth, also suggested devastation. If the land, which was stripped of its timber by speculative enterprise, should not be reforested, it meant the loss of a valuable national resource.

The discovery that the streams coming down from the mountains in the Piedmont would propel the machinery for the spinning of the cotton which grew in the fields of the South from the hill lands on down to the shores and islands of the sea, to obviate the sending of the crop to New England and Lancashire, may have seemed to require no especial insight.[1] But cotton mills were now a fact. One enthusiast, in North Carolina, computed that the streams of that state would develop three million horse power, which he thought was in excess of that of all the steam engines of this country or of Great Britain.[2] Another, in South Carolina, declared that there was enough power going to waste in the northern and western counties of that state to operate all the cotton factories in the United States.[3]

When water could not be used for power coal was at hand not many miles from the scene. Native enterprise, impelled by the active minds and the more cheerful hearts of the sons of those who had fought and lost the war, had started this new industry on the way to success, and in a little while to marked importance.[4] Only nine factories, employing some 1,400 persons, were in operation in South Carolina in 1879.[5] The number in the next year was given as 17, with 96,000 spindles and 1,933 looms.[6] Two years later these totals had nearly doubled. The capital invested in the business amounted

---

[1] Cf. Broadus Mitchell, Rise of Cotton Mills in the South, p. 137.
[2] App. Ann. Cyclop. for 1879, pp. 691-2.
[3] Ibid. for 1880, p. 669; cf. ibid. for 1882, p. 747; for Georgia see Report of Senate Com. on Ed. and Labor, 1885, vol. iv, p. 507.
[4] Holland Thompson, From Cotton Field to Cotton Mill, p. 81; M. A. Potwin, Cotton Mill People of the Piedmont, pp. 29, 30; Broadus Mitchell, Rise of Cotton Mills in the South, pp. 102, 105-11, 234-5.
[5] App. Ann. Cyclop. for 1879, p. 820.
[6] Ibid. for 1880, p. 669.

to nearly $5,000,000 and about 5,000 men, women and children found employment in the mills.[1]

Augusta and Columbus were the principal cotton manufacturing centers in Georgia. In the mills in and around Augusta in 1882 there were 128,000 spindles and 3,379 looms, consuming 57,000 bales of cotton annually. Within the walls of one factory in Columbus, with a capital of a million and a quarter, 46,000 spindles and 1,600 looms were at work.[2]

North Carolina in 1880 had had 49 cotton mills with 92,000 spindles. The number of mills in 1889 was 111 with 387,000 spindles and 7,851 looms, while, in the same time, Georgia had increased her spindles from 198,000 to 455,000 and South Carolina from 82,000 to 417,000.[3] The amount of money invested in cotton manufacturing in the South in 1870 had been, roughly, $11,000,000; in 1880 it was $17,000,000, trebling in the next decade to nearly $54,000,000.[4]

At first only coarse fabrics, such as shirting, sheeting and drilling, were woven, but skill increased. The principal mill in Augusta, Ga., was making, as early as in 1882, it was said, 100 kinds of materials derived from the fiber of the cotton plant.[5]

Competent labor was difficult to assemble. Negroes could not be used to any extent—at first it was believed that they could not be used at all [6]—and the poor whites,[7] many of them

[1] App. Ann. Cyclop. for 1882, p. 747.

[2] Ibid. for 1882, p. 344; cf. Report of Senate Com. on Ed. and Labor, 1885, vol. iv, pp. 495–500, 508 et seq., 684 et seq., 710 et seq., 721 et seq.

[3] R. H. Edmonds, The South's Redemption, p. 29.

[4] Broadus Mitchell, Rise of Cotton Mills in the South, p. 232.

[5] App. Ann. Cyclop. for 1882, p. 344; cf. Holland Thompson, From Cotton Field to Cotton Mill, p. 80; Report of Senate Com. on Ed. and Labor, 1885, vol. iv, pp. 527, 582–7.

[6] Cf. Holland Thompson, op. cit., pp. 249–68; M. A. Potwin, Cotton Mill People, p. 59; Broadus Mitchell, op. cit., pp. 213–23; Report of Senate Com. on Ed. and Labor, 1885, vol. iv, pp. 529, 538–9.

[7] Certainly they were "poor whites," if not "poor white trash." See Holland Thompson, op. cit., p. 113. The "trash" in the shape of "clay-eaters," "crackers," or whatever their local names, also presented themselves at the mills for employment.—M. A. Potwin, op. cit., pp. 50–51; Broadus Mitchell, op. cit., pp. 132–7, 162–4, 172; Horace Kephart, Our Southern Highlanders, pp. 429–31.

enticed out of the mountains,[1] were taught the intricacies of machinery.[2] Whatever the source, and in any case, it was, in all respects, an agricultural population which was to be drawn to, and made proficient in, industry.[3] This native people were quick of motion, tenacious and enduring.[4]

They were paid at the lowest rates and kept at their work for long hours. The wages in North Carolina in 1887 were, for men, from 50 cents to $1.50 a day, for women, 35 cents to $1, for boys and girls, 25 cents to 65 cents. Even foremen could be hired at wages rising from $1 to $2.66 a day.[5] Lodging places for them were found in cabins erected near the new factories.[6]

The working day was from 11 to 12½ hours, say from 6 o'clock in the morning until half past 5 in the afternoon, in summer until sunset, with a midday intermission of 50 minutes.[7] It was reduced by act of legislature in Georgia in 1889 to 11 hours,[8] and some ameliorations with reference to the hours of labor and the employment of children were attempted by the trades unions, as they strove to develop their influence in the South, but in the main, without effect.[9]

Some states, as South Carolina [10] and Mississippi,[11] exempted manufacturing establishments from taxation in order to bring capital and enterprise within their limits. Communities offered them similar advantages on the subject of local rates.

[1] M. A. Potwin, op. cit., pp. 53–7, 80–82; Broadus Mitchell, op. cit., p. 191.

[2] Cf. Writings of Carl Schurz, vol. iv, p. 377.

[3] Cf. Broadus Mitchell, op. cit., p. 173.

[4] Report of Senate Com. on Ed. and Labor, 1885, vol. iv, pp. 693, 725.

[5] Broadus Mitchell, op. cit., pp. 224–8; App. Ann. Cyclop. for 1887, p. 565. For South Carolina cf. ibid. for 1879, p. 820. For Georgia cf. Report of Senate Com. on Ed. and Labor, 1885, vol. iv, pp. 530, 535, 536, 591–2, 699, 728.

[6] App. Ann. Cyclop. for 1878, p. 820; Holland Thompson, op. cit., pp. 139–42.

[7] Senate Com. on Ed. and Labor, 1885, vol. iv, pp. 529, 533, 537, 700, 727.

[8] Sess. Laws of Ga. for 1889, p. 163.

[9] Potwin, op. cit., pp. 133–4; P. Blanshard, Labor in Southern Cotton Mills; M. S. Evans, Black and White, pp. 63–4.

[10] App. Ann. Cyclop. for 1882, p. 847; cf. Cotton Mills of S. C., published for the Dept. of Agriculture of S. C., 1880, p. 23.

[11] App. Ann. Cyclop. for 1882, p. 563.

Altogether the owners of mills in the South were so fortunate that their profits were large. The returns of cotton manufacturers in South Carolina were at times from 18 to 50 per cent.[1] In some cases dividends of from 40 to 60 per cent were paid in North Carolina.[2] It was said of a well known mill in Augusta that, since its foundation after the war, it had paid its stockholders cash dividends equal to two and a half times the capital invested in it, and there was a large undivided surplus.[3] The shares of the companies were selling at very satisfactory premiums.[4] D. A. Tompkins, a high authority on the subject, said that in a period of 20 years, preceding 1900, the average net profits in the cotton manufacturing business in the South had been 15 per cent.[5]

The North was compelled to note the advantages enjoyed by Southern competitors in the saving of transportation charges on raw materials, in lower taxation, in cheaper labor. The manufacturers of New England, who had felt themselves secure in the control of their trade, made visits of inspection and many of the most astute were not slow in determining to establish branches in Georgia or the Carolinas, or, perhaps, closed their plants in the North and took their entire capital into those states.

Piles of cotton seed lay rotting in the open air where it had been left by the ginners. Everywhere in a few years mills were built to convert what had been regarded as useless into oil, cattle food and fertilizer, a discovery in economy which was adding $30,000,000 annually to the value of the Southern cotton crop.[6]

The increase in the property assessments in Alabama, Arkansas, Florida, Georgia, Louisiana, Mississippi, Tennessee and

---

[1] App. Ann. Cyclop. for 1880, p. 669; cf. Cotton Mills in S. C., published for the Dept. of Agriculture of S. C., 1880, p. 22; Report of Senate Com. on Ed. and Labor, 1885, vol. iv, p. 794.

[2] Holland Thompson, op. cit., pp. 88-9.

[3] App. Ann. Cyclop. for 1882, p. 344.

[4] For North Carolina see Holland Thompson, op. cit., pp. 83-4.

[5] Ibid., p. 88.

[6] Cf. G. T. Winston, A Builder of the New South, chap. vii; D. A. Tompkins, Cotton and Cotton Oil, vol. i, p. 195; ibid., vol. ii, chap. xi.

Texas, eight states, in four years, was said to have been 495 millions of dollars, nearly one-third of the gain having occurred in Georgia alone.[1] In the whole South in 14 states, the 11 which had seceded from the Union, and Maryland, West Virginia and Kentucky, the increase was from 2,913 millions in 1880 to 4,220 millions in 1889.[2]

The cry, said a prophet of the New South, was no longer "Go West, young man!" but "Go South!"[3] Northern capitalists, journalists, politicians, travelers from Europe visited the country and gave the energy of the people high praise. With the unfolding of her great natural resources the South was "the coming El Dorado of American adventure," said the eloquent W. D. Kelley of Pennsylvania.[4] The country was full of the "music of progress."[5]

In 1886 it was said that there were over 3,000 manufacturing establishments in the old agricultural state of South Carolina with products in a year valued at $30,000,000, more than twice as much as in 1880.[6] North Carolina, which had been called the "Turpentine State" and later the "Peanut State," in 1882 had 3,800 factories which produced $20,000,000 worth of goods in a year.[7] Over $15,000,000 were invested in 43 factories in Columbus, Ga., whose population, in 1887, was nearly 30,000;[8] $8,000,000 in 99 factories, in 1885, in Chattanooga, Tenn., which gave employment to 8,500 persons.[9] New Orleans had come to have a population of nearly 250,000. Its position as a port, especially since the deepening of the channel as a result of Eads's jetties, led to a substantial increase in its commerce. More than $20,000,000 were invested in manufacturing in the city in 1888, four times as much as in 1870.

[1] N. Y. Tribune, Sept. 7, 1883.
[2] R. H. Edmonds, The South's Redemption, p. 9.
[3] Ibid., pp. 5, 6.
[4] W. D. Kelley, The Old South and the New, p. 162.
[5] Edmonds, The South's Redemption, p. 5.
[6] App. Ann. Cyclop. for 1886, p. 807; cf. ibid. for 1887, p. 738; N. Y. Nation, Jan. 6, 1887.
[7] App. Ann. Cyclop. for 1882, p. 634; cf. N. Y. Nation, Nov. 3, 1887.
[8] App. Ann. Cyclop. for 1889, p. 144.
[9] Ibid. for 1888, p. 161.

Over $8,000,000 were paid out in wages in a year.[1]   Atlanta
had trebled its population in ten years.   In 1886 eight railway
companies centered their lines in the city.[2]   Jacksonville in
Florida, Memphis in Tennessee, Mobile and Montgomery in
Alabama and many smaller towns, where sloth and somnolence
had been, felt the impulse of new life.

As for Texas and Arkansas beyond the Mississippi, filling
with men and women who displayed the spirit of the West
rather than of the South, their future was already clearly seen.
Even now these states were teeming with activity—bank deposits, money to be lent, new and prosperous developments
and undertakings, growing cities spoke of forgetfulness of what
had been and confidence in what was to come.

On January 1, 1878, the railway mileage in the eleven "Confederate" states was 15,652, and on January 1, 1885, it was
26,970.   In each of the three states, Louisiana, Florida and
Texas, it had nearly trebled in seven years.[3]   At the end of
the war Texas had had only 330 miles of railway in operation;
in 1884 there were in that state more than 6,000 miles.[4]   Engineers revived the old project of a ship canal across the peninsula of Florida to eliminate the tedious passage through the
straits, thus shortening the route from the Gulf of Mexico
to Europe and Northern coastal ports nearly 500 miles.[5]   Others
proposed the construction of a barge canal of less depth and
smaller dimensions.   A way for it would be found, it was supposed, over the same course, or, perhaps, farther south through
the Okeechobee swamp.[6]   In 1881 grants were secured
from the legislature of Florida by Northern capitalists permitting them to drain this swamp, reclaim the land and build
canals and railways.[7]   This work was begun promptly,[8] and
the governor said that its magnitude and its destined in-

[1] App. Ann. Cyclop. for 1888, p. 169.
[2] Ibid. for 1886, p. 159.
[3] Poor's Manual for 1885, p. xiv.
[4] Cf. App. Ann. Cyclop. for 1881, p. 835.
[5] Senate Ex. Doc., 47th Cong. 1st sess., no. 38.
[6] App. Ann. Cyclop. for 1879, pp. 377-8.
[7] Ibid. for 1881, p. 300; Sess. Laws of Florida for 1881, pp. 172-4.
[8] App. Ann. Cyclop. for 1882, p. 312.

fluence upon the future of the state could "scarcely be realized." [1]

The transformation from an agricultural to a manufacturing country, which the South was undergoing, was so swift that, while, in 1880, the value of products of her soil exceeded those of her factories by 200 millions, in 1900 manufactures had a value, in excess of farm products, of 190 millions, and, if the output of her mines were included, of nearly 300 millions of dollars. The value of the South's manufactured products increased in these 20 years from 458 to 1,463 millions of dollars.[2]

Such changes altered the views of the people on many subjects. They had hung the "latchstring" out, Mr. Grady said in his address on New England Day in New York. Both capital for manufacturing and labor to tend the machinery and run the mills were required. Men were brought from New England to instruct the native operatives in the cotton factories.[3] But wages in the North if they were low, hours if they were long, reckoned by the standards of this day, were still lower, still longer in the Southern mills. Men used to higher levels of living would not leave their homes without better prospects than removal offered them.[4] Nevertheless organized effort was made to open the streams of immigration on lines of longitude. Rather futile measures in this direction, with a view to supplanting the freedmen on the plantations, had been adopted by the reconstructed states immediately after the war. The movement was now widened—it had new purpose. In Florida an immigration convention, attended by delegates from all parts of the state, met and made its wants known. A "cordial welcome" was assured to "all foreigners" who might "settle" there. County societies should be formed, descriptive articles about the state should be printed, advantages should be offered to further the ends in view.[5] A "State

[1] App. Ann. Cyclop. for 1884, p. 332; W. D. Kelley, The Old South and the New, pp. 23–6.
[2] E. G. Murphy, Problems of the Present South, p. 102.
[3] App. Ann. Cyclop. for 1879, p. 820.
[4] Cf. N. Y. Nation, Oct. 26, 1882.
[5] App. Ann. Cyclop. for 1881, pp. 299–300.

Immigration Association" was formed; it held meetings annually.[1] A similar association was organized in Mississippi
"to swell the tide of the returning prosperity" of that "great
state." The governor promised those who should come to
Mississippi from other places just and fair treatment. They
would find themselves, he said, "on a perfect equality in all
respects with our own people."[2] The governor of Arkansas
issued a call for a convention to meet at Little Rock. A bureau
of immigration was established with a view to attracting farmers
and laborers to that state.[3]

On April 25, 1888, delegates from nearly all the Southern
states east of the Mississippi River met at Hot Springs, N. C.,
at the invitation of various railway and steamship companies.
The governors of Virginia, South Carolina and Georgia attended. It was resolved to establish an office in New York
with the object of having agents at hand to meet immigrants
coming from Europe and to direct them to the South instead
of the West, whither they now generally went.[4] Another
meeting, on December 13, 1888, at Montgomery, Ala., attended by 600 men from various parts of the South, many of
them of prominence and influence, created a Southern Interstate Immigration Bureau to inform the North and West
about the country. Various plans were proposed, among them
the lading of a railway car with Southern products to be
sent away on an advertising tour. Alabama prepared such a
wandering showroom, and to its travels the officer in charge
of it attributed value in forwarding the growth of the
state.[5]

These measures, if in the direction of a steady pressure
upon the country in the interest of a recognition of the South's
new claims, attracted less attention and had smaller outcome [6]
than its two expositions, the first in Atlanta in 1881, the other

[1] App. Ann. Cyclop. for 1888, p. 340.
[2] Ibid., p. 563.
[3] Ibid., p. 39.
[4] Ibid., p. 618; N. Y. Herald, April 26, 1888.
[5] App. Ann. Cyclop. for 1889, p. 8.
[6] Cf. Broadus Mitchell, Rise of Cotton Mills in the South, pp. 206–7.

in New Orleans in 1885.[1] These enterprises not only awakened
the consciousness of the Southern people, but also drew the
eyes of the nation and, in some degree, of the rest of the world,
to the natural resources and to human capacity in that part
of the republic. They were at once illustrative and prophetic,
an evidence of what was, though it might come as a surprise
to many, and of what would be.

The "International Cotton Exposition" at Atlanta was the
outgrowth of suggestions made by that interested friend of
American industry, Edward Atkinson of Massachusetts.[2] Some
$120,000 were subscribed and a large main building in the
form of a cross was erected in the state fair grounds on the
outskirts of the city. The outlay, all told, was only $160,000,
so that the result in mere bulk could not be expected to give
the exposition a high place among undertakings of the kind.
It was opened early in October and closed with the year, in
December, 1881, after having attracted to it nearly 300,000
persons. Within the grounds were displayed the various animal, agricultural and forest products of the South, natural
and manufactured. There were exhibits as well from the North
and some examples of foreign handiwork. The stated object
of the exposition was "improvement," and particularly with
reference to the cotton industry. The processes to be used
in the cultivation of the soil; the planting and gathering of
the crop; the ginning and the utilization of the seed in oil
mills; the cleaning, baling and compressing of the fiber; the
spinning and the manufacture of it into the greatest variety
of products, from the daintiest of muslins to the coarsest un-
bleached homespun, from delicate lace to tent canvas, from
the finest thread to cable rope, were impressively demonstrated
for the instruction of the people, so that they might more
clearly see their way into the future. The governor of the
state, catching and expressing the spirit of the occasion, appeared at the Exposition in the afternoon of one day in a suit

[1] The "Southern Exposition" in Louisville in 1883 was as much Western
as Southern.—App. Ann. Cyclop. for 1883, p. 464.
[2] Cf. Broadus Mitchell, Rise of Cotton Mills in the South, pp. 117–22.

of clothes made from cotton which had been picked from the stalk in the morning of that day.[1] Beside the products of the mills of Augusta and Columbus were shown those of the South's elder rivals in Lowell, Fall River and Providence. At the end the buildings and the land on which they stood were fittingly acquired by a company which converted them into another Georgia cotton mill.[2]

The New Orleans Exposition was projected on a much larger scale. Indeed it was, in point of the space occupied by its buildings, a greater "world's fair" than any which had yet been seen anywhere. A park covering about 245 acres (the site for the Atlanta Exposition had an area of less than 50 acres) was found for the use of a main building, extending over a space of 1,656,000 square feet, with aisles six miles in length. Other buildings, surrounding the principal structure, were of large size and all were set in grounds made beautiful by fountains, pools and gardens.

The project had originated in a resolution taken by the National Cotton Planters' Association to mark, in some fitting way, the centenary of the cotton industry in the United States. In 1784 six bags of cotton had been shipped from Charleston, the first appearance, it was said, of this commodity as an article of foreign trade. The "World's Industrial and Cotton Centennial Exposition" was incorporated by Congress, stock was sold, the governments of the city of New Orleans and the state of Louisiana each voted the enterprise $100,000, while the Federal government granted it as much as $1,000,000, thus providing the managers with a generous sum with which to bring the scheme before the public. Efforts were successfully made to interest foreign nations, in particular Mexico and the Central and South American countries. Exhibits came from many directions. Congress appropriated $300,000 more to meet the cost of a United States government building. Many states forwarded their products for display. The yet

---

[1] C. F. Pidgin, Cotton Manufactures in Massachusetts and the Southern States, p. 42.

[2] App. Ann. Cyclop. for 1881, pp. 260–71; Broadus Mitchell, Rise of Cotton Mills in the South, pp. 122–5.

new electric light was used at night not only within the buildings, but to illuminate the grounds by multiplied "candle
power." On December 16, 1884, President Arthur pressed an
electric key at the White House, the signal for the starting
of the engines which set the machinery in motion at New
Orleans. The improvement of processes in connection with
the growth and manufacture of cotton, rice and sugar were
emphasized and the instruction which was derived from the
exhibits before the doors were closed in the following June
must be accounted to have been an important factor, like
the exposition in Atlanta, in advancing the movement for
the industrialization of the South.[1]

Less and less was heard of the "negro question" except in
connection with the suffrage. The conviction deepened that
the freedmen were factors to be reckoned with permanently
in agriculture, indeed that any displacement of them, if it
were possible, was not to be desired. They were doing a work,
if awkwardly and inefficiently, which no other body of laborers
was at hand to do, or could be found on any side to do. They
had been trained for their job in slavery; they must be kept
at it in freedom. Landowners well enough realized the indispensable value of the negroes for farm labor in the presence of the fright which now and again came to them on the
subject of an "exodus." This plan for a general hegira into
some new land of Canaan attracted notice in the winter and
spring of 1879. It seems to have had its origin in many minds
and was promoted by various influences. There were preachers
and soothsayers among the negroes in the South who for some
years had cherished the thought of emigration. They had
loose organization, it was said, with traveling agents and
papers which spread the news of their plans.[2] The Liberian
state in Africa, to which many blacks had been carried by
philanthropists before the war, still beckoned.[3] That project
was still befriended by the American Colonization Society,

[1] App. Ann. Cyclop. for 1884, pp. 573–9.
[2] Senate Reports, 46th Cong. 2nd sess., no. 693, pt. 1, pp. 7–9; ibid., pt. 2,
pp. 101–10, 120–22, 125, 156–8.
[3] Ibid., pt. 1, pp. xxi, 287, pt. 2, pp. 158–9 and pt. 3, p. 520.

whose directors continued to meet from year to year, formulating their futile plans,[1] in spite of much testimony in pamphlet and newspaper as to the unhealthfulness of the country and the almost complete failure of the experiment.[2] The Liberian colonization agents could present no picture of prosperity and happiness in their distant land which would start the negroes from the American South.

But emigrant aid societies existed in Washington and in the North which had in view the movement of the negroes in some direction.[3] Land speculators were active[4] and even Governor John P. St. John of Kansas, who waxed rather eloquent about the broad acres of his state and the welcome which awaited all who should enter it,[5] played his part. Agents of railway companies with tickets to sell saw an opportunity to attract business to their lines and, therefore, encouraged the project.[6] Republican politicians, who had been telling the negroes of the persecutions which they had been suffering at the hands of the upper white class, and would have the colored people believe that their not too happy condition was attributable to prejudices of color and caste, found in the movement profitable occasion to emphasize the injustices and hardships of life in the South.[7] These men did what lay in their power to increase the unrest. If votes could not be cast and counted in the South the blacks might be made, after emigration, into actively useful Republicans in the North, especially in such states as Indiana, where majorities swung uncertainly from side to side.

[1] In 1891 it was said that, since the Civil War, 4,201 negroes had been forwarded by the society and altogether, since its establishment in 1816, 16,-209.—Seventy-fourth Ann. Report of the Am. Col. Soc., p. 3; cf. J. H. B. Latrobe, Liberia, Its Origin, Rise, Progress and Results; Benjamin Brawley, A Social History of the Am. Negro, chap ix; W. K. Roberts, An African Canaan for the American Negro.
[2] Cf. G. R. Stetson, The Liberian Republic as It Is.
[3] Cf. N. Y. Nation, April 10, 1879.
[4] Ibid., June 10, 1879.
[5] Senate Reports, 46th Cong. 2nd sess., no. 693, pt. 3, pp. 226, 228–9; cf. N. Y. Tribune, June 7, 1879.
[6] Senate Reports, 46th Cong. 2nd sess., no. 693, pt. 1, pp. xiv, 21–3.
[7] N. Y. Nation, April 10 and July 17, 1879; Senate Reports, 46th Cong. 2nd sess., no. 693, passim.

The truth was that the colored youth who had grown up since the war were restive under the isolation, poverty and hard work which were incident to plantation life.[1] Wages and the yields from profit sharing were even smaller than they had been.

Liens on live stock and crops of future growth, and a pernicious credit system, often involving payment in "orders" on stores at which exorbitant prices were exacted for the necessaries of life, accompanied by unfavorable returns from the soil, had disturbed the colored people and they were stubble for the flame.[2]

Furthermore existence for the negroes in many places was not too free from physical violence. No denials would avail the Southern white people on this point, and many of the blacks, apprehensive and demoralized by ill treatment, would betake themselves to happier lands.[3]

Circulars, handbills, papers, illustrated to feed the imagination, were distributed.[4] Swindlers appeared. The old forty acres, mules, money were again before the eyes of the ignorant and the credulous. Somewhere there were trees from which, if you would take hold of them and shake them, the dollars would come rattling down.[5] Negroes in the Gulf states were told that they could get free passage north on the steamboats, if they would go to the banks of the Mississippi.[6] Eighty of them on the plantation of a grandson of John C. Calhoun in Arkansas started for the river. In the preceding week two men had visited them and showed them the picture of a farm

[1] Report of Senate Com. on Ed. and Labor, 1885, vol. iv, pp. 49–51, 70–71, 122.

[2] They went to the landowner at the end of the year to get their profits and he would say, after some operations in arithmetic,
"Nought is a nought, figger a figger,
Figger belongs to me and nought to the nigger."
Senate Reports, 46th Cong. 2nd sess., no. 693, pt. 2, p. 252; App. Ann. Cyclop. for 1879, pp. 357, 634; N. Y. Nation, May 22 and June 5, 1879; Report of Senate Committee on Ed. and Labor, 1885, vol. ii, p. 526.

[3] Senate Reports, 46th Cong. 2nd sess., no. 693, passim.
[4] Ibid., pt. 1, p. 52 and pt. 3, p. 97.
[5] Ibid., pt. 3, p. 269.
[6] App. Ann. Cyclop. for 1879, pp. 357, 634; Senate Reports, 46th Cong. 2nd sess., no. 693, pt. 2, p. 293.

that General Grant had bought for them. Each one had paid $2 for a piece of pasteboard bearing the printed words, "Good for one trip to Kansas." [1]

In North Carolina there were blacks who implicitly believed that new suits of clothes and railway tickets awaited them in Washington if they could reach that city.[2] The newspapers were filled with accounts of a rising and a great march upon the West. Indiana had its advocates, but "Kansas" was the magic word; that was the promised land.[3] It was "Ho! for sunny Kansas,"[4] partly, perhaps, because some Tennessee negroes a few years since had established more or less successful colonies there.[5] It was "free soil"—it was associated with the name of John Brown. Why should that state not be the haven for these poor mishandled exiles from the South?[6] Many an old Abolitionist in New England, many a Quaker humanitarian in Pennsylvania and Ohio, convinced that the negro could not enjoy his liberties where he at present lived, looked with quiet, if not active, favor upon emigration.

The movement spread. Darkies sold their houses, mules and corn for a tithe of their worth,[7] abandoned their lands and crops and set forth;[8] and there were negroes without houses, or mules, or crops—they had less to lose by joining in the "exodus." Perhaps 1,000 or 1,500 reached Indiana out of North Carolina by way of Washington over the Baltimore and Ohio Railroad, which offered a bonus of one dollar a head to negro procurers,[9] and carried the emigrants to Indianapolis at a

---

[1] Report of Senate Committee on Education and Labor, 1885, vol. ii, pp. 178-9.

[2] Senate Reports, 46th Cong. 2nd sess., no. 693, pt. 1, p. 76.

[3] Ibid., pt. 3, pp. 363, 365; cf. C. K. Marshall, Address before Am. Col. Soc., 1880, p. 3.

[4] Senate Reports, 46th Cong. 2nd sess., no. 693, pt. 3, p. 362.

[5] Ibid., pt. 1, p. xiii; N. Y. Tribune, June 7, 1879; N. Y. Nation, May 1 and 22, 1879.

[6] The New York Tribune said that it was too cold for the negroes in Kansas; they should be settled in the Indian Territory. It was an injustice to reserve for a few thousand savages a region nearly twice as large as the state of Ohio.—Issue of June 3, 1879.

[7] T. Thomas Fortune, Black and White, p. 282.

[8] App. Ann. Cyclop. for 1879, p. 634.

[9] Senate Reports, 46th Cong. 2nd sess., no. 693, pt. 1, pp. xxiv, 73.

rate as low as $9.[1] It soon became quite clear that the "ex-
odusters," as the newspapers called them, were not welcome
in Indiana.[2] There no work or wages awaited them. They
were objects of charity from the time they left the railway
trains. Lest they starve to death [3] appeals must be sent out
to the people for money. It added nothing to the warmth
of the reception of the negroes to know that some who had
encouraged their coming had acted in this behalf with a view
to colonizing the state in the interest of the Republican party.
Employers of the "exodusters" were threatened, houses prepared for them were burned, laws against bringing paupers
into the state were invoked. Upon receipt of news that another trainload was on the way from Cincinnati a crowd
gathered at the railway station at Shelbyville to tell the
"damned niggers" that they could not stop at that place, and
they, on this account, must go on to Indianapolis, where most
of them seemed to be.[4]

From the Gulf states the negroes with the "emigration
fever" proceeded to the banks of the Mississippi and hailed
passing steamboats. At first the captains carried them at
low rates as deck passengers, afterwards raising the price of
tickets to $4 or $5 from New Orleans [5] and $3 or $4 from
Vicksburg to St. Louis,[6] where they must transship for Kansas,
at a cost of $2.50 or $3 more. The first party to come to St.
Louis were dumped out on the levee late in February, 1879,
while snow still covered the ground. The women in calico
dresses, the children in their bare feet, in tatters and rags,
directly from the cotton fields, some sick, others dying, all
destitute and helpless, they were thrown upon the charity
of the people. No other shelter being available the churches
were opened to them. Merchants sent pork and beans, crackers
and bread.[7] As the weeks passed and the arrivals increased

[1] Senate Reports, 46th Cong. 2nd sess., no. 693, pt. 1, p. 32.
[2] Ibid., pp. 80, 97, 180.
[3] Ibid., pp. 87, 89, 265, 276, 321, 338.
[4] Ibid., pp. 269–73, 276; pt. 2, pp. 287–8.
[5] Ibid., pt. 2, pp. 149, 161–2.
[6] Ibid., p. 291.
[7] Ibid., pp. 289 and pt. 3, pp. 36–7.

the facilities of white and negro relief committees were sorely taxed. Money was sought to send the exiles on to Kansas. They appeared in large numbers at Wyandotte, opposite Kansas City, at Atchison, at Topeka and at other places, and the hope was entertained that they would be "absorbed" in the population, so that they might become self-sustaining. Applications for laborers and offers of homes for the refugees reached the relief societies from sympathetic quarters, and some of the emigrants were forwarded to Illinois, Iowa, Nebraska and even to Colorado, where it was supposed that they might be useful in the coal mines.[1] Certain public land was secured in Kansas and a number of families were set upon it to try their experiment with Northern life.[2] Negroes coming from Texas and northwestern Louisiana used the "steam cars," or drove north over the wagon roads behind teams of horses. These were congregated, for the most part, at Parsons, a small town in the southeastern corner of Kansas and would be, it was expected, distributed in that part of the state.[3]

Such an influx of paupers and mendicants occasioned alarm and was met by expressions of popular indignation in Kansas, as it was in Indiana. Wherever the blacks came they were charges upon the community. Yellow fever and other diseases, it was believed, lurked in the packs of filthy clothing which they bore with them. At the end of April, 1879, 3,500 were encamped in the environs of Wyandotte, unable to go farther.[4] Atchison would proceed against them as paupers. No more could come to that place.[5] They were an offense in Emporia where the people shunned the dirty streets in which they were quartered.[6]

In Topeka barracks were hastily erected as a cover for the oncoming horde. The white people in that part of the city

[1] Senate Reports, 46th Cong. 2nd sess., no. 693, pt. 2, pp. 359–60.
[2] App. Ann. Cyclop. for 1879, p. 537.
[3] Senate Reports, 46th Cong. 2nd sess., no. 693, pt. 2, pp. 252–3, 361, 431 and pt. 3, pp. 268, 270.
[4] N. Y. Nation, May 1, 1879; cf. Senate Reports, 46th Cong. 2nd sess., no. 693, pt. 2, pp. 358–9; ibid., pt. 3, pp. 294–5.
[5] Senate Reports, 46th Cong. 2nd sess., no. 693, pt. 3, p. 23.
[6] Ibid., pp. 227–8.

in which the building was placed tore it down and threw the lumber into the river.[1] It was necessary to find a site in the fair grounds nearly a mile away, where from 300 to 500 were rudely sheltered.[2] A mass meeting was held to deplore the coming of the negroes to Topeka.[3] Governor St. John was seeking a reëlection; he was hard pressed [4] to explain why he had ever boasted of the state's rich soil, fine laws and hospitable temperament, when it was known that there was no more government land in Kansas except on a treeless, unwatered plain in the west,[5] that the labor market was overstocked, that the farmers who used machinery did not need the help of men who had never seen anything better than a shovel and a hoe, and that the "niggers" anyhow had not come to work but to quarter themselves in idleness on the white population.

The negroes, when places were found for them in the country, were soon in town again. They could be seen sunning themselves on the street corners any fine day.[6] Before the end of April, 1879, it was said that no less than 8,600 had already arrived in St. Louis;[7] a few months later the number had mounted to 15,000 or 20,000 [8] and the mayor asked that no more direct themselves thither, as they could not find food or lodging there, and no funds were at hand to forward them to other places.[9] The charitable societies urgently appealed to those responsible for the migration, whoever they might be, to divert the tide "to other and older states where the accumulated wealth and population" might afford facilities for the successful settlement of the race. Before August, 1879, 7,000 negroes, all in dire need, had come to Kansas,[10] and a few months later Governor St. John thought that the number which had

[1] Senate Reports, 46th Cong. 2nd sess., no. 693, pt. 3, pp. 98, 126, 406.
[2] Ibid., pp. 98, 99.
[3] Ibid., p. 120.
[4] Ibid., pp. 120, 126, 273, 361.
[5] Ibid., p. 121.
[6] Ibid., pp. 225, 227, 228.
[7] N. Y. Nation, May 1, 1879.
[8] Senate Reports, 46th Cong. 2nd sess., no. 693, pt. 2, p; 290; cf. ibid., pt. 3, p. 12.
[9] App. Ann. Cyclop. for 1879, p. 358.
[10] Ibid.

reached his state was not short of 15,000 or 20,000.[1] Others
spoke of 25,000.[2]

A state relief association, with St. John at its head, sought
contributions, but only a few thousand dollars were collected.[3]
Quakers, the unfailing friends of the negro and the Indian,
sent out appeals to all parts of the North and to England for
money, for clothing, for food and they mitigated much suffering.[4]

In spite of what was seen Thomas W. Conway, an old officer
of the Freedmen's Bureau [5] in the Gulf states, publicly espoused the cause of the emigrant and issued a call for funds.
The banks of the river were lined with negroes, eager to escape the miseries imposed upon them by the old slave owners
on the plantations.[6] If the Southern white people would not
let the darkies board the steamboats he would charter the
necessary shipping and take them up the river. "Ben" Butler,
he declared, had offered him 21,000 acres of land in Wisconsin.[7] Later Conway presented plans for settling the blacks in
New Mexico and Arizona, where they might be secure in the
enjoyment of their liberties.[8]

The motive forces behind the movement were not masked
at a colored men's convention which met in the hall of the
house of representatives in Nashville in the early days of May,
1879. Black agitators from the North, misled by white Republican politicians, were in attendance. The high note of
the meeting was prejudice and persecution. All comfortable
progress waited upon recognition of the social and political
equality of the negroes by the white people of the South. As
this could not be had the black man must seek a new home
and Congress was asked for a half million dollars to assist

---

[1] Senate Reports, 46th Cong. 2nd sess., no. 693, pt. 2, pp. 254–5; cf. ibid.,
pt. 3, p. 124.
[2] Ibid., pt. 2, pp. 360–61; ibid., pt. 3, p. 12.
[3] App. Ann. Cyclop. for 1879, p. 537; N. Y. Tribune, June 7, 1879.
[4] Cf. Senate Reports, 46th Cong. 2nd sess., no. 693, pt. 3, pp. 15, 292–3.
[5] Autobiography of Gen. O. O. Howard, vol. ii, p. 188.
[6] Senate Reports, 46th Cong. 2nd sess., no. 693, pt. 2, p. 293.
[7] N. Y. Tribune, June 10, 1879.
[8] Senate Reports, 46th Cong. 2nd sess., no. 693, pt. 3, pp. 433–49.

in the work of removing the race to states and territories in which they might enjoy the rights vouchsafed them by the Constitution and the laws. An "American Protective Society" would be formed for the black man's defense.[1]

The planters were aroused; the "exodus" must be stopped.[2] Delegates from a number of states met in a Mississippi Valley Labor Convention at Vicksburg on May 5, 1879. That some understanding might be arrived at negroes accounted to be spokesmen of the race were invited to come forward. The hope was expressed that, after stating their grievances, they would use their influence to allay the excitement. If the colored people wished to emigrate they should proceed "as reasonable human beings" without breaking labor contracts and disorganizing all industry, not going off before they had assembled enough money to carry them even as far as the steamboat landings at the river side.[3] A planter in Arkansas said that his negroes had left him owing him over $100,000.[4]

Repose was seen to be returning as the summer passed and the crops flowered, fruited and seeded again. Since boats, when they arrived in the North, were in many places forbidden to land,[5] and the captains at places in the South were afraid to take on the negroes assembled at the wharves, lest they feel the force of public disapprobation,[6] travel was no longer easy by way of the Mississippi. Sage counselors spoke and were heard.[7] Fred Douglass, the fugitive slave, the eloquent Abolitionist, now, by President Hayes's appointment, United States marshal of the District of Columbia, voiced his disapproval of the movement, as did many of the most intelligent negro preachers, editors and political leaders.[8]

---

[1] App. Ann. Cyclop. for 1879, pp. 357–8; N. Y. Nation, May 15, 1879; Senate Reports, 46th Cong. 2nd sess., no. 693, pt. 1, pp. 5–6, 13 and pt. 2, pp. 243–7.
[2] Cf. App. Ann. Cyclop. for 1879, pp. 634–5.
[3] Ibid., p. 357; cf. N. Y. Nation, May 8, 1879.
[4] T. Thomas Fortune, Black and White, p. 282.
[5] Senate Reports, 46th Cong. 2nd sess., no. 693, pt. 2, p. 149.
[6] Ibid., pt. 2, p. 293 and pt. 3, pp. 434–5.
[7] N. Y. Nation, May 15, 1879.
[8] Senate Reports, 46th Cong. 2nd sess., no. 693, pt. 1, pp. 69, 104, 140.

Not a few of the "exodusters" were returning to the South
to give accounts of their adventure. Their disappointment
was great. Nothing that had been said to them about this
fine, new, free land was true. They must work in Kansas as
they had worked at home. It were better to return afoot,
as long and weary as was the way, than to starve and freeze
in Wyandotte or Topeka. They never wanted to go again
"where they could not see cotton stalks and gin houses." [1]
One was on his way back "to give Kansas hell." [2] An old
man from Burleson county, Texas, who had accompanied some
of his people to Parsons, in Kansas, led the party home again.
He would not give Burleson county, he said, for the whole
state of Kansas. [3] John C. Calhoun of Arkansas said that the
negroes on his plantation, after their experiences in the North,
would have mobbed anyone who had dared to say "Kansas"
to them. [4]

Throughout the spring and summer of 1880 Senators Blair
and Windom, at Congressional committee hearings in Washington, were bulldozing witnesses and collecting testimony
concerning Southern "outrages" in an effort to revive the sectional issue for the oncoming Presidential campaign. [5] Apprehension of a renewal of the excitement in 1880 was felt
and expressed, but there was little ground for it. [6] Colored
industrial fairs were held annually in Raleigh. Here were
proofs of the progress of the negro and the harmony with which
the races dwelt together in at least one state of the South.
In 1880 Fred Douglass appeared on the platform with the
governor of North Carolina. In the preceding year hisses and
yells had greeted his name in some of the meetings organized
in the interest of emigration. [7] "A flea in a tar barrel without
claws," he said now in Raleigh, "was far better off than a

[1] Senate Reports, 46th Cong. 2nd sess., no. 693, pt. 2, p. 140.
[2] Ibid., pt. 3, p. 112; cf. ibid., pt. 1, p. 287.
[3] Dallas, Tex., Herald, quoted in Senate Reports, 46th Cong. 2nd sess.,
no. 693, pt. 2, pp. 431-2.
[4] T. T. Fortune, Black and White, p. 283.
[5] Senate Reports, 46th Cong. 2nd sess., no. 693.
[6] App. Ann. Cyclop. for 1879, p. 572; ibid. for 1880, p. 482.
[7] Ibid. for 1879, p. 357.

Southern darky up North without money." The "exodus" which the colored people wanted was "the exodus from ignorance, vice and lack of thrift." [1]

All the while Texas and Arkansas, with warmer air and some of the other qualities of the South, offered opportunities to the negro and a migration in that direction was in progress.[2] In 1879 the planters in Alabama complained of the inconvenience which they were suffering by reason of the efforts that were put forth to entice labor to Texas. Farmers from that state appeared in a number of counties, went about among the negroes, employed them and took them away. The legislature passed a law to prevent it. Any such emissary would hereafter need to secure a license costing $100; if he failed to pay it he would be fined three times that sum, or be subjected to imprisonment in the county jail.[3]

In 1881 an "exodus" alarmed the planters in South Carolina. In one week, about Christmas time, no less than 5,000 moved out of Edgefield county, leaving it practically without labor. Movements in other parts of the state worried the owners of land.[4]

In 1886 Mississippi was disturbed by the resolution of large numbers of negroes to seek new homes. Some crossed the river into Arkansas, but the movement was principally from the hills to the "Swamp," or " Yazoo Bottom." No railroad penetrated this region until 1883.[5] Protected from flood and overflow by new levees it was the delight of the lazy. It had been called "the cream jug of the continent." Every square foot rioted in vegetable life.[6] It was alleged that, by immigration, a district nearly as large as the state of Indiana was being Africanized. In 1886 there were almost a quarter of a million negroes in the Yazoo delta. They outnumbered the whites eight to one, on the other side of the Mississippi in Louisiana,

[1] App. Ann. Cyclop. for 1880, p. 585; see Geo. W. Williams, History of the Negro Race in Am., chap. xxviii.
[2] Cf. N. Y. Nation, Apr. 17, 1879.
[3] Sess. Laws of Ala. for 1878-9, p. 205.
[4] App. Ann. Cyclop. for 1881, pp. 812-3.
[5] A. H. Stone, The American Race Problem, p. 86.
[6] Ibid., p. 83.

ten to one, on adjacent land in Arkansas, four to one. In and around Greenville in Mississippi there were nearly a half million negroes, and a white population of only 60,000 or 70,000.[1]

Again in North Carolina in 1889 an "exodus" was in full swing. Some of the eastern counties of the state were so depopulated in respect of labor that the farmers despaired of cultivating their crops. Emigration agents from the West appeared, a convention in the interest of the movement met in Raleigh on April 25th, and the grounds of the negro's dissatisfaction with his condition were presented so strongly that at least 50,000, it was said, left the state, principally destined for Kansas, Arkansas and Texas.[2]

Liberty and enfranchisement, Mr. Grady had said, were the ultimate point to which law could carry the negro. The rest, he declared, must be left to those "among whom his lot is cast, with whom he is indissolubly connected and whose prosperity depends upon their possessing his intelligent sympathy and confidence."[3] These words from the orator might be taken more literally than his statement that the South had "planted the school house on the hill top and made it free to white and black."[4] Work for the love of it, where indolence had been, was excellent. But with awakened industry it was clear that there must be systematic attack upon ignorance in the middle and lower classes of the white population, as well as among the blacks.

It needed no particular inquiry to establish the fact that there were more unlettered persons in a hundred in the Southern than in the Northern states and the further facts that smaller sums of money, fewer teachers, less effective systems, in most cases, indeed, no systems at all, were employed in the effort to better conditions in this respect. Of about 2,751,000 negroes above ten years of age in twelve Southern states in 1870 no less than 2,383,000, or 87 per cent, were adjudged illiterate; 92 per cent were in this condition in Georgia. Of

[1] App. Ann. Cyclop. for 1886, p. 572; cf. ibid. for 1880, p. 530.
[2] Ibid. for 1889, p. 612.
[3] N. Y. Tribune, Dec. 23, 1886.
[4] Ibid.

4,306,000 whites of the same age in the same states in 1870 25 per cent were illiterate; 33 per cent in North Carolina could not read and write.[1]

No Southern state in 1870 had a free school system—there were schools which children might attend without charge only in isolated instances in some of the cities. The illiteracy of the people of the South, both white and black, was not improperly described as "appalling."[2]

The Freedmen's Bureau at the war's end had displayed some activity in the field of education and religious bodies were at work in feeble ways endeavoring to improve conditions.[3] But in the main nothing had been achieved. The country was prostrate; government had been destroyed, and was being reëstablished only with great difficulty. Charitable individuals of means large enough to enable them to forward social improvement were not at hand. The citizen and the state together had been left in impotency and ruin.

In this conjuncture one friend had appeared, George Peabody of Massachusetts, who had removed to, and had become a rich merchant in England, and who was devoting a great fortune to philanthropy. He had, in 1866, made a gift which, by later donations, reached a total sum of $3,500,000 for the promotion of the educational interests of the South, through which he had traveled and with which he had business connections. He placed the fund in the hands of trustees—men holding high places in the public confidence, among them Robert C. Winthrop, who was devoted in his attention to its interests;[4] Hamilton Fish, William C. Rives, Bishop McIlvaine, General Grant, Admiral Farragut and William M. Evarts. Dr. Barnas Sears[5] resigned the presidency of Brown University and accepted the post of general agent for the administration of what came to be known as the Peabody Edu-

---

[1] J. L. M. Curry, History of the Peabody Education Fund, p. 120.
[2] Ibid., p. 116.
[3] Cf. Senate Reports, 48th Cong. 1st sess., no. 101, p. 28; J. L. M. Curry, Education of the Negroes since 1860, Slater Fund, Occasional Papers, no. 3.
[4] R. C. Winthrop, Jr., A Memoir of Robert C. Winthrop, p. 320.
[5] Curry, Hist. of the Peabody Ed. Fund, pp. 68–71.

cation Fund, to be succeeded by an enlightened prophet of the "New South," J. L. M. Curry of Richmond, Va.,[1] a passage from New England, to sympathetic, native direction, since Curry, after having been for a time a representative in the Congress of the United States, had espoused secession and had sat in the Congress of the Confederate States.[2]

The trustees said that they would not found and maintain new schools, but would put the income at the disposal of Southern state authorities to enable them to accomplish the ends in view, particularly in the upbuilding of normal colleges for the training of teachers. There was at the time not one of these in all the South.[3] Primary and common school education would be encouraged. To this end the teachers who were to be fitted for service would be directed into work designed to benefit the masses, and principally in the towns and cities where greater numbers of children were congregated, and where, on that account, there were larger opportunities. Efforts would be made to establish departments of education in connection with the state governments; to form state associations of teachers; to organize "Teachers' Institutes" in which, for a few days annually, teachers might meet and hear pedagogical questions discussed, and to publish and distribute papers and magazines devoted to the discussion of such problems. The general agent conferred with state and local school officers, where there were these, addressed the legislatures in the interest of public education and kept astir, in whatever way he could, the cause of free instruction for the whole people. A few hundred dollars were bestowed here and a few hundred dollars there. The chief benefits were to flow, not from the sum given but from the incentive which might come from the gift in the shape of local supplementary appropriations. All was done with the aim of making the schools in each community self-supporting, when external stimulation could be withdrawn and like fostering care might be transferred to other points.

[1] Cf. Edgar G. Murphy, Problems of the Present South, pp. 5–6.
[2] E. A. Alderman and A. C. Gordon, J. L. M. Curry, A Biography, chap. xv.
[3] Curry, Hist. of the Peabody Ed. Fund, pp. 38, 121–2.

As one of the earliest manifestations in the North of a spirit of reconciliation and sympathy the South was moved by Mr. Peabody's philanthropy, and, if two of the states repudiated the bonds which they had issued and which Mr. Peabody had included in the trust, in the hope that they might see the advantage of honesty,[1] the principal which remained was large enough for the performance of useful and widely disseminated social service.[2] The disbursements from the fund from 1868 to 1884 inclusive amounted to $1,476,000.[3]

Other benefactions of a similar nature for the upbuilding of the South were inspired by Peabody's gift, such as John F. Slater's in 1882 of $1,000,000 for use among colored youth in the South.[4] Mr. Slater was an opulent textile manufacturer in Connecticut. This fund, too, was placed in the care of a number of eminent and respectable trustees and it was to be administered, like the Peabody fund, not for the construction of buildings and the establishment of new schools, but for the strengthening of existing educational facilities, especially with a view to training young negroes in the manual trades,[5] and in preparing them for the practice of medicine in the two or three schools which were open in the South to those who would serve as doctors to their race.[6]

There was no denying the fact that in many parts of the South there was latent, if not frank and outspoken, opposition to a public school system. The South had what was, in effect, a feudal society, wherein there could not be that competent respect for universal education which had come to be felt in other parts of the country. Knowledge had been looked upon

[1] Curry, Hist. of the Peabody Ed. Fund, pp. 141–6; N. Y. Nation, March 15, 1883.
[2] Curry, op. cit., p. 25; N. Y. Nation, March 15, 1883; Report of U. S. Com. of Ed. for 1879, pp. xlv–xlvi; ibid. for 1881, pp. xc–xci; Senate Mis. Doc., 48th Cong. 1st sess., no. 55, p. 10.
[3] Report of U. S. Com. of Ed. for 1884, p. lxiii; Curry, op. cit., p. 147.
[4] Curry, op. cit., p. 92.
[5] Diary and Letters of R. B. Hayes, vol. iv, pp. 42, 76, 88; Report of U. S. Com. on Ed. for 1883, p. lvi; Documents Relating to the Origin and Work of the Slater Trustees, Occasional Papers, no. 1, pp. 7–22.
[6] Report of U. S. Com. of Ed. for 1884, pp. lxiv–lxv; ibid. for 1888, pp. 993–7.

as for a few men of property, while the poor were put to one side as so much peasantry. As for the freedmen they were regarded as the slaves had been—they were meant for work; if they could not remain in their places as laborers it would be impossible to fit them into any kind of a tolerable social scheme.[1]

Moreover no man could be fairly charged for educating the children of another. As for the negroes, who in the main paid no taxes,[2] it was not the white man's duty to put them to school, especially since, by the process, they were spoiled as laborers.[3] Men were prone to say, if they accepted the principle of common schools at all, that the taxes paid by the whites should be used to educate white children and that the colored people should be left to take care of themselves.[4]

When a greater number of the white Southern people came to understand that a new order of things was at hand and that education was imperative if men were to have any degree of fitness as neighbors, as laborers, as voters and in the various social contacts, it was still quite plain that money was not available for the work. Public debts were being funded and scaled, even repudiated. Divers and sundry measures, honest and dishonest, as creditors lived to know, were adopted to assort "just" from "fraudulent" claims upon the treasuries

---

[1] The state superintendent of education in South Carolina said in 1884, "The slaves, of course, were not educated; it was not intended that they should be. Our social condition required that they should not be educated." —Senate Mis. Doc., 48th Cong. 1st sess., no. 55, p. 31.

[2] Not more than six per cent paid a property tax in South Carolina, said the superintendent of education in that state. (Ibid., p. 29.) Governor Gordon in Georgia said that in or around 1890 the negroes in his state were paying only 1/30 of the expense of educating their children—the rest of the burden, in so far as it had been assumed, was carried by the whites.— Thomas Nelson Page, The Negro, p. 277; cf. G. S. Merriam, The Negro and the Nation, p. 397.

[3] Report of U. S. Com. of Ed. for 1888, pp. 135–7; cf. Senate Mis. Doc., 48th Cong. 1st sess., no. 55, p. 30; N. Y. Nation, April 1, 1886; B. Sears, Objections to Public Schools Considered; Proceedings of the Trustees of the Peabody Fund, vol. ii, pp. 79–80; M. A. Potwin, Cotton Mill People, p. 116; Edgar G. Murphy, Problems of the Present South, pp. 68–9. Report of Senate Com. on Ed. and Labor, 1885, vol. iv, pp. 153, 564–5.

[4] Senate Mis. Doc., 48th Cong. 1st sess., no. 55, pp. 60–61; Report of Senate Com. on Ed. and Labor, 1885, vol. ii, p. 534; ibid., vol. iv, pp. 797–8.

and some time must necessarily elapse before the credit of the Southern governments, local and state, could be reëstablished. Meantime taxation yielded but small returns since there was so little property upon which to make the levies. Many states had large potential future wealth,—so much had become plain, but the requirements of the schools were immediate and what was to be done for the redemption of so hopelessly ignorant a population was of such importance that it could not be deferred. Arkansas, for instance, in 1880, had assessed values upon which taxes could be collected of only 86 millions of dollars, Florida only 30 millions, Mississippi 110 millions, South Carolina 133 millions, Louisiana, with New Orleans, 160 millions, Alabama, North Carolina and Georgia, with rising industrial interests, 122, 156 and 239 millions respectively, whereas Rhode Island had property of an assessed value for taxation of 252 and Massachusetts 1584 millions of dollars.[1]

In 1879 the total sum available for schools in Alabama was $387,000, in Georgia $465,000, in Louisiana $613,000, in Mississippi $739,000, in North Carolina $493,000, in South Carolina $304,000, in Virginia $670,000, in Arkansas $261,000.[2] The *per capita* expenditure for educational purposes for persons entitled to attend school in Virginia was only $1.06, in Georgia 95 cents and in North Carolina 80 cents, as compared with more than $15 in Massachusetts and $6.50 in New York.[3] It was $26 in Boston.[4]

The sources of income in the states were various. In some instances there was a state tax for school purposes. In Louisiana and Florida in 1880 it was one mill on each dollar's worth of taxable property; in Arkansas and South Carolina two mills.[5] Miscellaneous funds arising from public land sales, licenses

[1] Senate Reports, 48th Cong. 1st sess., no. 101, p. 24.
[2] Report of U. S. Com. of Ed. for 1879, pp. xviii–xix.
[3] Ibid., p. xx.
[4] Senate Mis. Doc., 48th Cong. 1st sess., no. 55, p. 15.
[5] Report of U. S. Com. of Ed. for 1879, pp. ccxxiii–ccxxv, 37, 85, 219; Senate Mis. Doc., 48th Cong. 1st sess., no. 55, pp. 29–30; App. Ann. Cyclop. for 1882, p. 744.

for the sale of liquor and for circuses and exhibitions, fines, escheats, poll taxes, etc.,[1] all yielding too little, would be put at the disposal of the public educational authorities. The state funds which were assigned to the counties with reference to the number of educable children in those counties might be supplemented by county taxes. But the amount of the local tax and, indeed, the laying of it at all were likely to be matters subject to local determination, so that this income was uncertain. In a number of counties in Mississippi no local tax was levied to eke out the scanty apportionment from the state.[2] Like neglect was observed in poor and niggard communities in Arkansas and in other places.[3] Parents must often pay a "supplement," say ten cents a week for each child, to the teacher who was told when he was engaged for the service that school would continue only "as long as the money lasts." Then he would be constrained to move on to another township where the fund, possibly, had not been expended, or return to clerking, farming or some other lucrative occupation until the small appropriation was again received from the state.[4]

Under the circumstances the growth of public education, which there were many to say lay at the very foundation of a new social structure, was gradual, even under the impulse provided by the Peabody fund and the forces which it and similar agencies awakened. Everywhere separate schools must be maintained for the whites and the blacks, separate teachers' institutes, separate teachers' training colleges, thus doubling the expense of the establishment.[5] Only Northern radicals who had been sent back to their homes essayed the task of instructing the children of the two races in the same schoolroom. The children in the farming districts, in the "piney

---

[1] For various curious sources of revenue in Georgia see Report of U. S. Com. of Ed. for 1882, p. 42; for Ala. see Sess. Laws of Ala. for 1878–9, pp. 117–8.

[2] Report of U. S. Com. of Ed. for 1879, p. 133.

[3] App. Ann. Cyclop. for 1881, p. 31; Report of U. S. Com. of Ed. for 1879, p. 10.

[4] Report of Senate Com. of Ed. and Labor, 1885, vol. iv, pp. 405, 465, 467.

[5] Senate Mis. Doc., 48th Cong. 1st sess., no. 55, p. 30.

woods" and in the mountains were gathered into buildings which gave little promise of large results. In the best case churches and unoccupied cabins were lent for the use. Men in a neighborhood might combine to erect a little schoolhouse.[1] Very often, however, log houses and abandoned outbuildings must serve the purpose. Indeed, as one Southern state superintendent of public instruction said, they were not log houses, but "log pens" or "log piles." The floors were of earth, the benches were roughly fashioned from round timber. Mere holes, without glass, served as windows, an unprotected opening as a doorway.[2] Parents were not able to clothe their children warmly enough to sit in such places. Those who did attend, a negro complained, must huddle together and keep their feet off the floor.[3] The estimated value of all the school property, owned by the commonalty, including sites, buildings, furniture, etc, in the state of South Carolina in 1879 was only $352,000, in North Carolina only $192,000, in Florida only $116,000.[4]

Everywhere only a small proportion of the children of school-going age were enrolled; still fewer attended since there were no compulsory regulations. Everywhere the period in which schooling was provided for the children was short. Everywhere the teachers were paid at a rate which furnished no assurance of competent service. Teaching under such conditions, of course, could not be a pursuit.[5] Members of local boards and other officers in charge of the subject were too frequently ignorant men, unfit for their trusts.[6] In joining a committee they had more interest in defeating a school tax or in giving a teacher's place to some dependent relation than in the common welfare.[7]

[1] Report of Senate Committee of Ed. and Labor, 1885, vol. iv, p. 199.
[2] Senate Mis. Doc., 48th Cong. 1st sess., no. 55, p. 35.
[3] Report of Senate Com. on Ed. and Labor, 1885, vol. iv, p. 625.
[4] Report of U. S. Com. of Ed. for 1879, pp. xviii–xix. For South Carolina cf. Senate Mis. Doc., 48th Cong. 1st sess., no. 55, p. 33.
[5] Report of Senate Com. on Ed. and Labor, 1885, vol. iv, p. 459.
[6] Ibid., p. 397; Report of U. S. Com. of Ed. for 1879, p. 133.
[7] Report of U. S. Com. of Ed. for 1888, p. 93; cf. ibid., pp. 143–4; Report of Senate Com. on Ed. and Labor, 1885, vol. iv, pp. 398–9.

The average time during which instruction was given in
the schools of Alabama in 1879 was only 84 days in the year.
Three years earlier the average teaching time in the schools
of the state had been only 60 days per annum.[1] In 1879 the
"school year" in Mississippi in the counties averaged 77½
days; in some country districts the term was only six weeks.
Conditions were better in the cities.[2] In South Carolina the
average time during which school continued was 73½ days
in a year, in Tennessee 69 days, in Texas 80 days and in North
Carolina 46 days.[3] In 1887–8 the averages were still very low,
with only 72 days in South Carolina, 65 in Georgia, 79½ in
Alabama, 84 in Mississippi, 89 in Louisiana and 63 in North
Carolina.[4] Scholars, a teacher observed, forgot all they had
learned "by the time they got around to school the next year."[5]
Often, when they came back, if they did return, they would
not know the alphabet.[6] They must go eight years to get two
years' schooling which, as a matter of course, another teacher
said, was of so little value that, when the child grew up, he
proved to have no education at all.[7]

The school population in Alabama in 1879 was, in round
numbers, 376,000; only 174,000 were enrolled and only 112,-
000, less than 1 in 3, attended school, even for the short period
during which instruction was given. In Arkansas, of 236,000
children, but 53,000 were enrolled—a still smaller, though un-
determined, number appeared before the teachers in the schoolhouses. The ratio of those who should have been at school
to those who really were there was less than 1 to 3 in
Georgia and Mississippi; 1 to 6 in Louisiana and 1 to 8 in
Virginia.[8]

[1] App. Ann. Cyclop. for 1880, p. 12; Report of U. S. Com. of Ed. for
1879, p. xiv, Senate Mis. Doc., 48th Cong. 1st sess., no. 55, p. 24.
[2] Report of U. S. Com. of Ed. for 1879, p. 133.
[3] Ibid., p. xv.
[4] Ibid. for 1888, p. 69.
[5] Report of Senate Com. on Ed. and Labor, 1885, vol. ii, p. 530; cf. ibid.,
vol. iv, pp. 577–8.
[6] Ibid., vol. iv, p. 579.
[7] Ibid., pp. 613–4.
[8] Report of U. S. Com. of Ed. for 1879, pp. xiv–xv. For Virginia see
App. Ann. Cyclop. for 1879, p. 844.

The average monthly pay of teachers in Alabama in 1879, including male and female, white and colored, was officially given as $18.70.[1] The average total sum paid to each teacher yearly in Alabama in 1881 was $85.30.[2] In Mississippi in 1878 some 4,700 teachers were employed at an average salary of $27 a month for negro and $28 for white teachers.[3] In North Carolina the rate of compensation was $22 a month and less.[4] The salaries of teachers in some of the counties of South Carolina were as low as $15 a month,[5] in Georgia $8.[6] The state superintendent of public instruction in North Carolina received $1,500 a year, with no allowance for traveling expenses.[7] The new school law of 1881 gave him $500 for this use and fixed the rate of pay of "third grade" teachers at $15 a month, and "second grade" teachers at $25. "First grade" teachers would receive salaries to be determined by the local school committees.[8] Teachers in the "back counties" in the South would now and again be paid in warrants which were "scalped" at a cost to the holder of from 15 to 40 per cent.[9]

The sum allotted by the state of Louisiana to the parish of Orleans, with 57,000 children to be educated, though only 15,000 attended, was $14,000.[10] About $200,000 were annually appropriated for the support of free schools by the city government in New Orleans.[11] The combined sum was so inadequate for the use that in 1882 teachers were being dismissed and the meager salaries of others were of necessity reduced.[12] Through neglect of duty on the part of the legislature and

[1] Report of U. S. Com. of Ed. for 1879, p. xvii.
[2] Ibid. for 1881, p. lvii.
[3] App. Ann. Cyclop. for 1879, p. 633; cf. ibid. for 1881, p. 597; Report of U. S. Com. of Ed. for 1879, p. 132.
[4] Report of U. S. Com. of Ed. for 1879, p. 132.
[5] Senate Mis. Doc., 48th Cong. 1st sess., no. 55, p. 30.
[6] Report of Senate Com. on Ed. and Labor, 1885, vol. iv, p. 577.
[7] App. Ann. Cyclop. for 1880, p. 584.
[8] Sess. Laws of N. C. for 1881, chap. 200.
[9] Cf. Report of Senate Com. on Ed. and Labor, 1885, vol. iv, p. 531.
[10] App. Ann. Cyclop. for 1880, pp. 484–5; Senate Reports, 48th Cong. 1st sess., no. 101, p. 22.
[11] App. Ann. Cyclop. for 1881, p. 518.
[12] Ibid. for 1882, p. 482.

litigation practically all the public schools in the state were closed during the winter of 1882–3.[1] The governor recommended the adoption of a new system. Local school precincts should be authorized to lay taxes for school use.[2] Little came of it, however. Buildings in which children were assembled to receive instruction were unworthy of the name. Even in New Orleans old, unsanitary houses were in use.[3] The term was short, the teaching was inefficient, illiteracy, it was said in 1887, was actually increasing.[4] More than one-half of the voters who went to the polls in the parishes were unable "to tell from their tickets for whom they were voting."[5]

In 1887, after ten years, the average duration of the school year in Alabama had not increased, nor had the proportion of educable children attending school undergone any marked change for the better. Still not so many as 1 in 3 persons of school age came under the influence of such teaching as was provided for them during a term of an average duration of only about three months. Teachers were paid only $22 a month. The state superintendent of education received a salary of $2,000 a year. The *per capita* disbursement by the state for its children of school age was only 70 cents.[6] One white and two colored normal schools were training teachers in 1880; the former received $7,500 from the state treasury, the two colored schools $4,000 and $2,000 respectively.[7] Another colored school, with an initial appropriation of $2,000 a year, was established at Tuskegee in 1881.[8] Two new schools for training white teachers, with an annual appropriation of $2,500 each, were authorized in 1883.[9]

---

[1] Report of Senate Com. on Ed. and Labor, 1885, vol. ii, pp. 528–9; Report of U. S. Com. of Ed. for 1883, p. xl; ibid. for 1884, pp. 104–6.
[2] App. Ann. Cyclop. for 1884, p. 454.
[3] Report of U. S. Com. of Ed. for 1881, p. 87.
[4] App. Ann. Cyclop. for 1887, p. 444.
[5] Report of U. S. Com. of Ed. for 1888, p. 112.
[6] App. Ann. Cyclop. for 1888, p. 8; Report of U. S. Com. of Ed. for 1888, pp. 79, 89–92; Sess. Laws of Ala. for 1878–9, pp. 117 et seq.
[7] App. Ann. Cyclop. for 1879, p. 19; ibid. for 1881, p. 7; Report of Senate Com. on Ed. and Labor, 1885, vol. iv, pp. 200–01.
[8] Sess. Laws of Ala. for 1880–81, pp. 395–6.
[9] Ibid. for 1882–3, pp. 520, 523.

The governor in 1883 expressed his satisfaction at the growth and improvement of the public school system in Mississippi. A state teachers' association had lately held a meeting which was largely attended; teachers' institutes in the counties were arousing interest in the work.[1] The state superintendent of public education noted a greater willingness on the part of the people to pay school taxes and a general desire to extend the school term beyond the constitutional limit of four months of twenty days each.[2] Though men who could not read and write and were otherwise incompetent continued to occupy places of trust on the local school boards, the cause of public education was unquestionably advancing. In 1888 the superintendent said that $200,000 had been expended upon new school buildings, and in some counties in that year the people would have "six months of free school."[3]

The state school authorities in Georgia were urgently pressing the claims of public education. The cause was forwarded by the meeting of the National Educational Association in Atlanta in 1881.[4] The fund should be large enough, the state "commissioner" said, to keep the schools open for six months in a year, and he asked for means to conduct teachers' institutes and to establish normal training colleges.[5] By diligent effort, with the assistance of the Peabody fund, conditions were improving. From an attendance in 1874 of 85,000 scholars, the number was increased in 1883 to 188,000,[6] and in 1887 to 226,000.[7] The "commissioner," now a "superintendent," in 1888 was still asking for funds with which teaching might proceed for six instead of three months. Additional taxation, both local and state, was recommended. He suggested an "educational local option" by which a community might,

---

[1] App. Ann. Cyclop. for 1883, p. 544.
[2] Con. of Miss. of 1868, art. viii, sec. 5; App. Ann. Cyclop. for 1884, pp. 529–30.
[3] Report of U. S. Com. of Ed. for 1888, p. 1108.
[4] Ibid. for 1882, pp. 308–10.
[5] App. Ann. Cyclop. for 1882, p. 343.
[6] Ibid. for 1884, p. 351.
[7] Ibid. for 1888, p. 360; Report of U. S. Com. of Ed. for 1888, p. 67.

with the approval of the voters, expend a larger sum upon schools.[1]

In North Carolina, where public education was on a very low plane, the governor, in 1880, desired that the school tax be trebled; instead of $8\,^1/_3$ cents on $100 worth of property it should be 25 cents; instead of 25 cents the capitation tax should be 75 cents.[2] The new school law of 1881 authorized some further levies with a view to lengthening the school term to four months,[3] but not enough money could be raised under its provisions to effect material reform. Half the districts remained without schoolhouses, or money to build them, or money, indeed, to hire a teacher for more than four weeks in a year.[4] "Confusion reigned supreme," said the state superintendent, "and the enemies of public schools increased." The authorities succeeded in 1881 in organizing five "normal schools" for white and five for colored teachers which, however, were mere teachers' institutes continued for four or six weeks in vacation time.[5] In 1886 about $750,000 were being expended upon the schools in North Carolina.[6] In 1888 the attendance comprised only 35 per cent of the school population and the average length of the period during which teaching continued was only 63 days, or 12 weeks. It was impossible, the superintendent observed, for the schools "to accomplish much in such short terms." The people of the state, he said, were not doing even what they could to advance the cause of public education. A large number of the schoolhouses were unsanitary; indeed they were unfit for use. Two-thirds of the buildings were

---

[1] Report of U. S. Com. of Ed. for 1888, p. 107.

[2] App. Ann. Cyclop. for 1880, p. 584.

[3] Ibid. for 1881, p. 664; Sess. Laws of N. C. for 1881, chap. 200; App. Ann. Cyclop. for 1882, p. 632.

[4] Report of U. S. Com. of Ed. for 1883, p. 193.

[5] App. Ann. Cyclop. for 1882, p. 632; Report of U. S. Com. of Ed. for 1881, p. 195.

[6] App. Ann. Cyclop. for 1886, p. 655. In 1902-3 $1,577,000 were used in connection with the public schools of North Carolina. During 1927-8 $26,580,000 were available for their support (L. H. Jobe of N. C. Dept. of Pub. Instruction in U. S. Daily, April 14, 1930), though still there were 300,000 children of school age who were receiving no instruction and there were 204,492 illiterate voters in the state.—U. S. Daily, July 21, 1930.

donated or hired for small sums. The average value of the other third, which were owned by the communities they served, was only $94 each.[1] The cotton manufacturers, after the mills were built, sometimes made contributions for the benefit of the schools in their neighborhoods,[2] as did the iron manufacturers in Alabama.[3] In the United States, at large, the average amount expended upon free common schools was $2 *per capita* of the total population; in North Carolina the rate was only 39 cents *per capita*.

Ten counties contained one-fourth of the whole colored school population of Virginia; in one of these, in 1884, only 22 per cent, in another only 28 per cent of the colored children were enrolled, and a much smaller number attended, betokening a distressing state of ignorance among the blacks.[4] Though nearly a million and a half dollars were expended upon public education in 1887–8, and there were 7,269 schools and 7,282 teachers, only 125,000 out of 345,000 whites and only 65,000 out of 265,000 blacks of school age made daily appearance at the schoolhouses during the short school year.[5] The superintendent despaired of getting better results without compulsory attendance laws, such as were in force in 24 states and territories, though he doubted the efficacy of such measures in Virginia where four-fifths of the people dwelt in sparsely settled rural communities.[6]

Arkansas had been reckoned among the most backward of the Southern states in regard to education. Conditions grew better. The increase of population and wealth, as the state participated in the expansion of the West, brought the income for schools from all sources to more than $1,000,000 annually. In 1869 the number of teachers employed had been 1,335; in 1888 there were 4,664. The number of schoolhouses in the same time increased from 1,453 to 2,452. In 1888 the superin-

[1] Senate Mis. Doc., 48th Cong. 1st sess., no. 55, p. 20.
[2] H. L. Herring, Welfare Work in Mill Villages, p. 27; Report of Senate Com. on Ed. and Labor, 1885, vol. iv, pp. 730, 796.
[3] Report of Senate Com. on Ed. and Labor, 1885, vol. iv, p. 475.
[4] App. Ann. Cyclop. for 1885, p. 778.
[5] Ibid. for 1889, p. 819; Report of U. S. Com. of Ed. for 1888, p. 1111.
[6] Report of U. S. Com. of Ed. for 1888, p. 1111.

tendent of public instruction could say that, in proportion to taxable property, no state in the Union expended more for education than Arkansas. The rate was 7 mills in addition to a poll tax, and it was "cheerfully" paid.[1]

Texas yet more rapidly advanced in material development, and at the same time in its ability to support free schools. In 1880 there were 5,800 schools scattered over 145 counties,[2] and in 1883 the sum available for school purposes was $1,375,000, or about $4.41 for each child entitled to free instruction.[3] The average school year in 1884 had been increased to five months in the country and nearly nine months in the cities.[4] Male white teachers in the counties were being paid an average salary of $56 a month, female white teachers $38 a month. In the cities men received, on an average, $90, and women $48 a month. In 1886 over $2,000,000 were being paid out in teachers' salaries in the state.[5] Communities, however, displayed unwillingness to impose local taxes under the "optional" system which prevailed. In many counties, the state superintendent said, in 1888, the value of the common jail exceeded that of all the school property in the county. The average value of the county schoolhouses in Texas, with sites and furniture, was not more than $300 each. Of 8,826 schools only 3,286 occupied buildings which were public property. In the rest, or 63 per cent, teachers and pupils met in churches, private homes, barns, shanties and huts which were secured at a small rental or were donated by charitable citizens for the use.[6]

Colleges, universities and institutions, whatever their name, which were concerned with higher education in the South also languished in poverty and weakness. The University of Geor-

[1] App. Ann. Cyclop. for 1889, p. 35; Report of U. S. Com. of Ed. for 1888, p. 92.
[2] App. Ann. Cyclop. for 1880, pp. 684–5.
[3] Ibid. for 1883, p. 760.
[4] Ibid. for 1884, p. 758.
[5] Ibid. for 1886, p. 814; cf. ibid. for 1888, p. 765.
[6] Report of U. S. Com. of Ed. for 1888, pp. 146–7. Many facts concerning the state of education in the South may be gleaned from the Proceedings of the Trustees of the Peabody Education Fund.

gia in 1888 had 316 students. It was supported on an income of about $30,000 a year. The University of North Carolina at Chapel Hill had 203 students. It received $12,000 from the state in 1882.[1] Its income in 1888 was less than $35,000. There were 229 students at the University of Mississippi in 1887–8, and about the same number in the University of Texas. The University of Alabama in 1887–8 had 238 students with an income of approximately $53,000 annually.[2] In the University of South Carolina, in 1887–8, there were 170 students. The cost of supporting the university and an agricultural college was about $65,000 a year. In the Louisiana State University there were 88 students. It received an annual appropriation of $10,000 from the legislature.[3]

Many a martyr, man and woman, died unhonored and unsung in the long war against illiteracy in the South.[4] The struggle to reduce the ratio of the children growing up to adult years who could not write, read, spell and do the simplest calculations in arithmetic seemed of too much magnitude to be faced in the presence of such indifference of public feeling, such want of the means of obtaining properly equipped teachers to advance the work in hand. The income of funds supplied by generous men in the North, the chief of which was the Peabody benefaction, was a mere bauble in comparison with what should have been available for instant use.

The education of the negro was a problem unlike any hitherto presented to our pedagogical men. To usher him into the higher regions of learning which saw its flower in the white race, building generation upon generation, was an utterly foolish design. A large part of the colored population of the South consisted of "plantation hands," a class of persons, as Carl Schurz observed, "entirely unknown in the North." Emancipation had found them "only a few removes from absolute barbarism."[5] As for the intellectual changes in the negro,

[1] App. Ann. Cyclop. for 1882, p. 632.
[2] Ibid. for 1889, p. 7.
[3] Ibid., p. 771; Report of U. S. Com. of Ed. for 1888, p. 626.
[4] Senate Mis. Doc., 48th Cong. 1st sess., no. 55, p. 8.
[5] Writings of Carl Schurz, vol. iv, p. 390.

the making of him into the white man's equal by quick processes
was only a dream of Northern enthusiasts who knew neither
the African and his history on the one side, nor the limitations
of teaching, even in more favored places than the American
South, on the other.[1] The turn which should be given to effort
for the improvement of the blacks, as well as the illiterate
white masses, was toward simple industrial and technical education, so that the young, after they had learned their letters,
might be put in the way of being practically useful to themselves
and to the communities in which they dwelt.[2]

So much was clearly seen and coeval with the development
of the elementary school system, attempts, if feeble, were
made to establish not only normal schools for the training of
teachers, but also agricultural and mechanical academies. Georgia in 1884 appointed a commission to visit the best technical
schools in the country and to report a plan for organizing similar
schools in that state. In the following year such an institute
was established as a branch of the state university.[3] At the same
time local boards of education were authorized to "annex"
departments of industrial education to the public schools.[4]
North Carolina was discussing the question,[5] and such schools,
in one form or another, ill equipped though they were and
the recipients of but mean allowances, appeared in nearly all
the Southern states.

Two institutions of this class, under unusual leadership, with
the aid of the North, which confidence in their heads inspired,
rose to preëminence. General Samuel C. Armstrong, born in
the Sandwich Islands, son of an American missionary, had
fought in the war, commanding a regiment of colored troops,
and at the end of it he was assigned by General Howard to
take charge of a large "contraband" camp at Hampton Roads,
formed under the shelter of Fortress Monroe. It was Arm-

---

[1] Cf. N. Y. Nation, March 19, 1885.
[2] Curry, History of the Peabody Fund, p. 110.
[3] Sess. Laws of Ga. for 1884-5, pp. 69-72.
[4] Ibid., pp. 72-3.
[5] N. Y. Nation, Dec. 11, 1884; Senate Mis. Doc., 48th Cong. 1st sess.,
no. 55, p. 49.

strong's task to break up this camp; such a pack of blacks could not be rationed by the government indefinitely. Those who could work he sent northward and southward. For the children he had a sympathy which he could not withhold. He felt the impelling need of educating them for useful pursuits. At once, with no capital but faith and enthusiasm, he laid the foundations of what soon became rather generally renowned as the Hampton Normal and Agricultural Institute. Four or five millions of ex-slaves were his bugle call. He was ready "to sail into a good hearty battle," to use his own words. He sang three verses, dipped his pen in the "rays of the morning light," and began the story of a memorable life.[1]

Armstrong was a happy mixture of zealot and business man.[2] Beginning with but two teachers and 15 pupils in the old barracks which had done service for the government during the war the number of his students in 1870 had increased to 50, and growth henceforward was rapid. His farm, his shops and mills were places for work as well as study. The pupils were fed and clothed by the organization which he created. Each one was credited with his labor at its market value and the sum was paid him in education, which he could, when he had finished, bring to bear upon his own life and the problems of his race.[3] In the normal school boys and girls were prepared for teaching; they went forth to impart the knowledge which they had gained to others whose needs were as great as theirs had been before they had enjoyed its civilizing care. A deficit remained after the operations of each year, even with the aid which was accorded the school by the Federal government in connection with the education of a certain number of Indians from the West, and by the legislature of Virginia which was induced to regard Hampton as a state agricultural college for negroes.

Armstrong's zeal was contagious. He felt happy only when all his powers of resistance were taxed.[4] "Doing what can't

[1] F. G. Peabody, Education for Life, The Story of Hampton, p. 107.
[2] R. C. Ogden, Life of Armstrong.
[3] Cf. M. F. Armstrong and H. W. Ludlow, Hampton and Its Students.
[4] Peabody, Education for Life, pp. 113–4.

be done," he would say to his students, "is the glory of living." [1] He gained the friendship of charitable rich men who took places on his board of trustees and who loyally supported him.

The fruits were soon seen. Hampton's young men and women, coming forth in increasing numbers, were eager to enter the service for which they were prepared and they were centers for radiating the good which had been put into them at the school, the most notable of the number being one who had been born a slave in Virginia, Booker Talliaferro Washington. Entirely poor and friendless he reached Hampton from the Kanawha Valley in West Virginia where he had worked in a salt furnace, in a coal mine and as a house servant. He had finished his course and he was teaching in 1881 when two or three citizens of Tuskegee, Ala., asked General Armstrong to commend to them a man who could establish a trades school in that place, in which manner he was introduced to his great opportunity. Neither land nor buildings were at first at his disposal. The state made a contribution of $2,000 annually for the support of the work,[2] which was increased the next year to $3,000, and he gathered together a few pupils in an old church and a shanty adjoining it where, however, they were not destined to remain. His knowledge of his people's needs, his facility and attraction as a platform speaker and his power to win public confidence in the North, as in the South, enabled him to leap into prominence in the kind of educational service which was performed at Hampton, the parent school, upon which he drew liberally for the assistance required to realize his ends.[3] His figure was more inspiring than Armstrong's because he himself was an example of what the race might come to be if it were subjected to proper influences. His aim was Armstrong's; he would not fill the heads of his people with Greek, Latin, philosophy and science, but teach them, first of all, to work,—make them into trained laborers and skilled

[1] Peabody, Education for Life, p. 138.
[2] Sess. Laws of Ala. for 1880–81, pp. 395–6.
[3] B. T. Washington, Tuskegee and Its People; Max B. Thrasher, Tuskegee, Its Story and Its Work; M. S. Evans, Black and White, chap. xiii.

artisans, and then let them advance, if they would and could, at their leisure, into other fields.

Still other problems were to be faced in the Appalachian Mountains. Here were settled an unfortunate people sunk in poverty, squalor and general benightedness. Of British stock, for the most part, they preserved interesting traces in speech, manners and customs, and in their household industries, of the England of the 18th century. Indeed some of their words and phrases, their dances and songs were Chaucerian in their antiquity. They had been caught in the spurs of the mountain ranges which separate the East from the West, the Atlantic plains from the Mississippi Valley. Without the spirit or power to go farther with the more ambitious groups which crossed and went down on the other side, they had stood motionless for generations in the recesses and defiles of the highlands.[1] Indeed they had deteriorated by inbreeding and for other causes, and they were in so distressing a social state that those who have wished to romance about them have been obliged to overlook much that must naturally fill the mind with compassion and disgust.

Their homes were in seven states. In rude log cabins through which the snow flew in winter, lazy, thriftless, unlettered and cruel, surrounded by some scrawny fowl, a few sheep or goats or, perhaps, a cow or two and a mule, which fed upon what they could glean in the copse, and the half wild razorback hogs, they were a pitiful part of our American citizenry. For kitchen utensils the women had gourds and bowls hollowed out of wood. Bread made from the meal of maize which grew in little patches among the rocks, and "sowbelly," were the principal articles of food. Parts of the hog and herbs depended from the rafters of their unfloored one-room huts. Food was cooked by, and heat came from, open wood fires kindled by friction. For light, when there was any, they were indebted to pine torches and yarns stuck in pig's grease. The women

---

[1] Horace Kephart, Our Southern Highlanders, pp. 444–7; John C. Campbell, The Southern Highlander and His Homeland; M. S. Evans, Black and White, pp. 62–3.

spun cotton at their wheels. They clothed themselves, their men and their numerous children in the jeans and linseys which they wove with their own hands. Lean and sinewy in figure, sly, suspicious and secretive of mind these mountain men carried ancient firearms to kill the wild animals which abounded around them, and for use in the fracases and feuds which their ignorant ways of life freely invited. They distilled intoxicants from corn in defiance of the revenue laws of the country which also involved them in riot and bloodshed. The "hill billies," or whatever they might be called in their neighborhoods, were as useless a part of the American white race as the poor white "trash" living on the lower lands of the South in nearer proximity to the plantations. Strangers to law and to religion, except as it was brought to them by circuit riders and revivalists, whose interest ended in "baptizing" them and "saving their souls," while they were left to controversy about some piece of theological doctrine, amid all their former illiteracies and vulgarities, two or three millions of people called for the Christian missionary, and for the school-house.

Brave and good men and women were appearing for the task. One of the first and one of the highest in repute of the good influences set to work upon this population was Berea College in eastern Kentucky. Amid local difficulties that only heroic devotion could surmount, assisted by generous hands in the North, this school stamped its good impress upon the Appalachian people, and, with the aid of other agencies, they were being put in the way, in some degree, of becoming more useful and honorable components of the national mass.[1]

The very disturbing conditions which prevailed in the South in respect of common intelligence, among the whites as well as the blacks, seemed to many persons to demand Federal intervention. President Hayes in his inaugural address in 1877 had said that "universal suffrage should rest upon universal education"; he had suggested that, "if need be," sup-

[1] Cf. J. A. Rogers, Birth of Berea College, especially chap. ii.

port given to free schools by the state governments of the South should be "supplemented by legitimate aid from national authority,"[1] and he had not failed, as his term of office advanced, to return to the subject in his annual messages to Congress.[2] Garfield, in his inaugural address, in 1881, befriended the cause,[3] and Arthur followed with recommendations for Federal appropriations in the interest of a higher rate of popular intelligence.[4]

Gustavus J. Orr, the commissioner of education in Georgia, who was waging a stubborn contest with illiteracy, eager for greater progress, called a number of Southern men to a conference in Atlanta in February, 1878. The wants of the Southern states, they agreed, were "immediate and pressing." They asked the Federal government to come to their assistance at once.[5] Another meeting was held in Louisville in September, 1883, during the progress of the exposition in that city. Delegates from all parts of the South attended upon the invitation of the governor of Kentucky. A committee was named to memorialize Congress for relief from a menacing national situation.[6] Representatives from the convention during the following winter appeared before Congressional committees and urged the enactment of the necessary legislation. In Georgia, North Carolina and other Southern states the legislatures indorsed the movement in resolutions which were sent to Washington.[7] The United States commissioner of education,[8] Southern state superintendents,[9] officers of the Peabody and Slater funds,[10]

[1] Richardson, Messages and Papers, vol. vii, p. 444.
[2] Cf. ibid., pp. 478, 479, 506, 579, 602-3.
[3] Ibid., vol. viii, p. 9.
[4] Ibid., pp. 58, 143-4, 184; cf. Senate Mis. Doc., 48th Cong. 1st sess., no. 55, pp. 86-7.
[5] Senate Mis. Doc., 48th Cong. 1st sess., no. 55, pp. 39-41.
[6] Ibid., pp. 3, 14, 42.
[7] House Reports, 48th Cong. 1st sess., no. 495, pp. 12, 22-3; Sess. Laws of N. C. for 1885, p. 680 and ibid. for 1887, p. 763; N. Y. Nation, March 4, 1886; Senate Mis. Doc., 48th Cong. 1st sess., no. 55, pp. 40-41; Chas. L. Smith, Hist. of Ed. in N. C., pp. 175-6.
[8] Cf. Report of U. S. Com. of Ed. for 1881, p. lxxxix.
[9] Cf. Bureau of Education, Circular of Information, no. 6, 1888, p. 147; Report of Senate Com. on Ed. and Labor, 1885, vol. iv, pp. 211, 672.
[10] Cf. Curry, Hist. of Peabody Fund, pp. 136-40.

educators generally in the South and in the North [1] gave the proposed measure their support.

Illiteracy, it was said, was increasing. Using the Census returns it appeared in 1880 that more than 6,239,000 persons in the United States above ten years of age, or one in eight, could not write. The number had been 5,658,000 in 1870,[2] a disgrace which was due, in the North, to foreign immigration, in the South, to backward and alarming native conditions. While in 1880 Massachusetts had about 5 per cent of illiteracy, nearly all foreign, Arkansas had 25, Florida 29, Mississippi, Georgia and North Carolina 33, Alabama 34 and South Carolina 37 per cent nearly all native.[3]

On the same basis, regarding every person above ten years of age who could not write as an "illiterate," about 7 per cent of the whites and nearly 50 per cent of the colored people of the United States in 1880 did not know their letters. The highest percentage of illiteracy for the whites in any Southern state, 22 per cent, was attributed to North Carolina. The highest percentage for the blacks in the South was in Alabama, Georgia and Louisiana, where it was more than 53 per cent; it was 51 per cent in the Carolinas, 49 in Mississippi, Arkansas and Virginia, 48 in Texas and Tennessee and 47 in Florida.[4]

---

[1] Cf. C. Meriwether, Hist. of Higher Ed. in S. C., pp. 78–80; T. Thomas Fortune, Black and White, pp. 54–6. Armstrong at Hampton was an exception. He believed in "self-help."—F. G. Peabody, Education for Life, pp. 203–4.

[2] Compendium of the Tenth Census, pt. ii, pp. 1645, 1654; Senate Mis. Doc., 48th Cong. 1st sess., no. 55, pp. 5–6, 9.

[3] Senate Reports, 48th Cong. 1st sess., no. 101, pp. 18–9. A distinction made by the statisticians between those who could not read and those who could not write, the latter class showing the higher totals, may be disregarded in arriving at conclusions as to "illiteracy." Percentages are computed by taking the number of those over ten years of age who could not write with reference to the whole population, including, therefore, children under ten. If the children were left out of account and the illiterates were set off against the population over ten the percentages would be much higher and still more impressively alarming. The computations used here are based on the returns of the Tenth Census in pt. ii of the Compendium, pp. 16, 45–56.

[4] Senate Reports, 48th Cong. 1st sess., no. 101, pp. 18–9; House Reports, 48th Cong. 1st sess., no. 495, p. 1; cf. Senate Mis. Doc., 48th Cong. 1st sess., no. 55, pp. 5–6.

In a population of 1,262,505 in Alabama 433,447 were illiterates over ten years of age; of 1,399,750 in North Carolina
463,975 could not read and write; of 1,542,180 in Georgia 520,-
416 were in the same unfortunate situation, and so on in all
the Southern states in a ratio of about 1 to 3, or 1 to 4.[1]

The people of the South were now taxing themselves "to
the very utmost of their ability." [2] The state superintendent
of public education in Alabama said that five-elevenths of
the entire income of his state was devoted to schools, but that
entire income was only $1,100,000.[3] While Massachusetts gave
to her schools $1 for about $400 of taxable property, South
Carolina declared that she was giving $1 for $250.[4] While
Boston was giving at the rate of 2½ mills for her complete
school establishment Charleston bore a tax of 3½ mills for her
primary schools alone.[5]

They had a school population of 5,000,000 in the South
and paid annually for common school education over $7,000,-
000.[6] While they expended one-tenth of the aggregate school
moneys of the country they had one-fifth of the population under
their care.[7] Federal aid was "indispensable," said Dr. Curry.
The South could raise only $7,000,000 a year and was using
it properly; to do what was to be done would require $30,000,000
or $40,000,000 which would mean taxation at three times the
rate laid at the time on property owners in Connecticut or New
York.[8]

For many years bills had been before Congress, which, if
they had passed that body, and had gained the approval of
the President, would have supplied the necessary means to
the faithful men in the South who were endeavoring, with

[1] Senate Reports, 48th Cong. 1st sess., no. 101, pp. 18–9; Senate Mis.
Doc., 48th Cong. 1st sess., no. 55, p. 66; N. Y. Nation, Jan. 21, 1886.

[2] Senate Mis. Doc., 48th Cong. 1st sess., no. 55, p. 7; cf. Report of U. S.
Com. of Ed. for 1883–4, pp. lx–lxi.

[3] Senate Mis. Doc., 48th Cong. 1st sess., no. 55, p. 24; cf. Bureau of
Education, Circular of Information, no. 6, 1888, p. 147.

[4] Senate Mis. Doc., 48th Cong. 1st sess., no. 55, p. 30.

[5] C. Meriwether, Hist. of Higher Education in S. C., pp. 77–8.

[6] Senate Mis. Doc., 48th Cong. 1st sess., no. 55, p. 7.

[7] Senate Reports, 48th Cong. 1st sess., no. 101, p. 27.

[8] Senate Mis. Doc., 48th Cong. 1st sess., no. 55, p. 85.

the feeble instruments at hand, to combat such intolerable conditions. It was proposed to create a "perpetual fund," derived from annual sales of Federal lands, patent office receipts, railroad revenues and other sources, the interest on which could be distributed to the states for education.[1] The hope of passing such a measure, which in 1880 had gained the approval of the Senate by a vote of 41 to 6,[2] was not abandoned, but assistance which would be immediate in its effect was required. It need not be a continuing benefaction but temporary aid should come from the Treasury by direct appropriation. The proposal took various forms, but that one which met with most favor, after 1881,[3] called for the outlay of a considerable sum, say 15 millions, at once, and further sums, diminished by a million annually, for ten years, at the expiration of which time the payments would cease, on the theory that thereafter the states and the local governments could sustain their schools without the further help of Congress.[4] The sum would be apportioned not to the South alone but to the various states and territories on the basis of illiteracy. More than one million dollars would pass from the Federal Treasury in the first year to the school authorities of each of five states—Alabama, Georgia, North Carolina, Tennessee and Virginia; only a little less than one million dollars to each of three states—South Carolina, Mississippi and Louisiana. New York's share would be $507,000 and Massachusetts's, $230,000.[5]

The scheme came to be associated with the name of Henry W. Blair, a member of the United States Senate from New Hampshire. He was an acrid and supple partisan who gave in fury what he lacked in discretion. With fennel in one hand and rue, for the South, in the other he was not a perfect advocate of the measure. The Southern educators who looked to him for

[1] Senate Reports, 48th Cong. 1st sess., no. 101, pp. 28–9; cf. McPherson's Handbook for 1886, pp. 163–4.

[2] McPherson's Handbook for 1882, pp. 37–9; cf. Report of U. S. Com. of Ed. for 1881, p. lxxxix.

[3] Senate Reports, 50th Cong. 1st sess., no. 4, p. 1.

[4] Senate Mis. Doc., 48th Cong. 1st sess., no. 101, pp. 29–30, 32–3. For another plan see House Reports, 48th Cong. 1st sess., no. 495, pt. 2.

[5] Senate Mis. Doc., 48th Cong. 1st sess., no. 101, p. 30.

friendly favors must hear themselves called "rebels" and forgive him for his inferences, if not forthright declarations, that, with education, communities which at the time were Democratic would see the light and become Republican.

The constitutionality of such a grant of Federal moneys to the South, even after it was agreed that all the states should be admitted to the benefits of the law, the moral obligation involved, the large social duty, the expediency of aiding those who ought to help themselves were for a long time discussed.[1] A powerful motive for Federal interposition was found in the need of guarding the franchise, of making the citizen, particularly the negro, fit to cast the ballot which had been put into his hands. The United States should guarantee to every state "a republican form of government"—this was a command of the Constitution. The republic could not continue to exist, if its vitals were sapped by ignorance.[2] It was stated, with statistical support, that there were 145,000 illiterate voters in Georgia, 131,000 in Virginia, 125,000 in North Carolina,[3] and more than 100,000 in each of five other Southern states—Alabama, Louisiana, Mississippi, South Carolina and Tennessee.

Over 75 per cent of the adult colored males in Georgia, Louisiana, Alabama, Mississippi, North Carolina, South Carolina, Texas and Virginia could not read and write.[4] More than half of those qualified to vote in South Carolina, white and black, were illiterates.[5] Of 1,580,000 illiterate voters in the United States, it was said, in 1881, that the Southern states furnished 317,281 white and 820,022 colored.[6] These men cast ballots the contents of which were unknown to them.

[1] Cf. N. Y. Nation, Jan. 21 and Feb. 25, 1886.

[2] Cf. Senate Reports, 48th Cong. 1st sess., no. 101, pp. 1–5.

[3] In 1884 the state superintendent of education in North Carolina said that there were 145,000 voters in his state who could not read the ballot which they cast on election day.—Senate Mis. Doc., 48th Cong. 1st sess., no. 55, p. 23.

[4] House Reports, 48th Cong. 1st sess., no. 495, pp. 19–20.

[5] Ibid., p. 8; cf. N. Y. Nation, Jan. 21, 1886.

[6] Senate Mis. Doc., 48th Cong. 1st sess., no. 55, p. 86. The aggregate vote of the United States at the Presidential election in 1880 was about 9,220,000.

They could not tell the Constitution of the United States from the code of Draco, said Senator Blair.[1] The influence of such a mass of ignorance, Dr. Curry said, "poisons society, corrupts the fountains of justice, sits like a juggling devil over the ballot box, makes elections a farce and a crime, causes demagogism and fraud to run riot, puts incompetence, conceit and villainy in high places and endangers the ark of our free representative institutions." [2]

When the Federal revenues exceeded the expenditures and this subject came to excite public attention in the Arthur and Cleveland administrations the way, it was believed, might be easier. The United States Treasury was bursting with a "surplus." Idle, unused, unneeded funds were its embarrassment.[3]

However much others may have deplored such an encroachment by the central government on state prerogatives, such enfeeblement of communities by doing for them what it was their business to do for themselves, Blair's enthusiasm continued. Ignorance was slavery, he said. "But for ignorance there would have been no slave. But for ignorance among the nominally free there would have been no rebellion." [4] Slavery would continue, he declared, until "intelligence, handmaid of liberty, shall have illuminated the whole land with the light of her smile." What was now to be done was "a part of the war." [5] "Secession and a confederacy founded upon slavery as its chief corner stone," he continued, were better than the future of the Southern states, if they were to become "the spawning ground of ignorance, vice, anarchy and every crime." [6] With education the United States and the world would "reach the millenium within one hundred years." [7]

In 1884 Blair succeeded in obtaining a majority in the Senate

[1] Senate Reports, 48th Cong. 1st sess., no. 101, p. 13.
[2] Senate Mis. Doc., 48th Cong. 1st sess., no. 55, p. 86; cf. Report of Senate Com. on Ed. and Labor, 1885, vol. iv, p. 669.
[3] Senate Mis. Doc., 48th Cong. 1st sess., no. 55, p. 8.
[4] Senate Reports, 48th Cong. 1st sess., no. 101, p. 6.
[5] Ibid., p. 28.
[6] Ibid.
[7] Ibid., p. 8.

for his bill. The vote was 33 to 11.[1] Again in 1886 the Senate
passed the measure in a slightly amended form, by a vote of
35 to 12,[2] and for a third time, with further amendments, in
1888, when the vote was 39 to 29.[3] But in no case, in spite
of "strenuous efforts," was progress made with it in the House,[4]
though Blair spoke of "suicidal delay." Every month thousands of illiterate youth, he reminded the nation, were passing
"beyond the reach of educational influences into the great
mass of American citizenship and cursing the land and the
world with their contribution to an ignorant and corrupted sovereignty." [5]

The New York Nation, although at first in favor of the
principle underlying the measure,[6] repeatedly described it as
"the bill to promote mendicancy." [7] Much of the hostility
to it was fairly attributed to the fanatical advocacy of it by
the man whose name it bore. It was seen to be a greater honor
to be arrayed in opposition to him than to be on his side and
public feeling set in strongly against the scheme.[8] The South
itself, the New York Nation said, had begun to "spurn the
humiliating idea of turning beggar and asking the authorities
at Washington to educate her children for her," [9] and a Northern senator dared to call it "an act of grand larceny on the
Treasury." [10] It was now a "New South"; much was heard
of its prosperity and the increase of taxable wealth. The Southern states might face their own future and solve their own
problems as they could without national aid.[11]

With all the civilizing forces which could be brought to

[1] Eight Southern Democrats voted against and 13 for the bill.—Mc-
Pherson's Handbook for 1884, p. 147.
[2] Ibid. for 1886, p. 160.
[3] App. Ann. Cyclop. for 1888, p. 234.
[4] Senate Reports, 50th Cong. 1st sess., no. 4, p. 1.
[5] Ibid., p. 4.
[6] N. Y. Nation, May 5, 1881.
[7] Cf. ibid., Feb. 18, May 27, 1886, and Aug. 25, 1887.
[8] Cf. ibid., March 4, 11, June 3, 1886, and Dec. 26, 1889.
[9] Ibid., Dec. 5, 1889; cf. ibid., Jan. 5, 1888.
[10] Ibid., Feb. 25, 1886.
[11] Cf. E. G. Murphy, Problems of the Present South, pp. 92–3; G. S.
Merriam, The Negro and the Nation, pp. 404–5; N. Y. Nation, Feb. 25,
1886.

bear upon Southern social conditions, on the plains as in the mountains, internally and externally, progress was in many directions disappointing. But there was encouragement in the fact that error was seen and remedy was in the public mind. The North, until it was invaded by great bodies of immigrants from Europe of inferior national stocks, and these elements congregated in large cities to complicate social relationships and demoralize political life, had attained standards of thought and action, in some regards, distinctly higher than those of the South. Slavery had given mastery to a few men of property. Democracy was a theory. Where work was done by a people of another race, imported for the service and held in absolute control, through fear of personal consequences, it was not the crown of social respectability for the white man to be industrious, nor was there assurance that social institutions in other respects would enjoy correct development and regulation.

Proof that the South remained in a primitive condition of thinking and feeling, and that it had not participated in the advancement of more highly developed communities had been plain to see before the war and traces of its rude feudal manners were still visible. The North's system of "Reconstruction" did nothing to eradicate it; indeed it had more firmly set opinions and magnified customs which were not admirable. The proneness of men, even among the well-born and more intelligent classes, to carry firearms, to resent insults by violence, to remember injuries and to avenge them, to rely upon individual prowess rather than a system of law for the maintenance of peace and order, as seen in whippings, lynchings, "street duels" and worse barbarities, indicated a very low notion of social behavior. Protest, especially if it originated in the North, was not greatly welcomed.[1] But the work was undertaken by many newspapers—more systematically and effectively, and more free from party or sectional animus by the New York Nation, later, after the union of the two papers, with the added influence of the New York Evening Post.

[1] N. Y. Nation, Nov. 2, 1882 and Jan. 4, 1883.

Mr. Godkin not only condemned such a state of manners as uncivilized, but pointed to it as a reason why labor and capital only slowly passed to the South [1] and, before he had said the last word on the subject, Southern people generally, if they had discernment, were brought to understand that they had rightly earned all that was being said about them.[2]

Any long recital of accredited instances of such a spirit of barbarity could be of no profit.[3] They were many and of swift recurrence on the plantations and in the hills and mountains, in the country and in the towns. "The curse and shame of the South," the New York Nation said without too much exaggeration, was the "constant presence in the minds of all males of all classes, from childhood up, of homicide as one of the probable contingencies of ordinary social life.[4]

In Atlanta a "colonel" sold an interest in a contract for convict labor. This action displeased a man who held another interest, so the two began shooting at each other in the state treasurer's office in the State House. One fell dead, the other was wounded. It was explained that the uncle of the murdered man had been killed in a duel, that a brother, the father of the murdered man, had then shot the surviving duellist in the street and that, to cap it all, the surviving duellist's brother had shot the man who had killed his brother.[5] A few days passed; the newspapers then told of a justice of the court of appeals in Kentucky who was shot dead in a public place by a defeated litigant. In Georgia a leading citizen was shot and killed for using a power of attorney for the sale of a contract. In Virginia a young man was killed while being fitted for a pair of boots, because he would not admit that he had insulted a lady whose name was not communicated to him. In Texas two actors were shot by a ruffian because they tried to afford protection to a

---

[1] Cf. N. Y. Nation, Dec. 14, 1882.
[2] Cf. ibid., Dec. 7, 1882, Jan. 4, 18 and Feb. 22, 1883.
[3] Many of them in and just prior to 1880 are particularly alluded to in H. V. Redfield, Homicide North and South.
[4] N. Y. Nation, Oct. 26, 1882; cf. ibid., Nov. 9 and 23, 1882; Redfield, Homicide North and South.
[5] N. Y. Nation, March 13, 1879.

woman, a fellow traveler.[1] So it was year after year, as in South Carolina in 1881, in the revolting murder of an elderly lawyer by a dissatisfied client which was called a "duel"; in Tennessee in 1882 when three men were killed as a result of a family feud in which two others had lost their lives some months earlier. All were men of prominence in their communities. Most of them answered to military titles suggesting service in the Confederate army. In the same year, in 1882, the speaker of the house of representatives of Mississippi was slain. He and his brother had thrashed a Baltimore merchant, whom they threatened to kill as soon as he got well of his injuries. The merchant hearing of their intentions rose from his bed at the first opportunity, went forth and shot the distinguished officer of the lower house of the state legislature.[2]

In Opelika, Ala., street fighting became so terrifying that the legislature repealed the charter of the town and in 1885 vested the government in a commission appointed by the governor.[3]

If the liberty of the individual to manufacture whiskey in the mountains was restrained by officers of the Treasury Department, who were commanded to collect a tax upon it, they would be shot. From Wheeling in West Virginia down the entire Appalachian mountain chain nearly to the Gulf of Mexico, a region which was penetrated only by foot paths and horse trails, the business of making corn in small copper stills into whiskey called "white lightning" had long proceeded without interference.[4] It is said that there were 3,000 of these, of a capacity of from 10 to 50 gallons a day, in the mountain counties of the South in 1877,[5] an estimate which was increased in the next year to 5,000.[6] The internal revenue laws required the payment of a tax upon the product and the government

[1] N. Y. Nation, April 3, 1879.
[2] Ibid., Dec. 13 and 28, 1882.
[3] Sess. Laws of Ala. for 1882–3, pp. 245 et seq.; ibid. for 1884–5, pp. 465 et seq.; N. Y. Nation, Jan. 11, 1883.
[4] Senate Reports, 47th Cong. 2nd sess., no. 981, pp. 3–4.
[5] Report of Com. of Int. Revenue for 1877 in Report of Sec. of Treas. for that year, pp. 120–21.
[6] Ibid., p. iii.

placed agents in the various states for the work. The resistance which they met was not lessened by the fact that some of the officers were "Yankees" from the North and that they, in too many instances, were identified with the Southern Republican party organizations. They were called "revenues," "revenooers," "spies," "whiskey smellers," "still-house nosers," "red-legged grasshoppers" who were eating at the vitals of the country, even "thieves." [1] Food and lodging were refused them at any price; their lives were threatened. The waylaying, beating and shooting of men who were but doing their duty, who were, perhaps, only suspected of being engaged in government service, or of being "informers" on the subject of the location of stills, were at times so close to riot and rebellion that the entire Federal establishment in the vicinity must be called upon for support. [2]

A party of 11 revenue officers in 1878 in the mountains of Tennessee who had taken refuge in a farmer's house, were fired upon by a mob throughout an entire night. In the morning they ran to a log inclosure where they could return the fire and where the siege was continued by some 200 men. Three of the officers were shot before relief arrived. [3] The Commissioner of Internal Revenue increased his force, armed his deputies with breech-loading carbines and organized posses in the hope of enforcing the law. He said in 1879 that in the past three years, for the seizure of 3,117 stills and the arrest of 6,431 persons, 26 of his men had been killed and 47 wounded. [4] He asked for larger appropriations so that he could cope with the situation, and for pensions for the widows and children of the dead.

The illicit distilling of grain into whiskey and of fruit into

---

[1] Senate Mis. Doc., 47th Cong. 1st. sess., no. 116, pp. 122, 191, 196. "Taxes cost mebbe three cents on the dollar and that's all right. But revenue costs a dollar ten cents on twenty cents worth o' liquor; and that's robin' the people with a gun to their faces."—A mountaineer to Horace Kephart in Our Southern Highlanders, p. 120.

[2] Cf. Geo. W. Atkinson, After the Moonshiners; Henry M. Wiltse, The Moonshiners.

[3] Report of Com. of Int. Revenue for 1878, p. iv.

[4] Ibid. for 1879, p. iii, xiv.

brandy was called "blockading," as was the manufacture of
tobacco upon which no tax was paid. Whiskey making was
defended by the mountaineers as a right which no one might
gainsay. It was their own grain; they were using it on their
own land.[1] The refuse was fed to the hogs. Selling "corn
juice" was not different from selling corn itself or bacon.[2]
It was a long task and a hard one to deal with an ignorant
people, entrenched in almost inaccessible fastnesses, with reference to this subject,[3] especially as local politicians, to gain
the votes of the "blockaders," encouraged them to think that
they were the victims of an oppressive system.[4] Even judges
on the bench openly took the side of the "moonshiners" with
the purpose of obstructing the enforcement of the law.[5] The
sentiment of the entire population was hostile.[6] Tickets at
elections were headed, "Down with the Revenue!" and campaigns were waged on this issue.[7] Resistance was most active
in a collection district embracing 34 counties lying west of
the Yadkin River in North Carolina, but the people were
almost as unruly in the mountains of Georgia, Tennessee and
South Carolina.[8]

Under such conditions when United States agents were killed
or wounded in their desperate work, it was practically impossible to secure the punishment of the offenders in the state
courts.[9] But progress was made by relentless pursuit, the
imposition of fines and the destruction of the distilling ap-
paratus, followed by suggestions to the people to buy licenses,
pay the tax and proceed with their business in a legal manner.[10]

[1] App. Ann. Cyclop. for 1880, pp. 308–9.
[2] Cf. Horace Kephart, Our Southern Highlanders, p. 122.
[3] Senate Reports, 47th Cong. 2nd sess., no. 981, pp. 2–3; Senate Mis.
Doc., 47th Cong. 1st sess., no. 116, pp. 231–2.
[4] Senate Reports, 47th Cong. 2nd sess., no. 981, p. 44; Senate Mis. Doc.,
47th Cong. 1st sess., no. 116, pp. 122, 191–4, 366–7, 450.
[5] Report of Com. of Int. Rev. for 1878, p. iv.
[6] Senate Reports, 47th Cong. 2nd sess., no. 981, p. 3; Senate Mis. Doc.,
47th Cong. 1st sess., no. 116, pp. 191, 352.
[7] Senate Reports, 47th Cong. 2nd sess., no. 981, pp. 124, 225.
[8] Ibid., p. 298.
[9] Report of Com. of Int. Rev. for 1878, p. ix.
[10] Senate Reports, 47th Cong. 2nd sess., no. 981, pp. 4, 30; cf. Senate
Ex. Doc., 47th Cong. 1st sess., no. 83; Report of Com. of Int. Rev. for

Disorder gradually diminished,[1] though in many of the remoter parts of the country it could not be entirely allayed,[2] nor is "moonshine" whiskey making an unknown pursuit in these fastnesses at this day.[3]

One family of mountaineers would lie behind walls and brush for members of another family, who were shot to satisfy some ignorant grudge. Boys were bred up for vengeance. "Clan" would fight "clan" with a view to its extermination.[4] In no other part of the country, not even on the plains and in the mining towns of the West, where men were frankly bandits and desperadoes, and there was no law, was human life so lightly esteemed as in our Southern states.

A computation was made in 1878. It appeared that there had been 734 homicides in Texas, Kentucky and South Carolina in that year, that 522 others had been shot or stabbed, though not fatally. There were, it was said, more homicides in Kentucky in 1878 than in the eight states of Maine, New Hampshire, Vermont, Massachusetts, Rhode Island, Connecticut, Pennsylvania and Minnesota with an aggregate population of ten millions; in South Carolina in the same year, more than in eight Northern states with a population of six millions. There had been, so it was alleged by a statistician of the subject, 40,000, perhaps 50,000 homicides in the South in the 13 years which had elapsed since the war. It was a record unequalled in any country on the earth which was held to be civilized.[5]

The truth is that a military spirit pervaded the people to a degree which was quite unknown in the North, as was attested by the general use of military titles and the large number of military schools to which the boys of old Southern families

1879, p. v; ibid. for 1880, pp. v–vi; Geo. W. Atkinson, After the Moonshiners; Henry M. Wiltse, The Moonshiners.
[1] Cf. Report of Com. of Int. Rev. for 1881, p. vii.
[2] Cf. Senate Reports, 47th Cong. 2nd sess., no. 981, p. 298.
[3] Cf. Horace Kephart, Our Southern Highlanders, chaps. v–viii.
[4] Cf. ibid., chap. xviii.
[5] Redfield, Homicide North and South, pp. 10–21; M. S. Evans, Black and White, pp. 65–6; N. Y. Nation, Nov. 23, 1882.

were sent to gain training in the use of arms, and to fit them, if not for war, to be "gentlemen," squeamish about their "honor" and ready to resent "insult." [1] Women in the South, in their hearts as a result of custom and by familiarity with such incidents, seemed to mantle the carrying of deadly weapons and the free use of them with the glamour of chivalry. [2] Even the religious press was silent in the face of such unusual conditions. [3]

There was force in the South's defense of its attitude toward its street encounters, its improvised duels and its feuds— that redress for grievances was not to be found in resort to the law. But it was true at the same time that Southern men had always regarded appeal to public judicatory agencies in the settlement of personal difficulties as a confession of cowardice. [4] As a matter of fact most of the affrays originated in incidents which were mere "insults," and of too vague and trifling a nature to be remediable by law. With such a body of opinion in the South it was not difficult to understand why taking the life of an "enemy" was not regarded as a crime to be punished as such. No white man was hanged for murder, [5] and the evil grew. The streets might be thronged when such a deed was done,—no hand would be raised against the perpetrator of it. The act, or the necessity of it, would be deplored and the family would be the recipients of public sympathy, but the killer moved about among his neighbors as before and went scot free. [6] It was an unwritten law that "You shall not suffer, if in a fair fight you kill." [7]

It was said, truly or not, that the arrest, trial, conviction and sentence to imprisonment for life of the man in Atlanta in 1879 who had killed a "colonel" in the State House was the only instance on record of so severe an expression of public

---

[1] N. Y. Nation, Jan. 4, 1883.
[2] Ibid., Jan. 4, 1883; cf. ibid., Oct. 26, 1882.
[3] Ibid., Jan. 18, 1883.
[4] A Southern correspondent in ibid., Feb. 22, 1883.
[5] Cf. Southern corr. in ibid., Jan. 18 and 25, 1883.
[6] Cf. Southern corr. in ibid., Feb. 22, 1883.
[7] A Southern corr. in ibid., June 28, 1883; another Southerner in ibid., Tan. 18, 1883 and another in ibid., Feb. 22, 1883.

reproof in such a case,[1] a severity which was justified, it seemed, because the "colonel" had not fallen in a "fair fight"—the prisoner had continued to shoot after the chambers of his adversary's revolver were empty. Yet this slayer, having served three years of his sentence, was pardoned by Alexander Stephens, the old Vice-President of the Confederacy, at the time governor of Georgia,[2] to become upon regaining his liberty, a possible target for the dead man's son.[3]

In the face of the changes which were in progress in the South it was inevitable that the absurdity of such conduct would be gradually understood and that evils which were so unfavorably remarked would disappear. The rise of a commercial and industrial civilization altered the popular outlook toward this as well as other subjects.[4] It was said in New Orleans, in 1883, that no "social" or "business" homicides had occurred in that city in several years and that they were becoming less frequent in all the larger commercial towns.[5] Influential citizens in many places formed boards of arbitration. Such committees assumed the duty of composing private differences in Savannah, Augusta, Macon and elsewhere, and the parties to injuries, as well as the communities in which they lived, respected the decisions of these peaceable intercessors.[6]

In the interest of better manners and in response to a developing public opinion laws had been passed to prohibit duelling, but the lying in wait and the whipping out of a revolver or a knife to kill an enemy on sight had taken its place.[7] Many legislatures passed acts forbidding the carrying of deadly weapons—pistols, dirks, daggers, bowie knives, brass knuckles, slung shot and the like, which were enumerated—if these were "con-

[1] A Southerner in N. Y. Nation, June 28, 1883.
[2] Ibid., Dec. 14, 1882. Stephens in the first eight weeks of his governorship pardoned 49 convicts, 12 of them being held for longer or shorter terms as murderers.—Ibid., Jan. 25, 1883.
[3] Ibid., Jan. 18, 1883.
[4] Cf. N. Y. Nation, Jan. 18, 1883.
[5] Southern corr. in ibid., Feb. 22, 1883.
[6] Southern corr. in ibid., June 28, 1883.
[7] Southern corr. in ibid., Feb. 22, and June 28, 1883.

cealed," or, to use the language of one of the laws in question,
if "hid from common observation." Penalties which comprehended fines of from $50 to $500, or hard labor for the county
for six months or a year, were prescribed.[1]

As the wearing of weapons was too general and was plainly,
if not at the root of the evil, a symbol and an expression of
it,[2] such measures, though the men in the capitols of the states
who adopted the laws and fixed the penalties had revolvers
in their hip pockets when they did so,[3] were the reflection of
a growing conviction that manslaughter must stop, both in
the interest of a higher civilization and for the purpose of
giving to Southern life a better reputation in the eyes of capitalists and laboring men in the North, who were so much desired for the economic advancement of the country.

The laws against duelling were operative. Proof of this
was found in the fact that Southerners of the old pattern were
deploring the abolition of the "Code," and the rise in its place
of unregulated murder.[4] Sooner or later the laws concerning
concealed weapons would be heeded and enforced. A Northern man who had ridden a horse through the wildest parts
of the South said that there was no more reason for wearing
arms there than in New England, where not one in a thousand
males did so.[5]

But amid such surroundings it is certain that in many communities life without such protection was not too safe, and
Southern men were not pleased to forego the privilege. In
the law in Mississippi there was exception for those who were
"threatened with," or had "good and sufficient reason to ap-

[1] Sess. Laws of Ala. for 1880–81, p. 38; ibid. of Miss. for 1878, pp. 175–6;
ibid. of S. C. for 1880, pp. 447–8; ibid. of Ga. for 1882–3, pp. 48–9; ibid.
of N. C. for 1879, p. 231; ibid. of Va. for 1881–2, p. 233, and for 1883–4,
p. 180; ibid. of Ark. for 1881, pp. 191–2.

[2] Men habitually carried arms in many neighborhoods. A witness in a
court of law in Virginia was asked if the prisoner had been armed and if
so how. "With the arms we all carry," he replied. "What are they?"
"A pistol and a knife."—Southern corr. in N. Y. Nation, Jan. 18, 1883;
cf. Report of Senate Com. on Ed. and Labor, vol. iv, p. 277.

[3] Redfield, op. cit., pp. 194–5, 203.

[4] Cf. Southern corr. in N. Y. Nation, Feb. 22, 1883.

[5] Redfield, op. cit., p. 193.

prehend an attack," or were "travelling (not being a tramp)"—
these might continue to carry pistols and knives.[1] In Arkansas,
too, a man, "upon his own premises," or "when upon a journey," was excepted from the prohibition.[2]

The first attempt to enforce the act in Mississippi was recorded in 1879.[3] The governor of the state in 1885 said that
the habit of going about armed was "too prevalent"; it was
"a fruitful source of crime." He asked for amendment of
the law; he would make the use of concealed weapons to kill,
or to attempt to kill, "a crime not admitting of defense."
If knives or pistols thus worn could not be "lawfully" employed
men, the governor thought, would cease to carry them.[4] Efforts
to enforce the law in Alabama were futile. The practice was
"sustained by public sentiment," a newspaper said; being apprehended, tried and convicted of the offense carried with it
"no opprobrium whatever."[5] In some states it was made
unlawful to sell weapons to minors or intoxicated persons. A
father would be made responsible for the conduct of a son under
16 years of age with respect to the carrying of arms; teachers
for the conduct in this regard of pupils under their care.[6] In
the "act to preserve the public peace and prevent crime,"
commonly called the "pistol bill," which the legislature of
Arkansas passed in 1881, when parts of that state were in
complete disorder, even the selling, keeping for sale, and giving
away of knives and revolvers were prohibited.[7]

A Southerner, writing to the editor of the New York Nation
in 1879, said that there could never be "any settled, contented
prosperity for the negroes" until their Northern friends should
cease to regard them "as a horde or clan for political purposes,
to be banded against their white neighbors."[8] Out of a situation which the North in unwisdom had created, without com-

[1] Sess. Laws of Miss. for 1878, pp. 175–6.
[2] Ibid. of Ark. for 1881, pp. 191–2.
[3] App. Ann. Cyclop. for 1879, p. 829.
[4] Ibid. for 1883, p. 545.
[5] Ibid. for 1885, p. 19.
[6] Cf. Sess. Laws of Miss. for 1878, pp. 175–6.
[7] Sess. Laws of Ark. for 1881, pp. 191–2.
[8] N. Y. Nation, June 5, 1879.

prehending the black man on the one side or the white people of the South on the other, came whippings, shootings, homicides, race riots and the more formal lynchings. These displays of power in the presence of the negro were gravely held to be necessary in many neighborhoods. The free "nigger" could not be kept at bay unless he were made to know that punishment for crime was sure and immediate.[1] If he killed a white man, raped a female, and for crimes less heinous, instead of being committed to the care of officers of the law for trial in the courts, a mob would be assembled and he would be hanged on improvised gallows, while men shot at his writhing body, or he would be tied with cords to a stake so that fagots might be burned around him, or he would be executed in some similarly horrible way, suggested by the cruel minds of his executioners as a lesson to other "niggers," and at the same time, as was too clear, to gratify a primitive native bloodthirst. When negroes were taken into custody the sheriffs would be intercepted on their way to the prisons. Jailers who held such offenders would be called out and at the point of a gun would be compelled to surrender their keys. Failing in this the insecure inclosures would be scaled, or broken down, or fired and the posses would lead the poor creatures, often merely suspects, without a hearing, to their terrible doom.

These outrages have been industriously compiled. One authority finds that in the South, from 1882 to 1903 inclusive, 1,985 negroes and about 600 whites were summarily executed. Mississippi in the 20 years had thus killed 294 negroes, Louisiana 232, Georgia 241 and Alabama 198.[2] The number underwent a sudden and disturbing increase after 1888, which brought the subject before the country more prominently than ever before,[3] and led to the adoption of measures for the correction of an evil which had become a national disgrace.[4]

[1] Cf. J. E. Cutler, Lynch Law, pp. 274–5.
[1] Ibid., p. 179.
[3] R. C. O. Benjamin, Southern Outrages, pp. 17–20; Thomas Nelson Page, The Negro, chap. iv; M. S. Evans, Black and White, chap. xix; A. H. Stone, Studies in Am. Race Problem, p. 93.
[4] The humorist, Mr. Dooley, said, "The negro has many fine qualities; he is joyous, lighthearted and aisily lynched."

It was such barbarity, aimed at the negroes, which the laws of Congress had been enacted to restrain. It had been predicted that when the Southern garrisons were withdrawn such injuries would be done the blacks. Republican editors and campaign speakers emphasized the frequency and barbarity of these outbreaks of mob rule with a view to holding in leash the negroes in the North and the old Abolitionist white element for political use. No palliation or excuse could be offered for such atrocities. They continued to be a disgrace to the Southern white people and their civilization, until the enforcement of law and order was given over to the agencies set up and established for that service.

The penal system, after sheriffs, prosecuting officers, judges and juries got through with their tasks in relation to crime, was, in the same way, a reflection upon the state of social culture in the South. The jails and penitentiaries, when these were used, were cheap, ill-contrived buildings which but poorly served counties or states for the confinement of prisoners, and the execution of sentences. Everywhere the convicts, or a great part of them, if they were able-bodied, were leased or sold to labor. This policy was advocated not so much as a deterrent upon crime, although the sight of men in clothing which marked them as criminals, watched over by guards, armed with shotguns, at work, perhaps, in chains in mines, on levees, on railways, on farms and in the roads, might be taken to be chastening in its influence upon the community. The truth of the matter was that this was accounted to be a thrifty course of conduct on the part of those charged with the management of public affairs. The use of the taxpayers' money for feeding and housing the wretches who were convicted of crime was prodigality when they might be made to work for their keep and, indeed, yield a return to the community. The labor of the convicts should be sold and the state could then wash its hands of them.[1]

The agreements were for five, ten or twenty years at the

[1] Cf. 2nd Ann. Report of Commissioner of Labor, 1886 (Convict Labor), pp. 381–2.

rate of, perhaps, $5 or $6 a month for each convict, with provision as to clothing and medical attendance. Those whose labor was not esteemed to be valuable would be farmed out for their "victuals and clothes," [1] or the arrangement might call for the payment of a round sum by the mine owner, railroad company or other bidder. Sometimes a group of politicians would take the contract and, with profit to themselves, sublet it. [2] The return in Florida was only $15 a year per man, [3] and, as the state had no penitentiary building, a speculator, seeing his opportunity, in 1884, demanded and received $8,500 a year for taking care of, and finding work for, the convicts. [4]

The contractors were made to call at the courthouse doors or at the gates of the prisons, where there were prisons, for the men who were then driven away on foot, or in wagons to the places of labor. If the distances were too great they were chained in box cars, and made their journeys in this plight under the sight of armed guards, [5] to be quartered in the usual case, upon reaching their destinations, when not at work, in camps behind stockades.

The governor of Alabama congratulated himself that in 1880, as a result of shrewd prison management, he would have a net sum of $27,000 to be paid into the state treasury. In two years the return was $45,000. Formerly the penitentiary had been "a constant drain" upon the taxpayers. [6] Georgia which had leased its convicts to three different companies, chartered for the business, would, in 20 years, the period of the agreement, make a "million clear." [7] Texas in 1882 announced that it was receiving $255,000 annually out of the leases for the labor of its two penitentiaries. [8]

---

[1] App. Ann. Cyclop. for 1881, p. 7.
[2] For the number of leases in force in the South in 1886 see 2nd Ann. Report of the Com. of Labor (Convict Labor), pp. 8 et seq.
[3] App. Ann. Cyclop. for 1880, p. 272.
[4] Ibid. for 1884, p. 333.
[5] Ibid. for 1879, p. 427.
[6] Ibid., p. 23; ibid. for 1881, p. 7; ibid. for 1884, p. 9.
[7] Ibid. for 1879, p. 427; cf. ibid. for 1880, p. 306; ibid. for 1882, p. 340.
[8] Ibid. for 1882, p. 797.

The sight of these convicts in transit and at work on the roads and in the fields, within the range of shotguns, was a revolting spectacle to persons of proper susceptibilities and was testimony of a low state of civilization. It added no pleasure to the scene to know, as most of the arrests and trials in the South were of negroes, that, consequently, most of the convicts were colored men.[1] In South Carolina in 1882 there were 824 convicts—778 were black and only 46 white;[2] in 1884 there were 956, of whom only 62 were white.[3] In Alabama in 1881, of 540 convicts, only 70 were whites.[4]

That scandals and abuses would arise from such a system of penal management might have been foretold.[5] But in a country which was accustomed to forced labor it met with too little protest. With few exceptions the convicts fell into the hands of inhuman contractors and overseers. Agreements, if there were any, were not kept. The men were held in insalubrious places, they were worked beyond their powers, they were not provided with medical attention in illness, they were improperly fed and inadequately sheltered, they were whipped and shot. Reformers faced wrongs in Northern prisons which they did not cease to condemn, but such conditions as were brought to notice in the South, and which were plain to see in mines and quarries, on railways, on roads and on plantations, aroused the deepest revulsion of feeling.[6]

In South Carolina, where 727 had been leased between November, 1878, and November, 1879, it appeared that 157 had died, 77 had escaped and several had been killed. In the service of a railroad company, to which the largest number of men, 285, had been sent, 128 had died, a rate of mortality exceeding 40 per cent, and 37 had fled the inhumanities to which they were subjected. The company had violated its

---

[1] Report of Senate Com. on Ed. and Labor, 1885, vol. ii, p. 527.
[2] App. Ann. Cyclop. for 1882, p. 745.
[3] Ibid. for 1884, p. 738.
[4] Ibid. for 1881, p. 7.
[5] Ibid. for 1887, p. 704.
[6] Cf. Report of Senate Com. on Ed. and Labor, 1885, vol. ii, pp. 529–30; ibid., vol. iv, p. 433.

contract, it appeared, at all points with respect to the treatment of the men committed to its care.[1]

The situation became so disturbing in Alabama in 1881 that the legislature appointed a committee to visit the convict camps.[2] The men were overworked, undernourished, improperly clothed and cruelly whipped. "The system," a prison warden in Alabama said, was a "training school for criminals." It was "a disgrace to the state and a reproach to the civilization and Christian sentiment of the age." [3]

Another legislative committee appeared in Mississippi, where the lessees had been subletting the men. Outrageous conditions were exposed. The system, it was said, reëstablished "a state of servitude worse than slavery." The average number of convicts out at labor under contract in 1886 and 1887 was 738. Of these 67, or more than 9 per cent, died in 1886 and 114, or more than 15 per cent, in 1887. That the blacks were mishandled to a greater degree than the whites was proven by the fact that their death rate in the Mississippi camps for a period of six years had been twice as great.[4]

The governor of North Carolina said that, in 1886, 142 of the convicts sentenced to the penitentiary in that state, and living under lease at railway camps, had died, a death rate of more than 10 per cent.[5] Even in Georgia, where the governors were boasting of the satisfactory arrangements which they had made with the leasing companies, charges of cruelty were preferred. Interposition became positively necessary. A legislative committee appointed to investigate the subject said that it was the duty of the state, in the interest of humanity and justice, to place an officer at each camp to protect the convicts from the greed and brutality of the contractors. The system, it was found and reported, had nothing in it which, by any possibility, could have been taken to be consonant

[1] App. Ann. Cyclop. for 1879, pp. 819–20; A. D. Oliphant, Evolution of the Penal System of S. C., pp. 6–7.
[2] Sess. Laws of Ala. for 1880–81, p. 26; ibid. for 1882–3, pp. 134 et seq.; ibid. for 1884–5, pp. 187 et seq.
[3] R. C. O. Benjamin, Southern Outrages, pp. 12–4.
[4] App. Ann. Cyclop. for 1888, pp. 562–3.
[5] Ibid. for 1886, p. 656.

with correct prison management. Old felons were chained to boys who, in proper surroundings, might have been reformed.[1] The legislature rose in some degree to the occasion. It authorized the appointment of an assistant keeper of the penitentiary at a salary of $1,200 a year. It would be his duty to visit each camp at least once a month and make report to the governor who, if occasion warranted, might terminate the lease of an offending contractor. No one might whip a convict except the regularly designated whipping boss, a man appointed by the lessees in each camp, subject to confirmation by the governor.[2] Again in 1887 the contractors were found to be violating the terms of their leases. The governor, upon a visit to the camps, discovered that prisoners were being cruelly punished and that excessive labor was being required of them. Two of the three companies were fined $2,500 each.[3]

To do away with such crying evils it was proposed that overseers and guards should be appointed and paid by the state, as in South Carolina.[4] It would be made the duty of grand juries of the counties in which the camps were situated, or members of the boards of supervisors of counties, or physicians, designated for the task, to make inspections in the interest of humanity.[5] In 1886 a special "board of control" was created to take over the management of the convicts of Mississippi.[6] The statute books of the Southern states during this period are burdened with legislative and administrative devices intended to improve conditions and to correct a system which, being essentially wrong, was incapable of correction.

There were hopeful signs here, however, as at other points in the South, real reason for the opinion that the country was coming out of itself and would, under new impulses, take its

---

[1] App. Ann. Cyclop. for 1881, p. 334.
[2] Sess. Laws of Ga. for 1881, pp. 106–7.
[3] App. Ann. Cyclop. for 1887, p. 318. For Texas, where not dissimilar conditions prevailed, see ibid. for 1879, p. 831, and for Ark. see ibid. for 1888, pp. 39–40.
[4] Ibid. for 1881, p. 813.
[5] Cf. Sess. Laws of Miss. for 1882, pp. 19–23; ibid. for 1884, p. 24; App. Ann. Cyclop. for 1882, pp. 240–41.
[6] Sess. Laws of Miss. for 1886, pp. 73 et seq.

place beside communities which were abreast of better public feeling. Governors, when they renewed contracts for the lease of convicts, did so with apology for the necessity of it, which they rested on economical grounds. The policy was objectionable; it was continued only because the state could not well afford to give up the income that came from farming out the labor of its prisoners and to assume the cost of keeping them within penitentiary walls.[1] Party platforms denounced such penitentiary systems as "a disgrace to the state and to the civilization of the age."[2] The "lease system" was making way for the "contract system," under which the contractor supplied the material and supervised the work of the convicts, while the state reserved to itself the business of guarding, feeding, clothing, housing and providing medical attention for them.[3]

The trades unions which were rising in the North and which were heard in protest against the use of convict labor in competition with "free labor" were a development of an industrial community. In the South they yet spoke in a small voice, which would reach louder utterance and would at length have its influence in breaking up the convict camps.[4] Counties, frugally inclined, would still empty their jails upon the public roads, or, indeed, entirely escape the charge of constructing prisons by sending convicts directly after sentence to the chain gangs. The members of labor unions had no wish to "work on the roads" and saw no damaging competition in service in this field.[5] To this day counties in the South with small revenues keep their prisoners on the public highways under armed guards, confining them at night, when other cover is

---

[1] As in Texas, App. Cyclop. for 1882, p. 797; Louisiana, ibid. for 1884, p. 455; South Carolina, ibid., p. 738; Alabama, ibid. for 1888, p. 809.

[2] Cf. ibid. for 1888, p. 564.

[3] Convict Labor for Road Work, U. S. Dept. of Agriculture, Bulletin no. 414, p. 3.

[4] App. Ann. Cyclop. for 1884, p. 455; ibid. for 1887, p. 514; ibid. for 1888, pp. 10, 40, 501, 619, 763, 764.

[5] Cf. National Anti-Contract Labor Association: Proceedings of Convention held at Chicago in 1886, p. 21; Report of Senate Com. on Ed. and Labor, 1885, vol. i, p. 581.

not provided, in movable cages which are allowed to disfigure an otherwise pleasing countryside.[1]

A patent impulse to crime and disorder in the South was provided by the free and unabated drinking of intoxicating liquor. It was sold everywhere in the towns; the country was drunken; raw "corn juice," "mountain dew," trickled down from the illicit stills in the hills. The unregulated consumption of spirits among a white people who seemed not to have control of themselves in the use of knives and firearms and, particularly among a great body of blacks just released from slavery, in which every precaution had been taken to keep them away from the inflaming dram, so that the maximum amount of work might be got from them and so that they might not be a menace to society, was on the point of becoming a matter of the gravest public concern.[2] The North was rising to grapple with the evil with demands for high license fees for the manufacture and sale of liquor; for prohibition in local communities, such as towns and counties; for proposals in the same interest for the amendment of state constitutions to be submitted to the people, which were adopted in Kansas in 1880 and in Iowa in 1882, and even for national prohibition by amendment of the Federal Constitution.[3] Men in the old South had loved their liquor—they were proverbial as generous users of it, but reform now seemed to most persons of clear sight to be an absolute social and economic necessity. The conviction spread that nothing less than the banishment of the trade, in so far as law could bring about this end, would give feasibility to life beside and among the free negroes,[4] though the Prohibition party, as a separate party, which was making some progress in the North was not useful in promoting the reform in the South, since, with the Reconstruction period fresh in mind,

[1] J. F. Steiner and Roy M. Brown, The North Carolina Chain Gang, 1927.

[2] Cf. Report of Senate Com. on Ed. and Labor, 1885, vol. iv, pp. 835, 837.

[3] Cf. App. Ann. Cyclop. for 1883, pp. 665–7.

[4] Report of Senate Com. on Ed. and Labor, 1885, vol. iv, pp. 158, 276, 277–8.

it was not deemed practicable for men, with the public welfare at heart, to leave the Democratic party on any account.

The restrictions at first were confined to areas around churches, schoolhouses, camp grounds and sometimes mines, factories and stores, and in rural neighborhoods. In a general law in 1879 the legislature of North Carolina named no less than 300 or 400 localities within which liquor might not be offered for sale. The business was prohibited within four miles of the University of North Carolina.[1] Several hundreds of places were named in another law in 1881,[2] more in 1883,[3] still more in 1885 and 1887.[4] A single act of the legislature of Alabama, in 1881, established prohibition in 150 places.[5] The citizens of towns asked that the sale of liquor therein should cease; these appeals were heeded by the legislature. When the representatives of the people were unwilling to proceed on their own responsibility they submitted the question to popular vote. General local option laws authorizing a referendum in townships, in towns and city wards upon the petition of a certain number of citizens were passed by the legislatures of some of the states, as South Carolina in 1882,[6] and Arkansas in 1879,[7] a system which was soon extended to counties.[8]

A State Temperance Convention met at Atlanta on July 4, 1881, and declared the manufacture and sale of intoxicating liquor in all its varieties to be "a nuisance and an unequalled curse to the people and state." There must be local organization everywhere in Georgia in the interest of the enactment by the legislature of a general local option law with the county as a unit. Men should go to the polls and choose by ballot between "Whiskey" and "No Whiskey." Only with and after popular approval should the trade be allowed to continue.

[1] Sess. Laws of N. C. for 1879, pp. 391–5;
[2] Ibid. for 1881, pp. 440–9.
[3] Ibid. for 1883, pp. 263–8.
[4] Ibid. for 1885, pp. 327–30 and 1887, pp. 444–7.
[5] Sess. Laws of Ala. for 1880–81, pp. 531–3.
[6] Sess. Laws of S. C. for 1882, pp. 893–5; Report of Senate Com. on Ed. and Labor, 1885, vol. iv, p. 838.
[7] Sess. Laws of Ark. for 1879, pp. 33–8.
[8] Cf. App. Ann. Cyclop. for 1883, pp. 667–8.

The General Assembly of the "grand old commonwealth" must "stay the tide and break and beat back the waves of ruin and sorrow that come like a flood in the wake of strong drink." There must be "everlasting redemption from the thralldom of the terrible monster that is blighting our fair land with drunkenness, ruin and infamy." [1]

The legislature did not immediately respond, but the progress of the movement through special acts was so rapid that the liquor dealers in Georgia in 1883 protested. They said that their business in a year had fallen off 50 per cent—two-thirds of the state was closed to them and the reformers were making appreciable advances in the smaller towns and cities. There were 137 counties—85 were "dry" and 30 others were partially so. In only 22 counties might the trade proceed without restraint. Men and women of both political parties, even the negro leaders, were enlisted in the movement for the general local option law, and a majority in the legislature in 1885, overriding the organized opposition, which drew its courage from a powerful lobby, enacted the measure. Henceforward, if citizens in any county in sufficient number should join in a request for an election it would be held—the voters might determine whether the business should continue therein. [2]

The battle was taken into Atlanta at once. By this time the sale of liquor was lawful in only 15 counties and all of these contained cities where the manufacturers and dealers had large property interests which were worth stubborn defense. As a result of a stirring campaign in Atlanta a majority of 225 was secured for prohibition and the leaders of the trade, exceeding wroth, appealed to the courts. [3] They were unsuccessful, but by stupendous efforts, at an election two years later, they regained the city for their business operations by a majority of a thousand votes. [4]

The movement made progress in other states. A conven-

[1] App. Ann. Cyclop. for 1881, pp. 333–4.
[2] Sess. Laws of Ga. for 1884–5, pp. 121–4; Report of Senate Com. on Ed. and Labor, 1885, vol. iv, p. 821.
[3] App. Ann. Cyclop. for 1885, pp. 409–10.
[4] Ibid. for 1887, p. 319.

tion met in Raleigh in January, 1881, with the purpose of preparing an appeal to the legislature of North Carolina in behalf of a prohibitory liquor law which was passed subject to approval by popular vote. As in Georgia citizens came together in the most fraternal spirit, meeting on "one common platform" with "only one aim," namely "the advancement of the material and moral prosperity of all the people" of the commonwealth, "the promotion of their health, wealth, liberty and happiness without any distinctions whatever." The liquor trade displayed unexpected activity on the opposite side, and, at the election in August, 1881, mustered a large majority against the bill. The negroes were aroused and were massed by cunning agents of the liquor interests.[1] The temperance party was beaten and it was obliged to return to prohibition by piecemeal under the local option system by authority of a general law.[2]

The sale of liquor in Alabama underwent increased restriction at every session of the legislature.[3] In 1887 the greater part of the state was "dry"[4] and in that year the legislature authorized further extension of the area under prohibition, subject to popular vote.[5] With the aid of a general local option law, which was passed by the legislature in 1886, the saloons in Mississippi had been closed in more than half the counties, it was said in 1889, and the prohibitionists were intent upon gaining control of the entire state.[6] The prevalence of violence and crime forwarded the movement in Arkansas.[7] Under a local option law, which was passed in 1881,[8] a number of counties extirpated the evil.[9] The prohibitionists in 1888 were rejoicing that at least half the state had been "redeemed from

---

[1] Cf. Daniel Dorchester, The Liquor Problem in All Ages, p. 493; App. Ann. Cyclop. for 1881, p. 667 and N. Y. Nation, May 5, 1881.

[2] Sess. Laws of N. C. of 1881, pp. 488–90.

[3] Cf. Sess. Laws of Ala. for 1886–7, pp. 665–715.

[4] App. Ann. Cyclop. for 1887, p. 9.

[5] Sess. Laws of Ala. for 1886–7, pp. 1024–6.

[6] Sess. Laws of Miss. for 1886, pp. 35–40; App. Ann. Cyclop. for 1889, p. 564.

[7] App. Ann. Cyclop. for 1888, p. 32.

[8] Sess. Laws of Ark. of 1881, pp. 132–3.

[9] App. Ann. Cyclop. for 1884, p. 42.

the presence of the saloon." [1] Similar laws in Virginia [2] and other states, permitting a specified number of voters in a county to call an election, and making the sale of intoxicating drink within its territorial limits depend upon the will of the people, was rapidly and certainly pressing the liquor trade out of the South.

At the same time the fees for licenses were raised to such a point as to be prohibitory in effect in some neighborhoods, and everywhere, even in cities, "high license" laws were crowding out the small dealers, and sensibly reducing the number of saloons. In 1884 a retailer in Alabama must pay $50 for a license; in the next year $100 and in 1887 from $125 to $250, according to the population of the town in which he would dispense his liquors.[3] In 1883 in Arkansas the charge laid upon a saloonkeeper by the state was $300, while the county often demanded from $300 to $500 more.[4] In Missouri the tax under a high license law, both state and county, might be as great as $1,200 per annum. The governor said, in 1888, that, of 87 counties, 50 had "local option." [5]

The conviction grew, too, that the suffrage must be restricted. The ballot had been put into the hands of the black man by the Northern Radicals without any regard for the interests of the Southern white people, frankly and patently, indeed, with the purpose of enlarging the negro's conception of his power. The scheme had been tried during long and sore years under Northern advice and it had wrought such havoc that safe, pleasant and prosperous existence, it is not too much to say, was no longer possible to the white race. The Radical newspapers had been filled with accounts of incidents indicative of an indisposition on the part of the whites to regard the negroes as their equals. Comment upon these evidences of a wish to do the black man injustice continued, though possibly with less bitterness than a few years since, and certainly without the incitement of the Northern people, even of the

---

[1] App. Ann. Cyclop. for 1888, p. 40.
[2] Sess. Laws of Va. for 1885–6, pp. 258–60.
[3] App. Ann. Cyclop. for 1887, p. 9.
[4] Ibid. for 1883, p. 668.
[5] Ibid. for 1888, p. 565.

old Abolitionist class, to the fury which they had earlier displayed. That the Southern whites did not wish to put their children to school with negroes, to go to church with them, to lie in graveyards after death with them, to sit at table with them at meals, or lodge in the same hotels, or ride in the same railway coaches, no longer appeared in the North to be a mark of savagery or even uncharitableness. Clearly, since, as the years passed and the Southern people who were in daily association with the negroes were seen to hold opinions which were quite unchanged on these subjects, and since in the North those who thought normally were of a not very different habit of feeling and conduct, when they came in contact with the negro, it was not necessary to keep alive a legend, which anyhow had served its use.

Political rights were apart from civil rights but they had close relationship. It was the more difficult to think kindly of the negro if it were known that he would visit the polls on election day and vote a "class ticket," as it was his wont, under a despised leadership, to do. Ignorant, without property, misdirected, he would not be admired in this rôle. He might be valued as a workingman, but it was assuredly not to his or to the white people's advantage that he vote upon subjects which he in no way understood, and that he attempt to make himself a force in the direction of the government. His holding this privilege was especially to be lamented, if, because of it, he was inflaming, and forfeiting the good opinion of the whites among whom he dwelt.[1] Half, if not more, of the violent crime in the South, since the war, could be fairly ascribed to the grave necessity, as many men believed it to be, though they may have had no direct part in such activity, of protecting society from such a menace. Negroes must be kept from the polling places on election day, by one method or another, and, after the Federal troops were withdrawn,

---

[1] "The weapon which the advocate of universal suffrage applauds himself for having helped to place in the negro's hands has been his destruction. It was a torch placed in the hands of a child, with which he has ravaged all about him, and involved himself in the general conflagration."—Thos. Nelson Page, The Negro, p. 123.

after "force bills" were no longer operative and after the Southern people were left to their own devices, plans for putting the negro aside as a voting citizen were meditated by men who preferred orderly and peaceful methods to fraud and violence.[1]

As a body it could be said, without danger of successful contradiction, that the blacks cared little about the franchise. Their first interest in it, which was induced by the not unselfish exertions of white men, had given way, a bishop of the African church observed, to thoughts of "hog and hominy." [2] Except for leaders who had their own ends in view, but slight resistance, it was surmised, would be encountered in the design to undo what was regarded as a great mistake. The zeal expended in advocacy of the "Blair bill" to give national aid to the Southern states for education, on the grounds that five or eight negroes in every group of ten could not read the letters on their ballots, and that this mass of illiteracy imperiled the "republican form" of government, spelling the destruction of our political institutions, might as well have been turned to negro suffrage itself. If the republic were endangered by the votes of ignorant men, local and state government, which touched the interests of the people in still closer ways, was also in jeopardy. Through the common schools the youth might in the course of time gain competency in forming political judgments and a genius for public affairs. But it would be a tedious process, and what of the present and the immediate future? Mr. Blair himself might not see the facts but it was certain that many who were associated with him in the promotion of his measure quite well understood that the cause of good, and even tolerable, government in the South was in the balance, with the weight heavily on the wrong side, so long as the polls could be crowded by a dumb rabble who were at the beck of any mountebank or thief.

So much had been said in the North about the suppression

---

[1] Cf. Writings of Carl Schurz, vol. iv, pp. 373–4.
[2] Report of Senate Com. on Ed. and Labor, 1885, vol. iv, p. 782; cf. ibid., p. 789; cf. A. H. Stone, The American Race Problem, pp. 357–8.

of the negro vote, there were so many carpetbaggers and scalawags in the South to furnish Northern Republican Radicals with testimony as to a purpose of the Southern white people to nullify, at the first opportunity, the amendments of the Federal Constitution, and the statutes passed by Congress to give them effect, that it required courage to approach the task. When it was seen, as time passed, that the North was growing. tired of the sectional issue and that the attention of the people was being turned in other directions, that, indeed, many were coming to be fairly well in accord with the Southern view of negro suffrage, the movement advanced.[1] In the North there were growing numbers of men who, when faced by the increasing immigration of foreign illiterates of disliked racial stocks, were ready to say that everywhere the exercise of the franchise should be restricted. The settlement of these obnoxious persons in groups in great cities, where they were the catspaws of political managers, to be passed about in blocks for the corruption of government, increased the conviction that something must be done to establish educational and other qualifications for voters. Sympathy for, and understanding of, the white man's position in the South were increased by knowledge that a distinct movement of the negro population toward the North was in progress. If each large city had its ghetto, its Italian, its Slavic and other quarters, wherein poverty, squalor and ignorance of our language and institutions reigned in disquieting degree, so were there blocks of houses in each city, growing in extent, which were being surrendered to the negroes, who were similarly crowded together in unwholesome masses.[2] Therefore it was, perhaps, that the South could go forward in a work of "high necessity"[3] with less and less fear of meeting Northern protest, or of suffering a resumption of Federal power.[4]

The situation excited the most alarm in Mississippi where the blacks outnumbered the whites by about 200,000, and in

[1] Cf. Thomas Nelson Page, The Negro, p. 124.
[2] Cf. Report of Senate Com. on Ed. and Labor, 1885, vol. iv, p. 51.
[3] Thos. Nelson Page, The Negro, p. 151.
[4] Cf. Fred Douglass, Why Is the Negro Lynched?, pp. 21–4.

South Carolina where they had a majority of 225,000. In 39 of the 75 counties of Mississippi there were more negroes than whites; in some cases the ratio was 8 to 1, and in one county, Issaquena, 15 to 1. In 26, all but nine, of the counties of South Carolina the negroes were in numerical ascendancy.[1] Their power could be controlled in Congressional elections in some degree by the arrangement of the counties in the apportionment bills. The states might be gerrymandered so that a black majority would be overbalanced by a white one and, when this could not be done, the negroes could be thrown together into districts, thus relieving other districts of their disturbing influence on election day. The black counties in the Yazoo delta in Mississippi were ingeniously joined to form what was familiarly known as the "Shoestring District," extending its length along the Mississippi River for a distance of about 300 miles, with an average breadth of but 20 miles.[2] To free Charleston of the great negro vote on adjoining plantations a new county, called Berkeley, containing nearly 50,000 negroes and less than 8,000 whites, was created in 1882 in South Carolina.[3]

Bills appeared in the legislatures, as in South Carolina, requiring all voters to be able to write their names.[4] Others hopefully viewed the possibilities of the poll taxes for the support of schools and, if possible, would have excluded the negroes from the franchise for failure to pay these charges. A registration law was passed in South Carolina in 1882 which disfranchised large numbers of the blacks,[5] and which proved to be profoundly disturbing to the men whose trade it had been to mass, and put to their own valuable use, the African vote. The law called for the appointment by the governor of "supervisors of registration," permanent officers, for each county before whom every person who desired to vote must appear at a specified time in 1882. Afterward, on one day in a month, for seven or eight months preceding future elections, the regis-

[1] By the Census returns of 1890.
[2] Lalor, Cyclopedia of Political Science, vol. ii, p. 368.
[3] Sess. Laws of S. C. for 1881–2, p. 682.
[4] App. Ann. Cyclop. for 1879, p. 819.
[5] Sess. Laws of S. C. for 1881–2, pp. 1110 et seq.

tration books would be reopened but only to admit the names of those who, because of their coming of age or of removal into the district or on some other good account, had subsequently become entitled to vote. A certificate was issued to each qualified elector. This he must exhibit at the polling place to the managers of the election. If he had brought this paper with him and was, at the same time, duly enrolled for voting he might cast his ballot. The registration days in 1882 were passed before the intricacies of the law were understood and the names of masses of men, particularly the ignorant blacks, who did not present themselves before the officers, were, as it proved, permanently excluded from the voting lists.

The law was designed, the politicians who had been exploiting the negroes said, with truth, to "suppress the will of the majority." It was "one of the most disgraceful acts ever placed upon the statutes of this or any other state." The Republican party convention in South Carolina in 1888 invoked the aid of the national government in doing away with "this obnoxious law." [1] Efforts were made to obtain from the supreme court of South Carolina an opinion declaring it null and void on the ground that it was a denial and abridgment of the guaranteed constitutional right of a citizen to vote. But an attempt to undo what had so greatly increased the feeling of popular security failed and the act remained in force, a precursor of other measures of the South's devising for gaining similar ends. [2]

In Edgefield county which had cast 9,380 votes in 1876 there were but 3,196 in 1888. Richland county with 6,286 votes in 1876 had only 2,360 in 1888. The number in Abbeville county fell from 8,057 in 1880 to 3,065 in 1888; [3] in Newberry from 5,791 in 1880 to 1,789 in 1888; in Barnwell from 8,903 in 1880 to 3,700 in 1888; in Beaufort from 9,803 in 1876 to 2,278 in 1888. [4] In

---

[1] App. Ann. Cyclop. for 1888, p. 744.

[2] Butler v. Ellerbe, 44 S. C., p. 256.

[3] By the census of 1890 there were 31,916 negroes and 17,340 whites in Edgefield county; 24,885 negroes and 11,933 whites in Richland county; 31,705 negroes and 15,142 whites in Abbeville county.

[4] There were more than 31,000 negroes in Beaufort county in 1890 and only 2,700 whites.

1876 the total vote of South Carolina for Presidential electors was 182,776; in 1888 it was only 79,561.[1]

Likewise in Mississippi the reduction of the number of voters in counties having a large negro population was striking. When the new code was adopted in 1880 it was proposed, amid outcry, to make the payment of a tax of 25 cents a condition for the exercise of the franchise.[2] Registration became more difficult.[3] Comparing 1876 and 1888 the number of votes cast in Noxubee county, where there were over 22,000 blacks and less than 5,000 whites declined from 3,059 to 846; in Yazoo, where there were nearly 28,000 blacks and less than one-third as many whites, from 3,674 to 1,203; in Panola from 5,307 to 2,771; in Wilkinson from 2,687 to 532.[4] In 1876 the total vote cast in Mississippi had been 164,778, while in 1888 it was only 115,807.[5]

[1] App. Ann. Cyclop. for 1888, p. 828.
[2] Senate Reports, 46th Cong. 2nd sess., no. 693, pt. 2, p. 266.
[3] Revised Code of Miss., 1880, chap. 4. Other methods which were employed to effect a disfranchisement of the negroes are discussed in F. A. Bancroft, A Sketch of the Negro in Politics.
[4] App. Ann. Cyclop. for 1888, p. 813.
[5] Ibid., p. 828.

CHAPTER XXXII

IN THE WEST

THE Union, after the admission of Colorado in the "Centennial year," comprised 38 states. Washington, Montana, Idaho, Utah, Arizona, New Mexico, Wyoming and Dakota retained territorial forms of government under governors appointed by the President. The population of the country by the Census returns in 1880 was 50,155,783—it had been 38,558,371 in 1870—it would be 62,622,250 in 1890. In 1870 more than 6,000,000 people dwelt in the states and territories located west of the Mississippi River, excluding Louisiana, which did not participate in Western expansion. In 1880 these same states and territories had come to have a population in excess of 10,000,000. In 1890 the inhabitants in the same area would number more than 15,000,000. From a little over one-sixth of the whole population of the country in 1870 the area beyond the Mississippi came, two decades later, to have nearly one-fourth. The "center of population" which in 1790, the first Census year, had been at a point 23 miles east of Baltimore was, in 1880, on the Ohio River, eight miles west of Cincinnati, and in 1890 it would be well within the boundaries of Indiana.[1]

In the decade ending in 1880 the frontier of settlement had moved westwardly at some points hundreds of miles, as in Nebraska, Kansas and Texas. In the Northwest, in Minnesota and on beyond to Dakota, where hardy and industrious families were planting the ground with wheat, the development was similarly rapid. When the limit of the lands which were watered from the sky was reached ribbons of settlement followed the lines of the streams still further into the west. The excitement attendant upon the discovery and opening up

[1] Report of Eleventh Census, pt. 1, p. xxxvii.

592

of mines brought more and more men into the mountains, while the Pacific coast went forward under the varied impulses which had led to its remarkable growth.

In another decade, in the ten years following 1880, all of Kansas was settled, nearly all of Nebraska, and Texas west to the Staked Plains. Large parts of Dakota, Montana and Colorado were under the dominion of man. Only Nevada failed to participate in a development which was marked, swift and general. The increase in population in the decade, 1870–80, for Washington was 213, Nebraska 167, Colorado 387 and Dakota 853 per cent; in the next decade, for Wyoming 192, Montana 237, Dakota 278 and Washington 365 per cent. The population of Kansas, which was 364,399 in 1870, was 996,096 in 1880 and 1,427,096 in 1890. Texas, in twenty years, advanced from 818,579 to 2,235,523, California from 560,000 to 1,208,000 and Nebraska from 122,993 to 1,058,910. Colorado which contained less than 40,000 inhabitants in 1870 had more than 400,000 in 1890. The population of Washington had grown in two decades from 24,000 to nearly 350,000, of Dakota, from 14,000 to more than 500,000.

Settlement followed the railroads, which, after the downfall of all speculative enterprise in this field in 1873, again in a few years resumed rapid construction. From a mileage of 70,000 in the United States in 1873 the length of the country's various lines had increased to 81,000 in 1878, or only 11,000 miles in five years. At the end of 1884, in six years, the number of miles which had been built was no less than 44,000, the total in the latter year standing at 125,000 miles.[1] More than two-thirds of this increase in the years 1879–84, or 34,000 miles, was made in the Western states and territories.[2]

In 1878 there was but one railroad between New York and Buffalo; five years later there were four. In a few years the number of lines connecting the East with Chicago was increased from three to eight.[3] The roads radiating from that city were extended into the West. The Burlington which owned

[1] Poor's Manual of Railroads for 1885, p. xiv.   [2] Ibid.
[3] N. Y. Tribune, Sep. 27, 1883.

1,300 miles of track had come, in 1884, to control 3,330 miles. That company ran trains into Denver. The Chicago, Milwaukee and St. Paul which covered Iowa and Dakota as well as Wisconsin and Minnesota with its tracks, operated 4,800 miles of road; the Chicago and Northwestern, in the same territory, 3,700 miles. Texas, in 1884, had come to have over 6,000 miles of railroads, Missouri nearly 4,800 miles, Kansas 4,200 miles and Iowa 7,500 miles.

The Union Pacific and Central Pacific roads, the first to cross the plains and scale the mountains, carrying passengers and goods from the East to the shores of the Pacific Ocean and fetching them back again, completed in 1869 by the favor of the Federal government in grants of public lands and guarantees given to construction bonds, held the field alone for more than ten years. Two powerful forces were acting in the country lying south of this line. The Atchison, Topeka and Santa Fé had closely followed the "southern branch" of the Union Pacific across the state of Kansas, piercing a lower tier of counties, on the course of the old Santa Fé trail, and opening them to settlement. The road was the dream of Cyrus K. Holliday, a native of Pennsylvania, who had early emigrated to Kansas with the "free state men," and who became one of the founders of Topeka.[1] Progress was slow, but, recovering from the panic of 1873, the railroad was carried steadily on into the West. While the Kansas Pacific passed through Colorado to Denver, the Santa Fé advanced toward Pueblo, a center for rich mineral, ranching and timber industries which demanded markets in the East. The line entered that place early in 1876.[2] The company, meanwhile, had secured an entrance to Kansas City, which by this time had distanced Atchison, as well as the other Missouri River towns, and was rapidly gaining commercial importance.

But it was the "Santa Fé Railroad," and it must reach that place. The company was controlled by prudent Boston capitalists and William B. Strong, a Vermont man who had risen

[1] G. D. Bradley, The Story of the Santa Fé, pp. 50-71.
[2] Ibid., p. 143.

by gradual stages to prominence in the management of various Western railways, became its vice-president and later its president. From La Junta, some fifty miles east of Pueblo, he would continue the road southwesterly through Colorado to Trinidad, where were coal mines, and cross the boundary over Raton Pass into New Mexico. A struggle with other interests to gain control of this defile, the only practicable route for a railroad, as it had been for the overland traffic by the trail, ensued. In the end Strong won. The railhead reached Las Vegas, 114 miles south of the Colorado boundary, on July 4, 1879, and in February of the next year a locomotive entered the old capital of New Mexico. The engineers, with their construction gangs, now moved rapidly down the valley of the Rio Grande to Albuquerque, from which place lines would soon be laid west toward California and south to old Mexico.[1]

In California another group of railway builders, headed by Collis P. Huntington, in the main the same as those who controlled the Central Pacific, were coming east with the railhead of the Southern Pacific.[2] It was their aim, at first, merely to connect San Francisco with Los Angeles and the southern part of California. The population of all Los Angeles county, in 1880, was only 33,000, of Santa Barbara county 9,000, of San Diego county 8,000, but the future of this region was seen, and, in 1877, the road was completed to Fort Yuma in the extreme southeastern portion of the state on the Colorado River. Crossing that stream it went on through Tucson, in southern Arizona, and New Mexico to El Paso in Texas, where connections were obtained, after 1883, with Mexico City.

Meantime Mr. Strong and the Santa Fé company who were extending their line down the valley of the Rio Grande, on March 1, 1881, met the completed Southern Pacific road at Deming, 466 miles from Yuma and 1,197 miles from San Francisco.[3] The Texas Pacific was reorganized and this road was moving in a westerly direction toward El Paso, joining the

---

[1] G. D. Bradley, The Story of the Santa Fé, p. 205.
[2] Poor's Manual for 1884, p. 901.
[3] G. D. Bradley, The Story of the Santa Fé, p. 207.

Southern Pacific at Sierra Blanca, 90 miles east of El Paso, on December 1, 1881, which gave New Orleans railway connections with the Pacific coast.[1] With the favor of the Southern Pacific, after October, 1882, the Santa Fé could use, for transcontinental traffic, a line which it had acquired in lower Arizona and Mexico terminating at Guaymas, a port on the Gulf of California.[2]

It was a year later, January 15, 1883, when the Southern Pacific secured by mergers a line to New Orleans completely under its own management, and March 1, 1885, when the great new Southern Pacific company, a consolidation of the Central Pacific and the Southern Pacific, was formed, with control over 4,700 miles of railway and 4,200 miles of steamship lines, under the presidency of Leland Stanford, the president of the Central Pacific, and the vice-presidency of Collis P. Huntington.[3]

The Santa Fé was no more content than the Southern Pacific to conduct a transcontinental business by leave of a rival.[4] Nothing of importance had come of the old Atlantic and Pacific railroad which, generously endowed with public lands by Congress, was to have proceeded to the Pacific coast from St. Louis, on or near the 35th parallel of latitude. The company, before 1873, had crossed Missouri and was at work in Indian Territory. The Santa Fé was confronted with the problem of laying rails from Albuquerque to California, and, by an arrangement with those into whose care the interests of the Atlantic and Pacific road had fallen, actual construction westwardly commenced in 1880. But the advance was to meet with obstruction. Huntington for the Southern Pacific and Gould, acting for the Texas and Pacific, which he now owned, were at one in a desire to keep the Santa Fé from entering California and, by purchasing control of the Atlantic and Pacific

---

[1] App. Ann. Cyclop. for 1881, p. 518; N. Y. Tribune, Aug. 25, 1883; Poor's Manual for 1884, pp. 819, 832.

[2] Bradley, The Story of the Santa Fé, p. 226; Fossett, Colorado, 2nd ed., p. 70.

[3] Poor's Manual for 1884, p. 877.

[4] Bradley, op. cit., pp. 207–8.

company (now called the St. Louis and San Francisco) which was nominally building the road through Arizona, they succeeded in checking the progress of Mr. Strong, who was obliged to accept Huntington's proposal that the Southern Pacific should construct a branch from its line at Mojave to the Needles on the Colorado River on the eastern boundary of California, to meet the Santa Fé's railhead. In August, 1883, the tracks were joined and another through route was opened to the Pacific coast. When the bridge across the river at the Needles was completed, in the summer of 1884, direct passenger train service over the Santa Fé line was inaugurated between San Francisco and Kansas City.[1]

But a traffic outlet over the Southern Pacific was not what the capable and enterprising managers of the Santa Fé had sought. They must have their own line to a California port in spite of Huntington, who was diverting freights, they said, from their road over his central and southern routes through Ogden and El Paso. They brought the Southern Pacific to terms by threatening to build an entirely new line of their own from the Needles to San Francisco, whereupon Huntington offered to sell them the road from Mojave to the Needles which he had built in the previous year. This arrangement became operative in October, 1884. The Santa Fé was still without rights or facilities beyond Mojave, except by favor of the Southern Pacific. One step more and a terminus at San Diego, by way of a road ready to fall into the company's control, which was extended by new construction to the Mojave line, afforded continuous trackage from the Missouri River to the Pacific coast. In the summer of 1887, by extensions in the East, the company was able to enter Chicago. From 28 miles in Kansas, in 1869, the Santa Fé in 18 years had been developed into a great railway system of 7,373 miles.[2]

Though the joint operations of the Santa Fé and the Southern Pacific in the Southwest, in running trains from Kansas City, by way of Deming, and from New Orleans, through El Paso, may be held to have resulted in giving us the second and,

[1] Bradley, The Story of the Santa Fé, pp. 236-7.   [2] Ibid., p. 271.

perhaps, a third transcontinental railway line in the years 1881-3, the honor of second place really belongs to the Northern Pacific. The completion of this road awakened national rejoicing and was held to be fairly comparable with the opening of the central line from Omaha to San Francisco in 1869.

The Northern Pacific to which Jay Cooke had lent his reputation and his fortune, only to succumb in 1873, rose out of the wreck of that year. Reorganization was difficult and slow. At the Pacific end of the line, Cooke, before his failure, had made some alliances with a company engaged in the navigation of the Columbia River. Here was a veritable empire in extent, containing unknown riches, in which the problems of transportation were to be solved, and it fell to the lot of Henry Villard, a young German, who had Americanized himself in a fine sense, to take the leadership in this service. After the crash of 1873 he had been intrusted by a group of his countrymen to represent their interests in the Northwest. In the construction of the Northern Pacific his strife with the government to gain the lands voted the corporation by Congress, the sale of bonds and the satisfaction of the holders of them, the actual work of leveling, bridging, tunneling and laying the track were similar to the experiences which Cooke had passed through a decade earlier. At one time, on the main line and its branches, over 25,000 men, more than half of them Chinese, were employed, requiring disbursements of $4,000,000 a month.

At last all obstacles were surmounted and the ceremonies in connection with the driving of the last spike were arranged for a day in September, 1883. Distinguished men from Europe, as well as America, were invited to be present. Special trains would convey them to the spot and no effort was spared to make the occasion memorable. General Grant, various members of the cabinet, and of the Senate and House of Representatives, the ministers at Washington of leading foreign governments attended. Charles Russell, a later Lord Chief Justice of England; the future Earl Grey; the future Lord Davey; "the great traveller and Radical professor, James Bryce, the man who has climbed to the summit of Great Ararat"; [1] Thomas Baring of the banking house of that name, and many others came from England. Germany sent several representatives of the learning of her universities. Georg Siemens of the Deutsche Bank headed a party of German financiers who crossed the ocean to be present on the occasion; German cities sent their official messengers of good will and congratulation. As the special trains reached the West the governors of states and the mayors of cities came forward to welcome Mr. Villard and his guests. Receptions in Chicago, feasts and processions in St. Paul and Minneapolis opened the proceedings.

President Arthur, after visiting the exposition at Louisville in Kentucky, had, with Secretary of War Lincoln and General Sheridan, made a journey to, and through, the Yellowstone Park. Riding in spring wagons from a station on the Union Pacific in Wyoming and then on horseback, provisioned by pack mules,[2] they, after a few weeks, reached the Northern Pacific tracks in Montana and came east over that railroad to join the westward-going party at Minneapolis.[3]

Proceeding west upon the line of the road Mr. Villard and his friends participated at Bismarck, the town beside the Missouri, where the work of construction had been halted by the crash of 1873, in the laying of the corner stone of a capitol building for Dakota. Farther on Indians were gathered to exhibit their strange dress, performing their war dances before the curious eyes of the European guests. At a point about 50 miles beyond Helena in western Montana, near the Mullen Pass, where a great tunnel was being constructed to carry the rails over the Rocky Mountains, all was in readiness for the ceremonies. A special train coming eastwardly had brought well-wishers of the enterprise from the Pacific coast. It was a goodly company which on Saturday, September 8th, met under a pavilion in a verdant meadow. With a military band playing, flags flying and cannon for a salute, it was a national and indeed an international celebration.

[1] N. Y. Tribune, Aug. 16, 1883.   [2] Ibid., July 24, 1883.
[3] N. Y. Nation, Sep. 6, 1883.

William M. Evarts was at hand to deliver the oration. The Secretary of the Interior, Mr. Teller of Colorado, and several foreign guests also spoke. A thousand feet of the line between the eastern and western track ends remained to be laid and 300 men were put to work to set the sleepers and the rails. The last spike was driven amid enthusiastic demonstrations. Those who must return to Chicago and the East did so, while Mr. Villard and a considerable number of his companions proceeded over the completed line to the Pacific coast. Public rejoicing continued at every place in which men dwelt on the way to Puget Sound. At Portland, Tacoma and Seattle a dream of many years had come true.[1] In a few days a through freight train of ten cars left Portland, Maine, for Portland, Oregon, over the new railway.[2]

The Northwest was at last open to settlement. No one could predict, said the New York Nation, "the rate of growth of the region now inviting the discontented of all the earth."[3] Another "iron-shod highway" crossed the continent, said the New York Tribune. The whole country was alive to an event which meant "so much for the common weal."[4]

The Union Pacific, not to be deprived of its share of the trade of the Northwest, projected the "Oregon Short Line," which left the main road in western Wyoming and crossed Idaho in the valley of the Snake River until it found connections with the Columbia Valley, a distance of 540 miles. It was nearly ready for use in November, 1884.[5]

Before Villard had turned his eyes toward the east, after the triumphal entertainments and celebrations in which he and his friends had indulged, the business of building and operating railroads again collapsed.[6] He was to fall from the heights of a great national reputation as Jay Cooke had fallen but ten short years before. Congratulation and praise would be

[1] Memoirs of Henry Villard, vol. ii, pp. 308–12; N. Y. Tribune, Sep. 10, 1883; N. Y. Times, Sep. 10, 1883.
[2] N. Y. Tribune, Sep. 18, 1883.
[3] N. Y. Nation, Sep. 13, 1883.
[4] N. Y. Tribune, Sep. 8, 1883.
[5] Poor's Manual of Railroads for 1885, p. 855.
[6] Cf. N. Y. Tribune, Sep. 28, 1883.

followed by blame and detraction.[1] The stocks, common and preferred, of the Northern Pacific, which had been selling in August at $49 and $89 were quoted on the day of his return to his office in New York, on September 26th, at $33 and $63. Deficits incurred in construction, obligations which must be met, importunate creditors, the desertion of friends intent upon saving themselves were his undoing. He knew that he was personally insolvent and that his roads were on the verge of bankruptcy before Christmas day had come. He resigned the presidency of his Oregon and the Northern Pacific companies and made an assignment for the benefit of his creditors.[2]

The wane of Henry Villard's star in the Northwest was accompanied by the rise of James J. Hill. This man, unlike Cooke and Villard, belonged to the country. He knew its byways and was a product of the soil. His parents, both of whom had come to Canada out of Ireland, lived in a log house where "Jim," as men generally knew him throughout his life, was born. Without a friend he appeared in 1856, at the age of 18 years, in St. Paul, then a village at the head of navigation on the Mississippi River, and from this place as a radius his activities in many kinds of business, which carried him north into the Red River Valley, and west and northwest, were marked by increasing success. His opportunity in railroading came after the panic of 1873. Jay Cooke had taken over the St. Paul and Pacific for incorporation into his Northern Pacific system. It ran hither and yon and often no whither in Minnesota, and, as its name would indicate, had been headed by hopeful promoters for the Western coast. Capital for its construction had come from Holland and, plucking the lines, a "pitiful heap of unrelated scraps," [3] from the ruins of the panic, Hill, with him who became Lord Strathcona, him who became Lord Mount Stephen and another, all Canadians, who were adventuring on this or that side of the border, raised the money and bought the property. With this as a begin-

[1] Memoirs of Henry Villard, vol. ii, p. 314.
[2] Ibid., pp. 317–8; N. Y. Tribune, Dec. 18 and 31, 1883, Jan. 5, 1884.
[3] Pyle, Life of J. J. Hill, vol. i, p. 162.

ning point were developed the plans which led to the building of a fifth transcontinental line of railroad in the United States, the Great Northern, and a sixth line, the Canadian Pacific, beyond our boundary, in British North America. The last spike on the Canadian Pacific was driven at Craigellachie in British Columbia on November 7, 1885.[1] Although the Great Northern did not reach Puget Sound until eight years later, Hill's western railhead was rapidly advanced. The St. Paul and Pacific became the St. Paul, Minnesota and Manitoba. When the Northern Pacific fell, with Villard, Hill's line had reached Devil's Lake in Dakota in the west. North it had been extended to the Manitoba boundary. On July 1, 1884, the company operated nearly 1,400 miles of road.[2] In 1886 the "end of track" was at Minot, 530 miles from St. Paul; in 1887 more than 8,000 men carried the tracks 550 miles farther, to the Falls of the Missouri in central Montana. Before winter had set in trains were running into Helena.[3] On through the Indian reservations, surmounting one obstacle and then another, political, financial and engineering, the road, under determined direction, was pressed toward the shores of the Pacific.

By this time the Western railroads were arranged in five distinct groups with reference to ownership and management. The Hill influence was rising in the Northwest. The system which Villard had constructed was ready for reorganization, coming in due time into Hill's possession. In the South the Santa Fé kept on an independent course under skillful and resolute direction. The Southern Pacific was in control of Huntington and the men in California, who had built the Central Pacific. They had been complete masters of the railway business in California and were extending their dominion.[4] Another prominent factor appeared in the person of Jay Gould who had made himself an active, restless and insistent influence in the situation. He, with or without Russell Sage and other men who joined him from time to time for their advantage, gave

[1] Pyle, Life of J. J. Hill, vol. i, chap. xv; N. Y. Nation, Nov. 3, 1887.
[2] Poor's Manual for 1885, p. 725; cf. ibid. for 1884, pp. 746–8.
[3] Pyle, vol. i, pp. 381, 383, 396–8.
[4] Cf. N. Y. Nation, Jan. 3, 1884.

his attention to bankrupt railroads. He bought them with no intention of holding them longer than his interest required. He slipped in and out of great properties by way of Wall Streęt. Without knowledge of the business, except as a speculator in corporate securities, without concern for the development of the country which his roads traversed or the welfare of its inhabitants, he gained a wide control of the American transportation system, at the same time doing much to add to the growing impression among the people that railroading was a kind of banditry for a few rich men. Low enough at best he distinctly reduced ethical levels in the conduct of corporate enterprise, and drove others, with better ideals, to the imitation of his ways.[1] An impression that his methods, since he had been the partner of Fisk in the management of the Erie Railroad, had improved was largely due to the mystery and skill with which his movements were executed and the awe which he inspired because of his increasing wealth.

In 1878, prior to the rise of industrial activity which set in with the resumption of specie payments, he and his friends had secured control of the Kansas Pacific, which had been built from Kansas City to Denver under government subvention, as a part of the first Pacific railroad system, and the spur connecting it with the Union Pacific at Cheyenne. It was a hastily constructed road; it had had inexpert management; in 1874 it had gone into the hands of a receiver. Gould saw his opportunity and the Kansas Pacific was soon in his possession. His object from the first seemed to be a consolidation with the Union Pacific, extending from Omaha to Ogden, in the stock of which he had earlier been operating for his advantage on an extensive scale,[2] and he rapidly put himself in a position to dictate his own terms. The Union Pacific, recently well managed, now found itself competing with a bankrupt line which, without interest charges, could cut rates

[1] Cf. A. D. Noyes, 40 Years of Am. Finance, pp. 62–4.
[2] Memoirs of Henry Villard, vol. ii, p. 281; Riegel, The Story of the Western Railroads, pp. 161–2; Senate Ex. Doc., 50th Cong. 1st sess., no. 51, pt. 1, p. 53; Report of Senate Com. on Ed. and Labor, 1885, vol. i, pp. 1066–7.

to a ruinous degree. The Union Pacific's margin of profit from earnings, over and above its indebtedness, had never been large and the officers were obviously disturbed.

Gould's proposal was not generous. He would put the stock of the Kansas Pacific, which he had bought for $12 a share or less, and which was then selling at $13, and of the Denver Pacific running from Denver to Cheyenne and the "Central Branch" running out of Atchison, worth still less, into a new company on a parity with Union Pacific stock, quoted on the exchanges at the same time at $68½. The Union Pacific earned $5,617 a mile, the Kansas Pacific $1,602 and the little road to Cheyenne $1,333. Naturally so audacious a plan was rejected. In this conjuncture Gould prepared himself for a threat, which he was right in believing might enable him to attain the object in view. He already owned the Wabash system, having for its original stem a corporation called the Toledo and Illinois Railroad Company, which, in 1853, or soon thereafter, laid tracks, 75 miles in length, from Toledo in Ohio, to the Indiana state line, and which, at the end of the war, under the name of the Toledo, Wabash and Western, owned 483 miles of track. This company and others affiliated with it Gould had lately consolidated under the corporate title of the Wabash, St. Louis and Pacific, with a capital of $40,000,000, for such a "milking" as the Erie had suffered while he and Fisk had controlled that road.[1] He acquired the Texas and Pacific, the ruins of Thomas A. Scott's ill-starred enterprise in the South, and, of more importance, the Missouri Pacific which gave him a line from St. Louis to Kansas City.[2] He now had continuous trackage from Toledo and Detroit to Denver,[3] and he was dallying with the Denver and Rio Grande. He said, in audible tones, that he would soon be in Salt Lake City, where he would meet the Central Pacific and gain a competing outlet to the coast.

[1] "A Chapter of Wabash," in North American Review, Feb., 1888; Trumbull White, The Wizard of Wall Street, pp. 142–4; Poor's Manual of Railroads for 1884, p. 655.

[2] Trumbull White, The Wizard of Wall Street, pp. 145–9.

[3] Murat Halstead, Life of Jay Gould, p. 80.

The managers of the Union Pacific believed that this was a very possible contingency and they could clearly see, too, the menace of the advances of Villard in the north, and of the Santa Fé and of Huntington's Southern Pacific in the south, which at no distant day would be rivals for the trade, all of which up to this time had been passing over their line. They were at his mercy; the roads were swept into a "mammoth combination,"[1] under the presidency of Sidney Dillon on a share for share basis.[2] Millions were in Gould's grasp and he could retire at his leisure, leaving the Union Pacific in embarrassment and on the way to final insolvency, under the burden of the unprofitable mileage which he had imposed upon it.[3] It was a performance, the New York Nation said, which had "never been surpassed in the annals of railroad witchcraft."[4] In 1884 the combined Union Pacific and Kansas Pacific systems covered 5,600 miles of line, the Missouri Pacific and Texas and Pacific together, 6,000 miles, the Wabash, 3,500 miles.[5]

While Gould, as every one knew, had no interest in his companies beyond profitable speculation in their securities,[6] he was obliged to hold some of his railroads for a longer time than he may have anticipated before he could withdraw with profit and leave the wreckage at the doors of other men. Those which remained in his hands were generally called "Gould roads," synonymous, as passengers, shippers and investors knew, with inept management, cheap and inadequate equipment, ill-paid and inefficient employees, as well as with machination in Wall Street.[7]

[1] Frank Fossitt, Colorado, 2nd ed., p. 44.
[2] Stuart Daggett, Railroad Reorganization, pp. 228-9; N. Y. Nation, May 26 and June 9, 1887.
[3] Report of Pacific Railway Commission, Senate Ex. Doc., 50th Cong. 1st sess., no. 51, pt. 1, pp. 54-65, and parts of testimony there cited; Daggett, op. cit., pp. 230-33; George Kennan, E. H. Harriman, vol. i, pp. 114-5; Memoirs of Henry Villard, vol. ii, pp. 281-3; J. P. Davis, Union Pacific Railway, pp. 233-4; N. Y. Nation, May 26, 1887.
[4] Issue of June 9, 1887.
[5] Poor's Manual for 1884.
[6] "Other men planned; he grabbed."—Trumbull White, The Wizard of Wall Street, p. 161.
[7] Cf. R. E. Riegel, The Story of the Western Railroads, chap. xi.

For some years now railway companies had been granted no subsidies. No longer did they share in the distribution of the public domain. Indeed it was difficult for them to obtain possession of the lands beside the tracks which a decade since had been so lavishly bestowed upon them and to which they seemed to have secure right. If grants had lapsed, if other irregularities in law could be discovered, if conditions of any kind in any manner permitted, it was loudly proclaimed, amid popular applause, that the land voted away to corporations and not yet claimed by them should be restored to the "people." [1]

The railroad companies, as we have seen, had encouraged immigration, often establishing agencies in Europe to advertise the attractions of the country penetrated by their lines, and offering enticements in rates of passage thither. The most extravagant merit would be ascribed to one or another place, at the time far beyond the limits of civilization, which offered, in fact, nothing but loneliness, denial and the hardest of work to those who could be persuaded to leave their homes, however mean, for our far frontier.

Settlement proceeded so rapidly that the supply of land in the Mississippi and Missouri Valleys, at the disposal of the railway companies, was exhausted during the speculative excitement of the 80's, though that less favorably situated, much of it held to be sterile, along the lines of the Pacific roads, remained in hand for distribution at a later day.[2]

At the same time the government land interspersed in quarter sections in the railway belts, and lying north and south of these areas, much of it inconveniently remote from lines of communication with markets, disappeared. Strife to obtain it, if it had any present or probable future value, was keen. It was rapidly surveyed for distribution. Title to 7,000,000 acres passed from the government in 1875.[3] Nearly 15,000,000

---

[1] Cf. Report of Pacific Railway Commission, Senate Ex. Doc., 50th Cong. 1st sess., no. 51, pt. 1, pp. iii–v.

[2] Cf. R. E. Riegel, The Story of the Western Railroads, pp. 278–84; Report of Sec. of Int. for 1883, vol. ii, pp. 653–6.

[3] Report of Sec. of Int. for 1875, p. 3.

acres were disposed of in 1880.[1] The withdrawals from the public domain to cover sales, entries and on other accounts reached a total of 19,000,000 acres in 1883, equal to the combined areas of New Hampshire, Massachusetts, Connecticut, Rhode Island and New Jersey, nearly two-thirds of it fertile land in Dakota, Kansas, Nebraska and Minnesota,[2] the largest annual distribution in the history of the public land system[3]—27,000,000 acres in 1884, or nearly enough to make another state of Pennsylvania.[4]

The area of the whole public domain in the various "land states and territories" (19 states and 11 territories) had been 1,818,462,000 acres,[5] and on June 30, 1880, the surveyed and unsurveyed lands still undisposed of by the government comprised, it was said, 1,270,708,000 acres.[6] But of this remainder 369,000,000 acres were located in Alaska, about which almost nothing was known, while at least 300,000,000 acres more were included in Indian reservations or would be taken under railway and other unpatented grants. As for the rest nearly all was declared to be "useless for agriculture by reason of altitude, lack of water or soil."[7] It was fit only for grazing; much of it was esteemed to be without value of any kind. In 1879 it was said that the government still held only about 25,000,000 acres of arable land, a tract approximately, therefore, no larger than the state of Ohio.[8]

The poor man for whose advantage our land system had been contrived was being cheated out of his portion by corporations.[9] The foreigner was begrudged his homestead. As a settler he was no longer so welcome as he had been. With the decrease in the amount of good land available for entry,

---

[1] Report of Sec. of Int. for 1880, p. 419.
[2] House Mis. Doc., 47th Cong. 2nd sess., no. 45, pt. 4, pp. 521-2.
[3] Report of Sec. of Int. for 1883, pp. 3-4; House Mis. Doc., 47th Cong. 2nd sess., no. 45, pt. 4, p. 521.
[4] Report of Sec. of Int. for 1884, vol. i, pp. xiv, 3, 4.
[5] House Mis. Doc., 47th Cong. 2nd sess., no. 45, pt. 4, pp. 10, 14.
[6] Ibid., p. 14.
[7] Ibid., pp. 25-6.
[8] Ibid., p. 22.
[9] "Land for the landless" had become "the demagogue's yelp."—N. Y. Nation, Aug. 6, 1885.

and the increase in immigration native Americans viewed jealously the arrival in the West of the "land hungry" from other countries. If many of those who reached the Atlantic coast cities remained there, to complicate the problems of urban life, very many others passed to the frontier. Almost one-third of the public lands were occupied, it was complained, by men, who, if some of them had declared their intention of being naturalized, were not citizens of the United States.[1]

The prodigal grants to the railroads and the various frauds practiced upon the government in securing possession of mineral, as well as farming land, excited public protest, but the greatest indignation was reserved for the ranchmen and the "timber thieves." Though the outer boundary of the arid tract, which was held to be valueless for agricultural purposes, was moving westward, and the herds of cattle which found free grass upon the public domain were being pressed toward the Rocky Mountains by the farmers of Kansas and Nebraska, our rancheros still reigned over an empire.[2] Cattle and sheep gleaned nutritious herbage on what were apparently desert plains. They could survive the winter's cold without shelter, though, when blizzards raged, they were sorely stricken[3]—the streams and water holes were frozen and many died a cruel death from thirst.[4] After the severe cold of the winter of 1880–81 carcasses lay rotting everywhere on the plains,[5] and again, in the winter of 1886–7, when prolonged freezing weather brought suffering to the herds, especially in Wyoming, Montana and the Northwest there was terrible mortality on the ranches.[6]

The herdsmen employed troops of "cowboys" to guard their property as well as it could be guarded in such a wilderness. They held national conventions, adopted resolutions and made

---

[1] House Mis. Doc., 47th Cong. 2nd sess., no. 45, pt. 4, pp. 22, 535–6.
[2] Forty-four per cent, it was said, of the total area of the United States.— Joseph Nimmo, Jr., Report on Internal Commerce for 1885, pt. 3, p. 95.
[3] Report of Sec. of Int. for 1886, p. 33.
[4] N. Y. Nation, Sep. 17, 1885.
[5] Report of Sec. of Int. for 1881, vol. ii, pp. 749–50.
[6] N. Y. World, March 16, 1887.

their appearance in the lobbies of state capitals and at Washington.[1] The business developed with an amazing rapidity, but the difficult conditions under which it was prosecuted made it profitable only if it were conducted on a large scale. Daring men accumulated substantial fortunes by selling their homeless and unnumbered herds to one another, and to those less experienced in such a use of capital.[2] More than a few young Englishmen, some of them bearing titles, were attracted to the business by its promise of adventure, as well as by the hope of gain, a fact which, in the state of feeling at the time with reference to foreigners, particularly to "Britishers," made it the more feasible to denounce the ranchmen as "cattle barons" and "bonanza cattle kings."[3] By the drilling of artesian wells, the building of reservoirs and the destruction of prairie dogs it was believed that, in at least some parts of the West, the number of cattle feeding upon the ranges might be doubled or trebled.[4] Promise of larger and more profitable markets was found in the development of refrigerating systems for the shipment of dressed beef over great distances by rail to the East, and even by sea to foreign countries.[5]

But the small herdsmen also had their rights and grazing as an occupation for him who would tend his own little flock on the edge of the frontier, or in favored spots in the "desert," became an increasingly difficult operation.[6] The owner of 20,000 or 30,000 head throve, while one who had 200 or 300, and could not lay his hands on these, was in sorry case. As the competition for grass developed among the large cattle men and they were confronted with parties of homesteaders who had "entered" the land over which the herds were

---

[1] Cf. Haynes, Life of J. B. Weaver, p. 238.

[2] Nimmo, op. cit., pp. 114–5; A. A. Hayes, Jr., New Colorado and the Santa Fé Trail, pp. 43–6; James S. Brisbin, The Beef Bonanza; E. S. Osgood, The Day of the Cattleman, chap. iv, on "The Cattle Boom."

[3] Cf. R. E. Riegel, The Story of the Western Railroads, p. 283; cf. N. Y. Tribune, Aug. 14, 1883; N. Y. Nation, July 2, 1885; House Reports, 48th Cong. 1st sess., no. 1325, p. 6.

[4] Nimmo, op. cit., pp. 113–4.

[5] Ibid., pp. 156–60.

[6] Cf. N. Y. Nation, July 2 and 16, Aug. 6 and 27, 1885.

roaming, many owners had the audacity to build fences around pasture ground, including water sources, thus greatly intensifying public feeling. Again they would dig ditches and turn entire streams into new courses for their own uses, driving away others whose lands were located in the same watershed.[1]

Settlers with a few head of cattle or sheep, in preëmpting land or locating a homestead in or near such seized areas, though their title be clear, well knew that they would subject themselves to molestation.[2] They would find themselves without water; their animals would be run off to be incorporated in a short while in the great herd nearby. Their land and whatever improvements had been lavished upon it were soon for sale and the purchaser, if there were one, was the "cattle king" who bought at his own price. Thousands of young men from the East who had wished to engage in grazing gave it up perforce. The nation lost what of worth they would have brought to the West and to our citizenship generally as they, courage gone, drifted into the dance halls and the gambling houses, picturesque features of our frontier life it may have been, but marks at the same time of the ruin of manhood which the government, by correct and intelligent administration of the public domain, could have turned to valuable purpose.[3]

When the great drovers of the plains indulged any scruples of conscience as to their rather free use of the public lands without compensation, or, for practical reasons of some kind, sought to establish a basis in law for their operations, they devised schemes for taking up adjoining quarter sections in bulk, or made leases with the Indians. The leases or pretended leases to gain right to graze in the Indian reservations for a payment not in excess, as a rule, of two cents an acre annually, were permitted by the Department of the Interior during the

[1] Report of Sec. of Int. for 1886, p. 15. J. W. Powell's Report on the Lands of the Arid Regions in 1878 suggested more just distribution and better use of the public lands.

[2] They avoided such localities as they would districts "stricken with a plague."—Report of Sec. of Int. for 1885, p. 205; cf. ibid., p. 210; House Ex. Doc., 50th Cong. 1st sess., no. 232, p. 2; N. Y. Tribune, Aug. 14, 1883.

[3] Cf. N. Y. Nation, Sep. 17, 1885; House Ex. Doc., 50th Cong. 1st sess., no. 232, passim; cf. Nimmo, op. cit., pp. 133–8.

Arthur administration.[1] It was clear that if the cattle men
were not allowed to make such agreements their herds would
graze on the land anyhow.[2] The Crows in Montana had leased
1,500,000 acres in their reservation to "stock growers." [3] The
Cheyennes and Arapahoes in the western part of the Indian Territory had made eight separate leases with cattle men, involving
the use of nearly 4,000,000 acres. The area retained by the
tribes for their own purposes was less than 500,000 acres.[4] In
1883 6,000,000 acres in the Indian Territory, had been leased
by the Cherokee "Nation" to a cattle company for a term of
five years at an annual rental of $100,000,[5] and this company,
it was alleged, had sublet the right to others for $500,000 a
year, reaping a profit of $400,000.[6] It was clear that such ar-
rangements at such a rate of compensation were more in the
interest of the "cattle barons" and the Indian agents, who
were fairly enough suspected of playing corrupt parts in per-
fecting the agreements, than of the Indians.[7]

The leases led furthermore to bickering and dissension among
the large graziers themselves. The Senate called upon the
Interior Department in December, 1883,[8] and again in December, 1884, for information, and the worst fears of the friends
of the Indians were confirmed.[9] Secretary Lamar made the
pertinent observation that, if the Indians were thus to lease
their lands, it should be under the supervision of the government. It were better, many said, if any tribe did not require

[1] Report of Sec. of Int. for 1884, vol. i, p. x; ibid. for 1885, vol. i,
pp. 14–9; Secretary Teller's defense of his course is in Senate Ex. Doc.,
48th Cong. 2nd sess., no. 17, pp. 1–9; Nimmo, op. cit., pp. 109–10; cf. Senate
Ex. Doc., 48th Cong. 2nd sess., no. 22 and Senate Ex. Doc., 48th Cong.
1st sess., nos. 54 and 139.

[2] Cf. Senate Ex. Doc., 48th Cong. 2nd sess., no. 17, pp. 1–2, 7.

[3] Report of Sec. of Int. for 1885, vol. i, p. 16; Senate Ex. Doc., 48th Cong.
2nd sess., no. 22, pp. 30–34; cf. ibid., 48th Cong. 1st sess., no. 139.

[4] Report of Sec. of Int. for 1885, vol. i, p. 14 and vol. ii, pp. 16–9.

[5] Ibid., vol. i, pp. 20–21; cf. ibid. for 1884, vol. ii, p. 33; ibid. for 1887,
vol. i, p. 31; ibid. for 1888, vol. i, p. iv; Senate Ex. Doc., 48th Cong. 2nd
sess., no. 17, pp. 8, 9, 16–8.

[6] Haynes, Life of J. B. Weaver, p. 236.

[7] Report of Sec. of Int. for 1885, vol. i, pp. 14–9; Senate Reports, 49th
Cong. 1st sess., no. 1278, passim.

[8] Senate Ex. Doc., 48th Cong. 1st sess., no. 54.

[9] Ibid., 2nd sess., nos. 17 and 22.

for its use the area assigned to it, that the surplus be made over to the United States to be opened to public settlement.[1]

President Cleveland's Attorney-General gave it as his opinion that without the consent of Congress the leases were illegal. Some were annulled, others abandoned and the reservations, when they could be, were cleared of cattle in the hope that the designated owners might learn to use the land themselves.[2]

Moreover, if filings and entries were made in the cattle country under the homestead, preëmption or desert land laws, they were likely to be fraudulent.[3] Men who would scorn the thought of committing a dishonest act in reference to another individual would eagerly listen to suggestion of schemes to evade the spirit and the letter of the settlement laws, and to cheat the government.[4]

In the East any policy giving to one individual more than a small piece of public land was regarded as "not only unrepublican but essentially unjust," [5] and it met with reprobation. Nevertheless law had been added to law and, by amendment and supplementation, the quarter section obtained by preëmption, or as a "homestead," to be plowed and seeded for harvest, while it was still the unit of the public land system, was no longer, in practice, the basis of distribution. It was a fact that any person, male or female, native or foreign, if he had filed his "first papers" in application for citizenship (always barring negroes and Chinese), could secure as much as 1,120 acres of land—160 under the homestead law, 160 under the preëmption law, which Congress had been repeatedly asked to repeal, 160 under the timber culture law and 640 under the desert land law of 1877.[6] He could buy a million acres of "offered" public land at $1.25 an acre in some Western and in

---

[1] Report of Sec. of Int. for 1885, vol. i, p. 19; cf. ibid. for 1886, vol. i, pp. 9–10.

[2] Ibid. for 1885, vol. i, pp. 18–9; ibid. for 1886, vol. i, p. 94.

[3] Cf. ibid. for 1883, vol. i, p. xxxi.

[4] Ibid. for 1885, vol. i, p. 202.

[5] House Ex. Doc., 46th Cong. 2nd sess., no. 46, p. vii.

[6] Cf. Report of Sec. of Int. for 1883, vol. i, pp. 7–8; House Ex. Doc., 46th Cong. 2nd sess., no. 46, p. ix; House Mis. Doc., 47th Cong. 2nd sess., no. 45, pt. 4, pp. 534, 535.

five Southern states.[1] Such methods of distribution, though
the original plan had been extended, were too intricate and
still in no way adapted to the requirements of the people of
the far West. Local agents of the Interior Department said
that in their districts only one-fourth, one-tenth and, in one
place, one-thirtieth of all the various kinds of claims to public lands were proper and honest, and the cattle men were
leading offenders. The entries were made to cover sources
of living water, adjacent to dry land belonging to the government over which the entrymen's stock grazed. If it were a
stream, and others were to be kept away from its uses, a hundred cowboys would be sent to the land office. The owners
advanced the money, the men gave their own or fictitious
names, presumptive title was gained to everything for miles
around. No houses were built, no land was plowed or planted,
no occupancy or residence was contemplated.[2] The "homesteads" all together fell into the hands of the cattle company
which then, perhaps, dismissed from service the men who had
made the entries, if, indeed, they had ever been employed for
any purpose except to defraud the government.[3] Even under the desert land law well-watered land was acquired by
the ranchmen. Under the swamp land act they secured desirable dry land.[4] If promise to irrigate the "desert," or to
drain the "swamp" were made, that promise was not remembered and kept. Live stock trod over it and ate the hay as
before. Altercations between ranchmen and settlers ensued.
Feuds between cowboys, attached to neighboring ranches, were
engendered and bloodshed resulted from rivalries to gain possession of that to which neither party had a shadow of right.[5]

---

[1] House Mis. Doc., 47th Cong. 2nd sess., no. 45, pt. 4, p. 535.
[2] Men, if they erected houses at all, would put up sod houses. The law
said that houses were to be 14 by 16—this was held to mean inches, not
feet. The "board floor" would be a "bored floor," and the "roof of shingles,"
two shingles, one hanging on each side of the ridge pole.—Report of Sec.
of Int. for 1885, vol. i, p. 204; cf. ibid., pp. 206–7.
[3] Ibid., pp. 208–9.
[4] See G. W. Julian, Our Land Policy, Atlantic Monthly, March, 1879.
[5] Cf. Report of Sec. of Int. for 1885, vol. i, p. 207; R. E. Riegel, The
Story of the Western Railroads, p. 150.

On the public lands outbreaks occurred also when men who grazed cattle met men who grazed sheep. In Colorado, New Mexico, Montana, California and in many other Western states and territories the flocks were so large as to put Ohio into the background in sheep raising except in the one matter of a demand upon the government for a high tariff on wool. The Western clip was large and valuable. But the sheep with their small, sharp hoofs trampled the grass. They cropped it too closely. They left a scent on the ground. Cattle would not feed where sheep had been.[1] The flockmasters said, with truth, that they had as fair a right in the public domain as the "cattle kings,"[2] who, however, had the greater wealth and power. Cowboys would drive the sheep together and ride over them if they came near a cattle range. Their throats were cut, shepherds were killed.[3]

There was another side to the question and the cattle man not unnaturally felt that his large new business should receive sympathetic consideration. Many of the graziers on the public domain would have willingly paid for "government grass," if a system should have been devised by which they might do so.[4] A farm of 160 acres and a cabin were well enough in Illinois or Minnesota, where land could be put to agricultural uses; it had little value in this great empire where acres were square miles and herd and herders made roof of the sky. It required the hay on from ten to 70 acres in this great dry belt, stretching from the Mexican border to Canada, to sustain a cow. Each sheep must run over from five to ten acres. If stock raising were to be a business on the plains the "Eastern land laws" should be revised to include provision for the lease, though it might not be the purchase, of ample and suitable tracts of land for pasturage, after the manner of systems prevailing in Canada and Australia.[5]

[1] House Ex. Doc., 46th Cong. 2nd sess., no. 46, pp. 286, 292.
[2] Ibid., p. 249.
[3] Cf. ibid.
[4] Cf. ibid., p. 286.
[5] Cf. House Ex. Doc., 46th Cong. 2nd sess., no. 46, pp. 247, 458; Report of Sec. of Int. for 1875, pp. 8–9; N. Y. Nation, July 2 and Aug. 27, 1885; Nimmo, op. cit., pp. 140–3.

As with the grazing lands so, too, was it with woodland in the public domain. Individuals and companies were doing with it as they would, without restraint. Steam sawmills were built in the forests. Wood was taken to make charcoal to be used in the smelters. Trees were felled for railway ties. The best portion of the log was removed and the rest was left to rot upon the ground. Forests near the railroads were scoured for telegraph poles. Every man owned all he could cut and destroyed what of it he did not carry away. Lumber was conveyed to the seacoast for export.[1] New Mexico was devastated to meet demands for timber in old Mexico. The shores of Puget Sound were invaded and bared that ships might be laden with lumber for transport to foreign countries.[2]

If they recoiled, perhaps, at thought of their effronteries and would have title to the land which they raided, the "lumber kings" sent gangs of their men to the land offices. For $1.25 and $2.50 an acre, the price of agricultural land, they acquired, by fraudulent methods, great tracts of standing timber worth from $25 to $100 an acre.[3] Others made desert land entries in afforested country, sank a well or two, cut the wood and then abandoned the claim.

It was not plain, as the commissioner of the General Land Office said, as early as in 1875, by "what rule of justice to the whole people a few were permitted to prey upon the common property."[4] The "indiscriminate destruction of our forests" met the angry reprobation of Carl Schurz, while he was Secretary of the Interior. He mightily forwarded, if he did not indeed crystallize, give form to, and start, the movement of public opinion in favor of guarding and preserving against depredation this great national resource.[5] Forests were disappearing with "appalling rapidity," we were living like "spendthrifts."[6] The

[1] Report of Sec. of Int. for 1880, vol. i, p. 36.
[2] Ibid. for 1881, vol. i, p. 377.
[3] Ibid. for 1880, vol. i, p. 575; ibid. for 1884, vol. i, pp. 18–9; ibid. for 1885, vol. i, pp. 205, 214–5, 225; cf. N. Y. Nation, Jan. 7, 1886.
[4] Report of Sec. of Int. for 1875, p. 18.
[5] Cf. ibid. for 1880, vol. i, pp. 34–5.
[6] Ibid., p. 38.

end could be seen. Such waste of public wealth must "inevitably result in incalculable and irreparable injury" to the economical interests of the West.[1]

The only defense which the offenders could offer for their depredations was that lumber was needed to build houses on the plains and in the mountains, and to support the tunnels in mines. The development of the West required timber and it was a public service to fell it, manufacture it and furnish it to the people at a reasonable price. Indeed, in some instances, the mill companies could point to legislation by Congress distinctly permitting the cutting of wood for local uses on government land.[2]

It was but puny obstruction to such brigandage that the government could interpose, whatever measure of protection for the public domain could be found in the law and however earnest and honest the agencies created for the task. The General Land Office at Washington in charge of this great subject was presided over by a commissioner who received $4,000 a year for his services. He had three employees to whom he might pay $2,000 a year each, and about 175 clerks compensated at the rate of from $1,000 to $1,800 annually each, largely useless party henchmen. They were performing their duties, in crowded apartments, in such manner as their poor abilities would allow. In spite of its extended and increasing responsibilities this bureau of the government was working under an organization which had undergone no essential change in 44 years.[3]

To investigate, punish and prevent trespasses on the timberlands in the various land states and territories Congress appropriated $12,500 in 1877, $25,000 in 1878 and $40,000 in 1879, the latter sum but enough to employ a force of fifteen special agents in a field covering two-thirds of the entire superficial area of the country.[4]

---

[1] Report of Sec. of Int. for 1879, p. 27.
[2] Cf. ibid., pp. 27–8.
[3] Ibid. for 1880, vol. i, pp. 412–3.
[4] Ibid. for 1879, pp. 26, 556–61; ibid. for 1880, vol. i, pp. 36, 574–82; ibid. for 1881, vol. i, p. 13.

Again and again the Interior Department had recommended changes in the land laws, some of which should have been repealed and others amended, but always without effect. In 1879, during Schurz's administration, Congress authorized President Hayes to appoint a Public Land Commission. It would be the duty of this body to codify the various and confusing laws bearing upon the survey and disposition of the public domain, to classify government lands and to propose such changes in the prevailing system as the best economic interests of the country were deemed to require for the advantage of "actual settlers."[1] The work was undertaken in a serious and responsible spirit and the study of the subject was extensive. The commission, either as a body or in detachments, visited all the states and territories west of Kansas and Nebraska, except Washington territory, and obtained a vast amount of interesting and valuable testimony. Fact and opinion thus assembled were presented in a report which reached Congress in 1880,[2] although two or three years more were occupied in observation, the fruits of which were incorporated in later statements and recommendations.[3] It was fairly clear that the system which had been contrived to govern the distribution of the lands in the old Northwest Territory[4] could not be well applied to the great tracts lying between the 100th meridian and the Sierra Nevada range, on the continental plateau out of which rose the Rocky Mountains.[5] One hundred and sixty acres on the rich prairies of the Mississippi Valley would furnish a homestead for a poor man who was asked to go West and extend the frontiers of the republic. They were of no value to one who went farther West to the dry plains. He could not plow and use it for agricultural purposes unless there were water at hand for irrigation, a method of farming which anyhow was as yet but little understood.

[1] House Ex. Doc., 46th Cong. 2nd sess., no. 46, p. v; Report of Sec. of Int. for 1879, p. 31.
[2] House Ex. Doc., 46th Cong. 2nd sess., no. 46; ibid., 46th Cong. 3rd sess., no. 47.
[3] House Mis. Doc., 47th Cong. 2nd sess., no. 45.
[4] House Ex. Doc., 46th Cong. 2nd sess., no. 46, p. vii.
[5] Ibid., p. 177; Report of Sec. of Int. for 1875, p. 7.

He would starve, as would his family and his domestic animals.[1]

The commission found that the people of the far West, unable to adapt the laws to their uses, had "framed customs" which took the place of laws. In other words they were "a law unto themselves." [2] It was a state of affairs which might furnish amusement to the adventurous visitor and incident in plenty for the romantic writer, but it was in no way worthy of a great government. The commission made recommendations. At the foundation of their system lay an assortment of the public lands into five classes—arable, mineral, irrigable, pastoral and timber lands. The different needs for law bearing upon these various kinds of land must be recognized by Congress, if attempt were to be made to reduce the system to order and secure the conformance of the people of the West to public regulation.[3] The General Land Office at Washington must be thoroughly reorganized. The manner in which it was left to be administered by ignorant clerks, Commissioner J. A. Williamson said, was "absolutely absurd." [4] A bill putting into form for enactment the valuable suggestions of the commission was prepared and presented to Congress,[5] which cast it away.[6]

Protest must continue. The commissioner of the General Land Office in 1884 spoke of the "vast and widespread violations of law," the "acquisition of great bodies of land in fraud of law by single individuals and corporations." The time was nearly come when the men who looked to the public domain for a cheap home could do so no longer. "Wastefulness in the disposal of public lands should cease" and "the portion

---

[1] House Ex. Doc., 46th Cong. 2nd sess., no. 46, p. 184.

[2] Ibid., p. ix.

[3] Ibid., pp. xix–xxii; House Mis. Doc., 47th Cong. 2nd sess., no. 45, pt. 4, pp. 533–51.

[4] Report of Sec. of Int. for 1880, vol. i, p. 415; cf. G. W. Julian, Our Land Policy, Atlantic Monthly, March, 1879.

[5] House Ex. Doc., 46th Cong. 2nd sess., no. 46, pp. xlix–c; Report of Sec. of Int. for 1880, vol. i, pp. 31–2.

[6] Cf. House Mis. Doc., 47th Cong. 2nd sess., no. 45, pt. 4, p. 1170; N. Y. Nation, July 2, 1885.

still remaining should be economized for the use of actual settlers only." [1] Thomas Donaldson, who had been authorized by Congress to continue the work of the Land Commission, declared in the same year that the "useless and vicious land laws" were at the root of the whole trouble. They were the "cancers" which were "eating up" the public domain. The "intelligent action of fair-minded men of the entire nation" should be directed to a revision of the system. [2]

Indignation was still more plainly expressed when Cleveland came to the Presidency. These truly scandalous things had been done under the Republican party's administration of the government. The Democrats would put the national house in order. Secretary of the Interior Lamar supported Commissioner Sparks who saw the situation at a glance. The "cattle kings" and the "transatlantic companies" were "parcelling out the country among themselves." They held unentered land by fences which were "defended by armed riders and protected against immigration and settlement by systems of espionage and intimidation." [3] The effect of such a domination of the far West, an honest inspector of the General Land Office said, was "the worst that can be imagined." "The best lands and practically all the waters," he continued, "are controlled by men who have no interest in the development of the country, evade taxation and, in many cases, owe no allegiance to our laws and government." [4]

"People are worth more to the state than steers," said the governor of New Mexico. [5] Babies are better than bullocks, said General Weaver, the Greenbacker. The "desert" might not be permanently arid; it should be held for those who would some day make their homes on these grazing grounds, and

---

[1] Report of Sec. of Int. for 1884, vol. i, pp. 17–8.
[2] House Mis. Doc., 47th Cong. 2nd sess., no. 45, pt. 4, pp. 534–5.
[3] Report of Sec. of Int. for 1885, vol. i, p. 201; cf. House Mis. Doc., 47th Cong. 2nd sess., no. 45, pt. 4, p. 539; House Ex. Doc., 50th Cong. 1st sess., no. 232.
[4] Report of Sec. of Int. for 1885, vol. i, p. 205. The cattle men overran and used millions of acres "without payment of scot or lot, taxes or rents." —N. Y. Nation, Sept. 17, 1885.
[5] Report of Sec. of Int. for 1885, vol. ii, p. 1010.

raise the unorganized territories and the new states reared on precarious foundations to the dignity of great commonwealths.[1]

The building of fences to inclose herds on pasture lands, especially if thereby water and trees, or other natural shelter, could be monopolized, had in truth become an abominable, as well as a prevalent, defiance of public rights. The commissioner of the General Land Office during the Arthur administration, N. C. McFarland, forcibly directed attention to conditions and called for action by which he might maintain "the supremacy of the laws and preserve the integrity of the public domain." The grazing of cattle was becoming an "individual and corporate monopoly"—it should be "equally free to the enterprise of all citizens, unembarrassed by attempts at exclusive occupation." [2] In 1884 he said that he had investigated reports concerning more than 4,000,000 acres and that other "immense tracts" were declared to be fenced in, though the means of corroboration of the many complaints reaching him were not at his disposal.[3] In 1884 in Colorado 300,000 acres in South Park alone were surrounded by fences.[4] Three-fourths of the grazing land in the Pueblo district, including all the water privileges, it was said, had been inclosed. Two Colorado ranges, embracing 1,000,000 acres each, had been brought within fences.[5]   Others of immense extent, surrounded by barbed wire, lay nearby.[6] There were extensive inclosures from the North Platte in Nebraska south through Kansas to, and into, the Indian Territory.[7] Entire counties were inclosed in Kansas. The governor of Texas asked the legislature of the state to release the courthouse town in Jones county. It was completely circumscribed by fences in which there were but two

[1] S. J. Buck, The Agrarian Crusade, p. 93; cf. Haynes, Life of J. B. Weaver, pp. 242–3.
[2] Report of Sec. of Int. for 1882, pp. 13–4; cf. House Reports, 47th Cong. 2nd sess., no. 1858; House Reports, 47th Cong. 1st sess., no. 1809.
[3] Report of Sec. of Int. for 1884, vol. i, p. 17.
[4] Ibid. for 1885, vol. i, p. 209.
[5] House Ex. Doc., 48th Cong. 1st sess., no. 119, p. 2.
[6] Report of Sec. of Int. for 1885, vol. i, pp. 209–10.
[7] Ibid., p. 205.

gates.[1] A "cattle baron" had strung wire for a distance of 250 miles at the head of the Red River; he was running a line from the western boundary of the Indian Territory across the Pan Handle and on into New Mexico to keep the Kansas herds from drifting down upon his pastures during the winter storms.[2] No less than 125 cattle companies were feeding their herds inside fences in Wyoming,[3] many of the owners being "titled gentlemen" from Europe, and Scotch, English and other foreign syndicates.[4]

The "long drive" from the ranches to the line of the Union Pacific was made unnecessary by the completion of other railroads, whereby cattle could be transported to the East. The business had undergone radical changes, but still often the cowboys must take their steers over the plains for hundreds of miles to find communication with Kansas City and Chicago, where the slaughter and packing houses were located.[5] They could not follow the nearest route to the railroad; they might not, on the way, find grass and water, now that grass land and streams were held under private lease from the Indians, or had been frankly seized for individual use by men who had no more right to these things than other drovers. The fences prevented free movement, even mail routes were closed,[6] another incitement to contention and violence. If the wires were torn down bloodshed was certain to ensue.[7] The old trails being obstructed breeders and graziers were urging Congress to establish a "National Cattle Trail" over which all alike might drive their herds.[8]

[1] E. S. Osgood, The Day of the Cattleman, p. 191.
[2] Ibid.
[3] Senate Ex. Doc., 48th Cong. 1st sess., no. 127, pp. 1–2; House Ex. Doc., 48th Cong. 1st sess., no. 119, p. 3; House Reports, 48th. Cong. 1st sess., no. 1325.
[4] House Reports, 48th Cong. 1st sess., no. 1325, p. 6; Nimmo, op. cit., pp. 138–9.
[5] Cf. App. Ann. Cyclop. for 1885, p. 733; Nimmo, op. cit., pp. 98, 117 et seq.
[6] House Reports, 48th Cong. 1st sess., no. 1326, p. 6.
[7] N. Y. Tribune, Aug. 14, 1883; R. E. Riegel, Story of the Western Railroads, pp. 148–9.
[8] Report of Sec. of Int. for 1885, vol. i, pp. 19–20; Nimmo, op. cit., pp. 117–8, 121–30.

The Land Office at Washington had been striving for some time to bring to book these bold outlaws, but it was necessary to act through the Attorney-General and the process involved examination, report and proof in court.[1] The House Committee on Public Lands called it a "monstrous evil."[2] "Not another nation on the earth would permit such outrages" to be perpetrated.[3] It was "intolerable" and a "disgrace," but seizures of the public property for private use had long continued with little check.[4]

In the final days of the Forty-eighth Congress, on February 25, 1885, an act had been passed which promised to make easier the task of coping with the situation. It authorized more summary procedure and put legal remedy in the hands of aggrieved citizens on the ground. President Cleveland, soon after he came to office, had issued a proclamation ordering cattle men who had built fences on public lands to remove them immediately in answer to the provisions of the new law, and, directing all Federal officers to cause his command to be obeyed.[5]

The response was reluctant. The General Land Office at Washington reported in December, 1886, 375 unlawful inclosures containing 6,410,000 acres, and this was an enumeration far from complete.[6] Secretary Lamar declared that "substantially the entire grazing country west of the 100th meridian" had been fenced in by "stock growers." How the "illegal occupation and possession of the public domain" had reached "such enormous proportions" was beyond his comprehension.[7]

Through the activities of the Interior Department,[8] enough

---

[1] Cf. Report of Sec. of Int. for 1883, vol. i, pp. xxxii, 30–31.
[2] House Reports, 48th Cong. 1st sess., no. 1325, p. 6.
[3] Ibid., p. 7.
[4] Cf. Senate Ex. Doc., 48th Cong. 1st sess., no. 143; House Ex. Doc., 48th Cong. 1st sess., no. 119.
[5] McPherson's Handbook for 1886, pp. 201–2; Report of Sec. of Int. for 1885, vol. i, p. 44.
[6] Report of Sec. of Int. for 1886, vol. i, p. 30.
[7] Ibid., p. 32.
[8] Cf. N. Y. Times, May 26, 1887.

fences were taken down in the first year of Secretary Lamar's administration to restore to the open country more than a million acres of land. Many cases were still pending and would receive later attention.[1] Inspectors were few. Railways were hundreds of miles from the ranges; travel was slow and difficult. Powerful combinations of capital impeded progress. Inclosures on railroad lands could not be touched. Ingenious fellows in Wyoming and Arizona bought the odd-numbered sections granted to the railroad company and zigzagged their fences around these tracts. They actually kept the posts and wires upon their own ground while impounding and gaining for their private use the alternate sections which lay inside, belonging to the government.[2] When the Cleveland administration was done the Secretary of the Interior declared that over 6,000,000 acres which had been inclosed had been cleared, and the "great evil" had been almost completely "redressed."[3] These "vast areas of the public heritage" were "restored to the people." Now only within the railway grants were there large inclosures, and these had been created by the "cunning device" of building fences around alternate sections.[4]

The cattle men justified their defiance of public authority. "Steve" Dorsey, after escaping the toils of the law for his corruptions in connection with the Star Route contracts, had become a cattle man in New Mexico. He declared that the fencing of the public lands was "unavoidable." The "stock grower" must evade the law or go out of business. Other men offered the same defense. If cattle were not bred on the plains what would the East do for beef?[5]

As desirable land in the public domain disappeared, either through entry or by theft, the pressure upon the Indian reservations increased. West of the Mississippi River there were 102 of these, containing, approximately, 224,000 representa-

[1] Report of Sec. of Int. for 1886, vol. i, p. 30.
[2] Ibid., vol. i, pp. 30–31 and vol. ii, p. 97; ibid. for 1887, pp. 12–6; ibid. for 1888, vol. i, pp. xvi–xvii; House Ex. Doc., 49th Cong. 2nd sess., no. 166.
[3] Report of Sec. of Int. for 1888, vol. i, p. xvi.
[4] Ibid. for 1887, vol. i, p. 13.
[5] Ibid. for 1886, vol. i, pp. 33–9.

tives of the aboriginal American race, who stood under the supervision of 68 agencies, reponsible to the Department of the Interior, and 37 garrisoned military posts.[1] Some of the reserves were large and some were small. The Utes held considerable tracts in Colorado. The Crows and other tribes were in possession of extensive areas over which they might roam in Montana. The Sioux ranged widely on land nominally theirs in Dakota.

West of Arkansas, south of Kansas and north of Texas 64,222 square miles had been designated as "Indian country" or "territory,"[2] which, in the struggle to find a solution of the Indian question, it had been benevolently intended might be the final home of many of the tribes. Some were happily located there; others, as need arose and the opportunity presented itself, might be transported to a place which would be their own in perpetuity.[3] In 1880 no less than 34 tribes found refuge on this ground.[4]

Nowhere was there an Indian reservation which was not encroached upon by miners, cattle men, timber thieves or by squatters, in wagons, with tents and farming tools, who hung around it as wolves at a sheepfold.[5] "For many years the people living in the vicinity of an Indian reservation," said Secretary of the Interior Teller in 1885, "have been accustomed to look upon the reservation as public property" and to pasture their cattle and to cut hay and timber on it "with little or no compensation" to the owners.[6] "Trespasses upon Indian lands," said Secretary of the Interior Kirkwood in 1882, "are of constant occurrence. Persons are daily entering upon Indian reservations in violation of law," frequently causing difficulties which "result in bloodshed and open war."[7]

As time passed the intruders grew more numerous and ag-

[1] Report of Sec. of Int. for 1881, vol. i, p. vi.
[2] See Senate Ex. Doc., 46th Cong. 1st sess., no. 20, pp. 16–8; House Mis. Doc., 47th Cong. 2nd sess., no. 45, pt. 4, pp. 458–62.
[3] Cf. Report of Sec. of Int. for 1885, vol. ii, p. 9; N. Y. Nation, Jan. 7, 1886.
[4] Senate Mis. Doc., 46th Cong. 2nd sess., no. 41, p. 6.
[5] Report of Sec. of Int. for 1879, pp. 104–7.
[6] Senate Ex. Doc., 48th Cong. 2nd sess., no. 17, p. 1.
[7] House Ex. Doc., 47th Cong. 1st sess., no. 145.

gressive.[1] Especially were covetous eyes cast upon the fine, fertile, well-watered tracts which enjoyed a mild climate in the "Indian Territory." The "Cherokee Strip," or "Cherokee Outlet," [2] remained the property of the Cherokees. By treaty with them in 1886 it was provided that such part of the reservation as lay west of 96 degrees of longitude should revert to the United States, at a price later to be agreed upon, for .assignment to Indians of other "nations" when it should be deemed advisable to remove them to this ground. The "Oklahoma lands," lying in the center of the "Territory," were ceded to the United States by the Creeks and Seminoles and comprised some 5,570,000 acres. This country was held with a similar purpose in view, namely the settlement upon it of "other Indians and freedmen." [3]

It was declared that but a short time would elapse before these lands would be taken from the Indians, surveyed and opened to entry. The tribes made no use of their vast acreage. They were leasing it to cattle companies. The "Territory" was so large that, if it were parceled out, each person in it might have 520 acres. Indeed, if the red race of the United States, men, squaws and children, were concentrated there, each one could be allotted 256 acres. Such canaille should be dispossessed anyhow, and the land over which they roved should be occupied by white men settled on homesteads.[4]

Statements, though unauthorized and wholly untrue, that these were, in fact, public lands were widely circulated, in some instances by design, notably by a man named Payne

---

[1] Cf. House Reports, 46th Cong. 1st sess., no. 13; House Mis. Doc., 46th Cong. 1st sess., no. 13.

[2] Called so because of the language of the treaty when the Cherokees were removed from the South and settled on this land. They were guaranteed, in addition to the area whereon they were to reside, "an outlet west, and a free and unmolested use of all the country lying west of the western boundary" of that area, as far as the sovereignty of the United States then extended.—Cf. Report of Sec. of Int. for 1888, vol. i, p. liv.

[3] Report of Sec. of Int. for 1884, vol. ii, p. 33; ibid. for 1885, vol. i, p. 32; Senate Reports, 48th Cong. 1st sess., no. 64; House Reports, 49th Cong. 1st sess., no. 1076, pp. xxxix–xliii.

[4] Report of Sec. of Int. for 1886, vol. i, p. 88; cf. ibid. for 1885, vol. ii, pp. 9–10.

who, beginning in 1879, put himself at the head of a series of expeditions into the Indian Territory. He formed what he called the "Oklahoma Colony," issued "certificates of membership" at $2.50 each and "land certificates" at $25 each, which, he let it be supposed, would entitle the buyer to 160 acres. Up to the year 1884 it was said that he had collected by his schemes about $100,000.[1]

Others who followed his example reaped still larger sums from the immigrants, some of whom, suffering from droughts in Kansas and the infertility of lands which they had taken in good faith, were deluded into thinking that they had a grievance against the government, and were easily drawn into what was, at ground, a huge swindle.[2]

In the spring of 1879, when news of the advance of parties of "land grabbers" from Missouri, Kansas and Texas reached Washington, President Hayes warned them away. Those who had crossed the line would be removed by the military. General Pope, from his headquarters at Fort Leavenworth, watched the development of events.[3]

Another invasion in 1880 met with another proclamation by the President in yet more vigorous terms.[4] In May of that year Payne and a number of his followers who were found in a camp on Indian lands were arrested and shown out of the territory. In July, having returned, they were again arrested and this time turned over to a United States marshal at Fort Smith, Ark. The leader was tried, convicted and fined $1,000, the maximum penalty prescribed by law, which, however, he did not pay, and he was soon at large projecting another scheme of invasion.[5]

[1] Report of Sec. of Int. for 1883, vol. ii, pp. 18–20; ibid. for 1884, vol. ii, p. 33.

[2] N. Y. Nation, Feb. 5, 1885, quoting a corr. of Bradstreet's in Indian Territory.

[3] Richardson, Messages and Papers, vol. vii, pp. 547–8; Senate Ex. Doc., 46th Cong. 1st sess., no. 20; Report of Sec. of Int. for 1879, pp. 14–5, 103–4, 294–5; Report of Sec. of War for 1879, pp. 80–81.

[4] Richardson, vol. vii, pp. 598–9.

[5] Report of Sec. of Int. for 1880, vol. i, pp. 97–8, 323; ibid. for 1881, vol. ii, pp. 46, 55; Report of Sec. of War for 1880, vol. i, p. 91; ibid. for 1881, vol. i, pp. 114–5.

Under Payne's experienced direction two more raids were organized in the summer of 1882. Twice he was captured by the troops and the last time, with some of his "colonists," was thrown into prison at Fort Reno and conveyed to Arkansas for another trial in a Federal court, where again a fine, which would be uncollectible, was imposed upon him.[1] The invasions were described by General Pope as merely "a series of processions to and from the Kansas line" for the amusement of the people of the frontier. By keeping troops in the field he could drive the "colonists" back, but it was an expensive as well as a foolish way of dealing with the subject.[2] The whole thing was a "farce," he said;[3] it was a "farce," said the commissioner of Indian Affairs, who had repeatedly asked Congress for legislation which would stop such performances. A prison sentence should be the penalty for conspiracy of this kind, with confiscation and forfeiture of the cattle, wagons and "outfits" of the intruders.[4] But Congress turned a deaf ear to suggestions manifestly so appropriate, though they were enforced from time to time by the urgent recommendations of the Secretary of the Interior and the President.[5]

The raids continued as before. Payne, in January, 1883, gathered together another lot of "boomers" who, armed with Winchester rifles and carbines, would proceed in several parties from Arkansas City, Coffeyville, Caldwell and places in southern Kansas. With wagons, provisions, tents and implements of husbandry, the men being accompanied by women and children, the movement was viewed with some alarm. The leaders indulged in verbal abuse of the government and the troops, which they knew would stand in the way of their

[1] Report of Sec. of War for 1882, pp. 98–9.
[2] Ibid., p. 99; ibid. for 1883, p. 13.
[3] Ibid. for 1882, p. 99; ibid. for 1883, p. 130.
[4] Report of Sec. of Int. for 1882, vol. ii, pp. 13–4; ibid. for 1884, vol. ii, pp. 33–4; ibid. for 1885, vol. ii, p. 29; Senate Ex. Doc., 47th Cong. 1st sess., no. 111.
[5] Cf. Report of Sec. of Int. for 1883, vol. ii, p. 18; House Ex. Doc., 47th Cong. 1st sess., no. 145; House Ex. Doc., 48th Cong. 1st sess., no. 17; Senate Ex. Doc., 47th Cong. 2nd sess., no. 58; House Ex. Doc., 47th Cong. 1st sess., no. 145; Senate Ex. Doc., 49th Cong. 1st sess, no. 14; Senate Ex. Doc., 50th Cong. 1st sess., no. 41; N. Y. Nation, June 1, 1882.

progress. Payne urged the people in the border towns to set fire to the grass and brush and to engage in general bushwhacking until the country should be opened to them. His followers paraded with banners on which were seen such inscriptions as "On to Oklahoma," "Oklahoma forever" and "We go this time to stay." [1] He had the effrontery to apply for an injunction in a Federal court to prevent the troops from interfering with his operations, and instituted suit against General Pope, the department commander, for arresting him, asking $25,000 damages.[2] Twice during 1883 he effected a lodgment in the territory, twice he must be removed "at great expense to the government." [3]

Notwithstanding the rulings of the Interior Department, the proclamations of the President and the declarations of the Federal courts that these lands were not a part of the public domain, and, therefore, not subject to preëmption and entry, Payne continued his activities. The number of persons whom he could deceive seemed to increase each year. In May, and again in June, 1884, he invaded the territory. On the last of these expeditions he, in eligible situations, located several settlements which were given names. Sutlers followed with groceries and liquors. On July 1st President Arthur issued a proclamation similar to President Hayes's.[4] General Hatch of the United States Army visited the camps of the "boomers" and induced many of them to withdraw from the country; Payne and other old offenders who remained were arrested for another journey to Fort Smith. The invasion was thought to have been participated in by as many, perhaps, as 2,000 persons. From 6,000 to 10,000 claims were staked out in the "Cherokee Strip" and in Oklahoma. The usual fine having been imposed, Payne ran back to the Kansas line and was at work organizing another expedition before the troops who had escorted him to Arkansas could return to the

[1] Report of Sec. of War for 1884, p. 118.
[2] Ibid. for 1882, pp. 98–9; Report of Sec. of Int. for 1883, vol. ii, pp. 19–20.
[3] Report of Sec. of Int. for 1883, vol. ii, pp. 17–20.
[4] Richardson, vol. viii, pp. 224–5.

scene.[1] But his course had been run; he died suddenly and a man named Couch succeeded him as the leader of the movement.

Couch was an experienced border runner and he entered the territory with a large body of armed men about Christmas time in 1884. He seemed to court collision with the military, thinking that bloodshed would awaken public sympathy for his crusade. The soldiers closed in upon the camp and the intruders surrendered at length to Hatch, who drove them back into Kansas and carried some of the ringleaders to Wichita to answer Federal warrants charging them with engaging in rebellion against the authority of the United States.[2] Even after the work of expulsion had been completed parties of men, many of them gamblers, horse thieves and other frontier desperadoes, hung about the border ready to cross it as soon as the troops should be withdrawn.[3]

Meantime petitions, numerously signed, came to Congress and the President. The demonstrations of the "boomers," if they were at first designed to line the pockets of Payne, were made possible by a knowledge that a large body of arable land, where the climate favored the planting and gleaning of crops, lay idle and by a belief that, if sufficient commotion were created and continued, the government might be hurried into opening it to settlement. General Miles but expressed the views of all, or nearly all the people of the Southwest, when he declared the Indian Territory to be "a block in the pathway of civilization," a refuge for outlaws of every color, race and national origin. Without courts of justice or public institutions, without roads, bridges or railways it was "a dark blot in the center of the map of the United States." [4]

[1] Report of Sec. of Int. for 1885, vol. ii, p. 58; Report of Sec. of War for 1884, p. 118.
[2] Report of Sec. of Int. for 1885, vol. ii, pp. 58–9.
[3] Ibid. for 1884, vol. ii, p. 32.
[4] Report of Sec. of War for 1885, p. 153. A clever rhymster addressed President Cleveland in poetic form. (Cleveland Papers.) These were some of the verses—

> "Tell the settler on his claim
> That the woodland, hill and plain
> Must be kept for cattle kings,
> British lords and money rings; (Continued on p. 630)

Unquestionably there was a "vast surplusage" of land in the territory, said the commissioner of Indian Affairs.[1] But rather than admit white men to the unoccupied "Oklahoma country," where they would be surrounded by Indians, he would remove the Kiowas, Comanches, Wichitas, Cheyennes and Arapahoes, living west of 98 degrees of longitude, eastwardly into that country, thus placing the various tribes in a compact area. The ground vacated, together with the Public Land Strip, or "No Man's Land," ceded to the United States by Texas in 1850, a rectangular tract lying farther west, north of Texas and south of Kansas,[2] might then be surveyed and put at the disposal of white settlers. There were nearly 14,-000,000 acres in the Indian Territory west of the 98th meridian and nearly 4,000,000 more in the Public Land Strip. It would be no mean addition to the area available for entry under the settlement laws.[3]

The hand of the Cleveland administration was not to be forced by "rapacity and lawlessness." More land had been set aside for the Indians than was needed "for their wants and accommodation," said Secretary Lamar. But such transgressions as those of the Oklahoma "boomers" were not to be met by surrender and reward. "Outlaws and depredators" must be shown that they could not "ride roughshod into possession of the lands of the Indian reservations."[4] The appointment of the commission authorized by Congress to

> That liberty is but a name
> And justice hangs her head in shame
> At Oklahoma.

> "Tell our leaders of today
> To right the wrongs while yet they may,
> To turn the current, stem the flood,
> And save the land from crime and blood.
> Justice is all the people ask,
> And justice they will have at last,
> And Oklahoma."

[1] Report of Sec. of Int. for 1886, vol. ii, p. 88.
[2] House Mis. Doc., 47th Cong. 2nd sess., no. 45, pt. 4, p. 462.
[3] Report of Sec. of Int. for 1886, vol. ii, pp. 13, 88–9; cf. ibid. for 1885, vol. ii, pp. 12–3.
[4] Ibid. for 1885, vol. i, p. 35.

open negotiations for changes in the treaties and for the cession of parts of the Indian Territory, therefore, would be deferred.[1]

Anyhow President Cleveland recommended a quite different course. He would have a permanent commission of six men, three drawn from the army and three from civil life, to take the Indian question under its care. One of the duties of this body would be to suggest reductions in the areas of reservations, when this policy should be deemed to be for the welfare of the race.[2] The time for the appropriation to the white man's use of the surplus lands in the Indian Territory was measurably near, but it was not yet at hand.

The Utes who, by covenant, held an immense tract in western Colorado had been dispossessed in 1873[3] of a part of their reservation containing rich mineral deposits. They still had nearly 12,000,000 acres, fully one-third of the arable land in the state, and a commission was appointed to visit them with a view to further cessions.[4] They were not receptive to the influences of civilization.[5] Their numbers, no less than their behavior, were not eloquent arguments in favor of their remaining in a place where, plainly, they were obstructing the development of the country.

The Utes stood under the oversight of two or three agencies, one of which had come into the charge of a man named Meeker. Agreements had not been kept, the Indians said, and they were irritated. In the summer of 1879 a party of young "bucks" went on the war path and were raiding herds and settlements. The soldiers came down from Wyoming—they were attacked and several men, including the commanding officer, Major Thornburgh, were killed. Meeker and a number of agency employees were brutally massacred. The excitement in Colorado

[1] Report of Sec. of Int. for 1885, vol. i, p. 34.
[2] Richardson, vol. viii, p. 357; Report of Sec. of Int. for 1885, vol. i, p. 27.
[3] Cf. House Ex. Doc., 45th Cong. 3rd sess., no. 84; Senate Ex. Doc., 46th Cong. 2nd sess., no. 29; G. W. Manypenny, Our Indian Wards, chap. xix; also vol. iii of this work, p. 387.
[4] Report of Sec. of Int. for 1878, p. 471; ibid. for 1879, pp. 96–8; Senate Ex. Doc., 45th Cong. 3rd sess., no. 62.
[5] Report of Sec. of Int. for 1879, p. 19.

was intense.[1] After the outbreak it was the easier to make progress with the design to set the Utes out of the state. It was proposed that they be removed to Arizona or the Indian Territory. The mining interests in Colorado were of so much importance and the need of land for the sustenance of the population engaged in the mineral industries was so pressing that action would be taken at once. The cry, "The Utes must go," grew louder and would be heard. Chiefs of the various bands were brought to Washington and a plan for the surrender of their entire reservation was laid before them. Some, at individual points, would remain on farms on the same terms of government as the white inhabitants of the state, while the rest, barring a few settled on a narrow oblong strip in the extreme south,[2] would be sent to the Uintah reservation in Utah. The United States would pay certain small annuities in return for their withdrawal from the country. A commission was appointed to visit the Indians in Colorado and to secure the ratification of the agreement by three-fourths of the adult males of the tribe, a work which was completed in the summer of 1880.[3]

The advance of the lines of Western settlement soon pressed upon the reservations in Dakota and Montana.[4] The Sioux had so lately been brought within narrower bounds, following the negotiations made necessary by the excited lust for the precious metals in the Black Hills, set in the very midst of their reservation, their spirit of resistance had been manifested so lately in the massacre of Custer and his men that the plan

[1] Report of Sec. of War for 1880, pp. 79–80, 82–3; Report of Sec. of Int. for 1879, pp. 16–8, 82–96; House Ex. Doc., 46th Cong. 2nd sess., no. 38; Senate Ex. Doc., 46th Cong. 2nd sess., no. 27; Senate Ex. Doc., 46th Cong. 2nd sess., no. 31; House Reports, 48th Cong. 1st sess., no. 693; cf. G. W. Manypenny, Our Indian Wards, pp. 421 et seq.

[2] It was the task of another commission in 1888 to remove this little band to Utah.—Report of Sec. of Int. for 1888, vol. i, pp. lxvi–lxvii; cf. Senate Reports, 49th Cong. 1st sess., no. 836; House Reports, 50th Cong. 1st sess., no. 861.

[3] Report of Sec. of Int. for 1880, vol. i, pp. 20–21, 101, 315–20; cf. ibid. for 1881, vol. ii, pp. 2, 27; Senate Ex. Doc., 46th Cong. 3rd sess., no. 31; Senate Ex. Doc., 46th Cong. 2nd sess., no. 114; House Reports, 46th Cong. 2nd sess., no. 1401.

[4] Cf. Nimmo, op. cit., pp. 112–3.

to take more of their land, it was foreseen, could not be contemplated pleasantly by them. But the case was urgent.[1] The Western members of Congress were driven forward by their "constituents." Congress authorized the Secretary of the Interior to proceed and in 1882 he appointed three commissioners to deal with the tribe.[2] The "Great Sioux Reserve" covered an area of more than 34,000 square miles, or about 22,000,000 acres,[3] and it contained only 24,000 Indians, or but one for nearly two square miles. In the entire reservation only 5¾ square miles, it was said, had been put to the plow and were planted in crops.[4] As a result of the labors of the commissioners some of the chiefs, purporting to represent the tribe, agreed, in 1883, to part with about 15,000 square miles, or nearly half their reserve, much of it land of the "finest quality."[5] The commission congratulated itself on having performed a valuable service. Secretary of the Interior Teller regarded the agreement "as favorable alike to the Indians and the government." President Arthur transmitted it to Congress.[6] Then the trouble began. Discussion and dissent in Congress, and among the Indians themselves, followed at once.[7] It was pointed out that the consent of three-fourths of the adult males required by the twelfth article of the treaty of 1868 had not been obtained. Deception and fraud had been practiced by the commissioners.[8] The agreement was sent back to the Indians for their signatures and a committee of the Senate, under the chairmanship of Mr. Dawes, was ap-

---

[1] House Reports, 47th Cong. 1st sess., no. 1536.

[2] Ibid., 48th Cong. 1st sess., no. 1724, p. 2; Report of Sec. of Int. for 1882, vol. ii, p. 41.

[3] House Reports, 47th Cong. 1st sess., no. 1536; Senate Reports, 48th Cong. 1st sess., no. 283, pp. i–ii.

[4] Report of Sec. of Int. for 1883, vol. i, pp. xvi–xvii; cf. ibid., vol. ii, p. 37. An opposite opinion is expressed in Senate Reports, 48th Cong. 1st sess., no. 283, p. ix; cf. Report of Sec. of Int. for 1885, vol. ii, p. 282.

[5] Senate Reports, 48th Cong. 1st sess., no. 283, p. viii.

[6] House Ex. Doc., 47th Cong. 2nd sess., no. 68.

[7] Report of Sec. of Int. for 1883, vol. i, pp. xvii–xviii and vol. ii, pp. 696–7; ibid. for 1885, vol. ii, pp. 50–51; Senate Reports, 48th Cong. 1st sess., no. 283.

[8] Senate Ex. Doc., 48th Cong. 1st sess., no. 70.

pointed to investigate the scheme,[1] which was denounced as
an attempt, in effect, if not in design, to impose upon and cheat
the tribe by methods in defiance of "express treaty stipulations." [2]

The plan would again be carried to the Indians. In 1884
it was revised in the hope of gaining the authority of Congress
for a renewal of the negotiation.[3] The House Committee on
Indian Affairs in 1886 said it was "monstrous and abnormal"
that 25,000 Indians, to the exclusion of white men and with
no benefit to themselves, should hold 22,000,000 acres of land
"against the pressing wants of our civilization." [4] The tribe
would be concentrated on six separate small reservations.[5]
The scheme of 1882, with amendment, was again approved
by Congress on April 30, 1888, and the way was opened for
the appointment of another commission, which visited the
various agencies and communicated the wishes of Congress to
the Indians.

The Sioux, under the advice which was always freely given
them at the agencies and by selfish persons settled on the frontier, acting under the guise of friends, demanded better terms.
Failure being in sight, 67 headmen, with their agents and in-
terpreters, were transported to Washington for a conference
with the Secretary of the Interior. They were given extended
hearings. They would have $2,000,000 instead of $1,000,000
as a quit payment, they said. They had been offered a sum for
each acre in the tract ceded to the United States, when it
should be taken by homesteaders, to be applied to the education and civilization of the tribe. This amount, they said,
should be materially increased. They were not anxious to
sell their lands, their crafty leaders averred. They made this
offer "to please the Great Father and his white children."
While some of the chiefs declared such demands to be "ex-

[1] Senate Reports, 48th Cong. 1st sess., no. 283.
[2] Report of Sec. of Int. for 1883, vol. ii, pp. 696–7, 701–2; Senate Reports
48th Cong. 1st sess., no. 283.
[3] House Reports, 48th Cong. 1st sess., no. 1724.
[4] Ibid., 49th Cong. 1st sess., no. 1227, p. 2.
[5] They were being cared for at six agencies—Standing Rock, Cheyenne
River, Crow Creek, Lower Brulé, Rosebud and Pine Ridge.

orbitant" and denounced them as "unreasonable and unjust
to a fatherly and kind government," this element was in the
minority. The gross sum asked for, it was said in Congress,
was in excess of what had been paid to France for the Louisiana
Territory. To accede would be to set a standard of price for
future Sioux and other transfers. Much of the land in any
case was inarable and practically valueless. To provide so
great a fund for the Indians would destroy any incentive for
personal effort which they might have, and this was now at
so low an ebb as to give the least possible prospect of their
early improvement and rise in the human scale. The proposals
were inadmissible. The Indians were sent home and the commission was directed to wind up its affairs.[1]

Better fortune was had in Montana. The Crows were in
possession of 20 square miles of "fine land" for each "buck,"
squaw and child in the tribe. It was "an empire as large as
all France."[2] In 1882 the Crows were divested of the western
part of their domain, some 1,500,000 acres, together with a
strip running from east to west entirely across their reservation, to accommodate the needs of the Northern Pacific Railroad.[3] It was believed that there were, all told, not more than
2,500 or 3,000 Crows. If 3,000,000 more acres were taken there
would still remain to them 600 acres of land for each individual
member of the tribe,[4] a further restriction of their estates
which was demanded in the West, and was warmly advocated
by the Indian Bureau and the Secretary of the Interior. The
various Indian reserves in Montana still comprised 45,000
square miles, which area, the governor of the territory said,
included 30,000,000 acres of the "finest agricultural and graz-

[1] Senate Ex. Doc., 50th Cong. 2nd sess., no. 17; Report of Sec. of Int.
for 1888, vol. i, pp. lvi–lxvi, cxlv–clxxviii; ibid., vol. ii, pp. lxxiii–lxxv; cf.
House Reports, 50th Cong. 2nd sess., no. 3645.

[2] House Ex. Doc., 46th Cong. 2nd sess., no. 46, p. 378; cf. N. Y. Nation,
Feb. 13, 1879, and April 15, 1880.

[3] Report of Sec. of Int. for 1882, vol. ii, p. 41; House Reports, 47th Cong.
1st sess., no. 311; Senate Ex. Doc., 47th Cong. 1st sess., no. 19; House
Reports, 48th Cong. 1st sess., no. 1724, p. 2; Senate Ex. Doc., 49th Cong.
1st sess., no. 49.

[4] Report of Sec. of Int. for 1883, vol. i, p. xxiv; cf. ibid., vol. ii, pp. 49–50;
ibid. for 1884, vol. i, pp. xiii–xiv and vol. ii, pp. 5–6.

ing lands to be found on the continent."[1] Nine-tenths of it was of "no use to the Indians," citizens of northern Montana declared in a mass meeting at Fort Benton.[2]

So rich a country would not long remain closed to the white man. Congress in 1886 opened the way. The Secretary of the Interior appointed a commission, usually called the "Northwest Indian Commission,"[3] whose labors resulted in the breaking up of the "Great Blackfeet Reservation" in northern Montana. The buffalo, which in dwindling herds were still seen in this region, had, in 1883, for the first time, failed to visit it. The Indians were in distress. They would starve if they were not fed by the government.[4] The commission persuaded them to withdraw from not less than 17,500,000 acres, leaving for their uses three smaller reservations containing about 4,150,000 acres. The price was $4,500,000 to be paid in annual installments and invested in cattle, clothing, and, when it should be necessary, subsistence in a manner to promote their well being.[5]

The Indians, in general, exhibited a degree of quiet in the sight of the cattle men and their herds, the builders of railroads and the advancing lines of settlement, which spoke either of their broken spirit, or a comprehension at last of their destiny in the presence of the white man. The Utes in Colorado, it is true, in 1879, before they were removed to Utah, had perpetrated outrages which nearly brought the tribe into a state of war. Only the influence of the intelligent Chief Ouray prevented a general rising of his people and disastrous clashes with the troops which, when Major Thornburgh and the Indian agent were killed, had been hurried to the scene.

Their residence in Utah, after their removal thither, gave

---

[1] Report of Sec. of Int. for 1885, vol. ii, p. 1000; cf. ibid., vol. i, p. 81; House Ex. Doc., 46th Cong. 2nd sess., no. 46, p. 378.

[2] Cleveland Papers.

[3] 24 U. S. Stat. at Large, p. 44.

[4] Report of Sec. of Int. for 1883, vol. i, pp. xxiv–xxv.

[5] House Ex. Doc., 50th Cong. 1st sess., no. 63, pp. 1–3, 4; Senate Ex. Doc., 49th Cong. 2nd sess., nos. 30 and 115; Report of Sec. of Int. for 1887, vol. i, p. 38 and vol. ii, pp. 27–8; ibid. for 1888, vol. ii, pp. lxxvii, 302; 25 U. S. Stat. at Large, p. 113.

them no happiness or content. The tribe was wild and ungovernable. At signs of a rising in 1886 a new military post was located in their vicinity. General Crook marched into the reservation with a body of troops and overawed the savages to such a degree that no further disturbances were apprehended.[1] But in the next year a band, led by a chief named Colorow, with fond memories of their old home, roamed with their horses, sheep and neat cattle into the pasture lands of Colorado, causing great excitement, though it did not appear that they were bent upon mischief. Posses were formed and commenced hostilities. The governor was asked to mobilize the militia, which he did. General Crook was importuned to use the Federal troops. The War Department was addressed. The President replied that the occasion, so far as he could perceive, was not at hand for a display of force. Colorow and his party would return peaceably to the reservation, if military activity were suspended.

Before the hands of the Coloradoans could be stayed Indian women and children were seized, their tents were burned, their ponies, sheep and goats were run off and stolen. Even while they were retiring they were attacked. The Indians were nearly within their reserve. Unable to make greater haste in their retreat they, on the night of August 24, 1887, were given permission to remain where they then were until the following day, with promise of immunity from harm. But at daybreak the next morning, while they were at breakfast, the militia and the desperadoes in the posse which for several days had been on the heels of the band treacherously fired upon the camp. Volleys continued to be exchanged for three and a half hours, the Indians meanwhile having removed their women and children inside the reservation, though not before two small girls and a baby boy were slain. They lost a number in dead and wounded, their entire winter's supply of dried meat, their robes and skins and, indeed, all their possessions. Only the coming of the Federal troops prevented the pursuit of Colorow and his party into the reservation and further attacks

[1] Report of Sec. of Int. for 1886, vol. i, pp. 127-9.

upon them by the militia and the mob. This outrage awakened nation-wide indignation and recalled the bloody blot upon the history of our Indian administration at Sand Creek.[1]

In the summer of 1885 the Cheyennes were under great excitement which was induced by leases for the grazing of cattle on their reservation in the Indian Territory. General Sheridan visited the tribe and, without recourse to hostilities, restored harmony, though the troops were concentrated in the neighborhood for action, if it should be necessary.[2]

A close approach to an "Indian war" was seen in the fighting with the Apaches in Arizona, one of the most active and cruel, and, withal, astute and crafty, of the various tribes of the American race.[3] Placed in a part of the country where they were brought into infrequent contact with the white population they remained unsubdued. They roved from Mexico over our border and back again, as their need or pleasure inclined, and they but recently had had homes set apart for their occupancy. In these they were not pleased to stay. Though for a time commended for their docility and industry, in a trice they were raiding herds, stealing horses, killing settlers and making themselves the terror of Arizona, New Mexico and the northern part of old Mexico, which were filling with white men who were interested in the ranches and the mines.[4]

They must be "hunted down in small detachments," said General Pope, and, because they ranged over so wide a region they gave the troops "more hard service and the government more expense than tribes ten times more formidable, both in numbers and warlike capacity."[5] Their reputation for endurance had long been celebrated. It was said that they could

[1] Report of Sec. of Int. for 1887, vol. i, pp. 41–3; ibid., vol. ii, pp. 76–80; Report of Sec. of War for 1887, pp. 128–32.
[2] Report of Sec. of Int. for 1885, vol. i, p. 6 and vol. ii, pp. 17–8.
[3] General Crook, after 32 years of contact as a soldier with our various Indian tribes, put the Apaches "at the very head" of them all "for natural intelligence and discernment."—Letter to Herbert Welsh in Harper's Weekly, Aug. 30, 1884.
[4] Cf. C. S. Fly, Scenes in Geronimo's Camp.
[5] Report of Sec. of War for 1879, pp. 82–3.

travel a hundred miles in a day—their lung power, General Miles averred, would enable them to start at the base of a mountain and run to the summit without pause.[1] They would conceal themselves near a trail so successfully that the most practiced eye could not detect their whereabouts until their shots were felt. Driven up the sides of high peaks they would subsist for days on field mice and the juice of the cactus plant.[2]

A chief named Victorio headed a band with which guerilla warfare continued for several years.[3] Closely pursued by competent border fighters, acting under the direction of Pope, this leader finally, in 1880, while in Mexico, was killed by an energetic commander of a military force of that republic, and such parts of his following as had not been slain or captured found their way back to the United States. He and his band in a year and a half had taken the lives of 400 persons.[4]

Though Victorio had disappeared the army was never without active employment with reference to savages as unpeaceable and murderous as he. A band led by Geronimo went on the "war path" in 1882. General Crook who had been recalled to the military department of Arizona, where he had earlier performed distinguished service,[5] after crossing the Mexican line, had corralled the hostiles in the Sierra Madre mountains and had brought them back to the reservation. The authorities at Washington, no less than the people of the Southwest, were surprised to hear of the return of such Indians to tribal life after so plain a display of their barbarity, and distrusted the judgment of Crook,[6] who was, in some degree, a composite of soldier and philanthropist, but, by reason of his knowledge of the situation, acceded to his plan on the condi-

[1] Nelson A. Miles, Serving the Republic, p. 219.
[2] Ibid., p. 220.
[3] Report of Sec. of War for 1879, pp. 86–9, 96–8, 104–10; Report of Sec. of Int. for 1879, pp. 98–100.
[4] App. Ann. Cyclop. for 1880, pp. 27–8; Report of Sec. of Int. for 1880, vol. i, pp. 25, 118; Report of Sec. of War for 1885, p. 172; N. Y. Nation, April 28, 1881.
[5] Cf. Harper's Weekly, August 30, 1884.
[6] General McCook wrote from Tucson to say that Geronimo should be punished; he was no "farmer."—To Lamont, Feb. 7, 1886, in Cleveland Papers.

tion that Geronimo and his friends be kept under the surveillance of the army rather than the agents of the Interior Department, as they had been before their departure for their southern lair.[1] Now, in May, 1885, in their rawhide moccasins, with their Springfield rifles, butcher knives and water canteens, they were gone again. They had betrayed their benefactor, and, before Crook could make good his pursuit, were once more "slipping around like coyotes" [2] in fastnesses from which they must once more be taken before there could be reassurance in the ranch houses and mining settlements of Arizona.[3] Throughout the summer, autumn and winter of 1885 on into the year 1886 their bloody deeds and the efforts of the army to stop their atrocities were in every newspaper. One small party of 11 hostiles, from November 15th to December 15th, killed 21 friendly Apaches on the reservation, and not less than 24 white men, women and children, for a loss of only one "buck." [4] On another occasion, on the line of a raid of 800 miles, with 5,000 troops, Mexicans and Americans, on duty, the Indians killed 25 persons and made their escape with only two casualties.[5]

It is certain that this tribe had been treated unfairly and had ample ground for resenting the injustices done them by the government and by the whites settled around them.[6] But they lived for pillage and bloodshed and were in all respects so stealthy, implacable and ferocious an enemy that it was resolved to send a number of them to the East for safe keeping and correctional training. In April, 1886, as many as 77 were carried to Fort Marion at St. Augustine in Florida, to be followed thither by many of their friends, who, though they remained

---

[1] Report of Sec. of War for 1883, pp. 5, 159–81; N. Y. Nation, June 14, July 5, 12, 26, Aug. 16, Sep. 13, 1883; John G. Bourke, On the Border with Crook, chaps. xxvi–xxvii; Robert Frazer, The Apaches, Report to Indian Rights Assoc. of Phila., 1885.

[2] General Crook in J. G. Bourke, On the Border with Crook, p. 475.

[3] N. Y. Nation, July 2, 1885.

[4] J. G. Bourke, An Apache Campaign, p. iv.

[5] Ibid., p. 11. For Apache outrages, cf. S. M. Barrett, Geronimo's Story of His Life.

[6] Cf. General Crook in Report of Sec. of War for 1883, pp. 159–69.

on the reservation, had been suspected of aiding and abetting the war party.[1]

Geronimo himself was still at large. During a year 140 persons had been killed by the Indians.[2] The people of Arizona and New Mexico were wildly excited. The commissioners of a county in New Mexico said that they would pay $250 for the scalp of "each and every hostile renegade Apache " killed by any citizen of that county.[3] General Crook who had been conducting the campaign [4] was succeeded by General Miles, and he, assisted by Captain, afterward General, Lawton, who lost his life at a later day in the Philippines, Leonard Wood and other energetic young officers, employing heliostatic signals which were flashed from crag to crag to the bewilderment of the Indians, finally secured Geronimo and the remnants of the band.[5] Miles was the recipient of many compliments for what he had done and he seemed to feel it no more than his due for exertions so "arduous" in a "remote and unsettled region." [6] Others were of a different mind. President Cleveland was greatly displeased with Miles for having negotiated a "surrender" instead of "capturing" the savages, "notwithstanding positive instructions" in another sense.[7] They should be treated as "prisoners of war"; he wished to hang the ruthless chief.[8]

There was fear of Geronimo's escape and a resumption of

[1] Cf. Senate Ex. Doc., 51st Cong. 1st sess., no. 83. Their part is taken by Crook's partisans and the "Indian Rights" men.—See Britton Davis. The Truth about Geronimo, and J. G. Bourke, On the Border with Crook.

[2] Report of Sec. of War for 1886, p. 165.

[3] Advertisement in Southwest Sentinel of Silver City, N. M., sent to President Cleveland by Mark Twain with his protest under date of Feb. 23, 1886, in Cleveland Papers.

[4] Report of Sec. of War for 1885, pp. 169–78; J. G. Bourke, On the Border with Crook, chap. xxviii.

[5] Senate Ex. Doc., 49th Cong. 2nd sess., no. 117, pp. 9–10, 18.

[6] N. A. Miles, Serving the Republic, pp. 223–9 and Personal Recollections, chaps. xxxv–xli; Miles to Lamar, March 19, 1887, in Cleveland Papers; Britton Davis, The Truth about Geronimo, pp. 218–35; cf. Senate Ex. Doc., 49th Cong. 2nd sess., no. 117.

[7] Drum to Endicott, Sep. 23, 1886, in Cleveland Papers.

[8] Senate Ex. Doc., 49th Cong. 2nd sess., no. 117, p. 4; Report of Sec. of War for 1886, pp. 164–81.

his operations, wherefore he was conveyed to San Antonio, from which place, after confinement for a few weeks, he was transported, with 14 of his associates in iniquity, "guilty of the worst crimes known to the law," to Fort Pickens in Florida.[1] The women and children in his party were forwarded to Fort Marion to join the colony of Apaches already established at St. Augustine, which had come now to number 470 souls,[2] to be removed later by the War Department to a more commodious military reservation in Alabama.[3] A few weeks after Geronimo's capture one of General Miles's officers brought in Mangus, another warring chief, and his retinue, who also were conveyed to Florida, thereby clearing the country.[4]

The keynote of the nation's Indian policy now was declared to be a system of humanitarianism.[5] The "home and the school" were to civilize the race whose rights we had extinguished and whose titles we had usurped, and whom we had so long, so notoriously and so wickedly mistreated. The protracted discussion as to whether the Indian should be under the surveillance of the War Department or the Interior Department, in the progress of which much fact had been adduced, and incidentally a great deal of angry rhetoric had been expended,[6] came to an end under some well directed strokes by the philanthropists. Their campaign had been untiring. The writing of a Massachusetts woman, who for some years had resided in Colorado, Helen Hunt Jackson, including her really terrible arraignment of the nation for its Indian policy, called "A Century of Dishonor," published in 1881, and a story,

[1] Senate Ex. Doc., 49th Cong. 2nd sess., no. 117, pp. 26–9.
[2] Report of Sec. of Int. for 1886, vol. i, pp. 17–8; cf. Senate Ex. Doc., 49th Cong. 2nd sess., no. 75; Senate Ex. Doc., 51st Cong. 1st sess., no. 88.
[3] Report of Sec. of Int. for 1887, vol. i, p. 40.
[4] Ibid. for 1886, vol. i, p. 18; Report of Sec. of War for 1887, p. 158. For later events in Geronimo's life see S. M. Barrett, Geronimo's Story and A. Mazzanovich, Trailing Geronimo.
[5] Cf. Senate Mis. Doc., 45th Cong. 3rd sess., no. 53, p. 227.
[6] Cf. House Reports, 45th Cong. 2nd sess., no. 241; Senate Mis. Doc., 45th Cong. 3rd sess., no. 53; Senate Reports, 45th Cong. 3rd sess., no. 693; House Reports, 45th Cong. 3rd sess., nos. 92 and 93; House Mis. Doc., 45th Cong. 2nd sess., no. 33.

"Ramona," which attracted much attention when it appeared in 1884, were not without a substantial influence in quieting those who espoused the cause of the War Department.[1] "The hand that feeds should punish," said the men in the army, who knew the Indian by long service on the plains.[2] But punishment henceforward should have little sting. The Indian must be taught to rise from his still too barbarous state over the paths of peace.[3]

Moralization about making the Indian drunk with "fire water" and supplying him with firearms continued. Intoxicating drink should be kept from his lips,[4] and he should be disarmed.[5] Laws on these subjects were passed, but they could not be enforced. Traders stood on the boundaries of, when they did not defiantly enter, the reservations. If the sale of whiskey could be stopped "peace and quiet" would exist among the tribes from the Mississippi River to the Pacific coast. It was "the one great curse of the Indian country."[6] Indian agents were still dishonest. Rations were not delivered punctually, nor were they of a good quality. Annuities were withheld. Sums pledged to the tribes in treaties were never paid, either in money or supplies.

The experiment with Indian police[7] was held to have justified itself. This constabulary force—there were nearly 900

[1] Cf. N. Y. Nation, Aug. 20, 1885 and Jan. 7, 1886. One of the last acts of Mrs. Jackson's life was to forward her books to President Cleveland through his friend, Lyman K. Bass, with a plea for just and humane treatment of the Indian. (Cleveland Papers.) Of some influence, too, was the book called Our Indian Wards by George Manypenny, published in 1880.

[2] Report of Sec. of War for 1885, p. 170.

[3] Still with the dissent of many men in the West as, for example, in the case of a "stock grower" of Nevada who informed the Public Land Commission that his "remedy" would be "to kill the Indians and Indian agents and annihilate the Indian Bureau, the curse of the entire frontier country as well as of the Indian himself."—House Ex. Doc., 46th Cong. 2nd sess., no. 46, p. 614.

[4] Cf. Report of Sec. of Int. for 1881, vol. ii, p. 24; ibid. for 1882, vol. ii, pp. 10–13; ibid. for 1883, vol. ii, pp. 2–4; ibid. for 1884, vol. ii, pp. 4–5.

[5] Ibid. for 1879, pp. 13–4, 70–73; ibid. for 1882, vol. i, pp. iv–vi; ibid. for 1883, vol. i, p. vi; ibid. for 1884, vol. ii, p. 27.

[6] Ibid. for 1882, vol. ii, pp. 11–3.

[7] Act of May 27, 1878, in 20 U. S. Stat. at Large, p. 86.

guards at 49 agencies in 1881[1]— was adjudged to be highly useful in combating vice and lawlessness on the reservations.[2] Compensated at the rate of $5 a month their pay, in consequence of urgent and frequent appeals of the Indian Bureau, was increased in 1885 to $8 a month. Officers received $10.[3] Under Schurz's administration of the Interior Department the government began to employ the Indians in hauling supplies to the agencies.[4] The Indian transportation service in 1880 had come to employ 2,000 freight wagons.[5]

A few Indians who had been left behind in the general migration to the West were making progress in self-support in the Eastern states, as were the so-called "civilized tribes"—Cherokees, Choctaws, Chickasaws, Creeks and Seminoles—numbering about 64,000 souls in the Indian Territory,[6] and it was the hope somehow to give. all of them occupational places in society so that, as soon as possible, the public dole might be replaced by work for wages and profits. The Indian service was costing the government $5,500,000 annually; the expense would increase if this people were not made to do something for themselves. They must be "transferred from the list of non-producers to that of producers" and the public must be "relieved from the burden of their support." [7]

But it must be admitted that their love of continuous labor was not marked. They would rove rather than remain in a fixed abode. Their rites, customs and superstitions were a fixed inheritance and could no more be conquered by the devices of the government than by those of the church, which

[1] Report of Sec. of Int. for 1881, vol. ii, p. 13.

[2] Ibid. for 1879, p. 13; ibid. for 1880, pp. 10–11, 88–90; ibid. for 1881, vol. ii, p. 13; ibid. for 1882, vol. ii, pp. 35–6; ibid. for 1884, vol. ii, pp. 12–3; ibid. for 1886, vol. i, p. 105; Senate Mis. Doc., 45th Cong. 3rd sess., no. 53, pp. 230–31, 273; House Reports, 46th Cong. 2nd sess., no. 1401, p. 4.

[3] Report of Sec. of Int. for 1885, vol. ii, pp. 23–4.

[4] Ibid. for 1880, p. 6; ibid. for 1881, vol. ii, p. 31; House Reports, 46th Cong. 2nd sess., no. 1401, p. 3.

[5] Report of Sec. of Int. for 1880, pp. 6, 90–91; ibid. for 1879, pp. 8–9, 74–5.

[6] Cf. ibid. for 1886, vol. i, pp. 81–7; ibid. for 1887, vol. i, pp. 24–5; Senate Reports, 49th Cong. 1st sess., no. 1278, pt. 1, pp. iv–xxvi.

[7] Report of Sec. of Int. for 1883, vol. i, pp. viii–ix; cf. House Mis. Doc., 45th Cong. 1st sess., no. 18.

had long borne its benison to them through the Christian missionaries. It was an ethnic problem and it must be solved in some way to accord with our national convenience. The Indian would disappear from the face of the earth if he should not allow himself to come under the influence of the new and stronger race settled about him to the point, at least, of living in quiet and order, in conformity with the manners of the white race.

The philanthropists still made their influence felt through the advisory board of Indian commissioners of which General Clinton B. Fisk was now the chairman, and a conference at Mohonk Lake in New York, organized in 1883 by Albert K. Smiley, a Quaker member of the board, and held annually thereafter for many years at his call and in response to his hospitalities.[1] They were a unit in advocating the policy of peace through kindness and civilization, through opportunity for education and work.

The education which was to be given the race would presuppose an interest, innate or to be acquired, in farming or grazing.[2] That they must dwell on homesteads set aside for them in the West to follow these pursuits was at the very root of all that was said and written about their future.[3] The allocation of individual tracts of land to some of the Indians at the agencies had developed a sense of personal responsibility in them.[4] If they could have permanent land titles they would welcome, it was said, a further development of the policy.[5] The reservation system had come to limit roaming and hunting and to set a doom on the tomahawk and the wigwam; but it in turn must go. For long the Indians had been herded by themselves on vast vacant spaces, where the wicked were mixed with the good. The reserves were "sinks of iniquity"

---

[1] Cf. Report of Sec. of Int. for 1887, vol. ii, pp. 957–1027; ibid. for 1888, vol. ii, pp. 776–834.

[2] Cf. ibid. for 1886, vol. i, pp. 96–9.

[3] Cf. ibid. for 1881, vol. ii, pp. 1–3; ibid. for 1883, vol. i, p. iv.

[4] Cf. ibid. for 1883, vol. ii, p. 111; House Reports, 45th Cong. 3rd sess., no. 165; House Reports, 49th Cong. 1st sess., no. 1076, pp. xxxi–xxxix.

[5] Report of Sec. of Int. for 1881, vol. ii, pp. 17–9; ibid. for 1883, vol. i, pp. 90–91.

which should be broken up. Their usefulness was past; China's wall had fallen, but America stood still.[1] So long as such conditions continued the philanthropists were without hope of making progress with their civilizing policies.

The subject was put upon a definite and certain basis finally by the land-in-severalty law, of February 8, 1887,[2] which provided for the cutting up of the reservations and the allotment of a certain number of acres to each member of the resident tribe, to be held in trust for him for 25 years, usually known as the "Dawes act," since Senator Dawes of Massachusetts was its prominent advocate.[3]

The new law was viewed very hopefully. No longer, when it was passed, would the Indian be a "ward of the nation," but "a member of the great family of American citizens," with introduction to their privileges, including the franchise.[4] As rapidly and as soon as could be, the race, not without governmental oversight and assistance, would be absorbed to become a part of the common population. Tribal organization would cease, the agency system would be brought to an end. The patenting of lands in severalty would teach the Indian the benefits of labor and induce him to follow civilized pursuits.[5] The day when the "Dawes bill" became a law, said the citizens' board of Indian commissioners triumphantly, was the "Indian emancipation day."[6] We stood at the end of "a century of dishonor," said Congressman B. M. Cutcheon of Michigan at a conference of Indian philanthropists at Washington; we were "at the threshold of one of great blessing."[7]

[1] Report of Sec. of Int. for 1885, vol. i, pp. 782–4; cf. N. Y. Nation, April 15, 1880.
[2] Cf. ibid. for 1879, pp. 12, 70; ibid. for 1880, vol. i, pp. 11–3, 94–5; ibid. for 1881, vol. ii, pp. 17–8; ibid. for 1883, vol. ii, p. 667; ibid. for 1884, vol. i, p. 26 and vol. ii, pp. 4–6.
[3] Ibid. for 1887, vol. ii, pp. 2–8; 24 U. S. Stat. at Large, p. 388.
[4] Report of Sec. of Int. for 1885, vol. ii, p. 7; cf. ibid. for 1887, vol. i, pp. 25–9; cf. N. Y. Nation, March 11, 1886.
[5] Report of Sec. of Int. for 1879, p. 70; cf. House Reports, 48th Cong. 2nd sess., no. 2247; T. J. Morgan, The Present Phase of the Indian Question, p. 7.
[6] Report of Sec. of Int. for 1887, vol. ii, p. 914.
[7] Ibid., p. 1046; F. E. Leupp, The Indian and His Problem, p. 34.

From education at the agencies in schools maintained by the government and by various religious societies,[1] the interest of those engaged in the improvement of the Indian passed to schools in proximity to the reservations and even, in a few notable cases, to institutions in the East which were adapted to the needs of the race. From the idea that the Indian might be taught to read and write in the English language came the rather general conviction that he should have industrial training. He should be taught farming processes, of course,—to be a farrier, a carpenter, a tinsmith, a baker or a tailor, to make boots and shoes and harness, to contrive and mend wagons. The girls should know how to cook, sew and perform the common domestic duties.

Again it was Schurz who made progress possible. In day schools on the reservations it was found that the children were not freed in the necessary degree of the influences from which it was the whole purpose, if possible, to emancipate them.[2] Therefore boarding schools were established at the agencies. Small—too small—sums were appropriated by Congress for the support of this work. Suitable buildings were few, the teaching was inefficient. In 1879 about 7,000 Indian children, excluding those of the "civilized tribes" in the Indian Territory, were enrolled. The number of Indian children of school-going age might be, it was supposed, 33,000,[3] an estimate later increased to 45,000 or 50,000.[4] In 1880 it was said that at only 15 of the 66 agencies had the government made adequate provision for education; at very few of the other 51 would the schools—boarding and day schools all taken together—accommodate fifty per cent of the children of the tribes.[5]

Clauses in the treaties definitely provided for education.[6] Children were pressing into the agencies asking for school accommodations, while Congress gave no more heed to this

[1] Cf. Report of Sec. of Int. for 1883, vol. ii, pp. 32, 298–302.
[2] Ibid. for 1880, vol. i, p. 7; ibid. for 1885, vol. ii, p. 112.
[3] Ibid. for 1878, p. 458; ibid. for 1879, p. 10.
[4] Ibid. for 1882, vol. i, p. 32.
[5] Ibid. for 1880, vol. i, p. 86.
[6] Cf. ibid. for 1883, vol. i, pp. ix–x; ibid. for 1884, vol. i, pp. vii–viii.

stipulation than to other pledges which the government had made with this sorely wronged race.[1] To have provided money for the establishment and support of Indian schools, as the commissioner of Indian Affairs pointed out, would have been no mark of generosity, merely "a tardy payment of an old debt." [2]

In 1878 the proposal that selected boys and girls should be brought to the East for instruction that would enable them, upon return to their homes, to become teachers and to serve as examples to their people, met the favor of the Department of the Interior, and it was determined to give the plan a trial under the enlightened direction of General Armstrong at the Hampton Normal and Agricultural Institute in Virginia, which had been founded primarily for the upbuilding of the negro, but which welcomed this opportunity to be useful in a related branch of social service.[3] The work of assembling the scholars was assigned to Captain R. H. Pratt, who had been detailed to duty in connection with certain refractory Indians transported to Florida at the instance of General Sheridan, and held as prisoners of war at St. Augustine. When these savages were released from custody by the government in May, 1878, largely through Pratt's influence in training them and reordering their lives,[4] he personally collected enough money from generous persons in the Northern states to place 17 or 18 of the number at Hampton,[5] and, with this act before the country as proof of the sincerity of his interest in the subject of Indian education, he was asked, when the occasion offered, in September, 1878, to visit the West with Mrs. Pratt and to fetch more youth to the same school.[6] While it had been said that parents would be disinclined to have their children go so far

[1] Report of Sec. of Int. for 1878, pp. 458–9; ibid. for 1881, vol. ii, p. 30; ibid. for 1882, vol. ii, pp. 33–4; ibid. for 1884, vol. ii, p. 683.
[2] Ibid. for 1882, vol. ii, pp. 33–4; ibid. for 1885, vol. ii, pp. 80–83; cf. ibid. for 1883, vol. ii, p. 667.
[3] Ibid. for 1878, p. iv; cf. ibid. for 1880, vol. i, pp. 304–7; House Reports, 46th Cong. 2nd sess., no. 752, p. 2; S. C. Armstrong, The Indian Question.
[4] R. H. Pratt, Drastic Facts, pp. 8–9.
[5] R. H. Pratt, Indians Chained and Unchained, p. 7.
[6] Report of Sec. of Int. for 1878, p. 473; F. G. Peabody, Education for Life, pp. 147–8.

away from them, Captain Pratt declared that he could have "gathered up" 3,000. He was limited to 50, choosing boys and girls in Dakota from 12 to 19 years of age whom he believed to be "good material" for the experiment,[1] which gave promise of being so successful that, in 1879, more Indians were brought on from the West to receive the advantages of training at Hampton. They at first were not too well pleased to be under the same roof with negroes. Nor did the negroes and their friends look with great favor on their association with "savages." This feeling vanished on both sides, however, under the influence of the zeal of General Armstrong[2] who made it one of Booker T. Washington's early tasks to act as "house father" to the young Indians.[3] Boys and girls "as wild as the chickens on the prairie" were being transformed into useful men and women,[4] a good work which was uninterrupted for many years.

But it was seen that the Indians must have their own training schools. The military barracks at Carlisle in southern Pennsylvania, no longer used by the War Department, were made over, at the request of Secretary of the Interior Schurz, to the Indian Bureau,[5] and no one seemed so likely to give the proposed undertaking intelligent management as Captain Pratt, who was again asked to visit the Indian agencies. He assembled 136 prospective pupils, three-fourths of them boys, and the school soon came to enjoy a national reputation.[6] Its sturdy young men appeared on the football fields of our principal Eastern colleges to be viewed curiously as specimens of the aboriginal American stock, and to come, in no long

[1] Report of Sec. of Int. for 1878, pp. 473, 669–71; F. G. Peabody, Education for Life, pp. 154–6; R. H. Pratt, Indians Chained and Unchained, pp. 8–9.

[2] R. H. Pratt, Indians Chained and Unchained, p. 9; Report of Sec. of Int. for 1879, p. 670; cf. ibid. for 1880, vol. i, p. 306; F. G. Peabody, Education for Life, pp. 148–9; B. T. Washington, Up from Slavery, pp. 97–9.

[3] B. T. Washington, Up from Slavery, pp. 97–9.

[4] F. G. Peabody, Education for Life, p. 157.

[5] R. H. Pratt, Indians Chained and Unchained, pp. 9–10.

[6] Cf. Report of Sec. of Int. for 1879, pp. 10–11, 73–4; ibid. for 1880, vol. i, pp. 300–03; House Reports, 46th Cong. 2nd sess., no. 752; House Reports, 47th Cong. 1st sess., no. 446.

time, to be sincerely respected by their adversaries for their athletic prowess. Already in 1880 Captain Pratt was exhibiting the handiwork of his pupils at a county fair.[1] Tin cups, shoes, harness and other products, even wagons, made at the school were shipped to the West for use at the agencies.[2] Those who had learned to set type were printing a school paper,[3] and the boys were marching to strains from their own brass band. Chiefs and headmen were brought from the reservations to see how it fared with their children and went home pleasantly impressed.[4] The Secretary of the Interior visited the school and expressed his warm approval of its work.[5] Captain Pratt's name came to be synonymous with Carlisle and with the cause of Indian education generally. When public grants were inadequate he appealed to philanthropic citizens, especially to the Quakers, for money and supplies to supplement the appropriations of the government. He persuaded families in the East to receive the pupils into their homes during the holidays. After their courses in school had ended, some were "planted out" for a time for bed, board and a low wage that they might become the better acquainted with civilized domestic life before they should return to their tribes.[6] Indian parents would soon be asked to leave their children in the East for five instead of three years.[7] In February, 1880, with an appropriation of $5,000 for the fiscal year, a similar school was opened, with 40 boys and girls, at Forest Grove, in Oregon, later removed to a site near Salem in the same state, for the advantage of the tribes settled on the Pacific coast and in Alaska.[8]

[1] Report of Sec. of Int. for 1880, vol. i, pp. 303–4.
[2] Ibid. for 1881, vol. ii, p. 27.
[3] Ibid. for 1880, vol. i, p. 302; R. H. Pratt, Indians Chained and Unchained, pp. 12–3.
[4] Report of Sec. of Int. for 1880, vol. i, pp. 9, 87.
[5] N. Y. Nation, June 29, 1882.
[6] Report of Sec. of Int. for 1880, vol. i, pp. 10, 87, 305; ibid. for 1882, vol. ii, pp. 28–9; ibid. for 1884, vol. ii, pp. 504–5; ibid. for 1887, vol. ii, pp. 15–6; R. H. Pratt, Indians Chained and Unchained, pp. 11–2, 13–4.
[7] Report of Sec. of Int. for 1882, vol. ii, p. 29.
[8] Ibid. for 1880, vol. i, pp. 8, 86, 300; ibid. for 1881, vol. ii, pp. 256–8. For progress of the work at Carlisle and similar schools see ibid. for 1882,

The development of the work thus far had been meagerly supported. The appropriation by Congress for Indian education had been only $60,000 in 1878, $75,000 in 1879, the same amount in 1880 and $85,000 in 1881. In 1881 the Secretary of the Interior was authorized to pay a salary not in excess of $1,000 annually to Captain Pratt, the first sum voted to him, though the school at Carlisle had been in operation under his management since November, 1879.[1] To make any progress recourse must be had to the so-called "civilization fund,"[2] which would be exhausted before the end of the fiscal year in June, 1882. Congress must act or the excellent schools which had been established by a few devoted persons would be compelled to close, and their pupils would be returned, perforce, to the reservations.[3]

Now that the American people were demanding "that Indians should become white men within one generation," the head of the Indian Bureau said in 1881, it was the more necessary that money should be provided for their education.[4] Secretary of the Interior Henry M. Teller, espoused the cause. In his first report, in 1882, he said that in the past ten years the cost of warfare upon the Indians and military protection against them on the frontier had been in excess of $223,000,-000. For subsisting them and keeping them from starvation the government spent $5,000,000 a year more. It were a better investment to lay out $5,000,000 or $6,000,000 annually to send the young to school where they might be made into peace-loving, self-supporting human beings.[5]

The commissioner of Indian Affairs in 1882 asked for a deficiency appropriation of $50,000 for that year, and for the next year, 1883, $150,000 for general Indian education, and $97,000 for use at Carlisle, Hampton and Forest Grove. To

vol. ii, pp. 237–50; ibid. for 1883, vol. ii, pp. 219–41, 670; ibid. for 1884, vol. ii, pp. 230–55; ibid. for 1885, vol. ii, pp. 114–8, 440–89; ibid. for 1887, vol. ii, pp. 316–53.

[1] Report of Sec. of Int. for 1885, vol. ii, p. 90.
[2] Cf. ibid. for 1882, vol. ii, p. 30; ibid. for 1885, vol. ii, pp. 79–80.
[3] Ibid. for 1881, vol. i, p. iv.
[4] Ibid. vol. ii, p. 27.
[5] Ibid. vol. i, pp. xiii–xvii.

his surprise Congress voted $300,000 for general education, $97,000 for use at the three manual training schools, $50,000 for two new schools of a similar type and $17,000 to support 100 Indian youth who should be placed in various existing white industrial schools in the states.[1] Public opinion had been awakened at last and there was recognition of the duty to give vocational and other instruction to the native American race.

Since at some schools notably good results were being obtained on the *per capita* contract system, money was provided for placing 200 children in Lincoln Institution, which had been established soon after the war to care for soldiers' orphans in Philadelphia.[2] The appointment of an inspector of Indian schools, the title of the office being changed in the following year to superintendent, was authorized, with promise of increased efficiency of administration,[3] though he was possessed of little executive power until further legislation was secured in 1888.[4]

There were those who declared that it was much trouble and great outlay of money for little gain, since the students, upon returning to their homes, relapsed into barbarous life.[5] They could not rise above their old surroundings. As a matter of fact many became practical missionaries for the social improvement of their families and their tribes. A movement so good was not to be arrested by unfortunate experiences in individual cases.

From the money appropriated by Congress in 1882 the Indian department was able to establish new trade schools at Genoa in Nebraska, on the old Pawnee reservation, and at

[1] Cf. Report of Sec. of Int. for 1884, vol. ii, p. 504.
[2] 18th Annual Report of the Lincoln Institution, 1884.
[3] Report of Sec. of Int. for 1882, vol. ii, pp. 30–31, 1011–28; ibid. for 1883, vol. ii, pp. 469–75; ibid. for 1885, vol. ii, pp. 90–92; Act of May 17, 1882, 22 U. S. Stat. at Large, p. 68.
[4] Report of Sec. of Int. for 1888, vol. i, p. xxxvii and vol. ii, pp. xxi–xxiii.
[5] Cf. ibid. for 1883, vol. ii, p. 102; ibid. for 1885, vol. i, pp. 782–3; ibid. for 1888, vol. ii, p. 722; House Reports, 46th Cong. 2nd sess., no. 1401, p. 4; House Reports, 49th Cong. 1st sess., no. 1076, p. xxi; Ten Years' Work for Indians at Hampton Institute, pp. 42 et seq.; Hampton Institute's Reply to a New Attack on Eastern Schools, 1890.

Chilocco in the Indian Territory, and to commence the construction of buildings for the Haskell Institute near Lawrence, Kansas—all opened for students in 1884,[1] and similar institutions were projected, with government aid, at Albuquerque in New Mexico for the Pueblos, Navajoes and Apaches, and at Grand Junction in Colorado for the Utes from the appropriations in 1884 and 1885.[2] Plainly the grants were still too small even with the supplementary gifts which General Armstrong, Captain Pratt and other men identified with Indian education were able to secure from individuals and charitable organizations.[3] In 1882 it was said that only 8,700 pupils could be crowded into all the school buildings which were available for use, and many of these were unfit for occupancy, especially during the winter months. Large numbers of Indian children were growing up in ignorance.[4] In 1887 14,000 were receiving instruction of some kind at schools supported entirely or in part by the government,[5] little more than a third of all who should be under this civilizing influence, and the philanthropists were pressing for larger grants.[6] The sum, General Fisk's board of Indian commissioners said, should be $2,000,000 in 1889, rising to $3,000,000 for 1890, $4,000,000 for 1891, and so on until all Indian children everywhere were provided with educational facilities suited to their needs.[7]

The disintegration of the tribal reservations and the absorption of the Indians by the general population under the Dawes land-in-severalty law was preparing the way for the creation of new states. Over the West strode giants who had prospered and who, like Abraham of old, were "very rich in cattle, in silver and in gold." Many more than two citizens in each ter-

---

[1] Cf. Report of Sec. of Int. for 1884, vol. i, p. lv; cf. ibid., vol. ii, pp. 14–5; ibid. for 1883, vol. ii, p. 27; House Ex. Doc., 48th Cong. 2nd sess., no. 38; House Reports, 49th Cong. 2nd sess., no. 1076, pp. x–xxii.

[2] Report of Sec. of Int. for 1885, vol. i, pp. 12–3 and vol. ii, pp. 106–7.

[3] For Hampton see Ten Years' Work for Indians at Hampton Institute, 1878–1888.

[4] Report of Sec. of Int. for 1883, vol. ii, p. 667.

[5] Ibid. for 1887, vol. ii, pp. 16, 757.

[6] Ibid., p. 919.

[7] Ibid. for 1888, vol. ii, p. 735. The appropriations are conveniently tabulated in T. J. Morgan, Indian Education, p. 19.

ritory looked forward to the day when they might descend
upon Washington with credentials which would give them
coveted places in the United States Senate. Moreover the
territorial system of government was ill suited to the people's
growing needs. Of law and public authority they had next
to none. "Road agents," mail robbers, cowboys and desperadoes of all descriptions roistered at will on the plains and in
the canyons of the truly "wild West" to meet restraint only
at the hands of the United States Army, stationed at places
so widely scattered that its power was little felt, and posses
of better disposed citizens who, as "Vigilantes," would resort
to the rude methods of the forces which, in the interest of
common safety, were to be repressed.

But the movement for statehood met with opposition in
many quarters. The failure of Nevada, which had been hastily
allowed to enter the Union during the war and which, in twenty
years, had furnished practically no reason for a recognition
so generous, was kept before the people.[1] It was pointed out
in a report to Congress that the creation of "immature" territories into states was unjust. To make a "petty community"
with undeveloped interests the political equal of the "grandest
commonwealth" in the Union was not less than "subvertive
of our system of government."[2]

The loudest demands came from Dakota where the people
were at a real disadvantage on the subject of government. The
territory was too large for the attainment of administrative
efficiency, especially since it was served by but one railroad
which crossed it in the north from east to west, while the capital remained at Yankton in the extreme southeast. It was
approximately 400 miles square, containing an area four times
that of the state of Ohio. The southeastern portion, which
was rapidly filling with settlers, was known as the "corn belt."
In the north, along the banks of the Red River, wheat was grown
on land which, the governor said, would yield more bushels
per acre of that grain of the best quality than any to be found

---

[1] N. Y. Nation, Jan. 28, 1886 and Jan. 5, 1888.
[2] House Reports, 47th Cong. 1st sess., no. 450, p. 6.

elsewhere on this continent.[1] In the west, in the Black Hills, another body of people were settled, drawn there by the recently discovered mines of gold and silver. Deadwood had supplanted Custer City. In this place, and in towns around it near the stamps, there was a more or less permanent population of 12,000 which was much increased by arrivals for sojourn during the summer months. It was 350 miles from Deadwood to Yankton—900 miles must be traversed over the most practicable route by a citizen in the Black Hills ere he could reach the capital of the territory for the transaction of public business. It cost that citizen more in money, and it consumed a greater time to make the journey than for a resident of Yankton to pass to the capital of the nation at Washington. To a letter dispatched from Deadwood to Yankton a reply could not be expected in less than ten days. It was, by an "air line," 400 miles from Yankton to Pembina in the northern part of Dakota, near the British line, but it was easier and cheaper to proceed from Yankton to Washington City.[2] The inhabited parts of the territory were rendered the more remote with reference to one another by the fact that the great Sioux reserve of 56,000 square miles lay athwart the way to prevent communication and settlement.

The interests, as well as the requirements, of these three sections, were so diverse that, in 1872, when Minnesota was developing at leaps and bounds, when the Northern Pacific Railroad was going west under the enterprising touch of Jay Cooke and the Red River country was being fast opened to settlement, a proposal appeared in Congress to create a separate territory which should be called Pembina. Men in and around the town bearing that name in the extreme northeastern part of the territory said that they must travel a distance of from 1,000 to 1,500 miles to reach Yankton, while judges and other officers, in connection with the performance of their duties in the north, found it equally difficult to pass in the opposite

---

[1] Report of Sec. of Int. for 1883, vol. ii, p. 518.
[2] Ibid. for 1878, p. 1097; Senate Reports, 45th Cong. 2nd sess., no. 110, p. 3.

direction.[1] The scheme was revived in 1881 when Congress
was rather confidently told that it was the "unanimous
wish" of the people of Dakota that the territory should be
divided, with a view to giving northern Dakota separate government.[2]

So, too, was it in the west. In 1878 it was suggested that
the Black Hills and the surrounding country in Dakota, together with parts of Montana and Wyoming, be embraced
in a new territory, with an area of about 108,000 square miles,
to be called the territory of Lincoln.[3] Indeed two new territories, to bear the names of Lincoln and Garfield, were in some
men's minds.[4]

Dakota was very truly undergoing rapid growth. New railroads had been built. Trains in 1884 were running on 2,475
miles, in 1887 on 4,200 miles of track. It was supposed in 1884
that the population was at least 400,000. In 1887 the wheat
crop was declared to have been not less than 40,000,000 bushels.
There were gleaned besides—oats, corn, barley and flax. The
governor said that Dakota was "the granary of the continent."[5]
Gold to the value of nearly $5,000,000 and silver worth $2,000,-
000 were shipped out of the Black Hills. On grazing lands
browsed herds of cattle and flocks of sheep. In the whole
territory, in 1878, there were no public buildings. Luna-
tics were sent to institutions in Minnesota and Nebraska,
convicts to a penitentiary in Detroit at so much expense for
transportation and subsistence, the governor told the Secretary of the Interior, that it absorbed almost all the public
revenue. Only by the building of a prison and an insane asylum,
said he, could the territory avoid "future bankruptcy."[6] But
in five years it had schools, colleges, universities, hospitals,

[1] Senate Reports, 43rd Cong. 1st sess., no. 195.
[2] Ibid., 46th Cong. 3rd sess., no. 864.
[3] Ibid., 45th Cong. 2nd sess., no. 110; Resources of the Black Hills,
a memorial to Congress printed by the Daily Deadwood Pioneer in
1878.
[4] House Mis. Doc., 47th Cong. 2nd sess., no. 45, pt. 4, p. 1180.
[5] Report of Sec. of Int. for 1884, vol. ii, p. 542; cf. ibid. for 1885, vol. ii,
p. 929.
[6] Ibid. for 1878, p. 1098.

penitentiaries and all kinds of necessary public institutions.[1] Its progress was "phenomenal." [2] The question of a more accessible site for the capital was solved by the tender of land, and a fund to erect public buildings upon it, in Bismarck, in the north, on the line of the Northern Pacific Railroad and the removal, in 1883, of the governor and the state offices to that place. This step was little calculated, however, to propitiate popular sentiment in the south and led naturally to an outburst of bitter sectional rivalry, followed by an appeal to the courts, and it tended rather to hasten the movement for a division of the territory. It was suggested that two states be formed, one north and the other south of the 46th parallel, each portion retaining "the famous name of Dakota" with a designating prefix.[3] Now and again the proposal to cut off the section containing the Black Hills mining districts was renewed; it should have territorial organization in preparation for admission to the Union at some later day.[4] Rival constitutional conventions, mass meetings, referenda, angry discussion on the platform and in the columns of the newspapers, which was extended to Congress, where the diverse projects had their advocates, reverberated through the land.[5]

The proposed state south of the 46th parallel, it was said in 1884, would have a population of 270,000 and that one north of this line 130,000. Each would have an area of 75,000 square miles; each would, therefore, be nearly twice as large as New York or Pennsylvania.[6] Judged by either one standard or the other—by the number of their inhabitants or by their

---

[1] Report of Sec. of Int. for 1883, vol. ii, pp. 520–21, 522–3; cf. ibid. for 1885, vol. ii, p. 937; App. Ann. Cyclop. for 1884, p. 241.

[2] Ibid. for 1883, vol. ii, p. 517.

[3] Ibid. for 1881, vol. ii, p. 964; cf. House Reports, 47th Cong. 1st sess., no. 450; Senate Reports, 47th Cong. 1st sess., no. 271; House Reports, 49th Cong. 1st sess., no. 2577.

[4] Report of Sec. of Int. for 1881, vol. ii, p. 964; cf. House Reports, 49th Cong. 1st sess., no. 2578.

[5] Cf. House Reports, 49th Cong. 1st sess., nos. 2578, 2580, 2779; House Mis. Doc., 50th Cong. 2nd sess., no. 39; Senate Reports, 50th Cong. 1st sess., no. 75; House Reports, 50th Cong. 1st sess., no. 1025, pp. 8–9, 28–39; House Mis. Doc., 47th Cong. 2nd sess., no. 45, pt. 4, pp. 1184–6.

[6] Report of Sec. of Int. for 1884, vol. ii, p. 541.

territorial extent—the two Dakotas were entitled to places in
that Federal community which the journalists called the "galaxy of states."[1]

West of Dakota lay Montana which, after the Indians were
brought within more restricted areas,[2] was a vastly rich region
for settlement. Its mines yielded the precious metals, copper
and coal. Its grasses fed cattle and sheep. Its beef, its mutton,
its wool clip drew to, and within, its boundaries a growing population. In 1883 the governor said that the territory had 80,-
000 inhabitants—the number had doubled in three years.[3]
There were 100,000 in 1885.[4] They traveled east or west over
Villard's new railroad. These people, though many had just
come to dwell in the valleys and on the plains and mountain
slopes of this northern land, coveted state government and
Federal relationships, equal to those enjoyed by the inhabitants
of older American communities.[5]

Still further west, under the British line, also in the belt
served by the new Northern Pacific Railroad, washed by the
ocean that stretched away to Asia, was Washington territory.
It had its mines and its ranches—more than this it had rivers
stocked with fish, well watered valleys in which cereals and
fruits would grow luxuriantly, forests of tall firs and other
trees for the lumber trade and for shipbuilding, coal deposits
which caused men to describe it as the "Pennsylvania of the
Pacific coast,"[6] and signally fine harbors for ships from the
seven seas, inviting the people to trade with all the world.[7]
In 1885 the governor said that there were 175,000 persons
settled in this territory.[8] They were "beseeching" Congress

[1] Cf. Report of Sec. of Int. for 1885, vol. ii, pp. 936–7.
[2] Cf. ibid., p. 1000.
[3] Ibid. for 1883, vol. ii, p. 541.
[4] Ibid. for 1885, vol. ii, p. 997.
[5] Cf. ibid. for 1883, vol. ii, p. 550; ibid. for 1884, vol. ii, p. 563; House
Reports, 49th Cong. 2nd sess., no. 3689, pp. 5–9; Senate Reports, 50th
Cong. 1st sess., no. 733; House Reports, 50th Cong. 1st sess., no. 1025,
pp. 9–11.
[6] Report of Sec. of Int. for 1885, vol. ii, p. 1065; App. Ann. Cyclop. for
1885, p. 780.
[7] Cf. House Reports, 47th Cong. 1st sess., no. 690, p. 2.
[8] Report of Sec. of Int. for 1885, vol. ii, p. 1046.

for admission to the Union. The House Committee on Territories recommended such a step as early as in 1882.[1] It could be no long time before the voices of the people of Washington were heard and they should become citizens of a "sovereign commonwealth."

Idaho had no seaboard and it was but little assisted in its progress by railroads. Much of its soil was infertile for want of a properly distributed rainfall and the tillage of large tracts waited upon the construction of canals and the development of other schemes of irrigation, which already claimed the attention of the people.[2] Such inconvenience in the matter of communication from place to place was suffered by the citizens of no other political jurisdiction in America. The narrow upper portion, sometimes called the "Pan Handle," was geographically entirely apart from the larger southern portion of the territory, and proposals were made, with the favor of the inhabitants, for its detachment from Idaho and its annexation by Washington, to which it "naturally" belonged.[3] The members of the legislature for one county in traveling to Boisé City, the capital, though the distance in a direct way would have been only 160 miles, collected "mileage" for 1,124 miles in each direction. In making the journey they were compelled to pass into three other territories—Montana, Wyoming and Utah. Another group of territorial lawmakers, when the legislative session called them from their homes, situated 130 miles from the capital, must traverse a distance of 610 miles.[4]

Freight carriage, without railroads, was even costlier than

---

[1] House Reports, 47th Cong. 1st sess., no. 690, p. 2; House Reports, 49th Cong. 2nd sess., no. 3689, pp. 1–5; Senate Mis. Doc., 49th Cong. 1st sess., no. 39; House Reports, 50th Cong. 1st sess., no. 1025; pp. 11–2; Senate Reports, 49th Cong. 1st sess., no. 61; House Reports, 49th Cong. 1st sess., no. 216; Senate Reports, 50th Cong. 1st sess., no. 585; Senate Mis. Doc., 50th Cong. 2nd sess., no. 55; House Mis. Doc., 47th Cong. 2nd sess., no. 45, pt. 4, p. 1184.

[2] Report of Sec. of Int. for 1884, vol. ii, pp. 550–51; ibid. for 1885, vol. ii, pp. 981–2, 991–3.

[3] House Reports, 49th Cong. 1st sess., no. 216; Senate Reports, 50th Cong. 1st sess., no. 585; House Reports, 50th Cong. 1st sess., no. 1182; N. Y. Nation, Dec. 9, 1886.

[4] Report of Sec. of Int. for 1878, p. 1104.

passenger transportation, and economic development was slow.
But the governor in 1884 spoke of the "boundless deposits
of mineral wealth" in Idaho.[1] He said that the value of the
output of the mines in a year was $7,000,000, and that no less
than $10,000,000 were invested by ranchmen in the "growing"
of cattle and sheep.[2]

Wyoming, within whose rectangular lines 100,000 square
miles of mountain and plateau were found, was kept from progress, like Idaho, by its inaccessibility as a place of settlement.
It was wanting in navigable water courses. Except for a belt
near its southern boundary, which was served by the first
Pacific railroad on its way from Omaha to San Francisco,
the territory was without communication with the rest of the
Union. It was said, in 1883, that its population was but 35,-
000, though it was known to contain coal, as well as the precious
metals, and flowing petroleum, the herald of untold wealth,
which was to come to many of the Western states and territories
from this source.[3] Hardy spirits pressed north into lands which
had known no white man and, driving cattle and sheep before them, "found nutritious grasses in the desert." In 1883
it was said that live stock roamed in every valley and drank
from every stream in the territory.[4] At a Mining and Industrial Exposition in Denver in 1882 Wyoming made a display
of its resources which attracted wide attention. Three years
later, in 1885, the population, the governor declared, was
65,000.[5] The Wyoming Stock Growers' Association said that its
membership had increased from ten men who owned 20,000
head of cattle valued at $350,000 in 1873, when it was organ-
ized, to 435 men, with 2,000,000 head, valued at $100,000,000,
in 1885. In addition the territory pastured 1,000,000 sheep.[6]

While law was but a poor thing in the north, and the
rude society developed in communities enforced its will as

---

[1] Report of Sec. of Int. for 1884, vol. ii, p. 547.
[2] Ibid. p. 550; cf. ibid. for 1885, vol. ii, pp. 984–6, 993–4.
[3] Ibid. for 1885, vol. ii, pp. 1158–61.
[4] Ibid. for 1883, vol. ii, p. 576.
[5] Ibid. for 1885, vol. ii, p. 1175.
[6] Nimmo, op. cit., p. 100; Report of Sec. of Int. for 1885, vol. ii, pp. 1181,
1186; cf. also Senate Reports, 50th Cong. 2nd sess., no. 2695.

pleased its fancy and convenience, even worse conditions prevailed in the south. New Mexico and Arizona had come out of old Mexico and adjoined that country, where order had little fame. Its desperadoes crossed our border, ours returned. So wide a playground for thieves and cutthroats, with so little certainty of retributive justice at the hand of competent established authority it were difficult to find elsewhere.[1] To these infamous elements were added bands of Apache Indians, so that settlement in either of the two southern territories went forward slowly. Both were of immense extent. Both were dry except in the valleys and must be watered by ditches before vegetation would prosper and crops could be harvested. Both had mineral deposits of unknown value—gold and silver, copper and lead. Three-fourths of the people in New Mexico spoke Spanish or its dialects, though the use of English was extending. In 1884 it was said that there were a million head of cattle and as many sheep on the ranches. The population was estimated to be 135,000, but it was in large degree a body of unenterprising, native people, with a high rate of illiteracy, under whose influence no notable advancement proceeded, and an obsolete land system, confused by old Spanish and Mexican grants, forbade the coming in of new settlers.[2] Nevertheless New Mexico's claims upon Congress for admission as a state were frequently considered with favor. Once a bill had been passed by both houses, and the territory seemed to be on the point of entering the Union with Colorado, but amendments called for further consideration, and adjournment came before they were adopted.[3] "Enabling acts" at later times made their way through one or the other chamber of the Federal legislature.[4]

Progress in Arizona was even slower than in New Mexico, but new mines were found and the zest for obtaining riches

[1] Cf. Report of Sec. of Int. for 1881, vol. i, pp. xliv–xlv.
[2] N. Y. Nation, Jan. 28, 1886.
[3] Cf. ibid. and ibid., Jan. 6, 1887.
[4] Cf. Senate Reports, 44th Cong. 1st sess., no. 69; House Reports, 43rd Cong. 1st sess., no. 561; House Reports, 44th Cong. 1st sess., no. 503; House Reports, 50th Cong. 1st sess., no. 1025, pp. 13–7; McPherson's Handbook of Politics for 1874, p. 220.

overnight induced much immigration and settlement. A place called Tombstone, which two years before was a piece of barren ground, had come in 1881 to have 7,000 inhabitants, though it was the center of such "violence and anarchy" as to induce the governor to call upon President Arthur for assistance in maintaining the peace.[1] It was destined to be, so men said, "one of the greatest mining camps ever discovered."[2]

The railroads from the east and from the west which were being joined to put Arizona and New Mexico on the trunk lines from California to Texas and New Orleans, and to Kansas City and St. Louis, with spurs, as the need arose, insured these territories a growth, which, as time passed, would make them successful suppliants for admission to places in the Union.

Utah was in very different case. It was the misfortune of this territory to include within its borders the settlements of a band of polygamous fanatics, the "Latter Day Saints of Jesus Christ," who, leaving the East, which could not countenance them and their works, had sought sanctuary among the savages and the beasts beyond the confines of civilization, which had now caught up with them.[3] Though their religion rested on a book whose leading characteristics, as an English visitor to Salt Lake said, were "blasphemy, rubbish and bad grammar,"[4] the Mormons had proven themselves, in some regards, an exemplary people. They were orderly and thrifty.[5] Their morals shamed the world, but they could point to the mining camps, to the "end-of-the-rail" towns, the murder unpunished except by new murder, the robbery and crime and vice of every kind which flourished on the fringe of the Christian civilization and wonder, indeed, as to the propriety of our presuming to act as their censors.[6] Men there were, be-

---

[1] House Ex. Doc., 47th Cong. 1st sess., nos. 58 and 188; Richardson, vol. viii, pp. 53–4, 101–2.

[2] Report of Sec. of Int. for 1883, vol. ii, pp. 505 et seq.

[3] Cf. ibid. for 1883, vol. ii, p. 630; House Mis. Doc., 48th Cong. 1st sess., no. 45, pp. 1–2.

[4] W. G. Marshall, Through America, p. 157.

[5] Cf. N. Y. Nation, Jan. 17, 1884; Phil Robinson, Sinners and Saints, p. 71.

[6] Phil Robinson, op. cit., pp. 72–3.

ginning with Lamech in the fourth chapter of Genesis, some of them well spoken of in the Scriptural writings, who had possessed a number of wives. It were, perhaps, no more unreasonable, if it were more mischievous, to take the Bible apart and to connect marriage to two or several women with a religious system, than so to use the statement that the world had been made in six days, that the first man had then risen out of the dust of the ground by the *ipse dixit* of the Creator, and that the first woman had sprung from one of his ribs. The Mormons were married to their various wives and owned and supported their begotten children. "Jim" Fisk and a thousand men in New York lived in loose relationship with many women to whom they were not married. The contrasting pictures were again not so advantageous to our Christian social order as men who engaged in polemic on the question might have desired, but the discussion proceeded without any merit being ascribed to the Latter Day Saints. The young journalist, eager to dip his pen in gall, was unrestrained by his employer on the subject of the Mormons, seen sitting in the midst of their Asiatic seraglios, who were not to be feared by the owner of the newspaper either as potential subscribers for, or as advertisers in, his sheet. Except in Utah, on local matters, they had no votes with which to intimidate the seeker for elective office. The Mormon was a pariah in the land and every hand was against him.[1]

Plural wiving was assuredly a repellant practice for which there could be no defense—it was the more opprobious when the responsibility for it was, through revelation, made to rest with God. While polygamy was a target for the reformer, because it was a gross indignity to womanhood, and for the clergy, because it offended religious teaching, it did as much affront to right-thinking persons generally, who held it to be, as Carl Schurz once said, "in direct opposition to the moral sense of the people of the country," [2] and who understood that monogamous marriage was necessary to well ordered so-

---

[1] Cf. N. Y. Nation, Dec. 15, 1881 and Dec. 20, 1883.
[2] Report of Sec. of Int. for 1880, p. 80.

ciety, which must have its root in happy and successful family life.

The new Republican party in its national platform in 1856 had joined slavery and polygamy as "twin relics of barbarism." In 1876 the makers of the party platform reiterated their determination to prohibit and extirpate this "relic of barbarism" in the territories.[1] They said again, in 1880, that, "slavery having perished in the states, its twin barbarity, polygamy, must die in the territories."[2] Garfield, when he took the oath of office in 1881, declared conditions in Utah to be "a reproach to the government."[3] Blaine, in accepting the nomination for the Presidency in 1884, denounced the Mormon claim of "right to destroy the great safeguard and muniment of social order and to practise, as a religious privilege, that which is a crime, punished with severe penalty, in every state of the Union."[4]

The problem had been mishandled from the first day. When Utah had been formed into a territory in 1850 President Fillmore appointed Brigham Young, the greatest Mormon of them all, who accumulated enough wives to shame the most uxorious sultan of the East, as governor. He was reappointed to the office by President Pierce and occupied the position until 1857, all the while strengthening the hold of the church upon the government and making more difficult the future task of disentanglement.[5] During the war, in 1862, the Republican leaders in Congress who were aiming blows at slavery, remembered the other unholy "twin," and laid a penalty, consisting of a fine of not more than $500 and imprisonment not in excess of five years, upon the man in a territory of the United States who, having one wife, should marry another.[6] The common law prior to that time had prohibited plural marriage.[7] Now it was condemned and was particularly named in a

[1] McPherson's Handbook for 1876, p. 211.
[2] Ibid. for 1880, p. 190.
[3] Richardson, Messages and Papers, vol. viii, p. 11.
[4] McPherson's Handbook for 1884, p. 205.
[5] House Reports, 48th Cong. 1st sess., no. 1351, p. 2; Report of Sec. of Int. for 1887, vol. ii, p. 1326; cf. ibid. for 1883, vol. ii, pp. 499, 628-9.
[6] Report of Sec. of Int. for 1883, vol, ii, pp. 499, 632-3.
[7] Ibid. for 1885, vol. ii, p. 1023; ibid. for 1887, vol. ii, p. 1327.

Federal statute. The Mormons who took any note of the enactment declared it to be unconstitutional, though, when a case came to the Supreme Court of the United States, calling for a judgment, they were differently advised.[1] They were undisturbed by this opinion for they had a "higher law," and they were safe from pursuit because Young, while he had been governor, had so organized the territory that such Federal officers as were in service in Utah were powerless to proceed with any practical system of enforcement.[2] In 1874 Congress, in the so-called "Poland law," aimed to strengthen the territorial courts for the transaction of criminal business, but, because of hampering restrictions in the local statutes, particularly in the matter of jury service, for which Mormons could still qualify,[3] there had been only three convictions under the act of 1862 in twenty years.[4]

The Mormons, in spite of their polygamy, had done little harm to other men so long as they isolated themselves by the Great Salt Lake, and they were separated from the rest of the country by days of travel behind plodding oxen. Utah was rich in mineral deposits; the output of the mines had a value of not less than $6,000,000 yearly,[5] but the people, under advice of the heads of the church, confined themselves to farming, grazing and local trade. Recruits were usually drawn from the ignorant classes of Europe through the efforts of agents who offensively confused religious proselytizing with their colonization schemes. Mormon immigrants were constantly coming to New York[6] and going through to the plains. Three-fourths of the inhabitants of Utah, it was said, were foreign-born, or of foreign-born parentage.[7]

[1] Reynolds v. United States, 8 Otto, pp. 161–7; cf. Report of Sec. of Int. for 1883, vol. ii, p. 502.

[2] Report of Sec. of Int. for 1883, vol. ii, pp. 633–5; ibid. for 1887, vol. ii, p. 1328; House Reports, 48th Cong. 1st sess., no. 1351, p. 2.

[3] Report of Sec. of Int. for 1885, vol. ii, p. 1030; ibid. for 1887, vol. ii, pp. 1326–7, 1328.

[4] Ibid. for 1883, vol. ii, p. 499.

[5] Ibid. for 1880, vol. i, p. 74.

[6] On one day, in the summer of 1883, 674 arrived.—N. Y. Nation, July 5, 1883.

[7] Report of Sec. of Int. for 1878, pp. 1115–7; N. Y. Nation, Dec. 20, 1883.

Before the Pacific railroad was built few Gentiles took up their abode in the territory. In 1878 non-Mormons were believed to constitute but a tenth part of the population,[1] a proportion which was increased with the development of the mines in the 80's to a sixth, or, perhaps, a fourth.[2] While they were undisturbed in their pursuits, barring the remark which frequently came to their ears that they were "outsiders," or, indeed, "cursed outsiders," [3] and a general indisposition to trade with them,[4] they were overborne by thê influences around them, which entirely controlled the local governments, except in a few mining communities, and the territorial legislature, subject of course to such a brake as could be put upon the wheel by the governor appointed from Washington,[5] and by the judicial system, also a Federal establishment.

In 1880 the population of the territory was about 145,000. Two years later it was supposed to be 150,000, and in 1887 it was, probably, 200,000.[6] The Gentiles, many of whom were associated with large new industrial enterprises, were paying one-third of the taxes in the territory.[7] While their number and their interest in the conduct of public affairs increased the Mormons, at the same time, were extending their influence and power. Four temples had been built, or were in process of construction, in Utah. Upon that one in Salt Lake, begun thirty years ago, two millions of dollars had been spent. In 1884 a new one had been opened with public ceremonies at Logan, in the northern part of the territory.[8] The prosperity of the church itself, which was wealthy, and of its directing heads, many of whom were canny and able,[9] grew with the

[1] Report of Sec. of Int. for 1878, p. 1116.
[2] Ibid. for 1882, vol. ii, p. 1003; ibid. for 1887, vol. i, p. 916; House Reports, 48th Cong. 1st sess., no. 1351, p. 1.
[3] Report of Sec. of Int. for 1887, vol. ii, p. 1324.
[4] Ibid., vol. i, p. 919; House Ex. Doc., 48th Cong. 1st sess., no. 153, p. 4.
[5] Cf. House Mis. Doc., 49th Cong. 1st sess., no. 238; Handbook of Mormonism quoting Judge McBride in International Review, pp. 92-3.
[6] Cf. House Reports, 49th Cong. 1st sess., no. 2568, p. 6; House Mis. Doc., 50th Cong. 1st sess., no. 104, p. 2.
[7] Report of Sec. of Int. for 1887, vol. ii, p. 1323; cf. ibid. for 1885, vol. ii, p. 1023.
[8] Ibid. for 1884, vol. ii, p. 518.   [9] Ibid. for 1886, vol. ii, p. 1066.

development of the country around them.[1] They found lucrative markets for their products in the active non-Mormon mining settlements. Tourists left money among them. Under such conditions polygamy exhibited a tendency to increase. At any time it was only for the well-to-do and for those who were, in their own sight, if they were not generally regarded as, holier than other men,[2] the poor being deterred from multiplying their domestic obligations for prudential reasons.

Time and the railroads, it had been said in the East, would solve the ugly question, and relieve Congress of responsibilities ,which it would have been glad to escape.[3] The issue might better have been faced at once. Twenty-five years had passed since the Republican party had linked polygamy with slavery, yet the evil continued to flourish more offensively and arrogantly than ever before, and in a territory (rather than a state) which, as all men knew, stood under the absolute control of the Federal government. Now that non-Mormon settlement was advancing and the colony exhibited a tendency to spread into Idaho,[4] Arizona [5] and the surrounding country,[6] and the prospect of making Utah into a state, with senators and representatives in Congress, was entertained, the time for action was seen to be at hand. If Congress, representing some tens of millions of people who fairly regarded polygamous relationships as a vice, were not to see their authority flouted by a preposterous little sect of religionists new measures must be devised. It is often said, and it may be a fact, that but for the active enlistment of some determined women in the work there would have been further delay. Because of the degradation which they were suffering as a sex under polygamy, enforced by some notorious instances of the deception

[1] Cf. Report of Sec. of Int. for 1887, vol. ii, pp. 1320–21.
[2] Cf. ibid. for 1885, vol. ii, p. 1038; North American Review, Jan., 1884, p. 5.
[3] Report of Sec. of Int. for 1883, vol. ii, p. 627.
[4] The governor of Idaho said that "the apostles of lechery" who had swarmed through the passes of southern Idaho with their "faith of filth" were imperiling the "commonwealth."—Ibid. for 1884, vol. ii, p. 553.
[5] Cf. App. Ann. Cyclop. for 1885, p. 43.
[6] North American Review for March, 1881.

used by the Mormons in enticing girls into their church for
marriage, a Women's Anti-Polygamy Society was formed, as
a result of a mass meeting held in Salt Lake in 1878, and
the activities of this band of faithful persons spread the truth
over the country and, indeed, over the civilized world.[1]

Many schemes were in the air—the withdrawal from Utah
of popular government through a legislature and its treatment as "a hostile dependency," [2] the partition of the territory
and the addition of its parts to the state of Colorado and to
neighboring territories,[3] even military occupation and the application of force through the army.[4] In Utah itself the non-
Mormons asked for government by a commission, the members of which should be drawn from their ranks.[5]

A bill which bore the name of Senator Edmunds of Vermont was passed by Congress and was approved by President
Arthur on March 22, 1882.[6] Its principal object was the capture of the government of Utah from the Mormons and the
punishment of some of the principal apostles, high priests,
bishops, elders, the "Lord's anointed," [7] or whatever they
might be called. The law of 1862 having declared it to be unlawful for a man already married to take another wife, was being
evaded by "simultaneous nuptials"; a Mormon would marry
several women at the same time by one inclusive ceremony.
The "Edmunds act" would bring this trickery to an end;
it prescribed punishment for "unlawful cohabitation." The
"saint" who lived with more than one woman would be subject
to a fine of $300 and imprisonment for six months, and hence-
forward there would be no escape for him except through failure
of the prosecuting and enforcement officers. In order to reform the local and territorial governments, the initial step
toward which would be a new territorial legislature, as well

[1] Cf. Handbook of Mormonism, pp. 65-6, 86-7.
[2] N. Y. Nation, Dec. 13, 1883 and Jan. 17, 1884.
[3] Ibid., Jan. 12, 1882.
[4] Ibid., Feb. 9, 1882.
[5] Handbook of Mormonism, pp. 87, 95; Governor Murray in North
American Review, April, 1882.
[6] 22 U. S. Stat. at Large, pp. 30-32.
[7] Cf. House Mis. Doc., 42nd Cong. 2nd sess., no. 208, p. 66.

as to penalize and discipline the polygamists, "all registration and election offices of every description" were declared vacant. New officers would be appointed by a Federal commission of five members; it would be their duty to supervise the election of a new legislative assembly, which, it was hoped and presumed, would enact such laws as would make a continuance of Federal intervention unnecessary. No man who was a polygamist, no woman (for women exercised the franchise in Utah to increase the Mormon power),[1] if she were living in polygamous relations, should vote in the future, or should be eligible to election or appointment to public office of any kind in the territory, or "under the United States." In a word political rights were withdrawn from Mormons who should refuse to renounce a practice so odious to the sense of the civilized world.[2] A "stigma" would be made to rest upon the polygamist, and, if the old could not be reformed, a "young Utah," ambitious and aspiring, not content to rest under such proscription, would, it was believed, emerge.[3]

The commission was assembled for organization at Chicago on July 17, 1882, and adjourned to meet in Omaha, after which it would proceed to Salt Lake City where the members arrived on the 18th of August. They would prepare at once for the election of a delegate in Congress in the ensuing November.[4] In consequence of their activities some 12,000 persons were deprived of the suffrage, and the commission had like success in excluding polygamists from the polls at the general election in August, 1883, for the choice of members of the legislative assembly and other territorial as well as local officers.[5] But it was very clear that the Mormon monogamists were at one, in doctrine and belief, with the polygamists, that the Mormon women had no quarrel with the Mormon men—all

[1] Cf. House Reports, 45th Cong. 2nd sess., no. 949, p. 2. Utah had woman suffrage so that the priests could "vote their submissive harems."—House Reports, 48th Cong. 1st sess., no. 1351, pt. 2, p. 54.

[2] Report of Sec. of Int. for 1883, vol. ii, p. 500.

[3] Ibid., vol. ii, pp. 501, 502; cf. views of Bishop Tuttle in House Ex. Doc., 48th Cong. 1st sess., no. 153, pp. 2–3.

[4] Report of Sec. of Int. for 1882, vol. ii, p. 1003.

[5] Ibid. for 1883, vol. i, pp. xlviii–xlix; ibid., vol. ii, p. 501.

together were under the complete influence of the priests. While three-fourths of the Mormons were actually living monogamously all seemed to entertain a conviction that polygamy, at least for the heads of the church, was an ordinance of God.[1] National questions which elsewhere divided men as Republicans and Democrats had remained of almost no interest to the inhabitants of Utah. The "saints" were associated in what was called the "People's party," while the "Gentiles" were known as "Liberals." The only issue was whether the Mormons or the Gentiles should control local affairs. Everywhere the "People's party" was overwhelmingly victorious. Officers of town and county governments, barring a few in the mountains, where the mining population dwelt, all the members of the legislative assembly in both branches, though they, in so far as it could be ascertained, were monogamists in practice, as the Federal statute required, were Mormons who subscribed to the doctrine of polygamous marriage as a Divine revelation.[2] The hope, if any entertained it, that the legislature would repeal old laws and enact new ones, expressive of a determination to bring the social system into conformity with that of the rest of the country, was vain.[3]

The legislative assembly instead prepared and forwarded "memorials" to Congress, reciting how the Mormons had trekked over the continent, living on wild roots and thistle tops, how they had redeemed the desert, how they had been persecuted from the first day unto this one, and reducing all their ills to sectarian animosity.[4] They protested against the governor's exercise of the veto power as a scheme to deprive the people of "every vestige of local self-government."[5] A small minority, the Gentiles, were involved in a "deep laid conspiracy" to wrest political control of the territory from a "large majority of its citizens," and were striving "to preju-

[1] Report of Sec. of Int. for 1884, vol. ii, p. 518; ibid. for 1885, vol. ii, p. 885.
[2] Ibid. for 1883, vol. ii, p. 503.
[3] House Ex. Doc., 48th Cong. 1st sess., no. 153, pp. 1, 5; House Reports, 48th Cong. 1st sess., no. 135, pt. 2, p. 53.
[4] House Mis. Doc., 48th Cong. 1st sess., no. 45.
[5] Ibid., 49th Cong. 1st sess., no. 238, p. 2.

dice the government and people of the United States against
Utah and its people." [1] The governor was denounced in a
"memorial" to Congress for his "atrocious falsehoods," "attempted usurpations" and "insolent messages," by which he
sought "to provoke a conflict between the people and the
Federal authority." [2] The Utah Commission was "cumber-
some, useless and expensive"; it should be abolished. [3]

The popular attitude, too, was hostile and defiant. [4] No
less than ten suits were begun by Mormons, complaining that
they had been unjustly deprived of the right to vote; [5] they
would see what religious freedom meant in the United States.
No threats availed. Warrants were issued and officers put
under arrest some of the principal patriarchs of Salt Lake
in proof that the government was in earnest, and that it would
imprison as well as disfranchise. Mormons for jury duty were
successfully challenged and the work of the courts proceeded. [6]
A man named Clawson, the son of a bishop, found guilty, was
fined $800 and sent to the penitentiary for four years. Another
named Evans was fined $250 and given a prison sentence of
three and a half years. Clawson's father, the bishop himself,
was jailed for six months and fined $300 for "unlawful co-
habitation." The "saints" were allowed to make speeches
to the court about their "celestial marriage." They might
regret that the laws of their country were in conflict with "the
laws of God," young Clawson said, but, whenever it was so,
he would "invariably" choose obedience to the laws of God.
The "Edmunds act" was "unconstitutional"; being so it
"could not command the same respect that a constitutional
law would." [7] There were only two courses for another polyg-

---

[1] House Mis. Doc., 49th Cong. 1st sess., no. 238, p. 1:
[2] Ibid., p. 2.
[3] Ibid., p. 6.
[4] Cf. Report of Sec. of Int. for 1883, vol. ii, p. 629.
[5] Ibid., p. 504; ibid. for 1885, vol. ii, p. 886. For cases reaching the Supreme Court, see 114 U. S., p. 15.
[6] Cf. Report of Sec. of Int. for 1884, vol. ii, p. 519; ibid. for 1887, vol. ii,
pp. 1326–7.
[7] Ibid. for 1884, vol. ii, p. 520. Affirmed as constitutional in Cannon v.
U. S., 116 U. S., p. 55; Mormon Church v. U. S., 136 U. S., p. 1.

amist who had got his head into the noose of the law, he said—
one was "prison and honor" and the other "liberty and dishonor." [1] John Nicholson had had families by numerous wives
beginning so long since as in 1871. He was in "excellent company," which included Moses. His purpose was "fixed and
unalterable." "I shall," he said, "stand by my allegiance to
God, fidelity to my family and what I conceive to be the Constitution of my country." [2]

The "First Presidency," the highest governing power of the
"polygamic empire" [3] set in the old "American desert," issued an "Epistle" to the "brethren and sisters." While acts,
they said, of "the most sickening depravity," the "most flagrant sexual crimes," among the non-Mormon population, were
matters of daily record in the newspapers, such sin, which
was spreading "with unblushing front through the land," went
unpunished. Enemies might well first cast the beam out of
their own eyes. They were "hypocrites." They could purge
and regenerate their own people, whose course of conduct so
loudly called for reform, instead of seeking "to destroy society in these mountains" by invading the quiet homes of
pious men and throwing unoffending followers of God into
the penitentiary to share the lot of thieves and murderers.
To "true saints" abuse and imprisonment were not "causes
of sorrow," but rather of "rejoicing." They must not yield
to an "oppressive and tyrannical government," if they were
to enjoy the "great hereafter" in the presence of "the son of
God, our Redeemer," of the prophets and apostles, of the
holy men and women of the ages, all of whom had suffered and
endured on this earth. It must be remembered that Jesus
Christ was "crucified between two thieves," to satisfy "Jewish
law." Upwards of 40 years had passed since God had "revealed" to the Latter Day Saints "celestial marriage." The
idea of a number of wives had been "naturally abhorrent"

---

[1] Report of Sec. of Int. for 1885, vol. ii, p. 1019.
[2] Ibid., p. 1021.
[3] For an account of the government of the church, see report of Utah
Commission in Report of Sec. of Int. for 1887, vol. ii, pp. 1318–22.

to the leading men of the church, but this "new and everlasting covenant" was before them "in language which no faithful soul dare disobey." Thousands had lived and died testifying that the command was "divine." They had made the "great sacrifice" in order to gain everlasting life. No one could have supposed that in a land of religious liberty a "counter law" would be passed and enforced. The "saints" had petitioned the President for a "redress of grievances." They had asked Mr. Cleveland to appoint a commission of inquiry. It was reasonable to expect that he would hear their plea. They waited. He had yet made no answer; if he should not do so, all they could say was that which the Lord had said, "Father, forgive them; they know not what they do."[1]

Nine polygamists were convicted in the year ending June 30, 1885, and 84 in the following year. Before pronouncing sentence freedom was proffered the men if they would promise the court that, upon release, they would obey the laws.[2] Only a very few were willing to do so and those who so pledged themselves went back to their homes to suffer the obloquy of the community.[3] A new governor who arrived at Salt Lake in 1886 visited the penitentiary—old brick houses surrounded by crumbling adobe walls entirely inadequate for the use, since the Mormon legislature would appropriate no money for its reconstruction or enlargement[4]— and proposed to those who were confined there that, if they would display penitence and put away their superfluous women, he would go to President Cleveland and endeavor to procure them pardons. All signed a paper declining the favor.[5] Those whose sentences had ended, when they issued from their prisons, received public welcomes from their friends.[6] All were "martyrs for religious

---

[1] Report of Sec. of Int. for 1885, vol. ii, pp. 1031–40. This Epistle was issued on October 6, 1885.
[2] Ibid. for 1885, vol. ii, p. 888.
[3] Ibid. for 1887, vol. ii, p. 1329; cf. ibid. for 1885, vol. ii, pp. 886–7.
[4] Ibid. for 1885, vol. ii, p. 1030; House Ex. Doc., 50th Cong. 1st sess., no. 224.
[5] Report of Sec. of Int. for 1886, vol. ii, p. 999; Senate Mis. Doc., 50th Cong. 1st sess., no. 201, p. 15.
[6] Report of Sec. of Int. for 1887, vol. i, p. 1330.

truth," and "patriots" who were suffering "in defense of the principle of religious liberty." [1]

It was said in Utah, and it was very plain, that the "saints" were still contracting bigamous and polygamous marriages, though they were acting stealthily, especially in Salt Lake City. The old apostles of the church were no longer seen in the streets, at the theaters and in public places with their women around them. [2] But in the interior, at the temples of Logan, a city in the extreme north, [3] and of St. George, in the extreme southern part of the territory, where they were under less observation, the "unusual condition of society" [4] prevailed as openly as before the enactment of the "Edmunds law." [5] Mormons, monogamists perhaps in their manner of life, but polygamists in their sympathies, still continued to occupy nearly all the offices and to administer the local and territorial governments. [6] All together were doing everything that was possible, at every opportunity, to thwart the Federal government and prevent the assertion of its authority. [7] Though they were a people usually little given to violent speech or action [8] they now often called the Gentiles around them "conspirators and adventurers." It had been a mistake to allow such intruders to gain a "foothold" in Zion. [9] No hope of acquiescence in the law or of reformation in the matter of marriage was to be found in any pronunciamento of the leaders. [10] The principal Mormon paper, the Deseret News, in Salt Lake

---

[1] Report of Sec. of Int. for 1885, vol. ii, p. 1037.

[2] Ibid. for 1887, vol. ii, p. 1329.

[3] Phil Robinson, Sinners and Saints, chap. x.

[4] The words of Governor Murray, Report of Sec. of Int. for 1883, vol. ii, p. 627.

[5] Ibid. for 1886, vol. ii, p. 1063.

[6] Ibid. for 1884, vol. ii, pp. 517-8. One Gentile, the first to enter the legislative assembly, was elected in 1885.—Ibid. for 1885, vol. ii, p. 885.

[7] Ibid. for 1885, vol. ii, p. 1017; ibid. for 1886, vol. ii, p. 1064.

[8] Efforts to connect them with the anti-Chinese outbreaks in Wyoming (Report of Sec. of Int. for 1885, vol. ii, p. 1034), or with Western Indian risings (Report of Sec. of War for 1883, p. 34) failed.

[9] Report of Sec. of Int. for 1887, vol. ii, p. 1324. Heber J. Grant, a well known apostle, on the occasion of a Mormon conference at Logan, indulged in angry abuse of the United States government.

[10] Report of Sec. of Int. for 1885, vol. ii, p. 890.

City, incited the people to insubordination and resistance. The flag of the United States on the 4th of July, 1885, was displayed at half-mast on the courthouse, the city hall and other public as well as church buildings in Salt Lake. Violence would have been done those who had moved to draw the banner of the country to the top of the pole. In Provo a Mormon newspaper bore the picture of a coffin with the epitaph, "Independence— Born July 4, 1776—Died July 4, 1885." [1] Mobs of Mormon rowdies were throwing containers filled with filth at the homes of the indomitable Federal officers whose unpleasant task it was to enforce the law.[2] Christian denominational school buildings were stoned and defiled. Women teaching in them were slandered and driven out of the country.[3]

To hold their members in leash, threats of everlasting damnation, did they fail to stand firm, issued from the mouths of the priesthood; even physical intimidation was employed to defeat the ends of the law.[4] But the work was advanced with an inexorable hand. Since the passage of the "Edmunds law" it was stated, in 1887, that 289 Mormons had been convicted of "unlawful cohabitation" and 14 were found guilty of, and given prison sentences for, contracting new polygamous marriages. Many had fled by the "underground" and were hidden by their friends in the interior, or had left the confines of the territory to escape the "martyrdom" which they earlier had courted and enjoyed. Women were spirited away to prevent their appearance as witnesses.[5] No less than 250 Mormons who had been indicted were in concealment or in exile.[6]

Nevertheless progress for the non-Mormons of Utah and for the rest of the country was too slow; the day of the final extinction of polygamy in the territory seemed yet far away.[7]

---

[1] K. D. Forgeron, Treason in Utah.
[2] Report of Sec. of Int. for 1885, vol. ii, p. 1023.
[3] Ibid., p. 1043.
[4] Cf. ibid., p. 1031.
[5] Senate Mis. Doc., 50th Cong. 1st sess., no. 201.
[6] Report of Sec. of Int. for 1887, vol. ii, p. 1329; cf. N. Y. Nation, Jan. 13, 1887.
[7] Cf. Report of Sec. of Int. for 1885, vol. ii, pp. 1017–8; N. Y. Nation, March 13, 1884.

The commission itself and the governor, while defending their activities in reference to the enforcement of the "Edmunds act," [1] did not conceal their disappointment at the results. The law should be amended. Secret marriages must be prevented; regulations making it necessary to perform the ceremonies in designated places and to register marriages should be required.[2] The law granting suffrage to women should be annulled by Congress.[3] The territorial militia was Mormon; the Federal military power must be made available for use at need in support of the civil authority in the execution of process and the preservation of the peace.[4] The penalty of six months' imprisonment and a fine of $300 for "unlawful cohabitation" was entirely inadequate.[5] The legislature elected by the people, which was "the creature of the church," [6] should be done away with and a council appointed by the President should be set up in its stead.[7] Presidents Hayes and Arthur recommended complete Federal control.[8] Idaho had dealt effectively with the Mormons who had come within her borders. There those who supported polygamy by counseling and defending its practice, or who belonged to any organization which subscribed to, or promoted, such doctrines were deprived of political rights, as well as the men who married and lived with two or more wives.[9]

The immigration into the United States of polygamists should be prohibited. President Cleveland favored such a law to "rid the country" of this "blot upon its fair fame." [10] The Constitution should be amended. The Mormons said that

[1] Cf. Report of Sec. of Int. for 1886, vol. ii, p. 1063.

[2] Ibid. for 1882, vol. ii, p. 1007; ibid. for 1883, vol. ii, p. 502.

[3] Ibid. for 1883, vol. ii, p. 503.

[4] Ibid. for 1882, vol. ii, p. 1007; ibid. for 1883, vol. ii, p. 628; ibid. for 1885, vol. ii, pp. 1001, 1023.

[5] Ibid. for 1885, vol. ii, p. 1023.

[6] Ibid. for 1887, vol. ii, p. 1343.

[7] Ibid., p. 1025.

[8] Richardson, vol. vii, p. 606, and vol. viii, p. 184; cf. House Reports, 48th Cong. 1st sess., pt. 2, pp. 40–51, 54–5.

[9] Report of Sec. of Int. for 1887, p. 1024; Davis v. Beason, 133 U. S., p. 333.

[10] Richardson, vol. viii, p. 362; Report of Sec. of Int. for 1886, vol. i, p. 71; ibid., vol. ii, p. 1065.

the laws of 1862 and 1882 were "unconstitutional." They might say this no longer, nor could they believe it, if a prohibition of polygamy were incorporated in the Constitution.[1] Senator Hoar suggested that the government take over the property of the church and sequester its funds.[2] Other suggestions appeared from time to time.[3]

Five years passed. A bill amending the "Edmunds act," which is usually described as the "Edmunds-Tucker bill," made its way through Congress[4] and became a law on March 3, 1887.[5] Now the women were disfranchised and they, as a body, were refused registration. A rigid test oath was prescribed to exclude those who, by their sympathy or advice, aided and abetted polygamy.[6] The corporations of the Mormon church were dissolved and the Attorney-General was authorized to commence proceedings looking to the forfeiture and escheat of their property to the United States for the benefit of the common schools in the territory.[7] The law in a number of ways really struck at the vitals of this rebellious little ecclesiastical despotism with which it was the government's imperative task to deal.[8] In 1886, 45,373 voters had been registered; the commission in 1887, after the enactment of the Edmunds-Tucker law, reduced the number to 20,790.[9]

---

[1] House Reports, 49th Cong. 1st sess., no. 2568; ibid., 50th Cong. 1st sess., no. 553; Report of Sec. of Int. for 1886, vol. ii, p. 1065; McPherson's Handbook for 1884, pp. 108, 110.

[2] House Reports, 48th Cong. 1st sess., pt. 2, pp. 24, 26.

[3] Cf. Report of Sec. of Int. for 1885, vol. ii, pp. 888–90; ibid. for 1887, vol. ii, pp. 1341–3; McPherson's Handbook for 1884, pp. 179–85; N. Y. Nation, Jan. 31, 1884.

[4] Cf. House Reports, 49th Cong. 1st sess., no. 2735.

[5] 24 U. S. Stat. at Large, pp. 635–41. Collis P. Huntington as president of a railroad which profited from the Mormons asked Cleveland to veto the bill. (Feb. 21, 1887, in Cleveland Papers.) Charles Francis Adams as president of the Union Pacific also spoke well of them.—See a letter of about the same date to Cleveland in ibid.

[6] Cf. Report of Sec. of Int. for 1887, vol. ii, pp. 1330–2, 1346–7.

[7] Senate Ex. Doc., 50th Cong. 2nd sess., no. 21; Richardson, vol. viii, p. 794; App. Ann. Cyclop. for 1887, p. 789; ibid. for 1888, pp. 831–2; Mormon Church v. U. S., 136 U. S., pp. 1–68.

[8] Cf. Report of Sec. of Int. for 1887, vol. ii, pp. 1352–3; N. Y. Nation, Jan. 20, 1887.

[9] Report of Sec. of Int. for 1887, vol. ii, p. 1340; cf. Senate Mis. Doc., 50th Cong. 1st sess., no. 201.

It was confession of complete defeat on the side of the Mormon politicians when they instituted a movement for statehood, though it betrayed no high estimate of the insight or temper of the rest of the country. The trick had been tried before.[1] A convention was assembled and a constitution was adopted—under it the Mormons would ask Congress for admission to the Union.[2] Such strategy, as a method of restoring their control, met instantly with expressions of distrust. Both the Republican and Democratic party organizations, which were being developed in Utah, declined having anything to do with the movement. The Methodist, Presbyterian and other sects which had secured a foothold in the territory [3] declared it to be a scheme to "blind" the people of the country to "the real object in view"; it would be surrendering Utah in perpetuity to Mormon rule.[4] The Utah Commission protested and said that the territory should not yet be allowed to enter the Union as a state.[5] The legislative assembly of Idaho viewed such a possibility as a "calamity," not only to the Gentiles, who would thus be put completely at the mercy of the "treasonable organization known as the Mormon church," but also to the people inhabiting adjacent states and territories,[6] wise counsel, since further chastening was required ere this people would be assimilable and proper parts of the nation.[7]

The entire northwestern corner of Wyoming, with strips of Idaho and Montana, some 3,000 square miles, taken by the Federal government to be brought, in 1872, into the Yellowstone Park, remained under the control of the Department of the Interior. This "peerless cliff and snow-encircled wonderland" [8]

[1] As in 1872 and 1882. House Mis. Doc., 42nd Cong. 2nd sess., nos. 165 and 208; House Mis. Doc., 47th Cong. 1st sess., no. 43.
[2] House Mis. Doc., 50th Cong. 1st sess., no. 104.
[3] Report of Sec. of Int. for 1887, vol. ii, p. 1324; cf. Handbook of Mormonism, pp. 78–86.
[4] Report of Sec. of Int. for 1887, pp. 1344–5.
[5] Ibid., pp. 1333–40.
[6] Senate Mis. Doc., 50th Cong. 2nd sess., no. 37.
[7] Report of Sec. of Int. for 1888, pp. cxxxi–cxxxii; Senate Mis. Doc., 50th Cong. 1st sess., no. 201; cf. Utah Statehood, Reasons Why it should not be Granted, Salt Lake City, 1887.
[8] Report of Sec. of Int. for 1878, p. 994.

continued to be inaccessible except by steamboat from Bismarck up the Missouri, and then by stagecoach and saddle horse south out of Montana, or by horse trails from the railhead of the Utah Northern Railroad, which left a junction point on the Union Pacific and pursued its way in a northerly direction into the wilderness. With the extension of the Northern Pacific westwardly and of the Utah railroad northerly in the 80's visitors found it more feasible to enter a country, which the accounts of explorers and returned travelers brought into public notice. In 1883, though the journey was still attended with hardship and adventure, the roster of those who pressed in to witness the steaming geysers, the boiling lakes, the leaping streams and the other scenic marvels which were crowded into the area included President Arthur, Secretary of War Lincoln, Chief Justice Waite, United States Senators Dawes, Edmunds and Logan, Roscoe Conkling, Carl Schurz, Generals Sherman and Sheridan and other public men of eminence in this country as well as of Europe. Though there were no railways, none but the crudest roads for stagecoaches and pack trains, and no hotels, many visitors were accompanied by ladies.[1]

Too little had been done not only with reference to the approaches, but also in the reservation itself. It was not enough to create a park and promulgate rules for its administration; a staff must be at hand with the will and power to enforce them. Buffalo, less than two hundred head, which here were making their last stand on American soil,[2] elk, deer, antelope, mountain sheep, beaver and many other animals were under the protection of the government. But, while General Sheridan was in the park in 1882, he was told that 4,000 elk had been killed in a recent winter and that, even under closer control, during the past year, 2,000 had been taken by the skin hunters on the borders of the reservation.[3] Many were shot for

---

[1] Cf. N. Y. Nation, Sep. 1, 1887.
[2] Report of Sec. of Int. for 1887, vol. ii, p. 1301; ibid. for 1888, vol. iii, p. 632; ibid. for 1885, vol. ii, p. 873; House Reports, 49th Cong. 1st sess., no. 1076, p. xlvi.
[3] Senate Reports, 47th Cong. 2nd sess., no. 911, pp. 4, 13; cf. House Reports, 49th Cong. 1st sess., no. 1076, pp. xlvi–xlvii, liii.

their antlers, the carcasses being left to rot upon the ground. Even buffalo to the number of 12 or 15, the superintendent said, had been killed for their "robes," or in "sport," in the winter of 1885–6.[1] Beaver were trapped for their skins, fish were destroyed in great numbers by the explosion of powder in the beds of the streams and lakes. The governor of Montana complained that this slaughter proceeded almost within sight of the superintendent's house at the Mammoth Hot Springs.[2] Even the Interior Department seemed to be in league with despoilers and speculators. While Teller was at its head he favorably entertained proposals for a lease of rights to the "Yellowstone National Park Improvement Company," organized by some promoters in New York, who were to build hotels, establish transportation lines and exploit the park generally. They would sell their stock in Europe as well as in this country.[3] Their "monopoly," Teller said, would "protect" the reservation with the "least possible expense to the government."[4] Sheridan and many others remonstrated.[5] Congress interceded to curb the Secretary of the Interior and the "Improvement Company."[6] The promoters built hotels which were unworthy of the park; they evaded the terms of their contracts with the government. Game continued to be shot so openly, said the superintendent whom Cleveland had appointed in 1885, that it was brought to the kitchen doors for sale and served at the public tables.[7] The hotel company itself was suspected and accused of complicity in the work of animal slaughter.[8] Stones, sticks, even logs, were thrown into the geyser basins. Men trampled on, indeed, rode and

[1] House Reports, 49th Cong. 1st sess., no. 1076, pp. xlvi–xlvii.
[2] Report of Sec. of Int. for 1884, vol. ii, p. 562.
[3] Senate Ex. Doc., 48th Cong. 1st sess., no. 10, p. 17.
[4] Ibid., pp. 1–2.
[5] Cf. Senate Ex. Doc., 47th Cong. 2nd sess., no. 48; Senate Reports, 47th Cong. 2nd sess., no. 911, pp. 6–11; Senate Ex. Doc., 47th Cong. 2nd sess., no. 10; Senate Reports, 48th Cong. 1st sess., no. 207; House Ex. Doc., 48th Cong. 1st sess., no. 139; Report of Sec. of Int. for 1888, vol. iii, pp. 634, 637.
[6] Act of March 3, 1883, 22 U. S. Stat. at Large, pp. 626–7.
[7] Report of Sec. of Int. for 1885, vol. i, p. 72; ibid., vol. ii, p. 873.
[8] Senate Ex. Doc., 48th Cong. 1st sess., no. 207, pp. 11, 12–3, 19.

drove their horses over, the beautiful silicious deposits. Others wrote or chiseled their names on every side, thus defacing the trees, the rocks and the incrustations,[1] or with hammers broke the most delicate tracery. Squatters, not a few of them highly disreputable persons,[2] in defiance of law built cabins within the reservation and turned out their cattle which, while grazing, trod upon and broke the rarest phenomena of nature. Wooden shacks and the débris of camping parties disfigured the landscape. Traders, in violation of the regulations, preyed upon visitors at the roadside and at hotel doors.[3]

Forest fires, carelessly lighted by tourists, who stopped to cook a meal, or maliciously started by evil white men, or by the Indians, constantly threatened damage and destruction.[4] When trappers, squaw men, old frontiersmen and other game poachers and skin hunters were ejected from the park they hugged the borders to catch and kill the animals which, by the cold in winter, were driven out of the mountains into the lower valleys.[5] They, in summer, would set fire to the wood and grass near the boundary lines to dislodge the game so that they might bring it within range of their guns.[6]

So much incompetency of administration was due less to the men appointed to superintend and police the park than to the failure of Congress to understand the nature of its trust. In no conceivable manner could the unrivaled objects within the reservation be protected against vandalism, in no way could the area be provided with roads, bridges, paths and conveniences necessary to tourists, without public appropriations. The grant, prior to 1882, was never more than $15,000 a year.[7] Only by the devoted and skillful service of a few men was that which had been done made possible. Scouts, woods-

[1] Cf. Report of Sec. of Int. for 1886, vol. ii, p. 1076.
[2] Ibid., p. 1079.
[3] Cf. ibid. for 1887, vol. i, p. 74.
[4] Cf. House Reports, 49th Cong. 1st sess., no. 1076, p. xiv.
[5] Cf. Report of Sec. of Int. for 1887, vol. ii, p. 1291.
[6] Ibid. for 1886, vol. ii, p. 1075; ibid. for 1882, vol. ii, p. 1001; ibid. for 1883, vol. ii, pp. 487, 489; ibid. for 1885, vol. ii, pp. 874-5.
[7] Ibid. for 1882, vol. ii, p. 1000; House Mis. Doc., 47th Cong. 2nd sess. no. 45, pt. 4, chap. xxxvi.

men, mountaineers, used to outdoor life in winter as in summer, were required in such a situation. They must have power to
arrest and punish offenders as well as to publish rules. But
there were no magistrates or courts.[1] The penal system of
Wyoming, which, with questionable validity, was extended to
the reservation by the territorial legislature, was soon withdrawn.[2] President Cleveland's appointee to the superintend-
ency in 1885 set about the performance of his duties earnestly.
He remained in the park throughout the year—[3] his predecessors had visited it for only a few weeks during the summer—and
endeavored to improve conditions. He had but $40,000 for
his use in the year ending with June, 1886.[4] He asked for $150,-
000 for the ensuing year.[5] Instead he received nothing. A
small sum was granted for road building, under the direction
of a United States army engineer, who was not available
until late in August, 1886.[6] His office having been abolished
the superintendent resigned, his force was scattered, since there
were no funds to pay the small wages of the guards, and the
Secretary of the Interior was compelled to ask the assistance
of the Secretary of War, who detailed a troop of cavalry to
take charge of the nation's property.[7] The commanding officer
repeatedly appealed for appropriations, the Secretary of the
Interior commended the subject to the attention of Congress,
and, though 5,000 visitors were registered at the hotels in
the summer of 1886,[8] and 10,000 in 1888,[9] no heed was taken
of the urgent pleas of those who could best form a judgment
of the needs of the park. Military protection was continued
perforce.[10] What a small band of soldiers with little knowledge

[1] Cf. Senate Reports, 50th Cong. 1st sess., no. 315.
[2] Report of Sec. of Int. for 1885, vol. ii, p. 875; ibid. for 1886, vol. ii,
pp. 1072, 1079; ibid. for 1887, vol. i, pp. 72–3.
[3] Ibid. for 1886, vol. ii, p. 1073.
[4] Ibid., p. 1071.
[5] Ibid. for 1885, vol. ii, p. 875; ibid. for 1886, vol. ii, p. 1073.
[6] Ibid. for 1886, vol. ii, p. 1076; cf. House Reports, 49th Cong. 1st sess.,
no. 1076, p. xlvii.
[7] Report of Sec. of Int. for 1886, vol. ii, p. 1073; ibid. for 1887, vol. i, p. 71.
[8] Ibid. for 1886, vol. i, p. 74.
[9] Ibid. for 1888, vol. i, p. cxii.
[10] Ibid. for 1887, vol. i, p. 71.

of frontiersmanship and woodcraft could do in such a place
was done, but the aspect of neglect which settled upon the
nation's "wonderland" was a source of mortification to the
officers in charge of it as well as to responsible citizens who
turned their faces toward it in summer vacation time, and entered its confines.[1]

After the purchase from Russia Alaska, for about ten years,
was under military administration, but, in view of the configura-
tion of the country, it was held to be a more appropriate task
of the Navy Department to give oversight to our interests
in this widely extended and quite remote new portion of the
national domain.[2] What its superficial extent really was no
one, in the absence of survey and calculation, could definitely
determine. It was roughly held to be greater than that of
21 states of the Union lying east of the Mississippi River—
it was nearly one-fifth of that of the entire contiguous continental area of the republic.[3] The population of the country
was also guessed at, since the settlements were scattered and
the groups of white, native and mixed peoples living here
were not accessible to the agents commissioned by the government to make the count of heads. In 1886 it was stated
to be 35,000, of whom only about 3,000 were whites, including
a considerable number of "Creoles," the descendants of Rus-
sians by native women.[4] The aboriginal inhabitants, it was
agreed, were superior to the American Indian—they were industrious, thrifty, self-supporting and yielded readily to civilizing influences.[5]

Likewise the resources of the country remained, after a
long period of American ownership and occupation, nearly as
great an enigma as when Seward had surprised the nation
by negotiating for, and announcing, the annexation of the
territory. It was alleged by observers on the ground that

[1] Cf. Report of Sec. of Int. for 1887, vol. ii, p. 1303.
[2] J. P. Nichols, Alaska, p. 59.
[3] Report of Sec. of Int. for 1886, vol. ii, p. 938.
[4] Ibid. for 1885, vol. ii, pp. 914–5; ibid. for 1886, vol. ii, pp. 938–41.
[5] Cf. ibid. for 1884, vol. ii, p. 638; ibid. for 1885, vol. ii, p. 915; ibid. for
1886, vol. ii, pp. 941–2.

ALASKA AND THE SEAL ISLANDS

there was enough arable land to make self-sustaining, in the matter of cereals and vegetable food, a population much larger than that now settled here.[1] It was reiterated, with the submission of detailed meteorological reports, that the climate, at least in and about Sitka, from which place such government as was given the country proceeded, was far more amiable in temperature, if not with reference to sunshine (for the rainfall was great), than was generally believed. At no time in the year ending in August, 1886, had the "glass" recorded weather colder than four degrees above zero (in January), with a maximum of 72 degrees in summer.[2] For the same period in 1884-5 the lowest temperature was 14, the highest 79 degrees.[3] Surely it was a mistaken assumption that Alaska was a "frigid waste." [4]

That the forests might yield a valuable supply of lumber was intimated, though this industry gained no headway. The fish which abounded, particularly cod, salmon and halibut, were being caught in great quantities and a number of canneries were established to prepare them for exportation.[5] The most of what was known about the country concerned the whale which had long been pursued off these coasts, and the fur seals which made their homes and bred from May to December on two small islands in the Bering Sea, a natural, if not a *de jure, mare clausum,* lying north of the long chain of Aleutian Islands, which extend from the mainland to the coast of Asia. These Pribylov Islands, called St. Paul and St. George, one containing 33 and the other 27 square miles, were located about 25 miles from each other.[6] They were distant some 200 miles north of Oonalaska, a coaling and trading station in the Aleutian chain, and 1,500 miles from Sitka.

[1] Report of Sec. of Int. for 1885, vol. ii, p. 916; ibid. for 1886, vol. ii, pp. 946-7.

[2] Ibid. for 1886, vol. ii, pp. 942-3.

[3] Ibid. for 1885, vol. ii, p. 915.

[4] Ibid. for 1886, vol. ii, p. 953; cf. Senate Ex. Doc., 49th Cong. 1st sess., no. 85; Sheldon Jackson, Report on Education in Alaska for 1886, pp. 8-10.

[5] Report of Sec. of Int. for 1886, vol. ii, pp. 944-5.

[6] Cf. House Ex. Doc., 44th Cong. 1st sess., no. 43; H. W. Elliott, Our Arctic Province, chap. ix.

The seal, wherever it had existed in nearly all other parts of the world, had been exterminated by unregulated slaughter. It survived here because Russia had intrusted the business of taking and skinning the animals to a company which stood under government control.[1] Patently, supervision must continue after American annexation,[2] and the two islands containing the rookeries were created by Congress into a special reservation for government purposes.[3] A successor to the Russian monopoly was found in a corporation called the Alaska Commercial Company, adjudged to be the most competent among several bidders for the lease, which would run 20 years from 1870. It was specified that no more than 100,000 skins should be taken in a year. The age and sex of the animals and the period within which the killing should proceed were named, as was the method of slaughter—the use of firearms was prohibited. In return for the company's profitable privileges responsibilities were laid upon it with reference to the sustenance and the education of the native inhabitants. A rental of $55,000 a year and royalties or taxes on the skins, equal to $2.62½ each, which, on the whole catch, would amount to $262,500 annually, were to be paid into the Treasury of the United States. Government agents resided on the islands to enforce the provisions of the contract.[4]

The company from the beginning received and probably merited criticism. The giving of this monopoly to "an unscrupulous ring of speculators," as General Jeff C. Davis, commanding the department of Alaska, described the men forming the company, was another corruption laid at the door of

[1] House Reports, 50th Cong. 2nd sess., no. 3883, p. ii.
[2] Cf. House Mis. Doc., 41st Cong. 2nd sess., no. 11; House Ex. Doc., 41st Cong. 2nd sess., no. 129.
[3] Act of July 1, 1870. 16 U. S. Stat. at Large, p. 180.
[4] Cf. House Ex. Doc., 41st Cong. 3rd sess., no. 108; House Reports, 44th Cong. 1st sess., no. 623; House Ex. Doc., 50th Cong. 1st sess., no. 296; Senate Ex. Doc., 45th Cong. 3rd sess., no. 59, pp. 133, 134–5; House Reports, 50th Cong. 2nd sess., no. 3883, pp. v–vii, 280–81; Nichols, Alaska, pp. 74–5; Sheldon Jackson, Report on Education for 1886, pp. 15–6; App. Ann. Cyclop. for 1882, pp. 6–10. For conditions as of 1874 see H. W. Elliott, Report on Alaska for the Treasury Dept., chaps. vi and vii and Our Arctic Province, by the same author, chap. ix.

the Grant administration. Merchants and shipping men in San Francisco did not cease to denounce the lease.[1] The company extended its operations from the seal islands to the Aleutian Islands and the mainland, and created them into a "principality of its own" over which it exercised "unbounded sway."[2] Its agents, it was said, were oppressing the native people, paying them at the trading stations too little for skins of the valuable sea otter,[3] and other fur-bearing animals, and charging them high prices for supplies.[4] It controlled transportation and merchandizing in a vast area and the unoffending Aleuts were at its mercy—they were its "serfs."[5] It supported a lobby at Washington which misrepresented and belittled the resources of the territory. It would have Alaska regarded as a wilderness, a mere "fur preserve" of no value to the United States, so that the profitable lease might not be questioned and, at its expiration, might be renewed.[6] The company was denounced by officers of the government at Sitka as a "blighting curse," a "deadly incubus." It should be shorn of its tyrannical power.[7] The lobbyists were "hired assassins" of the territory's "progress and welfare."[8] A few men, said the Alaska Free Press, "Jews and foreigners," had gained trading rights to the exclusion of 60,000,000 American

[1] A History of the Wrongs of Alaska, An Appeal to the People and Press of America by the Anti-Monopoly Association of the Pacific Coast, 1875; cf. J. L. McDonald, Hidden Treasure, pp. 33–9; W. H. Dall, Alaska and its Resources, pp. 493–7; A. K. Delaney to Cleveland, Oct. 7, 1887, in Cleveland Papers.

[2] House Ex. Doc., 50th Cong. 1st sess., no. 297, p. 2.

[3] H. W. Elliott, Report on Alaska, chap. v; ibid., Our Arctic Province, chap. vii.

[4] Report of Sec. of Int. for 1887, vol. i, p. 734.

[5] Senate Ex. Doc., 50th Cong. 2nd sess., no. 74, pp. 2–3. There were some compensations since they had been taught, and were singing, "John Brown's Body," "Marching Through Georgia" and strains from "Pinafore."—Ivan Petroff, House Ex. Doc., 46th Cong. 3rd sess., no. 40, p. 15.

[6] Cf. Nichols, Alaska, pp. 54–5; Senate Reports, 47th Cong. 1st sess., no. 457, pp. 38–9.

[7] Report of Sec. of Int. for 1887, vol. i, pp. 719–31; Senate Ex. Doc., 46th Cong. 2nd sess., no. 192, p. 4.

[8] Report of Sec. of Int. for 1886, vol. ii, p. 986; cf. ibid. for 1887, vol. i, pp. 710–11.

citizens.[1] William H. Seward had not purchased "Alaska for the Alaska Commercial Company, but for the whole people." The "arrogance and assumption" of this "huge monopoly" was "outrageous." [2]

On the other side it was said that the corporation had performed a distinct service to the natives in providing them with employment in the killing season, in purchasing from them skins for which they would not otherwise have had a market, in carrying them from place to place by ship and in satisfying their wants at the company stores.[3] The government would have been impotent in a work having to do with the protection of a valuable natural species of animal but for private mediation. The payment of $7,200,000 to Russia for Alaska had been denounced as an incredible and fantastic extravagance. The officers and friends of the company pointed to the fact that, up to the end of the fiscal year, on June 30, 1888, the lease had yielded the United States more than five and a half millions, and, if the further fact were considered that, on such part of the seal skins which were necessarily shipped to London to receive technical treatment, a secret in possession of one manufacturer, and which came back in finished form for use in the United States, four millions more were collected in customs duties, the return had been nine and a half millions, quite two millions in excess of the purchase price.[4]

It was even stated that the herds were increasing under the company's lease.[5] So much, as soon appeared, was quite untrue,[6] largely because of the onslaught by unauthorized persons, who, while the seals were going to and coming from the rookeries, shot them as they swam in the water. These "poachers" killed seven, or perhaps ten, for every one which

[1] Report of Sec. of Int. for 1887, vol. i, p. 734; Nichols, Alaska, pp. 47–9; Senate Ex. Doc., 46th Cong. 2nd sess., no. 192, p. 4.

[2] Senate Mis. Doc., 50th Cong. 1st sess., no. 78, p. 3; cf. Cong. Record, 48th Cong. 1st sess., p. 4123.

[3] Cf. House Reports, 50th Cong. 2nd sess., no. 3883, pp. xx–xxi.

[4] Ibid., pp. vii–viii, 3; House Reports, 44th Cong. 1st sess., no. 623, p. 11; House Ex. Doc., 55th Cong. 1st sess., no. 92, pt. 3, pp. 36–41, 295–300.

[5] House Reports, 50th Cong. 2nd sess., no. 3883, p. 371.

[6] Ibid., 63rd Cong. 2nd sess., no. 500, p. 2.

they skinned. One of the Treasury agents on the ground in 1887 said that for 30,000 skins taken by marauders in that year 300,000 seals had been killed.[1] Such reckless destruction naturally provoked protest on the part of the Alaska Commercial Company. It betokened the extinction of their business as well as of the seal itself.[2] Likewise public sentiment in the United States was awakened, and it was in some sections inflamed by the emphasis which was placed upon the nationality of the vessels engaged in the business. Many of the "poachers" were Canadians—they at any rate used the British flag as a cover for their operations—and international complications were imminent when the United States asserted its right to exclusive jurisdiction over the waters of Bering Sea, north of the Aleutian Islands and east of the 193rd meridian. Such general authority had been exercised by Russia—it had come to us by transfer on the day of purchase.[3] We should patrol these waters and, while some attempts to do so without clear right were put forth, the revenue cutters which visited Bering Sea from time to time were too few and ineffective to cope successfully with pelagic sealing.[4] The shots of the "poachers" could be heard on the seal islands— they ventured so near the shore. The *Corwin* in the summer of 1886, captured one American and three British schooners;[5] the *Bear* and the *Rush* in the following year seized eight American and six British ships,[6] which, if this were enough to create a diplomatic situation,[7] and, at the same time, stir certain

---

[1] Cf. Senate Ex. Doc., 50th Cong. 1st sess., no. 31, p. 9.

[2] House Reports, 50th Cong. 2nd sess., no. 3883, pp. ii–v.

[3] Ibid., pp. viii–x.

[4] House Reports, 50th Cong. 2nd sess., no. 3883, pp. 359–61; cf. Senate Ex. Doc., 48th Cong. 1st sess., no. 149; House Reports, 48th Cong. 1st sess., no. 802; House Ex. Doc., 48th Cong. 2nd sess., no. 252; Senate Ex. Doc., 50th Cong. 1st sess., no. 31; Senate Ex. Doc., 50th Cong. 2nd sess., no. 90; House Ex. Doc., 55th Cong. 1st sess., no. 92, pt. 3, pp. 318 et seq.

[5] Report of Sec. of Int. for 1886, vol. ii, pp. 981–2; Senate Ex. Doc., 49th Cong. 2nd sess., no. 7.

[6] Report of Sec. of Int. for 1887, vol. i, pp. 723–4, 737–51; House Reports, 50th Cong. 2nd sess., no. 3883, pp. xi–xvii; Senate Ex. Doc., 50th Cong. 1st sess., no. 31; House Ex. Doc., 50th Cong. 1st sess., no. 296, p. 5.

[7] Senate Ex. Doc., 50th Cong. 2nd sess., no. 106; J. H. Latané, Diplo-

American "fishermen" to protest,[1] little curbed the shocking
waste of seal life.[2]

But it was not sealing, or whaling, or fish canning which
led to increase of interest in "Seward's folly," nor yet was it
the discovery of seams of coal which it was said existed in
sufficient abundance to supply the whole Pacific slope "for
centuries";[3] it was the successful search for gold. A mountain
of quartz on Douglas Island, opposite Juneau, which, under
such impetus suddenly grew into a city, led to the erection of
stamp mills reported to be among the largest in the world.[4]
Miners from time to time had come down from the upper
Yukon with bags of gold dust, and sailed away. Clearly there
were El Dorados in the interior of the country. Stampedes such
as were familiar in the Western states and territories were
started hither and thither on reports of rich discoveries. Immigration was stimulated and, more than ever before, it was
plain that Alaska must have civil government. This measure
had been repeatedly urged upon Congress by the Secretary
of the Interior and the President.[5] In 1883 the appeal was
made with new earnestness.[6] The people, said President Arthur,
had been "expressly guaranteed" protection at the time of
the cession of the territory to the United States. The "prompt-
ings of interest," as well as "considerations of honor and good
faith," demanded "the immediate establishment of civil gov-

matic Relations of the U. S., pp. 461–6; T. W. Woolsey, America's Foreign
Policy, pp. 170–77.

[1] These men laid the blame at the door of the Alaska Commercial
Company. They should be allowed to pursue "their honorable business"
without being "treated as criminals and hunted down and seized and im-
prisoned by the piratical revenue cutters of the United States at the dictation and for the sole benefit of the Alaska Commercial Company."—
Senate Mis. Doc., 50th Cong. 1st sess., no. 78, p. 3.

[2] Cf. Senate Ex. Doc., 50th Cong. 2nd sess., no. 90, pp. 2–3, 4.

[3] Report of Sec. of Int. for 1888, vol. iii, p. 978; cf. Senate Ex. Doc.,
45th Cong. 3rd sess., no. 59, p. 103.

[4] Report of Sec. of Int. for 1884, vol. ii, p. 639; ibid. for 1885, vol. ii,
p. 917; ibid. for 1886, vol. ii, p. 951; ibid. for 1887, vol. i, p. 699; ibid.
for 1888, vol. ii, p. 969; Senate Reports, 47th Cong. 1st sess., no. 457,
p. 36.

[5] Cf. Richardson, Messages and Papers, vol. viii, pp. 64, 144.

[6] Report of Sec. of Int. for 1883, p. xlvii.

ernment." [1] There were in the whole land, after sixteen years, in spite of the repeated remonstrances of the people,[2] no laws except those in relation to seal taking on the islands in Bering Sea and some regulations as to customs collections and intercourse with the Indians, including a regulation prohibiting the manufacture and sale of intoxicating liquors; [3] no magistrates; no courts; no method of establishing and enforcing rights; no schools.[4] The country, indeed, had not been surveyed and was not open to settlement under the homestead and preemption laws. No man could acquire or transfer title to real estate. His house, his store, his shop, his cannery were on the undivided and indivisible public domain on which he remained a mere squatter. Mineral claims on the border were insecure, since the international boundary had never been located and the miners could not know whether they were on the American or the British side of the line.[5]

The Committee on Territories of the Senate in 1883 said that the obligation was "obvious and pressing." Ever since the treaty of purchase the inhabitants of the country had been "absolutely without the pale of the law and without any protection of life or property, except such as resulted from the temporary presence of some army detachment or the occasional visit of a vessel of war, or a revenue cutter." Such a condition of things was "no longer to be tolerated." [6]

Finally Congress was moved to action and, by a law approved on May 17, 1884,[7] Alaska was organized into a "district" which would have a governor and certain civil officers, who were to proceed to Sitka, where they arrived early in

---

[1] Richardson, vol. viii, pp. 184–5; cf. Cong. Record, 48th Cong. 1st sess., pp. 597–8.

[2] Cf. App. Ann. Cyclop. for 1879, p. 25.

[3] U. S. v. Nelson, 29 Federal Reporter, p. 202.

[4] Cf. Senate Reports, 47th Cong. 1st sess., no. 457, pp. 15, 23–4, 28, 29.

[5] Cf. Cong. Record, 48th Cong. 1st sess., no. 4121.

[6] Senate Reports, 48th Cong. 1st sess., no. 3, p. 1; cf. Senate Ex. Doc., 46th Cong. 2nd sess., no. 192, pp. 2–6; Senate Reports, 47th Cong. 1st sess., no. 457, p. 2; House Reports, 47th Cong. 1st sess., nos. 560 and 1106; House Reports, 48th Cong. 1st sess., no. 476.

[7] The bill passed the Senate Jan. 25 and the House May 13, 1884. See Cong. Record, 48th Cong. 1st sess., pp. 661, 4127.

September of that year. They were Republican politicians
with little qualification for, or interest in, their tasks. The
naval forces relinquished the exercise of civil authority. Though
Alaska would not have full "territorial organization," with
a legislative assembly—the new officers were to take with them
and enforce the laws of Oregon—and, though still only claimants
to mineral lands, not other kinds of real property, could obtain titles, through an office to be established at Sitka, it
was a beginning and more might later be expected.[1] Before
J. H. Kinkead, one time governor of Nevada, whom President Arthur had designated as the first governor of Alaska,
was fairly in place, news of the election of Mr. Cleveland was
received and, in the following year, A. P. Swineford, a journalist of varied experiences in the Northwest, went out with a
new staff of civil officers drawn from the Democratic party.
They had been preceded to their posts by a superintendent
of education, the Rev. Sheldon Jackson, an ardent Presbyterian missionary with a taste for politics, who had actively
interested himself for some time in Alaskan affairs,[2] and a
corps of teachers who were to establish and take charge of
the schools.[3]

The opportunities for service were few and the complaints
were open. Neither the military nor the naval administration
had brought protection to the handful of white people who
had cast their lot in Alaska—likewise the new government
would but little serve their needs. In the first place the governor was without facilities for even visiting and looking at
the country over which he had been made the executive officer.
He was confined to Sitka, where he found all the public buildings in partial or complete ruin,[4] and the ports in the "30
mile strip," lying in front of the British possessions in the

---

[1] Report of Sec. of Int. for 1884, vol. ii, p. 637; Cong. Record, 48th Cong.
1st sess., p. 597.

[2] Cf. Senate Ex. Doc., 47th Cong. 1st sess., no. 30; Nichols, Alaska, pp.
73, 109–10; Sheldon Jackson, Report on Education for 1886, p. 43; Swineford to Lamar, Oct. 13, 1885, in Cleveland Papers.

[3] Report of Sec. of Int. for 1885, vol. ii, pp. 912–4; R. L. Stewart,
Sheldon Jackson, chaps. xv and xvi.

[4] Report of Sec. of Int. for 1884, vol. ii, p. 638.

southeast, at which the mail steamer running to Port Townsend in Washington territory called,[1] a mere one-twentieth
part of the whole territory. There were no rail or wagon roads—
the widely scattered settlements could be reached only by
water, and not even a tugboat had been put at the governor's
disposal.[2] Not as much as a rowboat was at the service of
the collector of customs.[3] Such naval vessels as were at hand
from time to time were otherwise employed. The telegraph
did not extend beyond Port Townsend, the terminus of the
steamer line. If a letter were dispatched to Washington City
by Mr. Swineford, it would be three months before he could
receive a reply.[4] With Oonalaska, in the Aleutian Islands,
1,200 miles away, and the other islands in the chain, the ut-
termost being 850 miles still farther west,[5] and the sealing
grounds there was no communication from Sitka. Anyone
in those islands desirous of directing a prosecution, or of using
the new agencies of government in any way, must depend
upon the courtesies of boats occasionally bound for San Francisco, whence he might proceed to Port Townsend to meet
the monthly mail steamer, a distance of 4,000 miles. He could
not return to his home except in reverse in the same manner.[6]
Crime, which could not be punished, was committed every day
of the year.[7]

The governor asked for steamship lines and mails; he asked
for money for schools; he asked for surveys of land and the
establishment of boundary lines; he condemned the seal catching monopoly and deplored the want of government such as

[1] Report of Sec. of Int. for 1885, vol. ii, p. 911; ibid. for 1886, vol. ii,
pp. 937-8, 982-4; ibid. for 1887, vol. i, p. 691; Senate Ex. Doc., 49th Cong.
1st sess., no. 113.
[2] Report of Sec. of Int. for 1885, vol. ii, p. 922.
[3] A. K. Delaney to Cleveland, Oct. 7, 1887, in Cleveland Papers.
[4] Report of Sec. of Int. for 1886, vol. ii, p. 086.
[5] Senate Ex. Doc., 48th Cong. 1st sess., no. 149, p. 1; Senate Reports,
47th Cong. 1st sess., no. 457, p. 3. The Rush occupied six days in coming
from Oonalaska to Sitka "at its usual pace."—A. K. Delaney to Cleveland,
Oct. 7, 1887, in Cleveland Papers.
[6] Report of Sec. of Int. for 1884, vol. ii, p. 641; ibid. for 1885, vol. ii,
p. 921; Senate Reports, 47th Cong. 1st sess., no. 457, p. 30; Sheldon Jackson,
Report for 1886, p. 28.
[7] Report of Sec. of Int. for 1887, vol. i, pp. 726-7.

was given to Montana, Idaho and the other territories of the United States. Since the first day following the purchase, the white population of Alaska had urged upon Congress this convenience and right. They still were left without a legislature; without a delegate in Congress who could present their needs and defend their interests at Washington; without laws by which title could be taken to land except for mining.[1] Governor Swineford said that government was "little better than a ridiculous farce";[2] everywhere but in the small area in the southeast, accessible to Sitka, it was the "veriest myth."[3]

A problem of the South was also one for the West. The protection of lands bordering on the Mississippi from inundation, which so frequently recurred, and the use of the stream for navigation were matters of concern to the people of the entire watershed from the Alleghanies to, and far into, the Rocky Mountains. The river system, of which the Mississippi was the trunk channel, comprised 33 streams with 14,000 miles of waterway,[4] on which plied, in 1879, 3,000 vessels with a capacity of 500,000 tons, serving an area of about 2,000,000 square miles, or two-thirds of the republic, barring Alaska. A single tug would carry to New Orleans a tow of barges containing 600,000 bushels of coal. The number of boats was increasing in spite of the extension of railroads. The river and its tributaries floated the largest inland commerce in the world.[5] In the Mississippi Valley, it was said in 1880, 75 per cent of the cereal crops of the country were grown and gleaned; a difference of five cents a bushel in freight charges, which might easily result from water, as compared with land, carriage, would increase the income of the people

[1] Report of Sec. of Int. for 1885, vol. ii, pp. 923–6; ibid. for 1886, vol. ii, pp. 957, 961, 986–7; ibid. for 1887, vol. i, pp. 727–8; ibid. for 1888, vol. iii, p. 964.

[2] Ibid. for 1886, vol. ii, p. 983.

[3] Ibid. for 1887, vol. i, p. 726; cf. ibid., pp. 64–5; House Reports, 50th Cong. 1st sess., no. 1318. The act of 1884, the customs collector in Alaska said, was "a most crude, bungling and unsatisfactory piece of legislation." It gave the country "the mere shadow of civil government."—A. K. Delaney to Cleveland, Oct. 7, 1887, in Cleveland Papers.

[4] Cf. House Reports, 45th Cong. 2nd sess., no. 714, pp. 3–4.

[5] App. Ann. Cyclop. for 1879, pp. 635–6.

settled in the great mid-continental basin to the extent of $75,000,000 a year.[1]

Active interest in the subject began to be evidenced soon after the development of the steamboat, when the value of the river as an artery of trade became manifest. The wash from thousands of passing vessels battered down the soft earth banks,[2] and, breaking out, the stream roved over the prairie in wide shallows, without depth or velocity, to the damage of agriculture as well as the confusion of commerce. Moreover, with the settlement of the West, came a destruction of forests and other changes in conditions which affected the flow of the river and its feeding streams.[3]

Appropriations from the Federal Treasury for the improvement of the Mississippi were made early in the century. There were small grants at subsequent dates, more particularly for the advantage of the Ohio. But the beneficiaries of the government were usually quite insignificant streams, scarcely to be traced upon the map, which were favored with vociferous advocates in Congress, who would give their associates no rest until the wants of their particular communities were satisfied.[4] River and harbor bills were notorious compounds of small wastes and steals. The "pork barrel" of American politics was opened and greedy hands reached into it that members might be seen as great men in little neighborhoods. So, while it was pointed out that the United States took a revenue from the Mississippi, in the license fees of pilots and in steamboat taxes of various kinds, amounting to more than $1,000,000 annually, to say naught of the tax on cotton, which was produced in great quantities in the lower valley, when return was asked, even for obviously necessary uses, the most niggardly policy was pursued.[5]

[1] App. Ann. Cyclop. for 1879, pp. 534–5; cf. House Mis. Doc., 47th Cong. 1st sess., no. 56, pp. 6, 11.
[2] House Reports, 43rd Cong. 1st sess., no. 418, pp. 19–22.
[3] Senate Ex. Doc., 47th Cong. 1st sess., no. 10, pp. 124–5; Richardson, Messages and Papers, vol. viii, pp. 185–6.
[4] Cf. App. Ann. Cyclop. for 1880, p. 535.
[5] Ibid. for 1881, pp. 601–2; Senate Ex. Doc., 47th Cong. 1st sess., no. 159, p. 2.

Levees, or artificial earth parapets, on the river edges were built, of necessity, for the protection of the settlement at New Orleans as early as in 1720, and by 1763, they had been extended continuously on both banks of the stream 20 miles below and 30 miles above the city. By 1828 the dikes had been completed up to Red River Landing, except near Baton Rouge, where bluffs on the left bank rendered them unnecessary. North of Red River the system was in a very disconnected state.[1]

In 1849 and 1850 Congress donated swamp lands subject to overflow in Louisiana, Mississippi and other states to those states to be sold for the advantage of their levees,[2] and for a time notable progress was made in the construction of parapets. In 1850 Congress appropriated $50,000 for "a topographical and hydrographical survey of the delta of the Mississippi," and ordered investigations for the purpose of determining "the most practicable plan for securing it from inundation."[3] A like sum was granted in 1852 for a continuance of the inquiry, which was intrusted to the engineer corps of the army, in personal charge of Captain A. A. Humphreys. His observations covered ten years and they were incorporated in an exhaustive report,[4] which reached the Secretary of War in 1861, at the outbreak of hostilities between the sections.[5] Prior to the Civil War it was said that over $40,000,000 had been raised through local exertion for expenditure upon the river.[6] That struggle meant not only neglect of the levees, but also the actual destruction of many of them in the pursuit of military measures, and at its end the system was left in a state of general disorder.[7]

[1] House Ex. Doc., 46th Cong. 3rd sess., no. 95; House Reports, 43rd Cong. 1st sess., no. 418, pp. 5-6.

[2] House Reports, 43rd Cong. 1st sess., no. 418, pp. 6, 11; House Ex. Doc., 43rd Cong. 2nd sess., no. 127, p. 19.

[3] House Reports, 43rd Cong. 1st sess., no. 418, p. 11.

[4] Report upon the Physics and Hydraulics of the Miss. River, no. 4, in Professional Papers of the Corps of Topographical Engineers.

[5] House Reports, 43rd Cong. 1st sess., no. 418, p. 11; House Ex. Doc., 43rd Cong. 2nd sess., no. 127, p. 20.

[6] House Reports, 43rd Cong. 1st sess., no. 418, pp. 9-10.

[7] Ibid., p. 10; cf. House Ex. Doc., 43rd Cong. 2nd sess., no. 127, p. 19.

There were great floods in the valley in 1858 and 1874, with overflows of minor volume in 1862, 1865 and 1867.[1] In 1865 General Humphreys had been ordered to resume his work on the river and make further report to the War Department. He indicated a number of points at which repairs were "urgently required to prevent great injury" to agricultural interests as well as to commerce, and computed the cost at nearly $4,000,000.[2] Plainly no riparian owner, no union of owners, no local community or combination of communities, no state, especially in the period of poverty and maladministration in the South, following the war,[3] without national aid, could cope with such a situation. Congress had accepted the principle of Federal control,[4] officers completed surveys, committees made recommendations, bills were presented and discussed,[5] but legislation appropriating the necessary moneys was always deferred.[6]

Little of practical value having come of the investigations of General Humphreys, who was now chief of engineers of the army, Congress, after the flood of 1874,[7] authorized the appointment of a commission "to investigate and report a permanent plan for reclamation of the alluvial basin of the Mississippi."[8] Five men, three engineers from the army and two civilian engineers, were named by President Grant. They found and designated in the report, which they were ready to submit in January, 1875, a large number of crevasses—

[1] House Ex. Doc., 43rd Cong. 2nd sess., no. 127, p. 34. For the floods of 1862, 1865 and 1867 see Senate Mis. Doc., 41st Cong. 1st sess., no. 8.

[2] Senate Ex. Doc., 40th Cong. 1st sess., no. 8.

[3] House Ex. Doc., 43rd Cong. 2nd sess., no. 127, pp. 33, 70.

[4] Cf. House Reports, 43rd Cong. 1st sess., no. 418, p. 22.

[5] Cf. ibid., pp. 11–2; House Reports, 45th Cong. 2nd sess., no. 714, p. 3.

[6] The position of the South and West was simply stated by an intelligent man who dwelt upon the banks of the lower river: "We want the government of the United States to lay its strong arm on the hitherto uncontrolled waters of the Mississippi, to confine them within appropriate limits and to make them the servitors of the commerce and trade of the country."— House Mis. Doc., 47th Cong. 1st sess., no. 56, p. 4.

[7] For this flood see House Ex. Doc., 43rd Cong. 2nd sess., no. 127, pp. 38–49.

[8] Ibid., pp. 1–2.

these plainly must be closed,[1] in the interest of endangered
property, no less than in pity for unoffending and industrious
families, who periodically were driven from their homes on
the river banks and who, in distress, must be the recipients
of general sympathy and public relief. The commissioners
asked for more surveys, which they believed might occupy
three years.

Under the same impulse of public interest in the river Captain James B. Eads, an indomitable man, who had built ironclads for the government during the war and had thrown the
bridge across the Mississippi at St. Louis, was engaged, by
authority of an act of Congress of March 3, 1875, in spite
of violent opposition to his plan by other engineers, to build
jetties below New Orleans with a view to opening the South
Pass and creating a channel to the Gulf of a depth of 26 feet.[2]
By this time there were levees on both banks, which were in
a more or less serviceable condition, if they could be kept in
repair, of an average height of eight feet, rising in some places
to 30, 40 or even 50 feet, supplemented by hills where these
approached the river side, for a distance of 1,600 miles.[3]

In five years Eads's jetties were built. The parallel walls
of the work, set about 1,000 feet apart, extended for more
than two miles into the Gulf. The waves were bringing in
sand and sediment to form a natural-looking and permanent
embankment. The channel was deep enough—26 feet for a
width of 200 feet—to allow large ocean-going steamships to
come up to the wharves at New Orleans. The *Great Eastern*
might enter the harbor and it was proposed to employ this
capacious steamship in the export grain trade at New Orleans.[4]
But above the city the river was still little more than "a shift-
ing network of shoals and bars." [5] Captain Eads said, in 1882,

[1] Senate Ex. Doc., 47th Cong. 1st sess., no. 159, p. 3.
[2] Report of Sec. of War for 1879, pp. xvii–xix; E. L. Corthell, The Miss.
Jetties.
[3] House Ex. Doc., 46th Cong. 3rd sess., no. 95, pp. 35–6; Senate Ex. Doc.,
47th Cong. 1st sess., no. 10, p. 125.
[4] App. Ann. Cyclop. for 1880, p. 483; North Am. Review for March,
1884, p. 284.
[5] App. Ann. Cyclop. for 1880, p. 535.

that five, perhaps ten, per cent of the levees were down.[1] The entire alluvial basin must be deserted by man, if the holes in the banks were not filled.[2] The shoals, with snags in the bottom, all changing their position with the seasons, defied the navigator's art as well as the puny efforts put forth from time to time to remove them and clear the way even for boats drawing not more than four or five feet of water. At times in summer, in long periods of drought, no boats could run and the mail was carried from place to place in skiffs.[3]

Many of the crevasses had been deliberately opened in time of high water by owners of adjacent lands to turn the flood from the trembling embankments which protected their own property. There were some men who would visit disaster upon a neighbor; they would destroy, indeed, the crops, homes, lands of thousands of persons hundreds of miles away standing in the path of the released flood; they would permanently damage the whole levee system; they would imperil the navigation of the stream for months and years to come in order to gain temporary immunity for themselves. Again the banks would be cut by evil-minded persons to work revenge upon some planter who, they conceived, had done them injury. "Swampers" who had felled timber in the dry season opened the dikes so that they could get their rafts into the current and proceed to market. Muskrats, and other creatures which lived in the mud, were responsible for many a breach which, spreading, tumbled miles of the banks into the rushing torrent. After the crevasses were closed only sentinels, who were not at hand, and frequent, competent, authorized inspection would insure safety.[4]

As soon as the Radical leaders in the North abandoned the design of punishing their late military adversaries by leaving them indefinitely in helplessness and destitution, and conditions were seen to be damaging the West, as well as the South,

[1] House Mis. Doc., 47th Cong. 1st sess., no. 56, p. 54.
[2] Ibid., p. 62.
[3] Ibid., p. 64.
[4] House Ex. Doc., 43rd Cong. 2nd sess., no. 127, p. 23.

hope of progress increased. In 1879 Congress authorized the appointment of a permanent commission of seven members who should take the Mississippi under its care.[1] It was stipulated that a majority of the number should be army engineers and that one should be a river steamboat man. The President named General Quincy A. Gillmore, General C. B. Comstock and Major C. R. Suter, who was engaged upon surveys on the Missouri River, which had been authorized by recent river and harbor acts,[2] all of the United States army, and Henry Mitchell of the Coast and Geodetic Survey. The civilian appointees were James B. Eads, B. Morgan Harrod, a civil engineer from Louisiana, and Benjamin Harrison of Indiana. General Gillmore was chosen to be the president of the commission and it established its headquarters in St. Louis.

Garfield, when he accepted the nomination for the Presidency, in July, 1880, said that "the wisdom of Congress should be invoked to devise some plan" by which the river should "cease to be a terror to those who dwell upon its banks," and by which its shipping might "safely carry" the industrial products of 25 millions of people.[3] President Hayes in his last message, in December, 1880, in congratulating the country on the assurance which was given of the permanency of Eads's improvements at the mouth of the Mississippi, urged that the river generally, which was "the property of the nation," should receive the nation's care. A comprehensive policy in regard to a stream which was so strong a tie between the various sections of the country was of "transcendent importance." [4]

With public opinion unmistakably supporting them the new commissioners entered upon their stated tasks. They were to complete surveys already begun and to commence new ones with a view to correcting, permanently locating and deepening the channel, and protecting the banks of the river. They would aim to "improve and give safety and ease to navigation" and "prevent destructive floods." There had been long

[1] Act of June 28, 1879. 21 U. S. Stat. at Large, p. 37.
[2] House Ex. Doc., 46th Cong. 3rd sess., no. 92.
[3] App. Ann. Cyclop. for 1880, p. 701.
[4] Richardson, Messages and Papers, vol. vii, p. 619.

and acrimonious controversy as to the relative value of levees
and of "outlets," *i.e.*, artificial openings made at designated
points and maintained to deflect floods and send the water
away in other directions instead of keeping it in the stream
channel. One group of engineers, headed by the old chief
engineer of the army, General A. A. Humphreys, and the members of the commission of 1874, denied that confining the river
within artificial banks would increase the stream velocity and
scour the channel, though they accepted the levee as a necessity, in spite of its "fatal defects." [1]

Another group of authorities, following Captain Eads, gave
unqualified support to the theory that, with the closing of
the crevasses, and the maintenance of the embankments the
problem of controlling the floods, as well as of making the
channel navigable, would disappear.[2] It was Eads himself,
many of the river planters and steamboat men said, who had
made matters worse. By his jetty system at the mouth of the
Mississippi he had dammed up the water—of course it ran
back, since it could not escape, and flooded the lowlands of
Louisiana, Mississippi and Arkansas.[3] The commissioners were
to investigate the practicability of the "outlet system," the
"levee system" and the "jetty system," and to prepare estimates of the cost of their plans.

They made their first report on March 6, 1880. The "outlet system" was rejected as calculated to reduce the velocity
of the stream and develop shoals. The commission advocated

---

[1] House Ex. Doc., 43rd Cong. 2nd sess., no. 127, pp. 16–8. But see ibid.,
pp. 31, 148. For Humphreys see House Mis. Doc., 47th Cong. 1st sess.,
no. 56, pp. 65–77.

[2] House Mis. Doc., 47th Cong. 1st sess., no. 56, pp. 42–62; Senate Ex.
Doc., 47th Cong. 2nd sess., no. 32, pp. 10, 38, 42; House Ex. Doc., 48th
Cong. 1st sess., no. 37, pp. 18–9, 25.

[3] An old steamboat man who appeared before a committee of Congress
in 1882 said that Eads had "stopped up the mouth of the river." (House
Mis. Doc., 47th Cong. 1st sess., no. 56, pp. 64–5.) John Cowdon of New
Orleans was a leading advocate of outlets. If his plan were adopted levees—
"mud walls" he called them—would soon be rendered "useless"; in a few
years their "broken remains" would be regarded merely as "monuments
of human folly."—Ibid., pp. 16, 24; House Reports, 47th Cong. 1st sess.,
no. 848; cf. Senate Mis. Doc., 50th Cong. 1st sess., no. 155; House Mis. Doc.,
52nd Cong. 1st sess., no. 188.

the development of the "levee system" with a judicious use of jetties. The river should be kept within embankments in the interest of its use as a navigable waterway, as well as for the prevention of floods. Congress was asked for a sum in excess of $5,000,000 for the fiscal year ending June 30, 1881, to be expended in "closing existing gaps in levees" and for "initial works" in connection with channel contraction and bank protection.[1] This money would be applied to 184 miles of "bad navigation" between Cairo and Vicksburg, a reach covering about one-fourth of the distance from Cairo to Red River, all of which imperatively required the attention of the commission. To make the "initial works" in this reach permanent would mean an outlay of more than $8,000,000, or $45,-000 per mile. To improve the channel for the entire distance would call, at the same rate of cost, for appropriations aggregating about $33,000,000.[2]

The plans awaited the pleasure of Congress. A committee in 1880 visited the river and passed from St. Louis to New Orleans, returning with the firm conviction that the recommendations of the commission were judicious and should be adopted. This "great trunk line," they said, "this central highway of commerce" should not "remain blocked up, or permitted to convert itself into a shallow waste, useless and dangerous." [3]

But such counsel availed little. As could have been foreseen, perhaps, after much futile discussion, instead of even the $5,000,000 which were required for preliminary uses, Congress voted, on the last day of the session, March 3, 1881, $1,000,000 with which to proceed with the commission's plans.[4] How to expend so paltry a sum that it might usefully contribute to the attainment of the ends in view was far from clear.

[1] House Ex. Doc., 46th Cong. 2nd sess., no. 58.
[2] Senate Ex. Doc., 47th Cong. 1st sess., no. 10, p. 9; House Mis. Doc., 47th Cong. 1st sess., no. 56, p. 42; cf. North Am. Review, March, 1883. For projects affecting the upper Mississippi see House Ex. Doc., 45th Cong. 2nd sess., no. 49.
[3] House Reports, 46th Cong. 2nd sess., no. 1575; App. Ann. Cyclop. for 1881, p. 534.
[4] 21 U. S. Stat. at Large, p. 474.

If the money were to be frittered away at isolated points and the work should be carried on in a disjointed manner no estimate of the ultimate cost was possible.[1] It was determined, wisely enough, to concentrate effort upon two reaches,—one above Memphis, the other below that city; at both places there were shoals on which little more than four feet of water were found at low stages of the river.[2]

Disappointment in the West and South was great. For fifty years there had been conventions in the Mississippi Valley to discuss the needs of the people with reference to the river. In October, 1881, 656 men from 16 states and three territories met at St. Louis. The Mississippi and its tributaries had been "prepared by the Creator for the use of the people." The convention deplored the refusal of Congress to adopt the recommendations of the commission which it had established. This "great and indispensable work, national in every sense," should no longer be delayed; action by the government was a "manifest and imperative duty." A committee of 21 was formed to prepare a memorial. A committee of seven would lay the views of the convention before Congress.[3]

A Missouri River convention met at St. Joseph. The delegates urged the appointment of a Missouri River Commission that the work projected on the Mississippi might be extended in their direction.[4] The "Big Muddy," was, with the exception of the Ohio, the largest tributary of the trunk river. It was longer than any other stream in the United States, extending from its junction with the Mississippi for a distance of more than 3,000 miles to sources in the Rocky Mountains, and was navigated in some degree for nearly its entire length.[5] In a year it carried enough sediment, due to erosion and the caving of its banks, to cover a square mile of land to the depth

[1] Cf. House Ex. Doc., 46th Cong. 1st sess., no. 92, p. 10.
[2] Senate Ex. Doc., 47th Cong. 1st sess., no. 10, p. 4.
[3] House Mis. Doc., 47th Cong. 1st sess., no. 56, pp. 1–4; App. Ann. Cyclop. for 1881, p. 610.
[4] House Mis. Doc., 47th Cong. 1st sess., no. 56, pp. 9–14; App. Ann. Cyclop. for 1881, pp. 610–11.
[5] House Ex. Doc., 46th Cong. 3rd sess., no. 92, p. 2.

of 400 feet and threw this mass of silt into the Mississippi to make more difficult the problem in relation to the portion of the river below St. Louis.[1] Engineers desired $8,000,000 for the construction of mattress revetments, silt-catching devices and for other improvements, to be expended at the rate of $1,000,000 per annum.[2] In 1882 Congress voted the Missouri $850,000,[3] and in 1884[4] it created a Missouri River Commission of five members. The President assigned Major Suter, who had been giving special attention to this stream (a member since the beginning of the Mississippi River Commission), as chairman of the new board, which was to continue the work that he had begun. A small sum was appropriated by the same act for use south of Sioux City, and a smaller sum for the improvement of the channel up to Fort Benton in Montana.[5]

The Mississippi River Commission which had been dismissed by Congress with $1,000,000 in 1881 renewed its request for funds in 1882.[6] Disastrous floods in the spring of 1882 increased the conviction of need of action. The high water which pressed down the valley in the spring of that year swept through the old crevasses, and new breaks appeared.[7] It was, said the commissioners, a flood which, "for height, duration and widespread destruction," was "without a parallel." [8] More than 100,000 people were driven from their homes. Appeals were sent to Congress which voted money for the destitute. Up to the end of March army officers had issued over 2,000,000 rations at a cost to the government of more than $200,000.[9] The commission in 1882 doubled its estimates for

[1] House Ex. Doc., 46th Cong. 3rd sess., no. 92, p. 5.
[2] Ibid., p. 11.
[3] Senate Ex. Doc., 48th Cong. 2nd sess., no. 24, p. 3.
[4] Act of July 5, 1884.
[5] Senate Ex. Doc., 48th Cong. 2nd sess., no. 24, pp. 1–2; House Ex. Doc., 49th Cong. 2nd sess., no. 28, pp. 2–7.
[6] Senate Ex. Doc., 47th Cong. 1st sess., no. 10, p. 10.
[7] House Mis. Doc., 47th Cong. 1st sess., no. 56, pp. 7–14, 63, 65.
[8] Senate Ex. Doc., 47th Cong. 2nd sess., no. 32, p. 7.
[9] Senate Reports, 47th Cong. 1st sess., no. 254; Senate Ex. Doc., 47th Cong. 1st sess., no. 144; House Ex. Doc., 47th Cong. 1st sess., no. 126; ibid., no. 141.

the closure of gaps. The Secretary of War sent the recommendation to President Arthur and the President addressed Congress, urging an appropriation not only to satisfy temporary needs, but also in support of the general measures of the commission "for the permanent improvement of the navigation of the river and security of the valley." [1]

The work was now started and, under the impulse of the sentiment created by the flood, Congress voted over $4,000,000 for the levees and for other improvements on the river.[2] Another flood of dangerous proportions followed in 1883, and still another in 1884, preventing the prosecution of the plans of the commission, and wreaking further damage and destruction to property in the river valley.[3]

All that was needed to make their work successful, the commissioners declared in 1884, was money "liberally and promptly" supplied to them.[4] Partisan animosity at Washington during the next few years nullified every endeavor. Their work, the commission said in 1886, had been conducted under difficulties which could be "justly called extraordinary." There had been "a succession of floods without precedent." Twice the annual appropriation had been entirely withheld, and in no case, except once, did it reach the recommended amount. Costly work already begun at the two points chosen for improvement was deteriorating; the half completed works were exposed to injuries and, without money to finish them, even what had been already done, would be swept away.[5] The members of the commission could not visit the scene of their labors unless they did so at their own expense. The last appropriation for their benefit had been made in 1884; in 1888 the remainder in hand had been reduced to nineteen cents.[6] Without friends

---

[1] Senate Ex. Doc., 47th Cong. 1st sess., no. 159.

[2] Act of Aug. 2, 1882; Senate Ex. Doc., 47th Cong. 2nd sess., no. 32, p. 9; House Mis. Doc., 51st Cong 2nd sess., no. 127, p. 65.

[3] House Ex. Doc., 48th Cong. 1st sess., no. 37, pp. 4, 18; ibid., 48th Cong. 2nd sess., no. 64, p. 3.

[4] Ibid., 48th Cong. 2nd sess., no. 64, p. 4.

[5] Ibid., 49th Cong. 2nd sess., no. 66, pp. 2–3.

[6] Ibid., 50th Cong. 1st sess., no. 359; ibid., 50th Cong. 2nd sess., no. 64.

at Washington the people of the valley must act in their own defense. Locally between $8,000,000 and $9,000,000 were expended upon the levees in the years following the flood of 1882. When overflow threatened, the planters patrolled the banks, sprang to the breaches, and, with spade and sandbag, did their utmost to keep the angry water in its place.[1]

The completion of new transcontinental railroads in no way repressed the energies of men of large vision and busy enterprise, nor did it do aught to diminish public interest, with respect to a canal across the isthmus of Panama, or by some like available route. A shipway to join the Atlantic and the Pacific oceans on lines so often surveyed at various points in Panama, Nicaragua and Tehuantepec must one day be at the service of the world. To England it was important because of her great mercantile fleet and her preëminent position in the carrying trade. For the United States it had supreme interest because of the communication which it would establish between our Eastern and Western coasts. In 1872 President Grant had appointed a commission, headed by General A. A. Humphreys, for consideration of the subject. New surveys were made by government engineers,[2] and in 1876 a report was rendered in favor of the Nicaragua route.[3] The scheme to take ships across the continent at this point gained many friends, particularly as a large lake lay on the way. A canal only 17½ miles in length would carry vessels into this natural basin, another, about 36 miles in length, would bring them out of it and place them on the bosom of the Pacific. The work could be completed, it was said, for not more than half the estimated cost of a crossing at Panama.[4] This proposal was particularly associated with the name of A. G. Menocal, a Cuban, who had been, since 1872, in the service of the Navy Department as an engineer, who had accompanied a number

---

[1] House Mis. Doc., 51st Cong. 2nd sess., no. 127, p. 65.
[2] House Ex. Doc., 44th Cong. 1st sess., pt. 3, pp. 206–70.
[3] Senate Ex. Doc., 46th Cong. 1st sess., no. 15; cf. House Reports, 46th Cong. 3rd sess., no. 390; N. Y. Nation, July 31, 1879.
[4] House Mis. Doc., 46th Cong. 3rd sess., no. 16, p. 3.

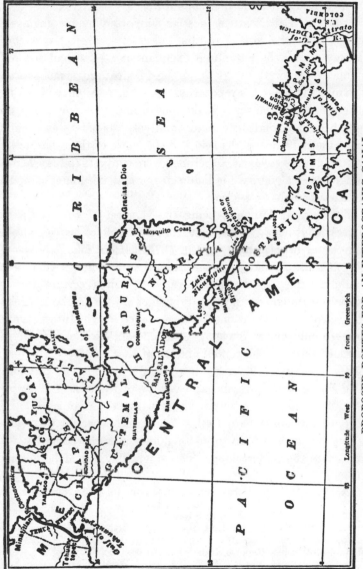

PROPOSED ROUTES FOR AN INTEROCEANIC CANAL

of expeditions to the south and who, convinced of its practicability, had prominently espoused it.[1]

James B. Eads, with a prestige supported by his engineering feats at the mouth of the Mississippi, projected a ship railway across the isthmus of Tehuantepec. He had secured a concession for the work from the Mexican government and was ready to stake his reputation upon the feasibility of taking a vessel out of the water in one ocean and of conveying it on rails behind powerful steam locomotives, "as safely as a child in its mother's arms," he said,[2] to the shore of the other ocean to continue its voyage.[3] Other men were converts to his scheme, and pressed Congress for indorsement and pecuniary support that work might be begun.[4]

The way at Panama, being the shortest of the suggested routes, continued, however, to hold first place in the public mind, and it was announced in 1878, not without expressions of solicitude in the United States, that a contract had been made by the Colombian government with a certain Lucien Napoleon Bonaparte Wyse, a Frenchman, who had been directing scientific explorations for a so-called Civil International Interoceanic Canal Society,[5] and who, in receiving the concession, acted as the representative of that society. The term of the grant was 99 years. It would be a monopoly privilege. The choice of a route and an estimate of the cost of the work should be submitted to an "International Commission" before, or not later than, 1881. The grantees would then have two years in which to form "a universal stock company" to prosecute the undertaking. This done they would be allowed

[1] House Mis. Doc., 46th Cong. 3rd sess., no. 16, p. 3; North Am. Review, Nov., 1880; N. Y. Nation, July 31, 1879.

[2] House Mis. Doc., 46th Cong. 3rd sess., no. 16, p. 60.

[3] App. Ann. Cyclop. for 1884, pp. 312-3; North Am. Review, March, 1881; House Mis. Doc., 46th Cong. 3rd sess., no. 16, pp. 59-70, 122-7; ibid., no. 13; House Reports, 46th Cong. 3rd sess., no. 322; Senate Reports, 47th Cong. 1st sess., no. 213; N. Y. Times, Oct. 20, 1929.

[4] Cf. Sess. Laws of Miss. for 1886, pp. 135-7; E. L. Corthell, The Atlantic and Pacific Ship Railway and An Exposition of the Errors and Fallacies of Rear Admiral Ammen.

[5] Cf. N. Y. Nation, Feb. 5, 1880.

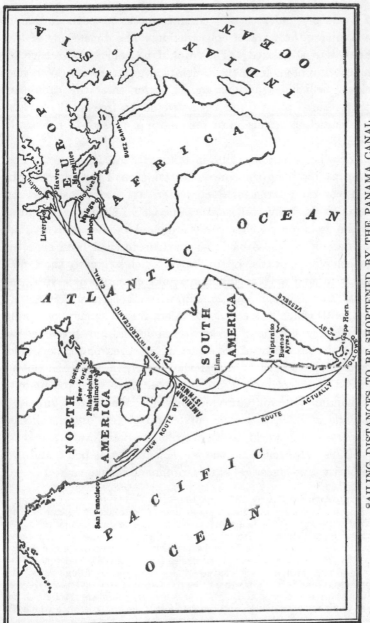

SAILING DISTANCES TO BE SHORTENED BY THE PANAMA CANAL

12 years or, under certain circumstances, 18 years in which to complete the work of construction. The dimensions of the canal were stipulated. Tolls would be collected, a share of these being payable to the Colombian government. War vessels of belligerent nations should never enter the canal—in other regards ingress and egress would be free to all, "without distinction, exclusion or preference of persons or nationalities."[1]

The scheme was not long in taking its intended form. The company receiving the concession, which had the outer marks of a neutral international character, at once transferred its rights to the Universal Interoceanic Canal Company in Paris, at the head of which stood Ferdinand de Lesseps, the old engineer upon whose name so much luster had been shed by the completion of the canal at Suez, which so greatly shortened routes to, and quickened commercial communication with, the East. A sanguine, magnetic man, with a good deal of imagination, with which was coupled a talent for diplomacy, he dominated every situation.[2] When those around him presumed to doubt the propriety of his exercising so much power he would quote Mehemet Ali to the effect that, if, in any great enterprise, there were more than one man, there were too many.[3] He had only one route in view, but he convened a "Congress" in Paris in 1879, to which public and private associations in all parts of the world, and governments, were invited to send delegates. He controlled the movements of this body, and the authority and prestige of his pronouncements caused it to

[1] App. Ann. Cyclop. for 1878, pp. 105–7.

[2] He made the following impression upon a journalist who saw him in San Francisco: "M. de Lesseps compels genuine respect at first sight. A man of middle stature, with white hair and gray mustache, piercing hazel eyes, which have an extremely kind expression, black eyebrows and a ruddy, healthy face, he combines the manners of a diplomatist and one of the vieux régime, with the best characteristics of a soldier of high rank. In conversation he is frank, eloquent, hearty and kind to a marvelous degree. His manner is energetic and his 74 years and gray hair are totally obliterated in his vigorous diction and the demonstrative gestures, with which his persuasive and gracious conversation is rendered all the more impressive." —San Francisco Examiner, March 17, 1880.

[3] House Ex. Doc., 46th Cong. 3rd sess., no. 16, p. 6.

choose, from seven or eight routes under discussion, that one running from Colon, or Aspinwall, to Panama, following, therefore, the course of the old Panama Railway and the Chagres River.[1] He asked for subscriptions amounting to 600,000,000 francs, or about $120,000,000.[2] It was given out that applications for two or three times as many shares as were available for sale had been received,[3] though so much seems not to have been true.[4] Something must be done to invigorate the scheme. De Lesseps visited Panama and, in February, 1880, on his way back to Paris, he came to the United States where it was suspected, with reason, that the undertaking was viewed with disfavor. Nothing daunted he sent home characteristically encouraging messages, induced by the complimentary dinners tendered him, because of his eminence and fame, and the friendliness of his receptions generally on a tour of the country which carried him to San Francisco in the interest of his "Canal de Chagres."[5] International banking houses with strong connections in New York were subsidized.[6] An American committee was chosen to create an impression of public sympathy. It was on this occasion that the use of Grant's name was sought in behalf of the scheme, and he was offered a tempting price if he would accept the chairmanship. When he declined it the place was offered to Colonel R. W. Thompson who retired from the cabinet of President Hayes for the service, as has been related in another place. By such devices the attitude of investors, especially in France, underwent some change and a considerable amount of money was raised by sale of the company's shares.[7]

---

[1] App. Ann. Cyclop. for 1881, pp. 510–11; N. Y. Nation, July 31, 1879, and Feb. 5 and 26, 1880; House Mis. Doc., 46th Cong. 3rd sess., no. 16, pp. 50, 93–7; North Am. Review, Sep., 1879, Jan., Feb. and July, 1880.

[2] G. Barnett Smith, The Life and Enterprises of Ferd. de Lesseps, chap. ix; F. de Lesseps, Recollections of Forty Years, chap. vii.

[3] App. Ann. Cyclop. for 1880, pp. 15–6. Millions were as ready to pour out at his call "as were the streams of Horeb at the touch of the rod of Moses."—San Francisco Examiner, March 18, 1880.

[4] House Reports, 52nd Cong. 2nd sess., no. 2615, p. 2.

[5] San Francisco Examiner, March 17, 1880.

[6] House Reports, 52nd Cong. 2nd sess., no. 2615, p. 5.

[7] Ibid., pp. 3–4.

At the first meeting of the stockholders in Paris in January, 1881, it was stated that engineers, superintendents, doctors to cope with the disease which lurked in the airs of so insalubrious a land, had already embarked for the isthmus, that contracts had been entered into for necessary machinery and that in a little while 8,000 laborers would be employed. Before the year 1881 should end the work would be well under way; it would be completed, it was believed, in 1888.[1]

On the surface all may have seemed well. But the management was sufficiently unfortunate, if not unintelligent. When the construction party arrived at Aspinwall, early in 1881, even the course of the canal had not yet been definitely fixed. Expensive machinery, as it arrived, found no shelter. Unceasing seasonal rains, disease which affected the men engaged in a work to which they were unused and imperfect preparation generally, already, two years after the inception of the undertaking, were prophecies of failure. It was to be a sea level canal without locks.[2] The French engineers, though a distinguished American consultant gave an opinion in opposition to theirs,[3] still believed that such a cut through swamp and mountain was practicable. De Lesseps continued to name 1888 as the year in which his plans would be realized, and reiterated that for $120,000,000 he could fulfill his promises to the stockholders and to the world. Others knew that the cost would be much in excess of the sum named; some said that it would be as great as $350,000,000 [4] and that the work would be far from complete at the mentioned date.[5]

The great "Culebra cut" involved the removal of an enormous amount of material, to which was added the danger of landslides. The Chagres River offered almost insuperable difficulties; the proposal for a dam which would impound its waters and effect a change in its course offered no certain solu-

[1] App. Ann. Cyclop. for 1881, pp. 714–5.
[2] Senate Ex. Doc., 48th Cong. 1st sess., no. 123, p. 11.
[3] Ibid., pp. 14–5.
[4] App. Ann. Cyclop. for 1885, p. 177.
[5] Ibid. for 1882, pp. 107, 814–5; Senate Ex. Doc., 48th Cong. 1st sess., no. 123, pp. 1–4, 14–5, 23–4.

tion of the problem, the character of which had received too
little prior examination.[1] Excavation and other labor could
proceed at the most advantageous pace only during the "dry
season," or from December to April. Then the temperature
was about 82 degrees Fahrenheit. Greater heat prevailed during
the months when rain fell and storms swept the land. Only
natives and negroes, drawn from Jamaica and other places
in the tropics, could effectively withstand the withering sun
and the fevers which were exhaled from the marshes.[2] Nevertheless some white men, as well as a number of Chinese, were
at times included in the force of laborers.[3] In 1883 no less than
10,000 men were at work upon the enterprise and in the following year 19,000 were in the company's employ.

Fire and flood prevented progress. An earthquake in 1882
created a panic which did not subside for some time. A native
insurrection called for the landing and intervention of American
troops. Financial troubles also beset the council of administration in spite of the stupendous efforts which were made to
give the work a favorable appearance.[4] Even a lottery was
suggested as a method of raising money and the quoted prices
of the company's shares and bonds underwent severe decline.[5]
Despite de Lesseps's many years—he was now 80—he invited
commercial bodies in this and other countries to meet him
at Panama in February, 1886, to inspect the work in the hope
of restoring confidence. He still predicted success, as he came
in October to attend the ceremonies attending the unveiling
of the French statue of "Liberty" in New York harbor,[6] even
while creditors were filing claims and obtaining judgments
against him.[7] It was very plain that failure was at hand. The

[1] App. Ann. Cyclop. for 1883, p. 308.
[2] Cf. G. Barnett Smith, op. cit., p. 266.
[3] Senate Ex. Doc., 48th Cong. 1st sess., no. 123, p. 3.
[4] Cf. App. Ann. Cyclop. for 1883, pp. 155-6, 315; ibid. for 1885,
pp. 177-9.
[5] Ibid. for 1885, p. 178; N. Y. Nation, July 29, 1886.
[6] N. Y. World, Oct. 29, 1886.
[7] Ibid., Nov. 23, 1886. For report of work in 1885 by a U. S. naval
officer see House Mis. Doc., 49th Cong. 1st sess., no. 395; for the same in
1886 see House Mis. Doc., 50th Cong. 1st sess., no. 599.

dazzling nature of the undertaking had blinded the venerable man to its hazards as a commercial enterprise and its perils to human life.[1] But surrender was a word not in his lexicon. He set forward the date of completion to 1890. He changed his plans; he turned from a sea level canal to locks and engaged the engineer, Eiffel, whose name is associated with a high tower in Paris, to build them.[2] Nearly $300,000,000 had been sunk without bringing the work appreciably near fruition.[3] The French government finally, as a last resource, authorized a lottery loan.[4] These bonds could not be sold. The company suspended payments in December, 1888, and work ceased, some 15,000 persons being thrown out of employment in Panama.[5] De Lesseps and his associates were compelled to resign and a committee was appointed by the French courts to settle the company's affairs,[6] with heavy and widespread losses, especially in France, to small investors, who could ill afford to suffer such disaster, and an outpouring of recrimination and scandal.[7] The costly machinery and the works generally, which had been brought to partial completion with so much human sacrifice, were abandoned, soon to be lost in a jungle of vegetable growth.[8]

As the prospect of a successful outcome disappeared the popular and official concern as to threatened encroachment upon the rights of the United States at the isthmus diminished. While there was some popular sympathy for de Lesseps, who had made a gallant attempt to perform a great task under the gravest difficulties, a measure of satisfaction was expressed, in political circles, that European interests would not control a transcontinental canal in America, as well as by those who cherished an interest in rival schemes for joining the two oceans.

[1] G. Barnett Smith, op. cit., p. 261; App. Ann. Cyclop. for 1886, pp. 191–2; N. Y. Nation, July 29, 1886, July 7 and Nov. 10, 1887.
[2] App. Ann. Cyclop. for 1888, p. 177.
[3] Ibid., p. 354.
[4] Cf. N. Y. Nation, Dec. 1 and 15, 1887 and May 3, 1888.
[5] App. Ann. Cyclop. for 1889, p. 221.
[6] Ibid. for 1888, pp. 178, 354.
[7] Ibid. for 1889, p. 165.
[8] Cf. John B. Henderson, Jr., American Diplomatic Questions, p. 75.

Eads was now dead, as was his ship-railway scheme in Mexico. Not so with the Nicaragua project which continued to have its active advocates.

The United States in 1846 had concluded a treaty with the republic of New Granada, which was binding upon its successor, the republic of Colombia. Reciprocal engagements concerning a canal were made by the two governments.[1] Four years later, in 1850, the Clayton-Bulwer treaty between the United States and Great Britain had been ratified; it contained provisions believed at the time to be of national advantage, binding the governments concerned to straightforward and honorable action, each with reference to the other, on the subject of an isthmian shipway.[2] The terms of these two treaties were reviewed with reference to the French scheme at Panama. The "Monroe Doctrine" was explained and reëxplained, its supposed relation to the canal was discussed.[3] The jingoes in Congress were under great excitement. The press fanned the flames. The national honor must be saved, come what might. Great Britain must renounce her claim under the treaty of 1850 to share in the guaranties which the United States had covenanted with Colombia four years before.[4] We would withdraw from a treaty providing for the joint protection of the canal in order that we might protect it ourselves.[5]

Congress in February and March, 1880, called for the correspondence of the Department of State with foreign powers on the subject of any and all isthmian canal schemes, and President Hayes, in communicating it to the Senate and the House, categorically protested the exercise of right by any European power in the premises. The canal must be "under American control" and the "American policy" would be defended.[6] It was our "right and duty," President Hayes re-

[1] App. Ann. Cyclop. for 1881, p. 716.
[2] Ibid., pp. 716–7.
[3] Cf. House Reports, 46th Cong. 3rd sess., no. 224; House Reports, 52nd Cong. 2nd sess., no. 2615, p. 4; North Am. Review, May, 1880; T. W. Woolsey, America's Foreign Policy, pp. 142–6.
[4] Cf. N. Y. Nation, Feb. 5, 1880.
[5] Ibid., Dec. 11, 1884.   [6] Richardson, vol. vii, pp. 585–6.

BLAINE AND THE CANAL

iterated in December, 1880, "to assert and maintain such supervision and authority" over the work as would "protect our national interests." [1] Hayes expressed the opinion privately that it must be "a canal under American control or no canal." European management of such a "thoroughfare between the different parts of the United States" was, in his sight, "wholly inadmissible." [2]

The question was passed on to Garfield and Arthur. Blaine's coming to the Department of State in March, 1881, was a signal for characteristic flings at England whose "intrusion" he declared to be uncalled for and unwanted. The United States refrained from activity of any kind in Europe; interference by Europe in the course of events on the American continent would be resented. We must be released from any obligation which we had entered into with Great Britain in the Clayton-Bulwer treaty. Its terms were unjust to this nation—we must be free to act in our own way, the treaty must be changed. It was "solely" an American question to be dealt with and decided by the governments of America. [3] Blaine's proposed Pan-American Congress of 1882 was seen to be an admonitory gesture to England, and to Europe generally, with reference to this continent, with no little bearing upon the canal question. [4]

Diplomatic communication between England and the United States on the topic continued during the administration of President Arthur, but our principal activity was displayed in a counter movement to build a canal of our own. Many schemes appeared. [5] The House of Representatives appointed

[1] Richardson, vol. vii, p. 611.
[2] Diary and Letters of Hayes, vol. iii, pp. 587-8, 589.
[3] Senate Ex. Doc., 47th Cong. 1st sess., no. 194; Senate Ex. Doc., 47th Cong. 1st sess., no. 78; cf. House Reports, 46th Cong. 2nd sess., no. 1121; Senate Ex. Doc., 46th Cong. 2nd sess., no. 112; Senate Ex. Doc., 48th Cong. 1st sess., no. 26; Senate Ex. Doc., spcl. sess., 1881, no. 5; Senate Ex. Doc., 47th Cong. 1st sess., no. 16; Senate Mis. Doc., 48th Cong. 2nd sess., no. 12; App. Ann. Cyclop. for 1881, pp. 718-21; ibid. for 1882, pp. 813-4; N. Y. Nation, Nov. 3, Dec. 15 and 22, 1881.
[4] App. Ann. Cyclop. for 1881, pp. 97-9, 130-31.
[5] House Reports, 46th Cong. 3rd sess., no. 390, pp. 1-2.

a committee of eleven members to choose a route. Various engineers, de Lesseps among the number, the hearings in 1880 coinciding with the time of his visit to America,[1] came forward and stated their views. The report, without advancing the controversy as to the most suitable site, completely discredited the project of de Lesseps and his company.[2]

The Nicaragua scheme was actively supported. A number of men had secured a concession from the government of that Central American state,[3] and, in 1881, with the name of General Grant, who was its advocate,[4] at their head, sought incorporation by Congress as the Maritime Canal Company of Nicaragua,[5] which, however, was not effected until 1889.[6] Indeed there were two groups of men with corporate organization who contended for the right to effect a crossing of the continent by ships over this route, and who asked for government guarantees so that they might sell their stock.[7] Their plans were well known before de Lesseps appeared with his scheme at Panama,[8] and they had not ceased to use their influences, as his work proceeded, to deprecate it and point out the impossibility of its successful prosecution.[9]

It was at their instance that the treaty with Nicaragua, which had made its appearance in the last year of Arthur's administration and which would set aside the much discussed Clayton-Bulwer treaty,—abrogate it by proclamation without further recourse to the ways of diplomacy—was nego-

[1] House Mis. Doc., 46th Cong. 3rd sess., no. 16, pp. 50–4; N. Y. Nation, March 11, 1880.

[2] House Reports, 46th Cong. 3rd sess., no. 390.

[3] Senate Reports, 47th Cong. 2nd sess., no. 952, p. 6; House Reports, 47th Cong. 1st sess., no. 1698, p. 4.

[4] Cf. North Am. Review, Feb., 1881.

[5] Cong. Record, 47th Cong. 1st sess., p. 136; Senate Reports, 47th Cong. 2nd sess., no. 952, pp. 1–4; cf. Senate Reports, 47th Cong. 1st sess., no. 368; House Reports, 47th Cong. 1st sess., no. 1698; Senate Reports, 49th Cong. 2nd sess., no. 1628; Senate Reports, 50th Cong. 1st sess., no. 221; House Reports, 50th Cong. 1st sess., no. 530; N. Y. Nation, July 27, 1882; App. Ann. Cyclop. for 1881, p. 662.

[6] Act of February 20, 1889.

[7] Cf. Senate Mis. Doc., 49th Cong. 1st sess., no. 139.

[8] Senate Reports, 47th Cong. 2nd sess., no. 952, p. 9.

[9] Cf. House Reports, 52nd Cong. 2nd sess., no. 2615, p. 4.

tiated.[1] In transmitting the paper to the Senate the President
said that the canal was "imperatively demanded by the present and future political and material interests of the United
States." By sea Europe and Africa were nearer to New York,
and Asia nearer to California than those two states of our
Union were to each other. Weeks by steam, months under
sail were consumed in transit around the Horn. The canal
must be built; it was primarily "a domestic means of water
communication" between our coasts. Nicaragua would contribute the territory and we would furnish the money.[2] The
Secretary of the Navy detailed Mr. Menocal, Robert E. Peary
and another engineer to visit the proposed canal zone and
make further surveys of the route.[3]

When Cleveland, upon coming to office in 1885, withdrew
the treaty from the Senate, on the ground that it was calculated
to bring us into "entangling alliances with foreign states," [4]
this scheme fell and the Nicaragua canal became a dream
even more shadowy than de Lesseps's. The realization of the
vision so hopefully seen by engineers, statesmen and the whole
world—a transcontinental canal through which, as Mr. Eads
said, "the commerce of the next century might pass unvexed
from ocean to ocean" [5] —must await a better day.

[1] N. Y. Nation, Dec. 18 and 25, 1884, Jan. 1, 8, 15 and 29, 1885.
[2] Richardson, vol. viii, pp. 256–60. For correspondence in connection
with this treaty see Senate Ex. Doc., 49th Cong. 2nd sess., no. 50.
[3] Senate Ex. Doc., 48th Cong. 2nd sess., no. 11; Senate Ex. Doc., 49th
Cong. 1st sess., no. 99; see also J. E. Nourse, Senate Ex. Doc., 48th Cong.
1st sess., no. 98, pp. 130–53.
[4] Richardson, vol. viii, pp. 327–8.
[5] Senate Mis. Doc., 46th Cong. 3rd sess., no. 16, p. 55.

INDEX

ADAMS, CHARLES FRANCIS, JR., 69, 175, 677.

Alabama, prosperity of, 507, 518; coal in, 510; iron in, 510–2; lumber in, 514; schools in, 541, 544, 545, 546, 549, 558, 559, 560, 561; lynchings in, 574; penal system in, 576, 577, 578; local option in, 582, 584; high license in, 585.

Alaska, area of, 607, 683; purchase of, 683; climate of, 685; seals in, 685–90; pelagic sealing in, 688–90; gold in, 690; absence of government in, 690–1; organized as a "district," 691–2; first governors of, 694.

Alaska Commercial Company, monopoly of, condemned, 686–8, 693; protests pelagic sealing, 689.

Aldrich, Nelson W., 156, 300, 490.

Aldrich, T. B., 176.

Allison, William B., silver views of, 30, 33; mentioned for place in cabinet, 104; opposes Chinese exclusion bill, 300; tariff views of, 487, 490.

Ambler, Jacob A., 146.

American Colonization Society, 525–6.

American Federation of Labor, 424.

American Free Trade League, 144.

American Iron and Steel Association, 143.

Ames, Oakes, 89–90.

Anarchists, bomb police in Chicago, 421–3.

Angell, James B., 295–6, 301, 492.

Anti-Monopoly Party, 176–7.

Anti-Saloon Republicans, 431.

Apaches, atrocities of, and war with, 638–42, 661.

Arizona, statehood for, proposed, 661–2; Mormons in, 667.

Arkansas, prosperity in, 518, 520; schools in, 541, 542, 550, 558; local option in, 584–5.

Armstrong, S. C., his work at Hampton Institute, 552–4, 648–9, 653.

"Arrears of Pensions" scheme, 352–3, 440, 444.

Arthur, Chester A., dismissed from customhouse, 52, 63, 89; nominated for Vice-President, 75, 76–7; nomination of, objected to by Independents, 79–80, 91; confers with Garfield, 96; charges Garfield with treachery, 102; attends Dorsey dinner, 107–8, 138; lackey for Conkling, 112; aids Conkling and Platt, 115; Guiteau names, 120; misgivings concerning, 120; becomes President, 120, 121; convenes Senate, 122; how he was nominated for Vice-President, 122–4; character of, 124–5; his cabinet, 125–7; deserts Stalwarts, 128–9; and civil service reform, 130–1; successor to, 132; his attitude toward Star Route frauds, 132–3, 136; his appointments, 140; vetoes River and Harbor bill, 142; recommends tariff reform, 146–7; recommends civil service reform, 151, 152–3; appoints Civil Service Commission, 154; signs tariff bill, 156; in campaign of 1884, 161–2; estimate of his administration, 161–2, 329; urges passage of bill to pension Grant, 168; Clayton deserts, 172; vote of delegates for, 172; unfriendly to Blaine, 210; vetoes Chinese exclusion bill, 300–03; labor leaders threaten, 303–4; signs ten year exclusion bill, 305; signs supplemental exclusion bill, 308; calls upon Cleveland, 327; and Indian lands, 340; his appointment of Chandler, 343–4; treaty with Nicaragua, 351–2, 717–8; appeal in behalf of Grant, 362; rec-

719

Schofield, General, 18.
Schoonmaker, Augustus, 447.
Schurz, Carl, urges Lodge to support Sherman, 76; his opinion of Garfield, 91; speaks for Garfield, 97; recommends Walker for Garfield's cabinet, 103; advises Garfield, 105; what he did for civil service reform in Hayes's administration, 107; purity of service of, 116; hears from Bayard, 124; editor of New York Evening Post, 141; addresses Independents in Brooklyn, 161; writes to Logan, 171; opposes Blaine, 176; addresses conference of Independents, 180; campaigning in 1884, 194, 196–7, 198; advises Cleveland about cabinet, 320–21; criticizes appointments of, 322, 330; favors tenure of office act, 369; informed about Cleveland, 458; his opinion of "Mills bill," 489; describes Southern negroes, 551; conservation of forests advocated by, 615; Indian policy of, 644, 649; his opinion of Mormons, 663; at Yellowstone Park, 679.
Scott, Thomas A., 16, 411, 604.
Scott, William L., contributor to Cleveland's campaign fund, 321; supports Cleveland's tariff policy, 485; deals unfairly for political reasons with Chinese, 501–2.
"Scratchers," see Independents.
Seals, haunts of, in Alaska, 685–6, 690; monopoly of catch of, 686–7; killed by poachers, 688–90.
Sears, Dr. Barnas, 537.
Seelye, President, 161, 176.
Seligmans, bankers, 3, 39, 40.
Seminoles, 625, 644.
Seward, George F., minister to China, 256, 294, 296.
Seward, William H., 224, 683.
Seymour, Horatio, 82, 83, 360.
Shapley, Rufus E., 146.
Shepherd, "Boss," 87, 90–91, 140.
Sheridan, General, in Louisiana, 84; pacifies Indians, 341, 638; in Yellowstone Park, 599, 679; orders Indians to Florida, 648.

Sherman, John, preparing for resumption, 8–9; his successor in Senate, 20; Congress checks operations of, 29; report of, as Secretary of Treasury, 29; against inflation, 30; wavering course of, 33–6, 78–9, 86, 365, 374; his adventures with silver, 36–7; on stump in 1878, 39; bringing gold into Treasury, 39–41; achieves resumption, 41; Presidential ambitions of, in 1880, 62–3; speaks for Cornell, 63; votes cast for, in convention of 1880, 71, 73; nominated by Garfield, 72–3; his defeat, 74, 75–6; invited to conference with Garfield, 96; speaks for Garfield, 97; hears from Garfield about tariff, 98; Conkling and Blaine oppose, 103–4; praises Hayes, 106; counsels Garfield, 109; his friends in convention of 1880, 122–3; tariff conferee, 156; business men for Arthur rather than, 163; Germans call him an "iceberg," 171; his advocates in 1884, 172; vote for, in convention, 172; on Blaine's popularity, 198; opposes Chinese exclusion, 305; reëlected senator, 358; president pro tem of Senate, 359; "bloody shirt" senator, 464; replies to Cleveland's tariff message, 484; his policy on Canadian fisheries question, 497.
Sherman, General W. T., compliments Arthur, 163; Germans describe, 171; boomed for President, 173; tries to help Grant, 361; denounces G.A.R. bigots, 465; his march to the sea, 507; hears Grady, 508; at Yellowstone Park, 679.
"Shoestring District," 589.
Siemens, Georg, 599.
Silver, mining of, in Nevada, 3–4; fall in price of, 4, 22–3, 24, 371; "demonetization" and "remonetization" of, 5–9, 26; free coinage of, 8–9, 24; commission to study, 8, 23–6; fanatical interest in, 20–22, 372–3; in Congress, 26–9; purchase law of 1878, 30–33; international conference, 31; not